THE MARINE OFFICER'S GUIDE

9TH EDITION

THE MARINE OFFICER'S GUIDE

9TH EDITION

COLONEL CHRISTIAN HALIDAY
UNITED STATES MARINE CORPS (RET.)

Naval Institute Press
Annapolis, Maryland

Naval Institute Press
291 Wood Road
Annapolis, MD 21402

Library of Congress Cataloging-in-Publication Data

Names: Haliday, Christian, author.
Title: The Marine officer's guide / Colonel Christian Haliday, United States Marine Corps (Ret.).
Description: Ninth edition. | Annapolis, Maryland : Naval Institute Press, [2023] | Includes
    bibliographical references and index.
Identifiers: LCCN 2022039618 | ISBN 9781682476055 (hardback)
Subjects: LCSH: United States. Marine Corps—Officers' handbooks. | BISAC: REFERENCE /
    Personal & Practical Guides | POLITICAL SCIENCE / Security (National & International)
Classification: LCC VE153 .E85 2023 | DDC 359.9/60973—dc23/eng/20220824
LC record available at https://lccn.loc.gov/2022039618

♾ Print editions meet the requirements of ANSI/NISO z39.48–1992 (Permanence of Paper).

Printed in the United States of America.

31 30 29 28 27 26 25 24 23   10 9 8 7 6 5 4 3 2 1

First printing

Photographs, unless otherwise indicated, are U.S. Department of Defense, U.S. Army, U.S. Marine Corps, U.S. Navy, U.S. Air Force, U.S. Space Force, or U.S. Coast Guard public domain. The appearance of DOD visual information does not imply or constitute DOD endorsement. Figures and tables, where not original, have been reproduced from various official publications.

To all Marine officers

Into whose keeping
The Corps is year by year entrusted.

Once a Marine, always a Marine.

Contents

Illustrations

Figures

Tables

Photos and Illustrations

Preface to the Ninth Edition

SINCE THE FIRST EDITION was published in 1956, *The Marine Officer's Guide* has no doubt helped legions of young officers and officer candidates take their places in this comradeship we know as the United States Marine Corps. I suspect that over the years it helped many enthusiastic young officers rapidly develop the knowledge, skills, and abilities to become fine leaders of Marines while hopefully avoiding some of the common pitfalls of inexperience; I know the fifth edition provided me such a head start. In a period of rapid and incessant change in global affairs, technology, the character of conflict, and the profession of arms, the *Guide* is a reassuring constant that offers its reader the resources to launch a promising Marine Corps career.

Why read a guidebook in an age of automation and computers? It is worth recalling the insight of Daniel J. Boorstin, American historian and twelfth librarian of Congress, on books in the information era: "A wonderful thing about a book, in contrast to a computer screen, is that you can take it to bed with you." While I am not necessarily advocating the *Guide* as bedtime reading, in book form it retains many attributes. It is more portable and durable than a computer. Unlike the screen of a smartphone, its printed page is gentle on your eyesight and comes without a low-battery indicator. And perhaps most importantly, the *Guide* offers a single, curated collection of information and wisdom on the Corps, which would require countless internet searches and careful vetting by an aspiring Marine officer who seeks the same information online. It thus seems a useful supplement to even the most modern sources of information on the Corps.

This ninth edition of *The Marine Officer's Guide* continues in the tradition of its predecessors. As Colonel Robert D. Heinl Jr., one of its originators, noted, the *Guide* aims "to assist new officers to learn the ropes as quickly as they can, to digest for all readers the continuing changes which have beset the Defense Establishment, and to help the entire officer corps keep professionally up to date."

I have completely reviewed and, where required, revised this edition. I have added new content that accounts for changes in the Department of Defense and Marine Corps, and I have updated many of the illustrations. This edition retains a similar general outline of chapters and appendices as in previous editions, although I have combined and shortened some chapters. Like the eighth edition, the work is organized into three parts. After the largely intact introductory chapter, part I addresses the Marine Corps as a military service, an institution, and (yes, to some degree) a bureaucracy. Its chapters touch upon the Corps' storied history; examine the service in the nation's defense and naval establishments, the treatments of which are completely updated; describe its mission, organization, and infrastructure; and reveal inter alia its culture, the sum of its beliefs, and its ways of thinking, working, and behaving. Part II turns to topics related to becoming and being an effective officer of Marines. Most important here are discussions of leadership and the profession of arms, but the updated and expanded chapters on such mundane but essential topics as unit and individual administration, pay and allowances, and military justice are also worth the effort. Part III provides useful information on personal, family, and social matters. In sum, this new edition is current and applicable to today's Corps.

I again thank Ken Estes, who prepared editions five through seven of *The Marine Officer's Guide.* I have profited greatly from our long association and friendship, which began more than four decades ago after I became a midshipman at Duke University, where he was the Marine officer instructor. To say he influenced me is an understatement. I believe he takes no small degree of pride in "stealing" me from the Navy by helping me change course as I entered my junior year and opted for a pathway into the Marine Corps. Ken has been a superb sounding board, mentor, supporter, and friend over these many years. He provided me invaluable advice throughout my own career. And he arranged for me to take the helm of this work, which I am finding a challenging and rewarding experience. I am in his debt.

I also thank the many officers and Marines with whom I have served over almost three decades and with whom I continue to interact since leaving active service. Fellow Marines—both seniors and juniors—shaped my understanding of and stoked my love for the Corps. They contributed to my successes in the Marine Corps and to my accumulation of the knowledge, expertise, and experience that has enabled me to complete this project. They have my gratitude.

And I am, of course, profoundly grateful to my wife, Anne, and our family, who supported me in this endeavor. Their encouragement, which kept me going, and indulgence, when I was perhaps not quite myself during the course of a year or so, contributed greatly to this revision of the *Guide*.

Finally, I express my appreciation to the Naval Institute Press and its acquisition, editorial, and production staffs, who have assisted and supported me during this edition's preparation over more than a year. Tom Cutler guided me expertly through the revision process. Kevin Brock applied a keen editorial eye, contributed his considerable writing expertise, and provided valuable feedback to improve the original manuscript. And I know that countless others worked behind the scenes to bring this project to fruition. Altogether, they were unsurpassed in their guidance, expertise, support, and, above all, patience as I researched and revised this new version of the *Guide*.

I welcome insights, comments, suggestions, and corrections from all readers, but particularly from those who are part of this work's primary audience: prospective and new Marine officers. Does this guidebook help you become a Marine officer and make a good start in your career? Does it answer your questions? Is it accurate and complete? What would make it better or more useful? Please send your suggestions to

Editor, *The Marine Officer's Guide*
Naval Institute Press
291 Wood Road
Annapolis, MD 21402–5034

With your help, these volumes will continue to improve and prepare future leaders to rapidly make their own contributions to the Corps.

Semper Fidelis, Marines!

—CHRISTIAN HALIDAY

Introduction to the First Edition

PREPARATION OF THIS BOOK was a project which began during my tenure as Commandant of the Marine Corps, and it was one to which I lent sympathetic attention. Now that I see the results, I am well satisfied that I helped to the extent that I did.

It is high time that the Marine Corps had a work of this kind.

Within the memory not of a few senior officers on the verge of retirement, but of the bulk of our most experienced field officers, the Corps has expanded immensely and has pursued its traditional role of national force in readiness on a vastly larger scale.

Thus, the Marine Corps is—or could be—in a time of transition. At such times it is all too easy to forget, depart from, or discard the well-tested ways which have brought us where we are. Fortunately, those ways are still with us, and such a book as *The Marine Officer's Guide* must be of the greatest value in keeping them with us.

As I write this to readers of *The Marine Officer's Guide*, I am reminded of what must be one of the earliest surviving "fitness reports" on a young Marine officer, submitted by Captain Daniel Carmick, USMC, in April 1799: "Lt Amory is very ignorant of Military duty, as he acknowledges, but he is a smart Gentleman and far preferable to the others." For the young officer of today who (like Lt. Amory) is not ashamed to admit the limits of his own experience and is intelligent enough to profit by the experience of others, *The Marine Officer's Guide* should prove indispensable.

—General L. C. Shepherd Jr.
United States Marine Corps (Ret.)

⁂{ 1 }⁂

THE UNITED STATES
MARINE CORPS

First to fight.
Retreat, hell! We just got here.
Gone to fight the Indians—will be back when the war is over.
Uncommon valor was a common virtue.
The Marines have landed, and the situation is well in hand.

PHRASES LIKE THESE say more about the United States Marine Corps than all the articles and books ever written. As you read this guide, remember that there is far more to the Marine Corps than can ever be expressed in a few—or even several—chapters. If you are fortunate enough to become a Marine, you will soon realize what the Corps is and what it represents.

⁂ WHAT IS A MARINE CORPS?

Beyond the statutes and official definitions, which you will encounter in later chapters, what is a marine corps?

To many observers, it is a military anomaly—a marine is a "soldier and sailor, too." But any cursory reading of military history tells us that navies, from their inception, have had a fundamental need for expert troops to guard ships and stations as well as to extend the force of naval power ashore.

Every world power has an army. Most powers have a navy and air force. Few throughout history have had a distinct marine corps, but more such corps, based on the examples of their eminent usefulness, have been formed since World War II. Almost fifty nations now field a marine corps or naval infantry units in their orders of battle: Argentina, Bolivia, Brazil, Cambodia, Chile, China, Colombia, Cuba, Ecuador, Finland, France, Greece, Honduras, India, Indonesia, Italy, Japan, the Republic of Korea, Kuwait, the Maldives, Mexico, Morocco, the Netherlands, Norway, Pakistan, Paraguay, Peru, the Philippines, Poland, Portugal, Romania, Russia, Saudi Arabia, Spain, Sri Lanka, Sweden, Syria, Taiwan, Thailand, Tonga, Turkey, Ukraine, the United Kingdom, Uruguay, Venezuela, and Vietnam (see appendix III to briefly explore the history, traditions, and organization of some of these marine corps). Several other countries have naval commando or coastal defense organizations that perform missions similar to those of marines.

Nowhere, however, has a marine corps attained the status of our own. This level of excellence was not foreseen when the Continental Congress, on 10 November 1775, formed two battalions of Marines. The Corps has gained its unique position through long evolution.

Much of the anomalous quality of the U.S. Marine Corps stems from the fact that the Corps possesses many individual attributes of the other services. As a result, you can usually discern something suggestive of the other services in the Marine Corps, which is only natural in an organization that has spent most of its time spearheading, supporting, or serving alongside the Army, Navy, and Air Force. But you can also see much more that belongs only to the Marine Corps.

Certainly, the Marine Corps' attitude is unique.

Fully as important as its attitude, however, is the Corps' fundamental mission. This primary mission—readiness—combined with the Marine state of mind makes the Corps what it is today: a national force in readiness, prepared in fact and required by law to "perform such other duties as the President may direct"—in other words, "ready for anything."

Most Americans, including some who know few specifics about the Corps, recognize Marines as the national force in readiness. Such tried-and-true phrases as "Call out the Marines!" and "The situation is well in hand" and "Tell it to the Marines" have entered the national lexicon and voice the country's attitude.

The existence of this nationwide feeling makes the Marine Corps a national institution.

As a Marine, therefore, you will represent an American institution whose standing and reputation are in your hands.

❯ WHAT THE U.S. MARINE CORPS STANDS FOR

The U.S. Marine Corps exists for one purpose—to fight. Whether the Corps is engaged in shipboard combat, landing operations, or a land campaign, this fundamental reason for its establishment remains unchanged.

The slogan "First to Fight" originally appeared on this World War I–era Marine Corps recruiting poster.

The qualities that the Marine Corps stands for might seem old fashioned. Nevertheless, these attributes have shaped the Corps since 1775, from Princeton to Belleau Wood, from Trenton to Chosin Reservoir to Khe Sanh, and from Granada to Fallujah. Here are some values that the Corps represents.

Quality and Competence. Simply stated, a Marine must be first rate. In the Corps, your best is just the acceptable minimum. It is expected, as a matter of course, that the technical performance of a single Marine or of a whole Marine outfit, whether on parade or in an attack, will be outstanding.

Discipline. Of all the principles of the Marine Corps, its insistence on discipline is the most unvarying and most uncompromising.

Valor. Displaying great courage in the face of danger or adversity is another Marine Corps hallmark. After the capture of Iwo Jima, Fleet Admiral Chester W. Nimitz epitomized the performance of the Marines who took the island. "Uncommon valor," wrote the admiral, "was a common virtue." Three hundred Medals of Honor—the highest U.S. military decoration—have been awarded to U.S. Marines. Valor is the Corps' stock in trade. The phrase "Retreat, hell! We just got here" was originally uttered in 1918 by a company commander of Marines.

Esprit de Corps. A Marine is intensely proud of the Corps, loyal to his or her comrades, and protective of the good name of the Corps. This spirit is nowhere better expressed than in a letter, written in 1800 by William Ward Burrows, second commandant of the Marine Corps, to a junior Marine officer who had been insulted by an officer in the Navy:

Camp at Washing., Sept 22, 1800

Lt. Henry Caldwell,

Sir—

When I answer'd your letter, I did not Know what Injuries you had received on board the *Trumbull*. . . . Yesterday the Secretary told me, that he understood one of the Lieutenants of the Navy had struck you. I lament that the Capt. of yr ship cannot Keep Order on board of her. . . . As to yourself I can only say, that a Blow ought never to be forgiven, and without you wipe away this Insult offer'd to the Marine Corps, you cannot expect to join our Officers.

I have permitted you to leave the Ship . . . that you may be on an equal Footing with the Captain, or any one who dare insult you, or the Corps. I have wrote to Capt. Carmick, who is at Boston to call on you & be your Friend. He is a Man of Spirit, and will take care of you, but don't let me see you 'till you have wip'd away this Disgrace. It is my Duty to support my Officers and I will do it with my Life, but they must deserve it.

On board the *Ganges*, about 12 mos. ago, Lt. Gale was struck by an Officer of the Navy, the Capt. took no notice of the Business, and Gale got no satisfaction on the Cruise: The moment he arrived he call'd the Lieut. out, and shot him; afterwards Politeness was restor'd. . . .

> Yr obdt Svt,
> W. W. Burrows
> LtCol Comdt, MC

Pride. Every Marine is intensely proud of Corps and country and does his or her utmost to build and uphold the Corps.

Loyalty and Faithfulness. *Semper Fidelis* (Always Faithful) is the motto of the Marine Corps. In addition, every honorable discharge certificate from the Corps bears the expression *Fideli Certa Merces* (A Sure Reward to the Faithful). Marines understand that these are not idle words. Absolute loyalty to the Corps is required of every Marine, as is devotion to duty. The percentage of Marines missing in action or taken prisoner by the enemy is minute. A good Marine places the interests of the Corps at the top of his or her list.

Individuality. The Marine Corps cherishes the individuality of its members and, although sternly consecrated to discipline, has cheerfully sheltered a legion of nonconformist, flamboyant individuals and extraordinary personalities. It is a perennial prediction that colorful characters are about to vanish from the Corps. They never have and never will. No Marine need fear that the mass will ever absorb the individual.

The Volunteer. Despite occasional acceptance of draftees in times of peak demand, as during World War II and the Vietnam War, the Marine Corps is a a "volunteer outfit." The Corps relies on those who want to be Marines. There is no substitute. As the old phrase goes, "One volunteer is worth ten pressed men."

The Infantry. The Corps is unique in that no matter what military specialty Marines acquire, be it combat, combat support, or combat service support specialty, either ground or aviation, they are all trained initially as riflemen. All officers, in addition, must be morally and professionally prepared to function as infantry officers.

Comradeship. A commandant of the Marine Corps once wrote, "The relation between officers and enlisted men should in no sense be that of superior and inferior nor that of master and servant, but rather that of teacher and scholar (that is, student). In fact, it should partake of the nature of the relation between father and son, to the extent that officers, especially commanding officers, are responsible for the physical, mental, and moral welfare, as well as the discipline and military training, of the young men under their command." These words stand as an enduring testimony to the comradeship among all Marines, whether officer or enlisted.

Tradition. Saint Paul's injunction "Hold the traditions which ye have been taught" could be a Marine motto. Respect for the traditions of the Corps is deeply felt. Every Marine adheres to the traditions that have shaped the Corps.

Professionalism. U.S. Marines are professionals who stand ready to fight any enemy, anytime, anywhere, as designated by the president and Congress, and to do so coolly and capably. They are not trained to hate, nor are they whipped up emotionally for battle or for any other duty the Corps is called on to perform. Patriotism and professionalism are their only two "isms."

Readiness. The Corps is perhaps most needed when the nation is demobilized and at peace. Marines are prepared mentally and physically for immediate employment, both as individuals and as trained units. A former secretary of state once remarked that as a crisis loomed, his first question to his staff was "Where are the Marines and the carriers?"

— ◆》 《◆ —

Above all, the public has maintained a consistent view of the Corps. That view is taken for granted, but all Marines could use it as a daily measure of effectiveness. It contains no sophisticated concept of national defense or the exercise of sea power but rather reflects the public appreciation of decades of consistent Marine Corps performance. It goes like this: First, wherever there is a crisis demanding U.S. military action, there will be Marines ready and able to go there in an instant. Second, once on the scene, those Marines will perform in a highly effective manner and restore the situation in our favor, without exception. Finally, the public believes that the Corps is a good thing to have around and consists of sound, energetic young men and women upon whom the national trust can be bestowed.

❧ COMMANDANT WRITES TO HIS OFFICERS

Major General John A. Lejeune, thirteenth commandant of the Marine Corps from 1920 to 1929, opened his heart to his officers in a collective letter.

TO THE OFFICERS OF THE MARINE CORPS:

I feel that I would like to talk to each of you personally. This, of course, it is impossible for me to do. Consequently, I am going to do the next best thing, by writing letters from time to time which will go to all the officers. In these letters, I will endeavor to embody briefly some of the thoughts which have come into my mind concerning our beloved Corps.

In the first place, I want each of you to feel that the Commandant of the Corps is your friend and that he earnestly desires that you should realize this. At the same time, it is his duty to the Government and to the Marine Corps to exact a high standard of conduct, a strict performance of duty, and a rigid compliance with orders on the part of all the officers.

You are the permanent part of the Marine Corps, and the efficiency, the good name, and the esprit of the Corps are in your hands. You can make or mar it.

You should never forget the power of example. The young men serving as enlisted men take their cue from you. If you conduct yourselves at all times as officers and gentlemen should conduct themselves, the moral tone of the whole Corps will be raised, its reputation, which is most precious to all of us, will be enhanced, and

Major General John A. Lejeune

the esteem and affection in which the Corps is held by the American people will be increased.

Be kindly and just in your dealings with your men. Never play favorites. Make them feel that justice tempered with mercy may always be counted on. This does not mean a slackening of discipline. Obedience to orders and regulations must always be insisted on, and good conduct on the part of the men exacted. Especially should this be done with reference to the civilian inhabitants of foreign countries in which Marines are serving.

The prestige of the Marine Corps depends greatly on the appearance of its officers and men. Officers should adhere closely to the Uniform Regulations, and be exceedingly careful to be neatly and tidily dressed, and to carry themselves in a military manner. They should observe the appearance of men while on liberty, and should endeavor to instill into their minds the importance of neatness, smartness, and soldierly bearing.

A compliance with the minutiae of military courtesy is a mark of well disciplined troops. The exchange of military salutes between officers and men should not be overlooked. Its omission indicates a poor state of discipline. Similarly, officers should be equally careful to salute each other. Courtesy, too, demands more than an exchange of official salutes between officers. On all occasions when officers are gathered together, juniors should show their esteem and respect for their seniors by taking the initiative in speaking to and shaking hands with their seniors. Particularly should this be done in the case of commanding officers. The older officers appreciate greatly attention and friendliness on the part of younger officers.

We are all members of the same great family, and we should invariably show courtesy and consideration, not only to other officers, but to members of their personal families as well. Do not fail to call on your commanding officers within a week after you join a base. On social occasions the formality with which all of us conduct ourselves should be relaxed, and a spirit of friendliness and good will should prevail.

In conclusion, I wish to impress on all of you that the destiny of our Corps depends on each of you. Our forces, brigades, regiments, battalions, companies, and other detachments are what you make them. An inefficient organization is the product of inefficient officers, and all discreditable occurrences are usually due to the failure of officers to perform their duties properly. Harmonious cooperation and teamwork, together with an intelligent and energetic performance of duty, are essential to success, and these attributes can be attained only by cultivating in your character the qualities of loyalty, unselfishness, devotion to duty, and the highest sense of honor.

Let each one of us resolve to show in himself a good example of virtue, honor, patriotism, and subordination, and to do all in his power, not only to maintain, but to increase the prestige, the efficiency, and the esprit of the grand old Corps to which we bel-ong.

With my best wishes for your success and happiness, I am, as always,

Your sincere friend,

John A. Lejeune,

Major General Commandant

Major General Lejeune's timeless and persuasive words make it evident that the Corps' reputation, its virtue, and indeed its future lie in the hands of its Marines—and particularly its officers. Read on to gain a deeper understanding of our Corps of Marines and what it takes to be an officer of Marines.

—» Part I «—

A CORPS
OF MARINES

⁂{ 2 }⁂

THE STORY OF THE MARINE CORPS

*Legend, tradition, history can drive a commitment to excellence
that raises people and has them perform at a level above anything
they ever dreamed they could do.*
— Captain Paul X. Rinn, U.S. Navy

THE MARINE CORPS dates from 10 November 1775. On that day, the Continental Congress authorized formation of two battalions of Marines.

Samuel Nicholas of Philadelphia was commissioned captain on 28 November 1775 and was charged with raising the Marines authorized by Congress to form part of the naval service. Nicholas remained senior officer in the Continental Marines for the duration of the American Revolution and is properly considered our first commandant.

⋗ THE CORPS IN ITS FORMATIVE YEARS

⋗ ⋗ *Marines in the Revolutionary War*

The initial Marine recruitment occurred at Tun Tavern in Philadelphia. By early 1776, the organization had progressed to the extent that the Continental Marines were ready for their first expedition. The objective was New Providence Island (Nassau) in the Bahamas, site of a British fort and a depot for large supplies of munitions. With Captain Nicholas in command, 234 Marines sailed from Philadelphia on board Continental warships. On 3 March 1776, Nicholas led his men ashore, took the fort, and captured the powder and arms for General George Washington's army.

For the first time in U.S. history, the Marines had landed, and the situation was well in hand.

During the succeeding years, Nicholas, promoted to major, commanded a battalion of Marines that fought in the Middle Atlantic campaigns of 1776 and 1777 at Trenton, Morristown, Assunpink, and Fort Mifflin. At sea (notably under John Paul Jones), shipboard Marines served as prize crews, sharpshooters, and landing forces (such as during the Penobscot Bay expedition in 1779).

❧ ❧ *Early Years, 1783–1811*

After the end of the American Revolutionary War in 1783, both the Continental Navy and the Marines waned into temporary obscurity. Although individual Marines continued to be enlisted to serve in the few U.S. armed vessels of the period (such as revenue cutters), no corps organization again existed until 1 July 1798, when Congress reconstituted the Marine Corps. Major William Ward Burrows, another Philadelphian with Revolutionary War experience, was appointed major commandant of the Corps.

During the decade that followed, the Naval War with France (1798–1800) and the campaign against the Barbary corsairs (1801–5) provided employment for the Corps. Other noteworthy events were the organization of the Marine Band in 1798, the relocation of Marine Corps Headquarters to Washington in 1800, and the retirement of Burrows as commandant in 1804.

The third commandant, Lieutenant Colonel Franklin Wharton, found approximately 65 percent of his small Corps on duty in the Mediterranean. There, in 1805, First Lieutenant Presley Neville O'Bannon led a mixed force, including Marines, six hundred miles across the desert in Libya to attack the fortress at Derna. O'Bannon's handful of Marines was the first U.S. force to hoist the Stars and Stripes over territory in the Old World. The Mameluke sword, carried by Marine officers to this day, memorializes O'Bannon's feat.

While events in the Mediterranean held the spotlight, Marines, together with Army and Navy forces, were active at home in Georgia, east Florida, and the lower Mississippi valley. In 1804, a 106-man Marine detachment was established at New Orleans.

✦✦ *The War of 1812*

During the first two years of the War of 1812, the main American achievements were at sea and on the Great Lakes. Marines fought in the great frigate duels of the war as well as at the Battle of Lake Erie (10 September 1813).

The outstanding record among seagoing Marines, however, was set by Captain John M. Gamble, who led the Marine detachment on board *Essex*, the raider that virtually destroyed England's Pacific whaling trade. He was the first Marine, and remains the only one known, to command a U.S. Navy ship. Late in 1813, Gamble, commanding the prize ship *Greenwich* with a crew of fourteen Marines and seamen, joined Captain David Porter in the Marquesas Islands and established a base where they could rest and refit over the winter. In the spring, Porter sailed for the coast of South America, leaving Gamble with twenty-two volunteers and six prisoners of war to man the base, should it be needed after a battle with the British, and safeguard the captured armed whalers *Seringapatam*, *Greenwich*, and *Sir Andrew Hammond*. In May 1814, a mutiny broke out on board the *Seringapatam*, and Gamble was put in a small boat with four others. He and his men then set fire to *Greenwich* before making it to *Sir Andrew Hammond*. When Marquesas natives attacked *Hammond*, Gamble, who had been wounded in the foot during the mutiny, hopped from cannon to cannon to fire them and beat off the attack. Gamble somehow got the ship under way with no charts and a crew of eight scarcely able to sail the vessel. He and his men made the Hawaiian Islands, only to be captured in 1814 by a British man-of-war. For all these exploits, Gamble was awarded a richly deserved brevet as lieutenant colonel.

In mid-1813, British forces under Rear Admiral George Cockburn and Major General Robert Ross began a campaign of raids against the Middle Atlantic Seaboard. A year later, in August 1814, a column of British soldiers, sailors, and marines advanced on Washington, D.C. On 24 August, after the federal government had fled to Frederick, Maryland, an irresolute force of American soldiers and militia under Brigadier General William H. Winder of the U.S. Army attempted to halt the much smaller British column at Bladensburg, just east of Washington. Reinforcing Winder's 6,000 soldiers was Commodore Joshua

During the War of 1812, sharpshooting Marine riflemen dominated the action between the U.S. Sloop of War *Wasp* and HMS *Reindeer* in 1814.

Barney's 114 Marines from the barracks at "Eighth and Eye" and a contingent of seamen gunners with five guns.

Winder's soldiers broke and ran at the first volley from the British, who advanced unconcernedly until they arrived at a piece of high ground occupied by Barney's men. Marine volleys and Navy gunnery forced the British (seven times stronger) to halt, deploy, and finally charge, three times in succession, at a cost of 249 men. After suffering a more than 20 percent casualty rate and being forced rearward by a double envelopment, the Marines and Sailors withdrew in good order, with at least a moral victory to their credit.

The British, having put Washington to the torch, were now determined to seize New Orleans.

Although a peace treaty was being signed in Europe, the British expedition forced its way up the Mississippi River. On 28 December 1814, the first enemy attack spent itself against an American line led by Major General Andrew Jackson, with Marines holding the center. Less than two weeks later, on 8 January 1815, the British tried again. Despite a courageous assault by the redcoats, Jackson's main battle position stood unbroken. As the British commander, Major General Sir Robert Pakenham, fell mortally wounded, the attack ebbed. New Orleans was saved, and the Marines shared in the glory when Congress recognized their "valor and good conduct."

➤ EPOCH OF THE "GRAND OLD MAN OF THE MARINE CORPS"

➤ ➤ *Archibald Henderson Takes Over*

Following the War of 1812, one of the most important events in the history of the Marine Corps took place, on 17 October 1820, when the adjutant and inspector, Archibald Henderson, succeeded Lieutenant Colonel Anthony Gale and became the fifth commandant. Gale's term as commandant had been cut short by a poorly timed dispute with Secretary of the Navy Smith Thompson that resulted in his removal and court-martial.

During the thirty-nine years and ten presidential administrations that followed, Henderson dominated the Corps and gave it the high military character it holds to this day. Had it not been for Henderson's firmness, reinforced by a sympathetic Congress, the Corps might well have been abolished in 1829, when President Andrew Jackson attempted (with connivance from certain influential naval officers) to transfer the Marines to the Army. After the smoke of controversy had cleared, Congress in 1834 placed the Corps directly under the Secretary of the Navy and increased its strength. This was the first instance of congressional redress and rescue for the Marine Corps—something that would recur repeatedly.

From 1836 through 1842, the Army, Navy, and Marine Corps collaborated to transfer the Creek and Seminole Indians of Georgia and Florida to new reservations in the West. Commandant Henderson spent part of this time in the field at the head of a mixed brigade of Army troops and a Marine regiment, the first organization of that size in the history of the Corps. At the Battle of Hatchee Lustee, Florida, in 1837, Colonel Henderson won one of the few decisively successful victories of the campaign and was thereupon breveted brigadier general—making him the first general officer in Corps history. Despite this success, as well as others

Archibald Henderson held the position of commandant
for thirty-nine years (1820–59), shaping the character of
the Corps in the nineteenth century.

against the Creeks, the Seminoles continued an obstinate resistance. When the
wars ended in 1842, most of the Seminoles still remained in Florida.

❯ ❯ *To the Halls of Montezuma*

The Mexican War included three distinct campaigns: one against Monterrey; one
against Mexico City; and one against California and the west coast of Mexico.
Marines took part in two of these and were, in fact, the first U.S. forces to set
foot on the soil of Mexico proper (at Burrita on 18 May 1846).

A battalion of Marines formed part of Major General Winfield Scott's column
that advanced from Veracruz, on the Gulf of Mexico, toward Mexico City.
The key to taking the Mexican capital was Chapultepec Castle, set on a crag

Marines participated in the campaigns against the Creek and Seminole Indians,
including service with the Navy's "Mosquito Fleet" of river-patrol boats.

commanding the swamp causeways into the city. For the assault on Chapultepec
on 13 September 1847, the Marines were divided into storming parties to head
the attack up the southern approach.

Under a hail of fire, the Marines moved out. Major Levi Twiggs, the battalion
commander, fell early in the attack, while Captain George H. Terrett, a company
commander, pressed home a separate assault toward the Mexican capital. After a
night on the outskirts of the city, the Marines marched through its gates in the
van of their division—the first U.S. troops to enter Mexico City—and occupied
the palace of the Montezuma on 14 September 1847. A new phrase had been
added to the annals of the Corps, and the exploit was later forever memorialized
in the first line of "The Marines' Hymn."

On the Pacific coast, Marines joined naval landing parties taking possession
of Monterey, Yerba Buena (San Francisco), Los Angeles, and San Diego. Around
this time, First Lieutenant Archibald Gillespie served as the confidential agent of

President James Polk in the diplomatic intrigues over California. He subsequently distinguished himself as a bold combat leader.

With California uneasily at rest but under U.S. control by 1847, Marines of the Navy's Pacific Squadron secured the Mexican west-coast ports of Mazatlán, Guaymas, Mulejé, and San José del Cabo. Marines garrisoned Mazatlán until June 1848, when peace was concluded.

❥ ❥ *Between the Wars*

The decade following the peace treaty with Mexico was hardly one of peace for the Marine Corps, despite its postwar reduction to approximately twelve hundred officers and men.

The opening of Japan in 1853–54 provided a setting for the historic landing of almost one-sixth of the Corps—six officers and two hundred Marines, commanded by Major Jacob Zeilin, a Mexican War hero and future commandant. In the best traditions of the Corps, Major Zeilin's Marines were the first U.S. armed forces to set foot on Japanese soil.

Hardly as peaceful were the landings in China at Shanghai (1854) and Canton (1856). In each of these, the conflicts represented trials of strength between the local Chinese and the Americans bent on "opening" China. At Canton's Barrier Forts, for instance, 176 Chinese cannon were taken and five thousand Chinese put to flight.

In subsequent years, Marines saw action a hemisphere away, in Nicaragua, Panama, Paraguay, and Uruguay. With the discovery of gold in California, the Panamanian isthmus assumed great importance in 1855, when Americans finally opened a rickety railroad across it. Soon, Panama became a hotbed of disorder, which led to several landings by Marines, ultimately including a brigade-sized force in 1885. In Uruguay and Paraguay, the story was the same—unsettled times, immature governments—and Marines protected U.S. interests.

At home, in Washington, Marines were called out in 1859 to stand off the Plug Uglies, a gang of Baltimore mobsters that operated with a loaded brass cannon for emphasis. While Marines and rioters faced each other across a downtown square, an old man, armed only with a gold-headed cane, stepped forward and placed his body across the muzzle of the mobsters' cannon. This gentleman was

Brevet Brigadier General Henderson, fifth commandant of the Marine Corps, now seventy-four years old. While the thugs milled about the steadfast old man, a squad of his Marines rushed the cannon, ending the confrontation.

❯ MARINES IN A NATION TORN ASUNDER

❯ ❯ *The Civil War*

For the Marine Corps, the opening shots of the Civil War sounded almost two years before the Confederate attack on Fort Sumter. On 17 October 1859, shortly after Colonel John Harris had succeeded Henderson as commandant, the president dispatched eighty-eight Marines to Harpers Ferry, Virginia, to recapture the U.S. Arsenal, which had been seized by the insurrectionist John Brown. Upon arrival, the Marine forces reported to Colonel Robert E. Lee, the senior U.S. Army officer present. When Brown refused to surrender, the Marines, led by First Lieutenant Israel Green, smashed their way under fire into his stronghold, wounded the abolitionist, and quelled the insurrection.

After 1861, the Marine Corps—like the regular Army—was never large enough to fill the demands upon it. A Marine battalion fought in the First Battle of Bull Run (Manassas), and other Marine forces served ashore in the Mississippi Valley and in the defenses of Washington. All along the Confederate-held seaboard, from Hatteras Inlet to Hilton Head and Fort Pickens, shipboard Marines, sometimes in provisional battalions, executed successful landings, which put teeth into the Union blockade. Only at Fort Fisher did Marines share with the Navy a bloody defeat.

By and large, the Corps did not gain in reputation during the Civil War. Its strength remained small, at only 4,161 officers and men. In addition, the Corps was not called on to perform either the readiness or amphibious tasks peculiar to the organization. Attempts to disband the Marine Corps and merge it into the Army in 1864 and in 1867 failed when Congress once again stepped into the breach to save it.

❯ ❯ *Post–Civil War*

Some have characterized the period from 1865 to 1898 as one of marking time by the Marine Corps, but this scarcely holds up. During these years, Marines landed to protect American lives and property in Egypt, Colombia, Mexico,

China, Cuba, the Arctic, Formosa, Uruguay, Argentina, Chile, Haiti, Alaska, Nicaragua, Japan, Samoa, and Panama.

In addition to these and many minor landings, in 1871 a combined Marine-Navy landing force of the Asiatic Fleet was sent to the west coast of Korea, where, after storming an elaborate system of forts along the Han River, it captured 481 guns and fifty Korean battle standards. In this fighting, two Marines tore down the Korean flag over the enemy citadel under intense fire and consequently were awarded Medals of Honor, the first of many to be conferred for action on the soil of the Hermit Kingdom.

Three able commandants—Jacob Zeilin, Charles G. McCawley, and Charles Heywood—did much to spark the Corps out of the Civil War doldrums. Despite its small strength, still below three thousand men, the Marine Corps was in excellent shape when the United States declared war on Spain in 1898.

❧ ❧ *War with Spain*

On the night of 15 February 1898, the battleship *Maine* (ACR 1) suddenly exploded and sank in Havana Harbor. Twenty-eight Marines were among the 266 casualties. During the attack, Private William Anthony, Captain Charles D. Sigsbee's orderly, intrepidly rescued the captain despite great personal danger, making Anthony the first U.S. hero of the impending war.

On 1 May, less than a week after the declaration of war, Commodore George Dewey destroyed the Spanish squadron in Manila Bay. Two days later, he landed Marine detachments to secure Cavite Navy Yard and settled down for a three-month wait until the Army could get troops to the Philippines.

Marines were first to land in the Philippines, and they were similarly the first U.S. forces to go ashore and fight in Cuba. On 10 June, an Atlantic Fleet battalion of Marines, commanded by Lieutenant Colonel R. W. Huntington, landed under cover of ships' guns at Guantánamo Bay, Cuba, and seized an advanced base for the fleet. Four days later at Cuzco Well, Huntington routed the remaining Spanish forces, destroyed their water supply, and completed the victory. The hero of the day was Sergeant John H. Quick, who was awarded the Medal of Honor for semaphoring while under U.S. and Spanish shellfire for an emergency lift of the naval bombardment.

After the war with Spain in 1898, Marines remained in the Philippines on guard duty, with the contingent eventually swelling to brigade size to assist in suppressing the Philippine Insurrection.

Huntington's battalion was not the conventional ship's landing party of the nineteenth century but rather a self-contained Marine expeditionary force that included infantry, artillery, and a headquarters complement of specialist and service troops. The battalion formed part of the fleet as a miniature fleet marine force whose primary mission was landing on hostile shores to secure an advanced base. It was a precursor to the modern Marine air-ground task force.

⤻ ADAPTATION, INNOVATION, AND EXPANSION OF THE CORPS AMID MODERN TOTAL WAR

⤻⤻ *"Our Flag's Unfurl'd to Every Breeze"*

Between 1899 and 1916, the Marine Corps participated in eight major expeditions or campaigns: the Philippine Insurrection, the Boxer Uprising, Panama, the Cuban Pacifications, Nicaragua, Veracruz, Haiti, and Santo Domingo (now the Dominican Republic).

Long oppressed by Spain, Filipinos in 1899 sought to make a clean break with colonialism and launched the Philippine Insurrection—or rather transferred the target of their insurrection from the Spanish to the Americans. The subsequent three-year campaign to quell the rebellion included the first modern Marine brigade. In addition, three exploits took place for which the Corps will be remembered: Major Littleton T. Waller's march across Samar, the storming of Sojoton Cliffs in Samar (where Captains David Porter and Hiram Bearss distinguished themselves in action, resulting in a Medal of Honor for each), and the pacification of the Subic Bay area on Luzon.

As 1900 dawned, China was experiencing one of its periods of xenophobia— this one known as the Boxer Uprising. In Tientsin and Peking, bloodthirsty Chinese mobs besieged foreign missions. In Peking, U.S. and British Marines joined forces and, together with other foreign garrisons, defended the beleaguered Legation Quarter throughout the summer of 1900. Later, the international relief column dispatched to relieve Tientsin and Peking included a U.S. Marine force commanded first by Major Waller—who in China befriended then-lieutenant Smedley Butler—and then by Major William P. Biddle, who eventually became the eleventh commandant of the Marine Corps.

At almost the same time, conditions in Panama began to threaten free transit across the isthmus. In 1903, on orders from President Theodore Roosevelt, a U.S. Marine brigade led by Major General George F. Elliott, the commandant, landed at Colón to protect U.S. rights during Panama's revolt against Colombia. Marines remained in the Canal Zone—the Panama Canal was still under construc-tion—until the situation became fully routine in 1911, when the Army took over.

First in 1906 and again in 1912, Marine brigades were sent to Cuba to restore order under the so-called Platt Amendment, by which the United States reserved the right to intervene in that newly liberated country. Marines occupied twenty-four towns in 1906 and twenty-six in 1912. Considerable fighting took place in eastern Cuba before peace was finally attained.

In response to circumstances like those in Cuba, Marine forces were also dispatched to protect U.S. interests and restore order in Nicaragua in 1912 and Santo Domingo in 1916.

When President Woodrow Wilson was obliged to protect U.S. rights, property, and citizens in Mexico in 1914, Marines from the Advanced Base Force, under development since 1901 and officially activated in 1913 (and described further below), were the first to land in the country, at Veracruz. Army forces followed. Veracruz provided the first field test of the Advanced Base Force, which it passed with flying colors.

Early in 1915, Haiti was wracked by revolution. Ship's detachments landed, but the situation called for reinforcement by units of the Advanced Base Force. The pacification of Haiti proved to be long and arduous. Bandits were firmly established in the north, where rugged mountains gave them every advantage. Under the dynamic leadership of Waller, now a colonel, and Butler, now a major, Marines finally brought the bandits to battle in their stronghold at Fort Rivière. During the storming of the fort, Butler displayed gallantry that led to his second Medal of Honor, having been awarded his first for actions at Veracruz. The resulting victory brought peace to northern Haiti. The Marines rebuilt civil government, and, for the time being, Haitians breathed easily.

All these deployments again dramatized the ability of the Corps to take effective action on short notice. But at least as important, and possibly more so, Marine developments and innovations during this period laid the foundation of U.S. amphibious-warfare techniques and ensured the future survival and growth of the Corps.

With the twentieth century, the Marine Corps began special training and developed organizations for the seizure and defense of advanced bases. Succeeding years saw increased use of battalions and regiments based in Navy transports as a means of projecting naval power beyond the shoreline. In 1910, at New London, Connecticut, Major General Elliott, the tenth commandant, established the Marine Corps Advanced Base School. For the first time in U.S. history, a military school had been created to focus the thinking of an entire service on the unsolved problems of amphibious warfare and to develop expeditionary readiness.

Hand in hand with the establishment of the Advanced Base School was the introduction of the Advanced Base Force in 1914, a Marine brigade containing all the necessary combined arms, maintained in readiness for immediate expeditionary service with the fleet. The Advanced Base Force was the prototype of the Fleet Marine Force (FMF).

By the end of 1916, the Corps had completed a major era of growth. It had become, in fact if not in law, a national force in readiness. Additionally over

Among the "First to Fight," the 4th Marine Brigade arrived in France during World War I and joined the Army's 2nd Infantry Division in 1918.

this period, Marines planted the seeds of amphibious-warfare doctrine, and the future leadership of the Corps gained experience in recurrent combat and expeditionary operations, which was destined to pay off for years to come.

❧ ❧ Marines "Over There"

Although Marines served faithfully around the globe, and their commitments in Cuba, Nicaragua, Haiti, and Santo Domingo remained little changed, the preeminent Marine story of World War I is that of the 4th Marine Brigade in France.

The 4th Brigade was the largest unit of Marines assembled up to that point in the Corps' history. Composed of the 5th and 6th Regiments and the 6th Machine Gun Battalion, it totaled 9,444 officers and men. Of the brigade's succession of notable actions—Belleau Wood, Soissons, Saint-Mihiel, Blanc Mont Ridge, and the Argonne—Belleau Wood was the most significant because it was the greatest battle, up to that time, in the history of the Corps. The casualties of the 4th Marine Brigade in assaulting the well-organized German center of resistance there were unmatched until the hardest-fought beach assaults of World War II. After Belleau Wood, German intelligence evaluated the Marine brigade as "storm troops"—the highest rating on the enemy's scale of fighting men.

By 11 November 1918, the 4th Marine Brigade and Marine aviation units in France had sustained more casualties in eight months of almost-continuous combat than had the entire Corps during the preceding 143 years. The grim total was 11,366 men.

Also noteworthy "over there" was Marine Corps aviation's baptism by fire. Founded in 1914 as part of the Advanced Base Force, Marine aviation was still in its experimental stages when World War I began. During the war, these aviation

For the first time, Marines in World War I faced a modern and well-trained adversary on a major scale.

units flew in combat over France and supported the fleet from an advanced base in the Azores. The spark plug of Marine participation in the air war was Major Alfred A. Cunningham, the Corps' first pilot. Starting from a strength of 7 officer pilots and 43 enlisted men in 1917, Marine aviation mustered 282 officers and 2,180 enlisted men by war's end. In the best traditions of the Corps, the 1st Aeronautical Company, destined for the Azores, was the first completely equipped aviation unit to leave the United States for service overseas.

In August 1918, the first women to wear the Globe and Anchor enlisted in the Marine Corps. They totaled 305 in all and were immediately nicknamed "Marinettes," an obvious derivative of the Navy's contemporary "Yeomanettes." Although the duties and scope of action of a Marinette—whose top possible rating was sergeant—were much more limited than those of today's female Marines, their spirit was similar.

❯ ❯ Expeditions between World Wars

The year 1919 found the Corps performing occupation duty along the Rhine while continuing or resuming security and stability operations in the Caribbean. Marines continued to occupy eastern Cuba, which was ultimately pacified in 1922. Two years later, in 1924, six hard-fought campaign years in Santo Domingo came to an end, and Marines were finally withdrawn.

Between 1918 and 1920, Haiti remained at a boil, with banditry again in full cry. Following the suppression of bandit forces in 1922, Brigadier General John H. Russell, an expert in Haitian affairs, was appointed U.S. high commissioner to administer the American protectorate over the troubled republic. It was not until 1934 that the 1st Marine Brigade hauled down its colors in Port-au-Prince and boarded ship for home.

The year 1927 was marked by trouble in both Nicaragua and China. Naturally, Marines were soon involved.

As early as 1912, Marines had landed in Nicaragua to preserve order. They were withdrawn in 1925. No sooner were they out, however, than the worst civil war in the history of Nicaragua erupted, and Marines (spearheaded by ship's detachments) were again dispatched in 1927 at the mutual request of the leaders of both warring factions. Marine occupation continued after an uneasy peace, its primary duty being the disarming of dissidents. The native Guardia

In the aftermath of World War I, more than three hundred women served in the Women's Reserve during the period 1918–19.

Nacional, much like the Marine-trained Gendarmerie d'Haiti, was organized under the Marines to police an unruly population that included thousands of demobilized revolutionary soldiers.

Marine aviation not only played a leading role in supporting ground operations in Nicaragua but also pioneered tactical and logistic air support on a scale hitherto unknown. The technique of dive-bombing, invented by Marine aviators in Haiti in 1919, was greatly refined. Practically all the isolated patrols and outposts in the

Major General John A. Lejeune (*left*) and Brigadier General
Wendell C. Neville returned from France in 1919 to lead
the Corps into its amphibious era as the thirteenth and
fourteenth commandants, respectively.

dense jungles of northern Nicaragua were maintained by air supply. To evacuate
Marine wounded, First Lieutenant Christian F. Schilt made ten landings and
takeoffs from a village street in Quilali in a fabric-covered scout plane under
murderous fire. Lieutenant Schilt was awarded the Medal of Honor.

When the Marines left Nicaragua in 1933, they turned over to that country's government a well-organized Guardia, a military academy, a system of

communications, and a first-rate public health service, plus many less obvious improvements.

As in Nicaragua, Marine embassy guards had been stationed in China for many years before 1927. There, too, civil disturbances of increasing violence reached a peak in 1927, and the United States rushed in additional forces—the 4th Marines to Shanghai and a brigade to North China. These precautions eased the threatening situation, and the brigade was withdrawn. The remaining units in Shanghai, Peking, and Tientsin faced crisis after crisis with Chinese warlords and the Japanese until World War II intervened.

❧ ❧ Guarding the U.S. Mail

In 1921, after a series of violent mail robberies, President Warren G. Harding directed the Marine Corps to guard the "United States mails." Within hours, armed Marines were guarding mail cars and trucks, with orders to shoot to kill. Not a single successful mail robbery took place against a Marine guard, and in less than a year they were withdrawn. Five years later, when mail robberies resumed, Marines were called in again; this time as well, the robberies ended at once.

❧ ❧ Amphibious Pioneering

In the early 1920s, it became clear to the Corps that a war with Japan would entail the amphibious seizure of a chain of advanced bases across the expansive Pacific. In 1921, the year after Marine Corps Schools opened at Quantico, the course of a possible war with Japan was forecast by Lieutenant Colonel Earl Ellis, who subsequently died while on an intelligence mission in the Japanese Palau Islands in 1923.

To Major General John A. Lejeune, thirteenth commandant, the prospect of amphibious warfare was bleak. The British failure at Gallipoli during World War I had convinced orthodox military thinkers that an amphibious operation could not succeed against strong opposition. Despite the forbidding nature of the problem, Commandant Lejeune set the Marine Corps to solving it.

Quantico became the focal point of U.S. fleet–centered amphibious development. Marine Corps Schools attacked the problem and, by 1934, had produced the first comprehensive U.S. manual of amphibious doctrine: *Tentative Landing Operations Manual*. This historic document was adopted intact by the Navy in

These primitive tactical exercises carried out by Marines during
the interwar years forged the vital amphibious doctrine that would
contribute to the defeat of Japan in World War II.

1938 as Fleet Training Publication 167, *Landing Operations Doctrine, U.S. Navy.*
In 1941, when the Army issued its first amphibious publication, Quantico's book
was again borrowed verbatim, even down to the illustrations, this time as War
Department Field Manual 31-5. Its tenets still constitute much of the basis for
current amphibious doctrine, and *Tentative Landing Operations Manual* served as
a model for the recently developed *Tentative Manual for Expeditionary Advanced
Base Operations.*

To deal with the matériel aspects of amphibious problems, the Marine Corps
Equipment Board was established in 1933. Most notable among the board's
pre–World War II achievements was the amphibian tractor, or LVT (Landing
Vehicle, Tracked), which joined the FMF in 1940.

During these pioneering years, the Advanced Base Force was redesignated
in 1921 as the East Coast Expeditionary Force. Then in 1933 it became the Fleet

Marine Force after Major General John H. Russell, later the sixteenth commandant, persuaded the Secretary of the Navy that Marine expeditionary troops should form an integral part of the U.S. Fleet. The FMF not only constituted a force in readiness but also performed an invaluable role in testing the doctrine and matériel evolved by Marine Corps Schools and the Equipment Board, respectively. From 1935, annual fleet landing exercises enabled the fledgling FMF to find its footing as well as to keep the thinkers at Quantico progressing along sound lines.

Two architects of amphibious victory, Commandant Thomas Holcomb (*left*) and future Pacific amphibious corps commander Brigadier General H. M. Smith (*right*), meet at Quantico in late 1940.

Because of its pioneering efforts during the 1920s and 1930s, the Marine Corps—ground and aviation—was ready for amphibious warfare. Marines were ready also to train others to wage it when the opening salvos of World War II rocked the world. Before the war had run its course, seven Army divisions, including the first three Army divisions ever to receive amphibious instruction, were trained in landing operations by the Corps.

❧ ❧ *Occupation of Iceland*

In 1941, under the seventeenth Marine Corps commandant, Major General Thomas Holcomb, the FMF demonstrated its capabilities.

Garrisoned by British forces, Iceland was critical in the Battle of the Atlantic. President Franklin D. Roosevelt, who well knew Iceland's strategic importance, agreed with British prime minister Winston Churchill that the island should be reinforced by U.S. forces to deny its use to Germany. The Army was unable to mobilize ready forces for the deployment, so the president turned to the Marine Corps. Less than one week later, on 22 June 1941, the 1st Provisional Marine Brigade embarked and sailed. On 7 July, more than four thousand Marines debarked at Reykjavik. Once again first on the spot, the Corps had proved itself the national force in readiness.

❧ ❧ *"Uncommon Valor"*

When the United States entered World War II in December 1941, the Marine Corps totaled some 70,425 men, organized into two divisions, two aircraft wings, and seven defense battalions (advanced-base artillery units). By 1944, the Corps included six divisions, four aircraft wings, and corps and force troops to support two amphibious corps, which were the FMF's highest formations. The Corps' top strength was 471,905 officers and Marines.

Despite differences in terrain and character of operations, the South Pacific and Central Pacific campaigns displayed two of the Marine Corps' unique attributes: those in the South Pacific highlighted *readiness*, and those in the Central Pacific showcased *amphibious assault virtuosity*.

The Guadalcanal Campaign not only typified the South Pacific but also, more importantly, dramatized to the American public the function of the Fleet Marine Force. In 1942, on the heels of valiant Marine defensive fighting at

Wake Island, Midway, and Corregidor, the need for a U.S. advance base in the southern Solomons became clear. Guadalcanal, where the Japanese were already building an airstrip, was the logical target. Despite high-level prophecies of disaster and recommendations that the assault be delayed until the following year—the earliest that Army troops could be trained to participate—the 1st Marine Division received the job of taking Guadalcanal and adjacent Tulagi. On 7 August 1942, the Marines landed.

Margins were never slimmer during the Pacific War than on Guadalcanal. But by late November 1942, when Army troops began to arrive in strength, battered Henderson Field had been firmly secured by Marine ground and air forces. In the inner councils of Japan, leaders already acknowledged that a turning point of the war had been reached. It was the first U.S. offensive of World War II; the long road in pushing back Imperial Japan had begun.

The lesson of the Guadalcanal campaign was that without a *ready* Marine Corps, the operation could never have taken place. Undertaken as a purely naval effort by fleet units and Marines, the campaign demonstrated the importance of fleet expeditionary forces to sea power as well as the degree to which the Corps had placed itself in readiness for just such an occasion.

If Guadalcanal and subsequent operations in the South Pacific—New Georgia, Bougainville, and Choiseul, all 1943, and New Britain in 1944—proved that the Marine Corps was ready for war, the campaign across the Central Pacific displayed its virtuosity in amphibious assault.

The succession of Central Pacific battles—Tarawa, 1943; the Marshall Islands, Saipan, Guam, Tinian, and Peleliu, 1944; and Iwo Jima and Okinawa, 1945—was by hard necessity mostly a series of frontal assaults from the sea against positions fortified with every refinement that Japanese ingenuity and pains could produce. To reduce such strongholds, the amphibious assault came of age.

On Iwo Jima toward the end of the campaigns, as on Tarawa at the beginning, the fighting ability of the individual Marine came into sharp focus. Each battle was one of frontal assault and close combat against fortified positions. Tarawa was the first combat test of the Marine Corps doctrine for amphibious assault, which was demonstrated to work. Two years later, at Iwo Jima—the largest all-Corps battle in history—Marines reaped the benefit of their Tarawa experience (and the experience of many other hard-fought assaults) in the form

As in other World War II Pacific battles, success on Tarawa during 20–23 November 1943 rested on the fortitude and fighting abilities of the individual Marine.

of a tested, combat-proven assault technique. Without Tarawa, Iwo would not have been possible. Without the Marine Corps (and without the years of study, experimentation, and development at Quantico), neither Tarawa nor Iwo (or the battles in between) could have succeeded, let alone taken place.

But the story of the Marine Corps in World War II was more than the great record of its seaborne assaults. Beginning on 7 December 1941 at Wake, Marine aviation was also in the war. During every engagement, Marine fliers again helped forge the concept of the air-ground team. And just as World War II matured the long-studied amphibious assault doctrine of the Corps, so too the war witnessed the introduction of Marine close air support. In the reconquest of the Philippines, four Marine aircraft groups working with Marine air liaison parties on the ground demonstrated the value of the Corps' tactical air support (in this case for Army comrades).

World War II was not only a period of tactical innovation in the Marine Corps but also a time of major social change, for it marked the beginning of the end of racial discrimination in the Corps. Although approximately a dozen Black Marines had fought during the Revolutionary War, the Corps had subsequently implemented a policy of racial discrimination, denying African Americans the opportunity to serve as Marines from 1798 to 1942. The growing power of the civil rights movement in the 1930s and early 1940s, together with the onset of World War II, proved transformative.

On 25 June 1941, President Franklin Roosevelt issued Executive Order 8802, prohibiting racial discrimination in federal departments, agencies, and the armed forces. The executive order compelled the Corps, despite initial objections by

Alerted to the sighting of approaching enemy aircraft, Marine pilots "scramble" to their Corsair fighters based at Bougainville in 1944. In the foreground, one mechanic helps a pilot onto the wing of his aircraft, while another inserts a starting cartridge. *National Archives photo by T/Sgt Douglas White*

Major General Holcomb and others, to begin recruiting Black Marines. In early 1942, the Corps established a camp at Montford Point, adjacent to Camp Lejeune, North Carolina, as a depot for the segregated training of Black enlistees. Recruiting began thereafter, and on 1 June 1942, Alfred Masters enlisted as the first African American in the Marine Corps. More than 900 other African Americans enlisted in the succeeding months, and they began arriving for recruit training at Montford Point on 26 August. From 1942 to 1949, the Corps trained approximately 20,000 recruits at this depot. Most of these Montford Point Marines, as they came to be known, went on to serve and fight in service-support units in the Pacific during World War II.

Despite the official end of racial discrimination by the Marine Corps, segregation was a prominent feature at Montford Point and beyond, as unofficial discrimination persisted well past World War II. For example, the Montford Point Marines were not allowed into neighboring camps without being accompanied by a white Marine. In 1948, President Harry S. Truman issued Executive Order 9981, bringing an official end to segregation in the U.S. armed forces. The Marine Corps deactivated Montford Point as a recruit training depot in 1949.

World War II also marked a breakthrough for women when the Corps organized a "new" women's component on 13 February 1943. On this date, Commandant Holcomb, by then a lieutenant general, authorized the creation of the Marine Corps Women's Reserve. The first officers and enlisted women were trained beside Navy WAVES (Women Accepted for Volunteer Emergency Service) in existing naval schools for women. By May 1943, 75 women had completed officer training in a special course at Mount Holyoke College, in South Hadley, Massachusetts, and 722 had weathered recruit training. Later in 1943, the Corps established at Camp Lejeune the Women Reserve Schools, where centralized recruit and officer candidate training took place. Also included were several specialist schools for the 18,000 enlisted women and 821 officers of the Women's Reserve, or WR, as it was soon short-titled.

It was an emphatic tradition of the new branch of the Corps that there would be no trick nicknames for the group. As far as female Marines are concerned, now and in the beginning, any cute or coy moniker, official or otherwise, merely demeans the Marine Corps emblem, which they proudly wear. Today, this tradition is stronger than ever, and since the late 1990s, Marines who happen to

One of the first Montford Point Marines, Corporal Edgar R. Huff, inspects a weapon during recruit training at Montford Point, Camp Lejeune, North Carolina. *U.S. Marine Corps photo from the National Archives*

be women are known simply as Marines (or female Marines when a distinction is relevant).

Much of the initial tone and standard of the Women's Reserve was set in ordinary course by the parent Corps, but quite as much, if not more, was due to the ability and effort of the first director of the WR, Colonel Ruth Cheney Streeter. Colonel Streeter made it her objective to integrate the women reservists into the framework of the Marine Corps. It was her vision that lifted the World War II women from clerical specialization—the World War I role of the Marinettes—into more than two hundred separate occupational specialties and billets at every major Corps base in the continental United States and ultimately overseas.

By the end of the war, the FMF, with aviation and ground units, was poised for the invasion of Japan—an operation rendered unnecessary after Japan's surrender on 2 September 1945. The Marine Corps had grown from 19,354 in 1939 to nearly 500,000 in 1945. The victories in World War II cost the Corps 86,940 casualties. In the eyes of the American public, the Marine Corps was second to none and seemed destined for a long future. Fleet Admiral Chester W. Nimitz's ringing endorsement of Marine fighting on Iwo Jima might very well be applied to the entire Corps during World War II: "Uncommon valor was a common virtue."

❧ ❧ *The Postwar Marine Corps*

Although the Marine Corps enjoyed high public prestige at the end of World War II and seemed here to stay, the years 1946–49 were devoted to a searching examination into the mission of (and behind closed doors in high quarters, even the need for) the Corps. These doubts were inspired, as two commandants testified before Congress, by the Army General Staff, whose long-term objective (since before World War I) had been the restriction of the development of the Marine Corps or, as some asserted, its reduction to a minor security and ceremonial unit. The question was firmly—and Marines hoped finally—resolved by the National Security Act of 1947 (discussed in the next chapters), which gave the Corps firm missions and reaffirmed its status as the service uniquely charged with primary development responsibility for amphibious tactics, techniques, and doctrine. Subsequently, the Douglas-Mansfield Act, enacted in 1952, afforded the commandant coequal status among the Joint Chiefs of Staff in all matters concerning the Marines and established the modern organization of the Corps.

In many respects, the Great Pacific War of 1941–45 truly cemented the Marine Corps as a unique armed service in the minds of the American public.

While the roles, missions, and status of the Marine Corps were being debated in both the executive and legislative branches of the federal government, the Corps maintained occupation forces in Japan and northern China while completing an orderly demobilization unmarred by indiscipline or untoward incident.

At the end of World War II, save for about one hundred women officers and enlisted women retained on duty at Marine Corps Headquarters under Major Julia E. Hamblet (later to become a director of female Marines), the Women's Reserve went home. In 1948, however, Congress passed the Women's Armed Services Integration Act, and a new chapter opened. Henceforth, each service would have a career cadre of female regulars in addition to the reservists.

To head the regulars (then called "WM" for women Marines), General Clifton B. Cates, nineteenth commandant, chose Colonel Katherine A. Towle, assistant dean of women at the University of California at Berkeley and wartime successor of Colonel Streeter. On 12 June 1948, the Women's Reserve ceased existence, and on the succeeding 4 November, the so-called women Marines, WM, came into being. Members of the former WR were reenlisted into the Marine Corps Reserve, and many became members of the Organized Reserve.

Ultimately, the postwar FMF comprised two major forces, Fleet Marine Force, Pacific and Fleet Marine Force, Atlantic, assigned respectively to the Pacific and the Atlantic Fleets. Each force embodied a Marine division and an aircraft wing (both on reduced manning for budgetary reasons) with supporting logistic units.

❯ CRISIS AND CONFLICT DURING THE COLD WAR

❯ ❯ *The Korean War*

The Marine Corps numbered approximately seventy-five thousand when, on 25 June 1950 (June 24 in the United States and Europe), North Korean troops, supported by the Soviet Union and China, attacked South Korea. The FMF was deployed in two shrunken divisions at Camps Pendleton, California, and Lejeune. Aviation, which had narrowly missed transfer to the Air Force by Secretary of Defense Louis Johnson, was even thinner: eighteen squadrons, divided into two wings at Cherry Point, North Carolina, and El Toro, California, but thirty fighter squadrons in the Marine Corps Reserve. The chairman of the Joint Chiefs of Staff, General Omar Bradley, had predicted publicly, hardly eight months before, that the world would never again see a large-scale amphibious landing.

On 2 July, faced with mounting catastrophe, General of the Army Douglas MacArthur sent his first request to the Joint Chiefs of Staff for help from the Marines. In the following days, MacArthur sent five more pleas, culminating in a request for a war-strength Marine division and a war-strength aircraft wing.

The requirement for reinforcements, of course, resulted in mobilization of the Marine Corps Reserve. And like other elements of the Reserve, women found themselves mobilized only days after the onset of war in Korea, with thirteen Organized Reserve women's platoons responding to the call.

Within two weeks, the 1st Provisional Marine Brigade was crossing the Pacific headed for the Pusan perimeter, where shaken U.S. Army and Republic of Korea units were already streaming rearward. On 3 August, Marine F4Us from USS *Sicily* (CVE 118) scored first blood for the Corps in an air strike over Inchon. Four days later and eight years after Guadalcanal, ground elements of the brigade began plugging holes in the Pusan perimeter, and, for the first time, helicopters were flown in support of ground close combat—by Marines.

In Tokyo, U.S. Marine and Navy planners were refining General MacArthur's vision to relieve Pusan and retake Seoul by an amphibious stroke to be delivered

Colonel Lewis B. "Chesty" Puller (*right*), who distinguished
himself during the Inchon landings, studies the terrain before
advancing to another objective beyond Inchon.

at the Korean west coast port of Inchon. Because of extreme tidal fluctuation,
15 September was the only suitable D-day until mid-October.

Despite unprecedented haste in preparation and numerous calculated risks of
enemy opposition, geography, and hydrography, the Inchon landing was almost
anticlimactic in its success. As favorable reports poured in throughout D-day,
General MacArthur signaled, "The Navy and Marines have never shone more
brightly than this morning." Largely because of the amphibious capability and

readiness of the Corps, the United Nations forces were able to rout the North Korean army south of the 38th parallel, leaving it all but destroyed.

Then, on 25 November, after an eerie lull, Chinese troops hit the right wing of the U.S. Eighth Army, routed and dispersed at least one Army division, and launched an entire army group, eight divisions, against the 1st Marine Division.

The blow fell while the division's forward elements were west of Chosin Reservoir at Yudam-Ni. It is enough to record that in the face of "General Winter" and of every weapon, artifice, and attack in overwhelmingly superior strength, the division concentrated promptly; rescued and evacuated surviving remnants of adjacent, less ready Army formations; and commenced one of the great marches of American history, from Chosin Reservoir to the Sea of Japan.

Following amphibious withdrawal and a short "breather," the 1st Marine Division spearheaded the IX Corps spring offensive of 1951. At the same time, the 1st Marine Aircraft Wing continued to provide the preponderance of all close air support sorties, nominally credited to the Fifth Air Force, under whose control the wing now operated. The two Marine elements fought on through 1952 until the armistice in 1953.

The Korean War tested the "new Marine Corps" in readiness and fighting quality, and the Corps was found wanting in neither. It demonstrated to doubters, in high places and low, that amphibious operations were anything but dead. Korea proved, as had World War II before it, the high caliber and readiness of the Marine Corps Reserve. Corps close air support distinguished itself as an unrivaled capability. Most of all, in a time of immense upheaval in military techniques, Korea underscored that the military principles for which the Marine Corps stood remained as sound in 1953 as in 1775.

❯ ❯ *Mid-Twentieth Century*

There was no demobilization after the Korean War. The Marine Corps maintained the structure of three divisions and three wings that Congress had established in 1952, with one of each on the East and West Coasts of the United States and the third in the Far East (split between Okinawa and mainland Japan). From these major forces, battalions deployed afloat with the U.S. fleets in the Mediterranean and the Far East and frequently in the West Indies as well. A thorough modernization of the war-tested amphibious doctrine of the Navy and Marine

Steadily improving helicopters, such as the Sikorsky CH-37 Mojave, in service from 1956 to 1970, brought a new dimension to postwar Marine amphibious doctrine.

Corps, originally conceived in Quantico in the late 1940s, gave these forces assault helicopters and specially designed helicopter carriers as transports. Blending these sophisticated and original methods with the tried-and-true ones of seaborne assault by landing craft and amphibious tractors, or amtracs, the amphibious assault now had even greater shock power and flexibility.

Following Korea, it became clear that despite the ever-present threat of nuclear war, the characteristic pattern of the Cold War was one of limited operations and politico-military guerrilla warfare—in short, the type of small war in which the Marine Corps had become so thoroughly versed during the first 150 years of its existence. In the Far East between 1955 and 1963, Marines landed in the Tachen Islands, Taiwan, Laos, Thailand, and South Vietnam in countermoves against Communist pressure.

In the Mediterranean, not only did Marines land at Alexandria, Egypt, to help evacuate U.S. and foreign nationals during the Suez incident of 1956, but also, on an appeal from the Lebanese government, Marines secured Beirut against a Communist coup in July 1958. A Marine brigade, subsequently reinforced by Army troops, stood by for ten weeks until completion of both peaceful elections and a constitutional change of government in Lebanon.

In the Caribbean, the nation's October 1962 confrontation over the Soviet's planned deployment of missiles on Communist Cuba saw the island ringed with floating Marine landing forces, while other FMF units ensured that Guantánamo Bay remained safe and secure against Fidel Castro's aggression.

On 24 April 1965, a military coup d'état morphed and escalated into an attempt by rebel factions to gain control of the Dominican Republic. In a five-day bloodbath, the government of Santo Domingo ceased to exist. Revolutionaries fired on or penetrated eight foreign embassies, including that of the United States. In the late afternoon of 28 April, President Lyndon B. Johnson ordered the landing of the 3rd Battalion, 6th Marines, at Ciudad Santo Domingo from USS *Boxer* (LPH 4), lying offshore. It had been thirty-nine years since Marines last landed in the Caribbean (at Bluefields, Nicaragua, in 1926).

Quickly augmented to brigade size, the landing force, despite sporadic resistance in some areas, established a demilitarized international zone protecting the U.S. and other embassies. When Army airborne units eventually arrived, the Marines came under command of the Army. Marine forces withdrew once pacification of the city was complete.

During the years ahead, female Marines continued as an increasingly important part of the Corps. By the time of Vietnam, they (on a strength of some two thousand) filled many key billets, which released other, male Marines for field service. A symbolic watershed for the WMs came in 1965, when, during the Dominican revolt, a staff sergeant on duty at the U.S. embassy earned the first combat campaign medal awarded to a female Marine.

❧ ❧ *War in Vietnam*

Meanwhile, on the other side of the globe, the dragging war in Vietnam heated up. Marine helicopter unit—flying half of the total U.S. armed forces sorties and flight hours with only 20 percent of the helicopter capability in the country—had been in Vietnam since 1962. So had Marine radio reconnaissance troops and a Marine advisory mission to train the Vietnamese marine corps.

A Marine Corps M50 Ontos light armored antitank vehicle,
mounting six recoilless rifles, maneuvers through the streets
of Hue City, Vietnam, in 1968.

According to longstanding contingency plans, elements of the 3rd Marine
Division, supported by squadrons of the 1st Marine Aircraft Wing, deployed in
1965 to a strategic enclave, centered around Da Nang and the existing airbase
complex, in the north of the Republic of Vietnam (South Vietnam). This area had
not been selected by chance: it had a port, independent of Saigon and others, to
the south; it had beaches; and it commanded defiles near the coastal road and rail
networks. Its main and enduring disadvantage was that it was adjacent to some
of the most hardcore Vietcong regions, both to the south and inland to the west.

On the heels of the 3rd Division followed the 1st Marine Division and Marine
Aircraft Group 36, being split between Vietnam and Okinawa. By the end of
1965, almost two-thirds of the combat units of the Marine Corps were committed
to the war in Vietnam.

Marines established another coastal enclave adjacent to Da Nang at Chulai, with the objective of not only protecting the important airbases at each but also pacifying a populous and productive region. They used the "oil-stain" tactics originated in this very region by France's master of colonial warfare, Marshal Louis-Hubert-Gonzalve Lyautey. Consolidated under Headquarters, III Marine Amphibious Force, they soon came to grips with the Vietcong. Late 1965 was marked by sustained patrols, ambushes, and intermittent battles to connect the Da Nang and Chulai enclaves. Not only did 1966 bring more of the same but also more troops. By the end of that year, approximately sixty thousand Marines—more than one-sixth of all U.S. forces in Vietnam—were ashore and in the field. These units included troops from the newly reformed 5th Marine Division, not seen on the active list since World War II. In hard fighting throughout I Corps area and especially along the 17th parallel demilitarized zone, separating North and South Vietnam, Marines repeatedly turned back stubborn North Vietnamese Army (NVA) units. They saw intense combat in 1968 during both the Battle of Hué City, involving thirty-three days of unrelenting, block-by-block urban fighting, and the Battle of Khe Sanh, during which U.S. forces dropped over 100,000 tons of bombs and fired more than 158,000 artillery rounds in support of the combat base there defended by two Marine regiments.

Yet even as successes in combat and pacification mounted for the U.S. forces and their allies, the war was being lost. The native Vietnamese government proved unsuited to gain and sustain the loyalty and obedience of its population. In the United States, the public grew weary of the war, amplified daily on television and in the printed media, to the extent that President Johnson chose not to pursue reelection and Congress began to apply halters to the war effort.

In mid-1969, as the South Vietnamese armed forces took on responsibility for fighting more of their own war, American troop withdrawals began. By October, the first-in 3rd Division and 1st Wing had been phased out. By this time, the Communists had transitioned almost completely to terrorism and guerrilla warfare. At the year's end, 90 percent of the population of the Marine-held northern provinces were living in secure areas. Even so, the 1st Division still had ample work holding NVA forays at arm's length from the vital Da Nang area. More and more, however, the Army of the Republic of Vietnam was out front, while the Marines were now in support.

One landmark Marine Corps achievement had been to forge the capable, high-spirited South Vietnamese marine corps, whose splendid fighting during the all-out Communist offensive of 1972 did so much to hold the northern provinces. Yet in the end it was all in vain: abandoned by the United States, which also cut off its weapons and supplies, South Vietnam was destined to fall to the unrelenting Communist aggression.

By that time, however (save for Marine landing forces that covered the final evacuation of the U.S. embassies in Phnom Penh, Cambodia, and Saigon), the Marines' long war was over. In the words of Commandant Robert E. Cushman in April 1972, "We are pulling our heads out of the jungle and redirecting our attention seaward, reemphasizing our partnership with the Navy and our shared concern in the maritime aspects of our national strategy. . . . With respect to our standards—we will maintain them: in appearance, discipline, personal proficiency, and unit performance. Without them, we would not be Marines."

❥❥ *End of a War, End of an Era*

With the signing of the Paris Peace Accords on 27 January 1973, U.S. involvement in the war in Vietnam officially ended. Not only a war, but also an era, was coming to an end.

The military draft was replaced by an all-volunteer policy for U.S. armed forces, and societal roles for women were changing rapidly. Both of these factors would soon be reflected in the increasing number and widening role of women in the armed services.

On 1 February 1973—almost thirty years to the day that the first director of female Marines was sworn in to office—Colonel Margaret A. Brewer became the seventh, and final director. The only director without World War II service, she had entered the Corps during the Korean War, immediately following graduation from the University of Michigan at Ann Arbor in 1952.

In many ways, her service career paralleled that of the previous directors. She was commissioned during a war, at a time of acute personnel shortages, and faced the unexpected demands that wartime service entailed. Colonel Brewer served as director during a period of sweeping change. In the post-Vietnam years, the Marine Corps took positive steps, within the limits of its combat mission and organization, to integrate women more fully. Many of the actions that occurred in the coming years stemmed from recommendations made by a specially formed ad hoc committee on increased effectiveness and utilization of women in the Corps. In November 1973, this committee's recommendations were approved by the commandant with the written comment "Let's move out!" Among the most significant recommendations were the establishment of a pilot program to train women for duty with selected stateside elements of the Fleet Marine Forces; the assignment of women to all occupational fields except the combat arms; and the elimination of the regulation that prohibited women from commanding any but female units.

In 1974, the commandant approved a change in policy permitting the assignment of women to specified rear-echelon elements of the FMF, on the condition that female Marines not be deployed with assault units or units likely to become engaged in direct combat. The decision came at the conclusion of a successful six-month pilot program and carried the provision "that such assignment [of female Marines] not adversely affect combat readiness." Three years later, out of a total of approximately 3,830 female Marines on active duty, 600 were serving in FMF assignments. Another major step was taken in the following year. The Corps approved the assignment of female Marines to all occupational fields except the four designated as the combat arms (infantry, artillery, armor, and pilot and air crew).

Of necessity, some assignment restrictions did remain, including the preservation of a rotation base for male Marines; the need for adequate facilities for women; the availability of nondeployable billets for women; and the legal restrictions prohibiting the assignment of female Marines to combat ships and aircraft.

As women became more fully integrated in the Marine Corps, the decision was made to disestablish the Office of the Director of Women Marines following thirty-four years of existence. Its functions were transferred to other Corps staff agencies.

⊁ THE CORPS AT THE CLOSE OF THE TWENTIETH CENTURY
⊁ ⊁ *The Cutting Edge of Sea Power*
In the aftermath of Vietnam, the Corps not only trained for conventional contingencies involving the reinforcement of the North Atlantic Treaty Organization (NATO) as well as South Korea but also found its operating forces in

the Sixth and Seventh Fleets involved in patrolling waters off the Middle East and west Asian hot spots. Middle East tensions brought Marines ashore in Lebanon again during 1983–84. This time in Beirut, they drew fire by interposing themselves between warring factions as part of a four-nation peacekeeping force. On 23 October 1983, 241 U.S. service personnel—220 Marines, 18 Sailors, and 3 soldiers— were killed by a terrorist truck bomb at a Marine compound in Beirut. Emerging undaunted from the rubble, the survivors and a relief battalion continued in their presence mission until withdrawn six months later.

Almost immediately after the Beirut disaster, other Marines played a successful role in the U.S. liberation of the island of Grenada that commenced on 25 October 1983, ousting the Cubans and radicals in control there. Marines exploited light resistance to dash across the island and relieve pressure on bogged-down Army paratroopers and rangers in a model ninety-six-hour intervention.

Expeditionary action short of war proved especially heavy and varied as Marine Corps units participated in the U.S. intervention in Panama to depose Manuel Noriega on 20 December 1989 and evacuated foreign nationals and secured the U.S. embassy in Liberia during a civil war there on 6 August 1990. Finally, the greatest U.S. deployment since the Vietnam War found the majority of the Fleet Marine Force in or afloat off Saudi Arabia as part of the international expedition sent to protect Saudi Arabia and subdue Iraqi forces in the 1990–91 Gulf War.

❧ ❧ *Gulf War and the Aftermath*

In wake of the Iraqi seizure of Kuwait in August 1990, the president of the United States ordered U.S. Central Command (USCENTCOM) to reinforce and defend Saudi Arabia and the other Persian Gulf states, in concert with a growing international coalition determined to resist and ultimately expel Iraqi forces. Among the first U.S. forces to arrive in Saudi Arabia for this purpose was the 7th Marine Expeditionary Brigade, which deployed to the key port and petroleum center of al-Jubayl, with its aviation based farther south on the Gulf of Bahrain. Offloading heavy equipment from its habitually linked Maritime Prepositioning Squadron 1, the brigade reported ready for operations on 25 August, a mere ten days after arrival in theater.

The brigade stood alone only for a few days, as the follow-on elements of the I Marine Expeditionary Force (I MEF) began to arrive. Eventually growing to a force of over ninety thousand Marines and attached Navy personnel, U.S. Marine Forces Central Command, the Marine component command for USCENT-COM, included two reinforced divisions, an enlarged aircraft wing containing most of the Corps' aircraft inventory, and the bulk of two force service support groups. Over twenty thousand Marines and Navy personnel of the 4th and 5th Marine Expeditionary Brigades remained afloat, while I MEF moved to the Kuwaiti-Saudi frontier.

This, the most rapid and complex strategic deployment in Marine Corps history, used all forms of transportation, including military and commercial aircraft, naval and merchant shipping, and the ferrying of hundreds of Marine Corps aircraft, from fighters to ubiquitous observation planes, from bases in Arizona, California, Hawaii, North and South Carolina, and Japan. Thousands of reservists and retired Marines were mustered to reinforce or augment the forces as well as to replace deployed units and personnel in their former garrisons. An infantry regiment and numerous battalions, squadrons, and smaller units of the Marine Corps Reserve participated in line with regular units in both combat and support echelons.

After long periods of training, marshaling, and waiting, the campaign began with an air offensive against Iraqi forces on 16 January 1991. Marine aircraft flying from Saudi bases and the amphibious ships in the Persian Gulf mainly struck targets in Kuwait, with Marine fighter and electronic warfare cover being provided to the coalition forces at large. After air superiority had been established, ground units assembled along the frontier and prepared for their assault. The two reinforced Marine divisions stood south of the Kuwaiti border, free from the observation of the Iraqi defenders, who were being pounded mercilessly by coalition air forces.

On 24 February, the 1st and 2nd Marine Divisions attacked inside Kuwait. They forced their way through Iraqi barriers and brushed aside the frontline resistance. Mounted in a variety of tanks, assault amphibious vehicles, light armored vehicles, and trucks, the attacking regiments destroyed or captured whole battalions of Iraqi troops and swept through burning oilfields toward the capital, Kuwait City. Artillery barrages and repeated strikes by fighter-bombers and attack helicopters supported the advance of the regiments. After one hundred hours of combat, Marines dominated southern Kuwait, and neighboring Arab coalition forces mopped up the capital. The cease-fire came too soon for many elements of the Marine force to come into play. The Marines of the landing force, afloat in the Gulf, raided a few islands, landed a tactical reserve in the MEF rear, and provided aviation support to their comrades ashore.

Even faster than their initial deployment to the crisis area, the withdrawal of Marines from the theater proved breathtaking. Except for the service support units needed to remove the bulk of the accumulated supplies, the I MEF returned to its bases in barely six weeks' time. A total of twenty-four Marines were killed and ninety-two wounded in action.

Marines in the same year found themselves on humanitarian support missions in Bangladesh, Iraqi Kurdistan, and Somalia. They would deploy in strength to Mogadishu, Somalia, on 9 December 1992 as the leading edge of a great United Nations effort to end starvation and lawlessness there. Later, a Marine expeditionary unit (MEU) formed the U.S. ground cutting edge for the NATO-led intervention in Kosovo, in 1998. An increased naval and Marine Corps presence in the Indian Ocean littorals also marked the decade.

❯ EXPEDITIONS AND EVOLUTION IN A NEW CENTURY

❯ ❯ *9/11 and the Aftermath*

The 9/11 al-Qaeda attacks led to the deployment of U.S. forces to Afghanistan, the organization's initial base, and then, after the widening of the prosecution of what came to be called the Global War on Terror, into Yemen and Somalia followed by the invasion of Iraq in 2003. These measures produced military defeats of the enemy in each case, but they also led to long-term campaigns in Iraq and Afghanistan to occupy, pacify, and conduct security and stabilization operations to help establish and support governments capable of leading the two nations back into the peaceful international community.

The initial Marine Corps contribution for the campaign in Afghanistan, called Operation Enduring Freedom, began on 7 October 2002 and consisted mainly of the deployment of two MEUs—the 15th MEU and 26th MEU—combined to form Naval Expeditionary Task Force 58 under Brigadier General James N. Mattis. This provisional Marine expeditionary brigade launched combat forces and supporting aviation hundreds of miles inland to envelop the southeast portion of the country around Kandahar. These actions, combined with U.S.-assisted antigovernment forces of Afghans in the north, caused the flight of the Taliban leaders and the terrorist bands they had sheltered. A U.S.-approved provisional government took office in December. After this, Marine Corps forces continued rotational deployments over twelve more years to conduct security and stability operations in Afghanistan, finally departing in 2014. The ensuing pacification and security assistance programs continued against a resurgent Taliban until 2021, when remaining U.S. forces commenced their final withdrawal.

Such an unusual campaign, harkening back to Marine Corps antibandit operations of the early twentieth century, paled in comparison to the Corps' major contribution to the invasion and occupation of Iraq, called Operation Iraqi Freedom, beginning on 20 March 2003. The Corps provided half of the initial U.S. assault forces and a third of the forces in the initial campaign. The I MEF employed the 1st Marine Division and a regimental task force of the 2nd Marine Division with a reinforced 3rd Marine Aircraft Wing and 1st Force Service Support Group to sweep into southeastern Iraq. Detaching British Army and Royal Marine contingents and the 15th MEU to take Basra and the Faw Peninsula, I MEF continued north, routing the Iraqi army in a fast-moving battle and pursuit between the Euphrates and Tigris Rivers, past Kut, and into Baghdad. As the Iraqi government and military collapsed, the collective Marine Corps and Army forces secured Baghdad. Meanwhile, a mobile Marine light armored task force swept northward to Tikrit and Kirkuk to prevent any consolidation by Iraqi remnant forces and to link up with U.S. and free Kurdish forces to complete the seizure of the country in a matter of five weeks. These operations remain unprecedented in scope and sweep for Corps forces.

Marine Corps forces then undertook the occupation of south-central Iraq, between Baghdad and Basra, for another six months while the United Nations sorted out an international coalition to relieve U.S. forces. In the end, a continuing American presence emerged as a requirement, and I MEF returned to Iraq in February 2004 after a brief absence. A continuous occupation of western Iraq by Marine Corps forces (I and II MEFs in rotation) ensued.

Fielding I MEF for combat operations in Operation Iraqi Freedom caused considerable reverberations in the operating forces and supporting establishment of the Marine Corps during 2002–3. The Corps mobilized some 22,000 reservists by 1 May 2003 and still retained over 10,500 on duty in mid-October. Up to

Marine rifle squads go into action from their
amphibious assault vehicles in Iraq, 2005.

10,000 would remain on active duty after March 2004 for augmentation and
reinforcement tasks through continued call-ups and demobilization of reservists.
Active duty end strength had also climbed because of the stop-loss and stop-move
directives, reaching a peak of 179,630 in July 2003 but then subsiding to 177,756
at the end of September before returning to the authorized 175,000 by March
2004. As security and stability operations continued in Afghanistan and the
insurgent conflict in Iraq deepened in intensity, however, authorized strength
of the Corps began to grow again, peaking at 202,441 in 2010.

The commandant's key decision and planning guidance on 27 November 2003
settled the future of Corps deployments to Iraq. U.S. Marine Corps Forces Central
Command would be provided with a reduced MEF (forward) for operations in
Iraq. In addition to the MEF command element, a reduced Marine division of
nine maneuver battalions would meet the Joint Staff and USCENTCOM requirement and would be accompanied by the doctrinal aircraft wing and force service

support group, both tailored for the smaller ground combat element envisioned. A seven-month unit rotation policy figured as the keystone of the planning guidance. Although the Army and other services earmarked their deployments to Iraq for a thirteen-month cycle, Marine leadership maintained the customary deployment of six to seven months as having the best chance of preserving the continuing operations and sustaining the health of the Corps in its global commitments.

As over twenty thousand Marines and Sailors of I MEF took up their new positions in Iraq during 2004, equipped as well as the hurried measures and changing military environment allowed, the age-old problem remained: Who is the enemy, where is he, and what are his intentions? Combat operations of the campaign beginning in 2004 were characterized by major urban battles in the cities of Fallujah and Ramadi, counterinsurgency operations—both rural and urban—all over al-Anbar Province, and a continuing effort to rebuild, protect, and nourish the native society and economy of a former enemy nation.

The Second Battle of Fallujah deserves special mention, as many regard it as the peak of conflict for Marine Corps forces during the Iraq War. In November and December 2004, Marine forces led the combined American, Iraqi, and British offensive—codenamed Operation Phantom Fury and Operation al-Fajr—against the stronghold of Iraqi insurgents in the city of Fallujah. This battle represented the second major operation in the city; in April 2004, coalition forces had fought the First Battle of Fallujah to capture or kill insurgent elements considered responsible for the gruesome murder of four civilian contractors that year.

After a period of time shaping the battlespace, coalition ground operations began during the night of 7 November 2004 as the Iraqi 36th Commando Battalion, supported by U.S. Army Special Forces advisers and other Army and Marine Corps units, attacked from the west and south. The main assault commenced on 8 November as the 1st Marine Division attacked with two Marine regimental combat teams, Regimental Combat Team 1 (RCT-1) and Regimental Combat Team 7 (RCT-7), along the northern edge of the city. Two U.S. Army heavy units, the 2nd Battalion, 7th Cavalry Regiment and the 2nd Battalion, 2nd Infantry Regiment (Mechanized), joined RCT-1 and RCT-7 in the attack. The British Army's 1st Battalion, known as the Black Watch, patrolled the main highways to Fallujah's east. While coalition forces achieved their principal objectives and most of the fighting subsided by 13 November, the operation continued until 23 December, when coalition forces neutralized the last pockets of resistance in the city.

This battle was the bloodiest of the entire Iraq War and the bloodiest one involving U.S. military forces since the Vietnam War. It was also notable for being the first major engagement of the Iraq War fought solely against insurgents rather than the forces of Saddam Hussein's Ba'athist Iraqi government, which coalition forces had deposed in 2003. Based on figures collected from multiple sources, coalition forces suffered 107 killed and 613 wounded during Operation Phantom Fury / al-Fajr. Most estimates place the figure for insurgent casualties in the range of 1,200–2,000 killed, with Red Cross estimates of around 800 noncombatant deaths. The Second Battle of Fallujah marked some of the heaviest urban combat for Marines since the Battle of Hué City in 1968.

After a relatively brief respite, insurgent activity in and around Fallujah resumed in 2005 and escalated in 2006. Tactics developed during this period of counterinsurgency operations—applied now on a wider scale in the surrounding areas, including Ramadi—led to what became known as the Anbar Awakening, whereby Sunni tribes that had previously tolerated and even supported the insurgency against the Shiite-led Iraqi government were persuaded to partner with U.S. forces to eject the insurgents from their communities. After four years of bitter fighting, Fallujah was ultimately turned over to Iraqi forces and provincial authorities during the autumn of 2007. Three years later, Marine Corps forces completed their planned withdrawal from Iraq.

✦ ✦ *Birth of Marine Corps Special Operators*

The intensification of global counterterrorism operations following 9/11 increased the demand for forces specifically organized, trained, and equipped for special operations. This focused attention on U.S. Special Operations Command (USSO-COM), headquartered at MacDill Air Force Base in Tampa, Florida. Since USSO-COM formed in 1986, the prospect of a Marine Corps service component had been a topic of recurring discussion and debate. Some held that the Marines must have a presence in this important combatant command, while others believed that the creation of such a service component would sap the Corps of critical organic capabilities. In October 2005, however, the secretary of defense effectively ended the debate, directing formation of a Marine service component at USSOCOM.

Marine Corps Forces Special Operations Command (MARSOC) activated in phases beginning on 24 February 2006 at Camp Lejeune. It initially comprised a small headquarters staff and the Foreign Military Training Unit, which in short order became the Marine Special Operations Advisor Group (MSOAG). MARSOC rapidly absorbed both the 1st and 2nd Force Reconnaissance Companies from I and II MEF during the year following its activation, and these two units grew to form the 1st and 2nd Marine Special Operations Battalions (MSOBs). As MARSOC's capabilities expanded, the MSOAG was redesignated the Marine Special Operations Regiment during April 2009, with the 1st, 2nd, and 3rd MSOBs as subordinate units. To round out its capabilities and achieve a degree of self-sustainability, MARSOC eventually formed the Marine Special Operations Support Group (MSOSG), providing organic combat support and combat service support to MARSOC, and also the Marine Special Operations School, responsible for screening, assessing, selecting, and training Marine special operators as well as reviewing, developing, and refining special operations doctrine for the Corps.

Almost a decade after its initial activation, MARSOC incorporated the word "raider" into the names of its subordinate operational units in June 2015. Thus, the Marine Special Operations Regiment became the Marine Raider Regiment; the MSOBs, Marine raider battalions; and the MSOSG, Marine Raider Support Group. "Raider" evokes the rich heritage of MARSOC's predecessors from World War II, the four Marine raider battalions first activated in February 1942 that operated as special, amphibious light infantry forces waging irregular warfare across the Pacific and often operating behind enemy lines.

MARSOC units first deployed six months after initial activation in August 2006. Since then, MARSOC has continuously deployed Marine special operations teams, which conduct foreign internal defense, and Marine special operations companies, which conduct not only foreign internal defense but also special reconnaissance and direct action.

❧ ❧ *Crisis Response and Coalition Warfare*

Concurrent with and following operations in Afghanistan and Iraq, Marines remained engaged and active around the globe. In addition to conducting scheduled deployments to execute forward presence and theater engagement missions in support of combatant commanders, Marine Corps forces continued to respond to crises worldwide. After a catastrophic magnitude 7.0 earthquake shook Haiti in January 2010, the Corps rapidly deployed both the 22nd and 24th MEUs to restore order, provide security, and distribute support. A year later, in 2011, Marines returned to the shores of Tripoli in support of Operation Odyssey Dawn in Libya. Positioned off the coast of Libya, Marines of the 26th MEU were among the first to enforce the no-fly zone over that troubled country, and the unit also conducted a successful tactical recovery of aircraft and personnel (TRAP) mission using its MV-22 Ospreys, CH-53E Super Stallions, and KC-130J Hercules aircraft.

In the western Pacific, Marines stationed in Okinawa responded with supplies and support to a magnitude 9.0 earthquake that resulted in a 124-foot tsunami that devastated parts of mainland Japan in 2011. With more than forty-five thousand buildings in ruins and a snowstorm dropping temperatures to 15° Fahrenheit, the 31st MEU joined forces with the Japan Self-Defense Forces to deliver vital water, heating fuel, and other supplies to displaced residents in difficult-to-reach areas.

In response to the 2012 attack on the U.S. consulate in Benghazi, Libya, the Marine Corps established Special Purpose Marine Air-Ground Task Force Crisis Response Africa (resulting in the rather awkward acronym SPMAGTF-CR-AF) in 2013 as a self-sustaining Marine air-ground task force (MAGTF) designed for response to a range of potential crises in Africa. Commanded by a colonel and operating from Morón Air Base in Spain, the unit comprises a command element, company-size ground combat element, robust aviation combat element (a reinforced Marine medium tiltrotor squadron providing, among other capabilities, extraordinary mobility), and compact logistics combat element. SPMAGTF-CR-AF participates in bilateral and multilateral training with regional partners while remaining ready to execute missions such as embassy reinforcement, noncombatant evacuation operations, TRAP operations, humanitarian assistance, and disaster relief.

While Marines supported coalition operations in Libya, responded to natural disasters half a world away, and conducted theater engagement and crisis response operations across Africa, a new threat emerged in the Middle East from the remnants of al-Qaeda in Iraq, which had faded into relative obscurity with the

U.S. troop surge into Iraq during 2007. Despite the surge, Iraq never achieved durable stability. Meanwhile, catalyzed by the Arab Spring, neighboring Syria descended into civil war. In this vacuum of effective governance, al-Qaeda in Iraq resurfaced in 2011 and capitalized on growing instability in Iraq and Syria, carrying out successful attacks and bolstering its ranks over the next few years. A new mission awaited the Marines.

Revealing its true ambitions in 2013, the terror group renamed itself the Islamic State of Iraq and Syria (ISIS), alternately known as the Islamic State of Iraq and the Levant and colloquially by its Arab-language acronym Daesh. ISIS soon became the object of serious global concern, having seized control of Fallujah and portions of Ramadi in 2013 and captured Mosul and Tikrit, Iraq, and Raqqa, Syria, in 2014. From its "capital" in Raqqa, the group proclaimed a worldwide caliphate that June and referred to itself as simply the Islamic State. As the group's strength and ambitions grew, reports of atrocities spread, refugees multiplied, and the threat of global terror intensified. U.S. and coalition forces undertook a campaign to contain and eventually defeat the group, beginning with air strikes against ISIS targets in Iraq during August and in Syria during September. The Pentagon named the campaign against ISIS Operation Inherent Resolve in October. By early 2015, the anti-ISIS coalition included Australia, Bahrain, Belgium, Canada, Denmark, France, Jordan, the Netherlands, Saudi Arabia, the United Arab Emirates, the United Kingdom, and the United States.

MARSOC was active against ISIS, and Marines assumed staff and advisory positions with the coalition, but perhaps the Corps' most visible contribution to Operation Inherent Resolve was the creation and deployment of Special Purpose Marine Air-Ground Task Force Crisis Response Central Command (SPMAGTF-CR-CC) beginning in November 2014. Commanded by a colonel, it operates from al-Asad Air Base, Iraq; al-Jaber Air Base, Kuwait; Sheik Isa Air Base, Bahrain; and several undisclosed locations. The still-active unit is essentially a land-based, reinforced MEU numbering 2,300 personnel. SPMAGTF-CR-CC performs a bilateral training and advisory mission while remaining ready to execute missions such as TRAP, embassy reinforcement, noncombatant evacuation, humanitarian assistance, and disaster relief. Its most recent operations include support to combat operations during the liberation of Mosul, Iraq, from ISIS during 2016 and 2017; reinforcement of the U.S. embassy in Baghdad, Iraq, when it was attacked by

On 31 March 2021, this MQ-9A Reaper unmanned aerial vehicle completed 10,000 flight hours in support of contingency operations by Marine Corps Forces, Central Command.

Iran-backed protesters in 2019; and the final evacuation of Kabul, Afghanistan.

Meanwhile, the story of the complete integration of women in the Marine Corps entered its final chapter during this period. In December 2015, Secretary of Defense Ashton Carter announced that all military occupations would be open to women. The Corps initially requested a waiver but eventually relented. A female Marine officer completed the Infantry Officer Course for the first time in September 2017. And the first wave of female Marines joined the Marine Combat Training course at Camp Pendleton for integrated training in March 2018, graduating in early April. By late 2018, a total of ninety-two women were working in a variety of traditionally male-only combat billets across the Corps, from rifleman to armored reconnaissance to combat engineers; females serving in the infantry numbered only one officer and eleven enlisted personnel.

As was the case with Iraq, stability proved elusive in Afghanistan in the face of a recalcitrant and reconstituted Taliban. In January 2017, the Corps deployed a task force to Afghanistan's unruly Helmand Province, with which Marines had grown intimately familiar during a particularly challenging period from 2009 to 2014. Security in this enduring Taliban stronghold had deteriorated following the withdrawal of U.S. forces from there in 2014. The three-hundred-person task force joined Operation Resolute Support to advise and assist units of the Afghan National Army and National Police in their efforts to reverse Taliban gains in the region. Staffed predominantly by more experienced senior personnel, Task Force Southwest, as it was named, for more than three years aimed to enhance the Afghan units' abilities to develop and interpret intelligence, integrate their operations, and sustain their forces.

Eventually, the United States decided to conclude its twenty-year military expedition to Afghanistan in 2021. Saying it was "time to end the forever war," President Joseph Biden announced on 14 April that all troops would depart Afghanistan by the symbolic date of 11 September 2021. Subsequently, the Biden administration ordered the U.S. military's in-country strength reduced dramatically, which led to abandoning Bagram Airfield, the largest, most capable airfield in Afghanistan, on 6 July and consolidating the remaining forces at Karzai International Airport in Kabul. Two days later, the president advanced the deadline for full troop withdrawal to 31 August. This series of decisions and events contributed to the acceleration of a Taliban offensive, to the collapse of the Afghan government and security forces, to an apparently rushed noncombatant evacuation operation, and to a withdrawal reminiscent of the fall of Saigon nearly fifty years earlier. During this final operation, thirteen U.S. servicemembers, including eleven Marines and one Navy corpsman, were killed in a suicide bombing at the airport.

❧ ❧ *Reinvention Redux*

Responding to the evolving geopolitical situation and military operating environment, the 2018 *National Defense Strategy* caused the Marine Corps to redirect its focus from countering violent extremists in the Middle East to preparing for competition and conflict with major powers. Geographically, the Corps' new emphasis would be the Indo-Pacific region. Such a profound shift in missions, from nonstate actor to nation-state competitor and from inland to littoral, necessarily required a substantial reexamination of how the Corps is organized, trained, and equipped. It also involved a reaffirmation and renewal of its historic partnership with the Navy.

Marine field artillery launches rockets from a High Mobility
Artillery Rocket System (HIMARS) during live-fire training
at Adazi Training Area, Latvia, 2019.

This has precipitated a period of institutional introspection and analysis—
still ongoing—evocative of the period from 1921 to 1941, when the Marine
Corps developed the original tactics, techniques, procedures, and equipment
for amphibious operations.

In 2019, General David H. Berger, thirty-eighth commandant of the Marine
Corps, issued his planning guidance, which made force design—or, perhaps
more precisely, force *redesign*—the top priority. The Marine Corps and the Navy
together had, by this time, already published two important new concepts, *Littoral Operations in a Contested Environment* (2017) and *Expeditionary Advance Base
Operations (EABO)* (2018), to drive innovation, experimentation, and doctrine
development. In 2020, General Berger issued *Force Design 2030*, which envisions
and charts a four-phase, ten-year process to transform the Marine Corps by 2030.

Central to this transformation is the EABO concept. EABO is "a form of
expeditionary warfare that involves the employment of mobile, low-signature,

operationally relevant, and relatively easy to maintain and sustain naval expeditionary forces from a series of austere, temporary locations ashore or inshore within a contested or potentially contested maritime area in order to conduct sea denial, support sea control, or enable fleet sustainment." All expeditionary operations imply overseas deployment under austere conditions to project power. EABO differs from other expeditionary operations, however, because the executing forces must operate persistently within reach of the adversary's lethal and nonlethal weapons. Therefore, the composition, distribution, and disposition of forces executing EABO must limit the adversary's ability to target them, engage them, and otherwise influence their activities.

The redesign and transformation of the Marine Corps remains a work in progress in 2022.

❧ ❧ *Ever Adaptive, Ever Present, Ever Ready*

In addition to the intense combat, security, and stability operations in Afghanistan and Iraq during 2001–21, the Marine Corps' more recent operational actions and its nascent efforts to reinvent itself for an uncertain future illustrate the continuity in its story. In every clime and place, Marines have stood vigil ashore and afloat. Readiness, versatility, amphibious expertise, prowess in expeditionary operations, and ferocity in combat remain hallmarks of the Corps. As long as our nation remains a maritime nation with global interests and global responsibilities, Marines will form its cutting edge.

⟫{ 3 }⟪

THE DEPARTMENT OF DEFENSE AND THE ORGANIZATION FOR NATIONAL SECURITY

The raising of that flag on Suribachi means a Marine Corps for the next 500 years.

— James Forrestal

NUMEROUS ORGANIZATIONS within the government play a role in U.S. national security. To set the stage for an explanation of the Marine Corps' role, it is important first to provide an overview of the principal individuals, organizations, and agencies responsible for decisions, policies, and plans affecting national security and military operations. The Department of Defense (DOD), the largest department of the federal government, is obviously central to this discussion, but we begin with the president of the United States and the National Command Authority.

⟩ THE PRESIDENT AND THE NATIONAL COMMAND AUTHORITY

⟩ ⟩ *Executive Office of the President*

The U.S. Constitution gives the sole power to declare war to Congress, but the president bears ultimate responsibility to protect national security. To fulfill this responsibility, the president is the commander in chief of the armed forces as set forth in Article 2, Section 2 of the Constitution. The cabinet and the

Executive Office of the President provide the broad support that the president needs to govern effectively. Several individuals, agencies, and offices within the Executive Office of the President provide direct and indirect support to the president in the national security domain. Among these entities, the National Security Council (NSC) and the Office of Management and Budget (OMB) are particularly important to the armed forces. Beyond the Executive Office of the President, we must also consider a third, the Office of the Director of National Intelligence (ODNI), at this high level.

Although the composition has varied over time, today the term "National Command Authority" (NCA) refers collectively to the president and the secretary of defense. The NCA signifies the constitutional authority to direct the armed forces in their execution of military action. As commander in chief, the president is the ultimate authority. The secretary of defense carries out NCA decisions and directives by tasking the military departments, combatant commands (CCMDs), and separate defense agencies.

Figure 3-1 shows the flow of authority and direction through the organization for national security, from the president as commander in chief to the secretary of defense and the three military departments, eleven unified CCMDs, and a multitude of separate defense agencies and field activities.

❯ ❯ *National Security Council*

The NSC was established by the National Security Act of 1947 and altered by the National Security Act Amendments of 1949. Later that year, as part of the reorganization plan, it was placed in the Executive Office of the President.

The NSC is the president's principal forum for considering national security and foreign policy matters with senior advisers and cabinet officials. Since its inception in 1947, the NSC's function has been to advise and assist the president on national security and foreign policies. It also serves as the executive's principal arm for coordinating these policies among various government agencies.

Statutory members of the NSC comprise the president, who chairs the council; the vice president; secretary of state; secretary of defense; secretary of energy; and secretary of the Treasury. Regular nonstatutory participants include the assistant to the president for national security affairs, commonly called the national security adviser; the deputy national security advisor; homeland security

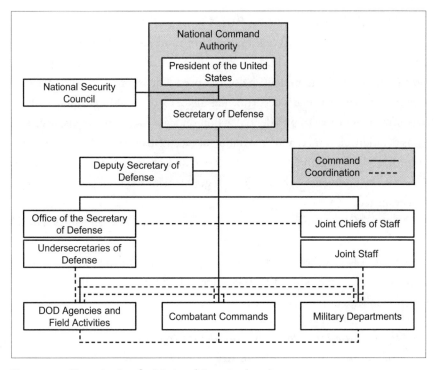

FIGURE 3-1. Organization for National Security (2021)

advisor; attorney general; and White House chief of staff. The chairman of the Joint Chiefs of Staff is the statutory military adviser to the NSC, and the director of national intelligence serves as intelligence adviser; subject to the direction of the president, they may attend and participate in NSC meetings. Secretaries and undersecretaries of other executive and military departments may serve as members of the council when appointed by the president and confirmed by the Senate. In addition, other government officials attend meetings as "standing request members" or on an ad hoc basis. The heads of other executive departments and agencies, as well as other senior officials, may attend meetings of the NSC when appropriate. The staff that supports the council is usually headed by a civilian executive secretary appointed by the president and includes officers and civilian officials primarily from DOD, the Department of State, and the five military services.

❧ ❧ *Office of Management and Budget*

Established in 1970, OMB has a number of functions. It helps the president prepare the government's budget, including the defense budget; supervises administration of the budget; helps the president improve governance and administration; coordinates departmental advice on proposed legislation, making recommendations as to presidential action on legislative enactments; assists in consideration, clearance, and preparation of executive orders and proclamations; improves, develops, and coordinates federal and other statistical services; and informs the president of the progress of government work proposed, initiated, or completed.

Thus, OMB is far more than is suggested by its title or even its mechanical functions. It functions, in fact, as a civilian "general staff" for the president. The power of the office—indeed, the ultimate power of the purse—and the continuity of its work give OMB considerable influence over DOD and the defense policies of the government.

❧ ❧ *Office of the Director of National Intelligence and the Intelligence Community*

The director of national intelligence (DNI), a position established in 2005, leads the ODNI. The DNI also functions as the head of the somewhat diffuse U.S. Intelligence Community, thus overseeing and directing the implementation of the national intelligence program and acting as the principal adviser to the president, the NSC, and the Homeland Security Council for intelligence matters related to national security. The president appoints the DNI with the advice and consent of the Senate. The director is assisted by a Senate-confirmed principal deputy director of national intelligence, recommended by the DNI and appointed by the president, and by several deputy directors and mission managers who lead various directorates, centers, and offices. Collectively, these compose the ODNI, whose overarching goal is to integrate foreign, military, and domestic intelligence in defense of the nation and of U.S. interests abroad.

The Intelligence Community is a coalition of agencies and organizations, including the ODNI, that work both independently and collaboratively to gather and analyze the intelligence necessary to conduct foreign relations and national security activities. In addition to the ODNI, the following seventeen organizations compose the Intelligence Community:

- Bureau of Intelligence and Research, Department of State
- Central Intelligence Agency
- Coast Guard Intelligence
- Defense Intelligence Agency, Department of Defense
- Intelligence Branch, Federal Bureau of Investigation, Department of Justice
- Marine Corps Intelligence
- Military Intelligence Corps (intelligence arm of the Army)
- National Geospatial-Intelligence Agency, Department of Defense
- National Reconnaissance Office, Department of Defense
- National Security Agency / Central Security Service, Department of Defense
- Office of Intelligence Analysis, Department of Homeland Security
- Office of Intelligence and Counterintelligence, Department of Energy
- Office of National Security Intelligence, Drug Enforcement Administration, Department of Justice
- Office of Naval Intelligence
- Office of Terrorism and Financial Intelligence, Department of Treasury
- Sixteenth Air Force (intelligence arm of the Air Force)
- Space Delta 7 (intelligence arm of the Space Force)

As the list above illustrates, the members of the Intelligence Community represent a diverse range of interests based primarily on the missions and functions of their parent organizations and the intelligence needs of their "customers." Several of these members merit further discussion given their relatively important roles in military intelligence, complementing the intelligence arms of each of the armed services.

The Central Intelligence Agency (CIA), established in 1947, is the civilian foreign intelligence agency responsible for providing national security intelligence to senior U.S. policymakers. A director heads the agency and, since 2005, reports to the DNI. This person is nominated by the president with the advice and consent of the Senate. The director and deputy director can be either military officers or civilians; if officers, they retain their rank and status on active duty but are otherwise exempt from normal military responsibilities. The director manages the operations, personnel, and budget of the CIA. Beneath the Office of the Director are five major directorates: Analysis, Operations, Science and Technology, Digital Innovation, and Support. Additionally, there are several mission centers, each with a specific geographical or functional orientation. Together, these directorates and centers carry out the "intelligence cycle," the process of collecting, analyzing, and disseminating intelligence information to top U.S. government officials.

The agency provides the president and senior advisers with accurate, comprehensive, and timely foreign intelligence relating to national security. It also conducts counterintelligence activities, special activities, and other functions relating to foreign intelligence and national security as the president may direct.

To fulfill its mission, the CIA performs several specific tasks:

- Collect, process, exploit, analyze, and disseminate foreign intelligence by employing a highly skilled, diverse workforce and state-of-the-art technical systems and devices.
- Protect intelligence sources and methods.
- Conduct research on, develop, and procure technical systems and devices;
- Protect the security of its installations, activities, and people.
- Provide necessary administrative and logistical support as well as services of common concern to the Intelligence Community.

The CIA does not possess police, subpoena, or law enforcement powers, nor does it deal with questions of internal security. In carrying out its functions, the CIA prepares national intelligence estimates, which are analyses of strategic intelligence that serve as the basis for policy decisions.

The Defense Intelligence Agency (DIA) is a combat support agency within DOD. With more than 16,500 military and civilian employees worldwide, DIA is a major producer and manager of foreign military intelligence. It collects, analyzes, and disseminates military intelligence to warfighters, planners, and policymakers in DOD and the Intelligence Community, thus supporting military planning, military operations, and weapon systems acquisition. DIA is led by a director, typically a military officer, who serves as principal adviser to the secretary of defense and to the chairman of the Joint Chiefs of Staff on matters of military intelligence. The director also chairs the Military Intelligence Board, which coordinates activities of the Intelligence Community's military members.

The National Geospatial-Intelligence Agency (NGA) provides civilian and military officials and organizations of the United States with geospatial intelligence about human activity on Earth derived from the analysis and exploitation of various forms of overhead imagery and geospatial information. NGA is a unique combination of intelligence agency and combat support agency. In fact, anyone who sails a U.S. ship, flies a U.S. aircraft, makes national policy decisions, fights wars, locates targets, responds to natural disasters, or even navigates with a cellphone relies on NGA.

The National Security Agency / Central Security Service (NSA/CSS) serves as the national cryptology organization. It coordinates, directs, and performs highly specialized activities to protect U.S. government information systems and produce foreign signals intelligence information. A high-technology organization, the NSA/CSS is on the frontier of communications and data processing. It is also one of the most important centers of foreign language analysis and research within the government.

≻ ≻ *Other Organizations*

Several other organizations, under direct control of the Executive Office of the President, relate to national security.

The Department of Energy (DOE) contributes to the nation's security and prosperity by addressing energy, environmental, and nuclear challenges. Specifically, it administers programs in the areas of energy production and distribution, energy science and innovation, and nuclear safety and security. The principal connection between DOE and DOD arises from their shared responsibilities for management of the nation's nuclear weapons stockpile.

The National Aeronautics and Space Administration (NASA) deals with problems of flight in space and planetary atmosphere, develops and operates space vehicles, and leads the nation's exploration of space.

The Selective Service System provides nationwide standby machinery for the registration and induction of individuals for military service—in other words, the draft.

The second largest of the federal government agencies based on total workforce, the Department of Veterans Affairs (VA) administers all laws authorizing benefits for former members of the armed forces and their dependent beneficiaries, together with all government insurance and health programs open to members of the armed forces. (For benefits and services of the VA, see chapter 20.)

The Department of Homeland Security (DHS) took form in the aftermath of the 9/11 al-Qaeda attack on the United States. The third largest of all departments, this extraordinary and debated entity comprises several agencies, offices, and directorates, including most notably the Management Directorate, National Protection and Programs Directorate, and Science and Technology Directorate. It also directs the field activities of numerous components and agencies, including, among others, the Coast Guard, Secret Service, Citizenship and Immigration Services, Customs and Border Protection, Immigration and Customs Enforcement, Federal Emergency Management Agency, and the Transportation Security Administration. DHS provides the unifying core for the vast national network of organizations and institutions involved in efforts to secure our nation, in the process executing five core missions: prevent terrorism and enhance security, secure and manage borders, enforce and administer immigration laws, safeguard and secure cyberspace, and ensure resilience in the face of disaster.

❯ DEPARTMENT OF DEFENSE

DOD is the largest agency in the federal government. Its central functions are to provide for the military security of the country and to support and advance the national policies and interests of the United States. It spends approximately one-sixth of the national budget in an ordinary fiscal year, not counting inevitable "supplemental" bills. In the six and a half decades since its creation, the department has grown to number roughly 1.4 million men and women on active duty and 800,000 in the reserves, supported by approximately 765,000 civilian personnel. The department is therefore the nation's largest employer.

DOD includes the Office of the Secretary of Defense (OSD); the Joint Chiefs of Staff (JCS) and supporting staff; the Departments of the Army, Navy, and Air Force and the five military services (Army, Marine Corps, Navy, Air Force, and Space Force) within those departments; the unified CCMDs; and such other agencies and field activities as the secretary of defense establishes to meet specific requirements (see figure 3-2).

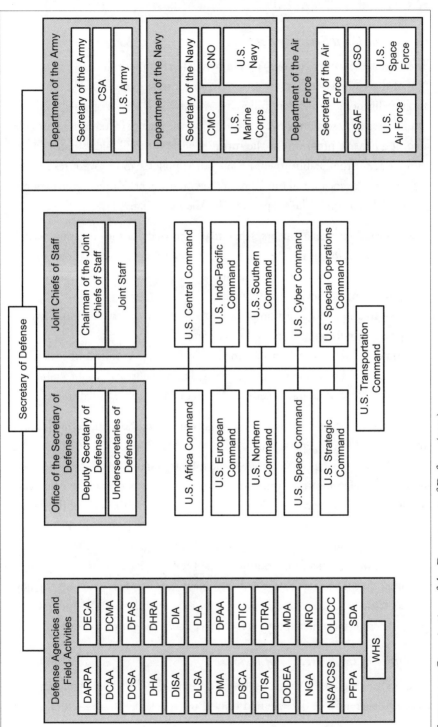

FIGURE 3-2. Organization of the Department of Defense (2021)

❯ ❯ *The National Security Act*

The National Security Act of 1947, as amended, is an important piece of legislation of the United States, for it directed a major restructuring of U.S. military and intelligence organizations following World War II, much of which endures today. The policy section of the act reads, "It is the intent of Congress to provide a comprehensive program for the future security of the United States; [and] to provide for the establishment of integrated policies and procedures for the departments, agencies, and functions of the Government relating to the national security." In so doing, the act provides for the following:

- three military departments, separately organized, for the operation and administration of the Army, the Navy (including naval aviation) and the Marine Corps, and the Air and Space Forces, with their assigned combatant and service components;
- coordination and direction of the three military departments and five services under a secretary of defense; and
- strategic direction of the armed forces, their operation under unified control, establishment of unified and specified commands, and the integration of the five services into an efficient team of land, naval, and air forces.

Two things it does not establish are a single chief of staff over the armed forces and an armed forces general staff.

The National Security Act unified the military establishment by giving the secretary of defense authority and virtual military control over the five services, although that person does not *directly* administer the Departments of the Army, Navy, and Air Force. He or she also has authority in procurement, supply, transportation, storage, health, and research and engineering. The secretary's greatest power lies in administration of the DOD military budgets.

Although the secretaries of the Army, Navy, and Air Force no longer enjoy cabinet status, each has the right to communicate directly to OMB and to Congress. He or she must first inform the secretary of defense of the intention to do so.

❯ ❯ *Office of the Secretary of Defense*

Since its inception, OSD has mushroomed from a handful of policymakers—in 1949, the secretary of defense had only three special assistants—to a major bureaucracy within the government. It serves as the principal staff element of the secretary of defense for planning, policy development, resource management, and program evaluation. OSD includes the offices of top civilian decision makers concerning defense personnel, weapons acquisition, research, intelligence, and fiscal policy as well as other offices the secretary may establish to assist in carrying out assigned responsibilities.

The secretary of defense, principal assistant to the president in all matters relating to DOD, is appointed from civil life by the chief executive with the advice and consent of the Senate. Under the president, the secretary exercises authority, direction, and control over DOD. The secretary is a member of the cabinet and the NSC.

The OSD includes the immediate offices of the secretary and deputy secretary of defense, undersecretaries of defense, assistant secretaries of defense, general counsel, special assistants to the secretary of defense, and such other agencies, offices, and positions as the secretary establishes to assist in carrying out assigned responsibilities. Several key positions within the office merit further discussion.

Deputy Secretary of Defense. Reporting directly to the secretary of defense, this person is delegated full power and authority to act for the secretary and is responsible for supervising and coordinating DOD activities.

Undersecretary of Defense for Research and Engineering. The principal adviser and staff assistant to the secretary of defense on matters relating to science, technology, and innovation, this individual serves as DOD's chief technology officer, tasked with ensuring the technological superiority of the U.S. military. He or she also exercises staff oversight of all research, development, and prototyping activities in DOD.

Undersecretary of Defense for Acquisition and Sustainment. This official is the principal adviser and staff assistant to the secretary of defense on acquisition and logistical matters. He or she exercises staff supervision over all acquisition and logistical activities in DOD and wields extensive coordinating and directive authority over virtually all matériel programs of the defense establishment.

Undersecretary of Defense (Comptroller). This individual serves as the principal adviser and staff assistant to the secretary of defense on all budgetary and financial matters, including the development and execution of the department's annual budget.

Undersecretary of Defense for Intelligence and Security. The principal adviser and staff assistant to the secretary of defense on intelligence, counter-intelligence, security, sensitive activities, and other intelligence-related matters, he or she exercises staff supervision on behalf of the secretary of defense over intelligence organizations within DOD, including NSA/CSS, DIA, NGA, and the National Reconnaissance Office.

Undersecretary of Defense for Personnel and Readiness. This official is the principal adviser and staff assistant to the secretary of defense for total force management as it relates to readiness; National Guard and Reserve component affairs; health affairs; training; and personnel requirements and management, including equal opportunity, morale, welfare, recreation, and quality-of-life matters.

Undersecretary of Defense for Policy. The principal adviser and staff assistant to the secretary of defense in matters of defense and security policy, including national defense strategy, national security requirements, regional security arrangements, and special measures for crises short of open warfare, he or she coordinates the formulation and translation of strategic concepts into military force programs and security policies.

Assistant Secretaries of Defense. Including the general counsel and certain special assistants, these officials are responsible to the secretary for policies, procedures, and activities in a variety of areas. In 2021, there were over a dozen of these areas, embracing such fields as health affairs, legislative affairs, program analysis, regional security affairs, public affairs, and intelligence oversight.

The agencies, offices, and positions that compose OSD are not fixed across administrations or over time. Each secretary of defense may periodically rearrange responsibilities and functions according to existing requirements.

❯ ❯ *Joint Chiefs of Staff*

To promote more personal control of the Army and Navy, to ensure direct access to the president for principal military advisers, and to improve coordination between the Army and Navy, President Franklin D. Roosevelt directed the organization of the JCS in 1942. With the passage of the National Security Act in 1947, it became a permanent part of the defense organization of the United

States. Today, the JCS consists of a chairman; a vice chairman; the service chiefs of the Army, Marine Corps, Navy, Air Force, and Space Force; and the chief of the National Guard Bureau.

Amended in 1949, the National Security Act authorized a chairman who would preside at JCS meetings and expedite the conduct of business. The president appoints the chairman from one of the five services with the advice and consent of the Senate. The chairman is the principal military adviser to the president, secretary of defense, and NSC; all JCS members are by law military advisers, however, and they may respond to a request or voluntarily submit, through the chairman, advice or opinions to the president, secretary of defense, or NSC. Taking precedence over all officers of the armed forces, the chairman serves as presiding officer for the JCS, provides the agenda for meetings, and manages the Joint Staff through its director.

The executive authority of the JCS has evolved. During World War II, the joint chiefs acted as executive agents in dealing with theater and area commanders, but the National Security Act of 1947 regarded the JCS as planners and advisers, not as commanders of combatant forces. Despite this, the 1948 Key West Agreement permitted JCS members to serve as executive agents for unified commands, a responsibility that allowed them to originate direct communication with the CCMD. Congress abolished this authority in a 1953 amendment to the National Security Act. Today, the joint chiefs have no executive authority to command combatant forces. The issue of executive authority was clearly resolved by the Goldwater-Nichols Department of Defense Reorganization Act of 1986, which established that the chain of command to a CCMD shall run from the president through the secretary of defense to the combatant commander (CCDR).

As principal military advisers to the president, secretary of defense, and NSC, the joint chiefs prepare strategic plans and provide strategic direction of the military forces; prepare joint logistic plans and assign logistic responsibilities in accordance with such plans; formulate policies for joint training of the armed forces and coordinate the education of servicemembers; review major matériel and personnel requirements of the military forces in accordance with strategic and logistic plans; and provide U.S. representation on the Military Staff Committee of the United Nations.

❧ ❧ *Organization of the Joint Chiefs of Staff*

The supporting establishment of the JCS comprises the Joint Staff and additional organizations and agencies that report directly to the JCS.

The Joint Staff assists the chairman of the JCS in accomplishing the responsibilities for the unified strategic direction of the combatant forces, their operation under unified command, and their integration into an efficient team of land, naval, and air forces. The Joint Staff comprises approximately equal numbers of officers from the Army, Navy and Marine Corps together, and Air Force. In practice, the Marines make up about 20 percent of the number allocated to the Navy.

The director of the Joint Staff, an officer of three-star grade, attends meetings of the JCS and serves, in effect, as the expediter and coordinator of the JCS organization. The Joint Staff is divided into the following directorates: Manpower and Personnel (J-1); Intelligence (J-2); Operations (J-3); Logistics (J-4); Strategy, Plans, and Policy (J-5); Command, Control, Communications, and Computers/ Cyber (J-6); Joint Force Development (J-7); and Force Structure, Resources, and Assessment (J-8). There are also various special assistants.

Other entities within the JCS organization, though not part of the Joint Staff, include the Joint Secretariat, the U.S. Delegation to the Inter-American Defense Board, the U.S. Delegation to the United Nations Military Staff Committee, the U.S. Representative at the North Atlantic Treaty Organization Military Committee, and various councils, boards, committees, and representatives.

❧ ❧ *Unified Combatant Commands*

Organized directly under the secretary of defense, with orders transmitted by the chairman of the JCS, are the unified combatant commands, predominantly located outside the United States and covering the geographic and functional areas of greatest strategic importance. A unified command has a broad continuing mission and comprises components of two or more services, all under a single commander. Each CCDR's staff includes representatives from all services. There are also subordinate "service component commanders" with authority over all units from their respective services within the CCMD.

There are eleven CCMDs. The following seven are oriented geographically, broadly responsible for military operations and activities within a designated region:

- U.S. Africa Command (USAFRICOM)
- U.S. Central Command (USCENTCOM)
- U.S. European Command (USEUCOM)
- U.S. Indo-Pacific Command (USINDOPACOM)
- U.S. Northern Command (USNORTHCOM)
- U.S. Southern Command (USSOUTHCOM)
- U.S. Space Command (USSPACECOM)

The remaining four CCMDs are oriented functionally, each responsible for global military operations and activities within a specialized functional area:

- U.S. Cyber Command (USCYBERCOM)
- U.S. Special Operations Command (USSOCOM)
- U.S. Strategic Command (USSTRATCOM)
- U.S. Transportation Command (USTRANSCOM)

❖ ❖ *Other DOD Agencies and Field Activities*

In addition to the CCMDs, several major agencies, field activities, and joint service schools come under the aegis of DOD or the JCS. These entities are established by the secretary of defense to perform an administrative, supply, or service activity common to more than one military department. Certain of them are of commanding size and stature and perform major functions for DOD that were once considered to be within the operating and administrative purview of the military departments. The list of defense agencies and field activities is extensive:

- Defense Advanced Research Projects Agency (DARPA)
- Defense Commissary Agency (DECA)
- Defense Contract Audit Agency (DCAA)
- Defense Contract Management Agency (DCMA)
- Defense Counterintelligence and Security Agency (DCSA)
- Defense Finance and Accounting Service (DFAS)
- Defense Health Agency (DHA) (formerly TRICARE Management Activity)
- Defense Human Resources Activity (DHRA)

- Defense Information Systems Agency (DISA)
- Defense Intelligence Agency (DIA)
- Defense Legal Services Agency (DLSA)
- Defense Logistics Agency (DLA)
- Defense Media Activity (DMA)
- Defense POW/MIA Accounting Agency (DPAA)
- Defense Security Cooperation Agency (DSCA)
- Defense Technical Information Center (DTIC)
- Defense Technology Security Administration (DTSA)
- Defense Threat Reduction Agency (DTRA)
- DOD Education Activity (DODEA)
- Missile Defense Agency (MDA)
- National Geospatial-Intelligence Agency (NGA)
- National Reconnaissance Office (NRO)
- National Security Agency / Central Security Service (NSA/CSS)
- Office of Local Defense Community Cooperation (OLDCC) (formerly Office of Economic Adjustment)
- Pentagon Force Protection Agency (PFPA)
- Space Development Agency (SDA)
- Washington Headquarters Services (WHS)

The joint service schools include the National Defense University (College of Information and Cyberspace, College of International Security Affairs, Dwight D. Eisenhower School for National Security and Resource Strategy, Joint Forces Staff College, and National War College) and over a dozen specialty schools, including the Defense Acquisition University, National Intelligence University, and Uniformed Services University of the Health Sciences.

For detailed, up-to-date information on the organization and functioning of the JCS, its supporting organization, and the unified and specified command structure, consult the current version of Joint Publication 1, *Doctrine for the Armed Forces of the United States.*

❯ DEPARTMENT OF THE ARMY

Established in 1947 by the National Security Act, which dissolved its predecessor, the Department of War (dating from 1789), the Department of the Army is one of the three military departments within DOD. It is the federal agency within which the U.S. Army is organized. It includes land combat and service forces as well as certain aviation, water transport, space, and cyberspace forces. These are organized, trained, and equipped primarily for prompt and sustained combat associated with operations on land. They also perform additional tasks assigned by the president, secretary of defense, and CCDRs and support the joint forces and other military services. The nation's principal land force, the Army is responsible for the preparation of forces necessary for the effective prosecution of war and other operations short of war, including military engagement and security cooperation. It contributes forces through a rotational, cyclical readiness model that provides flexibly organized units to the CCMDs and a surge capacity for unexpected contingencies.

The department is led by the secretary of the Army, who prescribes its regulations and directs its affairs subject to the limits of the law and the directions of

A fireball erupts from the muzzle of a U.S. Army M1 Abrams main battle tank during gunnery training.

the secretary of defense and the president. Department of the Army normally refers to the secretariat and headquarters, located near the nation's capital, and all field headquarters, forces, reserve components, installations, activities, and functions under its control or supervision.

❧ ❧ *Mission and Functions of the Army*

The Army's stated mission is "to deploy, fight, and win our nation's wars by providing ready, prompt, and sustained land dominance by Army forces across the full spectrum of conflict as part of the joint force." In addition to the functions common to all military services, it is responsible, per Department of Defense Directive (DODD) 5100.01, *Functions of the Department of Defense and Its Major Components*, to organize, train, equip, and provide forces with expeditionary and campaign qualities—as well as develop the appropriate concepts, doctrine, tactics, techniques, and procedures—to perform the following specific functions:

- Conduct prompt and sustained combined arms combat operations on land in all environments and types of terrain, including complex urban environments, to defeat enemy ground forces and seize, occupy, and defend land areas.
- Conduct air and missile defense to support joint campaigns and to assist in achieving air superiority.
- Conduct airborne, air assault, and amphibious operations (with primary responsibility for the development of airborne doctrine, tactics, techniques, and equipment).
- Conduct civil affairs operations.
- Conduct riverine operations.
- Occupy territories abroad and provide for the initial establishment of a military government, pending transfer of this responsibility to other authority.
- Interdict enemy sea, space, and air power and communications through operations on or from the land.
- Provide logistics to joint operations and campaigns, including joint over-the-shore and intratheater transport of time-sensitive, mission-critical personnel and matériel.

- Provide support for space operations to enhance joint campaigns in coordination with the other military services, combatant commands, and federal departments and agencies.
- Conduct authorized civil works programs, including projects for improvement of navigation, flood control, beach erosion control, and other water resource developments in the United States, its territories, and its possessions, and conduct other civil activities prescribed by law.
- Provide intratheater aeromedical evacuation.
- Conduct reconnaissance, surveillance, and target acquisition.
- Operate land lines of communication.

⋗ ⋗ *Organization of the Army*

Command flows from the president, through the secretary of defense and the secretary of the Army, to units and installations throughout the world. The Army comprises two distinct and equally important elements: the active component and the reserve component, which includes both the Army National Guard and the Army Reserve.

The Army's active component, the Regular Army, contains the forces capable of performing most of the its functions in both peacetime and wartime. It is also the framework upon which the nation builds wartime armies. The Army National Guard is part of the reserve component. In times of peace, the National Guard of any state can be called to active duty by its governor to perform emergency duties. Units or individual members of the National Guard can be called to active duty by the federal government only during war or national emergency or with their own consent in times of peace. Like the National Guard, units of the Army Reserve train in local armories and are subject to orders to active duty under similar conditions. Individual members are assigned to Army Reserve organizations in or near their hometowns.

Regardless of component, Army structure includes both operational and institutional elements. The operational Army consists of numbered armies, corps, divisions, brigades, and battalions that conduct operations around the world. A field army comprises a headquarters and two or more corps, each in turn composed of two or more divisions. The division is the smallest unit that permanently contains a balanced proportion of the combined arms and services and therefore is fully constituted to operate independently. Below division level, standing units are mainly composed of brigade combat teams and the separate arms or services of the Army.

The institutional Army supports the operational element. These organizations provide the infrastructure necessary to raise, train, equip, deploy, and ensure the readiness of all Army forces. Within this element, the training base provides military skills and professional education to every soldier as well as members of sister services and allied forces. It also allows the Army to expand rapidly in times of war. Complementing the training base, the industrial base provides equipment and logistics for the Army. Installations provide the platforms required to deploy land forces promptly to support CCDRs. Once those operational forces are deployed, the institutional Army provides the logistics needed to support them.

❧ ❧ *Major Army Commands and Activities*

The Army comprises the headquarters, commands, service component commands, and direct reporting units. Its service-retained forces—that is, those not assigned to a specific CCMD—reside within the following Army commands:

- U.S. Army Forces Command (FORSCOM), which trains, mobilizes, deploys, sustains, transforms, and reconstitutes assigned land combat forces
- U.S. Army Futures Command (AFC), which focuses on modernizing the Army—in terms of both organization and equipment—for the future
- U.S. Army Matériel Command (AMC), which provides superior technology, acquisition support, and integrated logistics to the Army's land forces
- U.S. Army Training and Doctrine Command (TRADOC), which recruits, trains, and educates the Army's soldiers and leaders; develops doctrine and standards; and builds the future Army

Assigned to and aligned under the CCMDs, Army service component commands exercise authority over assigned Army forces and provide continuous oversight and control of operations throughout the relevant CCDR's area of responsibility. Army service component commands include the following:

- U.S. Army Africa (USARAF)
- U.S. Army Central (USARCENT)
- U.S. Army Europe (USAREUR)
- U.S. Army North (USARNORTH)
- U.S. Army Pacific (USARPAC)
- U.S. Army South (USARSOUTH)
- U.S. Army Special Operations Command (USASOC)
- Military Surface Deployment and Distribution Command (SDDC), the Army service component command for USTRANSCOM
- U.S. Army Space and Missile Defense Command / Army Strategic Command (USASMDC), the Army service component command for USSTRATCOM
- U.S. Army Cyber Command (USARCYBER), the Army service component command for USCYBERCOM

Within the Army, direct reporting units provide broad, general support, usually within a specific functional area. They normally report to the Army secretary, Army chief of staff, or one of their principal staff officers. Army direct reporting units include the following:

- U.S. Army Medical Command (MEDCOM), which provides comprehensive medical, dental, and veterinary support to the Army and designated DOD organizations
- U.S. Army Intelligence and Security Command (INSCOM), which produces intelligence in support of the Army, the combatant commands, and the Intelligence Community
- U.S. Army Criminal Investigation Command (USACIDC), which provides broad criminal investigative support, including forensic support, to all Army organizations; conducts sensitive and special investigations; and provides personal protective services for designated officials
- U.S. Army Human Resources Command (HRC), which manages human resources, personnel programs, and personnel services throughout the Army
- U.S. Army Corps of Engineers (USACE), which provides engineering services and capabilities in support of national interests

- U.S. Army Military District of Washington (MDW), which provides administrative, logistical, and other support to Army organizations and other military services and federal agencies throughout the National Capital Region
- U.S. Army Test and Evaluation Command (ATEC), which plans, integrates, and conducts experiments, developmental and operational testing, and independent evaluations and assessments in support of acquisition officials
- U.S. Military Academy (USMA), which educates, trains, and inspires the Army's future commissioned officers
- U.S. Army Acquisition Support Center (USAASC), which supports Army matériel readiness and develops a professional acquisition workforce
- U.S. Army War College (AWC), which provides high-quality professional military education, conducts and publishes research, and orchestrates joint and service wargames
- Arlington National Cemetery (ANC), which lays to rest those who have served the nation with dignity and honor, treats their families with respect and compassion, and connects visitors to the rich tapestry of the cemetery's living history while maintaining the cemetery's hallowed grounds
- Civilian Human Resources Agency (CHRA), which provides comprehensive human resources services for the Army, enabling efficient and effective personnel support worldwide

❧ DEPARTMENT OF THE NAVY

The Department of the Navy, established in 1798, is one of the three military departments within DOD. It is the federal agency within which the U.S. Navy and U.S. Marine Corps are organized. Together, the Navy and Marine Corps are the nation's principal maritime force. They comprise naval, land, air, space, and cyberspace forces, including combat, combat support, and combat service support. By maintaining forward-stationed and rotationally based forces, they provide persistent presence, global reach, and operational flexibility to secure the nation from direct attack; secure strategic access and retain global freedom of action; strengthen existing and emerging alliances and partnerships; establish favorable security conditions; deter aggression and violence by state, nonstate, and

Wasp-class amphibious assault ships are one means
by which the Navy projects power across the seas.

individual actors; and, should deterrence fail, execute the full range of maritime
operations in support of U.S. national interests.

The department is led by the Secretary of the Navy, who prescribes the
regulations for and directs the affairs of both the Navy and the Marine Corps,
subject to the limits of the law and the directions of the secretary of defense and
the president. It encompasses the secretariat, Navy headquarters, and Marine
Corps headquarters; the entire operating forces of the Navy and the Marine
Corps, including naval aviation and the reserve components of such forces; all
field activities, headquarters, forces, bases, installations, activities, and functions
under the department's control or supervision; and the U.S. Coast Guard *when
operating as part of the Navy* pursuant to law.

Within DOD and the organization for national security (see figure 3-2), the
Department of the Navy occupies coequal status with the Department of the
Army and Department of the Air Force. The organization of the department,
the specific missions and functions of the Navy and Marine Corps, and the

place of the Marine Corps in the naval establishment are described in greater detail in chapters 4, 5, and 6.

❯ DEPARTMENT OF THE AIR FORCE

Established in 1947 by the National Security Act, the Department of the Air Force is one of the three military departments within DOD. It organizes, trains, equips, and provides air, space, and cyberspace forces for the conduct of prompt and sustained combat operations, military engagement, and security cooperation in defense of the nation as well as to support the joint forces and other military services. Established within the department, the U.S. Air Force and U.S. Space Force are the nation's principal military services oriented on the air and space domains and are responsible for the preparation of forces necessary for the effective prosecution of war. They provide the nation with global vigilance, reach, and power in the form of in-place, forward-based, and expeditionary forces. These forces possess the capacity to deter aggression and violence by state, nonstate, and individual actors and, should deterrence fail, to conduct the full range of military operations in support of U.S. national interests.

The Department of the Air Force is led by the secretary of the Air Force, who prescribes its regulations and directs its affairs, subject to the limits of the law and the directions of the secretary of defense and the president. It encompasses the secretariat and headquarters, located near the nation's capital, and all field headquarters, forces, reserve components, installations, activities, and functions under the department's control or supervision.

❯ ❯ *Mission and Functions of the Air Force*

The Air Force's stated mission is "to fly, fight, and win . . . airpower anytime, anywhere." It organizes, trains, and equips units to defend the United States against air attack, to gain and maintain general aerospace supremacy, to defeat enemy air forces, to control vital air areas, and to establish local air supremacy when required.

In addition to the functions common to all military services, the Air Force is responsible per DODD 5100.01 to develop concepts, doctrine, tactics, techniques, and procedures and to organize, train, equip, and provide forces to perform the following specific functions:

- Conduct nuclear operations in support of strategic deterrence, including provision and maintenance of nuclear surety and capabilities.
- Conduct offensive and defensive operations, including appropriate air and missile defense, to gain and maintain air superiority and, when required, air supremacy to enable the conduct of operations by U.S. and allied land, sea, air, space, and special operations forces.
- Conduct global precision attacks, including strategic attacks, interdiction, close air support, and prompt global strikes.
- Provide timely, global integrated intelligence, surveillance, and reconnaissance capability and capacity from forward-deployed locations and globally distributed centers to support worldwide operations.
- Provide rapid global mobility to employ and sustain organic air and space forces and, as directed, the forces of the other military services and USSOCOM, including airlift forces for airborne operations and air logistical support, tanker forces for inflight refueling, and assets for aeromedical evacuation.
- Provide agile combat support to enhance the aerospace campaign and the deployment, employment, sustainment, and redeployment of air and

A U.S. Air Force KC-10 Extender aerial tanker refuels an F-22 Raptor tactical fighter aircraft.

space forces and other forces operating within the air and space domains, including support to the other military services and USSOCOM beyond their organic capabilities.

- Conduct global personnel recovery operations, including theater-wide combat and civil search and rescue in coordination with the other military services, combatant commands, and DOD components.
- Conduct global integrated command and control for air and space operations.

❧ ❧ *Organization of the Air Force*

Command flows from the president, through the secretary of defense and the secretary of the Air Force, to Air Force units and installations throughout the world. Similarly to the Army's structure, the Air Force is composed, in its entirety, of the Regular Air Force, Air National Guard, and Air Force Reserve.

The basic organizational structure of the Air Force includes the headquarters—known as the Air Staff—major commands, direct reporting units, and field operating agencies.

Major commands (MAJCOMs), the principal Air Force subdivisions, are each assigned a primary part of the force's mission. MAJCOMs are directly subordinate to the Air Force chief of staff, and each normally includes the word "command" in its name. Their headquarters have the full range of functional staff. MAJCOMs may be further subdivided into any or all of the following:

- Numbered air force, an intermediate command echelon designed to control and administer a grouping of combat wings that can vary in size
- Wing, the smallest Air Force unit, manned and equipped to operate independently in sustained action
- Group, a flexible unit composed of two or more squadrons whose functions may be either tactical or administrative in nature
- Squadron, the basic unit in the organizational structure, manned and equipped to perform a specific military function, such as combat, maintenance, or communications
- Flight, the lowest tactical echelon in the Air Force (although not formally designated in the organizational structure), composed of a subdivision

of combat squadrons and providing the fundamental building block for combat formations and for training

Not all Air Force major commands follow this unit-oriented internal structure. Some, particularly those with an administrative or support focus, rely on alternate organizational structures. When this is the case, they are normally subdivided into centers, directorates or divisions, branches, and sections.

Direct reporting units, another subdivision of the Air Force, are—as the term implies—directly subordinate to the Air Force chief of staff. A direct reporting unit performs a mission that does not fit into any of the major commands but possesses many of the same administrative and organizational responsibilities as a major command.

Field operating agencies are directly subordinate to a functional manager at the Air Staff. Each performs field activities beyond the scope of any of the major commands and are specialized or associated with an Air Force–wide mission. They do not include functions performed in management headquarters unless specifically directed by a DOD authority. The word "agency" is usually part of their designation.

➢ ➢ *Major Air Force Commands and Activities*

Subordinate to the headquarters, nine major commands, three direct reporting units, and more than twenty-five field operating agencies represent the field organization of the Air Force. The following nine major commands are organized on a functional basis in the United States and on an area basis overseas:

- Air Combat Command (ACC), which is the primary provider of air combat forces to many of the CCDRs and the successor to the deactivated Tactical Air Command
- Air Education and Training Command (AETC), which recruits, trains, and educates airmen
- Air Force Global Strike Command (AFGSC), which is responsible for the nation's three intercontinental ballistic missile wings, the Air Force's entire bomber force and related programs, the Air Force's nuclear command, control and communications systems, and operational and maintenance support to organizations within the nuclear enterprise

- Air Force Matériel Command (AFMC), which conducts research, development, testing, and evaluation and provides the acquisition management services and logistical support necessary to keep Air Force weapons systems ready for war
- Air Force Reserve Command (AFRC), which provides operational capability, strategic depth, and surge capacity as an integrated total force partner in every Air Force core mission
- Air Force Special Operations Command (AFSOC), which provides operational units and serves as the Air Force component for USSOCOM
- Air Mobility Command (AMC), which provides global air mobility through airlift and aerial refueling for all the armed forces, including the Marine Corps, and serves as the Air Force component for USTRANSCOM
- Pacific Air Forces (PACAF), which provides operational units and serves as the Air Force component for USPACOM
- U.S. Air Forces in Europe and Air Forces Africa (USAFE-AFAFRICA), which provides operational units and serves as the Air Force component for USEUCOM and USAFRICOM

The three Air Force direct reporting units are:

- Air Force District of Washington (AFDW), which oversees Air Force operations in the National Capital Region
- Air Force Operational Test and Evaluation Center (AFOTEC), which is the Air Force's independent test agency responsible for testing, under operationally realistic conditions, new systems being developed for both its own and multiservice use
- U.S. Air Force Academy (USAFA), which offers a four-year program of education and experience designed to provide cadets the knowledge and character essential for leadership and the motivation to serve as Air Force officer

The complete list of Air Force field operating agencies is lengthy and covers wide-ranging functions, but representative among them are the following:

- Air Force Civil Engineer Center (AFCEC), which is responsible for providing responsive, flexible installation engineering services

- Air Force Inspection Agency (AFIA), which reports to the Department of the Air Force Inspector General and performs a range of inspection-related tasks to strengthen readiness and lethality at all levels
- Air Force Logistics Management Agency (AFLMA), which provides consulting support, conducts studies, and manages logistical participation in Air Force wargaming to promote solutions to logistical problems and develop new and improved concepts, methods, and systems
- Air Force Manpower Analysis Agency (AFMAA), which provides Air Force commanders the analysis and tools to help them identify manpower requirements, enabling the most effective and efficient accomplishment of Air Force missions
- Air Force Office of Special Investigations (AFOSI), which provides professional investigative services to commanders of all Air Force activities and identifies, investigates, and neutralizes criminal, terrorist, and espionage threats to Air Force and DOD personnel and resources
- Air Force Personnel Center (AFPC), which provides centralized personnel services to airmen worldwide
- Air Force Recruiting Service (AFRS), which inspires, engages, and recruits quality men and women from across the United States
- Air Force Research Laboratory (AFRL), which leads the discovery, development, and integration of warfighting technologies for the department's air, space, and cyberspace forces
- Air Force Safety Center (AFSEC), which develops, implements, and evaluates Air Force safety-related programs and policy
- Air National Guard Readiness Center (ANGRC), which performs operational and technical functions to ensure combat readiness of Air National Guard units and serves as a channel of communication between the National Guard Bureau and the states regarding the Air National Guard's operational activities

⋗ ⋗ Mission and Functions of the Space Force

Established in 2019, the U.S. Space Force "organizes, trains, and equips space forces in order to protect U.S. and allied interests in space and to provide space capabilities to the joint force." The Space Force's responsibilities include developing "guardians" (as servicemembers in the Space Force are known), acquiring military space systems, maturing the military doctrine for space power, and organizing space forces for and providing them to the CCMDs.

In addition to the functions common to all military services, the Space Force is responsible per DODD 5100.01 to develop concepts, doctrine, tactics, techniques, and procedures and to organize, train, equip, and provide forces to perform the following specific functions:

- Provide freedom of operation for the United States in, from, and to space.
- Protect the interests of the United States in space.
- Deter aggression in, from, and to space.
- Execute prompt and sustained space operations.

❧ ❧ Organization of the Space Force

Given the recent establishment of the Space Force in 2019, its organization is effectively a work in progress. Like the other military services, its headquarters is at the Pentagon. Staff members are currently focused on establishing a fully functioning headquarters; preparing to execute the full scope of service-oriented responsibilities involving organization, training, and equipment; and, in conjunction with the Air Force, developing a detailed plan to transfer personnel and equipment to the Space Force.

To significantly reduce costs and avoid duplication, the Space Force leverages the Department of the Air Force for more than 75 percent of its enabling functions. The department provides logistics, base-operating support, civilian personnel management, and information technology support, among others.

The Space Force operates with three different command echelons: field commands, "deltas" and garrisons, and squadrons. Led by a lieutenant general or major general, field commands align with specifically focused missions. Normally led by colonels, deltas and garrisons are organized around a specific function, such as operations or training in the case of a delta or installation support in the case of a garrison. Squadrons focus on specific tactics and are led by a lieutenant colonel.

❧ ❧ Major Space Force Commands and Activities

Subordinate to the headquarters, the field organization of the Space Force consists of one field command, with several subordinate activities, and one major center.

A U.S. Space Force Atlas V rocket carrying NASA's *Lucy* spacecraft lifts off from Space Launch Complex 41 at Cape Canaveral Space Force Station, Florida.

The Space Operations Command (SpOC), currently the Space Force's sole field command, is primarily responsible for space, cyber, and intelligence operations as well as the administration of bases. It also serves as the Space Force's service component for USSPACECOM.

SpOC exercises authority over the following nine space mission deltas and two garrisons:

- Space Training and Readiness Delta (Provisional), which handles the training and education of space professionals as well as the development of space-warfighting doctrine
- Space Delta 2, which maintains space domain awareness, monitoring and cataloging all man-made objects orbiting Earth
- Space Delta 3, which prepares forces to execute electronic warfare operations to dominate the space domain

- Space Delta 4, which provides strategic and theater missile warnings to the United States and its international partners
- Space Delta 5, which prepares and employs assigned and attached forces to achieve theater and global objectives
- Space Delta 6, which employs defensive cyberspace capabilities and maintains assured access to space through the satellite-control network
- Space Delta 7, which provides timely, useful intelligence for operations in space, including detection, characterization, and targeting of adversary space capabilities
- Space Delta 8, which provides satellite communications and the world's standard for position, navigation, and timing (PNT) signals through the Global Positioning System
- Space Delta 9, which conducts orbital warfare to protect and defend capabilities in orbit and, when necessary, deter and defeat orbital threats
- Peterson-Schriever Garrison, which provides a range of installation and logistic support and services to Space Force units operating at six separate sites
- Buckley Garrison, which provides installation support for the resident air operations, space-based missile-warning capabilities, space surveillance operations, and space communications missions at four separate sites

❧ COAST GUARD

On 4 August 1790, Alexander Hamilton, the secretary of the Treasury, created the Coast Guard's antecedent, the Revenue Cutter Service. It was initially a simple system employing cutters in U.S. ports. In 1915, the Revenue Cutter Service combined with the U.S. Lifesaving Service to form the U.S. Coast Guard. Today, the Coast Guard is a military service and a branch of the U.S. armed forces. It operates under the Department of Homeland Security during peacetime and under the Department of the Navy when directed by the president or upon a declaration of war. The service is the primary search-and-rescue agency in and around the nation's waters and the primary maritime law enforcement agency for drug interdiction and against maritime piracy and terrorism.

Although part of the Department of Homeland Security, Coast Guard personnel receive the same pay and benefits as men and women in the other armed forces,

Launched in 2006, *Bertholf* is the lead ship of the Legend class,
the first new class of national security cutters in twenty-five years.
Bertholf is the U.S. Coast Guard's largest ever patrol cutter.

and they are also subject to the Uniform Code of Military Justice. The service's
rank and rating system resembles the Navy's, except it contains fewer enlisted
ratings. It is led by the commandant of the Coast Guard, a four-star admiral.

❧ ❧ *Mission, Functions, and Organization of the Coast Guard*

Broadly stated, the mission of the Coast Guard is to ensure the nation's maritime
safety, security, and stewardship. It organizes and executes this mission in eleven
areas:

- Law enforcement, including enforcing fisheries laws and stopping drug
  smuggling

- Ports, waterways, and coastal security
- Drug interdiction
- Migrant interdiction
- Aids to navigation, including operating the nation's lighthouses, buoys, electronic navigation stations, and other vessel-traffic services
- Search and rescue
- Marine safety, including inspecting vessels for safety violations
- Defense readiness, including national security and military preparedness
- Living marine resources conservation and protection
- Maritime environmental protection
- Polar, ice, and Alaska operations, including tracking icebergs, operating icebreakers, and participating in the International Ice Patrol

To carry out its missions, the service operates 259 cutters larger than sixty-five feet, including 3 active icebreakers, and approximately 1,600 boats; runs hundreds of facilities, mostly small units, throughout the United States and a few abroad; and operates the world's seventh-largest naval air force, with 200 rotary- and fixed-wing aircraft.

The Coast Guard develops concepts, doctrines, tactics, techniques, and procedures as well as organizes, trains, equips, and provides forces to perform the following specific functions when providing direct or cooperative support to the Department of Defense:

- Conduct operations supporting coastal sea control, maritime interdiction, and air interception.
- Conduct operations to ensure maritime homeland security and counter-terrorism threats.
- Provide for port operations, security, and defense.
- Respond to maritime operational threats.
- Conduct operations to counter illicit trafficking.
- Conduct military environmental response operations.
- Conduct theater security cooperation operations.
- Conduct search-and-rescue operations.
- Conduct ice operations.
- Provide for marine safety, including aids to navigation.

The Coast Guard has recently assumed an increased military emphasis. It is the lead agency in the Maritime Defense Zone, which oversees the defense of the coastlines of the United States. In past wars, its resources have engaged in escort duties, antisubmarine warfare, cold-weather operations, riverine warfare, amphibious warfare, coastal security, port security, and much more.

The Coast Guard is organized into nine districts under a headquarters located in the nation's capital. Reporting to the commandant of the Coast Guard at headquarters are the deputy commandant for operations, the deputy commandant for mission support, the assistant commandant for resources, the director of governmental and public affairs, the director for civil rights, and the judge advocate general and chief counsel.

Responsible for Coast Guard operations and activities within designated geographic areas, the districts are organized under Atlantic and Pacific area commands, each led by a vice admiral. The following Coast Guard districts are in the Atlantic area:

- District 1, encompassing northern New Jersey, New York, Connecticut, Rhode Island, Massachusetts, New Hampshire, Vermont, and Maine
- District 5, ranging from South Carolina to New Jersey
- District 7, covering an area of 1.7 million square miles that includes Puerto Rico, the Florida Peninsula, Georgia, South Carolina, and thirty-four foreign nations and territories
- District 8, covering twenty-six states, with most of its activity in and near the coastlines of Texas, Louisiana, Mississippi, Alabama, and the Florida Panhandle
- District 9, encompassing the Great Lakes, the Saint Lawrence Seaway, and parts of the surrounding states, covering 6,700 miles of shoreline and 1,500 miles of the international border with Canada

These Coast Guard districts lie in the Pacific area:

- District 11, covering California, Nevada, Utah, and Arizona
- District 13, covering Washington, Oregon, Idaho, and Montana
- District 14, encompassing the Hawaiian Islands, Guam, American Samoa, Saipan, Singapore, and Japan

- District 17, with responsibility for the Alaskan maritime region, encompassing over 3,853,500 square miles and over 47,300 miles of shoreline throughout Alaska and the Arctic

Comparable to the Marine Corps motto, the Coast Guard motto is *Semper Paratus* (Always Ready).

⁘{ 4 }⁘

THE DEPARTMENT
OF THE NAVY

*Under all circumstances, a decisive naval superiority is to be
considered a fundamental principle, and the basis upon which
all hope of success must ultimately depend.*

— George Washington

SEVENTY-ONE PERCENT of the globe is covered by water, and the total
length of U.S. seacoast exceeds twelve thousand miles; these facts have long
caused the nation to appreciate the need for strong naval forces. The United
States is a maritime power, and its security strategy must always be fundamentally
maritime. In two world conflicts, superior sea power was vital to U.S. success.
Without maritime control, we could not have transported military forces, equipment, and supplies to distant battles, nor could we project our fighting power
from the seas onto the land.

Today, freedom of navigation and control of the seas are more important than
ever. The oceans connect the nations of an increasingly interdependent world.
The maritime domain—the world's oceans, seas, bays, estuaries, islands, coastal
areas, and littorals as well as the airspace above them—supports 90 percent of the
world's trade, which is vital to global prosperity and, by extension, the prosperity
of the United States. By maintaining control of the seas, we remain capable of
helping allied and friendly nations and confronting and defeating aggression far

The *Arleigh Burke*–class destroyer USS *Stockdale* steams in formation with other ships and aircraft from Carrier Strike Group 1, including the *Nimitz*-class aircraft carrier USS *Carl Vinson*.

from our shores. More important, we ensure the use of the seas for the offensive operations that victory requires. For all these reasons, we must maintain the nation's maritime forces. The Navy Department's *A Cooperative Strategy for 21st Century Seapower* (2015) highlights the importance of naval forces: "Seapower has been and will continue to be the critical foundation of national power and prosperity and international prestige for the United States of America. . . . Naval forces operate forward to shape the security environment, signal U.S. resolve, protect U.S. interests, and promote global prosperity by defending freedom of navigation in the maritime commons."

❖ MISSION, TASKS, AND ORGANIZATION OF THE DEPARTMENT OF THE NAVY

Under the Constitution, Congress is given the authority "to provide and maintain a navy . . . and to make rules for the government of the land and naval forces."

In the words of Supreme Court chief justice Charles Evans Hughes, "Congress provides; the President commands." Congress therefore enacts laws governing the role, mission, responsibilities, size, scope, and authority of the Navy and the Marine Corps. Congress also influences the department's organization by authorizing and providing funds for construction of ships and shore bases, procurement of weapons systems and equipment, and for conduct of all Navy and Marine Corps activities.

❧ ❧ *Mission and Tasks*

The National Security Act of 1947, as amended, details the mission and responsibilities of the Department of the Navy (DON):

> Sec. 206 (a) The term "Department of the Navy" as used in this Act shall be construed to mean the Department of the Navy at the seat of government; the headquarters, United States Marine Corps; the entire operating forces of the United States Navy, including naval aviation, and of the United States Marine Corps, including the reserve components of such forces; all field activities, headquarters, forces, bases, installations, activities, and functions under the control or supervision of the Department of the Navy; and the United States Coast Guard when operating as a part of the Navy pursuant to law.
>
> (b) The Navy, within the Department of the Navy, includes, in general, naval combat and service forces and such aviation as may be organic therein. The Navy shall be organized, trained, and equipped primarily for prompt and sustained combat incident to operations at sea. It is responsible for the preparation of naval forces necessary for the effective prosecution of war except as otherwise assigned and is generally responsible for naval reconnaissance, antisubmarine warfare, and protection of shipping.
>
> All naval aviation shall be integrated with the naval service as part thereof within the Department of the Navy. Naval aviation consists of combat and service and training forces, and includes land-based naval aviation, air transport essential for naval operations, all air weapons and air techniques involved in the operations and activities of the Navy, and the entire remainder of the aeronautical organization of the Navy, together with the personnel necessary therefor.

The Navy shall develop aircraft, weapons, tactics, technique, organization, and equipment of naval combat and service elements. Matters of joint concern as to these functions shall be coordinated between the Army, the Air Force, and the Navy.

The Navy is responsible, in accordance with integrated joint mobilization plans, for the expansion of the peacetime components of the Navy to meet the needs of war.

(c) The Marine Corps, within the Department of the Navy, shall be so organized as to include not less than three combat divisions and three air wings, and such other land combat, aviation, and other services as may be organic therein. The Marine Corps shall be organized, trained, and equipped to provide fleet marine forces of combined arms, together with supporting air components, for service with the fleet in the seizure or defense of advanced naval bases and for the conduct of such land operations as may be essential to the prosecution of a naval campaign. In addition, the Marine Corps shall provide detachments and organizations for service on armed vessels of the Navy, shall provide security detachments for the protecting of naval property at naval stations and bases, and shall perform such other duties as the President may direct. However, these additional duties may not detract from or interfere with the operations for which the Marine Corps is primarily organized.

The Marine Corps shall develop, in coordination with the Army and the Air Force, those phases of amphibious operations that pertain to the tactics, technique, and equipment used by landing forces.

The Marine Corps is responsible, in accordance with integrated joint mobilization plans, for the expansion of peacetime components of the Marine Corps to meet the needs of war. As of F[iscal] Y[ear] [20]17, the authorized active duty end strength is 182,000 Marines. However, the U.S. Congress could adjust this level year by year given the security environment or fiscal constraints.

The functions of the Navy and Marine Corps were further defined in the 1948 Key West Agreement, also referred to as the Functions Paper (see figure 4-1). Although the agreement's primary purpose was to amplify the functions of the Army and Air Force, it also assigned collateral functions to the Navy

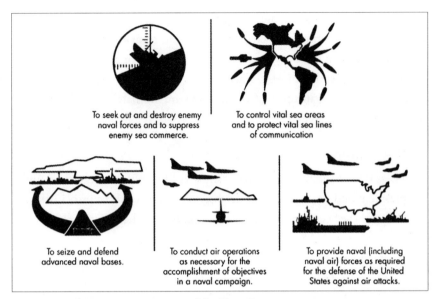

FIGURE 4-1. The Primary Functions of the Navy Department
as Set Forth in the Functions Paper

and the Marine Corps and spelled out some basic functions in more detail. Nonetheless, the primary source for Marine Corps functions is the National Security Act, not Key West.

To accomplish its mission, DON capitalizes on the global reach, persistent presence, and operational flexibility of Navy and Marine Corps forces to accomplish six principal tasks. It postures the Navy–Marine Corps team to

- limit a regional conflict with forward-deployed, decisive maritime power;
- deter a major power war;
- win the nation's wars as an integral part of the joint force;
- contribute to homeland defense in depth;
- foster and sustain cooperative relationships with an increasing number of international partners; and
- prevent or contain local disruptions before they affect the global system.

Critical to accomplishing these tasks is the maintenance of a powerful fleet— ships, aircraft, and shore-based fleet activities, together with multipurpose Marine

Corps forces—capable of controlling the seas, projecting power ashore, and protecting friendly forces and civilian populations from attack.

As you reflect on these key features of the nation's maritime forces, remember the words of General Lemuel C. Shepherd, twentieth commandant: "Both the functions and the future of the Marine Corps are intimately linked with those of the U.S. Navy."

❧ ❧ *Organization*

DON, as one of the military departments within DOD, is organized under the president and the secretary of defense. It consists of three principal parts: the Office of the Secretary of the Navy, also known as the Navy secretariat; the U.S. Navy; and the U.S. Marine Corps (see figure 4-2).

The Navy secretariat supports the secretary of the Navy in exercising the authority, under Title 10 (Armed Forces), U.S. Code, to conduct all the affairs of DON. It includes the secretary of the Navy and his or her personal staff; the undersecretary of the Navy; the assistant secretaries of the Navy; and several additional chiefs, deputies, and directors who assist the secretary in the administration of the department.

The U.S. Navy is one of two uniformed services within DON, and it comprises the Navy headquarters, the Operating Forces, and the Shore Establishment. The Navy headquarters encompasses all of the offices, boards, and agencies reporting to and performing duties for the Chief of Naval Operations, and these are collectively referred to as the Office of the Chief of Naval Operations (OPNAV). The Operating Forces of the Navy include the service components assigned to the combatant commands; the several fleets, including the Fleet Marine Forces and other assigned forces of the Marine Corps; the Navy Reserve forces; several specialized commands; and such other Navy field activities and commands as are assigned by the Secretary of the Navy. The Shore Establishment consists of all activities of the Navy not assigned to the Operating Forces and not a part of OPNAV. These include various commands, centers, and groups that primarily provide administrative, matériel, technical, and training support to the Operating Forces.

The Marine Corps, the second of two uniformed services within DON, includes Headquarters, U.S. Marine Corps (HQMC); the Operating Forces Supporting

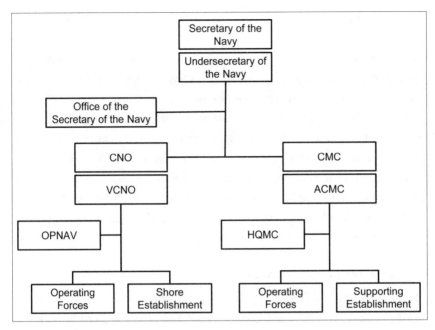

FIGURE 4-2. Organization of the Department of the Navy (2021)

Establishment; and the Marine Corps Reserve (see chapters 5 and 6 for more detailed discussion of the roles, missions, and organization of the Marine Corps).

❧ THE SECRETARIAT

❧ ❧ *Secretary of the Navy*

The Secretary of the Navy (SECNAV) heads DON and is responsible for the direction, control, and policies of the department. Subject to the authority, direction, and control of the president and secretary of defense, the SECNAV has the responsibility and authority to "conduct all affairs of the Department of the Navy," including recruiting; organizing; supplying; equipping, including research and development; training; servicing; mobilizing; demobilizing; administering, including the morale and welfare of personnel; maintaining; constructing, outfitting, and repairing military equipment; constructing, maintaining, and repairing buildings, structures, and utilities; and acquiring real property and interests in real property to support the department's activities.

As far as practical, the SECNAV discharges these responsibilities through civilian executive assistants and other military and civilian assistants. The secretary, however, normally retains personal direction over activities relating to legislation and to Congress and maintains relationships with the secretary of defense, other principal government officials, and the public.

The SECNAV is responsible for the formulation and implementation of policies and programs that are consistent with the national security policies and objectives established by the president and the secretary of defense.

The secretary recommends to the secretary of defense and the president appointments, removals, or reassignments of the legally constituted positions of DON. At his or her own discretion, the SECNAV controls the selection and assignment of all other principal officials of the department.

❧ ❧ *Undersecretary of the Navy*

The undersecretary of the Navy is the deputy and principal assistant to the SECNAV and acts with the secretary's authority in managing DON. He or she serves as the department's chief operating officer and must promptly and fully inform the SECNAV regarding any matter or action taken involving or affecting DON. The undersecretary is supported by two assistants: a deputy undersecretary of the Navy and an assistant for administration.

Deputy Undersecretary of the Navy (DUSN). This deputy serves as the principal civilian adviser to the secretary and undersecretary on defense and foreign policy; sensitive activities, intelligence, and intelligence-related support activities; policy implications of emerging naval capabilities and concepts; military readiness; and special operations and irregular warfare.

Department of the Navy Assistant for Administration (DON/AA). This assistant to the undersecretary serves as a senior adviser on business systems, information technology, information management, administrative services, innovation initiatives, and management processes. Notably, DON/AA oversees the administration and management of the Navy secretariat.

❧ ❧ *Civilian Executive Assistants to the Secretary of the Navy*

The Navy secretariat also includes civilian executive assistants who are authorized and directed to act for the secretary and undersecretary within assigned areas of responsibility. They also supervise all functions and activities internal to their offices and to any designated field activities. These principal civilian executives, whose responsibilities are summarized below, exercise top management, oversight, and coordination over the bureaus and offices of DON.

Assistant Secretary of the Navy (Research, Development, and Acquisition). The ASN(RD&A) supervises all research, development, engineering, test, evaluation, and procurement efforts within DON, naturally including the Marine Corps. Assisting in the execution of the duties of the ASN(RD&A) are two principal deputies, one military and one civilian. Among several agencies under this assistant secretary is the Office of Naval Research, with which the Marine Corps interacts regularly.

Assistant Secretary of the Navy (Financial Management and Comptroller). As the SECNAV's principal financial adviser, the ASN(FM&C) is responsible for all matters relating to financial management and comptrollership within DON, including budgeting, accounting, financing, progress and statistical reporting, and auditing. No other office or entity may be established or designated therein to perform these responsibilities.

Assistant Secretary of the Navy (Energy, Installations, and Environment). The ASN(EI&E) supervises all matters relating to the acquisition and disposal of real property; construction and maintenance of installations; improvement of energy efficiency and security; protection, safety, and occupational health of DON's military and civilian personnel; environmental protection, planning, and restoration ashore and afloat; and conservation of natural and cultural resources.

Assistant Secretary of the Navy (Manpower and Reserve Affairs). The ASN(M&RA) supervises all manpower and reserve matters, including the development of programs and policy related to military personnel (active, reserve, and retired), their family members, and the civilian workforce, including morale- and performance-related matters; the tracking of the contractor workforce; and the oversight of DON's human resources systems. Various naval personnel boards function under the ASN(M&RA). Several of these affect Marines, including the Board for Correction of Naval Records, Naval Clemency and Parole Board, Navy Discharge Review Board, and Naval Physical Disability Review Board.

General Counsel of the Department of the Navy. As DON's chief legal officer, the GC also heads the Office of the General Counsel (OGC), which furnishes legal services in the field of commercial law. The GC is responsible for legal aspects of procurement, contracts, property disposition, and renegotiation. The GC maintains a close working relationship with the Navy's judge advocate general and the staff judge advocate to the commandant of the Marine Corps on all matters of shared interest.

In the event of death, incapacitation, or resignation of the SECNAV, the order of succession as acting secretary is as follows: the undersecretary of the Navy; assistant secretaries, either in the order prescribed by the secretary and approved by the secretary of defense or, if no order is prescribed, then the seniority in office of the respective assistant secretaries; the GC; the Chief of Naval Operations; and the commandant of the Marine Corps.

Within the Office of the Secretary of the Navy, there are also several staff assistants who support the SECNAV in the leadership and direction of DON. Within assigned areas of responsibility, they supervise all functions and activities internal to their offices and to assigned field activities, if any. Several of these staff assistants and their offices within the Navy secretariat merit special mention:

- Chief of legislative affairs, who leads the Office of Legislative Affairs, advises and assists the secretary and all other principal military and civilian officials of DON in connection with legislative affairs and congressional relations.
- Chief of information (CHINFO), who leads the Office of Information, oversees the performance of public information and public relations functions for DON and the Chief of Naval Operations.
- Chief of naval research (CNR), who directs the Office of Naval Research and assigned shore activities, is DON's science and technology executive.
- Judge advocate general, who leads the Office of the Judge Advocate General, supports both the SECNAV and the Chief of Naval Operations by providing legal and policy advice.
- Inspector general, who leads the Office of the Inspector General, conducts independent investigations and inspections on behalf of the SECNAV and formulates policies and procedures governing the conduct of the same at lower levels within the department.

- Director of the Department of the Navy Sexual Assault Prevention and Response Office serves as the SECNAV's direct source of subject matter expertise on sexual assault prevention and response.

⇴ *Uniformed Naval Executives to the Secretary of the Navy*

Two senior naval officers support the SECNAV in his or her leadership of the department.

Chief of Naval Operations (CNO). The CNO, an admiral, is the senior officer of DON and principal naval adviser to the president and to the SECNAV. The CNO commands the U.S. Navy and is responsible to the SECNAV for its operation and administration. As Navy member of the JCS, the CNO is responsible additionally to the president and secretary of defense for certain duties external to DON.

Per Title 10, U.S. Code, and subject to the authority, direction, and control of the SECNAV, the CNO is principally responsible for

- presiding over OPNAV;
- transmitting the plans and recommendations of OPNAV to the SECNAV and advising the secretary about such plans and recommendations;
- putting plans and recommendations into effect after their approval;
- supervising, as the SECNAV determines and consistent with the authority assigned to commanders of unified or specified CCMDs, the service-members and organizations of the Navy;
- performing prescribed duties relating to membership on the Armed Forces Policy Council, to acquisition-related functions for service chiefs, and to certain other provisions of law;
- performing prescribed duties as a member of the JCS; and
- performing such other military duties, not otherwise assigned by law, as may be assigned by the president, the secretary of defense, or the SECNAV.

Commandant of the Marine Corps (CMC). The CMC, a general and the senior officer in the Corps, commands the U.S. Marine Corps and is directly responsible to the SECNAV. The commandant has additional responsibility to the CNO for the forces of the Corps assigned to the Operating Forces of the

Navy, to the civilian executive assistants for matters related to them, and to the president and secretary of defense for certain duties external to DON.

Per Title 10, U.S. Code, and subject to the authority, direction, and control of the SECNAV, the CMC is principally responsible for

- presiding over Headquarters, U.S. Marine Corps;
- transmitting the plans and recommendations of Headquarters, U.S. Marine Corps, to the SECNAV and advising the SECNAV about such plans and recommendations;
- putting plans and recommendations into effect after their approval;
- supervising, as the SECNAV determines and consistent with the authority assigned to commanders of unified or specified CCMDs, the service-members and organizations of the Marine Corps;
- performing prescribed duties relating to membership on the Armed Forces Policy Council, to acquisition-related functions for service chiefs, and to certain other provisions of law;
- performing prescribed duties as a member of the JCS; and
- performing such other military duties, not otherwise assigned by law, as may be assigned by the president, the secretary of defense, or the SECNAV.

The commandant of the Coast Guard is a uniformed naval executive to the SECNAV when the Coast Guard is attached to the Navy in a time of war or emergency (see chapter 3).

❯ THE UNITED STATES NAVY

As provided in the National Security Act, the U.S. Navy, within DON, includes naval, land, air, space, and cyberspace forces, both combat and support, not otherwise assigned, to include those organic forces and capabilities necessary to operate and support the Navy and Marine Corps, the other military services, and joint forces. Together with the Marine Corps, the Navy constitutes the nation's principal maritime force. Providing global reach, persistent presence through forward-stationed and rotationally based forces, and operational flexibility, the Navy helps secure the nation from direct attack, ensures strategic access to vital areas and global freedom of action, strengthens existing and emerging alliances and partnerships, establishes favorable security conditions, deters aggression and violence, and, should deterrence fail, conducts the full range of military operations in support of U.S. national interests.

❧❧ *Mission and Functions of the Navy*

The United States is a maritime nation, and the U.S. Navy protects it and its interests at sea. Alongside U.S. allies and partners, the Navy executes its mission to "defend freedom, preserve economic prosperity, and keep the seas open and free." It accomplishes this by executing directives under Title 10, U.S. Code, to include organizing, training, and equipping forces for the conduct of prompt and sustained combat operations on, above, below, and in proximity to the sea and by performing additional tasks assigned by the president, secretary of defense, and CCDRs.

In addition to the functions common to all military services, the Navy is responsible per DODD 5100.01 to develop concepts, doctrine, tactics, techniques, and procedures and to organize, train, equip, and provide forces to perform the following specific functions:

- Conduct offensive and defensive operations associated with the maritime domain, including achieving and maintaining sea control and covering subsurface, surface, land, air, space, and cyberspace operations.
- Project power through sea-based global strike, including nuclear and conventional capabilities; interdiction and interception capabilities; maritime and/or littoral fires, including naval surface fires; and close air support for ground forces.
- Conduct ballistic missile defense.
- Conduct oceanic, hydrographic, and river survey and reconstruction.
- Conduct riverine operations.
- Establish, maintain, and defend sea bases in support of naval, amphibious, land, air, or other joint operations as directed.
- Provide naval expeditionary logistics to enhance the deployment, sustainment, and redeployment of naval forces and other forces operating within the maritime domain, including joint sea bases, and provide sea transport for the armed forces other than that which is organic to the individual military services, USSOCOM, and USCYBERCOM.

- Provide support for joint space operations to enhance naval operations, in coordination with the other military services, CCMDs, and U.S. government departments and agencies.
- Conduct nuclear operations in support of strategic deterrence, including providing and maintaining nuclear surety and capabilities.

Command flows from the president through the secretary of defense and the SECNAV to Navy units and installations throughout the world. The Navy is composed of regular and reserve components. It does not include national guard forces like the Army and Air Force.

The Navy's basic organization structure includes OPNAV, the Operating Forces, and the Shore Establishment (see figure 4-3).

❧ ❧ *Office of the Chief of Naval Operations*

OPNAV assists the SECNAV in carrying out his or her responsibilities. It includes the CNO, whose role and responsibilities have been discussed; the vice chief of naval operations; deputy chiefs of naval operations; assistant chiefs of naval operations; and other special staff officers. OPNAV is analogous to Headquarters, U.S. Marine Corps. Within it, several individuals perform critical functions in support of the CNO.

❧ ❧ ❧ *Vice Chief of Naval Operations*

The vice chief of naval operations (VCNO) acts for the CNO on all matters not specifically assigned solely to the CNO, performs the duties of the CNO during the chief's absence, and is principal adviser to the CNO. Under the VCNO are the special assistants for Public Affairs (No9C), Safety Matters (No9F), Inspections (No9G), Legal Services (No9J), Legislative Support (No9L), Naval Investigative Matters and Security (No9N), and Material Inspections and Surveys (No9P).

There is also a director of the Navy staff (DNS) who functions on behalf of the CNO and VCNO as the coordinator among the deputy chiefs of naval operations and the field activities reporting directly to the CNO. The latter include the surgeon general of the Navy (No93), chief of Navy Reserve (No95), and the chief of chaplains of the Navy (No97).

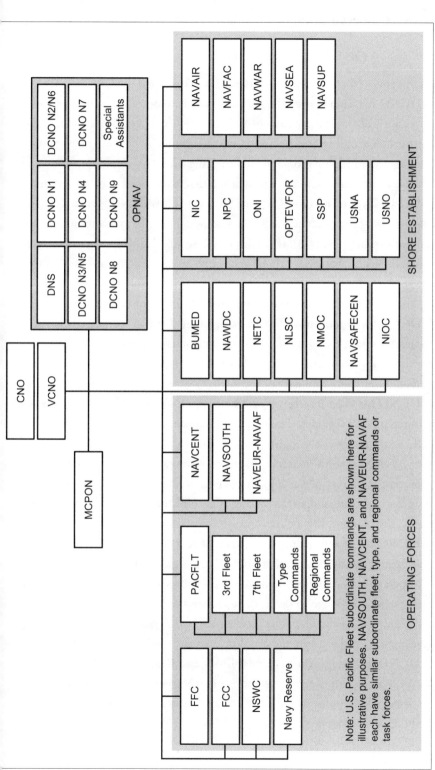

FIGURE 4-3. Organization of the U.S. Navy (2021)

❖ ❖ ❖ *Deputy Chiefs of Naval Operations*

Seven deputy chiefs of naval operations (DCNOs) assist the CNO.

DCNO for Total Force (N1). This deputy is responsible for ensuring that sailors are ready for the myriad jobs and tasks they must undertake in the Navy. This includes finding and recruiting talented individuals, managing training pipelines and education programs, and ensuring that Navy ships, squadrons, and submarines are fully manned. This officer also serves as chief of naval personnel.

DCNO for Information Warfare / Director of Naval Intelligence (N2/N6). Exercising staff responsibility for battlespace awareness (N2) and communications and network matters (N6), this officer oversees the Navy's primary office for resourcing such capabilities as intelligence, cyberwarfare, command and control, electronic warfare, battle management, oceanography, and meteorology. He or she also serves as the deputy chief information officer for DON.

DCNO for Operations, Plans, and Strategy (N3/N5). This deputy has cognizance over the monitoring of daily operations and readiness of the Navy, service planning for present and future military strategy, and working with the Joint Staff on the numerous military policy matters that occupy the Washington scene.

DCNO for Fleet Readiness and Logistics (N4). This deputy serves as the resource sponsor for operational logistics and supply chain support, exercising staff cognizance over the logistic requirements of the Operating Forces of the Navy, including ships' matériel readiness, shore facilities programming, and inspection and survey of warships. The N4 determines requirements and allocates resources to provide support in such areas as combat logistics, ordnance, supply, energy, distribution, tug, rescue, and salvage platforms.

DCNO for Warfighting Development (N7). Responsible for the Navy's strategy, this officer integrates, prioritizes, and aligns its strategic efforts to solve key operational problems. He or she aims to develop and ensure the Navy's warfighting advantage to deter, dissuade, and deny or defeat adversaries by undertaking three broad, interrelated efforts: "warfighter development, warfare development, and warfighter corps development."

DCNO for Integration of Capabilities and Resources (N8). This deputy plans the allocation of resources, providing a Navy-wide perspective and independent analysis. He or she assesses strategy, requirements, and resources during the budget formulation process.

DCNO for Warfare Systems (N9). This deputy determines, validates, and integrates requirements and resources for manpower, training, sustainment, safety, modernization, and procurement of the Navy's air, surface, undersea, and expeditionary warfare systems (both manned and unmanned). The N9 establishes requirements, sets priorities, and supervises overall planning and programming for such domains as expeditionary warfare, surface warfare, undersea warfare, air warfare, and unmanned warfighting systems. Key divisions include Program Integration (N91); Naval Research (N94); Expeditionary Warfare (N95), which is notably led by a Marine major general; Surface Warfare (N96); Undersea Warfare (N97); and Air Warfare (N98).

❖❖ *Operating Forces of the Navy*

The Operating Forces, as the name implies, conduct naval operations around the world in support of the CCDRs. The Navy's Operating Forces comprise the following major commands:

- U.S. Fleet Forces Command
- U.S. Pacific Fleet
- U.S. Naval Forces Central Command
- U.S. Naval Forces Southern Command
- U.S. Naval Forces Europe-Africa
- U.S. Fleet Cyber Command
- U.S. Naval Special Warfare Command
- U.S. Navy Reserve

Collectively, these commands encompass the seven active "numbered" fleets, seagoing forces, district forces, shore activities, and such other forces as may be assigned by the president or the SECNAV. The fleet commanders and commanders in the Operating Forces function under a dual chain of command. Administratively, they report to the CNO and provide, train, and equip naval forces. Operationally, they provide naval forces and report to the appropriate component commanders of the CCMDs.

Technically, the fleets in the Navy serve as force providers. They do not carry out military operations independently; rather, they train and maintain naval units that will subsequently be provided to the naval forces component of each CCMD. Practically speaking, however, the fleet commander is often also dual-hatted as the naval forces component commander.

All naval units within the major fleets are also organized into categories by type (for example, aviation, submarine, and so forth), reporting administratively to an appropriate type commander. Aircraft carriers, aircraft squadrons, and air stations are under the administrative control of an appropriate commander, Naval Air Forces. Submarines come under a commander, Submarine Forces. Other ships and Navy units fall under a commander, Surface Forces. Marine forces, when assigned, report to their own type commander, a commanding general, Fleet Marine Forces. The purpose of this "type organization" is to prepare and provide forces for operations—not to conduct operations.

❧ ❧ ❧ *U.S. Fleet Forces Command*

U.S. Fleet Forces Command is a large, unique operational and administrative command that merits more detailed examination. It was originally established as U.S. Atlantic Fleet on January 1, 1906, by combining the Navy's North Atlantic and South Atlantic Squadrons. Since then, the command has undergone several reorganizations and redesignations. Today it continues to perform its mission to support national defense by providing strategic deterrence with ready forces in the right place at the right time.

This command has a fourfold mission:

- Train, certify, and provide to the CCDRs combat-ready Navy forces that can conduct prompt and sustained naval, joint, and combined operations in support of U.S. national interests.
- Command and control subordinate Navy forces and shore activities during the planning and execution of assigned service functions in support of the CNO.
- Provide operational planning and coordination support to the commanders of USNORTHCOM and USSTRATCOM.
- Command and control subordinate forces during the planning and execution of joint missions as commander of U.S. Naval Forces Northern Command in support of USNORTHCOM.

Fleet Forces Command comprises the Second Fleet, which operates in the northern Atlantic Ocean and along the East Coast of the United States; the five type commands Naval Air Force Atlantic, Naval Surface Force Atlantic, Submarine Force Atlantic, Navy Expeditionary Combat Command Atlantic, and Navy Munitions Command Atlantic; Naval Information Forces, which staffs, trains, equips, and certifies combat-ready information warfare forces for the Navy; Navy Warfare Development Command, whose mission is to "develop and integrate innovative solutions to complex naval warfare challenges to enhance current and future warfighting capabilities"; Military Sealift Command, which serves the Navy and the entire DOD as an ocean carrier of equipment, fuel, ammunition, and other goods essential to the smooth function of U.S. armed forces worldwide, also doubling as the Navy component command of USTRANSCOM; and several smaller "niche" commands, centers, and offices with very focused missions.

Notably, Fleet Forces Command also includes Task Force 80, the designation for its major maritime headquarters and task force. Task Force 80 is the lead organization within Fleet Forces Command for all predeployment training, evaluation, and readiness of assigned naval units. It comprises Strike Force Training Atlantic; Carrier Strike Groups 2, 8, 10, and 12; Expeditionary Strike Group 2; and several smaller groups and squadrons specialized in coastal patrol, riverine operations, explosive ordnance disposal, and other disciplines.

As units of the Navy deploy from the continental United States, where they are under the control of Fleet Forces Command, and enter an area of responsibility of a CCMD and the associated Navy component commander, they are operationally reassigned to the appropriate Navy component and numbered fleet.

❯ ❯ ❯ *Major Component Commands*

In addition to U.S. Fleet Forces Command, the Navy's Operating Forces include several component commands that typically exercise administrative and operational control over one or more of the numbered fleets and other assigned forces. Each of these is oriented either geographically or functionally in support of a CCMD.

U.S. Pacific Fleet, which is the Navy component of USINDOPACOM, comprises the Third Fleet, which operates in the northern, southern, and eastern Pacific Ocean, as well as along the West Coast of the United States; the Seventh Fleet, the largest forward-deployed U.S. fleet, which operates in the western Pacific and the Indian Ocean, stretching to the Persian Gulf and including much

An F/A-18F Super Hornet multirole fighter aircraft launches
from the aircraft carrier USS *Harry S. Truman*, operating
in the Fifth Fleet's area of responsibility.

of the east coast of Africa; and the four type commands Naval Air Force Pacific,
Naval Surface Force Pacific, Submarine Force Pacific, and Navy Expeditionary
Combat Command Pacific.

U.S. Naval Forces Central Command, which is the Navy component of
USCENTCOM, contains the Fifth Fleet, which operates in the Persian Gulf,
Red Sea, Gulf of Oman, and parts of the Indian Ocean, and several specific
task forces separate from the Fifth Fleet.

U.S. Naval Forces Southern Command, which is the Navy component of
USSOUTHCOM, centers on the Fourth Fleet, which operates in the Caribbean
basin and portions of the Atlantic and Pacific Oceans adjacent to Central and
South America. The Fourth Fleet performs a variety of missions, including
contingency operations, counter-narcoterrorism, and theater security cooperation
activities.

U.S. Naval Forces Europe-Africa, which serves as the Navy component for both USEUCOM and USAFRICOM, includes the Sixth Fleet, which operates in the eastern half of the Atlantic Ocean from the North Pole to Antarctica as well as in the Adriatic, Baltic, Barents, Black, Caspian, Mediterranean, and North Seas. U.S. Naval Forces Europe-Africa also includes a number of specific task forces.

Because of their proximity to many of the world's hotspots, the Fifth, Sixth, and Seventh Fleets in the Persian Gulf, Mediterranean, and Far East, respectively, represent the cutting edge of American sea power in these vital regions. Each ordinarily includes one or more Amphibious Ready Groups with embarked Marine Expeditionary Units (MEUs), task-organized combined arms units built around a reinforced Marine infantry battalion.

U.S. Fleet Cyber Command centers on the Tenth Fleet, which has operational control of Navy cyber forces that execute the full spectrum of computer network operations, cyberwarfare, electronic warfare, information operations, and signals intelligence capabilities and missions across the electromagnetic spectrum and the space and cyber domains. Tenth Fleet also coordinates with and supports other fleet commanders, providing guidance and direction to ensure coordinated, synchronized, and effective defense and response capability in cyberspace. Fleet Cyber Command serves as the Navy component command for USCYBERCOM.

U.S. Naval Special Warfare Command serves as the Navy component of USSOCOM. It provides vision, leadership, guidance, resources, and oversight to ensure component maritime special operations forces are ready to meet the operational requirements of CCDRs.

The U.S. Navy Reserve exists to "provide strategic depth and deliver operational capabilities to the Navy and Marine Corps team and joint forces, in times of peace or war." Its purpose and general organization are described in additional detail later in this chapter.

These major component commands and fleets are normally regarded as too large to execute specific operational missions, while individual ships, submarines, and aviation squadrons are usually too small. So below the level of component commands and fleets, naval forces are further organized—in decreasing size, scope, and capability—into task forces, task groups, task units, and task elements. Because the Operating Forces of the Marine Corps integrate with this organizational construct, it is discussed in chapter 9.

❧❧ *Shore Establishment of the Navy*

The Shore Establishment provides training, administrative, and logistical support to the Operating Forces. It comprises all field activities of DON except shore activities assigned to the Operating Forces of the Navy, including various systems and engineering commands, education and training commands, and several other commands, centers, groups, and offices providing specialized services and support.

Shore commands provide capabilities and facilities for the repair of ships, aircraft, machinery, and electronics; communications centers; training areas and simulators; intelligence and meteorological support activities; storage areas for repair parts, fuel, and munitions; and medical and dental facilities. Major shore commands include the following:

- Bureau of Medicine and Surgery (BUMED)
- Naval Aviation Warfighting Development Center (NAWDC)
- Naval Education and Training Command (NETC)
- Naval Legal Service Command (NLSC)
- Naval Meteorology and Oceanography Command (NMOC)
- Naval Safety Center (NAVSAFECEN)
- Navy Information Operations Command (NIOC)
- Navy Installations Command (NIC)
- Navy Personnel Command (NPC)
- Office of Naval Intelligence (ONI)
- Operational Test and Evaluation Force (OPTEVFOR)
- Strategic Systems Programs (SSP)
- United States Naval Academy (USNA)
- United States Naval Observatory (USNO)

Systems commands oversee the Navy's technical requirements; manage the design, development, acquisition, repair, storage, and distribution of weapon systems, equipment, and supplies; and manage the design, construction, and maintenance of facilities. The Navy has five systems commands:

- Naval Air Systems Command (NAVAIR)
- Naval Facilities Engineering Systems Command (NAVFAC)
- Naval Information Warfare Systems Command (NAVWAR)

- Naval Sea Systems Command (NAVSEA)
- Naval Supply Systems Command (NAVSUP)

The activities of the Shore Establishment are generally distributed along the coasts, where they can best serve the Operating Forces. Many activities for which such proximity to the sea is not essential (notably air, ordnance, and supply) are based inland.

❯ ❯ ❯ Navy Installations Command

Established in 2003, Navy Installations Command is responsible for Navy-wide shore installation management. It serves as a single organization for this activity and focuses on installation effectiveness and improving the shore installation community's ability to support the fleet. Commander, Navy Installations Command, has overall management responsibility for shore installations and leads installation policy and program execution oversight.

Navy Installations Command is organized worldwide into the following ten regionally oriented subordinate commands and activities:

- Naval District Washington
- Navy Region Europe, Africa, and Southwest Asia
- Navy Region Hawaii
- Navy Region Japan
- Navy Region Korea
- Navy Region Mid-Atlantic
- Navy Region Northwest
- Navy Region Southeast
- Navy Region Southwest
- Joint Region Marianas

Within their geographic areas of responsibility, these commands oversee clusters of naval bases, naval stations, naval shipyards, naval weapons stations, naval air stations, naval air facilities (which are like naval air stations but provide fewer capabilities, serve an auxiliary function, or are geographically situated within a sovereign allied nation), and smaller naval support activities, fleet support activities, and naval support facilities.

❯ ❯ ❯ Naval Bases and Stations

A naval base or station centralizes in one command's activities that support the fleet. At each major naval base or station, a single, designated officer normally exercises command over all fleet support activities. A naval base or station may include a shipyard and/or an air station. Commanders of naval shipyards are technically qualified officers who are skilled in industrial and matériel management.

Commanding officers of the component activities of a naval base or station receive instructions on support and technical matters directly from the responsible agencies in DON.

❯ ❯ ❯ Naval Air Stations

A naval air station typically comprises the various Shore Establishment activities that furnish aviation logistic support to the Operating Forces of the Navy. Commanding officers of component activities of naval air stations are subject to the command of their air station commander. As with naval bases and stations, support of such activities stems directly from DON.

❯ ❯ Components of the United States Navy

❯ ❯ ❯ The Regular Navy

The active component of the Navy is often referred to as the Regular Navy. It includes all naval combat and service forces, including organic aviation, that are organized, trained, and equipped—and do not require formal *mobilization*—for prompt and sustained combat incident to operations at sea. The active component encompasses the Navy's aircraft carriers and carrier air wings, cruisers, destroyers, frigates, submarines, amphibious warships, littoral combat ships, mine countermeasures ships, and patrol craft; crews; squadron, group, and fleet staffs; and supporting naval forces, organizations, and infrastructure.

Officers of the Regular Navy (and, for that matter, the Navy Reserve) are divided among the following communities: unrestricted line, restricted line, staff corps, limited duty officer, and warrant officer.

Unrestricted Line. The community of unrestricted line officers comprises aviation, surface warfare, nuclear (both surface and submarine) warfare, naval special warfare, and explosive ordnance disposal. These individuals are commissioned

Ohio-class ballistic missile submarine USS *Alaska* returns to home port following a strategic deterrence patrol. The boat can carry up to twenty submarine-launched ballistic missiles with multiple warheads.

officers of the U.S. Navy, both Regular Navy and Navy Reserve, who are not restricted in the performance of duty and are qualified to command at sea the Navy's combatant units, such as warships, submarines, aviation squadrons, and naval special warfare teams. They are also qualified to command at higher echelons, such as destroyer and submarine squadrons, aviation wings and groups, and naval special warfare groups.

Although not eligible to command at sea or to command a Navy base or station, commissioned Marine officers are nevertheless unrestricted line officers of the naval service and have been held, legally, to be naval officers.

Restricted Line. The community of restricted line officers covers the following disciplines: aerospace engineering duty, aviation maintenance duty, cyberwarfare engineering, engineering duty, foreign area, human resources, information professional, cryptologic warfare, intelligence, public affairs, oceanography, and permanent military professor. Restricted line officers of the Regular Navy and

Navy Reserve perform duties only within their specialties. They have limited authorization to command ashore but are not eligible for combatant command at sea, which remains strictly within the purview of unrestricted line officers.

Staff Corps. The Navy's Staff Corps include the Medical Corps, Dental Corps, Nurse Corps, Medical Service Corps, Chaplain Corps, Supply Corps, Civil Engineer Corps, and Judge Advocate General Corps (see figure 4-4). Officers, both Regular and Reserve, of the Navy's staff corps are specialists as described below:

- *Medical.* This corps is composed exclusively of doctors of medicine who treat the ill, injured, and wounded and administer the hospitals, dispensaries, sick bays, and other medical units of the naval establishment. Medical and dental services for the Marine Corps are provided by Navy doctors, dentists, and hospital corpsmen.

- *Nurse.* Navy nurses are commissioned officers in the Nurse Corps. They serve in hospitals and dispensaries at home and on foreign installations and in hospital ships and transports at sea.

- *Medical Service.* This corps is composed of specialists in optometry, pharmacy, and such allied sciences as bacteriology, biochemistry, psychology, and medical administration and statistics.

- *Dental.* Composed of dental surgeons, this is a separate corps whose members serve at hospitals and dispensaries and on board larger ships. The Dental Corps, like the Medical, Nurse, and Medical Service Corps, comes under BUMED.

- *Chaplain.* Ordained ministers of various denominations, officers of the Chaplain Corps conduct religious services and promote the spiritual and moral welfare of the Navy and Marine Corps. The chief of chaplains heads the corps. The deputy chief of chaplains also serves as the chaplain of the Marine Corps.

- *Supply.* This is the business branch of the Navy that administers the Navy supply system and receives and disburses funds for supply and for pay, subsistence, and transportation.

- *Civil Engineer.* This corps is composed of formally educated and licensed civil engineers, normally restricted to shore duty, who supervise buildings, grounds, and plants at shore installations as well as the construction of buildings and the layout of shore bases and stations. This corps conceived,

Specialty Insignia — Staff Corps

Medical Corps

Dental Corps

Nurse Corps

Medical Service Corps

Chaplain Corps
(Christian)

Chaplain Corps
(Jewish)

Chaplain Corps
(Muslim)

Supply Corps

Civil Engineer
Corps

Judge Advocate
General's Corps

Specialty Insignia — LDO and Warrant

Boatswain

Engineering

Repair

Ordnance

Diving Officer

Aviation Boatswain

Aviation Ordnance
Technician

Aviation Electronics
Technician

Air Traffic
Control
Technician

Ship's Clerk

Data Processing
Technician

Cryptologic
Technician

Aerographer

Security
Technician

Aviation Maintenance
Technician

FIGURE 4-4. Specialty Insignia of Navy Staff Corps,
Limited Duty, and Warrant Officers

organized, and commanded the Navy construction battalions (Seabees) that served so illustriously beside Marines during World War II, Korea, and Vietnam.

- *Judge Advocate General.* This corps consists of Navy lawyers who have been duly certified to practice law and perform staff legal and judicial duties under the judge advocate general and within the system of military jurisprudence.

Members of certain staff corps, such as the Medical, Supply, and Civil Engineer Corps, may command shore activities and units (such as Seabees) under the cognizance of their respective bureaus.

Limited Duty Officer (LDO). As officer technical managers of the line or staff corps, LDOs serve specifically within broad technical fields, such as administration, cryptology, electronics, ordnance, and supply, that are related to their former enlisted ratings. At the level of ensign through captain, they fill leadership and management positions that require technical background and skills not attainable through the normal development of unrestricted line officers. Under varying circumstances, LDOs may serve as division officers, department heads, officers in charge, executive officers, and commanding officers.

Warrant Officer (WO). Today, LDOs, WOs, and chief warrant officers (CWOs) are qualified by extensive experience and knowledge and possess the authority to direct the most complex and exacting operations within a given occupational specialty. Warrant officer specialties include, among others, acoustics, aviation maintenance, nuclear power, food service, and oceanography. Although intended primarily as technical specialists, WOs and CWOs may serve as division officers, department heads, and officers in charge.

Enlisted Persons. Enlisted men and women of the Navy and Coast Guard are divided into rating groups (as illustrated in figure 4-5). Just as we expect Navy officers to recognize and identify Marine noncommissioned officers, so should a Marine officer be able to identify Navy petty officers in the various ratings.

❯ ❯ ❯ *The Navy Reserve*

The Navy Reserve, as the name implies, is the reserve component of the Navy. Its mission is to "provide strategic depth and deliver operational capabilities to

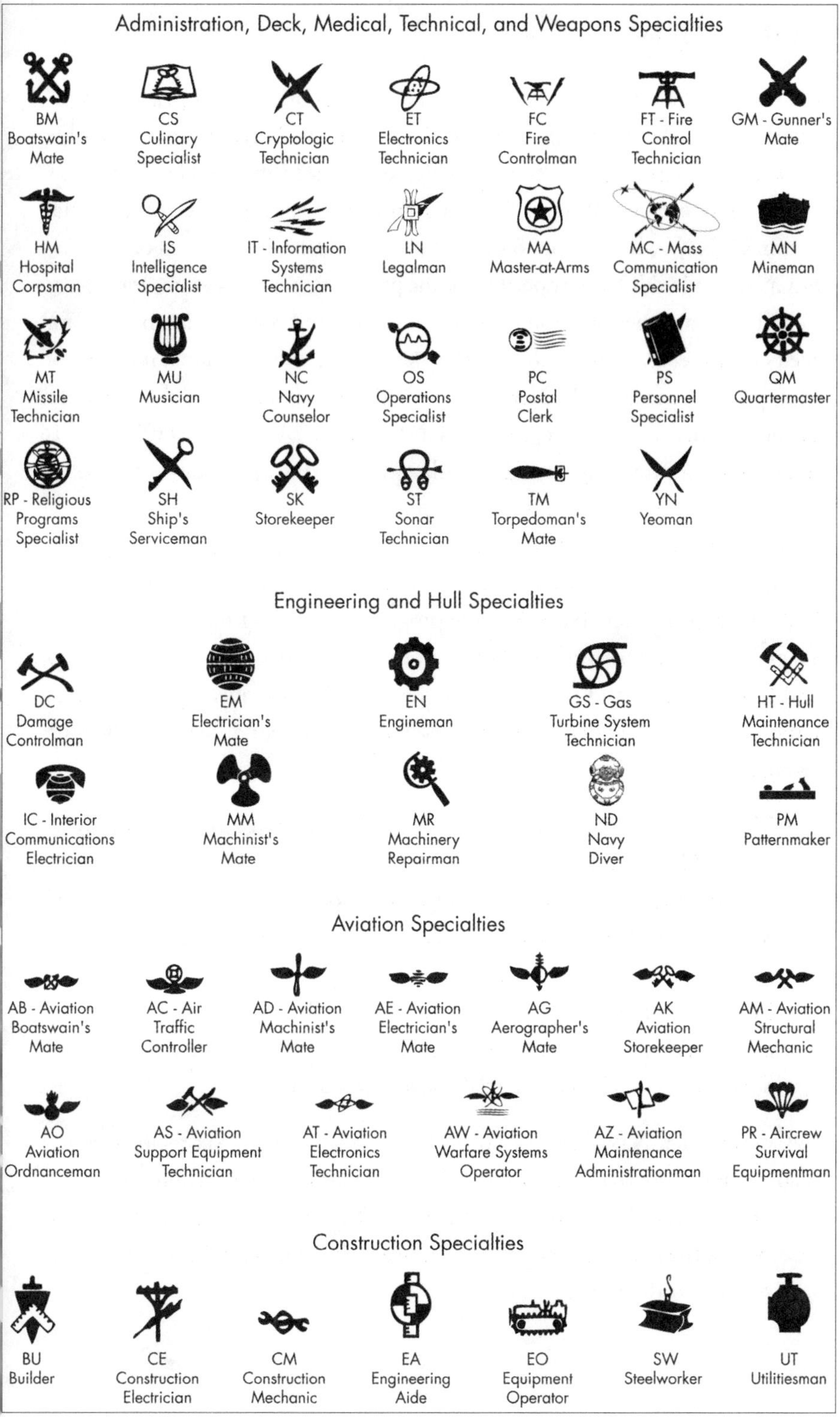

Administration, Deck, Medical, Technical, and Weapons Specialties

 BM Boatswain's Mate

 CS Culinary Specialist

 CT Cryptologic Technician

 ET Electronics Technician

 FC Fire Controlman

 FT - Fire Control Technician

GM - Gunner's Mate

 HM Hospital Corpsman

IS Intelligence Specialist

IT - Information Systems Technician

LN Legalman

MA Master-at-Arms

MC - Mass Communication Specialist

MN Mineman

 MT Missile Technician

MU Musician

NC Navy Counselor

OS Operations Specialist

 PC Postal Clerk

PS Personnel Specialist

 QM Quartermaster

 RP - Religious Programs Specialist

SH Ship's Serviceman

SK Storekeeper

ST Sonar Technician

TM Torpedoman's Mate

YN Yeoman

Engineering and Hull Specialties

DC Damage Controlman

 EM Electrician's Mate

EN Engineman

GS - Gas Turbine System Technician

HT - Hull Maintenance Technician

 IC - Interior Communications Electrician

 MM Machinist's Mate

MR Machinery Repairman

 ND Navy Diver

PM Patternmaker

Aviation Specialties

 AB - Aviation Boatswain's Mate

 AC - Air Traffic Controller

 AD - Aviation Machinist's Mate

 AE - Aviation Electrician's Mate

 AG Aerographer's Mate

 AK Aviation Storekeeper

 AM - Aviation Structural Mechanic

 AO Aviation Ordnanceman

 AS - Aviation Support Equipment Technician

AT - Aviation Electronics Technician

 AW - Aviation Warfare Systems Operator

 AZ - Aviation Maintenance Administrationman

PR - Aircrew Survival Equipmentman

Construction Specialties

 BU Builder

 CE Construction Electrician

 CM Construction Mechanic

 EA Engineering Aide

 EO Equipment Operator

 SW Steelworker

 UT Utilitiesman

FIGURE 4-5. Specialty Insignia of Navy Enlisted Ratings

the Navy and Marine Corps team and joint forces, in times of peace or war." The purpose, classification, and organization of the Navy Reserve resemble those of the Marine Corps Reserve, which is discussed in detail in chapter 7.

The chief of Navy Reserve (CNR), normally a vice admiral, is the official within OPNAV who, subject to the authority, direction, and control of both the SECNAV and CNO, is responsible for the preparation, justification, and execution of the personnel, operation and maintenance, and construction budgets for the Navy Reserve. As such, the CNR is the director and functional manager of appropriations made for the Navy Reserve in these areas. He or she also functions as commander, Navy Reserve Force (CNRF or COMNAVRESFOR), and is responsible for providing strategic depth and delivering operational capabilities to the Navy–Marine Corps team and joint force.

Reporting to the CNR/CNRF is the deputy CNRF, who is also dual-hatted as commander, Navy Reserve Forces Command. Normally a rear admiral, this individual administers Navy Reserve programs, including management of all assigned resources; performs other functions or tasks directed by both the CNO and CNR/CNRF; and performs additional duties prescribed by Fleet Forces Command. Commander, Navy Reserve Forces Command, has the following responsibilities:

- Manage, train, and administer the Navy Reserve Force as prescribed by the CNO and CNRF.
- Manage and execute assigned budgetary resources.
- Monitor the effectiveness of resource management, training, and administration of the Navy Reserve.
- Ensure the mobilization readiness of the Navy Reserve to meet requirements, taking corrective action when necessary to remedy shortcomings.
- Serve as a general court-martial convening authority.

Commander, Navy Reserve Forces Command, operates six regional headquarters and more than one hundred Navy operational support centers located in all fifty states, Puerto Rico, and Guam. The support centers generate the readiness of the Navy Reserve by providing administrative, training, and readiness support to Reservists.

Within the structure of the Navy Reserve are three major organizational categories that further define a member's service responsibilities and commitment status: Ready Reserve, Standby Reserve, and Retired Reserve. Each Reservist falls into one of these categories based on details such as military experience, military status, and individual situation.

Ready Reserve. This provides trained officers and enlisted Reservists who, added to qualified personnel from other sources, complete the war organization of the Navy. Members of the Ready Reserve are in an active status. It is composed of the Selected Reserve (SELRES), whose members drill regularly for pay, and the Individual Ready Reserve (IRR), whose members are not in a pay status but may drill in a voluntary training unit or be assigned to the nondrilling active status pool. Members of the Ready Reserve are eligible for involuntary recall to active duty in time of national emergency or when authorized by law.

Standby Reserve. This component provides a force of qualified and partially qualified officers and enlisted persons who have transferred from the Ready Reserve after fulfilling certain requirements established by law. Most common are those who have been deemed key civilian employees by a government agency. Within the Standby Reserve, members are further categorized as either active or inactive.

Active Standby Reservists are eligible to participate in a Navy Reserve program without pay for retirement point credit only. They may not receive pay, allowances, or travel allowances for any duty performed. All officers continue to be eligible for promotion consideration. Enlisted members in this category are eligible for advancement only under certain circumstances. Active members of the Standby Reserve are subject to involuntary recall to active duty only in time of war or national emergency.

Inactive members of the Standby Reserve are not eligible to participate in a Navy Reserve program for pay or for retirement points. They also are not assigned to a Navy Reserve organization. They may not be considered for advancement or promotion, but they are subject to recall as authorized by law.

Retired Reserve. This includes those who are drawing retired pay or are qualified for retired pay upon reaching sixty years of age. Members of the Retired Reserve are liable for active duty only in a time of war or an emergency declared by Congress, when otherwise authorized by law, or in the event sufficient qualified personnel are not available in the Ready Reserve and Standby Reserve.

❖ ❖ *Education of Officer Candidates*

There are several paths to becoming a candidate for a commission in the Navy.

United States Naval Academy. The Naval Academy was established in 1845 at old Fort Severn, located at the mouth of the Severn River in Annapolis, Maryland, to train naval officers.

The strength of the Brigade of Midshipmen is maintained by appointments from U.S. senators, representatives, and territorial delegates; by competitive appointments from regular and reserve enlisted men and women of the Navy and Marine Corps; and by appointments at-large by the president and vice president. The so-called presidential appointments are made on a competitive basis from among the children of regular and reserve officers as well as children of any members of the armed forces killed or disabled in the line of duty. In addition, the children of Medal of Honor winners are admitted to the academy upon passing the usual mental and physical examinations.

The academy is commanded by a superintendent of flag rank. The staff includes officers of all the services as well as civilian professors. The course is four years and leads to a B.S. degree regardless of major.

Since the 1880s, the Marine Corps has annually commissioned some Naval Academy graduates as second lieutenants. At present, approximately 20–25 percent of the midshipmen per graduating class are permitted Marine commissions; the competition for these vacancies is keen.

Naval Reserve Officers Training Corps (NROTC). The NROTC offers the opportunity for young men and women to qualify for Navy and Marine Corps commissions while attending college. The path to a commission as a Navy officer via the NROTC program resembles that described in chapter 12 for those pursuing a commission in the Marine Corps.

NROTC units are located at more than sixty institutions throughout the country. Individuals interested in this program may find complete information and application instructions at the NROTC website (https://www.netc.navy.mil/NSTC/NROTC/).

Officer Candidate School. Located at the Naval Training Center, Newport, Rhode Island, the Navy's Officer Candidate School trains young college graduates as Navy officers. Upon completing the thirteen-week course, successful candidates are obligated to serve three to five years on active duty as commissioned officers and to continue in the Reserve a total of six years. Meritorious enlisted persons selected for integration as Regular Navy officers also attend Officer Candidate School.

⁂{ 5 }⁂

ROLES, MISSIONS, AND STATUS OF THE MARINE CORPS

The Marine Corps is the Navy's police force and as long as I am President that is what it will remain. They have a propaganda machine that is almost equal to Stalin's.
— Harry S. Truman to Representative Gordon L. McDonough

I sincerely regret the unfortunate choice of language which I used in my letter of August 29 to Congressman McDonough concerning the Marine Corps.
— Harry S. Truman to General Clifton B. Cates

EVERY AMERICAN respects the Marine Corps (well, almost every American), but a surprising number of people are quite hazy on what the Corps really is and does. Every Marine officer should thus possess precise knowledge of and be skillful at explaining the roles, missions, and status of the Corps.

⁍ MARINE CORPS ROLES AND MISSIONS
⁍ ⁍ *The Law*
The statutes of the United States include many provisions that affect the Marine Corps. All these provisions have been codified under Title 10 (Armed Forces), U.S. Code, as they have been for the others services.

The "charter" of the Marine Corps, however, has evolved from three laws: An Act Establishing and Organizing a Marine Corps, signed 11 July 1798; An Act for the Better Organization of the United States Marine Corps, passed 30 June 1834; and the National Security Act of 1947, as amended.

The National Security Act, which unified the armed services, is the controlling military legislation of the United States. For Marines, though, the Douglas-Mansfield Act of 1952 (Public Law 416, 82nd Congress, 2nd Session) has particular importance. This law amended the National Security Act as it regards the Corps, and the debates and hearings regarding it (1951–52) contain a trove of information.

To summarize, the National Security Act as now amended (see Sections 307 and 401) makes the following provisions for the Marine Corps:

- It reaffirms the Corps' status as a service within the Department of the Navy.
- It provides for Fleet Marine Forces, ground and aviation.
- It requires that the combatant forces of the Corps be organized based on three Marine divisions and three Marine air wings, establishing a peacetime ceiling of 400,000 personnel for the Regular Corps.
- It assigns the Corps the missions of seizure and defense of advanced naval bases as well as land operations incident to naval campaigns.
- It gives the Corps primary responsibility for development of amphibious warfare doctrines, tactics, techniques, and equipment employed by landing forces.
- It seats the commandant of the Marine Corps on the Joint Chiefs of Staff.
- It affords the Corps appropriate representation on various joint Defense Department agencies, notably the Joint Staff.
- It assigns the Corps collateral missions of providing security forces for naval shore installations, providing ships' detachments, and performing such other duties as the president may direct.

In taking stock of Marine Corps missions found in law, it is important not to overlook the short phrase "and shall perform such other duties as the President may direct." This phrase, which the Unification Act quotes directly from the 1834 Marine Corps law, stems in turn from similar language in the Act of 1798. It validates in law those functions that transcend the Corps' purely naval missions. In mid-1951, the House of Representatives Armed Services Committee highlighted the significance of this clause in a trenchant summary:

It is, however, the Committee view that one of the most important statutory—and traditional—functions of the Marine Corps has been and still is to perform "such other duties as the President may direct."

The campaign in Korea, in which the 1st Marine Division and the 1st Marine Air[craft] Wing are presently participating, can hardly be called a naval mission. Practically every war involving the United States has found the Marine Corps performing duties other than naval. Indeed, the first two battalions of Marines raised in this country were raised specifically for service before Boston with General Washington's army.

Many Marine activities in the War of 1812 involved only land fighting; in the 1840s the Marines saw "the Halls of Montezuma" while fighting with the Army in the War with Mexico; in the early 1900s Marine activities in Central America were repeatedly entirely of a land nature; their participation in the fighting in the Boxer Uprising in China in 1900 likewise was of a land nature; certainly when in May 1917 President Wilson ordered the 4th Marine Brigade to serve as part of the Army's 2d Division in the Battles of Belleau Wood, Aisne-Marne, St. Mihiel, Blanc Mont, and Meuse-Argonne, and later in the occupation forces, these can hardly be described as naval missions; nor can the activities of Marine Maj. Gen. John A. Lejeune, in commanding for a time the Army's 2nd Division in France, be called a naval function; nor could the service of Marine aviation in France during 1918 be accurately termed a naval activity.

It is difficult to see how the sending of Marines as the initial force to hold Iceland prior to the last war, until relieved by Army troops, could accurately be called a naval mission; how the reinforcing of Corregidor by the 4th Marine Regiment sent from China just before war broke out, could be accurately termed a naval action; and if the actions of the 1st Marine Division on Guadalcanal, commencing the first American attack of the war on August 7, 1942, can accurately be called a naval action, then in the same fashion the activities of Army divisions in this area must likewise be so termed. It further is worthy of note that on Mindanao and Luzon in the

Embodying the maxim "Any Clime and Place," which paraphrases a line from "The Marines' Hymn," U.S. Marines patrol to a rally point during an exercise in mainland Japan in 2020.

Philippines, in the last ground action against the enemy in World War II, Marine Air Groups 12, 14, 24, and 32, gave close air support to the 24th, 31st, and 41st Infantry Divisions—an activity that appears to the Committee to be only distantly related (if at all) to exclusively naval activities.

The Committee must also call attention to the fact that, after V-J Day, the V Amphibious Corps, USMC, was part of the forces sent to occupy the Japanese Home Islands; the III Marine Amphibious Corps was sent to North China to accept the surrender of Japanese troops there; that a Marine division, with other forces, was kept in China until the summer of 1947 during the attempt of the United States to settle civil war between the Chinese Government and Chinese Communists. It is a strained construction, indeed, of military activities to characterize such employment of the United States Marines as essentially naval in character.

In line with the foregoing, Marines were on several occasions temporarily detached by executive order of the president to service under the secretary of war. The last occasion on which Marines were detached to service under the Army was in July 1941, when the 1st Provisional Marine Brigade in Iceland was assigned to the Army by President Franklin D. Roosevelt. Note the distinction between administrative transfer of Marines to Army duty, which can only be effected by order of the president, and operational attachments under unified command, which occur routinely—as was the case throughout the greater part of the Korean and Vietnam Wars as well as the conflicts in the Persian Gulf and Afghanistan.

So much, then, for the main provisions of law that give the Marine Corps its roles and missions. While those roles are carefully spelled out, the law nevertheless allows employment of Marines anywhere on any service the president may desire.

❖ ❖ *The Functions Paper*

Originally known colloquially as the Key West Agreement of 1948 (see chapter 4), the Department of Defense directive that outlines the functions of that department and of its major components is now usually referred to as the Functions Paper. Its main provisions are currently embodied in DODD 5100.01, *Functions of the Department of Defense and Its Major Components.* The directive is essentially a compilation of interservice agreements dating from 1948, revised from time to time, as to how the provisions of the National Security Act are to be implemented with respect to roles and missions. It also establishes several service relationships and common functions within DOD that affect the Marine Corps equally with the other services.

In addition to the functions common to all, the Marine Corps, within the Department of the Navy, is responsible per DODD 5100.01 to develop concepts, doctrine, tactics, techniques, and procedures and to organize, train, equip, and provide forces—normally employed as combined arms air-ground task forces—to serve as an expeditionary force in readiness and to perform the following specific functions:

- Seize and defend advanced naval bases or lodgments to facilitate subsequent joint operations.

- Provide close air support for ground forces.
- Conduct land and air operations essential to the prosecution of a naval campaign or as directed.
- Conduct complex expeditionary operations in the urban littorals and other challenging environments.
- Conduct amphibious operations, including engagement, crisis response, and power projection, to assure access. The Corps has primary responsibility for the development of amphibious doctrine, tactics, techniques, and equipment.
- Conduct security and stability operations and assist with the initial establishment of a military government pending transfer of this responsibility to another authority.
- Provide security detachments and units for service on armed vessels of the Navy, provide protection of naval property at naval stations and bases, provide security at designated U.S. embassies and consulates, and perform other such duties as the president or the secretary of defense may direct. These additional duties may not detract from or interfere with the operations for which the Marine Corps is primarily organized.

Although many of the foregoing provisions stem directly from and include language of the National Security Act, you should never confuse the Functions Paper, only a departmental directive, with the National Security Act, which is the law and thus governs in any disagreement. Additionally, you should note that the Marine Corps, though repeatedly overruled, has consistently opposed inclusion of the meaningless "second land Army" phrase in the Functions Paper since nothing could be further from its objectives or interests.

In addition to what may be considered its primary missions, the Corps is assigned several collateral missions.

Department of State Guards. Under authority of the Foreign Service Act of 1946, the Marine Corps has a collateral mission to provide security guards for U.S. embassies, legations, and consulates. For this duty, which demands the highest discretion and trust, the Corps furnishes over a thousand Marines, both officer and enlisted, who are distributed throughout more than 110 Department of State overseas stations.

White House Duties. Dating from 1798, the scarlet-coated Marine Band has been called "The President's Own" because of its privilege of providing the music for state functions at the White House. Similarly, Marines have established and guarded presidential camps at Rapidan, Virginia; Warm Springs, Georgia; Camp David, Maryland; and elsewhere, while Marine helicopters were the first to carry a president and still routinely do so.

Unwritten Missions. Nowhere do the statutes say that the Marine Corps is the national force in readiness, yet our history demonstrates clearly that this is and always has been a fundamental mission. To quote former assistant secretary of the Navy John Nicholas Brown: "Readiness, the capacity to move anywhere immediately and become effective, is always needed and at the present juncture of events is especially necessary. This is the daily bread of the Marine Corps."

In close corollary to this traditional mission is the Corps' worldwide service, in times of nominal peace, as "State Department Troops" for enforcement of foreign policy and protection of U.S. nationals—or their evacuation—under direction of the Department of State.

⋗ MARINE CORPS STATUS

"The Marine Corps is sui generis" (something "of its own sort"), ruled a federal judge when construing the legal status of the Corps. This is probably the best one-sentence characterization of the Corps.

The Marine Corps is one of the services—along with the Army, Navy, Air Force, and Space Force—that with the Coast Guard, when attached to the naval establishment in a time of war, compose the armed forces of the United States. It is important to be aware of this since you may sometimes encounter "the three services," an erroneous reference to the three *departments* within DOD, and so far as the Corps is concerned, a term excluding it.

Side by side with the Navy, the Marine Corps is one of two military services in the naval establishment, under direct control and supervision of the SEC-NAV. Although discussed in some detail below, the relationship of the Marine Corps to the Navy is encapsulated in the words of Representative Carl Vinson, distinguished former chairman of the House Armed Services Committee: "The fact is that the Marine Corps is and always has been, since its inception 175 years ago, a separate military service apart from the United States Army, the United States Navy, and the United States Air Force."

Still, a brief account of the evolution of the status of the Marine Corps is useful knowledge for you as a Marine officer.

✦ ✦ *Evolution and Clarification*

The act signed on 11 July 1798 reconstituting the Corps after its post–Revolutionary War hiatus provided for a corps of marines "in addition to the present military establishment." In line with this thinking, although the Corps' distinct status from the Navy was never questioned, it would take nearly forty years for it to be firmly dissociated from the Army. During this time, while on shore, U.S. Marines (like the British marines) were promoted, paid, rationed, and disciplined under Army Regulations—practices sanctioned not only by custom but also by express rulings handed down from time to time by the attorney general of the United States.

To clarify the status of the Marine Corps, Congress in 1834 affirmed the Corps as a separate service but placed it unequivocally under the SECNAV and therefore under Navy Regulations "except when detached for service with the Army, by order of the President."

For more than a century, the Acts of 1798 and 1834 governed the status of the Marine Corps. In 1947, the National Security Act became law. As amended by Public Law 416 of 1952, it not only spells out the missions of our Corps today but also defines the Corps in declaratory language as one of the four services given statutory missions. In the first years of unification, there was some tendency to assume that the National Security Act had intended to organize the armed forces on a three-service basis, with the Marine Corps merely a specialist branch of the Navy. This misconception was set to rest with emphasis in the debate and hearings on Public Law 416, during which Congress avowed that the Marine Corps was not a mere appendage but a service in its own right.

House Report 970 (84th Congress) contains a final and legally definitive ruling on the foregoing point. This is the report by the House of Representatives on the codification of Title 10, U.S. Code. It states, "The legislative history of Public Law 432, the National Security Act of 1947, and Public Law 416 of the

A Marine Corps MV-22B Osprey tiltrotor aircraft takes off from Marine Corps Air Station Iwakuni, Japan, in support of earthquake relief efforts in 2016.

82nd Congress . . . clearly indicate that the Marine Corps is legally a separate and distinct military service within the Department of the Navy, with individually assigned statutory responsibilities, and that the Commandant directs and administers the Marine Corps under delegated command of the Secretary of the Navy."

The status of the Marine Corps can be summed up thus:

- The Marine Corps is a separate military service possessing distinct statutory roles and missions prescribed by the National Security Act.
- The Marine Corps is a part of the naval establishment (or DON) and falls directly under the SECNAV.

- The CMC commands the Corps as a whole and is directly responsible to the SECNAV in a well-defined historical and legal relationship for the total performance, administration, readiness, discipline, and efficiency of the Corps.

❯ THE MARINE CORPS AND THE DEPARTMENT OF THE NAVY

The brotherhood between the Marine Corps and Navy is so longstanding, so close, and so normally smooth in operation that the casual observer may be readily pardoned the erroneous conclusion that the Corps is part of the Navy.

As we have seen, this is not the case. To quote General C. B. Cates, nineteenth commandant from 1948–51,

> The partnership between the Navy and Marine Corps had its legal birth more than 150 years ago when Congress placed both Services—which were then some 25 years of age—under a newly created Secretary of the Navy. The partnership was a close one initially, and it grew even closer with the passage of time. Today it is so close that only a handful of people—inside the Naval Services as well as outside—realize that technically the Navy and Marine Corps are separate Services under the command of the Secretary of the Navy. Practically speaking, the Navy and Marine Corps have lived, worked, and fought together since their inception.

To understand the place of the Marine Corps in the naval establishment, you must first understand exactly what constitutes the Department of the Navy, or, as it was called for many years in the past, "the naval establishment." As stated in Navy Regulations, and in chapter 4 of this guide, the naval establishment (that is, DON) embraces all activities committed to the care of the SECNAV and thus includes the Marine Corps. This does not make the Corps a part of, but rather a partner of, the Navy proper.

❯ ❯ *The Marine Corps and Public Law 432*

The law that defines the position of the Chief of Naval Operations in the Navy is Public Law 432, 80th Congress (or H.R. 3432).

Casual reading of parts of this law by a person not conversant with the intent of Congress in framing it (or of DON in seeking it) might suggest that it places the Marine Corps under the command of the CNO. To save confusion on this, it is enough to quote from an official letter by Secretary of the Navy John L. Sullivan, dated 17 December 1947, to General A. A. Vandegrift, eighteenth commandant:

> The Commandant of the Marine Corps is informed that it is not the intent of the Navy Department, in seeking enactment of H.R. 3432 [Public Law 432], to alter the Commandant's direct responsibility to the Secretary of the Navy for the administration and efficiency of the Marine Corps.
>
> The Navy Department interprets neither Executive Order 9635 [an earlier directive defining the wartime position of the CNO] nor H.R. 3432 as interposing the Chief of Naval Operations in the administrative chain of responsibility between the Secretary and the Commandant, or as otherwise modifying the historical relationship between the Secretary and the Commandant.

❭ ❭ *The Marine Corps as a Naval Service*

Attempts are sometimes made to show that the term "naval service" has a specific organizational meaning that includes both the U.S. Navy and the U.S. Marine Corps so that together they may be said to constitute one military service—that is, the "naval service." The claim that this term has such a meaning is baseless.

The phrase "naval service" originated as a matter of convenience for the SECNAV in issuing orders affecting all military personnel under his jurisdiction. It has occasionally been used for comparable specific purposes in statutes dealing with personnel administration or discipline and with no general or consistent construction or definition of the term in question. That Marines, within the meaning and purposes of these statutes and regulations, are "members of the naval service" has long been accepted without dispute, but as the codification of Title 10, U.S. Code, underscores, the Corps is a legally distinct and separate military service. Therefore, the best usage when this term arises in connection with Marines or the Corps is to pluralize it as the "naval services," for there are always two naval services—the U.S. Navy and the U.S. Marine Corps—

within DON and, when the Coast Guard is assigned in time of hostilities, sometimes three.

❖ ❖ *Working Relations between the Marine Corps and Navy*

Although the emphasis here has been on the legally and essentially separate status of the Marine Corps within the naval establishment, this standing has not prevented harmonious working relations between the Corps and the Navy.

Not only do individual Marines serve as part of Navy commands and vice versa, but units are likewise freely interchanged. Every Navy staff of any consequence includes at minimum one Marine, officer or enlisted, while all major Marine units and bases have Navy doctors, dentists, chaplains, and hospital corpsmen. In addition, Marine Corps forces often include naval gunfire liaison officers—Navy line officers who, as staff officers, help obtain gunfire support.

Each major combatant ship of the fleet once had a Marine detachment, and each major Navy shore installation boasted Marine barracks or detachments for security purposes, although with reductions in Corps end strength, this is no longer universally the case. On the other hand, to this day Navy units such as Seabees, naval beach groups, and so on are frequently assigned to Marine Corps formations.

At higher levels, Marine Corps forces best exemplify the close relationship between the Corps and Navy. There, major Marine Operating Forces are assigned by the SECNAV on a continuing basis to duty with the fleets and, while so assigned operationally under the CNO, are just as much part of a fleet as its ships or aircraft. Side by side with this operational relationship, however, the CMC retains full control over the administration, readiness, and military efficiency of the units concerned. All hands, Marines and Sailors, are governed alike by Navy Regulations. In the words of former secretary of the Navy Robert B. Anderson, "They are, in every sense of the word, a team."

❖ SUMMARY

The missions and status of the Marine Corps are prescribed in the National Security Act as amended. Public Laws 432 (80th Congress) and 416 (82nd Congress) supplement and affirm the act, as does the Functions Paper (even though without statutory standing). For a detailed discussion and analysis of the tortured struggle of the Corps to achieve its statutory position, read Lieutenant General Victor H. Krulak's *First to Fight* (Naval Institute Press, 1999).

The status of the Corps within DON can best be summarized in the words of Vice Admiral O. W. Colclough while serving as judge advocate general of the Navy: "The Marine Corps has been held for years to be a separate Service, although it operates with the Navy, and under the Secretary of the Navy."

Over and above its usual status and duties within the naval framework, the Marine Corps may be, and frequently has been, assigned other duties and status elsewhere in the executive branch under the plenary powers that the president possesses regarding the Corps.

⊰{ **6** }⊱

ORGANIZATION OF THE
MARINE CORPS

Fighting spirit is not primarily the result of a neat organization chart nor of a logical organization set-up. The former should never be sacrificed to the latter.
— Ferdinand Eberstadt

MAJOR GENERAL W. S. "BIGFOOT" BROWN, one of the Marine Corps' most beloved old-timers, began a lecture at a service school with these words: "Well, gentlemen, they've given me the job of describing the organization of the Marine Corps. This surprised me somewhat, because I never knew we had any organization." Despite this prologue, the Corps does have an organization (see figure 6-1), and comprehensive knowledge of it is one of the first things a Marine officer must acquire.

The Marine Corps, within the Department of the Navy, is organized as a general purpose "force in readiness" to support national needs. Deploying for combat as combined arms Marine air-ground task forces, the Corps provides the National Command Authority with a responsive force that can conduct operations across the spectrum of conflict.

Two parallel chains of command—service and operational—exist within the Marine Corps. The service chain begins with the president and progresses sequentially through the secretary of defense, Secretary of the Navy, and commandant of the Marine Corps. The operational chain runs from the NCA (see chapter 3) directly to combatant commanders for missions and forces, including Marine forces, assigned to their commands. Marine Corps component commanders provide operational forces to the CCDRs and other operational commanders as required.

The Marine Corps is made up of land combat, combat support, combat service support, and security forces; aviation combat and support forces; and reserve forces. In many ways, its organization resembles that of the Navy. The Corps is organized into three broad categories: Headquarters, U.S. Marine Corps, and supporting activities; Marine Corps Operating Forces (active and reserve); and Marine Corps Supporting Establishment. Marine aviation is included across these categories, being necessary to carry out the missions of the Corps.

The complete organization of the Marine Corps is detailed in the most current version of Marine Corps Reference Publication 1-10.1, *Organization of the United States Marine Corps*, which contains an extensive and authoritative discussion of this chapter's topic and is available online.

The chapter here describes the *current* organization of the Marine Corps. But you should be aware that the Corps is experiencing a period of extraordinary innovation and change comparable to the period between World Wars I and II. It is currently exploring, wargaming, and experimenting with several new concepts that may soon lead to changes in the Corps' structure, particularly in the Indo-Pacific region. Details of the organizational changes currently under consideration remain classified, therefore, the *Guide* is unable to address them. Aspiring and serving Marine officers, however, will have the opportunity to learn the details of these coming changes as decisions are made, new structures are implemented, and reports of these begin to appear in the defense media.

❯ HEADQUARTERS, U.S. MARINE CORPS

Headquarters, U.S. Marine Corps (HQMC) serves as the Corps' executive. It consists of the commandant of the Marine Corps, assistant commandant of the Marine Corps, deputy commandants, staff judge advocate to the commandant, directors, members of the Navy and Corps assigned or detailed to it, and civilian employees in DON assigned or detailed to it. HQMC is distributed among the Pentagon, Henderson Hall (located on Joint Base Myer–Henderson

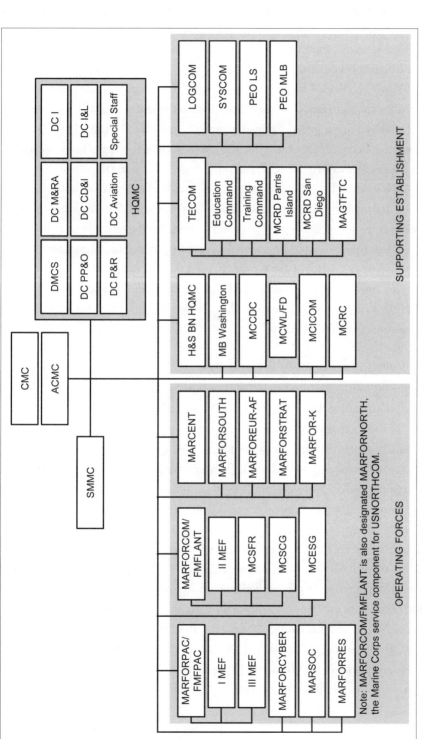

FIGURE 6-1. Organization of the U.S. Marine Corps (2021)

Hall), Marine Barracks Washington, Marine Corps Base Quantico, and the Washington Navy Yard.

HQMC is divided (from largest to smallest) into departments, each led by a deputy commandant (DC) in the grade of lieutenant general; divisions, typically led by a major general, brigadier general, or civilian member of the Senior Executive Service; branches, typically led by a colonel or federal civil servant (in the grade of GS-15); sections; and units. Figure 6-1 charts the organization of HQMC at its highest level and its relationship to the field activities of the Corps.

Under the authority, direction, and control of the CMC, HQMC prepares for the employment of Marine forces and orchestrates the recruiting, organizing, supplying, equipping, training, servicing, mobilizing, demobilizing, administering, and maintaining of the Corps. It assists in the execution of any power, duty, or function of the CMC. The function, composition, and general duties of HQMC are defined in Title 10, U.S. Code, Subtitle C, Part I, Chapter 806, "Headquarters, Marine Corps."

❧ ❧ *Commandant of the Marine Corps*

Reporting to the SECNAV, the CMC leads the Marine Corps as well as HQMC. One commandant defined his responsibilities in these simple terms: "I want each of you to feel that the Commandant of the Corps is your friend and that he earnestly desires that you should realize this. At the same time, it is his duty to the Government and to the Marine Corps to exact a high standard of conduct, a strict performance of duty, and a rigid compliance with orders."

Phrasing those responsibilities today, we can say that the commandant is directly responsible to the SECNAV for the readiness, total performance, and administration of the Marine Corps as a whole, including the Reserve. He commands all Marine forces and activities except those specifically assigned to the naval operating forces, unified commands, or elsewhere. For the readiness and performance of those elements of the Corps assigned to the Operating Forces of the Navy, the commandant is also responsible to the CNO.

With the advice and consent of the Senate, the president appoints the commandant from among the active four-star general officers of the Corps for a four-year term. Under certain conditions, the commandant may be reappointed for more than four years. Archibald Henderson, fifth commandant, served for thirty-nine years, the longest tenure to date.

The principal duties of the commandant extend, but are not limited, to procurement, discharge, education, training (individual and unit), and distribution of the officers and enlisted personnel of the Corps; all matters of command and discipline; and capabilities, requirements, readiness, organization, administration, equipment, and supply of Marine Corps organizations and units. Appendix II lists the commandants from the Corps' inception to the present.

❧ ❧ Assistant Commandant of the Marine Corps

The second-highest-ranking officer in the Corps, the assistant commandant of the Marine Corps (ACMC) is a general and discharges the duties of the commandant during the latter's absence or disability as well as performs such duties as the CMC may direct. For example, because of the vital importance to the force of operational risk management and safety, the CMC has directed that the ACMC directly supervise the activities of the Safety Division within HQMC.

❧ ❧ Director, Marine Corps Staff

Either a major general or lieutenant general, the director of the Marine Corps staff (DMCS) is the commandant's executive officer. He or she directs, supervises, and coordinates staff activities of HQMC. In the commandant's absence, the DMCS also performs the duties of the ACMC while that officer performs the duties of the CMC.

❧ ❧ Deputy Commandants

There are seven deputy commandants (formerly called deputy chiefs of staff) who lead HQMC departments, most of them situated in the Pentagon, and assist the CMC in managing the day-to-day affairs of HQMC.

The deputy commandant for manpower and reserve affairs (DC M&RA), a lieutenant general, has authority over matters related to manpower assignment, planning, programming, and budgeting policies; manpower information systems; military and civilian manpower management and administration; equal opportunity policies, programs, and activities; civilian personnel policy;

Marine and family programs, including the Wounded Warrior Regiment; the Semper Fit program and exchange services; and assignment and distribution of Reserve component military assets. The office of the DC M&RA is situated at Marine Corps Base Quantico.

The deputy commandant for plans, policies, and operations (DC PP&O), a lieutenant general, is the operations deputy for the CMC; is responsible for coordinating the development and execution of service plans and policies related to the structure, deployment, and employment of Marine forces in general; serves as the focal point for the interface between the Corps and the joint and combined activities of the JCS, CCMDs, and various allied and other foreign defense agencies; has cognizance over unit training and readiness, amphibious doctrine, and other doctrinal and policy matters; and acts for the DMCS in his or her absence. On behalf of the CMC, the DC PP&O exercises staff supervision over the activities of the Marine Corps Embassy Security Group, which screens, trains, assigns, and oversees operational readiness, administration, logistical support, and discipline of Marines assigned to provide security to Department of State diplomatic missions.

The deputy commandant for aviation (DC Aviation), a lieutenant general, has responsibility for matters related to Marine Corps aviation. The DC Aviation is tasked to develop, integrate, and supervise plans, policies, and budgets for all aviation assets and aviation expeditionary enablers (for example, aviation command and control, aviation ground support, and unmanned aviation systems). On behalf of the CMC, the DC Aviation exercises staff supervision over the activities of Marine Helicopter Squadron 1, which provides helicopter transportation and contingency support for the president of the United States, vice president of the United States, members of the president's cabinet, and foreign dignitaries and also supports planning, execution, and reporting for independent operational test and evaluation of helicopters and related systems.

The deputy commandant for installations and logistics (DC I&L), a lieutenant general, has cognizance over matters related to logistical plans, policy, and management; contracting policy and contract management; and facilities and installations. On behalf of the CMC, the DC I&L exercises staff supervision over Marine Corps Logistics Command, which provides worldwide, integrated logistical, supply chain, and distribution management; maintenance management; and

Marines with 1st Battalion, 7th Marine Regiment, part of Marine Rotational Force Darwin, dismount two MV-22B Ospreys while conducting air assault training with the Australian Defense Force in 2021.

strategic prepositioning capability in support of the Corps' Operating Forces and other supported units.

The deputy commandant for combat development and integration (DC CD&I), a lieutenant general, commands the Marine Corps Combat Development Command and holds staff responsibility for analysis, development, and integration of Marine warfighting capabilities, including development of future operational concepts and determination of how to best organize, train, and equip the Corps of the future.

The deputy commandant for programs and resources (DC P&R), a lieutenant general, has cognizance over Marine Corps fiscal requirements; fiscal planning, programming, and budgeting; and systems and cost analysis. This officer also represents the Corps in certain external functions related to these areas.

The deputy commandant for information (DC I), a lieutenant general, acts on behalf of the CMC in matters relating to operations in the information environment (OIE) and provides the Marine Corps with a service-wide approach to policy and management of OIE. The newest deputy commandant, the DC I supervises the activities and operations of several special staff members, offices, activities, and centers:

- *Director of intelligence* (DIRINT), a brigadier general, who has cognizance over intelligence, counterintelligence, cryptology, and electronic warfare and, as a service intelligence chief, maintains liaison with other government intelligence agencies, exercises staff cognizance over the Marine Corps Intelligence Activity (MCIA), and disseminates intelligence information within HQMC.
- *Director, command, control, communications, and computers*, a brigadier general, has responsibility over all Marine Corps automated information systems and programs, command and control systems, and telecommunications and communications security.
- The *Marine Corps Information Operations Center* (MCIOC) provides general support to the Corps across a full range of information operations planning and execution.

❧ ❧ Special Staff and Directors

There are several additional important positions at HQMC with which you should be familiar.

Sergeant Major of the Marine Corps (SMMC). The sergeant major is the senior noncommissioned officer (NCO) of the Corps and, by virtue of this billet, is senior to all other enlisted Marines. This NCO advises and assists the commandant in all matters relating to enlisted Marines as well as in other matters within his or her cognizance.

Counsel for the Commandant of the Marine Corps. The counsel, through the main office and field offices, provides comprehensive legal advice and support to the commandant, headquarters staff agencies, and the Marine Corps Operating Forces and Supporting Establishment in the areas of business and commercial law, environmental law, land use, civilian personnel law, procurement and fiscal law, government ethics, and all other matters under the cognizance of the general counsel of the Navy.

Chaplain of the Marine Corps. The Navy's deputy chief of chaplains serves as chaplain of the Marine Corps, advising the CMC on religious ministry matters in reference to personnel, plans, programs, policies, support, and facilities within the Corps.

Medical Officer of the Marine Corps. This officer advises the CMC and HQMC staff on all matters regarding health care and serves as the functional expert in working with the appropriate agencies for determining health service and field medical requirements, doctrine, policies, procedures, and programs.

Legislative Assistant to the Commandant of the Marine Corps. This assistant, normally a brigadier general, is the commandant's principal adviser in legislative matters, including liaison with Congress. He or she prepares comments on legislative proposals referred to, or affecting, the Marine Corps (except cases falling within the province of the DC P&R).

Inspector General. The inspector general (IG) reports to the naval IG, the commandant, and the SECNAV as a deputy naval IG for Marine Corps matters. It is the IG's eagle-eyed responsibility to conduct inspections and investigations as directed by the commandant; to coordinate the readiness programs of the Corps; and to maintain liaison with the inspection authorities of the other defense agencies. Although an "IG inspection" invariably begets unease, the mission of this officer is to help and to improve by constructive inspection.

Director, Special Projects. Working under the cognizance of the DMCS, this officer plans, supports, and conducts events, conferences, symposia, and foreign visits and prepares speeches and articles for the CMC, the ACMC, the SMMC, or as directed by the DMCS.

Director, Administration and Resource Management Division. This officer has cognizance over administration and management services for HQMC, headquarters security, transportation, internal communications services, and military and civilian personnel for the headquarters.

Director, Judge Advocate Division. Normally a major general, this person serves as staff judge advocate for the commandant and has cognizance over all legal matters (except certain questions of business or budgetary law, which fall to the legal counsel or to the fiscal director).

Director, Office of Marine Corps Communication. Formerly the director of public affairs, this brigadier general heads the Office of Marine Corps Communication. It is his or her delicate, exacting, and sometimes thankless job to represent the Corps to the public. The director is responsible for planning, coordinating, and implementing communication strategies designed to build understanding, credibility, trust, and mutually beneficial relationships with domestic and foreign publics. He or she maintains liaison with DOD and other government public affairs agencies as well as with national public affairs and news media. The director also represents the Marine Corps within the entertainment and publishing industries; controls the trademark and licensing activities for the Corps; and exercises staff supervision over field activities that disseminate public-affairs information.

Director, Safety Division. This colonel is the senior adviser to the CMC and ACMC for all safety matters and reports directly to the ACMC. The director aims to enhance the Corps' consistent posture of combat readiness by aligning doctrine and policy with risk-management principles in order to foster a climate and culture of force preservation.

❯ ❯ *Manpower and Reserve Affairs Department*

Of all the HQMC agencies , this department has more directly to do with you as an officer on an enduring basis than any other throughout your career.

Manpower selects and "procures" you (just as it recruits enlisted Marines). It gives you your commission and administers you from the moment you are sworn in until you rest beneath the trees in Arlington National Cemetery (or elsewhere). It assigns you, manages your career, promotes you, and retires you. With one hand, if need be, M&RA disciplines you, while with the other it attends to your welfare. It maintains your records at HQMC as it maintains similar records on every officer and enlisted Marine in the Corps. If you become a casualty, M&RA notifies your next of kin, sends you your Purple Heart, and sees that you receive the decorations and medals you are awarded.

❯ MARINE CORPS OPERATING FORCES

The Operating Forces are the heart of the Marine Corps. They provide the forward presence, crisis response, and combat power that the Corps makes available to CCDRs. The majority of Operating Forces are held in five permanent commands, all headquartered in the United States:

- U.S. Marine Corps Forces Command (MARFORCOM)
- U.S. Marine Corps Forces Pacific (MARFORPAC)
- U.S. Marine Corps Forces Reserve (MARFORRES)
- U.S. Marine Corps Forces, Special Operations Command (MARSOC)
- U.S. Marine Corps Forces Cyberspace (MARFORCYBER)

Before drilling into the details of some of these commands and discussing how the Operating Forces organize to conduct military operations, it is important to introduce the concept of *componency*.

❧ ❧ *Componency and Marine Corps Components*

As discussed in chapter 3, the president of the United States establishes CCMDs to execute broad and continuing missions at the strategic level using forces of two or more military departments. These commands typically have geographic responsibilities (for example, USEUCOM, with responsibility for military operations in the specifically delineated European theater) or functional responsibilities (for example, USTRANSCOM, with responsibility for strategic transportation and distribution supporting the whole of DOD). The CCDR exercises command authority over all assigned or attached forces.

CCMDs normally include subordinate service component commands (that is, Army, Marine Corps, Navy, and Air Force components). Service component commanders organize their forces to accomplish missions assigned by the CCDR. Service component commanders normally exercise operational control (OPCON) of forces assigned or attached to their CCMD, or they may be limited under certain circumstances to only tactical or administrative control of these forces. The Marine Corps component commander is responsible for accomplishing assigned missions, providing forces, and performing operational-level administrative and logistical tasks on behalf of or in support of assigned or attached Marine forces.

Marine Corps Operating Forces are generally assigned to CCMDs by the SECNAV through the secretary of defense's annual "Forces for Unified Commands Memorandum," published in "Global Force Management Implementation Guidance." With the disestablishment of U.S. Joint Forces Command in 2011, some operational forces are retained within the OPCON of the services until assigned to a CCMD for a specific mission.

❧ ❧ *Marine Corps Forces*

The Marine Corps organizes MAGTFs (described in detail later in the chapter) from forces that are organizationally either situated within the straightforwardly named Marine Corps forces (MARFORs) assigned to a specific CCMD, where they function as the service component command, or retained by the Corps under the CMC and available for missions globally. MARFORs constitute a balanced force of combined arms. They consist of a headquarters group, comprising command and control, service and support, and other specialized capabilities; one or more Marine divisions or brigades; one or more Marine aircraft wings; and one or more Marine logistics groups. MARFORs are organized, trained, and equipped as MAGTFs for

- service with the unified commands in seizure and defense of advanced bases as well as for land operations related to naval campaigns;
- development of amphibious tactics, techniques, and equipment;
- training the maximum number of Marines for war or emergency expansion; and
- immediate expeditionary service where, when, and as directed.

Collectively, the active component MARFORs today include three headquarters groups, three combat divisions, three aircraft wings, and three logistics groups. Based on combat experience, the ratio of one aircraft wing to support one Marine division is the fundamental proportion in the air-ground logistics team.

U.S. Marine Corps Forces Command. The Marine Corps retains control of MARFORCOM, headquartered in Norfolk, Virginia. The CMC, via the JCS global force management process, maintains II MEF and other unique capabilities under the Commander, MARFORCOM.

U.S. Marine Corps Forces Pacific. The Commander, MARFORPAC, is assigned to the Commander, USPACOM; functions as the Marine service component commander for USPACOM; and provides I MEF and III MEF to USPACOM. The MARFORPAC headquarters is in Honolulu, Hawaii.

Marines embark a combat rubber-raiding craft during reconnaissance scout swimmer training at Marine Corps Training Area Bellows, Hawaii, in 2021.

U.S. Marine Corps Forces Reserve. MARFORRES, headquartered in New Orleans, Louisiana, maintains trained Reserve units and qualified Reservists for active duty service in times of war, national emergency, or in support of contingency operations. The Commander, MARFORRES, also functions as the service component commander for USNORTHCOM. The unique nature of MARFORRES is addressed in greater detail in chapter 7.

U.S. Marine Corps Forces, Special Operations Command. The Commander, MARSOC, is assigned to the Commander, USSOCOM, and provides assigned forces to this CCMD. The MARSOC headquarters is located at Camp Lejeune, North Carolina.

U.S. Marine Corps Forces Cyberspace. Finally, the Commander, MARFORCYBER, is assigned to the Commander, USCYBERCOM, which is a subunified command under USSTRATCOM. The MARFORCYBER head-quarters is near Fort Meade, Maryland.

These assignments reflect the peacetime disposition of the Marine Corps Operating Forces. The majority of the Operating Forces reside in one of the five aforementioned MARFORs. Others are allocated for contingency planning to the remaining geographic and functional CCMDs: USSOUTHCOM, USCENTCOM, USEUCOM, USAFRICOM, USSTRATCOM, and U.S. Forces Korea (USFK). The secretary of defense provides Marine forces to these commands as required to meet the demands of theater security cooperation, forward presence, and crisis response.

It is worth mentioning here that there are additional MARFORs, but unlike the five already detailed, they are typically headquarters with few, if any, significant forces assigned on a *permanent* basis. These include U.S. Marine Corps Forces South, which is designated as the Marine service component for USSOUTH-COM; U.S. Marine Corps Forces Central Command, for USCENTCOM; U.S. Marine Corps Forces Europe and Africa, for USEUCOM and USAFRICOM; U.S. Marine Corps Forces Strategic Command, for USSTRATCOM; and U.S. Marine Corps Forces Korea, for USFK and United Nations Command.

When Marine Corps units are assigned to the unified commands or to the Operating Forces of the Navy, they report to the senior Marine commander. For the unified command, the MARFOR component commander (COM-MARFOR) exercises operational control. That OPCON does not include administration and training responsibilities, which remain under the CMC's purview. COMMARFORs have important strategic and budgetary planning activities, under the unified commanders, that contribute substantially to the determination of the size and composition of the Marine Corps Operating Forces in total.

❥ ❥ *Marine Air-Ground Task Force*

The Marine Corps normally organizes and employs its Operating Forces as MAGTFs, which are integrated, combined arms teams that include air, ground, and logistics units under a single commander, thereby obtaining unity of command and effort. MAGTFs are the fundamental building blocks of the Operating Forces and are how the Corps reliably delivers the NCA and CCDRs an

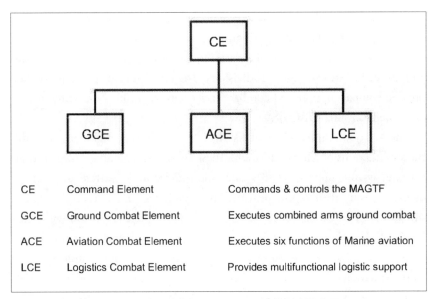

FIGURE 6-2. Organization of a Generic Marine Air-Ground Task Force

operational capability that is rapidly deployable, responsive, versatile, flexible, expandable, and sustainable. They are organized, trained, and equipped primarily from the forces of MARFORCOM, MARFORPAC, and MARFORRES. As depicted in figure 6-2, a MAGTF normally comprises four principal elements: a command element, ground combat element, aviation combat element, and logistics combat element.

The command element (CE) is the MAGTF's headquarters. It comprises the commander and a headquarters with an executive and special staff, command and control capabilities, and service support capabilities. The establishment of a single headquarters over the ground, aviation, and logistics elements provides the command, control, and coordination capability essential for effective planning and execution of operations. In amphibious operations, when Marines constitute the preponderant force, the MAGTF command element serves also as the landing force headquarters. Also capable of operating as the core of a joint task force (JTF) headquarters, the CE enables the MAGTF commander to be appointed a JTF commander, exercising tactical control over both the embarked MAGTF and the associated elements of other services.

The ground combat element (GCE) is a task organization tailored, as the name implies, for the conduct of ground combat. It is constructed around a ground combat infantry unit and varies in size from a reinforced battalion to a reinforced Marine division or divisions. The GCE also includes appropriate organic combat support and combat service support units. Normally, there is only one GCE in a MAGTF.

The aviation combat element (ACE) is normally task organized to fulfill the six functions of Marine aviation. These roles—air reconnaissance, anti-air warfare, assault support, offensive air support, electronic warfare, and control of aircraft and missiles—are provided in varying degrees based on the tactical situation and on the size of the task force. Usually, there is only one ACE in a MAGTF. It includes those organic aviation command (including air control agencies), combat, combat support, and combat service support units required by the situation.

The logistics combat element (LCE) provides the primary combat service support to all elements of the MAGTF beyond each element's organic capabilities. Depending on the mission, it is task organized to satisfy any or all of the following functions: supply; maintenance; transportation, including material handling and landing support; combat and deliberate engineering, including limited construction capabilities; health services, including medical and dental support; military police; automated data processing; personnel services; food services; disbursing support; and financial management. It can provide smaller task organizations for support of MAGTF operations as required.

The MAGTF is unique to the Marine Corps. It is trained and equipped not only for expeditionary operations and amphibious warfare but also for a variety of combat and noncombat situations. Its structure and its emphasis on strategic mobility make the MAGTF exceptionally useful in a wide array of crises. Its organization by task enables the commander to tailor the force to a specific contingency. The MAGTF can fight well and harmoniously within a joint or combined task force in a land campaign or provide a one-service force of combined arms for a variety of situations.

When employed in other than amphibious operations, MAGTFs are capable of functioning as self-sustaining forces under the command of the unified, subunified, or JTF commander. Their organization and training for amphibious warfare, which the Marine Corps pioneered and continues to perfect, enhance their capability to deploy rapidly by any means.

There are permanent MAGTFs—for example, a standing Marine expeditionary force—but the MAGTF is not necessarily a permanent organization; it is often organized for a specific mission and, after completion of that mission, is dissolved in accordance with prearranged plans. A MAGTF headquarters is structured to control whatever forces are assigned; thus, the Marine Corps can rapidly converge forces from any or all of its base locations to form a composite task force without regard for parent administrative organization.

The current and planned uses of MAGTFs reflect an understanding by the NCA of the unique role expeditionary and amphibious operations can play in a limited or worldwide war. To provide a peacetime presence and rapid-response capability that contributes to deterrence and forward defense strategy, Marine expeditionary units (described below) are continuously deployed on amphibious ships in the waters of the Mediterranean Sea, Arabian Sea, Persian Gulf, and Pacific Ocean, and they routinely visit the littoral areas of the Caribbean Sea and Indian Ocean.

Deployed MAGTFs provide the means to rapidly project power in support of vital U.S. interests anywhere in the world. Able to move on and be supported from the sea, MAGTFs, with associated amphibious shipping and carrier battle groups, are free from dependence on basing or overflight rights and provide an effective force presence without political commitment. During peacetime, they provide assurance to our allies and demonstrate resolve to our adversaries.

Although a MAGTF is a task organization tailored to accomplish a specific mission, they come in three standard types: the Marine expeditionary unit (MEU), the Marine expeditionary brigade (MEB), and the Marine expeditionary force (MEF). There is also the designation of special purpose MAGTF (SPMAGTF) for any task organization that differs markedly from the standard task force in size or configuration.

Marine Expeditionary Unit. The MEU is the standard, forward-deployed MAGTF (see figure 6-3). Its mission is to provide the NCA and CCDRs with a forward-deployed, sea-based, rapid-response capability to execute military operations. The MEU is commanded by a colonel. It is a self-contained, general purpose operating force capable of a range of military missions of limited scope and duration, including selected maritime special operations, such as reconnaissance and surveillance; tactical recovery of aircraft and personnel; seizure/recovery of selected personnel or matériel; and visit, board, search, and seizure of vessels. The MEU typically numbers approximately 2,200 Marines and Sailors and may be viewed as a forward-deployed extension of the MEB or MEF.

There are seven MEUs: the 11th, 13th, and 15th MEUs are sourced from I MEF; the 22nd, 24th, and 26th MEUs are sourced from II MEF; and the 31st MEU is part of III MEF. These deploy from their home bases on a rotational basis to conduct forward presence, theater engagement, and crisis response operations in the regions of the Mediterranean Sea, Pacific Ocean, Indian Ocean, or Arabian Gulf. Each MEU is organized with up to fifteen days of sustainment and includes

- a standing CE;
- a GCE, a battalion landing team consisting of an infantry battalion reinforced with artillery, reconnaissance, engineer, light armored reconnaissance, assault amphibian units, and other detachments as required;
- an ACE, a composite squadron built around a medium tiltrotor squadron reinforced with detachments from a heavy helicopter squadron, light-attack helicopter squadron, attack squadron, unmanned aerial vehicle squadron, air traffic control detachment, wing support squadron, and aviation logistics squadron; and
- an LCE, a combat logistics battalion organized to provide the MEU's other elements with multifunctional combat service support, encompassing supply, maintenance, transportation, engineering, health care, and other services.

The MEU undergoes an intensive twenty-six-week standardized predeployment training program. To gain certification, the unit must demonstrate competence across a range of designated capabilities, be able to plan and execute any assigned mission within six hours of notification, and be able to conduct multiple missions simultaneously.

On board the ships of a Navy amphibious ready group (ARG), a deployed MEU provides a CCDR or other operational commander with a quick, versatile, sea-based reaction force. In many cases, the MEU embarked on amphibious warships may be the first U.S. forces at the scene of a crisis, and it can conduct enabling actions for larger follow-on forces.

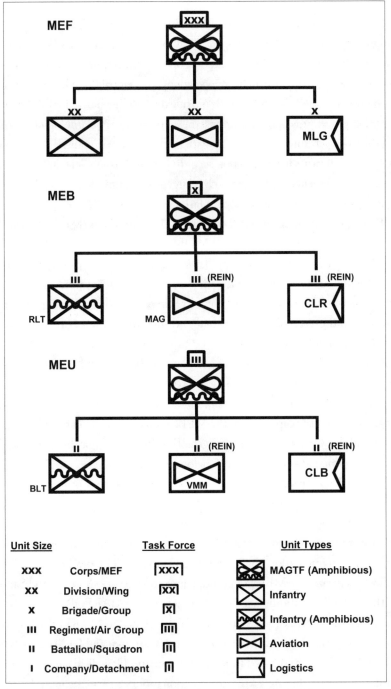

FIGURE 6-3. Organization of a Marine Expeditionary Force, Marine Expeditionary Brigade, and Marine Expeditionary Unit

Marine Expeditionary Brigade. The MEB is a midsized MAGTF that accomplishes larger, more demanding operational missions than the MEU. Its mission is to conduct major security cooperation operations, respond to larger crises or contingencies, or participate in major operations and campaigns. A brigadier general normally commands this unit. MEBs provide the building blocks for forcible entry and other power projection operations, the landing forces for amphibious assault, and the fly-in echelons that marry up with prepositioned equipment and supplies. Although each varies in composition according to the mission, it includes the same subordinate elements—although each is larger—as configured for the MEU and typically numbers upward of 15,000 Marines and Sailors.

There are three standing MEB command elements: the 1st MEB is embedded in the I MEF staff, while 2nd and 3rd MEBs are stand-alone organizations within II MEF and III MEF, respectively. These standing MEB CEs do not all have permanently assigned forces; instead, they maintain structured relationships with associated Marine divisions, aircraft wings, and logistics groups through planning and exercises. When formed and mobilized, the MEB is capable of full-spectrum operations and self-sustainment for thirty days.

As an expeditionary force, the MEB is capable of rapid deployment and employment via amphibious shipping, strategic airlift marrying up with maritime prepositioning force assets, or any combination thereof. If the scope of operations expands beyond the capability of the MEB, additional forces can readily deploy to expand the presence to MEF strength. Thus, the MEB may become—and is usually regarded as—the forward echelon of the MEF.

Marine Expeditionary Force. The MEF is the Marine Corps' largest, most capable, and principal warfighting MAGTF. It is capable of missions across a range of military operations, including amphibious assault and sustained operations ashore in any environment. The MEF is commanded by a lieutenant general. With appropriate augmentation, the MEF CE may serve as a JTF headquarters. While each varies in size, the MEF can number upward of 40,000 Marines and Sailors.

There are three standing MEFs: I MEF, assigned to MARFORPAC and based in southern California and Arizona; II MEF, assigned to MARFORCOM and based in Virginia, North Carolina, and South Carolina; and III MEF, assigned to MARFORPAC and based in Japan, Guam, and Hawaii. Each consists of a permanent CE, including a MEF information group; a permanent GCE, which

Marines and Sailors operate a landing craft, air cushion, from USS *Kearsarge*, a *Wasp*-class amphibious assault ship, during Large Scale Exercise 2021

is one Marine division (MARDIV); a permanent ACE, one Marine aircraft wing (MAW); and a permanent LCE, one Marine logistics group (MLG). These major subordinate commands (MSCs) constitute the primary reservoir of combat, combat support, and combat service support capabilities from which other MAGTFs are sourced.

Special Purpose Marine Air-Ground Task Force. A SPMAGTF is a task force formed to conduct a specific mission, normally when one of the three aforementioned MAGTFs is either inappropriate or unavailable. A SPMAGTF is organized, trained, and equipped to conduct a wide variety of missions that include crisis response, regionally focused training exercises, and peacetime missions.

The MAGTF may be seen as the culmination of over one hundred years of Marine Corps evolution from a ship's police force to a standing ready force. Its genesis lies in the Huntington Battalion of 1898 (Guantánamo), modified by the development of the air weapon, the requirements of the Pacific War of 1941–45, and joint forces and combined arms experiences since the Korean War.

❧ ❧ *Major Subordinate Commands*

The MEF is the principal Marine Corps warfighting organization and the principal (though not exclusive) repository of the Marine Corps Operating Forces. Within each MEF, these forces are held in one of four MSCs: MEF information group, MARDIV, MAW, and MLG. Each MSC fulfills a unique role in the MEF and thus has a unique mission and set of characteristics.

MEF Information Group (MIG). The MIG supports the MEF headquarters with a variety of capabilities; detaches these capabilities, when required, in support of other MAGTFs; and coordinates, integrates, and conducts operations in the information environment, such as electronic warfare and cyberspace initiatives.

Each MEF has one MIG that normally includes the following subordinate units: headquarters company; MEF support battalion; separate communications, intelligence, and radio battalions; air naval gunfire liaison company (ANGLICO); and expeditionary operations training group (EOTG).

The MIG retains administrative control of the communication, intelligence, and radio battalions; ANGLICO; and EOTG. Operational command of these subordinate battalions is retained by the MEF commanding general and exercised through the MEF CE staff.

Marine Division. The MARDIV is the ground combat organization of the Marine Corps. Its mission is to provide forces for and to execute amphibious operations, expeditionary operations, and other operations as may be directed. The division is a balanced force of combined arms, although it depends respectively on the MAW and MLG as primary sources of aviation and logistical support.

Each MEF currently has one MARDIV, although a MEF could feasibly contain multiple divisions. MARDIVs are not identical, but the typical division (see figure 6-4) comprises a headquarters battalion, three infantry regiments (the division's cutting edge), an artillery regiment, and separate assault amphibian, light armored reconnaissance, reconnaissance, and combat engineer battalions.

Today, the Marine Corps includes three active component divisions and one reserve division, but during World War II the Corps reached an all-time high of six divisions.

Marine Aircraft Wing. The MAW is the main tactical unit of Marine aviation, just as the division is the major ground unit. It is organized to provide

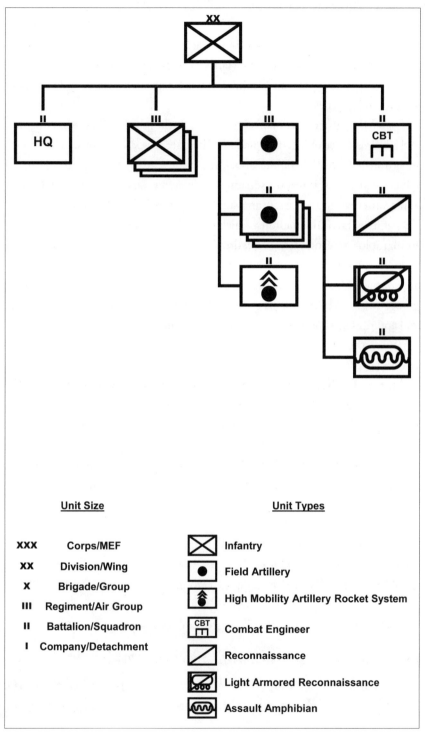

FIGURE 6-4. Organization of a Marine Division (2021)

flexible and balanced aviation capabilities across the full range of aviation operations, including all six functions of Marine aviation: offensive air support, anti-air warfare, assault support, air reconnaissance, electronic warfare, and control of aircraft and missiles.

Each MEF currently contains one MAW. Within the MAW, the basic tactical and administrative unit is the squadron. There are attack squadrons, fighter attack squadrons, all-weather fighter attack squadrons, air control squadrons, aerial refueler squadrons, transport squadrons (tiltrotor, rotary wing, and fixed wing), and a variety of headquarters and support squadrons for the groups and wing. Two or more tactical squadrons, which normally fly aircraft that are functionally similar, plus a headquarters squadron, aviation logistics squadron, and wing support squadron constitute the Marine aircraft group. Marine aircraft groups are normally organized as either fixed-wing or rotary-wing groups. Two or more groups, with a Marine wing headquarters squadron, Marine air control group, and appropriate supporting and service units, make up a MAW (see figure 6-5).

Today, the Marine Corps includes three active component MAWs and one reserve MAW.

Marine Logistics Group. The MLG provides tactical logistics above the organic capability of supported units to all elements of the MEF. In addition, it serves as the MEF's link to operational- and theater-level logistic agencies capable of supporting the MEF.

Each MEF has one MLG (see figure 6-6), which normally consists of a headquarters battalion necessary to provide administrative and logistical support internal to the MLG as well as selected logistical services externally to the other elements of the MEF; two multifunctional combat logistics regiments; and separate, functionally organized engineer support, supply, maintenance, medical, and dental battalions. In this respect, it is structured to support, in garrison or deployed, a MEF configured around one MARDIV and one MAW. All units of the MLG are structured to provide task-organized units to support independently deployed MAGTFs or geographically separated units in garrison.

❯ ❯ *Marine Corps Aviation and the Air-Ground Team*

Aviation in the Marine Corps differs from its counterparts elsewhere in DOD. The primary role of Marine aviation in the air-ground team is to support MAGTF

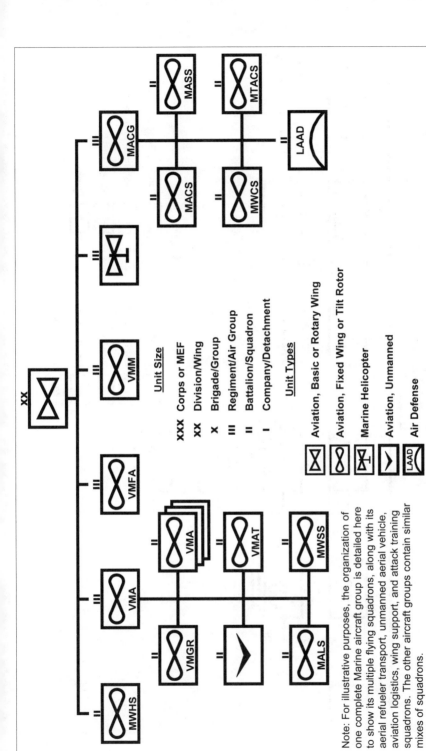

Note: For illustrative purposes, the organization of one complete Marine aircraft group is detailed here to show its multiple flying squadrons, along with its aerial refueler transport, unmanned aerial vehicle, aviation logistics, wing support, and attack training squadrons. The other aircraft groups contain similar mixes of squadrons.

FIGURE 6-5. Organization of a Marine Aircraft Wing (2021)

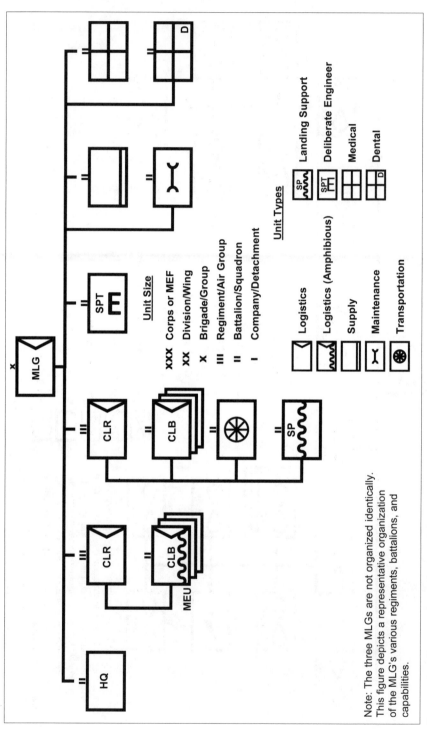

Note: The three MLGs are not organized identically. This figure depicts a representative organization of the MLG's various regiments, battalions, and capabilities.

FIGURE 6-6. Organization of a Marine Logistics Group (2021)

operations by close and general tactical air support and air defense. Secondarily, Marine aviation may be called on to replace or augment squadrons for duty with the carrier air groups of the Navy.

In many respects, aviation is the part of the Corps that most nearly lives up to Rudyard Kipling's "Soldier and sailor, too," because Marine aviation is very closely related to Navy aviation. This relationship stems not only from the long partnership between the Corps and Navy but also from the fact that most Marine fixed-wing squadrons are organized and equipped for carrier operations and regularly perform tours of duty afloat. In addition, Marine pilots undergo flight training at Naval Air Station Pensacola and earn their wings as naval aviators.

The most noteworthy characteristic of Marine aviation, however, is that it forms an inseparable part of the combined-arms team (that is, the MAGTF) operated by the Corps. Thus, the special role of Marines in the air is to support their teammates on the ground. The kind of close air support that Marines are accustomed to demands complete integration of air and ground forces. Pilot and platoon leader wear the same color uniform, share the same traditions and a common fund of experience, and go to school side by side at Quantico. Beachhead and battlefield liaison between air and ground is accomplished by Marine pilots who share frontline fighting positions with the riflemen while directing Marine aircraft onto targets just ahead. This makes for maximum reliance by ground commanders on aviation and for maximum desire by aviators to assist the ground combat units.

Probably the most outstanding demonstration of this tradition in Marine aviation took place during the defense of Wake Island in 1941. Marine Fighting Squadron 211 provided a heroic air defense of Wake until no more airplanes were left. Then the officers and men of the squadron calmly donned helmets, picked up their Model 1903 rifles, and went down to glory as infantry.

Organization of Marine Corps Aviation. The CMC controls the administration, individual training, and organization of Marine aviation. The CNO, however, prescribes (via the commandant) the aeronautical training programs and standards for Marine aviation units. And the aviation matériel used by Marine squadrons comes from the same Navy sources as does that used by Navy squadrons.

The organization of Marine Corps aviation resembles the organization of the Corps as a whole:

Two F-35B Lightning joint strike fighters conduct
aerial maneuvers over the Atlantic Ocean.

- Headquarters, in the form of the Aviation Department (known colloquially as "Aviation Hallway") at HQMC under the direction of the DC
  Aviation, which plans and supervises matters relating to the organization,
  personnel, operational readiness, and logistics of Marine aviation;
- Operating Forces, in the form of the MAWs embedded in the MEFs, which
  constitute the combatant part of the Corps' aviation organization; and
- Supporting Establishment, in the form of the air stations and naval
  aviation depots supporting Marine aviation.

Aviation is also represented in staff and planning billets throughout the ground
organization and through the tactical air-control parties that form part of the
battalion, regimental, and division headquarters of MARFORs.

❯ ❯ *Marine Corps Security Forces Regiment*

Part of the Operating Forces, Marine Corps security forces (MCSF) are organized, trained, and equipped to support CCDRs and naval commanders by

conducting expeditionary antiterrorism and security operations and by providing security for strategic weapons and vital national assets. Formerly made up of dozens of Marine barracks and detachments, these declined in number over the years and then reformed in 1986 into MCSF companies, monitored by a single battalion headquarters.

These forces are now organized as the Marine Corps Security Forces Regiment under MARFORCOM. Headquartered at Naval Weapons Station Yorktown, Virginia, this unique regiment includes

- a headquarters company, collocated with the regimental headquarters at Naval Weapons Station Yorktown;
- a training company, located in Chesapeake, Virginia;
- two MCSF battalions, one based at Kings Bay, Georgia, and the other at Bangor, Washington;
- one MCSF company, permanently located at Naval Station Guantánamo Bay, Cuba;
- three fleet antiterrorism security team (FAST) companies permanently assigned within the continental United States (CONUS), two head-quartered in Norfolk, Virginia, and one collocated with the regimental headquarters in Yorktown; and
- three FAST companies forward deployed in support of geographic CCDRs and stationed in Rota, Spain; Manama, Bahrain; and Yokosuka, Japan.

The FAST platoons or their detachments are "task organized security forces to augment Navy security to protect against terrorist acts at designated installations, units, ships, and critical assets, and perform other emergency security operations." Since their first deployment in February 1998, when afloat Marine detachments ceased operating, the platoons have conducted installation and airfield security, reinforcement of bombed U.S. embassies, and protection of ships and flagships.

❱ ❱ *Marine Corps Embassy Security Group*

Marine Corps Operating Forces also include the Marine Corps Embassy Security Group (MCESG), which provides, through its detachments, internal security at designated U.S. diplomatic and consular facilities and protection for U.S. citizens and government property located within designated U.S. diplomatic and consular premises. Aligned under HQMC and reporting to the CMC via the DC PP&O, the commanding officer (CO) of MCESG exercises command, less operational supervision, of personnel assigned to Marine security-guard detachments around the globe.

❧ ❧ *Final Thoughts on the Operating Forces*

Because the president can assign Marines to any duty, Marine Corps Operating Forces can be, and frequently have been, detached for service outside the naval establishment, under unified commands, independently, or even under other executive departments (such as the Marine embassy or mail guards). Command of Marine units not otherwise assigned by the president or the SECNAV remains with the CMC.

Tables of organization (T/Os) spell out the organization of every Marine unit, right down to the individual Marine and his or her duties, rank, specialist qualifications, and personal weapons. Tables of equipment (T/Es) list the organizational equipment required by each unit. When you are assigned to the Operating Forces, know your unit's T/O and acquire more than a passing knowledge of your T/E. Similarly, learn the organization of adjacent and related Marine units with which you are likely to interact.

❧ MARINE CORPS SUPPORTING ESTABLISHMENT

The Marine Corps Supporting Establishment consists of those personnel, installations, and activities that provide, train, maintain, and support the Marine Corps Operating Forces. The Supporting Establishment thus executes a sizable chunk of the commandant's organize-train-equip mission. Its infrastructure includes nineteen major bases and stations in the United States and Japan and all the personnel, equipment, and facilities required to operate them—approximately 30,000 Marines and Sailors. It also encompasses several smaller camps, training centers, and support facilities. But it is more than just bases and stations; the Supporting Establishment also comprises all the Marine Corps activities and agencies that support the Operating Forces.

Specifically, the Supporting Establishment consists of the following significant commands and organizations as well as several miscellaneous smaller activities:

- Headquarters and Service Battalion, HQMC
- Marine Barracks Washington
- Marine Corps Installations Command
- Marine Corps Combat Development Command, notably including the Marine Corps Warfighting Lab / Futures Directorate among others
- Marine Corps Recruiting Command
- Marine Corps Training and Education Command
- Marine Corps Logistics Command
- Marine Corps Systems Command and Program Executive Offices

All Marine officers begin their careers as part of the Supporting Establishment: the first post-commissioning assignment for every officer is The Basic School, part of Training and Education Command (TECOM). Later, officers typically return to the Supporting Establishment in between tours with the Operating Forces. Familiarity with it is thus useful to every officer.

❧ ❧ Headquarters and Service Battalion, HQMC

Situated on board Joint Base Myer–Henderson Hall in Arlington, Virginia, Headquarters and Service Battalion provides operational, administrative, supply, and logistical support for Marine Corps personnel, both military and civilian, assigned within the Washington metropolitan area to HQMC, other departments and agencies of the federal government, joint and other service schools, and for Marine Corps personnel within the Washington metropolitan area who are assigned to duty under instruction; hospitalized; awaiting assignment, separation, or transportation; or in a disciplinary status.

The CO of Headquarters and Service Battalion reports to the CMC through the DMCS.

❧ ❧ Marine Barracks Washington

Occupying a unique place in the Supporting Establishment and in the history of the Corps, Marine Barracks Washington, also known as "Eighth and Eye," is the oldest active Marine base. It was founded in 1801 by President Thomas Jefferson and Lieutenant Colonel William Ward Burrows, second commandant.

Located on the corners of Eighth and I Streets in southeast Washington, D.C., the Barracks supports both ceremonial and security missions in the nation's capital.

The Barracks is home to many nationally recognized units, including the Marine Corps Silent Drill Platoon, the Marine Band, the Marine Drum and Bugle Corps, the official Marine Corps Color Guard, and the Marine Corps Body Bearers. It is also the site of the home of the commandant, which, along with the Barracks, is a registered national historic landmark.

Marine Corps Silent Drill Platoon. A unique organization in the Supporting Establishment is the Marine Corps Silent Drill Platoon, a twenty-four-man rifle platoon that performs a unique precision-drill exhibition. This highly disciplined platoon exemplifies the distinctive professionalism associated with the Marine Corps. It first performed in the sunset parades of 1948 and received such an

Marines with the Silent Drill Platoon, Marine Barracks Washington, execute their long-line sequence at the Golden Gate Bridge, San Francisco, California, in 2019.

overwhelming response that the platoon soon became a regular part of the parades at Marine Barracks Washington.

Marine Band. The United States Marine Band is also a part of Marine Barracks Washington. This 120-piece military band is not only the best but also the oldest—established in 1798–of the armed forces musical organizations. It has the privilege of providing music for all White House and official state functions in Washington in addition to its normal duties in military parades and ceremonials. By long custom, the director of the band is ex officio musical director of two of Washington's traditional dining clubs, the Gridiron Club (for Washington correspondents) and the Order of the Carabao (military and naval).

✦ ✦ *Marine Corps Installations Command*

Marine Corps Installations Command (MCICOM) is, in many ways, the embodiment of the Supporting Establishment. It portrays itself as the "platform" from which the Operating Forces launch into overseas expeditions. MCICOM provides, manages, and maintains the training ranges and areas that the Operating Forces use to hone their warfighting skills. It also provides the day-to-day support essential to Marines and their families as they live and work on board the Corps' installations.

Discussed in greater detail in chapter 8, MCICOM oversees base and station operations, develops and coordinates relevant policy, and prioritizes resources for the support of Marine Corps installations. While MCICOM is headquartered at the Pentagon, Marine installations span the globe.

✦ ✦ *Marine Corps Combat Development Command*

In 1917, the Marine Corps established Marine Barracks Quantico, where thousands of Marines subsequently trained during World War I. The courses and training activities conducted during that time assumed more formal status when Major General John A. Lejeune established the Marine Corps Schools in 1920. Training and innovation continued at Marine Corps Schools through the first half of the twentieth century until the organization was redesignated the Marine Corps Development and Education Command on 1 January 1968. From this tradition, the Marine Corps Combat Development Command (MCCDC) emerged on 10 November 1987, cementing its central role in leading the combat development process; developing Marine Corps concepts, doctrine, and capabilities; and training and educating the Corps' Marines.

Today's MCCDC is the intellectual and developmental heart of the Corps. Normally commanded by a lieutenant general, it serves as the central agency responsible for the training, concepts, and doctrine development necessary for all types of operations by Marine forces. Its commanding general also serves as the DC CD&I and, as such, is also part of the HQMC staff, charged with the responsibility of leading integration of the Corps' warfighting capabilities. This arrangement makes MCCDC/CD&I a bit of a hybrid organization—part field command, part headquarters department.

In addition to the general and special staffs typical of a major command, MCCDC/CD&I comprises four significant commands and directorates: Marine Corps Warfighting Lab/Futures Directorate, Capabilities Development Directorate, Joint Capabilities Directorate, and Operations Analysis Directorate.

Marine Corps Warfighting Lab/Futures Directorate (MCWL/FD). The Lab seeks to improve naval expeditionary warfighting capabilities across the spectrum of conflict for current and future Marine Corps Operating Forces. MCWL/FD encompasses four divisions: Concepts and Plans, which develops naval concepts and coordinates for the Corps on joint concepts and planning; Wargaming, which conducts wargames to gain insights on new concepts, tactics, techniques, procedures, and equipment; Science and Technology, which identifies and assesses cutting-edge technologies for potential use by the Corps; and Experiment, which designs, coordinates, and executes live-force experiments of new concepts and technologies.

Capabilities Development Directorate (CDD). This directorate operates at the heart of capabilities development, identifying and validating gaps in Marine Corps doctrine, organization, training, matériel, leadership and education, personnel, and facilities and then developing integrated solutions to overcome these capability gaps. Five divisions tend to the key capability development responsibilities carried out by the directorate: the MAGTF Integration Division, Command Element Integration Division, Ground Combat Element Integration Division, Aviation Combat Element and Naval Integration Division, and Logistics Combat Element Integration Division. CDD also includes the Total Force Structure Office, which is the keeper of the Corps' force structure (simplistically, the T/

Os and T/Es for all Marine units), and the Expeditionary Energy Office, which works closely with the combat and technology development communities and serves as the proponent for expeditionary energy in the force development process.

Joint Capabilities Directorate (JCD). JCD is the organization through which MCCDC/CD&I connects to the Joint Capabilities Integration and Development System, which is the formal DOD system that defines and develops acquisition requirements and evaluation criteria for future defense programs. JCD ensures that new Marine Corps capabilities are conceived and developed in a joint warfighting context and are ultimately consistent with the integrated joint force.

Operations Analysis Directorate (OAD). Enabling and assuring sound assessment and analysis of potential solutions to capability gaps, OAD executes and provides oversight for the Marine Corps on all matters pertaining to operations analysis and modeling and simulation. The Corps' service-level activity responsible for studies and analyses, OAD serves as its lead for modeling and simulation, manages the Marine Corps Studies System, assists the Operating Forces and other Corps agencies with operations analysis support, and represents the Corps at modeling and simulation events across DOD.

❖❖ *Marine Corps Recruiting Command*

Headquartered at Marine Corps Base Quantico, the Marine Corps Recruiting Command (MCRC) has one of the most challenging missions in the Marine Corps. Accountable to the CMC, the commanding general of MCRC is responsible for the procurement of qualified individuals in sufficient numbers to meet the established personnel strength levels, officer and enlisted, of the Corps, for both its active and reserve components.

The MCRC divides the United States into two regions: the eastern recruiting region (covering districts east of the Mississippi River) and the western recruiting region (covering districts west of the Mississippi). Each is then divided into three districts, with each district covering several states. The districts then are subdivided into recruiting stations for large metropolitan areas, recruiting substations that cover smaller cities and rural areas, and even smaller satellite offices known as permanent contact stations.

Among a wide range of miscellaneous additional duties, recruiting district directors maintain liaison with corresponding agencies and headquarters of the other three services, state adjutants general, other federal field agencies, schools and colleges, and veterans' associations and military societies.

❖ ❖ *Marine Corps Training and Education Command*

Commanded by a lieutenant general, TECOM tends to the responsibilities of the commandant for training and education concepts, policies, plans, and programs, including their execution. The principle subordinate activities include the following commands:

- Training Command, which is responsible for fifteen formal schools, including the Officer Candidates School, Basic School, Weapons Training Battalion, School of Infantry (East and West), and Marine Corps Center for Lessons Learned—to highlight just a few—as well as forty-two detachments with other service schools
- Education Command, which is responsible for Marine Corps University, including enlisted professional military education programs, Expeditionary Warfare School, Command and Staff College, School of Advance Warfighting, Marine Corps War College, College of Distance Education and Training, and Center for Advanced Operational Culture Learning
- Marine Corps Recruit Depot Parris Island
- Marine Corps Recruit Depot San Diego
- MAGTF Training Command (at Twentynine Palms), which is responsible for the Marine Corps Air-Ground Combat Center, Mountain Warfare Training Center Bridgeport, Marine Aviation Weapons and Tactics Squadron 1 (MAWTS-1), Expeditionary Warfare Training Group (East and West), and several smaller training groups and activities

As a Marine Corps officer, you will most frequently encounter Marine Corps University out of all these commands. Its president, a general officer, also serves as the commander of Marine Corps Education Command, the lineal successor to the fabled Marine Corps Schools. The Corps established its first formal military school in 1891, when the School of Application opened to become the first residential training program for Marine officers. This evolved into the Officers Training School in 1909 and became the nucleus of Marine Officer Instruction at Quantico following World War I. Realizing the benefits that would be obtained through further education of officers as they progressed through their careers, additional courses of instruction were created. The first of these, the Field Officers Course, welcomed its first students in October 1920, and the second course, the Company Grade Officers Course, convened its first class in July 1921. These, along with the basic Marine Corps Officer Training School, formed the foundation for Major General Lejeune's Marine Corps Schools. It was this beginning that formed the basis of Marine Corps University as it exists today.

The resident schools at Quantico constitute the principal intellectual activity of the Corps. The following schools provide for the education of officers:

- Basic School is the place where newly commissioned lieutenants and warrant officers receive their initial training and are made into officers of Marines.
- Expeditionary Warfare School is a career-level course of instruction for captains. It prepares them for command at the company level and battalion-level staff work in the Operating Forces.
- Command and Staff College, a nine-month course for majors and lieutenant colonels, is an intermediate-level school. It includes the first phase of joint professional military education in its curriculum.
- School of Advanced Warfighting (SAW) is a follow-on school for selected graduates of the Command and Staff College. SAW lasts another year, during which students hone their expertise in operational art and planning. These officers are joined by several of their peers from other service staff colleges.
- Marine Corps War College is a top-level school and convenes annually a class of a dozen colonels or lieutenant colonels, including peers from other services.

The Staff Noncommissioned Officers' Academy provides advanced NCO training for staff sergeants and sergeants selected for promotion to staff sergeant. The academy also conducts an annual Sergeants Major Seminar. It also validates curricula for similar academies operated at other bases.

In addition to The Basic School, the recruit depots are the foundation of the Corps. The Marine Corps has two recruit depots—at Parris Island, South Carolina, and San Diego, California. Each trains and equips the fledgling Marine, or "boot." Recruits from eastern states go to Parris Island, while those from western states go to San Diego. "Boot camp" transforms the average young American into a Marine. Highly qualified officers and veteran enlisted drill instructors emphasize the elements of obedience, esprit, and the military fundamentals all Marines must master before taking their places in the fighting elements of the Corps. After boot camp, the new Marines graduate to advanced individual training at other schools of the Corps or others services.

Within the Supporting Establishment and connected to MCCDC are other entities and roles that support the education and training of Marines and merit mention here:

- The Library of the Marine Corps provides resources and data to the entire Corps from a building located across the street from Marine Corps University. It contains a research library, archives, telecommunications media, and conference seminar spaces.
- The director of Marine Corps History Division has cognizance over all of the Corps' historical programs, serving under the president of Marine Corps University.
- The director of the Museums Division and the National Museum of the Marine Corps has cognizance over all Marine Corps museums as well as maintenance of related historical and material references and library functions.

❯ ❯ *Marine Corps Logistics Command*

The Marine Corps' logistical activities provide comprehensive support for the Corps. Military logistics is the discipline of planning and carrying out the movement and maintenance of military forces. In its most comprehensive sense, it encompasses those aspects of operations that involve the design, development, acquisition, storage, distribution, maintenance, evacuation, and disposition of matériel. Additionally, logistics involves the sustainment of the personnel who employ and maintain this matériel.

From its position in the Supporting Establishment, Marine Corps Logistics Command (MARCORLOGCOM or, more simply, LOGCOM), headquartered at Albany, Georgia, plays a central role in the ongoing logistical support of the

Marines with Combat Logistics Battalion 8, 2nd Marine Logistics
Group (Forward), convoy to the wreckage of a downed French
F-2000 Mirage aircraft for a recovery operation in Helmand
Province, Afghanistan, in 2011.

Corps. It provides worldwide, integrated logistical, distribution, and supply
chain management; maintenance management; and strategic prepositioning
capability in support of the Operating Forces, Supporting Establishment, and
other supported units to maximize their readiness and sustainability.

It is perhaps simplest to provide some insight into what this major command does to support the Marine Corps by briefly describing its organization.
LOGCOM consists of a headquarters element and three or more subordinate
commands. The headquarters element includes staff directorates and offices,
integrating operations and providing command support, and four distinct centers:

- Weapon System Management Center, which manages the lifecycle
  sustainment of ground weapons systems
- Supply Chain Management Center, which plans, manages, improves,
  executes, and integrates the Marine Corps supply chain and related
  logistical programs
- Maintenance Management Center, which monitors and analyzes depot
  maintenance programs for ground weapons systems

• Quality Management Center, which promotes and strengthens a culture of quality, innovation, compliance, and continuous process improvement throughout the command

LOGCOM also directs the activities of three permanent subordinate commands. Marine Depot Maintenance Command, headquartered in Albany, Georgia, rebuilds, modifies, and performs depot-level maintenance on ground weapons systems and equipment through its two industrial production plants in Albany and Barstow, California. Blount Island Command, located in Jacksonville, Florida, manages, maintains, and provides logistical support for the Corps' strategic ashore and afloat prepositioning programs. Marine Force Storage Command, headquartered in Albany, with storage battalions in Albany and Barstow, stores combat-ready equipment capability sets to support expeditionary readiness of the Operating Forces.

In addition, upon request by the MARFORs, LOGCOM provides worldwide supply, maintenance, distribution, and prepositioning support through task-organized contact teams, technical assistance advisory teams, and other support teams up to a forward-deployed subordinate command.

You may note that the preceding discussion of Logistics Command has focused on the support of ground weapons systems and equipment. Supporting Marine aircraft and aviation systems is outside the scope of the LOGCOM mission, and discussing it in any detail is outside the scope of the *Guide*. It suffices to say—and this is a colossal understatement—that Marine aviation supply and support to Marine aviation units are complicated endeavors. Marines in aviation units get their clothing, individual equipment, rations, weapons, and pay from the Marine Corps. Yet they receive their aircraft, armament, aviation munitions, flight gear, aviation ground support equipment, and most training aids and manuals from the Naval Air Systems Command.

— ❖❖ ❖❖ —

Through the 1980s and 1990s, the Defense Logistics Agency (DLA) emerged as the overall Defense Department manager of matériel. As America's combat logistics support agency, it provides the Army, Marine Corps, Navy, Air Force, other federal agencies, and partner-nation armed forces with a full spectrum of logistics, acquisition support, and technical services.

DLA sources and provides nearly all the consumable items that U.S. military forces need to operate—food, fuel, energy, uniforms, medical supplies, construction material, and almost anything else required. Among its diverse collection of logistical missions, the agency also supplies nearly 90 percent of the military's spare parts and manages the reutilization of military equipment. And DLA Troop Support Clothing and Textiles provides clothing, textiles, and equipment to U.S. servicemembers and federal agencies, outfitting every Soldier, Sailor, Airman, and Marine around the world from their first day of service at basic training to camouflage uniforms worn on the battlefield to service dress uniforms worn in garrison.

DLA and its multiple depots, centers, and activities worldwide are staffed by officers from each of the services. Thus, if you enter the supply field, you may reasonably expect to be detailed at some time to one of these joint agencies.

❖ ❖ *Marine Corps Systems Command and Program Executive Offices*

Marine Corps Systems Command, Program Executive Office for Land Systems, and Program Executive Office for Manpower, Logistics, and Business Solutions together outfit U.S. Marines with virtually every major piece of equipment and technology they drive, shoot, employ, and wear. Their focus is the Marine in harm's way, protecting warfighters and equipping them to execute the mission. In a few words, these organizations of the Supporting Establishment provide the gear that Marines rely on to accomplish their missions.

Marine Corps Systems Command (MARCORSYSCOM). MARCORSYS-COM serves as DON's systems command for Marine Corps ground weapon and information technology system programs. The command's program managers aim to equip and sustain Marine forces with current and future warfighting capabilities. It manages programs in many areas: ammunition; command and control; communications; cyberspace operations; engineer systems; fire support systems; infantry combat equipment; infantry weapons; intelligence; light tactical vehicles; long-range fires; medium/heavy tactical vehicles; supply and maintenance systems; training systems, including synthetic, range, and sustainment and support services; and wargaming capability.

MARCORSYSCOM additionally directs the operations of the Marine Corps Tactical Systems Support Activity, which provides test and evaluation, engineering, and deployed technical support for the Corps and joint service command, control, computer, and communications systems throughout all acquisition lifecycle phases.

Program Executive Office for Land Systems (PEO LS). PEO LS is a separate command, reporting directly to the assistant secretary of the Navy (research, development, and acquisition), although it works in concert with MARCOR-SYSCOM. PEO LS manages programs in five areas: advanced amphibious assault; air command and control and sensor netting; ground/air task-oriented radar; ground-based air defense; and light armored vehicles.

Program Executive Office for Manpower, Logistics, and Business Solutions (PEO MLB). PEO MLB oversees the collection of Marine Corps–wide information technology programs designed to enable common business processes for Sailors ashore or at sea and Marines in garrison or in the field. PEO MLB currently manages programs in two areas: Marine Corps Enterprise Network applications and integrated information solutions for logistics.

❯ MARINE CORPS STAFF ORGANIZATION, PROCEDURE, AND RELATIONSHIPS

❯ ❯ *Staff Organization*

The general framework of Marine Corps staff organization resembles that employed by the U.S. Army. A complete description of the latter organization and associated staff functions can be found in Field Manual (FM) 6-0, *Commander and Staff Organization and Operations*; it is well worth the effort to be familiar with this invaluable manual. It perhaps seems odd, at this point, that a guide for Marine Corps officers refers to Army doctrine, but there is a time-honored tradition among Marines of unashamedly adopting best practices, regardless of the source, and Army doctrine in this matter is among the best. Equally important is knowledge of the current edition of Marine Corps Warfighting Publication (MCWP) 3-40.1, *Marine Air-Ground Task Force Command and Control*. This publication imbeds within several of its chapters and appendices what is effectively the Corps' staff manual.

To suit differing functional needs of the Marine Corps (particularly in amphibious operations), we modify some of the staff functions described in

FM 6-0. Moreover, the Corps has evolved several special staff functions peculiar to MARFOR operations that do not appear in FM 6-0. These along with other staff functions, are described below.

The Marine commander's staff normally consists of three subdivisions: a general (or executive) staff, a special staff, and a personal staff.

As we discuss the staff, one principle should be kept in mind: regardless of how much help the commander receives from the staff, *the commander alone is responsible* for all that his or her unit does or leaves undone. This is a basic principle of command.

General Staff. The general, or executive, staff is a coordinating staff group that plans and supervises all the basic functions of command. At divisions, wings, logistics groups, or higher headquarters, it is the *general staff*; in units below this level, it is known as the *executive staff*. Except for scale, the functions and duties of general and executive staffs are identical.

The basic functions of command are personnel, intelligence, operations and training, logistics, planning, and communications and information systems. These six functions are referred to by number, in the order given; for example, personnel is "1," intelligence is "2," and so forth. If the staff is a general staff, the numbers are prefixed by the letter "G"; in an executive staff, the numbers are prefixed by the letter "S."

The general staff, which is concerned with these command functions, is headed by a chief of staff, or executive officer in the case of an executive staff, who may be assisted by a deputy chief of staff and by a staff secretary. This last staff officer acts as office manager for the commander, the chief, and the deputy chief of staff. At the major command level, general staff officers are designated as assistant chiefs of staff (AC/S) for their respective functional areas: AC/S, G-1, personnel; AC/S, G-2, intelligence; AC/S, G-3, operations and training; AC/S, G-4, logistics; AC/S, G-5, plans; and AC/S, G-6, communications and information systems (CIS). The staffs of all major commands also include a comptroller, or financial management officer, who is considered to be a member of the general staff.

The commander, assisted by the chief of staff, determines the number, type, and function of general staff sections. If desired, he or she may organize additional principal staff sections based on requirements. Specifics on the organization, functions, and responsibilities of a particular command's staff are normally delineated in its published orders, directives, and standard operating procedures (SOPs).

At lower echelons, the executive staff is similarly organized. Executive staff officers are designated S-1, personnel officer; S-2, intelligence officer; S-3, operations officer; S-4, logistics officer; and S-6, CIS officer. Given the military penchant for acronyms and abbreviations, Marines typically refer to these principle staff officers by their alphanumeric moniker. Thus, the unit operations officer is the "S-3," or often simply "the 3."

You will find detailed descriptions of the duties of each of the foregoing officers in the current edition of MCWP 3-40.1, with alternate Army interpretations in FM 6-0.

Special Staff. The special staff includes all the staff who are not members of either the general (or executive) staff or the personal staff (described below). This is a body of specialist advisers and assistants to the commander who provide technical advice, information, and supervision. Within their respective fields, special staff officers act as advisers, planners, supervisors, and coordinators. They are authorized to have direct access to the chief of staff or the executive officer and direct liaison with other staff sections in matters of interest to those sections. Special staff officers in some commands or in certain specialties may enjoy direct access to the commander regarding matters that relate *directly* to their specialties. But special staff officers normally operate under the staff cognizance of either the chief of staff/executive officer or a member of the general/executive staff.

These specialists are often organizationally situated in one of the principal staff sections; in some cases, a special staff officer may reside in his or her own separate office and enjoy the support of several assistants.

Special staff sections can be organized at will by the commander to fill a particular need, although commanders should be careful to avoid staff "bloat." Existing sections can be consolidated or inactivated. Thus, the following list of special staff officers is illustrative rather than exhaustive or fixed: adjutant; air officer; aircraft maintenance officer; fire support coordinator or fires officer; aviation supply officer; chaplain (Chaplain Corps, USN); dental surgeon (Dental Corps, USN); disbursing officer; embarkation officer; engineer; food services officer; headquarters commandant; inspector general; civil affairs officer; naval gunfire officer; nuclear, biological, and chemical officer; public affairs officer; special operations officer; staff judge advocate; supply officer; surgeon (Medical Corps, USN); and weather or meteorological officer.

When a command has no special staff representation within a particular specialty or discipline and it gains an attached unit with that specialty, the attached commander acts as adviser to the gaining commander on matters pertaining to his or her units' capabilities and employment.

Personal Staff. The personal staff consists of the staff officers whom the commander wishes to coordinate and administer directly rather than through the chief of staff. The personal staff thus includes such officers and noncommissioned officers as aides-de-camp, sergeants major, and, for certain purposes, selected members of the special staff, such as the public affairs officer or the inspector.

The relationship between the commander and the personal staff is direct and confidential. These staff members perform only such duties as the commander personally directs.

❧ ❧ *Staff Procedure and Relationships*

Although this chapter deals mainly with Marine Corps organization, it is impossible to discuss staff organization without a few words on staff procedure and relationships. The fundamentals of these are staff supervision and completed staff work. As a junior officer, you will probably not be assigned to staff duties for a while. Nevertheless, you ultimately face assignment on a staff and, meanwhile, will be on the receiving end of staff coordination and supervision. It therefore behooves you to become familiar with the following fundamentals.

Above all, you must bear in mind the status of the staff. No staff officer ever exercises command in his or her own right. Thus, the orders voiced by a staff officer are those of the commander—whether or not the commander is aware of them at the time when issued. Regardless of how much authority the commander allows the staff, the commander alone retains responsibility.

Staff supervision consists of advising other staff officers and subordinate commanders of the policies and desires of the commander, interpreting those policies when necessary, and reporting back to the commander how and to what degree the policies and desires are being carried out. This supervision does not extend to command.

Completed staff work is the most important working principle of the staff. This has been variously defined by many commanders and by official or semiofficial publications. The following serves as one of the best and most generally quoted definitions of this principle:

> Completed staff work is the study of a problem and presentation of a solution, by a staff officer, in such form that all that remains to be done by the commander is to indicate his approval or disapproval of the completed action. The more difficult the problem is, the greater the tendency to present the problem to the chief in piece-meal fashion. It is your duty, as a staff officer, to work out the details. You should not burden your chief in the determination of those details, no matter how perplexing they may be. You may and should consult other staff officers. The product, whether it enunciates new policy or modifies established policy, should, when presented to the commander for approval, be worked out in finished form.
>
> It is your job to advise the commander what he ought to do, not to ask him what you ought to do. He needs answers, not questions. Your job is to study, write, restudy, and rewrite, until you have evolved a single proposed course of action—the most advantageous course of all that you have considered. The commander then approves or disapproves.
>
> Do not worry your commander with long explanations and memoranda. Writing a memorandum to your chief does not constitute completed staff work, but writing a memorandum for him to send to someone else does. Your views should be placed before him in finished form, so that he can make them his own views simply by signing his name. In most cases, completed staff work produces a single document prepared for the commander's signature, without accompanying comment. If the document stands on its own feet, it will speak for itself; if the commander wants further comment or explanation, he will ask for it.
>
> Completed staff work usually requires greater effort for the staff officer, but it results in greater freedom and protection for the commander. Moreover, it accomplishes two results:
>
> 1. The commander is protected against half-baked ideas, voluminous memoranda, and immature oral presentations.

2. The staff officer who has a valid, important proposal can more readily find receptive consideration.

The final test of completed staff work is this: If you yourself were the commander, would you be willing to sign the paper you have prepared? Would you stake your professional reputation on its being right?

If your answer would be "No," take the paper back and rework it, because it is not yet completed staff work.

This should not suggest, however, that the staff officer operates in a vacuum. Properly prepared, he or she understands the commander's methods, character, and desires and acts in that spirit. Commanders give their appreciation of the situation at hand and should indicate their intentions to their staffs. *Staff work reflects the commander's intent* and not the personal whims of the staff officer concerned. When staff officers conceive of other arrangements, they should present them to the commander as clearly identified alternative. In higher headquarters, this takes the form of a decision brief; at the regimental or small-unit level, the presentation may be less formal.

Ultimately, highly proficient and complete staff work is an essential and unavoidable part of any military career. Successful Marine officers excel during their staff assignments.

⊰{ 7 }⊱

MARINE CORPS RESERVE

In its outstanding service to our Corps, the Marine Corps Reserve
has earned the right to be called our "Secret Weapon."
— General Lemuel C. Shepherd Jr.

THE MARINE CORPS RESERVE has proved itself repeatedly to be a vital component of the Marine Corps. The highly motivated, well-trained, and characteristically spirited Marine Corps Reserve assists the active component in maintaining its position as the national force in readiness. Over the years, complementary and seamless integration with the active component of the Corps has been a constant aspiration of the Reserve, which distinguishes it from its counterparts in the other services.

⋗ STORY OF THE RESERVE

⋗ ⋗ *Inception and Early Years*

The Marine Corps Reserve came into being in 1916, while Major General George Barnett was twelfth commandant, with an initial strength of three officers and thirty-three enlisted men. Like many other steps forward during the period, the Reserve was, in fact, the product of the foresight and imagination of Barnett's assistant, Colonel John A. Lejeune, who would later become thirteenth commandant. Despite its eventual importance, the Reserve played no significant role in World War I. Indeed, it nearly died in the early 1920s due to fiscal starvation. But for the loyalty and single-mindedness of the pioneer Reservists of that decade, there might not be a Marine Corps Reserve today.

Following enactment by Congress of the Navy Reserve Act of 1925, the Marine Corps Reserve began to thrive. This legislation permitted individual training duty with pay as well as the organization of drilling units in pay status. Training programs were instituted, and units sprang up in 1927. This prosperity was short lived, however, as the Great Depression years of 1929–33 found the Reserve again without funds. During that lean period, most units continued to drill and train without pay—even buying their own uniforms. The Reservists themselves again saved the organization from oblivion.

The Reserve was finally able to stand fully on its own feet in 1935. Three developments occurred that crucial year: (1) appropriations for training an organized and volunteer Marine Corps Reserve (ground and aviation), which totaled almost 10,000 officers and enlisted Marines; (2) inauguration of the Platoon Leaders Classes to obtain a steady input of well-trained, carefully selected junior reserve officers from colleges not participating in Army or Navy Reserve Officer Training Corps; and (3) dawn of the Reserve pilot program for Marine Corps aviation, an extra dividend of the Naval Aviation Cadet Act of 1935.

In 1938, Congress updated the 1925 Navy Reserve Act in many aspects—perhaps the most important being the provision, of a charter of rights and benefits for the Reserve. Included in this were hospitalization, death, and disability benefits; equitable promotion; retirement with pay for active service; and the right to participate in the formation of Reserve policy.

✦ ✦ *The Reserve Proves Its Mettle*

The solid success of the peacetime Reserve was amply attested in 1939, when individual Reservists were brought to active duty after President Franklin D. Roosevelt's proclamation of a limited national emergency in September and a year later, in 1940, when mobilization of the remainder of the Reserve brought 15,138 additional Marines to the colors. The extent to which the Reserve had hewn its place in the Corps was proved in 1945 by the fact that of 471,000 Marines on active service, the largest number in the Corps' 170-year history, approximately 70 percent were Reservists.

Much of the Reserve's effectiveness throughout World War II stemmed from the philosophy behind its mobilization, which today is as strong as ever. Although the 1940 Reserve was built around thirty-six hometown battalions and squadrons, each with its own distinctive personality, comradeship, and local associations, Major General Thomas Holcomb, seventeenth commandant, took the position that no Marine, Regular or Reservist, should, while on active duty, claim any home but the Corps. Thus, as Reserve units reached mobilization points, they disbanded and their members simply became individual Marines headed for service in the expanding Regular formations of the Fleet Marine Force. To drive home the significance of this decision and to emphasize that every man privileged to wear the Eagle, Globe, and Anchor was a Marine, no more and no less, Holcomb decreed that except where required by law for administrative purposes, the word "Reserve" and its corresponding abbreviation "R" following the "USMC" would not be used. All hands, Reserve and Regular, were Marines.

Following World War II, the postwar buildup of Marine Reserves was one of the great achievements of the Corps. Through good leadership (both Regular and Reserve), through willingness to invest capable personnel in the Reserve program, and because of the unflagging loyalty of Marine alumni—"Who ever saw a sorehead ex-Marine?" asked a prominent journalist—the Reserve was in unmatched readiness to back up the attenuated Regular Corps when the Korean War flared.

In the field in Korea, as in the Pacific battles before then, it was literally impossible to distinguish Reservist from Regular. Once again, as always, all hands were Marines. Among those who had originally started as Reservists, it is worth noting that, in World War II and Korea, fifty-seven were awarded Medals of Honor.

❯ ❯ *Toward the Total Force*

Soon after the end of the Korean War, Congress passed the Reserve Forces Act of 1955, which continues to exercise a profound effect on the reserve components of all the armed forces, including the Marine Corps. This law provided for the so-called Special Enlistment Program, whereby young men, after receiving not less than twelve weeks of hard training with and by Regular forces, enter the Ready Reserve for a prescribed period of years of obligated service. The Reserve was reorganized on 1 July 1962 to provide a distinct unit-mobilization structure, embodied in the 4th Marine Division, 4th Marine Aircraft Wing, and 4th Force Service Support Group. These were to be mobilized and employed as units, yet the Ready Reserve still maintained additional units whose function is to provide trained individual Marines for fleshing out Regular and Reserve units.

When U.S. forces deployed to the Arabian Peninsula and its seas during 1990–91 for the liberation of Kuwait from Iraqi occupation, Marine Corps forces moved in the vanguard. As the conflict deepened and the eventual campaign took shape, some 30,000 Marine Reservists deployed to augment and reinforce deployed Marine forces and to operate the bases nearly vacated in the United States. The 2002–3 Afghanistan and Iraq operations saw the Corps mobilize some 22,000 Reservists by 1 May 2003. A maximum of 8,000 would remain on active duty after March 2004 for augmentation and reinforcement tasks by means of continued call-up and demobilization of Reservists.

Today, the Department of Defense Total Force Policy integrates active, reserve, and National Guard forces into all military planning, especially major campaigns requiring more than the forward-deployed segment of the active forces. The Marine Corps reflected this sea change by establishing the position of commanding general, Marine Forces Reserve, to command the Reserve's various major elements under the direction of the commandant.

❯ MISSION, COMPOSITION, AND ORGANIZATION

❯ ❯ *Mission of the Reserve*

The mission of the Marine Corps Reserve, both organized Reserve units and individual Reservists, is to augment and reinforce active component Marine forces in times of war, national emergency, or contingency operations; provide personnel and operational tempo relief for the active forces in peacetime; and provide service to the community.

For decades, the Reservist maintained this capability with the stance of the "weekend warrior," drilling monthly on weekends and for two weeks in the summer with his or her unit to maintain the required individual skills and unit capabilities. That routine was judged adequate to provide readily available additional forces with the capability to mobilize and prepare for eventual operations at the side of active duty forces. Convention generally gave Reservists a "grace period" of sixty days upon mobilization to prepare for such operations.

Operations at the end of the twentieth century, however, ushered in an era of increasing dependence on the day-to-day readiness of the Reservist and quick reinforcement by Reserve units. The expenses of maintaining active duty forces, their typical worldwide commitments, and the difficulty of providing certain skills all have demanded an unconditional readiness of the Reserve and an increasing willingness to put it into action in situations short of declared war. Thus, today's Reservists train with the knowledge that their commitments to operations might be required in mere days rather than months.

Two concepts dominate the doctrine for preparing and deploying the Reserve. *Augmentation* brings units and selected individuals to join the active forces as required for operations, national emergency, or war. *Reinforcement* provides depth, replacement, and capabilities not resident in the active forces for operations, national emergency, or war.

❧ ❧ *Composition of the Reserve*

The Marine Corps Reserve includes individual categories for mobilization planning and assignment that vary according to the needs of the Corps and the preferences and background of the Reservist. Thus, it affords various opportunities for activity, which can usually be adjusted to the desires of anyone qualified to be a Marine. The Marine Corps Reserve is composed of the Ready Reserve, Standby Reserve, and Retired Reserve.

Ready Reserve. This encompasses both Reserve units and individual Reservists who are liable for immediate active duty during war or national emergency. The Ready Reserve is divided into the Selected Reserve and the Individual Ready Reserve.

The Selected Reserve describes the portion of the Reserve that is most ready to reinforce the active component. It is composed of Selected Marine Corps Reserve units, Individual Mobilization Augmentees, and members participating in the Active Reserve program.

- *Selected Marine Corps Reserve* (SMCR). SMCR units include the 4th Marine Division (4th MARDIV), 4th Marine Aircraft Wing (4th MAW), 4th Marine Logistics Group (4th MLG), and Force-level units of MARFORRES. All SMCR units remain under the administrative and operational control of the MARFORRES commanding general until activated. Currently there are 160 Reserve training centers located in forty-seven states, Washington, D.C., and Puerto Rico.

- *Individual Mobilization Augmentee* (IMA). IMA Marines are members of the Selected Reserve but are not members of an SMCR unit. They are normally preassigned to an active component unit billet that must be filled to meet the unit's requirements to support mobilization. The IMA program provides a source of trained and qualified individuals to fill a time-sensitive portion of the active component wartime structure.
- *Active Reserve* (AR). Reservists on active duty with this program normally serve in full-time active duty billets that support the organization, administration, recruiting, retention, instruction, and training of the Marine Corps Reserve. The program may also permit a Marine Reservist to serve on a full-time basis in various billets to help support the active component.

Members of the Individual Ready Reserve (IRR) consist of individual Marines who are available for mobilization, have had training, and have previously served in the active forces or in the Selected Reserve. IRR Marines are not actively drilling, nor are they affiliated with the SMCR. A Reservist in the IRR falls into one of three categories: (1) one who has not completed his or her mandatory service obligation (MSO); (2) one who has completed his or her MSO and remains in the Ready Reserve by voluntary agreement; or (3) one who has not completed his or her MSO (that is, a mandatory participant) but is transferred to the IRR.

All are deployable. Current law authorizes the president, without a prior declaration of war or a national emergency, to order not more than 200,000 Reserve servicemembers (of all branches of the armed forces) to active duty for not more than ninety days for purposes other than training.

Standby Reserve. This second broad category of the Reserve consists of Marines who are unable to meet the participation requirements of the Ready Reserve but desire to maintain their affiliation. They may also be bound by a remaining contractual obligation. The Standby Reserve is organized into two categories: Standby Reserve–Active Status List and Standby Reserve–Inactive Status List. These Reservists are not required to train and are not members of units, but they are subject to mobilization to satisfy manpower requirements for specific, often unique, skills.

Retired Reserve. Finally, this third category of the Corps' Reserve consists of Marines who have requested and been approved for retirement. Its members may be recalled to active duty under certain, usually rare, circumstances. The four categories of Retired Reserve Marines are Fleet Marine Corps Reserve (FMCR), Retired Reserve Awaiting Pay, Retired Reserve in Receipt of Retired Pay, and Regular Retired List.

❖ ❖ *Organization of the Reserve*

The Marine Corps Reserve today is organized and maintained under the Armed Forces Reserve Act of 1952, amended in 1955; it superseded the 1938 Navy Reserve Act. This law incorporated the basic principles of its predecessor but modernized the Reserve. Since 1969, legislation has provided annual strength authorizations for the Reserve just as in the case of the active component. In 2020, the authorization for the Marine Corps Reserve stood at 38,500 servicemembers.

Because the Reserve is a component of the Marine Corps as a whole, its command and administration stem directly from the commandant. Thus, the departments and offices of Marine Corps Headquarters bear the same relationships and responsibilities toward the Reserve as they do toward the rest of the Corps.

The Reserve Branch, situated within Manpower Department, HQMC, monitors the current operations and budget actions of the Reserve for the commandant. The headquarters staff, however, no longer enters directly into the chain of command of the Reserve.

❖ ❖ *Marine Corps Forces Reserve*

Reporting to the commandant, the commanding general, U.S. Marine Corps Forces Reserve, exercises command of the elements of the Reserve under the Total Force Concept. With headquarters and staff located at New Orleans, Louisiana, the commanding general exercises command over the 4th MARDIV, 4th MAW, 4th MLG, IRR, and Force Headquarters Group, which supports the commanding general's exercise of command and also contains an assortment of units providing functional and specialized capabilities, such as supporting arms liaison, civil affairs, and reserve mobilization (see figure 7-1).

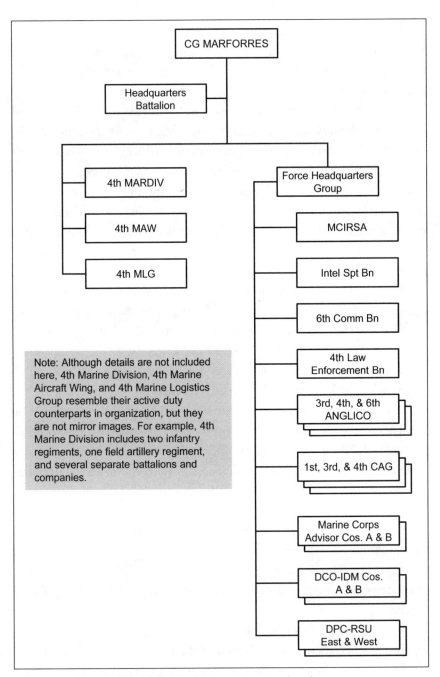

FIGURE 7-1. Organization of the Marine Corps Reserve (2021)

❥ ❥ *Marine Corps Reserve Units*

More than many Marines realize, the Corps entrusts its readiness to the units of the SMCR. They are the backbone of the Reserve and constitute the mobilization backbone of the Corps.

Leaving out the mobilization training units (discussed below), organized units of the Marine Corps Reserve are formed almost entirely from the SMCR. Both ground and aviation units are mainly organized at or below the battalion/squadron level. These units parallel—but do not necessarily mirror—like units in the active Marine Corps Operating Forces. Thus, in the ground portion of the Selected Reserve, you will find infantry, artillery, assault amphibian, reconnaissance, engineer, and air naval gunfire liaison company units. Reserve aviation likewise follows the active component pattern and includes, in various cities, most of the principal operating units of a MAW: fighter-attack squadrons, aerial refueler transport squadrons, helicopter squadrons, unmanned aerial vehicle squadron, and wing headquarters as well as service units. Reserve logistical units also resemble their active component counterparts.

Because Selected Reserve units follow the active Marine Corps Operating Forces pattern, their administration and functions are carried on in the same way as in similar units in the Regular establishment.

Selected ground units, typically battalion and below, are commanded by Reserve officers who have been selected for their professional experience and background. Like all commanding officers, they must administer, train, and maintain the readiness of their commands. In addition, they must stimulate and promote whatever recruiting is needed to keep their units up to strength. Reserve COs usually serve for a two-year tour, which may be extended under certain circumstances. This gives them adequate experience in command and ensures the advantages of healthy rotation.

Aviation squadrons, like ground units, are commanded by Reserve officers whose responsibilities are much like those of ground unit COs in the Ready Reserve.

Because of the large amount of technical training, the paramount requirement for safe flight operations, and the quantities of expensive matériel (including aircraft) required by a Reserve aviation unit, the inspection instruction organization (see the section on this topic below) for Reserve aviation outfits differs somewhat from that used with ground units.

The home station of each Reserve aviation unit has a parent Marine Air Reserve training detachment (MARTD). This detachment is commanded by a regular Marine Corps aviator and includes assistant instructors and maintenance crews to support the reserve squadron. The reserve unit's commander comes under the authority of the CO, MARTD.

Staff groups permit drill pay and Organized Reserve status for more senior Reserve officers for whom mobilization requirements exist but who cannot train with other Organized Reserve units. Staff groups attend paid drills and annual field training.

As part of the Force Headquarters Group, the Marine Corps Individual Reserve Support Activity (MCIRSA) plays a key role in managing and supporting the Reserve organization. It provides support to HQMC for the involuntary recall of IRR Marines and to conduct administrative screening of them so these Reservists can augment and reinforce the active component. Additionally, it administers the Mobilization Training Unit Program.

Mobilization training units (MTUs) are not part of the Selected Reserve but provide training in staff and command functions, both ground and air, for Reserve officers and enlisted men and women ordinarily not associated with a unit who want to stay with the Corps, keep up professional training, and amass credits for Reserve retirement.

Each MTU is made up of six or more servicemembers (officer or enlisted) of any military specialty or combination of specialties. Most units train under a specified syllabus provided by Marine Corps Training and Education Command, but some specialize in given fields when all members hold the same or related military occupational specialties. Each MTU is assigned an adviser, usually the nearest inspector-instructor (I&I) or CO, MARTD.

Members of the Reserve who are not affiliated with a unit or who live in a locality without a local unit obtain support and maintain contact with the Corps via the district director's office applicable to the member's geographical region. Those who wish to join the Reserve but have no hometown unit may also obtain advice and help from the district director.

The Reserve Branch, HQMC, administers Marine Reserve affairs outside the United States.

❧ RESERVE TRAINING

❧ ❧ *The Inspector-Instructor*

To ensure that Reservists have the benefit of coordinated and professional up-to-date training, advisory personnel from the active Marine Corps are detailed to duty with the Reserve.

Each SMCR unit has a Regular Marine officer who is known as the inspector-instructor (I&I). This title describes the job exactly. With the help of a small staff, the I&I must, as instructor, provide training assistance and general guidance to the unit. As inspector, however, he or she must make certain that the unit is up to the standards set by HQMC. I&Is for Reserve ground, aviation, and service support units are under the direct command of the respective commanding generals of the 4th MARDIV, 4th MAW, and 4th MLG. For certain Reserve aviation units, functions comparable to those of the I&I are performed by the CO, MARTD.

The I&I's job (and any duty in connection with the Reserve) calls for top-tier leadership, imagination, and tact. Responsibilities are heavy (much heavier than they look on paper). Authority, meanwhile, is slight, as Reserve units have their own Reservist commanders and staffs. Nevertheless, the job presents great challenges and can deliver corresponding rewards. In most cases, the I&I alone represents the active Marine Corps in the community. That officer's conduct, example, and loyalty to the ideals of the Corps inform and shape the local community's impression of Marines and, by extension, the whole Corps. The I&I, working with the leadership and members of his or her Reserve unit, thus serves as a crucial link between the Marine Corps and the nation's communities from which the Corps draws its support.

❧ ❧ *Training Opportunities in the Reserve*

Every Selected Reserve unit must complete a carefully planned annual training cycle. In addition to this unit training program, the individual Reservist may avail himself/herself of volunteer periods of training duty as well as a wide selection of gratis home-study courses, typically provided by the Marine Corps

Reserve Marines with 1st Battalion, 24th Marines, 4th Marine Division conduct live-fire training during Integrated Training Exercise 4-16 at Marine Corps Air Ground Combat Center, Twentynine Palms, California, in 2016.

College of Distance Education and Training (see chapter 14). Reserve training offers opportunities to fit the goals and interests of every individual.

Selected Reserve Training. Training of the average SMCR unit consists of twelve paid weekend drill or flying periods and two weeks' annual active duty training.

Reserve training is as challenging and meaningful as human effort can provide. It involves realistic field training. The amount of air-ground and combined arms training can be considerable, with two or more neighboring units joining in weekend exercises. Selected Reserve field artillery units (generally located near Army or Marine Corps bases with range facilities) conduct live firing throughout the year.

The hometown Selected Reserve training cycle culminates annually in two weeks' training by the unit at a Marine Corps base or station. It follows a cycle to include desert, mountain, jungle, amphibious, air-ground, combined arms, and specialist training. When possible, the Marine Corps arranges the movement of SMCR outfits to and from annual training by military airlift or in amphibious shipping. This increases the adaptability, experience, and professional know-how of the units and Marines concerned.

Members of the Selected Reserve receive drill pay for each drill session attended as well as for summer training. This can provide a welcome augmentation for one's primary income.

Individual Ready Reserve Training. Members of the IRR do not have to attend drills but may be required to perform training duty not exceeding fifteen days a year. (Enlisted personnel meeting certain criteria must perform thirty days' active duty annually.) There are also many open opportunities to train with Ready Reserve units or mobilization training units on one's own initiative, with or without pay. Reservists who aim to maintain high levels of professional proficiency and to accrue credits for Reserve retirement with pay (discussed below) can keep up to date by periodic spells of training duty and through courses from the College of Distance Education and Training.

A typical training cycle for an Individual Ready Reservist might include completion of a correspondence course, a two-week Reserve summer staff course at Quantico, and perhaps a few days' training duty without pay with an active duty unit or activity to brush up in a specialty. By remaining professionally up to date, an IRR Marine may earn additional rewarding training opportunities.

❯ INDIVIDUAL ADMINISTRATION PERTAINING TO RESERVISTS

Administration of the Marine Corps Reserve is controlled by statute and is relatively complex. The latest edition of *Marine Corps Reserve Administrative Management Manual* contains the most complete and accurate information on Reserve administration. The following paragraphs summarize some of the more salient points.

❯ ❯ *Privileges and Perquisites of the Marine Reservist*

A Marine recruiting poster, alleged to date from Revolutionary War days, recounts the privileges and perquisites of the Marine of 1776:

You will receive SEVENTEEN DOLLARS BOUNTY, And on your arrival at Head Quarters, be comfortably and genteelly clothed—And spirited young boys of a promising Appearance, who are Five Feet Six Inches high, WILL RECEIVE TEN DOLLARS, and equal advantages of PROVISIONS and CLOTHING with the Men. In fact, the Advantages which the MARINE possesses, are too numerous to mention here, but among the many, it may not be too amiss to state—That if he has a WIFE or aged PARENT, he can make them an Allotment of half his PAY; which will be regularly paid without any trouble to them, or to whomsoever he may direct that being well Clothed and Fed on Board Ship, the Remainder of his PAY and PRIZE MONEY will be clear in Reserve, for the Relief of his Family or his own private Purposes. The Single Young Man, on his Return to Port, finds himself enabled to cut a Dash on Shore with his GIRL and his GLASS, that might be envied by a Nobleman.

Clearly, times have changed. Today, the preeminent privilege one gains as a member of the Marine Corps Reserve is the right to wear the Eagle, Globe, and Anchor and call oneself a Marine. There are, however, other noteworthy privileges and perquisites.

Pay. A short but important word, "pay" is certainly a perquisite of the Reservist. For each regular drill or equivalent, one draws one day's pay, according to rank. This also applies to all active or training duty, unless performing it in nonpay status.

Uniforms. Reservists, of course, wear Regular Marine Corps uniforms. They are worn, or may be prescribed, during drills and instruction and on other appropriate occasions, such as military ceremonies, dinners, or balls. When wearing a Marine Corps uniform, it is imperative that a Reservist be indistinguishable from the most squared-away active component Marine.

Reserve officers must purchase and maintain their own uniforms, but they receive an initial allowance to help with this expense when first reporting for active duty.

Every Reserve officer must possess a required kit meeting minimum requirements but may, in addition, purchase other uniforms, such as dress uniforms and accessories, if one desires them and can find proper occasions to wear them. HQMC publishes lists of uniforms that Reserve officers must have.

It always bears emphasizing that wearing Marine Corps uniforms is a *privilege*, one that members of the Reserve have always treasured. When wearing the uniform, Reservists must hold themselves *accountable* to every *high standard* of the Corps and its *discipline*.

Clubs and Messes. These centers of Marine Corps social life extend a hearty welcome to the Marine Corps Reserve officer, whether active or inactive. Thus, Reserve officers will always find a friendly greeting (and, likely as not, old comrades) in the open mess at the nearest Marine Corps or Navy base or station.

Exchanges and Commissaries. Privileges at military exchanges and commissaries are unlimited for Reservists *during drill periods*. Commissary privileges are available on a limited basis for those on duty less than seventy-two hours. When a duty period exceeds seventy-two hours, Reservists rate the same exchange and commissary privileges as a Regular Marine.

Promotion. Promotion opportunities afford Reservists the chance to gain responsibility, expand their contributions to the nation, and, of course, to be eligible for increased retirement pay.

Decorations and Medals. Marine Reservists may be awarded decorations and medals just as any other Marine—strictly as earned. They are worn on the uniform or, on certain occasions, with civilian clothes in the same way as by Regulars (per the current edition of *Marine Corps Uniform Regulations*).

Government Insurance Benefits. Marine Reservists may qualify for Servicemembers' Group Life Insurance, Veterans' Group Life Insurance, and, for those completing twenty years of satisfactory federal service for entitlement to retired pay, the Reserve Component Survivor Benefit Plan.

Employment Protection. The Universal Military Training and Service Act (Public Law 632, 86th Congress), as amended, protects Reservists against loss of seniority, status, pay, and vacation while they are away from their civilian jobs on Reserve training duty. Also, those who unfortunately become disabled while training and unable to perform the duties of their jobs are entitled to reemployment for assignment to other jobs whose duties they may be able to perform. If a Reservist is hospitalized due to training duty, he or she may delay reemployment application for a period up to one year. On the other hand, the law requires the Reservist to request leave of absence from his or her employer before going on training duty and to report back to work immediately on completion of training.

Reserve Marines with Charlie Company, 4th Reconnaissance Battalion, 4th Marine Division conduct search-and-rescue operations with members of the Texas Highway Patrol and Texas State Guard in the wake of Hurricane Harvey in 2017.

Additionally, federal employees, if in the Reserve, rate up to fifteen days' extra leave with pay per year to cover periods spent on training duty. They are also protected by law against "loss of time, pay, or efficiency rating" while availing themselves of this additional special leave for training. Government employee Reservists ordered to active duty must, by law, be restored to the job they held before being called up.

The Marine Corps Association, which publishes the professional magazine of the Corps, *Marine Corps Gazette*, is open to membership by officers and enlisted members of the Reserve. So is the U.S. Naval Institute, which publishes *Proceedings*, the professional journal of the naval services.

⇥ ⇥ *Reserve Retirement*

Members of the Marine Corps Reserve are eligible to earn retirement benefits. In general, the fundamental prerequisite for Reserve retirement with pay is twenty or more years of qualifying service. Although one may achieve Reserve retirement under various provisions of law, the principal one affecting most Reservists is a section of Public Law 810, 80th Congress, which makes retirement pay available to all Marine Reservists who accumulate sufficient "retirement points" (credits earned by service, training, and professional military education). The number of retirement points one chalks up also determines the amount of retired pay one earns.

To qualify for Reserve retirement, a Reservist must earn at least fifty points a year for a minimum of twenty years, although these years need not be consecutive. He or she must earn at least fifty points in a year to have that year count toward Reserve retirement. The amount of retired pay one receives is determined by the total number of points accumulated. The number of points earned depends largely on the amount of effort put into training, distance learning, and other types of equivalent instruction: the more one gives as a Reservist, the more one receives in return.

After satisfying all the requirements, a Reservist normally becomes eligible for Reserve retirement pay the first month after his or her sixtieth birthday. Reserve retirement pay is computed based on a formula that factors in both total retirement points earned during the Reserve career and the prevailing retirement pay for an active duty retiree with comparable service and longevity. Since retirement policies may change from time to time, it is always wise to consult the latest edition of *Marine Corps Reserve Administrative Management Manual.*

Amendments to Title 10, U.S. Code, created a pair of special cases affecting eligibility for Reserve retirement and calculation of Reserve retirement pay. First, the law now authorizes a reduction of retirement age for a member of the Ready Reserve (excluding those in the AR) who serves on active duty for ninety days or more after 28 January 2008. This provision is not retroactive. For each aggregate period of ninety days on active duty in any fiscal year, the eligibility age for Reserve retirement will be reduced below sixty years of age by three months. A day of duty may be included in only one aggregate ninety-day period. In any case, the eligibility age may not be reduced below fifty years of age for a member entitled to retired pay for non-Regular service.

Second, Marines who entered service after 7 September 1980 and who elected discharge after completing twenty years of Reserve service instead of passing to the Retired Reserve will use the average of the three highest years of basic pay earned during the serving years.

In addition to all the foregoing, physical disability retirement rules that govern Regular Marines extend with equal force to Reservists who incur service-connected disabilities.

❖ ❖ *Additional Information on Reserve Matters*

The Marine Corps Reserve can supply more detailed information on the Reserve not only to Marines but also to prospective Reservists and friends. The Reserve Branch, HQMC, is always glad to answer individual queries and to assist Reservists in solving professional problems. But before contacting HQMC, it is always wise to search online for a local Marine Corps activity, either Regular or Reserve. A nearby Marine officer—whether I&I, NROTC instructor, officer selection officer, or recruiting district director—is always a ready and willing resource, and he or she may be able to provide the best advice on where to find desired information on the Marine Corps Reserve.

⸬{ 8 }⸬

MARINE CORPS
INSTALLATIONS

Our flag's unfurl'd to every breeze, from dawn to setting sun.
— "The Marines' Hymn"

ONLY THE GLOBE ITSELF—trademark of the Corps—limits the number of places where Marines may serve over the course of their careers.

The major permanent bases and stations of the Corps are the places where, between expeditions, deployments, and periods of service at sea, Marines will spend much of their careers honing their craft. The following describes not only the organization and general conditions at a typical Marine Corps installation but also the facilities and services that a typical base or station offers to Marines and their family members.

⸥ BASICS

In addition to installations with missions directly reflected in their titles (such as recruit depots or training centers), the Marine Corps has several types of bases and stations.

The Marine Corps base (MCB) and Marine barracks (MB) are the basic permanent installations for support of ground units of the Corps. Both are administratively autonomous and wholly or partially self-supporting. MCBs, along with similar installations sometimes labeled "camps," are devoted to field training and support of major tactical units, whereas MBs perform security missions.

A Marine Corps air station (MCAS) is the aviation counterpart of the MCB. Like a base, air stations are also permanent, autonomous, and self-supporting. Each MCAS has a common mission: support of Marine aviation units. When an aviation installation is not self-supporting, it is normally known as a Marine Corps air facility (MCAF).

Marine Corps installations whose focus is to host organizations dedicated to higher levels of support, such as procurement, depot maintenance, strategic distribution, or administrative support to high-level headquarters, are the Marine Corps logistics base (MCLB) and Marine Corps support facility (MCSF).

Finally, there are Marine detachments in several locations. These are the smallest organizations of the Corps that, in some ways, function like installations. A Marine detachment (MARDET), however, depends administratively and logistically on some larger organization (for example, a joint base or a naval station) and often does not have the permanent status enjoyed by other Marine activities.

› A TYPICAL MARINE CORPS INSTALLATION

› › *Organization of a Typical Base or Station*

With allowances for different missions, locations, and sizes, most Marine Corps installations follow a similar—though certainly not identical—organization. Figure 8-1 depicts the organization of a typical base or station.

Command. The commanding officer is in charge of the installation. (If the commander is a general, then he or she is instead referred to as the commanding general.) The CO is responsible for all that the command does or leaves undone.

The executive officer (XO) is the line officer next junior in rank to the CO. As the CO's alter ego, the XO relieves the commander of administrative detail and succeeds to command in the latter's absence. On a base commanded by a general, instead of an executive there is typically a chief of staff, who in turn may be assisted by a deputy. Given the turnover every two to three years of an installation's active duty leadership, many bases and stations will also have a civilian executive director or executive deputy who provides continuity as well as specific expertise in the intricacies of installation management.

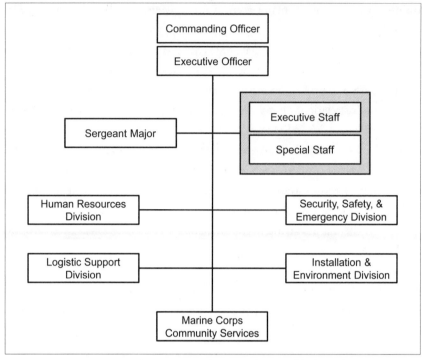

FIGURE 8-1. Organization of a Typical Marine Corps Installation

Staff. Just as in tactical units, an installation commander is assisted by an executive and special staff (much like those described in chapter 6). The executive staff typically includes assistants for administration, operations and plans, logistics and facilities—though in some instances facilities functions may lie in a distinct staff section—and communications and information systems, which together manage the full range of services that bases and stations must provide. In addition, most have a few special staff functions that differ materially in scale or scope from similar Marine Corps forces staff jobs, where administrative functions and business operations are not quite so important as on a base or station.

While the command and staff sections coordinate, Marine Corps installations typically conduct operations through several subordinate departments, divisions, and offices. These are most often functionally oriented, and their number and configuration vary among installations. But a typical base or station would include the following departments or divisions.

Security, Safety, and Emergency Services. This department or division normally provides law enforcement and security, fire protection, and emergency medical services to protect life and property, preserve good order and discipline, and promote quality of life. It may also be responsible for management of the installation's safety program, although this function might be organized in a separate installation safety center.

Within this department or division, you will normally find the provost marshal. This is the installation's "chief of police" or "sheriff," responsible for public safety, traffic control, criminal investigation, internal and external security, regulation of pets, and law and order in general. Law-abiding members of the community usually encounter the provost marshal in connection with registration of vehicles, pets, and personal firearms or when obtaining passes for guests and family members.

Installation and Environment. Often led by an active-duty or retired Navy Civil Engineer Corps officer, this department or division plans, oversees, and coordinates the construction, renovation, modernization, maintenance, and demolition of installation facilities and utilities. This organization bears responsibility for minor construction, repair, and upkeep of the physical plant of the base or station as well as its cleanliness and shipshape appearance. Additionally, it typically manages the installation's environmental programs.

Installation residents are most likely to interact with this organization through a bachelor or family housing office, whose operations usually fall within its purview, or by submitting a request for facility maintenance or repair.

Logistics Support. This department or division of the installation normally provides supply support, which may include military clothing issue and operation of "stores" (commonly called ServMart) that provide office supplies, tools, and other consumables; transportation support, including operation and maintenance of motor vehicles and material-handling equipment; and other logistics support.

Human Resources. The human resources and administration functions may reside in a department or division of the installation. This is often true at larger bases and stations with substantial numbers of civilian employees. In other cases, these functions may reside wholly at the staff level within the S-1 or G-1.

Marine Corps Community Services (MCCS). Every major base or station includes a department or division that manages Marine and family programs, recreation and leisure programs, and health and fitness programs and operates the associated facilities and activities. Additionally, MCCS operates retail-shopping and service outlets, including the Marine Corps exchanges and annexes, dining establishments, and commercial lodging facilities.

Policies require that MCCS generate revenue to cover its activities, which is to say that most MCCS operations are not supported by funding appropriated by Congress. Instead, income from retail shopping, dining, and lodging—along with some fee-for-service activities—provides the primary revenue supporting MCCS.

Smaller Offices. In addition to the larger departments or divisions, most installations include several smaller offices, such as the Office of the Comptroller, Office of the Staff Judge Advocate, Office of the Chaplain, Base Inspector's Office, Public Affairs Office or Communications Strategy Office (sometimes Office of Community Plans and Liaison when having a wider mandate), and Business Performance Office.

Boards and Councils. To advise the commander and sometimes supplement the staff, most installations include one or more standing boards or councils. Some are required by regulations, while others exist to meet local needs. Board and council membership often includes representatives of both the installation staff and the supported community. Typical examples include an exchange council, recreation council, athletic and sports council, school advisory board, and housing advisory board.

⁂ *Facilities and Services at a Typical Base or Station*

In many ways, an installation resembles a small town. Most if not all the facilities and services you could expect in such a community have counterparts on a Marine base or station. But just as with small towns, bases and stations of varying age, locality, and mission exhibit considerable local disparities. Thus, what you find on one installation may not exist at another.

Marine Corps bases and stations typically offer the following facilities and services.

Medical and Dental Care. Virtually every Marine installation includes health-care activities for the health and welfare of all its personnel and their families. These activities—normally tenant activities commanded, managed, and operated by the Navy—may range from a dispensary (sick bay) to a clinic (dispensary with limited facilities for inpatient care) or, on the largest installations, a naval hospital that can handle any medical or surgical emergency. Often, a smaller base or station will have a branch clinic that operates as a satellite of a regional naval medical center.

Commissary. Most installations host a commissary, the military equivalent of a grocery store or supermarket, which, since 1991, has been operated by the Defense Commissary Agency. If a commissary does not exist, however, there is normally one located at an adjacent base or station. Stock and services available in commissaries vary somewhat according to the size of the installation and the quality of nearby civilian facilities. Their prices are slightly lower than those charged by grocers in the local community, although so-called big-box retailers provide real competition for commissaries, which nevertheless provide good value and win on convenience.

The privilege of making purchases at commissaries is limited to active duty and retired personnel, to Reservists on active or training duty, and to certain government civilians. Family members of anyone entitled to such privileges may also use the commissary, but all must present appropriate identification to do so. Use of the commissary is a privilege, not a right, and all purchases must be for your own use and that of your household.

Marine Corps Exchange. Marine Corps exchanges—or MCX, as they are commonly known—and/or exchange annexes operate at most bases and stations. Moreover, these operations, along with the welfare, recreation, and other beneficial activities described below, have been centralized under the MCCS department or division of each installation. Since 1999, they have operated under the headquarters-staff cognizance of the deputy commandant for Manpower and Reserve Affairs.

Military exchanges, originally called post exchanges and still called that today on Army installations, go far back in U.S. military history. During the nineteenth century, when the Army pushed our frontier westward, each isolated post had its "post trader," or sutler, authorized to keep a store at the post. One of the trader's perquisites was the right of trading with area Indians, trappers, and hunters, and from this arose the title "post exchange." After the frontier vanished, the name remained, carrying over from the old Army into the old Marine Corps. In early times, the perquisite of keeping the post trader's stores at the various MBs was awarded to the widow of some officer or senior NCO. The modern post exchange system was established by Major General Charles Heywood, the ninth commandant. As part of a Corps-wide rebranding effort beginning in the late 1990s, the Marine Corps exchange system began using the MCX moniker exclusively.

Today's exchange is really the installation's general store. On large bases and stations, it approximates a small department store, but the size of an exchange depends on the size of the installation it serves and the accessibility of civilian shopping centers. Marine Corps exchanges aim to provide military personnel (including family members) convenient retail access, at reasonable prices, to articles necessary for health, comfort, and well-being.

Eligibility to shop on base at the exchange, like the commissary, is a privilege that extends only to active or retired service personnel, to their eligible family members and surviving spouses, and to Reservists on active or training duty.

DOD extended, in 2017, limited privileges to all *honorably discharged* veterans to shop online at military exchanges, with the shopping benefit taking effect beginning on Veterans Day 2017. While shopping privileges exclude the purchase of uniforms, alcohol, and tobacco products, they cover the majority of the online retail environment of the exchange services. This "win-win" policy both recognizes the service of honorably discharged veterans and provides additional financial support to morale, welfare, and recreation programs at military installations.

Welfare Activities. In addition to welfare services provided by the chaplain, special services officer, and legal assistance officer, most large bases have representatives of the American Red Cross, Navy–Marine Corps Relief Society, and Navy Mutual Aid Association. The assistance furnished by these groups is described in chapter 20.

Educational Programs and Facilities. Many installations have their own public schools for the children living on the installation. In some regions (mostly overseas), these are operated by the highly regarded Department of Defense Education Activity (DODEA), while in other regions schools on board Marine Corps installations are part of a surrounding or adjacent civilian school district.

Every installation has a free library open to Marines and their family members. HQMC provides the books. A few large bases have museums.

Even the smallest station and detachment features an Education Office, charged with providing information on educational opportunities available on and off base, including correspondence courses. Many of these programs lead toward various types of college degrees. The same office will advise you of tuition aid, veteran's assistance, and loan and scholarship programs.

Fitness and Recreation. Most bases and stations feature excellent on-station physical fitness, athletic, and recreational activities, and the Semper Fit program, operated by MCCS, offers virtually unlimited opportunities. Facilities for athletic activities and hobbies are open to all. Frequently, instruction in various sports and hobbies will be available at little or no cost—you and your family would do well to avail yourselves of the opportunity to acquire new skills and hobbies for present and future enjoyment. Depending upon space and demand, Marine Corps bases and stations may have golf courses, tennis courts, marinas, gymnasiums, skeet and small-arms ranges, swimming pools, stables, flying fields, and various workshops. Take advantage of these resources!

One key to gaining the most benefit from the military community resides in the single Marine programs, family programs, and family service centers managed and operated by MCCS at all bases and activities. Family service centers provide a single point of reference for Marines as they change location. Specialists provide the latest information on new duty stations and civilian communities: housing, schools, employment, child care, vehicle and firearms registration, and non–Marine Corps activities.

The programs and centers offer seminars and orientation courses on the many aspects of personal and family development. Trained counselors and social workers provide guidance and referrals to outside agencies. Also offered are employment counseling for family members and retirement preparation for Marines, services often not available in communities except at considerable expense. If assigned to another service's installation, Marines and their families may also us that installation's similar programs and centers.

⟩ MARINE CORPS INSTALLATIONS COMMAND

Established in 2011 to consolidate and improve the management of Marine installations worldwide, Marine Corps Installations Command oversees base and station operations, develops and coordinates relevant policy, and prioritizes resources for the support of the Corps' installations. MCICOM is commanded by a major general, who also functions as the assistant deputy commandant for installations and logistics (facilities) within HQMC. MCICOM is located at the Pentagon.

Central reasons for establishing MCICOM included unburdening the Operating Forces from having to manage bases and stations and creating an organization with a singular focus on providing installation support that directly, effectively, and efficiently advances the Marine Corps' warfighting mission. This reorganization enabled operational commanders at all levels to concentrate their efforts on preparing their forces for deployment and employment across the full spectrum of operations.

Marine Corps installations are an essential component of the nation's defense establishment, for they are the "force projection platforms" that enable the readiness, mobilization, training, sustainment, deployment, redeployment, and reconstitution of the Operating Forces.

❯ ❯ *Mission and Organization of Marine Corps Installations Command*

The MCICOM mission reads, "As the single authority for all Marine Corps installation matters, MCICOM exercises command and control of regional installation commands, establishes policy, exercises oversight, and prioritizes resources in order to optimize installation support to the Operating Forces, tenant commands, Marines, and family members." MCICOM continually aims to apply its capabilities and capacities to the highest priorities of the operational and training commands located on board Marine Corps bases and stations.

MCICOM consists of a headquarters situated in the Installations and Logistics Department at HQMC, and four subordinate regional commands:

- Marine Corps Installations National Capital Region (MCINCR)
- Marine Corps Installations East (MCIEAST)
- Marine Corps Installations West (MCIWEST)
- Marine Corps Installations Pacific (MCIPAC)

As depicted in figure 8-2, the MCICOM organization provides for oversight of base and station operations in support of tenant organizations and coordination

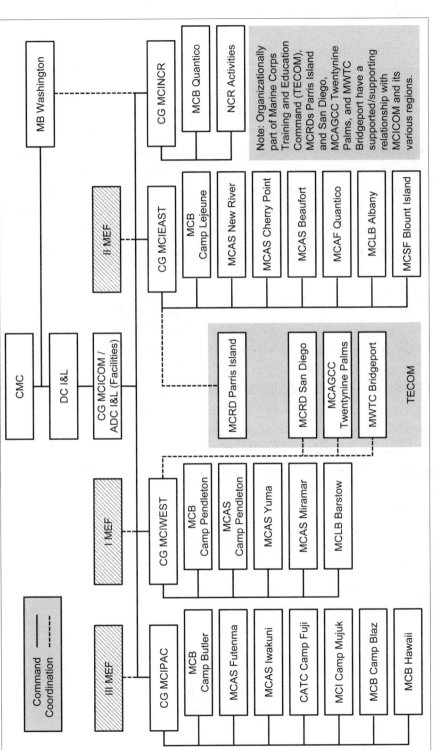

FIGURE 8-2. Organization of Marine Corps Installations Command (2021)

with both the Marine Forces and key training commands, which fall under the separate cognizance of the Marine Corps Training and Education Command.

MCICOM's more than 33,000 personnel oversee twenty-four Marine Corps installations, 2.3 million acres of land, and 283 training ranges. Included within these installations are eleven air stations, air facilities, and expeditionary airfields. MCICOM also provides operational support aircraft for transporting passengers and cargo in support of contingency operations, training exercises, and operational commanders. To accomplish its mission, MCICOM manages a budget of approximately $2.7 billion each year, providing a broad spectrum of services and support across seven functional areas: command and staff support, installation protection, training and operations support, logistic support, facilities support, information technology, and Marine, family, and community services.

❯ ❯ *Marine Corps Installations National Capital Region*

This regional installation command is headquartered at MCB Quantico, Virginia. MCINCR encompasses the bases, stations, and activities located in the Washington metropolitan area.

Marine Barracks Washington. Situated in southeast Washington, D.C., at the intersection of Eighth and I Streets and colloquially known as "Eighth and Eye," MB Washington is the oldest active installation in the Marine Corps. It is famous for its weekly Evening Parades, and it provides ceremonial troops for official occasions in the nation's capital, supports the U.S. Marine Band and the Marine Corps Drum and Bugle Corps, and provides Marines for special security duties in and about Washington and in the Navy Yard.

Marine Corps Base Quantico. Situated on the Potomac River, approximately thirty-five miles south of Washington, D.C., MCB Quantico is the "Crossroads of the Marine Corps" because of its significant role supporting training, education, and combat development in the Corps. It is home to the Marine Corps Combat Development Command, Marine Corps Systems Command, Marine Corps Intelligence Activity, Marine Corps Network Operations and Security Center, Marine Corps Warfighting Laboratory, Marine Corps Air Facility Quantico, and Naval Medical Clinic.

Other activities in the national capital region include Henderson Hall (named for Archibald Henderson), located on the southern edge of Arlington National

Marine officer candidates navigate a portion of the Combat Course at Officer Candidates School on Marine Corps Base Quantico, Virginia—the "Crossroads of the Corps." The Combat Course aims to challenge candidates with an environment they may encounter on the battlefield.

Cemetery and now part of Joint Base Myer–Henderson Hall, and Marine Corps Detachment Fort Meade, located in Laurel, Maryland, and host to Marine Corps Forces Cyberspace Command.

❯ ❯ *Marine Corps Installations East*

Located on board MCB Camp Lejeune, MCIEAST is the regional command that oversees the activities of assigned Marine Corps bases and stations located in the eastern United States. It develops and implements strategies, plans, and policies for installation management; directs and oversees installation activities; prioritizes allocation of resources; and provides regional services and support through assigned bases and stations to support the Operating Forces and tenant commands and activities. MCIEAST is commanded by a brigadier general, who also serves as the commanding general for MCB Camp Lejeune.

MCIEAST encompasses a headquarters and the following bases and stations.

MCB Camp Lejeune. Located near Jacksonville, North Carolina, it is the East Coast base for the ground units of the FMF and accommodates the II MEF CE, 2nd MARDIV, and 2nd MLG; 22nd, 24th, and 26th MEUs; MARSOC; several training centers and specialty schools; and the Naval Hospital.

MCAS New River. Adjacent to and partially integrated with MCB Camp Lejeune, it is the East Coast home to Marine Corps tilt-rotor and rotary-wing aviation. It primarily hosts elements of 2nd MAW, in particular Marine Aircraft Group 26, Marine Aircraft Group 29, and other units dedicated to aviation support.

MCAS Cherry Point. Near Havelock, North Carolina, it is the largest MCAS in the world and is one of the best all-weather jet bases. MCAS Cherry Point is home to the 2nd MAW Headquarters, Marine Aircraft Group 14, Marine Air Control Group 28, the only Marine Corps–operated Fleet Readiness Center, and the Naval Health Clinic.

MCAS Beaufort. Adjacent to Beaufort, South Carolina, it is home to the Marine Corps' East Coast fixed-wing fighter-attack aircraft assets. It is a major jet base and currently hosts elements of the 2nd MAW, primarily Marine Aircraft Group 31, and the Naval Hospital. It is also close to Marine Corps Recruit Depot (MCRD) Parris Island.

MCAF Quantico. A tenant facility located on board MCB Quantico in Virginia, it is the home to Marine Helicopter Squadron 1 (HMX-1), established there in 1947 as an experimental unit to test and evaluate military helicopters. Founded to develop tactics, techniques, and procedures, as well as to test equipment, HMX-1 is perhaps most widely known for supporting helicopter transport of the president of the United States. MCAF Quantico is organizationally distinct from MCB Quantico, which is part of MCINCR. The air facility, however, is dependent on MCB Quantico for virtually all base-support functions.

MCLB Albany. Located just outside Albany, Georgia, it provides the full range of base support to LOGCOM and several other tenant organizations, including a distribution center of the Defense Logistics Agency. Notably, the base boasts some of the finest storage capability within DOD, encompassing more than 3.8 million square feet of closed storage in nineteen warehouses and more than 7.7 million square feet of open storage lots.

The large live oak tree affectionately known as Dubber's Oak is located just outside Marine Corps Logistics Base Albany's main gate. The historical landmark is dedicated to Colonel A. E. Dubber, who from March 1951 to July 1955 oversaw planning and construction of the installation, originally named the Marine Corps Depot of Supplies, Albany, Georgia.

MCSF Blount Island. Located in the vicinity of Jacksonville, Florida, it serves as the hub of the Marine Corps' worldwide prepositioning programs and as the home of Blount Island Command, which manages these programs in support of the MARFORs. Both Blount Island Command and the support facility operate with relatively few Marines on staff, relying instead on sizable contingents of federal civil servants and defense-contractor partners. As a result, base support at MCSF Blount Island is limited.

MCRD Parris Island. Located along the South Carolina coast, this depot is not organizationally part of MCIEAST; instead, it is part of TECOM. But as an installation, it is included here because of its geographic location and its supporting-supported relationship with MCIEAST. More than one million recruits have been trained on Parris Island since "boot camp" was established there in 1915. The depot commanding general, a brigadier general, is also commanding general for the Eastern Recruiting Region.

❧ ❧ *Marine Corps Installations West*

Located on board MCB Camp Pendleton, MCIWEST is the regional command that oversees the activities of assigned Marine Corps bases and stations located in the western United States. Like its counterpart on the East Coast, MCIWEST develops and implements strategies, plans, and policies for installation management; directs and oversees installation activities; prioritizes allocation of resources; and provides regional services and support through assigned bases and stations to support the Operating Forces and tenant commands and activities. It is commanded by a brigadier general, who also serves as the commanding general for MCB Camp Pendleton.

MCIWEST comprises a headquarters and the following bases and stations.

MCB Camp Pendleton. Wedged between San Clemente and Oceanside, California, it is the prime amphibious training base in the Corps. It serves as the major West Coast base for ground units of the FMF and provides facilities and support for the 1st MARDIV, the 1st MLG, and I MEF CE. Camp Pendleton also completely envelopes MCAS Camp Pendleton. Recruits from MCRD San Diego complete weapons training at Camp Pendleton's Edson Range and Weapons Field Training Battalion, and the base also hosts several other formal schools and smaller organizations.

MCAS Camp Pendleton. Situated on MCB Camp Pendleton, it supports the operations of Marine Aircraft Group 39, with several medium tilt-rotor and light rotary-wing aircraft squadrons. As part of MCIWEST, MCAS Camp Pendleton is organizationally distinct from MCB Camp Pendleton. The air facility, however, is dependent on MCB Camp Pendleton for virtually all base-support functions.

MCAS Yuma. Adjacent to Yuma, Arizona, it is one of the newest of the Marine Corps air stations. It has a 13,300-foot main runway, an instrumented range, and some of the finest flying weather to be found. The air station is home to Marine Aircraft Group 13, Marine Aviation Weapons and Tactics Squadron 1, Marine Operational Test and Evaluation Squadron 22, and several tenant units involved in aviation, aviation training, and aviation support.

Commonly referred to as the "white house," this historical headquarters building at Marine Corps Base Camp Pendleton, California, has been the workspace for numerous commanding generals and staff of the 1st Marine Division.

MCAS Miramar. Located north of San Diego, California, it has become one of the Marine Corps' largest aviation facilities, following its reversion from Navy to Corps control in 1997. It hosts a large complement of the Corps' fixed-wing and tilt-rotor aircraft based on the West Coast. It is home to the 3rd MAW Headquarters, Marine Aircraft Group 11, Marine Aircraft Group 16, and Marine Air Control Group 38 as well as several other tenant organizations.

MCLB Barstow. Just outside of Barstow, California, it takes advantage of a confluence of transportation routes and the Mojave Desert's hot, dry climate, which inhibits deterioration of stored material. Covering more than six thousand acres, Barstow generally supports all Marine organizations west of the Mississippi River and in the Far East by operating a substantial industrial and storage complex, including a ten-acre repair shop—the largest building in the Marine Corps.

MCRD San Diego, Marine Corps Air-Ground Combat Center (MCAGCC), and **Marine Corps Mountain Warfare Training Center** (MWTC). These are not organizationally part of MCIWEST but are instead part of TECOM. Yet they are discussed here because of their geographic locations and their supporting-supported relationships with MCIWEST.

The primary mission of MCRD San Diego, located in central San Diego on the Pacific Highway, is twofold. First is the recruiting of new Marines from the Western Recruiting Region, composed of the 8th, 9th, and 12th Marine Corps Districts. Second is the training of Marine recruits using facilities at San Diego and Camp Pendleton, California. Also located at the MCRD is the Recruiters' School and the West Coast Drill Instructors' School. The depot commanding general, a brigadier general, is also commanding general for the Western Recruiting Region.

Covering 932 square miles, twice the size of Los Angeles and big enough to encompass MCBs Pendleton, Lejeune, and Quantico with room to spare, MCAGCC is not only the largest installation in the Marine Corps but also a primary training and experimental center for Marine artillery and guided missiles. It is also the location of the Communication-Electronics School and has facilities for most elements of the 7th Marine Regiment (Reinforced). The base also includes the Tactical Exercise Evaluation and Control Group, which exercises the combined arms capabilities and readiness of operational units in a live-fire environment.

The MWTC is located within the Humboldt-Toiyabe National Forest, twenty-one miles north of Bridgeport, California, and twenty-two miles south of Coleville, California, on Highway 108 in Pickel Meadow. For over sixty-two years, the Marine Corps has conducted training in partnership with the U.S. Forest Service at this location. The training center hosts unit and individual training courses to prepare Marine Corps, joint, and allied forces for operations in mountainous, high-altitude, and cold-weather environments. MWTC also develops tactics, techniques, procedures, and specialized equipment for use in mountain and cold-weather operations.

❧ ❧ *Marine Corps Installations Pacific*

Headquartered at MCB Camp Smedley D. Butler in Okinawa, Japan, MCIPAC is the regional command that oversees the activities of assigned Marine Corps bases and stations located outside the continental United States in Hawaii and the western Pacific. Like its counterparts in the continental United States, MCI-PAC develops and implements strategies, plans, and policies for installation management; directs and oversees installation activities; prioritizes allocation of resources; and provides regional services and support through assigned bases and stations for the Operating Forces and tenant commands and activities. MCIPAC is commanded by a brigadier or major general, who also serves as the commanding general for MCB Camp Butler.

MCIPAC is composed of a headquarters and the following bases and stations.

MCB Camp Butler. Located on the island of Okinawa, Japan, it is not a single installation but actually encompasses a cluster of Marine installations and facilities on Okinawa, including several smaller camps (Camps Foster/Lester, Courtney/McTureous, Gonsalves, Hansen, Kinser, and Schwab). The MCB Camp Butler headquarters is located on board Camp Foster. The III MEF CE, 3rd MARDIV, 1st MAW, and 3rd MLG are all headquartered at one of the camps within the Camp Butler complex.

MCAS Futenma. Positioned in southern Okinawa, this station is capable of safely handling the largest commercial and military cargo planes in the world. It primarily hosts propeller-driven and tilt-rotor aircraft, however, for Marine units on Okinawa. Marine Aircraft Group 36 and Marine Air Control Group 18 are headquartered on board the air station. MCAS Futenma's future is uncertain, as it has become a focal point of Okinawan opposition to the U.S. military presence on the island. As part of MCIPAC, it is organizationally distinct from MCB Camp Butler. But the air station shares most base-support functions and services with Camp Butler, excluding air station operations.

MCAS Iwakuni. Situated southwest of Hiroshima on the island of Honshu, Japan, it is the home station of all tactical jet aircraft units of the 1st MAW (whose headquarters is at MCB Camp Butler) and of Japanese naval aviation units as well.

Combined Arms Training Center Camp Fuji. Sited on the southeast slope of Mount Fuji on the island of Honshu, Japan, it occupies ground that was reportedly used to train samurai warriors long before the Marines arrived. As far back as AD 1198, the Kamakura feudal government trained more than 30,000 samurai warriors on the same ground that Fuji Marines use today. The Fuji Maneuver Area, which consists of the 12,000-acre northern area and 22,000-acre eastern

Station fire department members douse a simulated burning
aircraft as part of an airport rescue firefighter course at
Marine Corps Air Station Iwakuni, Japan.

area, is jointly used by U.S. forces and the Japan Ground Self Defense Force
(JGSDF). It contains live-fire ranges as well as maneuver areas. The camp itself is
an exclusive-use, full-service, 309-acre U.S. facility designed to support U.S. forces.

Marine Corps Installation Camp Mujuk. Located just outside Pohang,
South Korea, it supports Marines, other U.S. military personnel, and foreign
military personnel who deploy to the Korean Peninsula for bilateral training
and exercises with the South Korean armed forces. Like Camp Fuji, and due to
Camp Mujuk's remote location and distance from other U.S. military installations capable of providing services to support families, assignment to Camp
Mujuk is a one-year, dependent-restricted tour of duty.

MCB Camp Blaz. Located at Dededo, Guam, a U.S. territory in the Micro-
nesia subregion of the western Pacific, it is the Marine Corps' newest installation,
activated in 2020. This officially marked the initial operational capability of the

base, which will eventually host III MEF units as part of a realignment of forces according to an international agreement with the government of Japan. This will help guarantee a Marine Corps posture in the Indo-Pacific region that is geographically distributed and operationally resilient.

MCB Hawaii. Headquartered at Kaneohe Bay on the island of Oahu, it reflects the 1994 consolidation all of Marine Corps installations and activities in Hawaii, including MCAS Kaneohe Bay, Camp H. M. Smith, Molokai Training Support Facility, Manana Family Housing Area, Puuloa Range, and the Pearl City Warehouse Annex. The headquarters (and nerve center) of Marine Forces Pacific is at Camp H. M. Smith, overlooking Pearl Harbor. Because of its superb site and outstanding facilities, Camp Smith is also home to U.S. Pacific Command, which is a tenant activity. In addition to Camp Smith, there is MCAS Kaneohe, on the "windward" side of the island, home station of the 3rd Marine Littoral Regiment, Marine Aircraft Group 24, 3rd Radio Battalion, and a variety of other units. Here, both ground and air units of the Operating Forces train and operate as an integrated air-ground team.

❥ SMALLER ACTIVITIES AND DETACHMENTS

In addition to the large installations just described, the Marine Corps maintains numerous smaller units, activities, and detachments at various sites around the globe. These generally operate as tenant organizations on another installation or installation complex managed by another service or executive agent.

❥ ❥ *Marine Activities in the Vicinity of Norfolk, Virginia*

Although the Norfolk–Hampton Roads area includes no major Marine Corps installations, Camp Allen (formerly Camp Elmore) is in Norfolk, Virginia, and home to both MARFORCOM and two FAST companies of the Marine Corps Security Force Regiment. Overall, nearly 3,500 Marines reporting to ten local Marine commands call the Norfolk–Hampton Roads area home.

Other Marine commands in the area—many of which are tenants on board the area's numerous Navy installations—include the Marine Corps Security Cooperation Group, Expeditionary Warfare Training Group Atlantic, various detachments, and the School of Music. Thus, Norfolk and the surrounding area can be considered a Marine Corps base of importance.

❖ ❖ *Marine Corps Embassy Security Group*

The Marine Corps maintains Marine security guard (MSG) detachments at designated Department of State diplomatic and consular facilities around the world. These detachments provide protection to mission personnel and prevent the compromise of national security information and equipment. The Marine Corps has no responsibility in which individual quality and outstanding performance are of higher importance than the MSG program, which the Corps administers and operates for the Department of State.

The MCESG, which is headquartered at Quantico, Virginia, and commanded by a colonel who reports directly to the CMC, exercises command, excluding operational supervision, over the MSG detachments through subordinate regional commands:

- Region 1, covering Eastern Europe and Eurasia and situated in Frankfurt, Germany
- Region 2, covering South Asia and the Middle East and based in Abu Dhabi, United Arab Emirates
- Region 3, encompassing East Asia and the Pacific and based in Bangkok, Thailand
- Region 4, covering South America and located in Fort Lauderdale, Florida
- Region 5, covering Western Europe and Scandinavia and located in Frankfurt, Germany
- Region 6, including East Africa and southern Africa and based in Johannesburg, South Africa
- Region 7, encompassing North Africa and West Africa and situated in Frankfurt, Germany
- Region 8, covering Central Europe and situated in Frankfurt, Germany
- Region 9, covering North America and the Caribbean and located in Fort Lauderdale, Florida

Under this program, some 1,500 carefully selected Marines maintain the internal security of American embassies, legations, missions, and consulates throughout the world. All of these vitally important security posts are under the independent command of staff NCOs. Apart from recruiting duty and drill instruction at the recruit depots, the Corps has no other program that depends so directly and singly on the loyalty, military character, self-discipline, good sense, and devotion to duty of its NCOs.

❖ ADDITIONAL INFORMATION

While this chapter provides a limited overview of Marine Corps bases and stations, an officer transferring to a new and unfamiliar duty station will desire significantly more detailed information about his or her future professional home. You can find two good sources of current, detailed information online: My Base Guide (https://mybaseguide.com/) and Base Directory (https://www.basedirectory .com/). For each installation, both sites contain a variety of resources, including information on transportation, quarters, schools, child development, health, recreation, and commissary and exchange services.

❊{ 9 }❊

NAVAL INTEGRATION AND
SERVICE AFLOAT

*I should not deem a man-of-war complete without a body of
Marines . . . imbued with that esprit that has so long characterized
the "old Corps."*

— Commodore Joshua R. Sands

SEA DUTY—dating from the Athenian fleets of the fifth century BCE and
carrying on through Roman times, when separate legions of *milites classiarii*
(soldiers of the fleet) were assigned to duty afloat—is the oldest and original duty
of marines. In the seventeenth century, when the British and Dutch organized
the first modern corps of marines, it was for duty as ship's detachments, and it
was for this same purpose that U.S. Marines were first employed. The anchor
in the Marine Corps emblem today symbolizes that the Marine is first and
foremost a maritime soldier whose natural medium is the sea.

Since World War II and the Korean War, and even more so today, the expansion of the Corps, coupled with an increased demand for Marines elsewhere,
contributed to the elimination of permanent Marine detachments on Navy ships.
As a result, sea duty has virtually disappeared for Marines. That said, should you
receive orders to report on board the USS *Makin Island* (LHD 8) for duty with
Combat Cargo, not only are you embarking upon a tour for which previous
experience has little prepared you, but you also cannot turn to a contemporary

in your outfit for advice. Embarked Marine units will nonetheless experience service afloat, which is approximately equal to the old sea duty and one of the most rewarding tours that can come your way.

❯ NAVAL INTEGRATION

On 7 December 1933, Secretary of the Navy Claude A. Swanson issued General Order 241, establishing the Fleet Marine Force, successor to the Advanced Base Force discussed in chapter 2, under the operational control of the fleet commander. This generated unity of effort and operational agility, and it contributed to the integrated application of Navy and Marine Corps capabilities throughout the maritime domain. The 1986 Goldwater-Nichols Act, however, removed most of the FMF from fleet operational control, created separate Navy and Marine Corps components within joint forces, and thereby altered the longstanding relationship between the Navy and Marine Corps. Over time, Navy and Marine officers tended to view their operational roles as separate and distinct, rather than as intertwined and complementary.

The nadir of naval integration within the Department of the Navy may best be exemplified by a scene from the classic 1992 film *A Few Good Men*. In this scene, Navy lawyer Lieutenant Daniel Kaffee, played by Tom Cruise, interviews Marine Corps infantryman Second Lieutenant Jonathan Kendrick, played by Kiefer Sutherland:

> Kaffee: Lieutenant Kendrick . . . can I call you Jon?
> Kendrick: No, you may not.
> Kaffee: Have I done something to offend you?
> Kendrick: No, I like all you Navy boys. Every time we've gotta go someplace
> to fight, you fellas always give us a ride.

Ironically, Columbia Pictures released *A Few Good Men* near a pinnacle of U.S. naval power, even if parts of the film seem to depict a low point in naval integration. With the end of the Cold War and dissolution of the Soviet Union in 1991, the U.S. Navy was unchallenged on the high seas and seemingly had few real operational worries beyond "giving Marines a ride" to places to fight or, more commonly, to hand out ready-to-eat meals during humanitarian crises. Shortly thereafter, however, America's adversaries "went to school" on several strikingly successful U.S. military operations during the 1990s and the first decade of the twenty-first century and began to develop ways to neutralize the U.S. military's advantages.

Over the succeeding two decades, the nation's adversaries advanced their intelligence, surveillance, and reconnaissance capabilities; developed sophisticated anti-access and area-denial systems; and acquired lethal long-range precision weapons to challenge the U.S. Navy, even far from the world's coastlines. This rise of both land- and sea-based threats in the global commons changed the operating environment for naval forces. Navy and Marine Corps leaders have recognized a need to reestablish a more integrated approach to operations in the maritime domain. To this end, the Corps plans to reinvigorate the FMF by assigning more Marine forces to the fleet, redesign portions of the force to contribute to sea-denial and sea-control operations, assign Marines to the fleet Maritime Operations Centers, and emphasize naval integration in its training, education, and supporting-establishment activities.

Ultimately, the changing environment in which naval forces operate makes closer naval integration an imperative. This means Marine officers need a deeper understanding of how naval forces organize and operate and how Navy staffs and ships function.

❧ ❧ *The Task Force Principle*

The task force principle refers to the Navy–Marine Corps system of organizing forces for given missions while preserving a separate administrative organization for training, management, and housekeeping details. This is the fundamental organizational principle of the nation's naval Operating Forces.

Type Organization. All forces in the U.S. fleets are grouped into the type organization of the fleet, which is based on kinds of ships or forces. Note that the FMF is a type command since it comprises all Marine Corps tactical units—air and ground—assigned to the fleet. The type organizations are principally responsible for ensuring that assigned forces are prepared to conduct operations.

Task Organization. The other facet of fleet organization is the task organization, which conducts operations using units the type organizations prepare and provide. Taking the Pacific Fleet as an example, it includes several permanent task forces. Certain of these, such as antisubmarine warfare (ASW) forces, might

Two Marine F-35B Lightning IIs, two Navy F-35C Lightning IIs, a Navy EA-18G Growler, and a Navy F/A-18E Super Hornet conduct midair refueling training, displaying the integration and interoperability of naval aviation.

be task organized from aviation, surface, and submarine forces to perform a specific mission—in this case, to maintain control of the sea.

This system provides for a flexible structure, consisting of fleets further subdivided into task forces, groups, units, and elements. Each of these descending subdivisions has a numbered designation and appropriate communication call signs. When a fleet commander receives a mission from higher authority, he or she can then assign necessary forces to do the job by tailoring a unique organization of ships and units. Such a task organization is adaptable to operations of any magnitude, ranging from campaigns of entire fleets in general war to a single ship on a temporary mission. For example, an LHD (landing helicopter dock) amphibious assault ship might be given a task designation simply to steam across the Chesapeake Bay for a Navy Day visit; on conclusion of that job, the task designation would cease.

Within the Seventh Fleet, a typical (hypothetical) task fleet numbering system would be one in which the commander, Seventh Fleet, would assign the fleet's major forces to numbered task forces (TFs), such as Battle Force, TF 70; Navy

Special Warfare Force, TF 71; Patrol and Reconnaissance Force, TF 72; and so forth. Amphibious forces might be designated Amphibious Force, TF 76, with assigned Marine forces perhaps designated Landing Force, TF 79.

Within each force, the commander would then assign logical subdivisions of that force as task groups (TGs), such as TG 70.1, Carrier Group; TG 70.2, Gunfire Support and Covering Group; and so forth.

Within each task group would be task units (TUs). For example, TG 70.1, Carrier Group, might be divided into TU 70.1.1, Carrier Unit, and TU 70.1.2, Screen Unit.

Note the fashion in which components of a task organization are designated by the addition of decimal separators and successive numbers. This enables you to determine immediately the place of a given unit in an operational command.

Significance. The simultaneous organization of the fleets by types and task is obviously complex. Nevertheless, it is a system precisely adapted to any given job, large or small, temporary or permanent. Moreover, it is flexible and economical.

❯ ❯ *Organization and Functions of an Operational Naval Staff*

Naval staffs are organized and function like other military staffs, as they, in practice, include personal, executive, and special components.

This discussion is important because Marine officers serve in some capacity on every significant naval staff. The operational naval staff (as in the amphibious group headquarters) is of primary interest to Marine officers. You will find that other naval staffs, ashore or afloat, are organized along much the same lines, with special functions as appropriate.

The typical large naval staff is organized much like OPNAV (see chapter 4). This organization comprises the personal staff and the coordinating staff, which is equivalent to the executive staff in the Marine Corps.

Personal Staff. The duties of a Navy personal staff essentially resemble those listed in chapter 6 for the Marine personal staff, although titles differ somewhat.

The chief of staff not only carries out the functions the title implies but also is the admiral's personal assistant. He or she is the senior officer on the staff and coordinates all of its activities, thus serving as a member of the coordinating staff as well. In Navy commands headed by officers below flag rank, this billet instead bears the title of chief staff officer.

The flag secretary serves as the admiral's administrative aide and confidential secretary. Like the chief of staff, the flag secretary also has dual status as a member of the coordinating staff, in which he or she heads the administrative section.

The flag lieutenant, in addition to providing personal services to the admiral, supervises salutes, honors, awards, official calls, uniforms, social protocol, and transportation for the admiral and the staff (barge, staff gig, helicopter, and staff cars). The flag lieutenant keeps the staff duty officer, as well as other members of the staff and interested officers of the flagship, apprised of the movements and intentions of the admiral.

Coordinating Staff. The organization of a coordinating staff varies considerably and may comprise as many as nine sections or, in larger staffs, directorates, each headed by an assistant chief of staff or director.

The Total Force Section (N1), principally responsible for personnel and administration, is headed by the flag secretary. The section combines in a single entity the shore functions associated with several sections of a Marine Corps staff: AC/S G-1, staff secretary, adjutant, and legal officer.

The Intelligence and Information Operations Section (N2/N39) performs naval intelligence functions analogous to those performed by Marine Corps AC/S G-2 ashore, and it is typically also responsible for information operations. In some Navy staffs, the intelligence officer may have cognizance over public affairs. Marine officers may serve in Navy intelligence sections—primarily in connection with amphibious intelligence.

The Operations Section (N3) performs planning (separated into N5 in larger staffs), training (separated into N7 in larger staffs), and operations functions comparable to those of the Marine Corps AC/S G-3. In addition, the naval Operations Section often has responsibility for matters affecting readiness, and, in amphibious staffs, deals with and conducts the ship-to-shore movement. A Marine frequently serves in the Operations Section, not only as plans officer but also as military operations officer; both titles are self-explanatory.

The Logistics Section (N4) has all the functions of the AC/S G-4 section in a Marine Corps staff. It is principally responsible for supply, maintenance, ordnance, and engineering. In addition, this section typically plans availability for the overhaul of ships, screens work requests, and administers funds for repair and alterations.

The Communications and Information Systems Section (N6) is sometimes a separate section and sometimes part of the N1 section. The communications officer not only supervises communications but also controls classified publications for the staff. In amphibious staffs, a Marine communication officer usually forms part of the section.

Larger commands may have separate sections or directorates to handle Warfare Requirements, Resources, and Force Structure (N8) and Warfighting Assessments and Readiness (N9). Very large naval commands may also incorporate an additional staff layer to alleviate a commander's potential span of control challenges. For example, the current Pacific Fleet staff includes a director, Maritime Headquarters (N03), who oversees N1, N4, N8, and N9, and director, Maritime Operations (N04), who oversees N2, N3, N5, N6, and N7. Both report to the fleet commander (N00) via a deputy fleet commander (N01).

Specialist Officers. Although the Navy staff organization does not routinely include a special staff, it does, of course, have certain specialists who, in effect, compose a special staff. While the specialties are not as numerous as on a Marine staff, the duties are quite similar. The following specialist officers would be included in the typical Navy staff: air officer, weapons officer, surgeon, chaplain, and judge advocate or legal officer.

❯ ❯ *Marine Duties on Navy Staffs*

Nowhere more than on a Navy staff is a Marine expected to be "soldier and sailor, too." Thus, when assigned to the Navy, never be surprised, regardless of what duty you find yourself performing. Your only concern should be to see that that duty is well done so that, as a Marine representative, you set an example to your Navy colleagues.

Subject to the foregoing, Marines are usually assigned to one or several of the following staff duties.

Staff Marine Officer. As division, squadron, force, or fleet Marine officer, you exercise staff supervision over Marine personnel and matters within your command. In practice, this boils down to coordination of landing force activities involving Marines, inspection of embarked Marine detachments, advice and assistance as needed for other Marine commanders, and supervision of the flag Marine detachment (or "flag allowance"), if one is provided. Naturally, the staff

Marine officer is usually selected to maintain liaison between his or her staff and any Marine or Army staffs in the vicinity. The senior Marine officer on any Navy staff, regardless of other duties, performs all these functions as well.

Military Operations Officer. The military operations officer has cognizance over all military operations ashore in which the naval staff may be involved. In essence, the job of the Marine military operations officer is to provide the Navy staff expertise in matters of land warfare and organization.

Combat Cargo Officer. As a member of a Navy staff or ship's crew, the combat cargo officer performs the duties of troop loading, billeting, and landing associated with embarkation functions in the Marine staff ashore.

Other Duties. The foregoing jobs are those to which Marine representatives on Navy staffs are usually assigned. But according to your capabilities, your experience, and the needs of the organization, you might also find yourself serving as security officer, logistics officer, intelligence officer, air officer, or plans officer. In any case, never acquiesce in the bad old practice (still occasionally encountered) of allowing yourself to be assigned duty in a staff section headed by a Navy officer junior to you. Your lineal precedence, based on date of rank, is as binding on a Navy staff as anywhere else.

❯ ❯ *Staff Duty Officer Afloat*

Senior line officers (including Marines) take turns as staff duty officer (see chapter 16) in Navy organizations.

In port, the staff duty officer takes a day's duty, receives routine reports, acts on routine matters in the absence of officers having staff cognizance, regulates the use of staff boats, and tends the side on occasions of ceremony. In an emergency, the staff duty officer must be prepared to make decisions when the admiral and chief of staff are unavailable.

Under way, the staff duty officer stands watch on the flag bridge and represents the admiral in the same way that the officer of the deck represents the captain. He or she makes routine reports and signals, supervises navigation and station keeping of the force, keeps the staff log, and oversees the watch on the flag bridge. To perform efficiently, the staff duty officer must keep informed of current operations, expected hazards, conditions of readiness, launching and recovery of aircraft, joining and detaching of units, fueling and provisioning, and so on.

The state of relations between the staff and flagship depends in considerable measure on the attitude and consideration of the staff duty officer.

❧ THE SHIP AND SHIPBOARD LIFE

Given that there may be little experience with service afloat among your peers, some research and reference reading is wise. The nominal cost of a copy of the current edition of *The Bluejacket's Manual* (Naval Institute Press, 2022) and *Watch Officer's Guide* (Naval Institute Press, 2020) will be repaid many times over. In addition, obtain a copy of the invaluable *Naval Ceremonies, Customs, and Traditions* (U.S. Naval Institute, 2004) and locate and review, if possible, the discontinued Marine Corps Education Center Pamphlet 1-17, *Service Afloat*. You may gain a historical perspective from an excellent article on sea duty by Major W. M. Cryan in the September 1961 issue of the *Marine Corps Gazette* and from a similar article in the June 1927 issue by Captain L. C. Shepherd Jr.—still useful and containing much excellent advice. Both articles are in the *Marine Corps Gazette* archives at the Library of the Marine Corps, Alfred M. Gray Marine Corps Research Center; *Gazette* subscribers may search the online archives at the Marine Corps Association and Foundation website.

Whether you join a ship as part of the crew, afloat staff, or embarked unit of the Marine Corps Operating Forces, it remains an important mark of your professionalism that you understand the Navy and shipboard life.

❧ ❧ *Reporting On Board*

Although Marines seldom form part of a ship's company, they certainly do deploy or "go on float" on board U.S. Navy ships. With the continuing deployment of Marine expeditionary units, establishment of the Expeditionary Strike Group concept, and naval integration of tactical aircraft, Navy–Marine Corps integration in today's naval services figures more importantly than ever. Thus, Marine officers and staffs have continued to embark Navy ships for complete deployments, sometimes exceeding six months' duration.

If reporting as an individual, your orders will name a specific ship and, in peacetime, the port in which you are to meet it. When this is impossible for security reasons, you will be directed to report to some shore command, such as a naval base, a naval shipyard, or a naval district. This headquarters will further

Sea duty remains the oldest and original duty of U.S. Marines. Seagoing Marines played traditional roles as security detachments, prize crews, landing parties, and gunners throughout U.S. history. Today, permanently embarked Marine detachments are no longer routine.

direct you where and when to join your ship. Arrive in the specified port at least as early as the night before you are expected to report.

Your ship may be pierside or at anchor. Ships in port but not pierside periodically send boats to the regular fleet landings. Coordinate with the appropriate headquarters to ascertain the schedule for your ship's launch. Plan to have your baggage and yourself at the appropriate pier or landing at least fifteen minutes before the designated time.

After you complete any formalities at the pier or on board the ship's launch, ensure you pay attention to protocol when boarding your ship. As you reach the top of the gangway or accommodation ladder, come to a halt, face aft, and salute the national flag—also known as the Color—flown at the ship's stern from 0800 to sunset. Then face and salute the officer of the deck (OOD), saying "I request permission to come aboard, sir/ma'am" and identifying yourself.

The OOD will return your salute, probably shake hands, greet you with a "Welcome aboard!" and then ask for a copy of your orders for the log. The OOD's assistant or messenger will escort you below to the command duty officer or a designated representative. After reporting to the command duty officer, you will ordinarily accomplish the following tasks:

- Report to the first lieutenant, or the Marine commander of troops, as appropriate, to obtain your stateroom or berthing assignment. The first lieutenant, the "housekeeper" of the ship, assigns the rooms, if not already turned over to the commander of troops. On nonamphibious ships, the supply officer controls the rooms.
- See the mess treasurer and pay your mess entrance fee, known as the "mess share," to join the ship's wardroom, where you will take your meals (see below as well as chapter 21 for additional information).
- Begin to orient yourself to the ship.

Plan to make a reporting call on the captain within forty-eight hours if you are a senior officer or the commander of troops for embarked units; the officer next in your chain of command will arrange the time. At the designated time, ascertain that the captain is in. Remove your cover before entering the cabin. Be alert for the captain's dismissal; this call will usually last no longer than ten minutes.

›› *Ship's Organization*

One of your first tasks should be to learn the ship's organization. Each ship prepares its own organization book, but all have certain essentials in common (see figure 9-1).

The captain of a naval vessel, the senior line officer assigned to the ship's company, has full command of and responsibility for the ship and exercises authority and precedence over all persons serving on board. Also, this officer is charged with the supervision of all persons temporarily embarked in the ship. The captain's authority, responsibility, and duties are described in Navy Regulations, which every officer going to sea should study.

The executive officer is the executive arm of the commanding officer. As such, he or she is the captain's direct representative and is responsible for the prompt and efficient execution of orders. The XO works through the heads of departments, who assist in organization, administration, operation, and fighting on board the ship. In addition to these general responsibilities, the XO directly oversees such administrative functions as morale, welfare, berthing, training, religious accommodations, and legal matters.

Under the XO, the tasks of the ship are divided among the departments and activities and then further subdivided into divisions.

›› *Ship's Orientation*

Usually in a binder located in the wardroom, you will find the "Ship's Organization and Readiness Manual" (SORM) and "Commanding Officer's Standing Orders" (the captain's continuing orders to all hands), which contain indispensable information as to the organization and administration of the ship and its departments and divisions. The ship's secretary or the aide to the XO will issue them. Study them carefully; these regulations will answer many questions and save much embarrassment.

Study the ship's plans, a copy of which can be borrowed from the vessel's first lieutenant. Supplement them with a tour of the ship. If no guide is provided for a new officer's tour, ask your roommate or some friendly officer to show you around. Visit the bridge, forecastle (pronounced "foc'sle"), combat information center, central control station, ship control stations, plotting rooms, handling rooms, crew's quarters, galley, and one engine room.

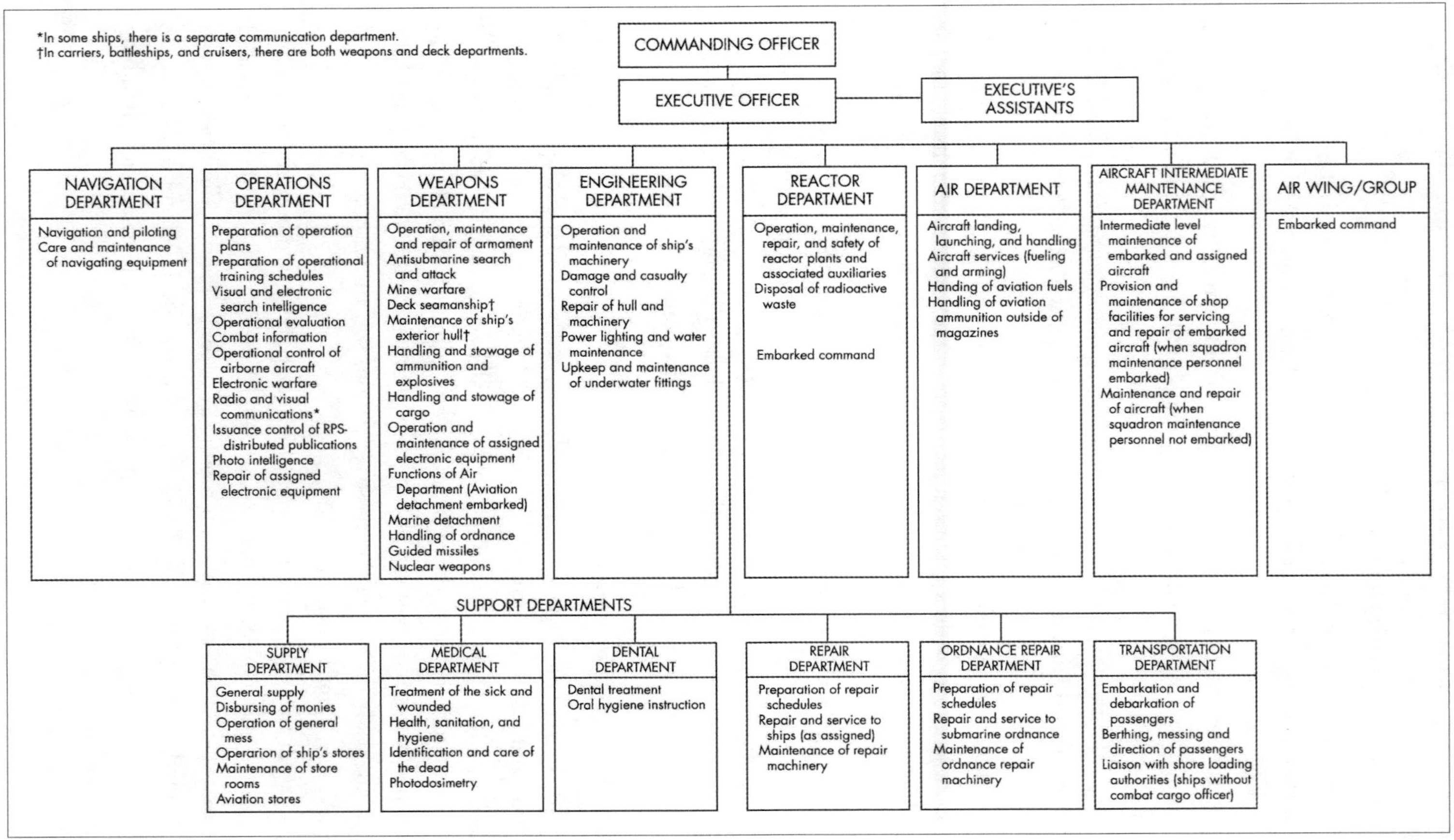

FIGURE 9-1. Typical Organization of a Large Ship of the U.S. Navy

*In some ships, there is a separate communication department.
†In carriers, battleships, and cruisers, there are both weapons and deck departments.

COMMANDING OFFICER

EXECUTIVE OFFICER

EXECUTIVE'S ASSISTANTS

NAVIGATION DEPARTMENT
Navigation and piloting
Care and maintenance of navigating equipment

OPERATIONS DEPARTMENT
Preparation of operation plans
Preparation of operational training schedules
Visual and electronic search intelligence
Operational evaluation
Combat information
Operational control of airborne aircraft
Electronic warfare
Radio and visual communications*
Issuance control of RPS-distributed publications
Photo intelligence
Repair of assigned electronic equipment

WEAPONS DEPARTMENT
Operation, maintenance and repair of armament
Antisubmarine search and attack
Mine warfare
Deck seamanship†
Maintenance of ship's exterior hull†
Handling and stowage of ammunition and explosives
Handling and stowage of cargo
Operation and maintenance of assigned electronic equipment
Functions of Air Department (Aviation detachment embarked)
Marine detachment
Handling of ordnance
Guided missiles
Nuclear weapons

ENGINEERING DEPARTMENT
Operation and maintenance of ship's machinery
Damage and casualty control
Repair of hull and machinery
Power lighting and water maintenance
Upkeep and maintenance of underwater fittings

REACTOR DEPARTMENT
Operation, maintenance, repair, and safety of reactor plants and associated auxiliaries
Disposal of radioactive waste

Embarked command

AIR DEPARTMENT
Aircraft landing, launching, and handling
Aircraft services (fueling and arming)
Handling of aviation fuels
Handling of aviation ammunition outside of magazines

AIRCRAFT INTERMEDIATE MAINTENANCE DEPARTMENT
Intermediate level maintenance of embarked and assigned aircraft
Provision and maintenance of shop facilities for servicing and repair of embarked aircraft (when squadron maintenance personnel embarked)
Maintenance and repair of aircraft (when squadron maintenance personnel not embarked)

AIR WING/GROUP
Embarked command

SUPPORT DEPARTMENTS

SUPPLY DEPARTMENT
General supply
Disbursing of monies
Operation of general mess
Operation of ship's stores
Maintenance of store rooms
Aviation stores

MEDICAL DEPARTMENT
Treatment of the sick and wounded
Health, sanitation, and hygiene
Identification and care of the dead
Photodosimetry

DENTAL DEPARTMENT
Dental treatment
Oral hygiene instruction

REPAIR DEPARTMENT
Preparation of repair schedules
Repair and service to ships (as assigned)
Maintenance of repair machinery

ORDNANCE REPAIR DEPARTMENT
Preparation of repair schedules
Repair and service to submarine ordnance
Maintenance of ordnance repair machinery

TRANSPORTATION DEPARTMENT
Embarkation and debarkation of passengers
Berthing, messing and direction of passengers
Liaison with shore loading authorities (ships without combat cargo officer)

Plan of the Day. This is an important document, issued daily by the XO, giving the next day's schedule of routine work or operations and highlighting any unusual variations. The Plan of the Day promulgates the orders of the day, drills and training, duty and liberty sections, working parties, and movies or recreational events. In recent years, it has become a "for official use only" or sometimes confidential document and cannot be removed from the ship.

Boat Schedule. This is promulgated when in port and not lying alongside a dock or pier. Obtain a copy and keep it with you, especially when going ashore.

›› *The Quarterdeck*

The quarterdeck is a portion of the ship's main deck (or occasionally a prescribed area on another deck) set aside by the captain for official and ceremonial functions. Certain parts of the quarterdeck (usually the starboard side) are reserved for the captain or for an admiral if embarked. The remainder is reserved for the ship's officers. In years past, the detachment parade of the Marines was typically on or immediately adjoining the quarterdeck. The rules, traditions, and etiquette of the quarterdeck are among the most venerable in the Navy, and their strict observance by all hands is the mark of good sea manners:

- Never appear on the quarterdeck unless in the uniform of the day, except when crossing to enter or leave the ship, or when otherwise required by duty.
- Do not be seen on the quarterdeck with hands in pockets and do not linger on the quarterdeck if in civilian clothes.
- Salute the Color every time you come on board.
- Do not clown around or engage in recreational sports on the quarterdeck.
- Remain clear of those portions of the quarterdeck reserved for the captain or admiral.

›› *The Wardroom*

The wardroom is the mess cabin of naval commissioned officers. The term also refers collectively to the individuals who have the right to make use of the space. It provides a place for recreation as well as dining. The wardroom is your home—and your club. It is also used on smaller ships as a meeting or conference room. Here you meet and get to know your fellow officers; it is up to you to make them shipmates.

In Navy messes, tradition is important, and seniority is well recognized. Seats for the captain and XO will be designated, usually at the head of the senior table. Some ships may assign the seats of other officers, such as the supply officer, "Bull" ensign (senior in grade O-1), or "JORG" (most junior O-1).

Unless you are on duty under arms, remove your cover when entering the mess. Although it may seem an anachronism, never unsheathe your sword—either literally or figuratively—in a mess. Save your quarrels for elsewhere (see chapter 21).

This does not mean that the silence of a library need be maintained in the wardroom. A noisy mess is often the sign of a happy mess. Between meals, you gather in the wardroom to relax for a moment, discuss problems, watch a video, play a card game, or enjoy a quiet cup of coffee. It is also often a place for fun, on a Mess Night, when spouses and dates are entertained, or for a ship's party. It can be all these things, or it can just be a place to eat. It depends upon you and the other members of the mess.

Do not loaf about the wardroom during working hours. If you have nothing else to do, catch up on your professional reading and study the ship's organization and regulations. Also be sensitive to the fact that naval officers assigned to ship's company typically work odd schedules due to irregular watches and rarely manage more than six hours of sleep a day. Therefore, they are seldom afforded the opportunity to lounge in the wardroom. As a result, if embarked Marines are regularly socializing there for extended periods while the Sailors only enter for meals and meetings, unnecessary tensions may emerge due to a perception that Marines are monopolizing the wardroom. Awareness of the issue and good manners should be sufficient to avoid this undesirable situation.

Officers' messes (see chapter 21) are organized as business concerns, with a mess fund to which you contribute your share on joining. Monthly assessments are made, from which costs of food, periodicals, decorations, and other essentials and conveniences are paid. The senior Navy line officer (usually the XO) is mess president. A mess treasurer administers this fund. In addition, on board some ships a junior officer—it could be you—is designated as "mess caterer" and put in charge of menu planning, detailed supervision of meal service, and so on. A good way to get this job is to complain about any of these matters; avoid doing so unless you have better ideas that you would like firsthand experience implementing.

Enlisted mess specialists crew the wardroom, pantries, and officers' galleys, and they may take care of senior officers' staterooms.

Wardroom country is "out of bounds" to enlisted persons except when on duty or in special circumstances. Do not use your stateroom as an office. See that enlisted persons have little need to enter wardroom country. When they do, require that they uncover (unless under arms), keep quiet, and refrain from profane language.

❧ ❧ *Wardroom Etiquette*

Be punctual for meals. You should be in the wardroom prior to the assigned meal hour. When the CO enters, he will invite all those assembled to eat. If unavoidably delayed, address the CO, express your regrets, and "request permission to join the mess" (although this custom may be dispensed with as impractical on large ships such as LHDs). If the CO is not present, make your request to the most senior officer present. If necessary to leave before the senior member has risen, ask to be excused using the phrase, "Request permission to depart the mess." Although this custom is not observed in all ships today, this does not excuse you from showing ordinary politeness and deference.

You should never be on a ship out of uniform unless transiting to or from liberty or for physical training. Do not hang around the wardroom out of uniform.

Introduce guests to as many wardroom officers as possible, and always to the senior member and those at your own table. Entertain only such guests as your messmates and their families will be happy to meet.

Each guest is considered a guest of the wardroom. Be friendly and sociable with all guests. When a visiting officer enters, introduce yourself, and try to help the visitor in any way you can.

Except on mess or party nights, officers' guests should leave the ship by four bells of the first watch (that is, 2200).

Do not take meals in your stateroom unless ill. This does not preclude your having a cup of tea or coffee in your cabin when you are working there.

Do not loiter in the wardroom during working hours. It bears repeating: if you have nothing else to do, catch up on your professional reading and study the ship's organization and regulations.

Avoid rowdy, disruptive behavior in the wardroom; be considerate of your messmates.

Observe mess rules—for example, not to talk shop at meals, not to talk religion or politics, not to play music during meals—whatever they may be.

Be fair and pleasant in your dealings with mess specialists; make complaints to the mess treasurer. Additionally, do not assign the watch mess personal tasks. This specialist is there to serve all officers.

Finally, pay your bills promptly. Within twenty-four hours of reporting, pay the mess treasurer your mess bill and mess share in advance.

❧ ❧ Adjusting to Life at Sea

Your stateroom may be small or, if large, crowded. Junior officers are usually doubled or quadrupled up. But the CO of an embarked Marine unit is normally assigned his or her own stateroom.

Space will be cramped regardless. You may have an upper bunk, comfortable but not luxurious, a share in a desk with drawers for stowing clothing, a chest of drawers or part of one, and some hanging space. Some rooms have portholes, but most are force ventilated or air conditioned.

A mess specialist will supply you with bed linen, blankets, and towels and will pick up laundry. Deal with the mess specialist tactfully but firmly.

Get to know your roommates and, if possible, to like them. Being in cramped quarters on board ship requires effort and adjustment to live in harmony with several other positive personalities.

If one of few Marines embarked, you can expect considerable good-natured teasing based on healthy interservice rivalry. Marines at sea traditionally get a certain amount of teasing harassment from Navy shipmates. Remember it is in fun, do not let it get under your skin, and do not hesitate to slip in your own digs as targets present themselves. Make a definite effort to get along. It is a matter of give and take; be sure you give more than you take.

❧ EMBARKED MARINE UNITS

With the extinction of seagoing Marine Corps detachments on board Navy ships, the most common type of service afloat for Marine officers comes with the embarkation of your unit for deployment or for exercises, usually with an afloat Marine air-ground task force or an aircraft squadron ordered to a carrier air group. Such duty reflects the essence of the modern Corps, which has provided landing forces for the fleet throughout its history.

❖ ❖ *Navy–Marine Corps Team*

When under way together, the Navy and Marine Corps form a team, but a typical set of misconceptions can cloud the experience of embarkation for all. This is the notion of some uninitiated Marines (as exemplified by the Second Lieutenant Kendrick character from *A Few Good Men*) that the U.S. Navy exists primarily as a taxi service for Marines and should conduct itself in an appropriately service-oriented manner. At the other extreme is the occasional Sailor who thinks that Marines exist solely to interrupt a ship's routine, clutter spaces, and make a mess of the paintwork on vehicle and cargo areas. Neither concept could be further from the truth. The amphibious force and naval aviation doctrines of the Navy–Marine Corps team provide one of the most striking military capabilities in the history of warfare, primarily through the unique concepts of teamwork, cooperation, and integration that have evolved over decades of training and operations.

Your first charge as an officer embarking with your troops must be to create an atmosphere of teamwork and demonstrate the desired symbiotic relationship with Navy counterparts. Accordingly, be prepared to redress thoroughly all instances of actual or imagined friction that can rise from untrained and inexperienced personnel reacting to the obvious conditions of shipboard life.

❖ ❖ *Commanding Officer of Troops*

Under Navy Regulations, the authority of a ship's captain governs embarked personnel and units as well. To ensure the maximum cooperation and under-standing for mutually satisfying results, the ship's CO requires embarked units to organize themselves under a single troop commander, responsible to the captain for all ship-related matters pertaining to them.

This CO of troops, or more often commander of troops (COT), therefore functions with respect to the ship's organization as another department head, reporting for the embarked detachments to the CO and XO of the ship. Musters, duty assignments, working parties, and the all-important needs of the troops for training and maintenance support on board ship require much attention from the COT. Many of the duties of the COT also approximate those of the commander of the Marine detachments of yesteryear, so your conduct places you equally at the forefront of tradition and an exemplar of Corps virtues to our sister service.

Shipboard collateral duties for Marine officers embarked with their units may include the following: team embarkation officer, ship's platoon commander, troop officer of the day / guard officer, troop billeting officer, troop mess officer, officer's mess treasurer, and troop communications officer. These and other requirements are made clear by the ship's captain before embarkation occurs, mainly through liaison with the advance party that your unit will have sent to the ship. Your unit will provide a standing working party (ship's platoon), cooks, and messmen on a fair-share basis to assist in the functioning of the ship, which will be your collective home for the period of embarkation.

Your embarked unit also will be responsible for the care and cleaning (but not repair) of assigned berthing and working spaces. The daily cleanliness of a ship is of paramount concern to all, especially considering the obvious closeness of shipboard life. Do not let your personnel be found lacking. Above all, cultivate the respect of the ship's XO by following the standards to the letter and never quibbling over them. Be a good guest as well as an effective professional. Your conduct, camaraderie, and demeanor should make you indistinguishable from a valued ship's company officer.

Shipboard routine soon becomes second nature to embarked personnel. Training periods and maintenance of troop weapons, equipment, and cargo will take up most of each day, but these will be supplemented as required by ship drills and exercises that involve you and your Marines. Be familiar with the various Watch Bills and Emergency Bills, particularly for general quarters, man overboard, abandon ship, and fires. Know the rules for movement through the ship during general quarters, and ensure your Marines know these as well. Learn your way around, and memorize the compartment numbering system so that you can locate yourself and ship spaces.

Many areas will be designated as "restricted spaces," both to afford requisite security for sensitive equipment and documents and to keep the limited space from becoming overcrowded. These restrictions largely apply to enlisted personnel. Embarked officers should feel free to include these spaces in their familiarization tours, being sure to ask the assigned Sailors kindly to explain their duties and the capabilities of their equipment.

❧ ❧ *Guard Duty for Embarked Marines*

When a Marine Corps unit not part of the ship's company goes to sea, the guard duty required is a combination of that maintained ashore and that required for the exigencies of service afloat.

Bear in mind two principles of command relations. First, the captain of a ship has paramount authority and responsibility for safety, good order, and discipline over everyone embarked, even if not under the captain's direct military command. Second, the COT embarked in a ship retains his or her military command authority and responsibility for his or her officers and enlisted persons, subject only to the overriding authority and responsibility of the captain.

Consistent with the foregoing principles, the captain can call upon the embarked troop units to establish a guard to assist in maintaining the security and safety of the ship as well as by performing any other necessary guard duties. For internal order, security, and control of embarked units and equipment, the COT, with the concurrence of the captain, may establish any posts he or she considers necessary. In general, the troop commander organizes the guard like an interior guard ashore and provides an officer of the day as his or her direct representative for supervising the troop guard and carrying out troop orders, ship's regulations, and special instructions of the ship's captain.

All orders to embarked troops, including instructions for the troop guard, are transmitted through the COT.

❧ ❧ *Housekeeping Afloat*

Much advice and information presented in chapter 15 applies to Marine units on board ships. The COT thus has additional duty as department head, a status roughly analogous to that of a company commander ashore, although department heads on a carrier or amphibious assault ship may be in the grades of commander or lieutenant commander. The Marines man and maintain certain equipment and have their own part of the vessel (where the unit lives, works, and maintains its headquarters—styled, Sailor-fashion, as "the Marine office").

The term "housekeeping" refers to the tasks that one must accomplish regularly for an organization or system to function efficiently, including all routine tasks associated with the care, cleaning, maintenance, and management of spaces, property, equipment, and services. The term has no exact equivalent afloat. "Ship's work," or "keeping the ship," includes some housekeeping functions but does not encompass all shoreside connotations of the phrase. Some of the similarities and differences in examining housekeeping for Marines at sea are noted here.

Police. Police, in the Navy sense, means the ship's police force. Under the command master at arms, each division, other than the Marines, details a master at arms whose job is to act as a kind of military policeman in enforcing good order and ship's regulations. It is a popular misconception that Marines perform this function and act as "the Navy's police force" on board ship. Nothing could be further from the truth.

Within the embarked Marine unit, however, the term "police" has its normal meaning, as in chapter 15, and the police sergeant performs the duties usually associated with that title anywhere in the Corps.

Subsistence and Mess Management. Subsistence and food service are functions under the oversight of the ship's XO. The supply officer and assistants perform the duties that ashore would fall to the food service officer, as described in chapter 15. In most ships, a central enlisted mess, called "the mess decks," operates in a manner resembling a cafeteria. Among enlisted persons, only chief petty officers have a separate mess. For messing purposes, Marine gunnery sergeants and above are treated as chief petty officers on board ship.

Embarked units provide a fair share of messmen, detailed from privates, privates first class, and, when necessary, lance corporals of the Marine unit on the basis provided by Navy Regulations. Mess stewards in the Navy are now called culinary specialists. Never detail an NCO as a messman. If the embarked units include rated cooks, they should be assigned to duty in the ship's galley. But if this occurs, never lose sight of the detailed cook as a Marine.

Ship's Store. The ship's store is the seagoing equivalent of a Navy exchange ashore. It is operated by the supply officer and stocks stationery, candy, toiletries, clothing, insignia, and the usual selection of exchange supplies, including, in most ships, "pogey bait" and "gedunk" as found ashore. Obviously, the Marine officers and NCOs must prevent Marines from improper wearing of Navy articles of uniform in lieu of prescribed Marine items of similar type.

Ship's Welfare and Recreation. On board ship, Welfare and Recreation embraces the gamut of activities associated with Special Services ashore. Both as individuals and as an embarked unit, Marines take part in the ship's athletic and recreation programs. A ship's special services officer administers the funds for these purposes. Be tactful, but be sure the Marine unit gets its share based on the period of time embarked. This matter includes a deposit of a pro rata share of the store profits to the unit's community services or similar welfare and recreation fund before debarking the ship.

❥ ❥ *Shipboard Cleanliness and Upkeep*

For its spaces on board ship, the Marine unit embarked usually has berthing compartments, a storeroom, an office, and occasionally topside deck space. The cleanliness and upkeep of these spaces and structures are the responsibility of the Marine unit's CO and ultimately the COT in his or her capacity as a division officer. Each unit performs its own minor repairs; more extensive repair, when needed, is the job of the ship's company based on "work requests" submitted by the COT.

As ashore, your unit will have a police sergeant. Instead of a police shed, though, he or she will have a gear locker. In lieu of a police gang, the police sergeant will levy on every Marine in the unit to keep the ship's "Marine country" a model space, spotlessly clean, an example to the Bluejackets.

In your responsibility for upkeep and cleanliness of the ship, you should assign certain "cleaning stations" to your NCOs and, if you are in command, to your junior officer(s) to supervise.

❥ COURTESY, ETIQUETTE, AND HONORS

❥ ❥ *Shipboard Courtesy and Etiquette*

Often during your career, you will find yourself serving or embarked in naval vessels, on a Navy staff, as part of the ship's company, or as a passenger. Because of this and because, as a Marine officer, you are a member of the naval services, you must comply meticulously with the courtesies and customs practiced on board Navy warships.

Ladders and Gangways. The starboard accommodation ladder is reserved for officers; if there are two starboard ladders, one ladder may be designated for flag and general officers. The port ladder is for enlisted persons. When a ship is alongside a dock, the officers' gangway usually leads to the quarterdeck; the gangway for enlisted persons, if separate, is forward or aft of this.

Coming on Board and Leaving a Warship. You will board via a gangway or accommodation ladder. On reaching the quarterdeck, halt, face aft (or toward the National Ensign), and salute the Color (if displayed). Immediately afterward, render a second, distinct salute to the OOD, and say, "Sir/Ma'am, I request permission to come aboard." When it is time to leave the ship, render the same courtesies in reverse order, saying, "Sir/Ma'am, I request permission to leave the ship," or alternately, "Sir/Ma'am, I request permission to go ashore." If you are a member of the ship's company, you report to the OOD as follows: Upon coming on board, "I report my return on board, sir/ma'am," and on leaving the ship, "I have permission to leave the ship, sir/ma'am."

If the ship is at anchor, you will reach it by boat. Observe boat etiquette. Defer to senior officers in the boat, and introduce yourself.

As a Marine officer, you should seize every opportunity to visit each type and class of ship so that you may increase your seagoing knowledge. If the vessel is docked, there will usually be little complication to arranging a visit other than perhaps the timing. The Navy is rightly flattered by such visits and will do everything possible to make your stay pleasant and instructive. Always pay your respects to the senior Marine watch officer when visiting a ship that has Marines embarked.

Boat Etiquette. When boarding a small boat, juniors embark first and sit forward, leaving the stern sheets for seniors, who embark last. The most senior officer in the boat sits farthest aft, at the centerline, or elsewhere as he or she wishes. When disembarking, personnel do so in order of rank beginning with the senior officer (see figure 9-2).

Rise and salute when a senior officer boards or debarks.

Rise and yield seats to seniors when a boat is crowded. If there are not enough seats, take the next boat.

Do not rise and salute a senior officer who passes close aboard either in another boat or ashore. The senior officer and the coxswain render hand salutes, unless to do so would be dangerous or impracticable.

Remain in place and do not salute during Colors when your boat under way passes within sight or hearing of the ceremony. The coxswain (or boat officer, if embarked) stands and salutes unless dangerous to do so.

FIGURE 9-2. Senior Officers Are First to Leave the Boat when Disembarking

Marine officers and officers of the Navy staff corps, when senior in a boat, receive and return salutes and are otherwise accorded the deference due individuals of their seniority, but they are never in charge of the boat. The senior Navy line officer or petty officer in the boat, regardless of how junior he or she may be, is in charge and is responsible for its navigation and for the safety of personnel and matériel embarked. This is provided by Navy Regulations and should be remembered by you as a Marine officer should you inadvertently be directed to act as a boat officer.

Shipboard Amenities and Saluting. In general, the amenities and rules for saluting set forth in chapter 11 apply on board ship, but the following special points should be observed.

Except when attention is called or when a passageway must be cleared, personnel at work, at games, or at meals are not required to rise when an officer other than the captain, a flag or general officer, or an officer senior to the captain passes. It is customary for all officers to uncover when entering a sick bay or space in which food is being prepared or served; when a senior officer does so, this indicates that he or she does not desire the people present to be brought to attention.

Juniors give way to seniors in ships' passageways and particularly when going up and down ladders.

"Gangway!" is a command given by anyone who sees an officer or civilian dignitary approaching a gangway, ladder, or passage that is blocked. Never use "Gangway!" except for an officer or senior civilian. For others, "Coming through!" is appropriate. The senior officer, NCO, or petty officer present must clear passage after "Gangway!" has been given.

The ship's captain, any officer senior to the captain, all flag and general officers, the XO, and inspecting officers are saluted at every meeting except in officers' country, heads, and messing compartments.

On the first meeting of the day, salute each officer senior to you; thereafter, salutes are dispensed with except when an officer is directly addressed by a subordinate or in the cases of the senior officers noted above.

Sentries at gangways salute all officers coming on board or leaving the ship. Sentries posted on the topside also salute officers passing close aboard in boats.

When passing honors are being exchanged between men-of-war or when ruffles and flourishes are sounded on the quarterdeck, all personnel on weather decks, not in formation, come to attention and salute.

Navy (but not Marine) formations on board ship are dismissed with the command "Post" or "Dismissed" (always issued from attention), whereupon all members of the formation salute, the officer in charge returns the salute, and all hands fall out.

Ship's sentries posted on the dock, when a ship is moored alongside, carry out normal saluting procedures for sentinels ashore.

When colors go in port and the ship is in port, all hands on weather decks or on the pier (if the ship is berthed alongside) face aft and salute.

❧ ❧ *Display of Personal Flags and Pennants Afloat*

On Board Ship. A flag officer or unit commander afloat displays his or her personal flag or command pennant from the flagship but not from more than one ship at a time. If two flag officers are embarked in the same ship, only the senior's flag flies. When a civil official who rates a personal flag is embarked for passage in a naval vessel, his or her flag is flown, but if an officer rating a personal flag or command pennant is also on board, both the officer's flag and that of the civilian are displayed.

In Boats. A flag officer in command, when embarked officially in a naval boat, flies his or her personal flag from the bow. Officers who rate neither display a commission pennant. Officers who rate a personal flag may display a miniature of such flag or pennant from the vicinity of the coxswain's station when embarked on other than official occasions. Civilian officials display their flags, if any, from the bow, when embarked in a naval boat.

⃗ ⃗ *Official Visits and Calls on Board Ship*

Official Visits. Insofar as practical, the same honors and ceremonies are rendered for an official visit afloat as for one ashore. In addition, however, on board ship the compliments mentioned in chapter 11 are added, such as manning the rail and piping and tending the side.

If Navy Regulations call for a gun salute on departure of the visitor, it is fired when the visitor is clear of the side, and the flag or pennant (if that person rates one) is hauled down with the last gun of the salute.

Official Calls on Board Naval Vessels. The procedure for receiving official callers on board U.S. Navy ships is more formal than ashore. According to the rank of the visitor, and the occasion, the side may be piped; side boys, guard, and band are paraded; and certain officers attend the side. If you or your ship are on the receiving end of the call, you can find the details (and should check these carefully in advance) in such publications as *The Watch Officer's Guide* or *The Naval Officer's Guide*, both of which will be readily available on board, as well as in Navy Regulations. For a table of honors to be rendered for the various military and civil officials of the United States and foreign countries, see chapter 11.

⃗ FINAL THOUGHTS

Glossary for Seagoing Marines. See *Dictionary of Naval Terms* (Naval Institute Press, 2005) for commonly used shipboard terms and phrases that every Marine should know. By using and understanding these, you will prove to Navy shipmates that Marines can be, and are, just as salty as any Sailor.

Navy Ratings and Navy Abbreviations. The Navy's system of ratings (that is, petty officer ranks and specialties), with its many different abbreviations, may at first appear confusing but is something seagoing Marines must understand. Navy abbreviations, like those in the Marine Corps, can also be mystifying. *Dictionary of Navy Abbreviations* (Naval Institute Press, 2005) is a good source for decoding Navy shorthand.

⁌{ **10** }⁍

TRADITIONS, FLAGS, DECORATIONS, AND UNIFORMS

Old breed? New breed? There's not a damn bit of difference so long as it's the Marine breed.
— Lieutenant General Lewis B. Puller

THE TRADITIONS of the Marine Corps, its history, its flags, its uniforms, its insignia—*the Marine Corps way of doing things*—make the Corps what it is and set it so distinctly apart from other military organizations and services. These traditions give the Corps its flavor and are the reason Marines cherish its past, its ways of acting and speaking, and its uniforms. These things foster the discipline, valor, loyalty, aggressiveness, and readiness that make the title "Marine" "signify all that is highest in military efficiency and soldierly virtue."

And remember, whenever the Corps is impoverished by the death of a tradition, Marines are generally to blame. Traditions are preserved not by books and museums but by faithful adherence on the part of all hands—*you especially.*

⋗ MARINE CORPS TRADITIONS AND CUSTOMS

⋗ ⋗ *Marine Corps Motto*

Semper Fidelis (Always Faithful) is the motto of the Corps. That Marines have lived up to this motto is proved by the fact that there has never been a mutiny, or even the thought of one, among U.S. Marines.

Semper Fidelis was adopted as the motto about 1883. Before that, there had been three Marine Corps mottoes, all traditional rather than official. The first, antedating the War of 1812, was *Fortitudine* (With Fortitude). The second, By Sea and by Land, was obviously a translation of the Royal Marines' *Per Mare, Per Terram*. Until 1848, the third motto was To the Shores of Tripoli, in commemoration of Lieutenant O'Bannon's capture of Derna, Tripoli, in 1805. In 1848, after the return to Washington of the Marine battalion that took part in the capture of Mexico City, this motto was revised to From the Halls of the Montezuma to the Shores of Tripoli—a line now familiar to all Americans. This revision has encouraged speculation that the first stanza of "The Marines' Hymn" was composed by members of the Marine battalion who stormed Chapultepec Castle.

For years, the Marine Corps shared its motto with England's Devonshire Regiment, the 11th Foot, one of the senior infantry regiments of the British Army until it merged with the Dorset Regiment in 1958. The Devonshire Regiment's sobriquet was the "Bloody Eleventh."

❧ ❧ *Eagle, Globe, and Anchor*

When Major General Smedley Butler, two-time recipient of the Medal of Honor, was a lieutenant in the Philippines in 1899, he decided to get himself tattooed: "I selected an enormous Marine Corps Emblem to be tattooed across my chest. It required several sittings and hurt me like the devil, but the finished product was worth the pain. I blazed triumphantly forth, a Marine from throat to waist. The emblem is still with me. Nothing on earth but skinning will remove it."

It turns out Butler's bold final assertion was somewhat premature. Within a year, during the storming of the Tartar Wall in Peking, a Chinese bullet struck him in the chest and gouged off part of his emblem. The rest of it accompanied him to the grave forty years later.

Whether you are a private or general is secondary compared to the shared privilege of wearing the emblem. The Globe and Anchor—today, often called the Eagle, Globe, and Anchor—is the most important insignia you have.

The Marine Corps emblem (never "logo") as we know it today dates from 1868, when Brigadier General Jacob Zeilin, seventh commandant, introduced it to the Corps. Until 1840, Marines wore various devices, mainly based on the spread eagle or foul anchor. In 1840, two Marine Corps devices were accepted.

The current Marine Corps emblem, the Eagle, Globe, and Anchor, was adopted by Brigadier General Jacob Zeilin, seventh commandant, in 1868.

Both were circled by a laurel wreath, likely borrowed from the Royal Marines' badge; one had a foul anchor inscribed inside, and the other bore the letters "USM." In 1859, a standard center was adopted—a U.S. shield surmounted by a hunting-horn bugle, within which was the letter "M." This type of bugle was the nineteenth-century symbol for light infantry or jager—so called because they were recruited from the ranks of foresters, gamekeepers, and poachers, all renowned as skirmishers and riflemen.

In 1868, however, Brigadier General Zeilin felt that a more distinctive emblem was needed. His choice fell on another device borrowed from the British marines: the globe. King George IV had conferred the globe on the Royal Marines in 1827. Because it was impossible to recite all the achievements of marines on the corps color, said the king, "the Great Globe itself" was to be their emblem, for marines had won honor everywhere.

Zeilin's U.S. Marine globe displayed the Western Hemisphere (the "Royals" emblem featured the Eastern Hemisphere). The eagle and foul anchor were added to leave no doubt that the Corps was both American and maritime.

❧ Marine Corps Seal

The official seal of the Corps, designated by General Lemuel C. Shepherd Jr., twentieth commandant, consists of the Marine Corps emblem in bronze, the eagle holding in its beak a scroll inscribed "Semper Fidelis," against a scarlet-and-blue background, encircled by the words, "Department of the Navy—United States Marine Corps."

❧ Marine Corps Colors

The colors of the Corps are scarlet and gold. Although associated with U.S. Marines for many years, these colors were not officially recognized until Major General John A. Lejeune became thirteenth commandant. Today you will see scarlet and gold throughout Marine bases—on signboards; auto tags; bandsmen's drums, pouches, and trumpet slings; military police brassards; officers' hat cords and aiguillettes; and, it sometimes seems, simply everywhere.

In addition to scarlet and gold, forest green enjoys semiofficial standing as a Marine color. Forest green comes from the same source as the light infantry bugle—the ranks of foresters—that was once part of the Corps' nineteenth-century badge. Since 1912, when forest green was adopted for the service uniform, it has become the standard color for such equipment as vehicles, weapons, and organizational chests and baggage. In addition, it is a distinguishing color of marines throughout the world, being worn as a service uniform by the British, Dutch, and Korean corps, among others.

❧ Marine Corps Bulldog

Since World War I, the bulldog has been associated with the Corps. A male English bulldog has been the official mascot at "Eighth and Eye," and therefore top dog of the Corps, since the 1920s. Prior to World War II, he was always named Jiggs. Subsequently, in an appropriate tribute to one of the Corps' bravest officers, Lieutenant General L. B. "Chesty" Puller, the canine's name has been Chesty.

The Marine Corps seal, designed by General Lemuel C. Shepherd Jr., twentieth commandant, was approved by President Dwight D. Eisenhower in 1954.

✧ ✧ "The Marines' Hymn" and "Marine Corps March"

"The Marines' Hymn" (see appendix I) is the oldest of the official songs of the armed services, and as the name implies, it is the hymn of the Marine Corps. Every Marine knows the words, but the hymn's origin is obscure. The words date from the nineteenth century, but the author remains unknown. The music comes from an air, "Gendarmes of the Queen," in Jacques Offenbach's opera *Geneviève de Brabant*, first performed in November 1859. Regardless of its origin, however, all Marines *rise to their feet and stand at attention* whenever "The Marines' Hymn" is played or sung.

"Semper Fidelis," the Corps' official march, was composed by John Philip Sousa in 1888 during his tour as leader of the Marine Band. "Semper Fi," as the troops know it, is habitually rendered for parades and reviews with Marines.

❧ ❧ *Birthday of the Corps*

The Marine Corps was founded by the Continental Congress on 10 November 1775. The resolution that created the Corps reads as follows:

> *Resolved.* That two Battalions of Marines be raised consisting of one Colonel, two lieutenant Colonels, two Majors, & Officers as usual in other regiments, that they consist of an equal number of privates with other battalions; that particular care be taken that no persons be appointed to office, or inlisted into said Battalions, but such as are good seamen, or so acquainted with maritime affairs as to be able to serve to advantage by sea, when required. That they be inlisted and commissioned for and during the present war with Great Britain and the colonies, unless dismissed by order of Congress. That they be distinguished by the names of the first and second battalions of American Marines, and that they be considered as part of the number, which the continental Army before Boston is ordered to consist of.

Chapter 21 explains how Marines celebrate the Marine Corps' birthday. Although the Corps joins the other services each May in observing Armed Forces' Day, 10 November remains the Marines' own day—a day of ceremony, comradeship, and celebration.

❧ ❧ *"Leathernecks"*

The Marines' longstanding nickname, "Leathernecks," goes back to the leather stock, or neckpiece, that was part of the uniform from 1775 to 1875. One historian wrote, "Government contracts usually contained a specification that the stock be of such height that the 'chin could turn freely over it,' a rather indefinite regulation, and, as one Marine put it, one which the 'tailors must have interpreted to mean with the nose pointing straight up.'"

Although many justifications have been adduced for the leather stock, the truth seems to be that it was intended to ensure that Marines kept their heads erect—"in battery," the artillery would say—a laudable aim in any military organization, any time.

Descended from the stock is the standing collar, hallmark of Marine blue dress and evening dress uniforms. Like its leather ancestor, the standing collar regulates stance and posture and thus proclaims the wearer as a modern-day "Leatherneck."

❥ ❥ *First to Fight*

The slogan First to Fight has appeared on Marine recruiting posters ever since World War I.

Marines have been in the forefront of every American war since the founding of the Corps. Marines entered the Revolutionary War in 1775, before the Declaration of Independence was signed. They helped defend the *Chesapeake* against the British fleet at the outset of the War of 1812. Before the Civil War, Marines captured John Brown at Harpers Ferry. They were among the few U.S. Regulars who fought in the First Battle of Manassas in 1861. In 1898, Huntington's Fleet Marines were the first U.S. troops to occupy Cuban soil, and Admiral Dewey's Marines were the first to land in the Philippines.

The tradition continued into the twentieth century. In World I, the 5th Marines formed part of the first American Expeditionary Force contingent to sail for France. When Iceland had to be occupied in 1941, Marines, the only U.S. troops who were ready, were the first to land. In World War II, at Pearl Harbor, Ewa, Wake, Midway, Johnston, and Guam, Marines formed the ready forefront of our Pacific outpost line. At Guadalcanal in August 1942, they launched the first U.S. offensive of the war. In the Korean War, the first reinforcements to leave the continental United States were the 1st Provisional Marine Brigade. Marines were the first to land in Lebanon in 1958 and first to fight in Santo Domingo in 1965. In Vietnam, the first U.S. ground unit to be committed to the war was the 3rd Marine Division. In the Persian Gulf War, Marines opened the ground war, in 1991.

On this record of readiness, First to Fight constitutes the Marine's pride, responsibility, and challenge.

❥ ❥ *"Tell It to the Marines!"*

In his book *Fix Bayonets!*, Captain John W. Thomason Jr. gives the popularly accepted version of the origin of the phrase "Tell it to the Marines!":

> They relate of Charles II that at Whitehall a certain seacaptain, newly returned from the Western Ocean, told the King of flying fish, a thing never heard in old England. The King and court were vastly amused. But, the naval fellow persisting, the Merry Monarch beckoned to a lean, dry colonel of the sea regiment, with seamed mahogany face, and said, in

With James Montgomery Flagg's iconic 1917 recruiting poster, the Marine Corps recast an insult as a challenge.

effect: "Colonel, this tarry-breeks here makes sport with us stay-at-homes. He tells of a miraculous fish that foresakes its element and flies like a bird over water." "Sire," said the colonel of Marines, "he tells a true thing. I myself have often seen those fish in your Majesty's seas around Barbados—" "Well," decided Charles, "such evidence cannot be disputed. And hereafter, when we hear a strange thing, we will tell it to the Marines, for the marines go everywhere and see everything, and if they say it is so, we will believe it."

This yarn (for such it is) was for many years credited to Samuel Pepys, although scholars have dismissed it. In *They Never Said It: A Book of Fake Quotes, Misquotes, and Misleading Attributions*, Paul F. Boller and John George assert that the original meaning of the phrase is pejorative to the Marines, implying that they are gullible. And in the introduction to *Semper Fidelis: The History of the United States Marine Corps*, Allan R. Millett not only includes the Pepys version but also allows that the alternate interpretation, "preferred by everyone but marines," is not particularly kind to the Corps.

Whatever the truth, the Corps turned the phrase to its favor in fine Marine fashion when it was incorporated into a 1917 recruiting poster. The poster implied that, when an outrage needs avenging, one should "Tell That to the Marines!" because they will do something about it. In any case, the Marine Corps has embraced the phrase, which is an old one and can be found in print as early as 1726.

❖❖ *"And St. David"*

During the Boxer Uprising at Tientsin and Peking at the dawn of the twentieth century, the Marine battalion in the international relief column was brigaded with the Royal Welsh Fusiliers (23rd Foot), one of Britain's most renowned regiments. The resulting fellowship between the two organizations is symbolized each year on St. David's Day (1 March, the Welsh national holiday), when the commandant of the Marine Corps and the colonel of the Fusiliers exchange by dispatch the traditional watchword of Wales: "And St. David."

❖❖ *First on Foot and Right of the Line*

Marines form at the place of honor—head of column or on right of line—in any naval formation. This privilege was bestowed on the Corps by the Secretary of the Navy on 9 August 1876.

❖❖ *The President's Own*

Founded in 1798—more than a century before the bands of the other three services—and especially favored by Thomas Jefferson, the Marine Band has performed at White House functions for every president except George Washington. Because of its traditional privilege of performing at the White House, the band is known as "The President's Own." President John F. Kennedy epitomized its special position when he remarked in 1962, "I find that the only forces which cannot be transferred from Washington without my express permission are the members of the Marine Band."

The Marine Band has been present at many of the most memorable and cherished moments in U.S. history, including the dedication of the National Cemetery at Gettysburg when Lincoln gave his immortal address. Among its many traditions, including leadership for twelve years by John Philip Sousa, is the scarlet, full-dress blouse of band members, the only red coat worn by American forces since the Revolutionary War. (In 1956, the Marine Corps Drum and Bugle Corps was likewise granted the privilege of wearing red coats.)

The Marine Band tours the country each year and has done so ever since Sousa commenced the practice in 1891, although one section always remains in Washington to fulfill its traditional primary mission: "To provide music when directed by the President of the United States, the Congress of the United States, or the Commandant of the Marine Corps."

⋗ ⋗ *Evening Parade*

From May through early September, the ceremonial Evening Parade is held each Friday evening after nightfall at the Marine Barracks Washington, "Eighth and Eye." This colorful ceremony, executed under searchlight illumination, features the Marine Band, Marine Corps Drum and Bugle Corps, a special exhibition drill platoon, and a battalion of Marines from the barracks. Evening Parades were first held in 1957 after a Marine Corps ceremonial detachment participated in the Bermuda International Searchlight Tattoo. They became a fixed Marine Corps custom following similar participation by a larger Marine detachment in the famed Edinburgh Searchlight Tattoo in Scotland in 1958.

Evening Parades are open to the public, and any officer who desires to attend with a reasonable number of guests can usually obtain reserved seats by contacting the Barracks adjutant.

⋗ ⋗ *Need-to-Know Traditions*

The Commandant's License Plate. If, when in Washington, D.C., you ever bump into a car bearing plate "1775," climb out of the wreckage at attention. That license plate is set aside for the official sedan of the CMC.

Rum on New Year's Day. Every New Year's Day since 1804, the Marine Band has serenaded the commandant at his quarters and received refreshments in return.

❖ ❖ *Traditions of the Marine Corps Uniform and Accoutrements*

Marine Corps uniforms—both officer and enlisted—are rich in tradition, and every Marine officer should be familiar with the history behind and significance of several unique features of the Corps' uniforms and accoutrements.

Collar Emblems. Although officers have worn collar emblems since the 1870s, enlisted Marines did not rate this privilege until August 1918, when Franklin D. Roosevelt, then assistant secretary of the Navy, visited the 4th Marine Brigade in France shortly after Belleau Wood. In recognition of the brigade's victory, Roosevelt directed on the spot that enlisted Marines would henceforth wear the emblem on their collars.

Scarlet Trouser Stripe. Officers and noncommissioned officers have intermittently worn scarlet stripes on dress trousers since the early days of the Corps. Often repeated but unsubstantiated is the assertion that the right to wear scarlet stripes was conferred on the Corps as a battle honor after the Mexican War. (Actually, the uniform trousers issued after reconstitution of the Corps in 1798 had scarlet piping).

Headgear. Two Marine traditions center on headgear. The *quatrefoil*—the cross-shaped braid atop officers' frame type ("barracks") cover—has been worn since 1859. The design, of French origin, is a distinguishing part of the Marine officers' uniform.

The campaign cover, once called the field hat, is a broad-brimmed felt hat with a high crown, pinched symmetrically at the four corners. It was the rugged, picturesque expeditionary headgear of the Corps from 1898 until 1942. Although the hat became outmoded during World War II, General Clifton B. Cates, the nineteenth commandant, authorized its use on the rifle range in 1948 and took steps to issue this universal favorite to all medalist shooters in Marine Corps matches. Subsequently, in 1956, General Randolph McCall Pate, the twenty-first commandant, directed that campaign covers be worn by all recruit drill instructors, and the headgear—later copied and adapted by the Army for the same purpose—has become a symbol of Marine Corps recruit training.

Mameluke Sword. The sword that Marine officers carry goes back to the *Uniform Regulations* of 1826 (with a hiatus from 1859 to 1875). Records of the day, however, indicate that swords of this pattern were worn by Marine officers before the War of 1812.

The Mameluke sword gets its name from the cross-hilt and ivory grip, both used for centuries by the Muslims of North Africa and Arabia. The Marine Corps tradition of carrying this type of sword dates from Lieutenant O'Bannon's assault on Derna in 1805, when he is said to have won the sword of the governor of the town.

Aside from its use on parade, many Marine Corps rituals center around your sword. You wear it when you get married and cut your wedding cake with it. The sword is both worn and employed in cake-cutting ceremonies around the world on the birthday of the Corps.

Never unsheathe your sword inside a mess or wardroom. If you do, custom decrees that you must buy a round of drinks for all present. This tradition goes back to stringent rules against dueling in the early days of the Navy and Marine Corps.

Swagger Sticks. The tradition of the swagger stick originated in the British Army and goes as far back as 1790. In the Marine Corps, the stick came into vogue in the latter part of the nineteenth century and was virtually a required article of uniform until World War I. Its origin lay in the whips or batons carried by mounted officers of the eighteenth century. Once carried with relish by many Marine officers, swagger sticks were prohibited in 1960 and adorn only a few mantles in hopes that they might gain favor again.

Ties. Also once popular was a Marine Corps tie with "regimental" colors, scarlet-and-gold stripes over a forest-green background. If you can find it, that tie, and equivalent cummerbund, may be worn with civilian attire.

❧ ❧ *Traditional Marine Talk and Terminology*

Marines have a uniquely naval—and Marine—way of communicating. The 4th Marine Brigade's admired Army commander at Belleau Wood, Lieutenant General James G. Harbord, was quick to note and record the salty Marine way of saying things:

> In the more than a month that the Marine Brigade fought in and around the Bois de Belleau, I got a good opportunity to get the Marine

psychology. . . . The habitual Marine address was "Lad." . . . No Marine was ever too old to be a "lad." The Marines never start anywhere: they always "shove off." There were no kitchens: the cooking was done in "galleys." No one ever unfurled a flag—he "broke it out."

Toward the end of the *Guide*, there is a glossary of Marine terms. Become familiar with them, and never feel self-conscious about using them. Encourage subordinates to use them.

❧ ❧ *Conduct in Action*

Beyond the competence, resolution, and courage expected of every Marine in battle, Marines in action traditionally leave no wounded or dead Marine on the field or unattended, regardless of the cost. As for surrender, the Marine Corps code is a tenet expressed by Napoleon: "There is but one honorable mode of becoming prisoner of war. That is, by being taken separately; by which is meant, by being cut off entirely, and when we can no longer make use of our arms."

❧ ❧ *Last to Leave the Ship*

Marines are always or should be the last—other than the ship's captain—to leave a ship being abandoned or put out of commission. Although the tradition is an old one, it first appears in Navy Regulations of 1865: "When a vessel is to be put out of commission, the Marine officer with the guard shall remain on board until all the officers and crew are detached and the ship regularly turned over to the officers of the Navy Yard or station."

❧ ❧ *Traditions at Religious Services*

Religious services for Marines should include the Marine Corps Prayer (written at the suggestion of General Shepherd, twentieth commandant, by Bishop Sherrill, twentieth presiding bishop of the Episcopal Church and hero in World War I):

> O Eternal Father, we commend to Thy protection and care the members of the Marine Corps. Guide and direct them in the defense of our country and in the maintenance of justice among nations. Protect them in the hour of danger. Grant that wherever they serve they may be loyal to their high traditions and that at all times they may put their trust in Thee; through Jesus Christ our Lord. Amen.

If your chaplain is unfamiliar with the prayer, it is a good idea to draw his or her attention to it.

It is also customary for Marine Corps religious services to conclude with the traditional naval hymn "Eternal Father, Strong to Save." When no chaplain is available, the commanding officer, following the traditions of the sea, may conduct divine services, including funerals. When a chaplain is present, some commanders may choose to read the lesson, another traditional prerogative of the CO. This is arranged beforehand with the officiating chaplain.

❧ ❧ *Marine Corps Museums*

"The scrapbook of the Marine Corps," as it was sometimes described, was the Marine Corps Museum. Now rebuilt and rededicated as the National Museum of the Marine Corps and consolidated outside Quantico at Triangle, Virginia, it remains the central repository of awards, battle honors, historical flags, and other objects of lasting sentimental significance to the Corps. The museum collection documents Marine Corps history from 1775 to the present day. On display is an extensive array of uniforms, weapons, artifacts, equipment, prints, and paintings giving tangible substance to the proud traditions of the Corps. Every Marine Corps officer should become thoroughly familiar with this museum, which now surpasses the best military and naval museums in the United States.

Additionally, there are excellent repositories of Marine Corps history around the country. In a restored building from pre–Revolutionary War days in Philadelphia, the New Hall Military Museum contains an outstanding collection dealing with the early days of the Corps and its origins in Pennsylvania. Part of the Independence Seaport Museum, the nearby relic cruiser *Olympia* contains an exhibit depicting Marines of the Spanish-American War. Finally, several battleships and aircraft carriers maintained as monuments around the country also usually include exhibits concerning their Marine detachments.

❧ COLORS, FLAGS, AND STANDARDS

A Parris Island recruit once asked his drill instructor, "Sergeant, who carries the flag in battle?"

Came the unhesitating reply, "Son, *every* Marine carries the flag in battle!" As the soldier's proverb says, "The flag is a jealous mistress," and any Marine will fight and die rather than permit the National Color or an organizational color to be dishonored.

Colors or standards must never fall into enemy hands. If capture seems inevitable, they should be burned. Unserviceable colors or standards, or those from disbanded units, are turned in to the supply system. The latter in turn forwards flags of historical value to the National Museum of the Marine Corps, which is the Corps' repository for historical flags as well as for flags and war trophies captured by Marines. Soiled, torn, or badly frayed flags, if not historical, are destroyed privately by burning.

› › *Types of Flags*

Marine Corps terms that deal with flags are precise, and it behooves you to learn to distinguish the various kinds of flags and to speak of them in the correct terminology.

National Color or Standard. This is the U.S. flag. When the flag is displayed over naval installations or ships, its official title is the National Ensign. When carried by Marine organizations, it is called the National Color (except when borne by a mounted, mechanized, motorized, or aviation unit, when its title becomes the National Standard). This technical distinction between a color and a standard also applies to the battle colors and organizational colors described in the following paragraphs.

The National Color is carried on all occasions of ceremony when two or more companies of a unit are present. When not in the hands of troops, it is entrusted to the adjutant. With the Marine Corps Color (discussed below), the National Color is usually displayed in the office or before the tent of the CO. Whenever the National Color is carried in the open, it is escorted by a color guard composed of selected Marines, and the Color itself is borne by an outstanding NCO, the color sergeant.

The National Ensign, displayed over ships and shore installations, comes in three sizes:

- *Post flag*: size ten feet by nineteen feet, flown in fair weather except on Sundays and national holidays
- *Storm flag*: size five feet by nine feet, six inches, flown during foul weather

• *Garrison flag*: size twenty feet by thirty-eight feet, flown on Sundays and national holidays as provided in the *Marine Corps Flag Manual*, but never from a flagpole shorter than sixty-five feet

For more information on display of the National Color or Ensign, refer to Navy Regulations and to the *Marine Corps Flag Manual*.

Marine Corps Colors and Standards. The commandant issues to every major Marine unit or organization a distinguishing flag, which is carried beside the National Color. These unit flags are called Marine Corps colors (or standards). A Marine Corps color bears the emblem and motto of the Corps and the unit title and follows the color scheme of the Corps, scarlet and gold.

The Marine Corps color of a Fleet Marine Force unit is called the unit battle color; the color authorized for an organization in the Supporting Establishment (such as a Marine barracks) is called the organizational color. No unit smaller than a separate battalion or regiment receives a battle color, nor does a temporary or provisional unit unless specially authorized by the commandant.

Certain units of the Marine Corps Reserve are likewise authorized to carry organizational flags, but these bear a Reserve designation.

Guidons. These are small rectangular flags, made in the Marine Corps colors, carried by companies, batteries, or detachments or used as marker flags for ceremonies. Organizational guidons carry the Marine Corps emblem and the title of the unit. Dress guidons (used as markers) simply bear the initials "USMC."

Personal Flags. Every active general officer in command displays a personal flag. Marine Corps personal flags consist of a scarlet field with white stars, the number according to the general officer's rank, arranged in the same manner as the stars on Navy personal flags. Regulations governing personal flags are in Navy Regulations.

Miscellaneous Flags. In addition to the aforementioned flags, the Corps employs several miscellaneous flags and pennants described in the *Marine Corps Flag Manual*. Examples are the United Nations flag, Geneva Convention flag, church pennants, and heat condition flags.

⯈ ⯈ *Flag Accessories*

Different accessories, such as streamers, bands, cords, tassels, and staff ornaments, adorn Marine colors, standards, flags, and guidons. Streamers denote participation in combat or award of a collective citation or decoration conferred on the unit as a whole. A silver band is attached to the staff of a Marine Corps color or standard for each streamer awarded. When the unit or organization does not rate streamers or bands, a cord and tassel, woven in the Corps colors, are substituted. Finally, the heads of staffs bear the following staff ornaments: colors and standards bear a silver lance head; personal flags, a silver halberd; and guidons, a plain silver cap.

❧ ❧ *Battle Color of the Marine Corps*

The Corps has one battle color, called the Battle Color of the Marine Corps. This color is entrusted to the senior post of the Corps, Marine Barracks Washington. Attached to it are all the battle honors, citations, battle streamers, and silver bands that the Corps has won since 1775. At the time of writing, these fifty-five honors are as follows:

1. Presidential Unit Citation (Navy) Streamer with six silver and three bronze stars
2. Presidential Unit Citation (Army) Streamer with one silver oak leaf cluster
3. Joint Meritorious Unit Award
4. Navy Unit Commendation Streamer
5. Valorous Unit Award (Army) Streamer
6. Meritorious Unit Commendation (Navy–Marine Corps) Streamer
7. Meritorious Unit Commendation (Army) Streamer
8. Revolutionary War Streamer
9. Quasi-War with France Streamer
10. Barbary Wars Streamer
11. War of 1812 Streamer
12. African Slave Trade Streamer
13. Operations against West Indian Pirates Streamer
14. Indian Wars Streamer
15. Mexican War Streamer
16. Civil War Streamer
17. Marine Corps Expeditionary Streamer with twelve silver stars, four bronze stars, and one silver "W"

18. Spanish Campaign Streamer
19. Philippine Campaign Streamer
20. China Relief Expedition Streamer
21. Cuban Pacification Streamer
22. Nicaraguan Campaign Streamer
23. Mexican Service Streamer
24. Haitian Campaign Streamer with one bronze star
25. Dominican Campaign Streamer
26. World War I Victory Streamer with one silver and one bronze star, one Maltese Cross, and Siberia and West Indies Clasps
27. Army of Occupation of Germany Streamer
28. Second Nicaraguan Campaign Streamer
29. Yangtze Service Streamer
30. China Service Streamer with one bronze star
31. American Defense Service Streamer with one bronze star
32. American Campaign Streamer
33. European–African–Middle Eastern Campaign Streamer with one silver and four bronze stars
34. Asiatic-Pacific Campaign Streamer with eight silver and two bronze stars
35. World War II Victory Streamer
36. Navy Occupation Service Streamer with Europe and Asia Clasps
37. National Defense Service Streamer with three bronze stars
38. Korean Service Streamer with two silver stars
39. Armed Forces Expeditionary Streamer with five silver stars
40. Vietnam Service Streamer with three silver and two bronze stars
41. Southwest Asia Service Streamer with three bronze stars
42. Kosovo Campaign Streamer with two bronze stars
43. Afghanistan Campaign Streamer with one silver and one bronze star
44. Iraq Campaign Streamer with one silver and two bronze stars
45. Inherent Resolve Campaign Streamer with two bronze stars
46. Global War on Terrorism Expeditionary Streamer
47. Global War on Terrorism Service Streamer
48. Philippine Defense Streamer with one bronze star

49. Philippine Liberation Streamer with two bronze stars
50. Philippine Independence Streamer
51. French Croix de Guerre Streamer (Fourragère) with two palms and one gilt star
52. Philippine Presidential Unit Citation Streamer with two bronze stars
53. Korean Presidential Unit Citation Streamer
54. Republic of Vietnam Armed Forces Meritorious Unit Citation of the Gallantry Cross with Palm
55. Republic of Vietnam Meritorious Unit Citation Civil Actions Streamer with Palm

❧ DECORATIONS, MEDALS, AND UNIT CITATIONS

"A soldier will fight long and hard for a bit of colored ribbon," said Napoleon, who originated the awarding of personal decorations. Napoleon's conqueror, the Duke of Wellington, in turn introduced all-hands campaign medals, the first of which went to British troops who fought at Waterloo. Both Wellington and Napoleon realized that decorations and medals not only express national gratitude to individuals but also stimulate emulation and esprit in battles to come.

Today, Marine Corps awards fall into three classes: personal and unit decorations; commemorative, campaign, and service medals; and marksmanship badges and trophies. The *Navy and Marine Corps Awards Manual* gives details on all of these.

❧ ❧ *Personal and Unit Decorations and Medals*

The United States confers numerous military decorations. These range from the Medal of Honor at the top of the hierarchy to a campaign ribbon in junior position. Certain military decorations are awarded only under special conditions: for heroism only (denoted below by *), for either heroic or meritorious acts (**), or for heroism not in combat (***). In order of precedence, the personal or unit decorations that Marines might receive or might have received are as follows:

1. Medal of Honor (Navy)*
2. Navy Cross*
3. Defense Distinguished Service Medal
4. Homeland Security Distinguished Service Medal

5. Distinguished Service Medal (Navy)
6. Silver Star Medal*
7. Defense Superior Service Medal
8. Legion of Merit**
9. Distinguished Flying Cross**
10. Navy and Marine Corps Medal***
11. Bronze Star Medal**
12. Purple Heart
13. Defense Meritorious Service Medal
14. Meritorious Service Medal
15. Air Medal**
16. Joint Service Commendation Medal
17. Navy and Marine Corps Commendation Medal**
18. Joint Service Achievement Medal
19. Navy and Marine Corps Achievement Medal**
20. Combat Action Ribbon*
21. Presidential Unit Citation*
22. Joint Meritorious Unit Award
23. Navy Unit Commendation**
24. Navy Meritorious Unit Commendation
25. Navy "E" Ribbon
26. Prisoner of War Medal
27. Marine Corps Good Conduct Medal
28. Selected Marine Corps Reserve Medal
29. Marine Corps Expeditionary Medal
30. China Service Medal
31. American Defense Service Medal
32. American Campaign Medal
33. Europe–Africa–Middle East Campaign Medal
34. Asiatic-Pacific Campaign Medal
35. World War II Victory Medal
36. Navy Occupation Service Medal
37. Medal for Humane Action
38. National Defense Service Medal

39. Korean Service Medal
40. Antarctica Service Medal
41. Armed Forces Expeditionary Medal
42. Vietnam Service Medal
43. Southwest Asia Service Medal
44. Kosovo Campaign Medal
45. Afghanistan Campaign Medal
46. Iraq Campaign Medal
47. Global War on Terrorism Expeditionary Medal
48. Global War on Terrorism Service Medal
49. Korean Defense Service Medal
50. Armed Forces Service Medal
51. Humanitarian Service Medal
52. Military Outstanding Volunteer Service Medal
53. Navy Sea Service Deployment Ribbon
54. Navy Arctic Service Ribbon
55. Navy and Marine Corps Overseas Service Ribbon
56. Marine Corps Recruiting Ribbon
57. Marine Corps Drill Instructor Ribbon
58. Marine Security Guard Ribbon
59. Armed Forces Reserve Medal
60. Marine Corps Reserve Ribbon (obsolete)
61. Philippine Presidential Unit Citation
62. Korean Presidential Unit Citation
63. Vietnam Presidential Unit Citation
64. Republic of Vietnam Meritorious Unit Citation Cross of Gallantry
65. Vietnam Civil Actions Service Medal
66. Philippine Defense Ribbon
67. Philippine Liberation Ribbon
68. Philippine Independence Ribbon
69. United Nations Service Medal (Korea)
70. United Nations Medal
77. NATO Medal for the Former Yugoslavia
72. NATO Medal for Kosovo

73. NATO Medal for Operation Active Endeavor
74. NATO Medal for Operation Eagle Assist
75. NATO Medal for the Balkans
76. NATO Medal for NATO Training Mission–Iraq and International Security Assistance Force
77. Multinational Force and Observers Medal
78. Inter-American Defense Board Medal
79. Republic of Vietnam Campaign Medal
80. Kuwait Liberation Medal (Saudi Arabia)
81. Kuwait Liberation Medal (Emirate of Kuwait)
82. Republic of Korea War Service Medal

Among the foregoing, the Medal of Honor merits special mention as the highest military decoration conferred by the United States. Ordinarily, it is awarded only for gallantry and intrepidity in combat, at the risk of one's life, above and beyond the call of duty. Since the Civil War, when the award was established in 1861 by President Abraham Lincoln, U.S. Marines have received almost three hundred Medals of Honor.

Medal of Honor recipients receive several special privileges and benefits, including, to list just a few, a special Medal of Honor pension in addition to any earned military pension; a 10 percent increase in retired pay; commissary and exchange privileges (including for eligible dependents); admission for qualified children to any of the U.S. service academies, without nomination or quota requirements; entitlement to special motor vehicle license plates in several states, sometimes with registration fees waived; and finally, entitlement (though not officially recognized) to a salute from all hands regardless of rank.

❧ ❧ *Unit Decorations*

Marine Corps units have earned all of the top U.S. unit decorations, or unit citations, as well as several foreign unit citations. If you are a member of an organization when it earns a collective citation, you are entitled to wear that citation ribbon or device as a personal decoration.

The French Fourragère is the senior unit award (and first collective award) won by Marines. The Fourragère dates from Napoleon's time; it was awarded to the 4th Marine Brigade in 1918 in lieu of awarding all hands the Croix de

The Silver Star is awarded to servicemembers who display conspicuous gallantry in action and is the third-highest award for heroism that can be given to members of the U.S. armed forces.

Guerre. Members of the 5th and 6th Marines still sport the green-and-scarlet cord of the Fourragère on their left shoulders.

The Presidential Unit Citation is the highest service unit award. It was also the first American collective award, having been personally instituted by President Franklin D. Roosevelt as a citation for the defenders of Wake (1st Defense Battalion and Marine Fighting Squadron 211) in December 1941. The Presidential Unit Citation is considered to represent unit attainments that would warrant award of the Navy Cross if the recipient were an individual.

The Navy Unit Commendation (NUC) ranks next in the naval service after the Joint Meritorious Unit Award. Like the latter, the NUC may be won by extremely meritorious service in support of, but not participation in, combat operations. When awarded for combat performance, the NUC is comparable to the Silver Star for an individual; for noncombat meritorious service, this commendation is comparable to the Legion of Merit.

Following the NUC in precedence is the Navy Meritorious Unit Commendation. To be eligible for this award, a unit must have performed service of a character comparable to that which would merit the award to an individual of a Bronze Star in a combat situation or similar achievement in a noncombat situation.

Other unit decorations awarded for collective achievements of valor or merit include the Army Valorous Unit Award, Air Force Outstanding Unit Award, and Joint Meritorious Unit Award (which actually ranks in precedence above the NUC).

❧ *Campaign Medals*

The Marine Corps issues campaign or service medals to all hands who take part in particular campaigns or periods of service for which a medal is authorized. In addition to those for specific campaigns, Marines may be awarded the Marine Corps Expeditionary Medal for service ashore on foreign soil, against opposition, for which no other campaign medal is authorized. For similar joint operations in which the Army or Air Force is involved, the Armed Forces Expeditionary Medal may be substituted. Campaign medals are often embellished by clasps or bronze stars, which denote participation in specific battles or phases of the campaign.

As a general policy, the Department of Defense does not permit U.S. military personnel to accept service medals from foreign governments. There are, however, exceptions. The Republic of Vietnam Campaign Medal, Kuwait Liberation Medal (Saudi Arabia), Kuwait Liberation Medal (Kuwait), Republic of Korea War Service Medal, and selected service medals awarded by the United Nations are the only foreign service medals authorized for wear without specific individual authorization. Those eligible shall wear these decorations in the manner prescribed in applicable uniform regulations.

In addition to campaign and service medals, certain commemorative medals have been struck to honor noncombat but notable achievements, such as polar expeditions or pioneer flights.

❧ *Wearing Decorations and Medals*

The Marine Corps has strict rules that govern the wearing of decorations and medals; they are provided in the *Marine Corps Uniform Regulations*. You should familiarize yourself with these regulations, but here are a few noteworthy highlights.

Uniform Regulations details the manner of wearing and mounting larger numbers of awards by specific numbers and rows. For example, large medals may not be worn more than seven (five for women) per single row; miniatures, not more than ten (eight for women). Marines with eight or more ribbons of any type may wear them in rows of four rather than three, thus avoiding a top-heavy stack.

When medals are prescribed instead of ribbons, unit citations and other ribbons for which no medal has been struck are worn centered on the right breast.

Decorations and medals are part of your uniform and must be worn, but the wearing of ribbons on khaki shirts is the individual's option unless the unit commander prescribes that they must be worn. If the individual opts to wear ribbons on the khaki shirt, as is typical, there are two permitted options: wearing all authorized ribbons or wearing only personal U.S. decorations with U.S. unit awards and the Good Conduct Medal. The wearing of campaign ribbons is optional.

Most decorations, and all campaign medals, have half-size miniature reproductions known as miniature medals. You wear "miniatures" with evening and mess dress as well as with civilian full dress or dinner jacket when appropriate. The Medal of Honor, however, is never represented in miniature, and when miniatures are worn, it is suspended in the normal fashion about the collar.

With every U.S. decoration (and many foreign ones, too) you receive a lapel device to wear with civilian clothes. This may be worn in the left lapel of your civilian suit when you think fitting.

Marksmanship badges are not to be worn with the evening dress, blue dress "A," blue-white dress "A," camouflage utility, or camouflage maternity work uniforms. Commanders may prescribe marksmanship badges for wear on all other uniforms. Unless otherwise prescribed by the commander, wearing marksmanship badges is at the option of the individual. That said, by current custom, the wearing of marksmanship badges is normally confined to the coats of the service "A," blue dress "B," and blue-white dress "B" uniforms. Incidentally, you are limited to a ceiling of three badges of your choice, if you rate more than three. The *Marine Corps Uniform Regulations* contains detailed guidance on precedence and placement.

When soiled, faded, frayed, or otherwise unserviceable, the ribbons of decorations and medals should be destroyed by burning rather than thrown away, not only to prevent reuse by unauthorized persons but also because these ribbons symbolize the bravery, devotion, and sacrifice of U.S. Marines.

❧ ❧ *Initiating an Award*

One of your responsibilities as a combat leader is to see that your Marines are promptly recommended for awards you believe they have earned. During active operations, it is usual for every unit, from battalion up, to maintain a board of awards. This panel evaluates and passes on recommendations for decorations that originate within the organization, but you must see that the board of awards promptly receives recommendations that are accurately stated in whatever form may be required.

Few leadership derelictions are more reprehensible than failure to submit proper recommendations for awards, then to see an award fail because you were too lazy to recommend it in the right form and with the detailed information required.

Marine Corps procedure for initiating awards is described in the *Navy and Marine Corps Awards Manual.*

❧ UNIFORMS, INSIGNIA, AND PERSONAL GROOMING

"It is proverbial," wrote one commandant, "that well-dressed soldiers are usually well-behaved soldiers." The Marine Corps has always set course by that axiom and has enjoyed success and repute on both counts. As a Marine officer, it rests squarely with you to maintain the Corps' reputation for smart, soldierly, and correctly worn uniforms.

Marine Corps Uniform Regulations is the "bible" on uniforms, insignia, and grooming. You must know *Regulations*, set an example by rigid compliance, and enforce its rules meticulously.

In *Uniform Regulations*, there are two essential compilations: the listing of required articles of uniform for all officers and the table showing types and combinations of uniforms authorized for officers (see tables 10-1 and 10-2). They provide a complete checklist of articles (for male and female officers, respectively) that should, or should not, be worn as part of each prescribed uniform combination.

❧ ❧ *Wearing the Uniform*

The current version of *Marine Corps Uniform Regulations*, totaling almost 250 pages, provides official policy and guidance on wearing Marine uniforms.

Covering these regulations completely is beyond the scope of the *Guide*, but the following paragraphs provide a general orientation and summarize important rules and information that govern uniform wear.

Uniforms designed to be buttoned *must* be worn buttoned.

Wear headgear whenever under arms or on watch, except when in a space where a meal is being served or divine service is being conducted, when in quarters (if on watch), or when specifically excused from remaining covered. Always remain covered when outside or on topside spaces on board ship. See chapter 9 for further shipboard ground rules.

"Mixed uniform"—components of two different uniforms worn simultaneously, for example, blue blouse and utility trousers—is strictly *forbidden* unless specifically authorized in *Uniform Regulations*.

The combat utility uniform, colloquially "utilities," is the quintessential work uniform across the Marine Corps, especially in the Operating Forces. Commanders may prescribe the utility uniform as the uniform of the day. It is authorized for parades, reviews, ceremonies, and informal social functions on base.

During the summer season, Marines wear utilities with the sleeves rolled up above the elbow. The uniform is worn with the sleeves rolled down during the winter season. The utility coat may be removed only for physical training and work details.

Utilities are not appropriate for wear in a civilian environment. *Uniform Regulations* authorizes their wear while commuting to and from work via privately owned vehicle. Yet en route stops while off base are not authorized except for bona fide emergencies, such as medical emergencies, vehicle breakdown, or vehicle accidents, and when patronizing certain drive-through services.

The service uniform, in its various forms, corresponds to civilian business attire. The service "A" uniform, with service coat, may be prescribed for parades, ceremonies, social events, and as the uniform of the day. It is normally worn when reporting to a new duty station, unless otherwise prescribed by the commander. It is also normally prescribed for the following official military occasions: (1) when assigned as a member of courts-martial, unless otherwise designated by competent authority; (2) for official visits and calls of, or to, U.S. civil officials, officers of the U.S. armed forces, and officials of foreign governments according

TABLE 10-1. Types and Components of Authorized Uniforms for Male Officers

Designation	Cap	Coat or Jacket	Shirt	Necktie	Trouser/Belt
Evening dress "A"	Dress	Evening w/strip collar & white waistcoat	White w/pique placket	None	Evening (suspenders optional)
Evening dress "B"	Dress	Evening w/strip collar & scarlet waistcoat or cummerbund (c)	White w/pique placket	None	Evening (suspenders optional)
Blue dress "A"	Dress	Blue w/strip collar	White plain front	None	Sky blue (d) w/web belt or suspenders
Blue-white dress "A"	Dress	Blue w/strip collar	White plain front	None	White w/web belt or suspenders
Blue dress "B"	Dress	Blue w/strip collar	White plain front	None	Sky blue (d) w/web belt or suspenders
Blue-white dress "B"	Dress	Blue w/strip collar	White plain front	None	White w/web belt or suspenders
Blue dress "C"	Dress	Blue sweater (optional)	Khaki long sleeve	Khaki w/clasp	Sky blue (d) w/web belt
Blue dress "D"	Dress	Blue sweater (optional)	Khaki short sleeve	None	Sky blue (d) w/web belt
Service "A"	Garrison/ frame	Green	Khaki long sleeve	Khaki w/clasp	Green w/web belt
Service "B"	Garrison/ frame	Green sweater (optional)	Khaki long sleeve	Khaki w/clasp	Green w/web belt
Service "C"	Garrison/ frame	Green sweater (optional)	Khaki short sleeve	None	Green w/web belt
Utility uniform	Utility	Utility	Green undershirt optional	None	Web belt or martial arts utility belt

a. If required or prescribed.
b. Black gloves always worn or carried with all-weather coat during winter uniform period. Optional when coat not worn.
c. Scarlet waistcoat for general officers only. Scarlet cummerbund for all other officers.
d. Dark blue trousers for general officers.
e. Green scarf optional for wear with all-weather coat/tanker jacket during winter months.

Gloves	Footwear	Outer Coat (a)	Insignia Bofs	Medals/Ribbons	Badges	Sword
White (b)	Black shoes & socks	AWC/ optional boatcloak	Dress collar/cap	Miniature medals	Not worn	Not worn
White (b)	Black shoes & socks	AWC/ optional boatcloak	Dress collar/cap	Miniature medals	Not worn	Not worn
White (b)	Black shoes & socks	AWC/ optional boatcloak	Dress collar/cap	Large medals (ribbons worn per para. 5205.3)	Not worn	(a)
White	Black shoes & socks	AWC/ optional boatcloak	Dress collar/cap	Large medals (ribbons per para. 5205.3)	Not worn	(a)
White (b)	Black shoes & socks	AWC/ optional boatcloak	Dress collar/cap	Ribbons	Optional (a)	(a)
White (b)	Black shoes & socks	AWC/ optional boatcloak	Dress collar/cap	Ribbons	Optional (a)	(a)
(b)	Black shoes & socks	AWC or tanker jacket	Dress cap	Ribbons optional (a)	Optional (a)	(a)
(b)	Black shoes & socks	AWC or tanker jacket	Dress cap	Ribbons optional (a)	Optional (a)	(a)
(b)	Black shoes & socks	AWC (e)	Service collar/cap	Ribbons	Optional (a)	(a)
(b)	Black shoes & socks	AWC or tanker jacket (e)	Cap	Ribbons optional (a)	Optional (a)	(a)
(b)	Black shoes & socks	AWC or tanker jacket (e)	Cap	Ribbons optional (a)	Optional (a)	(a)
(b, d)	Combat boots/socks	AWC (e) or ECWCS	Emblem decal/name & service tapes	Not worn	Not worn	Not worn

TABLE 10-2. Types and Components of Authorized Uniforms for Female Officers

Designation	Cap	Coat or Jacket	Shirt	Necktie	Skirt/Slacks	Handbag/Purse
Evening dress "A"	Dress	Evening w/ cummerbund (e)	White pleated front	Black	Long black skirt	Black purse
Evening dress "B"	Dress	Evening w/ cummerbund (e)	White pleated front	Black	Long/short black skirt	Black purse
Blue dress "A"	Dress	Blue	White plain front	Scarlet w/skirt, black w/slacks	Blue skirt/ slacks	Black purse or handbag optional
Blue-white dress "A"	Dress	Blue	White plain front	Scarlet w/skirt, black w/slacks	White skirt/ slacks	Black purse or handbag optional
Blue dress "B"	Dress	Blue	White plain front	Scarlet w/skirt, black w/slacks	Blue skirt/ slacks	Black purse or handbag optional
Blue-white dress "B"	Dress	Blue	White plain front	Scarlet w/skirt, black w/slacks	White skirt/ slacks	Black purse or handbag optional
Blue dress "C"	Dress		Khaki long sleeve	Black	Blue skirt/ slacks	Black handbag optional
Blue dress "D"	Dress	None	Khaki short sleeve	None	Blue skirt/ slacks	Black handbag optional
Service "A"	Green service/ garrison	Green	Khaki long or short sleeve	Green	Green skirt/ slacks	Black handbag optional
Service "B"	Green service/ garrison	Green v-neck sweater (optional)	Khaki long sleeve	Green	Green skirt/ slacks	Black handbag optional
Service "C"	Green service/ garrison	None	Khaki short sleeve	None	Green skirt/ slacks	Black handbag optional
Maternity service uniform	Garrison service/ garrison	Green tunic (see para 3016)	Khaki long or short sleeve	Green (a)	Green skirt/ slacks	Black handbag optional
Utility uniform	Utility	Utility	Green undershirt optional	None	Web belt or martial arts belt	Not worn

a. If required or prescribed.
b. Black gloves always worn or carried with all-weather coat during winter uniform period. Optional when coat is worn.
c. Oxford/flats may be worn per paragraph 3010.
d. Green scarf optional for wear with all-weather coat/tanker jacket during winter uniform period.
e. Evening Dress with scarlet waistcoat and plain front shirt worn by general officers.

Gloves	Footwear	Outer Coat (a)	Insignia Bos	Medals/Ribbons	Badges	Sword
White (b)	Black pumps (cloth/suede)	AWC/ optional cape	Dress collar/cap	Miniature medals	Not worn	Not worn
White (b)	Black pumps (cloth/suede)	AWC/ optional cape	Dress collar/cap	Miniature medals	Not worn	Not worn
White (b)	Black pumps (c)	AWC/ optional cape	Dress collar/cap	Large medals (ribbons per para. 5205.3)	Not worn	(a)
White (b)	Black pumps (c)	AWC/ optional cape	Dress collar/cap	Large medals (ribbons per para. 5205.3)	Not worn	(a)
White (b)	Black pumps (c)	AWC/ optional cape	Dress collar/cap	Ribbons	Optional (a)	(a)
White (b)	Black pumps (c)	AWC/ optional cape	Dress collar/cap	Ribbons	Optional (a)	(a)
(b)	Black pumps (c)	AWC or tanker jacket	Dress cap	Ribbons	Optional (a)	(a)
(b)	Black pumps (c)	AWC or tanker jacket	Dress cap	Ribbons optional (a)	Optional (a)	(a)
(b)	Black pumps (c)	AWC or tanker jacket (d)	Service collar/cap	Ribbons	Optional (a)	(a)
(b)	Black pumps (c)	AWC or tanker jacket (d)	Service cap	Ribbons (a)	Optional (a)	(a)
(b)	Black pumps (c)	AWC or tanker jacket (d)	Service cap	Ribbons optional (a)	Optional (a)	(a)
(b)	Black pumps/ oxfords or flats	AWC (d)	Service cap	Ribbons optional (a)	Optional (a)	Not worn
(b)	Combat boots/ socks	AWC or ECWCS	Emblem decal/ name & service tapes	Not worn	Not worn	Not worn

to Navy Regulations; or (3) when visiting the White House, except in a tourist capacity or when an individual is specifically invited on either a social or an official occasion for which another uniform is indicated on the invitation.

A variation of the service uniform, the service "B" uniform is the same as the service "A" uniform except that the service coat is not worn. This uniform may be worn as the uniform of the day and may be prescribed for formations at parades or ceremonies. It will not be worn for formal or semiformal social events.

The short-sleeve khaki shirt with appropriate service trousers, skirt, or slacks is designated as the service "C" uniform. It is worn under circumstances similar to the service "B" uniform, particularly in warmer climates.

The blue dress uniform, in its various forms, is equivalent to civilian formal and semiformal attire. Blue dress "A" uniform (blues with medals and, when prescribed, sword) may be worn for parades, ceremonies, and formal or semiformal social functions as appropriate to the season or those occasions requiring uniformity with NCOs and below. It is normally worn for the following official military or social occasions: (1) parades, ceremonies, reviews, solemnities, and entertainments when the commander or senior officer present desires to pay special honors to the occasion; (2) official visits of, or to, U.S. civil officials, officers of the U.S. armed forces, and officials of foreign governments according to Navy Regulations; (3) receptions given by, or in honor of, officials or officers as listed in Navy Regulations; or (4) at daytime formal or semiformal occasions.

Blue dress "B" uniform may be worn for parades, ceremonies, informal social functions as appropriate to the season or those occasions requiring uniformity with NCOs and below. It may also be worn as the uniform of the day for those commands that receive the appropriate clothing allowance. Blue dress "B" is normally worn for the following official military or social occasions: (1) official visits of, or to, U.S. civil officials, officers of the U.S. armed forces, and officials of foreign governments, according to Navy Regulations; or (2) at informal daytime receptions to which a Marine is invited in an official capacity. Dress "B" uniforms consist of the same items as the corresponding dress "A" uniforms except that ribbons are worn in lieu of medals. Shooting badges may be prescribed.

The blue dress uniform with long-sleeve khaki shirt (without coat) and tie for male Marines or tab for female Marines is designated as blue dress "C." Commanders may prescribe blue dress "C" as the uniform of the day for specified occasions or duties or for honors, parades, and ceremonies on and off the military installation.

The blue dress uniform with short-sleeve khaki shirt (without coat) is designated as blue dress "D." Commanders may prescribe this uniform for honors, parades, and ceremonies where climatic conditions preclude the comfortable wearing of the other blue dress uniforms.

The blue-white dress "A" and "B" uniforms are prescribed when appropriate to the season for the same types of official military or social occasions for which the equivalent blue dress uniform is prescribed as discussed above. The blue-white dress "A" and "B" uniforms consist of the same items as the blue dress "A" and "B" except the trousers, skirt, or slacks are white. The blue-white dress uniform is not normally worn in ceremonies with enlisted Marines who are not authorized white trousers.

Evening dress is worn on formal evening occasions when civilian full dress is prescribed (such as the Marine Corps Birthday Ball) or on semiformal evening occasions. Evening dress will be prescribed for official or military-sponsored events, either formal or semiformal. Any evening function that you attend as an official representative of the Marine Corps is an occasion for evening dress. Evening dress is an optional uniform for company-grade officers, but its possession becomes mandatory upon promotion to major.

While the boat cloak is optional, male officers should feel free to obtain and, more important, wear this handsome, traditional garment. The boat cloak, made of dark blue broadcloth material lined with scarlet wool broadcloth, may be worn with evening dress and blue dress "A" or "B" uniforms for official and social functions. Female officers may wear the similar dress cape. Neither will be worn when the blue dress uniform is worn as the uniform of the day.

You must buy and maintain in good condition all articles of uniform that the commandant prescribes for officers as listed in *Uniform Regulations*. You must keep your full assignment of uniforms with you at all times except when in the field.

As you acquire clothing, mark each article as reflected in *Uniform Regulations*. Stencil your baggage and personal kit appropriately. Inside each piece of baggage, stencil or affix the same information in a permanent manner. You can purchase clothing-marking sets at the Marine Corps exchange. Once deployed to or off foreign shores and using field or ship's laundry services, it is too late to mark your clothing properly.

The law prohibits anyone not in the armed forces from wearing the uniform or any distinctive part thereof (10 U.S. Code 771, 772; 18 U.S. Code 702). This does not apply to retired Marines, who may continue to bear the title and, on occasions similar to active and reserve component personnel, wear the uniform of highest rank held. Persons who served honorably *during wartime* and whose most recent service was terminated under honorable circumstances may wear the uniform in public, but only for military funerals, memorial services, weddings, and inaugurals; parades on national or state holidays; or other parades or ceremonies of a patriotic character in which any active or reserve U.S. military unit is taking part. In other words, previous service *alone* does not grant a universal right to wear the uniform for former servicemembers.

Wearing the uniform is prohibited in connection with nonmilitary commercial or business activities or in any circumstances that might compromise the dignity of the uniform or the Corps.

No Marine (including retired or Reserve personnel) may wear the uniform while attending (unless on duty) or participating in any demonstration, assembly, or activity, the purpose of which is furtherance of personal or partisan political, social, economic, or religious issues. In other words, public events of dubious dignity or outright demonstrations and the Marine Corps uniform or emblem do not mix.

Rules on body markings and piercings ebb and flow with the times. By 2007, with increased influence of civilian trends, Corps policies became more restrictive, and they were reinforced to prohibit tattoos or brands on the neck and the head as well as on the arm and viewable in short sleeves. In 2016, the Marine Corps published new guidelines, clarifying and easing somewhat the policies governing tattoos and piercings. Body markings on the head or neck, including in or around the mouth area, remain prohibited. *Marine Corps Uniform Regulations* contains very specific policy concerning body markings on the upper and lower arms, upper and lower legs, and hand, finger, and wrist. In all areas of the body, tattoos or brands that are prejudicial to good order, discipline, and morale, or are of a nature to bring discredit upon the Marine Corps, are prohibited. Tattoos, body piercings, and nondental tooth crowns are identified as body art, and commanders are tasked with upholding current regulations regarding eccentric appearance.

❧ *Uniform Accessories*

Marine Corps uniforms come with far more accessories than comparable civilian attire, and it thus takes some effort before their proper wear becomes habit. The following rules concern the wearing of uniform accessories. Once again, you are wise to refer regularly to the current *Marine Corps Uniform Regulations.*

Belts. Belts are worn with buckle centered and aligned. Belt buckles (except on 782 gear) must be brightly polished. Since the introduction of the Marine Corps Martial Arts Program, Marines have the option of substituting a color-coded rigger's belt for the web belt worn with the combat utility uniform. During 2008, this option became a requirement owing to the requirement for all hands to achieve the tan belt during basic training.

Gloves. During the winter uniform period, Marines may wear or carry black, midweight triblend gloves with leather palms when an outer coat is worn with the service uniform. Optional certified black dress gloves may be worn. The all-leather black gloves issued prior to the current poly-blend leather gloves may be worn only until no longer serviceable. Black gloves may also be worn or carried with the service "A" uniform or service uniform with sweater or tanker jacket at the individual's option. Local commanders will designate whether gloves will be worn by troops in formation.

Marines may wear black gloves with the utility uniform.

White cloth gloves may be worn or carried with evening dress, blue dress, or blue-white dress uniforms during summer and winter uniform seasons. When an outer garment is worn during the winter uniform season, black gloves may be worn or carried. During the summer season, black gloves may be worn or carried when the all-weather coat is worn as the outer garment. White gloves are worn or carried when the boat cloak or dress cape is worn as the outer garment.

Shoes. With the service uniform, Marines must wear approved, commercial black shoes of natural or synthetic leather in semigloss or high-gloss (patent) finishes. For male Marines, they must be either oxford shoe or chukka boot in style without fancy stitching. Depending on the uniform and occasion, female Marines wear black pumps, dress flats, or oxfords; *Uniform Regulations* includes a lengthy discussion of the policies and choices. Socks must match shoes in color.

Swords. Swords may be prescribed with all uniforms except evening dress, and they must be carried in line with troops in dress uniforms. Officers must possess swords, but no longer must have their names engraved on the blade. A Marine officer may carry a parent's sword, provided it is sized correctly.

"Sam Browne" Belt. The service, or "Sam Browne," belt may be worn at ceremonies, parades, honor guards, and reviews when the sword is prescribed or when deemed appropriate by the commander. It may be worn with the blue dress "A" or "B," blue-white dress "A" or "B," and service "A" uniforms. It is not to be worn with the all-weather coat.

Jewelry. Marines in uniform may wear jewelry with limitations. The following are authorized: inconspicuous rings, only one per hand except for engagement and wedding rings, which count as one when worn on a single finger; a necklace if not visible in uniform; an inconspicuous wristwatch; a regulation tie clasp; and sunglasses of conservative design, but never when in line with troops unless by medical requirement.

Females are authorized to wear a single pair of small earrings (one per ear), and they may carry umbrellas when in service or dress uniform.

Religious Jewelry and Apparel. Marines may wear neat and conservative religious jewelry and apparel items as follows: (1) articles of religious apparel that are not visible or apparent when worn with the uniform; (2) visible articles of religious apparel with the uniform while attending or conducting divine services or while in a chapel or other house of worship; and (3) visible articles of religious apparel with the uniform that do not interfere with or replace required uniform articles.

❧ ❧ *Civilian Clothes*

As an officer you are expected to maintain a high standard of civilian dress. Your clothes should be conservative in cut and color, of the best quality, and well maintained. When off duty, wear civilian clothes. If on duty abroad, however, be sure to check local directives on wearing of plain clothes. Unless you have permission, you may not wear a uniform when on leave outside the United States or its territories.

While dressed in civilian clothes, wear no distinctive articles of a uniform (exceptions: certain items not exclusively military and authorized in *Uniform Regulations*, such as sweater, gloves, socks, and so forth).

Never forget, incidentally, that your general neatness and grooming at all times are marked on your fitness report. This includes not only uniform but civilian clothes as well.

❖ ❖ *Grooming and Appearance*

The following rules guide the maintenance of the good grooming and professional appearance for all officers:

- Most military grooming has simply reflected society's standards through history, but Marines since the 1950s have stressed neat and close trimming of hair. Although three inches is the maximum permissible length on top for males, hairstyles approaching the maximums are regarded as somewhat foppish by many Marine officers and insubordinate by more than a few others. Therefore, the *Guide* must, in good faith, encourage more junior male officers to resist "pushing the envelope" in terms of hair length. Females may wear their hair in short, medium, or long styles. *Uniform Regulations* contains extensive, detailed discussion of hairstyles and grooming for both men and women.
- Male Marines must keep clean-shaven except for a mustache, if desired. Eccentric moustaches are not acceptable.
- All smooth leather must be maintained in very high polish.
- To keep shirt collars trim and neckties in place, wear a collar stay.
- Keep the overlap of your khaki web belt within the prescribed 2–4 inches, for coat belts, 2¾–3¾ inches.
- Although your uniforms contain many pockets, the safest rule is to carry nothing in them. Specifically, you should never place anything in exterior pockets of a dress or service uniform (exceptions: a pencil out of sight in a shirt pocket, notebook in hip pocket, or wallet and handkerchief kept flat in trouser pockets).
- With all uniforms, keep a vigilant eye out for visible stray threads— known colloquially as "Irish pennants"—and remove them carefully. They detract from a military appearance.

- To wear utility trousers properly with combat boots, attach blousing bands near the top of each boot and turn up the trousers to form interior cuffs with a blousing band inside each interior cuff. This produces a neat overhang approximately one inch below the top of the boot. Most Marine Corps exchanges stock bands for this purpose. In a pinch, a strong rubber band or section of inner tube will do the job.
- At least two weeks before the seasonal change from summer to winter uniform variants and vice versa, break out the forthcoming uniform, have it cleaned and pressed, and check it for completeness and repair.
- Bottom line: read and follow the advice in *Uniform Regulations* on marking, care, and wearing of uniforms.

⑪

MILITARY COURTESY, HONORS, AND CEREMONIES

A compliance with the minutiae of military courtesy is a mark of well-disciplined troops.

— Major General John A. Lejeune

COURTESY IS said to be "the lubricant of life." Military courtesy, the traditional form of politeness in the profession of arms, similarly eases the way along well-worn, customary paths. Sharing many elements with courtesy in civilian life, military courtesy nevertheless stems firmly from a more traditional code of rules and customs. The life and discipline of military service are formal; so too is its form of courtesy.

⟩ MILITARY COURTESY

Military courtesy embraces much more than the salute and other rituals, important as these are. Courtesy is a disciplined state of mind. It must be accorded to all ranks and on all occasions. Courtesy toward a senior indicates respect for authority, responsibility, and experience. Courtesy toward a junior shows appreciation and respect for his or her support and for that person as a fellow Marine. When paid to the Color and to the national anthem, it expresses loyalty to the United States and to the Constitution, which we are sworn to uphold and defend.

A prerequisite to discipline, military courtesy promotes the willing obedience and unhesitating cooperation that make a good unit "click." When ordinary acts of military courtesy are performed grudgingly or omitted, discipline suffers. Discipline and courtesy alike stem from and contribute to esprit de corps. The Marine Corps has always stood at the top of the services by full and willing observance of the twin virtues of soldierly courtesy and discipline.

❧ ❧ *Pointers on Military Courtesy and Etiquette*

The Marine officer should be familiar with several important Marine Corps and Navy customs, courtesies, and points of etiquette—some written, others unwritten.

The CO's "Wishes." When your CO says, "I wish," "I desire," "I would like," or similarly phrased expressions, these have the force of a direct order and should be complied with on that basis. Given this custom, commanding officers at every level, including platoon leaders, must take care when expressing their "wishes," lest they find themselves in the predicament of having given an order they did not actually intend.

Acknowledging Orders. When a Marine officer or enlisted Marine receives orders or instructions, he or she replies, "Aye, aye, sir," or "Aye, aye, ma'am." This phrase, which descends from the earliest days of the Marine Corps and Navy, is used in both services. It means "I understand the orders received and will carry them out." Never permit a subordinate to acknowledge an order by "Very well," "All right," "Yes," or "Okay."

Accompanying a Senior. The position of honor for one's senior is on the right. Therefore, in company with a senior, you walk, ride, or sit on the left. When entering a vehicle or a boat, juniors embark first and take the less desirable places in the middle, on "jump," or front seats (or forward in a boat). When debarking, the senior leaves first, while juniors follow in order of rank.

When a senior is inspecting, in most cases he or she is followed by the immediate commander of the unit being inspected, who remains on the senior's left, one pace to the rear. But during inspection of troops in formation, the immediate commander remains on the right of the inspecting officer and precedes him or her. For additional details on inspections, see chapter 15.

Meeting a Senior Indoors. When you meet a senior indoors, in a passageway or doorway or on a stairway or ladder, give way smartly and promptly. In such an instance, it is customary to exchange greetings, initiated by the junior individual. Observe this practice on board ship as well.

Senior Entering a Room. When a senior enters a room or passes nearby unorganized groups either indoors or outside, the senior officer or NCO of the group or groups commands, "Attention on deck!" or simply "Attention!" All hands come to attention and remain so until the senior passes or orders "As you were." If out of doors and covered, all hands salute.

Permission to Speak to Senior Officers. When one of your enlisted people wishes to speak to the company or detachment commander, the enlisted person first obtains permission from the unit's senior enlisted person (see chapter 15). If he or she desires to speak to an officer of still higher rank or position, the enlisted person must in turn have the company or detachment commander's permission.

Similarly, as a junior officer, you obtain your immediate CO's permission before you seek an official interview with any higher officer. The reason for this is that the senior enlisted person or CO can probably solve the problem satisfactorily without the matter having to go higher.

Entering an Office. Enlisted Marines entering any office should be required to observe the following procedure, regardless of whether an officer is present: knock, enter and stand at attention immediately inside the doorway uncovered (unless under arms), identify oneself by name and rank, and then state one's business.

Although the foregoing sequence is not mandatory for officers, it is a prudent procedure for junior officers to bear in mind, especially when entering the office of one who is appreciably senior. In general, however, an officer should not "freeze" on entering. Having once made an entrance, the junior officer should distinctly come to the position of attention (to signify respect for the senior) and then, once recognized, assume a less formal stance of alert composure.

If you are a smoker, never enter the office of a senior while you are smoking, and do not smoke in the senior's office or presence unless invited to do so.

On the Telephone. Use moderate and respectful tones and identify yourself and your organization. Be brief. For example, answer a phone call as follows: "Company B, 5th Marines, Lieutenant Griffith." Never answer by simply saying, "Hello."

Mounted Juniors. Juniors mounted in vehicles or equipment (or, in days past, on horses) dismount before addressing or reporting to seniors except when in the field. Even then, however, dismount if practical.

Uncovering under Arms. The only exception to the rule that Marines under arms never uncover is at a religious service, such as a wedding, when officers may wear swords and still uncover. You do not unsheathe your sword inside a church, however, unless express authority is granted by an appropriate religious functionary.

❧ ❧ *Military Titles, Phraseology, and Address*

When interacting with other Marines and members of the other services, knowing and employing proper military titles and forms of address are a mark of professionalism.

Addressing Seniors. Never forget that "sir" or "ma'am" is an important word when addressing or in conversation with anyone senior. You may not be reprimanded on the spot for omitting "sir" or "ma'am," but this omission is quickly noted and usually remembered. This norm applies whether in uniform or not, whether on duty or off.

Speaking to Juniors. To help promote subordination and respect among your juniors, address them by their proper titles and their names. Follow the leadership principles discussed in chapter 15, and be wary of overly casual use of first names or nicknames. Formality in speaking to a subordinate is never wrong, whereas informality can be risky and may compromise your position. In particular, never allow casual or even unintentionally disrespectful reference to an absent third person, particularly a senior individual, by one of your juniors.

Shortcuts. It is acceptable to use shortened titles in conversation or unofficial correspondence. Table 11-1 shows the correct military forms of address on official and unofficial occasions and when dealing with civilians.

While it is never wrong to address servicemembers by their complete ranks and names, here are some commonly used informal alternatives:

- A male officer is addressed as "sir," whereas a female officer is addressed as "ma'am." Both may be addressed by rank, such as "Yes, Major," or "Good morning, Lieutenant."
- At one time, custom sanctioned a second lieutenant's being addressed or spoken of as "Mr." or "Ms." But this practice has fallen into disuse. Today,

it is normal and preferable to use "Lieutenant," especially in the presence of enlisted people. Do not be surprised to hear warrant officers addressed as "Mr." or "Ms."—especially in the Navy—although addressing them by their proper rank is never wrong.

- Lieutenant colonels are often addressed simply as "Colonel."
- Generals and admirals of any rank are spoken to as "General" or "Admiral," respectively.
- Medical and dental officers below the rank of commander may be addressed simply as "Doctor."
- Any chaplain may be addressed by another officer as "Chaplain" or "Padre" and Roman Catholic chaplains of any rank (and Episcopal chaplains who so prefer) as "Father."

In general, address enlisted personnel by rank and last name. As an indicator of respect and professionalism, you should address sergeants major and master gunnery sergeants using their complete titles, although after some time working together in a close-knit unit, "Master Gunny" becomes appropriate for the latter.

The first sergeant of a company, battery, or detachment should be addressed by officers of the unit as "First Sergeant." The title "top sergeant" is not used in the Marine Corps. Yet officers commonly address master sergeants as "Top" and gunnery sergeants as "Gunny," neither of which implies any disrespect.

Navy chief petty officers are habitually spoken to as "Chief," although it is wise to address the more senior chief petty officers using the longer forms, such as "Senior Chief" and "Master Chief," corresponding to their actual ranks.

Avoid the unfortunate practice, which has occurred in some instances, of referring colloquially to enlisted Marines as "troopers." This is an Army—not a Marine or Navy—term going back to horse cavalry and more recently used to refer to paratroopers. It is inappropriate for Marines (and sounds like a reference to the highway patrol). Marines should be referred to collectively as "Marines" or less formally in the traditional Corps usage as "people" (as in the injunction, "You people, square yourselves away").

Being at ease with the proper military titles and forms of address relies on thorough familiarity with the rank structures of the armed forces and the insignia that denote rank. Insignia of rank appear in figures 11-1 and 11-2.

TABLE 11-1. Correct Forms of Address for Naval and Military Personnel

Person Addressed or Introduced	To Military Personnel		To Civilians	
	Introduce as:	Address as:	Introduce as:	Address as:
Marine, Army, or Air Force Officer	Major (or other rank) Smith	Same	Major Smith[a]	Same
Naval Officer	Captain Smith	Same	Captain Smith[a]	Same
Navy Staff Corps Officer	Commander Smith[b] Chaplain Smith	Same Same	Commander Smith[b] Chaplain Smith	Same Same
Coast Guard and Coast and Geodetic Survey Officers	Same as for same rank in Navy[b]	Same	Same as for same rank in Navy[b]	Same
U.S. Public Health Service Officer (M.D. or D.D.S.)	Dr. Smith[c]	Same	Dr. Smith of the Public Health Service	Dr. Smith
U.S. Public Health Service Officer (Sanitary Engineer)	Mr. or Ms. Smith[c]	Same	Mr. or Ms. Smith of the Public Health Service	Mr. or Ms. Smith
Commissioned Warrant Officer[d]	Chief Warrant Officer Smith[d]	Same[d]	Chief Warrant Officer Smith[d]	Same

TABLE II-I. (continued)

Person Addressed or Introduced	To Military Personnel		To Civilians	
	Introduce as:	Address as:	Introduce as:	Address as:
Midshipman or Cadet	Midshipman (or Cadet) Smith	Mr. or Miss Smith	Midshipman (or Cadet) Smith	Mr. or Miss Smith
Warrant Officer[d]	Warrant Officer Smith[d]	Same[d]	Warrant Officer Smith[d]	Same[d]
Staff NCO or Chief Petty Officer[e]	Sergeant Major Smith,[e] Master Chief Gunner's Mate Smith	Sergeant Major or Chief	Sergeant Major Smith, Master Chief Gunner's Mate Smith	Sergeant Major or Chief
Noncommissioned Officer or Petty Officer	Corporal Smith or Gunner's Mate Smith	Same	Corporal Smith or Petty Officer Smith	Same
Private or Seaman	Private (or Seaman) Smith	Smith	Private (or Seaman) Smith	Smith

a   When not in uniform, an officer should be introduced as "of the Navy" or "of the Marine Corps" to distinguish the rank from similar-sounding ranks in the other armed services. Suggested phraseology: "This is Lieutenant Smith of the Marine Corps." Such a form of introduction indicates the officer's rank, service, and the proper form of address.

b   Add "of the Medical Corps," "of the Civil Engineer Corps," or the other corps, when helpful to indicate status of officer. If a senior officer of the Medical or Dental Corps prefers to be addressed as "Doctor," such preference should be honored. Some senior members of the Chaplain's Corps prefer to be addressed by their rank, but it is always correct to address a chaplain of any rank as Chaplain.

c   In any case where there is reason to believe that the officer's insignia might not be recognized, it is correct to add, "of the Public Health Service," "of the Coast Guard," or "of the Coast and Geodetic Survey."

d   Male Marine Corps warrant officers appointed in certain occupational fields bear the title of (Chief) Marine Gunner, addressed as "Gunner."

e   All staff NCOs (that is, those with rank of staff sergeant and higher) are addressed by their particular titles, such as "Gunnery Sergeant Hayes," "Master Sergeant Wodarczyk," or "Staff Sergeant Basilone."

PAY GRADE	ARMY	AIR FORCE	SPACE FORCE	MARINE CORPS	NAVY	COAST GUARD
W-1	BLACK — SILVER WARRANT OFFICER (WO1)	NOT APPLICABLE	NOT APPLICABLE	SCARLET — GOLD WARRANT OFFICER (WO)	BLUE — GOLD WARRANT OFFICER (WO1)	NOT APPLICABLE
W-2	CHIEF WARRANT OFFICER 2 (CW2)	NOT APPLICABLE	NOT APPLICABLE	SCARLET — GOLD CHIEF WARRANT OFFICER 2 (CWO2)	BLUE — GOLD CHIEF WARRANT OFFICER 2 (CWO2)	GOLD — BLUE CHIEF WARRANT OFFICER 2 (CWO2)
W-3	CHIEF WARRANT OFFICER 3 (CW3)	NOT APPLICABLE	NOT APPLICABLE	SCARLET — SILVER CHIEF WARRANT OFFICER 3 (CWO3)	BLUE — SILVER CHIEF WARRANT OFFICER 3 (CWO3)	SILVER — BLUE CHIEF WARRANT OFFICER 3 (CWO3)
W-4	CHIEF WARRANT OFFICER 4 (CW4)	NOT APPLICABLE	NOT APPLICABLE	SCARLET — SILVER CHIEF WARRANT OFFICER 4 (CWO4)	BLUE — SILVER CHIEF WARRANT OFFICER 4 (CWO4)	SILVER — BLUE CHIEF WARRANT OFFICER 4 (CWO4)
W-5	BLACK — SILVER CHIEF WARRANT OFFICER 5 (CW5)	NOT APPLICABLE	NOT APPLICABLE	SCARLET — SILVER CHIEF WARRANT OFFICER 5 (CWO5)	BLUE — SILVER CHIEF WARRANT OFFICER 5 (CWO5)	NOT APPLICABLE

Figure 11-1. Officer Insignia of Rank

PAY GRADE	ARMY	AIR FORCE	SPACE FORCE	MARINE CORPS	NAVY	COAST GUARD
O-1	GOLD — SECOND LIEUTENANT (2LT)	SECOND LIEUTENANT (2dLt)	SECOND LIEUTENANT (2dLt)	SECOND LIEUTENANT (2ndLt)	ENSIGN (ENS)	ENSIGN (ENS)
O-2	SILVER — FIRST LIEUTENANT (1LT)	FIRST LIEUTENANT (1stLt)	FIRST LIEUTENANT (1stLt)	FIRST LIEUTENANT (1stLt)	LIEUTENANT JUNIOR GRAD (LTJG)	LIEUTENANT JUNIOR GRADE (LTJG)
O-3	SILVER — CAPTAIN (CPT)	CAPTAIN (Capt)	CAPTAIN (Capt)	CAPTAIN (Capt)	LIEUTENANT (LT)	LIEUTENANT (LT)
O-4	GOLD — MAJOR (MAJ)	MAJOR (Maj)	MAJOR (Maj)	MAJOR (Maj)	LIEUTENANT COMMANDER (LCDR)	LIEUTENANT COMMANDER (LCDR)
O-5	SILVER — LIEUTENANT COLONEL (LTC)	LIEUTENANT COLONEL (LtCol)	LIEUTENANT COLONEL (LtCol)	LIEUTENANT COLONEL (LtCol)	COMMANDER (CDR)	COMMANDER (CDR)

FIGURE II-I. (*continued*)

PAY GRADE	ARMY	AIR FORCE	SPACE FORCE	MARINE CORPS	NAVY	COAST GUARD
O-6	COLONEL (COL)	COLONEL (Col)	COLONEL (Col)	COLONEL (Col)	NAVY BLUE — CAPTAIN (CAPT)	COAST GUARD BLUE — CAPTAIN (CAPT)
O-7	BRIGADIER GENERAL (BG)	BRIGADIER GENERAL (BrigGen)	BRIGADIER GENERAL (BrigGen)	BRIGADIER GENERAL (BGen)	REAR ADMIRAL LOWER HALF (RDML)	REAR ADMIRAL LOWER HALF (RDML)
O-8	MAJOR GENERAL (MG)	MAJOR GENERAL (MajGen)	MAJOR GENERAL (MajGen)	MAJOR GENERAL (MajGen)	REAR ADMIRAL UPPER HALF (RADM)	REAR ADMIRAL UPPER HALF (RADM)
O-9	LIEUTENANT GENERAL (LTG)	LIEUTENANT GENERAL (LtGen)	LIEUTENANT GENERAL (LtGen)	LIEUTENANT GENERAL (LtGen)	VICE ADMIRAL (VADM)	VICE ADMIRAL (VADM)
O-10	GENERAL (GEN)	GENERAL (Gen)	GENERAL (Gen)	GENERAL (Gen)	ADMIRAL (ADM)	ADMIRAL (ADM)

FIGURE 11-1. (*continued*)

PAY GRADE	ARMY	AIR FORCE	SPACE FORCE	MARINE CORPS	NAVY	COAST GUARD
E-1	NO INSIGNIA PRIVATE (PVT)	NO INSIGNIA AIRMAN BASIC (AB)	SPECIALIST 1 (Spc1)	NO INSIGNIA PRIVATE (Pvt)	NO INSIGNIA SEAMAN RECRUIT (SR)	NO INSIGNIA SEAMAN RECRUIT (SR)
E-2	PRIVATE (PV2)	AIRMAN (Amn)	SPECIALIST 2 (Spc2)	PRIVATE FIRST CLASS (PFC)	NAVY BLUE SEAMAN APPRENTICE (SA)	COAST GUARD BLUE SEAMAN APPRENTICE (SA)
E-3	PRIVATE FIRST CLASS (PFC)	AIRMAN FIRST CLASS (A1C)	SPECIALIST 3 (Spc3)	LANCE CORPORAL (LCpl)	SEAMAN (SN)	SEAMAN (SN)
E-4	CORPORAL (CPL) / SPECIALIST (SPC)	SENIOR AIRMAN (SrA)	SPECIALIST 4 (Spc4)	CORPORAL (Cpl)	PETTY OFFICER THIRD CLASS (PO3)	PETTY OFFICER THIRD CLASS (PO3)
E-5	SERGEANT (SGT)	STAFF SERGEANT (SSgt)	SERGEANT (Sgt)	SERGEANT (Sgt)	PETTY OFFICER SECOND CLASS (PO2)	PETTY OFFICER SECOND CLASS (PO2)

FIGURE 11-2. Enlisted Insignia of Rank

PAY GRADE	ARMY	AIR FORCE	SPACE FORCE	MARINE CORPS	NAVY	COAST GUARD
E-6	STAFF SERGEANT (SSG)	TECHNICAL SERGEANT (TSgt)	TECHNICAL SERGEANT (TSgt)	STAFF SERGEANT (SSgt)	NAVY BLUE — PETTY OFFICER FIRST CLASS (PO1)	COAST GUARD BLUE — PETTY OFFICER FIRST CLASS (PO1)
E-7	SERGEANT FIRST CLASS (SFC)	MASTER SERGEANT (MSgt)	MASTER SERGEANT (MSgt)	GUNNERY SERGEANT (GySgt)	CHIEF PETTY OFFICER (CPO)	CHIEF PETTY OFFICER (CPO)
E-8	MASTER SERGEANT (MSG) / FIRST SERGEANT (1SG)	SENIOR MASTER SERGEANT (SMSgt)	SENIOR MASTER SERGEANT (SMSgt)	MASTER SERGEANT (MSgt) / FIRST SERGEANT (1stSgt)	SENIOR CHIEF PETTY OFFICER (SCPO)	SENIOR CHIEF PETTY OFFICER (SCPO)
E-9	SERGEANT MAJOR (SGM) / COMMAND SERGEANT MAJOR (CSM)	CHIEF MASTER SERGEANT (CMSgt) / COMMAND CMSgt	CHIEF MASTER SERGEANT (CMSgt)	SERGEANT MAJOR (SgtMaj) / MASTER GUNNERY SERGEANT (MGySgt)	MASTER CHIEF PETTY OFFICER (MCPO) / COMMAND MCPO	MASTER CHIEF PETTY OFFICER (MCPO) / COMMAND MCPO
E-9	SERGEANT MAJOR OF THE ARMY (SMA)	CHIEF MASTER SERGEANT OF THE AIR FORCE (CMSAF)	CHIEF MASTER SERGEANT OF THE SPACE FORCE (CMSSF)	SERGEANT MAJOR OF THE MARINE CORPS (SMMC)	MASTER CHIEF PETTY OFFICER OF THE NAVY (MCPON)	MASTER CHIEF PETTY OFFICER OF THE COAST GUARD (MCPOCG)

Note: The Air Force master sergeant, senior master sergeant, and chief master sergeant rank insignia with a rhombus—also referred to as a "lozenge"—in the center of the blue field denotes a first sergeant by billet who, on behalf of the commander, focuses specifically on readiness, health, morale, welfare, and quality-of-life issues within his or her organization.

FIGURE II-2. (*continued*)

Finally, in addition to the brief discussion of the traditional Marine way of saying things in chapter 10, the glossary contains a lengthy list of Marine Corps terms. Know, employ, and enforce the use of those terms.

⋗ ⋗ *Conduct toward Members of Other Services*

The minutiae of military courtesy vary little from service to service and from nation to nation. As a Marine (and therefore, as a professional), you must learn the meaning and traditions behind the badges, insignia, and titles of the officers and enlisted personnel of other military services, both American and foreign.

When you go to duty with another service or in another country, make it a particular point to know and, in most instances, defer to the customs and traditions of that service or country (see, for example, the section below on hand salutes). But never forget that you are a Marine. And never feel self-conscious about adhering to Corps standards of uniform or to the Marine way of doing and saying things.

⋗ ⋗ *The Military Salute*

Saluting is a military custom observed by all who follow the profession of arms. It is a matter of pride among Marines, from general to private, to salute willingly, promptly, smartly, and proudly. The good Marine stands out from the other services by a smart, correct, and cheerful salute, which is as much a hallmark of the Corps as the Eagle, Globe, and Anchor. When you render or receive a salute, you mark yourself as a Marine who has pride in self and Corps.

As a junior officer, you must recognize and teach that the salute is a privilege enjoyed only by military people and is a mutual acknowledgment of comradeship in the profession of arms.

Origins of Saluting. Over the centuries, men-at-arms have rendered fraternal and respectful greetings to indicate friendliness. In early times, armed men raised their weapons or shifted them to the left hand (while raising the empty right hand) to give proof of amicable intentions. During the Middle Ages, knights in armor, on encountering friendly knights, raised their helmet visors in recognition. If they were in the presence of feudal superiors, the helmet was usually doffed. In every case, the fighting man made a gesture of friendliness—the raising of the empty right hand. This gesture survives as today's hand salute, which is the traditional greeting among soldiers of all nations.

Like the original hand salute and doffing of the cap, the discharge of weapons, presentation of arms, and lowering of the point of the sword have all signified good will. In every case, the one so saluting momentarily rendered himself incapable of using his weapon offensively. The descendants of these earlier gestures are the modern sword salute, present arms, and gun salutes.

Whom to Salute. Those entitled to salutes include

- all commissioned and warrant officers of the Army, Marine Corps, Navy, Air Force, Space Force, and Coast Guard, of the reserve components of those services, and of the National Guard;
- officers of friendly foreign powers; and
- by service custom, though not by regulation, any high civilian official who is entitled to honors by Navy Regulations.

The junior person initiates the salute. Enlisted Marines salute other enlisted Marines only in formation when rendering reports.

Prisoners may not salute or, for that matter, wear the Marine Corps emblem.

Definitions. The following definitions apply to Marine Corps saluting procedure.

Out of doors means "in the open air; or the interior of such buildings as drill halls and gymnasiums when used for drill or exercises of troops; or on the weather decks of a man-of-war; or under roofed structures such as lanais, covered walks, and shelters open at one or both sides to the weather." It is synonymous with "on the topside" when used afloat.

Indoors means "the interior of any building ashore, other than a drill hall, gymnasium, or armory."

Between decks means "any shipboard space below a weather deck, other than officers' country."

Covered and *uncovered* mean, respectively, "when and when not wearing headgear."

Under arms is a term indicating that a Marine is carrying a weapon in his or her hand, is equipped with side arms, or is wearing equipment pertaining to an arm, such as a sword sling, pistol belt, or cartridge belt. Any Marine wearing an "MP" (military police) or "SP" (shore patrol) brassard is considered under arms.

Saluting distance means "the maximum distance within which salutes are rendered and exchanged," prescribed as thirty paces. Insignia, colleagues, and acquaintances are normally recognizable at this distance. The salute should be rendered when six paces from the person (or Color) to be saluted. If the parties obviously will not pass within this distance, the salute is rendered at the point of nearest approach.

❧ ❧ *Pointers on Saluting*

You must return all salutes received unless you are uncovered or unless both hands are completely occupied. If physically unable to return a salute, you should acknowledge it verbally and, if possible, excuse yourself to the individual who rendered the salute. If you are uncovered or in any circumstance when you cannot render a correct salute, you should, if standing still, come to attention.

When wearing civilian clothes, you should use the civilian salute for salutes to the Color, salutes to the National Anthem, and salutes during military funerals. If wearing headgear, remove it and hold it with the right hand over the left breast. Without headgear, execute the civilian salute by placing the right hand over the left breast with fingers extended and joined and thumb streamlined alongside.

If salutes are to be properly exchanged, both junior and senior must be alert. The junior must spot the approaching senior, and the senior must respond with enthusiasm. The attitude of seniors toward salutes has a profound effect on the spirit with which any salute is rendered. Enlisted persons are discouraged from saluting (and rightly so) if you overlook their courtesy or seem not to observe them. Such an attitude on your part as a Marine officer is both discourteous and insulting.

You can do much to foster correct rendering of salutes by inviting them. A pleasant, direct look at an approaching junior generally alerts that person and encourages the junior to salute with goodwill. It is an old trick, when a junior officer seems to need a reminder in saluting manners, for the senior to salute the junior first, with a solicitous greeting, thus extending a courteous reprimand.

Here is the proper way to render a salute:

- Begin your salute in ample time (at least six paces away).
- Hold your salute until it is returned or acknowledged.
- Look squarely at the person or Color being saluted.
- Assume the position of attention.

- Have thumb and fingers extended and joined.
- Keep hand and wrist in same plane, not bent.
- Incline forearm at 45 degrees.
- Hold upper arm horizontal while hand is at salute.

But be sure to avoid making the following mistakes:

- Salute with blouse or coat unbuttoned.
- Salute with cigarette, pipe, or cigar in mouth.
- Have anything in your right hand.
- Have your left hand in a pocket.
- Salute when in ranks, at games, or part of a working detail.
- Salute at crowded gatherings, in public conveyances, or in congested areas unless addressing or being directly addressed by a senior.
- Salute when doing so would physically interfere with performance of an assigned duty.

One of the most unmilitary habits encountered among some Marines, both while saluting and even in ranks, is the cartoonish and ludicrous habit of literally leaning over backward in an exaggerated effort to stand straight. This swaybacked stance, with stomach and pelvis thrust forward, jaw jutting out, and shoulders too far back, is a caricature of the position of attention.

❭ ❭ Individual Saluting Etiquette

Whether to Salute Once or Twice. After an officer has been saluted initially, no further salutes are required if that officer remains nearby and no conversation takes place.

When a junior is spoken to by, or addresses, a senior officer, he or she salutes initially, and again when the interaction ends. Throughout the conversation, the junior stands at attention unless otherwise directed by the senior. It should be an instinctive military courtesy on your part, as an officer, to give your subordinates "at ease" or "carry on" during any extended conversation.

Reporting when Indoors. When you report indoors to an officer senior to you, unless under arms, you uncover, place your cover under your left arm, visor forward (or, if a soft cover, hold it smartly in your left hand), knock, and enter when told to do so. Two paces in front of the senior, halt and report, "Sir/

Ma'am, Lieutenant Neville reporting." Remain at attention unless told to stand at ease, carry on, or be seated. On being dismissed, take one backstep, halt, and then face about and march out. If under arms, remain covered, and salute on reporting, and again on being dismissed. The latter salute is rendered after completion of the backstep.

The foregoing procedure also applies to enlisted Marines who report to you.

Enlisted Marines Not in Formation. When an officer approaches enlisted Marines who are not in formation, the first to recognize him or her calls the group to attention as soon as the officer comes within ten paces. Out of doors, if covered (as they should be), all hands turn to face the officer and salute when he or she is within six paces. The salute is held until returned. The group remains at attention until the officer passes or commands "Carry on," which an officer should be quick to do under informal circumstances.

Learn from the example of Major General John A. Lejeune, later the thirteenth commandant, during the Meuse-Argonne battle in 1918. Lejeune approached a group of Marines, whom an NCO called to attention. As the men sprang to their feet, the general checked them, saying: "Sit down, men. It is more important for tired men to rest than for the division commander to be saluted."

Overtaking. When you overtake an officer senior in rank proceeding in the same direction, draw abreast on the senior's left, saluting as you do so, and say, "By your leave, sir." The senior officer acknowledges the salute and replies, "Granted." Remember, if approaching at double time, first slow to quick time.

When you overtake a Marine junior to you, pass on the right. As you come into view, abreast, salutes are exchanged.

Indoors. Marines not under arms do not salute indoors. In an office, however, Marines need not cease work when an officer enters unless called to attention, which is normally the case for a CO who enters. When addressed by an officer, the person addressed should rise.

In the Mess Hall. At meals, do not rise when called to attention but stop eating and keep silent. If spoken to directly by an officer, an enlisted person gets to his or her feet and stands at attention until placed at ease. If not under arms, be sure to uncover when entering a galley, mess hall, or ship's messing compartment.

In Sick Bay. Formal military courtesies are neither rendered nor required in a sick bay. Always uncover when you enter a sick bay or ward.

In Vehicles. Except when on board public conveyances such as buses and trains, officers in vehicles are saluted as if afoot. Other passengers salute or return salutes as necessary.

During Games. Games are not interrupted at the approach of an officer. Spectators do not rise or salute unless individually addressed by an officer.

On Guard. Saluting while on guard duty merits special discussion. *When armed with the rifle*, sentries salute by presenting arms. A sentry walking post halts, faces the officer being saluted, and comes to the present. When the officer (or any other person) addresses the sentry, he or she executes port arms and holds this position throughout the conversation. If speaking with an officer, the sentry does not interrupt the conversation to salute another officer unless the one with whom he or she is speaking likewise salutes; if so, the sentinel presents arms. At the end of the conversation, the sentry presents arms again.

During hours of challenging, a sentry armed with a pistol, shotgun, or carbine does not initially salute. While challenging, a sentry armed with the pistol remains at raise pistol; one armed with a shotgun or carbine remains at port arms. The salute or present arms is rendered after the officer has been duly advanced and recognized, as described in chapter 16.

When not armed with the rifle, a sentry renders hand salutes in the usual way.

If circumstances are such that payment of compliments interferes with a sentry's performance of duty, the sentry does not salute.

Prisoner guards ("chasers") do not salute except when addressed directly by an officer. If marching prisoners, the chaser halts them and takes necessary precautions for their security before rendering the salute. If armed with the rifle, a chaser executes a rifle salute but does not present arms. Prisoners may not salute at any time. Note that you must never pass between a guard and prisoners, and be sure you correct any guard who permits you or any other person to do so.

When in Doubt. If you are uncertain as to whether a salute is required, always salute. For a well-trained Marine, there should never be any doubt. Should a doubtful situation arise, however, do not go out of your way to avoid saluting. Having made up your mind to salute, do so properly and smartly. Never give a hesitant, half-hearted salute, which plainly reveals a lack of knowledge or professionalism. Remember, it is better to render five unnecessary salutes than to omit one that you should give.

❖ ❖ *Group Saluting Etiquette*

Troops in Formation. Troops in formation salute on command only. Officers and NCOs in command of formations render salutes for their units. Before doing so, the person in command brings the unit to attention. Individuals armed other than with the rifle (and officers and NCOs whose swords are not drawn) execute the hand salute.

If an officer speaks to an individual in ranks when the unit is not at attention, the person spoken to comes to attention. At the end of the conversation, the person resumes the position of the others in the unit.

Troops at Drill and on the March. Troops drilling do not render compliments. The person in command salutes for the unit. An officer in a formation is saluted only if in command of the entire formation, and that officer alone returns all salutes. NCOs in charge of detachments or units do not exchange salutes with other units so commanded except at guard mounting, when doing so is part of the formal guard turnover.

Troops marching at ease or route step are called to attention on the approach of a senior entitled to a salute, and the individual in command renders compliments for the unit.

As an aside, Marine units always begin and end a march at attention. March your unit at attention while within barracks and central areas and on main roads of your base. No matter how tired you are after a day or a night in the field, bring your outfit home covered and aligned, at regulation cadence, and at attention. This is the Marine Corps way.

Working Parties. The NCO in charge renders salutes for the entire detail. Individuals come to attention and salute if addressed directly by an officer, but they do not interrupt work at the approach of an officer unless the detail is called to attention.

Formations in Vehicles. Members of formations embarked, as units, in military vehicles do not salute individually. The senior person in each vehicle renders and acknowledges salutes. Only the hand salute is employed.

Groups of Officers. When officers are walking, standing together, or embarked in a vehicle, all render and return salutes as if each were alone.

While Honors Are Being Rendered. During ruffles and flourishes by the band or field music, while honors are being rendered, the guard presents arms to the recipient of honors. All persons in the vicinity but not in formation come to attention and salute, following the motions of the guard (for example, hand salute on present arms; terminate salute on order arms). If ruffles and flourishes are followed by a gun salute, persons in the vicinity stand fast at attention until the last gun has fired.

On board ship, all hands on the quarterdeck salute while an officer is being piped over the side. If the guard is paraded, follow the motions of the guard in your hand salute.

At Military Funerals. The basic rule for saluting at military funerals (for further details, see the section on military funerals below) is to salute each time the body bearers move the coffin and during volleys and "Taps." If you are wearing civilian clothes, uncover and, with your right hand, hold your headgear over your left breast.

During prayers, stand at parade rest without arms, head bowed. During the firing of volleys, come to attention and salute.

Body bearers remain covered, both indoors and outdoors, when carrying the coffin. When the remains are lowered into the grave, body bearers do not salute but stand at attention, holding the flag waist high over the grave.

When a military funeral cortege passes, all hands come to attention and salute the remains, using the hand salute if in uniform or uncovering in the civilian salute if wearing civilian clothes.

❯ ❯ *Hand Salutes*

In some services, the hand salute has been deemphasized almost to the vanishing point based on an erroneous perception that rendering a salute signifies inferiority and subservience, rather than being an act of courtesy and soldierly recognition. Nothing could be further from the truth. In civil life, it is customary to show deference and render courtesy to individuals who occupy more senior positions in an organization. Similarly, a junior Marine salutes his or her senior. The senior in turn returns the salute as a comrade in arms. Thus, the exchange of salutes is a two-way street.

The manner and enthusiasm with which you render or receive a salute indicate the state of your training, your individual esprit, the discipline of your outfit, and your quality as a Marine. Proper saluting habits characterize a good Marine.

Hand salute

How to Execute the Hand Salute. Salute only while stationary or at quick time. If you are at the double and must salute or receive a salute, slow to quick time. Stand or walk at attention. When halted, come to attention distinctly as a preliminary motion to the salute. Look directly at the person or Color you are saluting. If walking or riding, turn your head smartly toward the person being saluted, and catch that person's eye. Execute the first movement, holding position until the salute is acknowledged, then complete the salute by bringing your hand down smartly. When doing this, keep your fingers extended and joined, your thumb streamlined alongside—taken together, your hand, fingers, and thumb should form a single straight "blade." In returning a salute, execute the two counts at marching cadence.

In the Marine Corps and Navy, it is customary to exchange a greeting with a salute. The junior should always say, "Good morning (or evening), sir (or ma'am)," and the senior should unfailingly reply in the same vein—with a smile.

In the Marine Corps and Navy, one does not salute when uncovered—that is, when not wearing headgear. The rare exception to this rule is that one *may* salute uncovered when in a special circumstance where not to salute might cause serious misunderstanding or undesired friction. For example, when serving with the Army or Air Force (who *do* salute uncovered), you may, if good judgment and good relations dictate, depart from the naval procedure. But beware of adopting this as habit. In today's environment of increased "jointness" among the services, knowledgeable Army and Air Force officers are familiar with naval customs concerning salutes and do not normally expect or require Marines to salute when uncovered.

How Not to Salute. A sloppy, grudging salute—or a childish pretense not to notice someone who merits a salute—indicates unmilitary attitude, lack of pride in self and Corps, and plain ignorance. Avoid—and, as an officer, never tolerate—trick salutes. Here are the most common (and a few rare) and unacceptable aberrations:

- Right wrist bent
- Left elbow stuck out at exaggerated, unnatural angle
- Palm turned inward, knuckles kept forward
- Fingers on right hand bent and flexed inward
- Right thumb extended away from fingers
- Hips thrust forward, shoulders swayed back
- One hand in a pocket, a blouse unbuttoned, or headgear not squared away

When you encounter a Marine doing any of these things, no matter how hard he or she seems to be trying, correct the Marine on the spot and see that he or she knows and practices the right way to salute.

❧ ❧ *Rifle Salutes*

Any individual armed with a rifle executes a rifle salute from the following positions: right or left shoulder arms, order arms, trail arms, and present arms. Only a Marine with a rifle at "sling arms" executes a hand salute.

In its four forms, the rifle salute is rendered as follows under the conditions given:

- *Right* or *left shoulder arms* is rendered when out of doors at a halt or at a walk.
- *Order arms* is rendered when at a halt, either indoors or out of doors.
- *Trail arms* is rendered when at a walk, indoors or out of doors.

- *Presenting arms* is a special compliment, as a Marine at present arms represents the authority of the nation. The privilege of saluting by presenting arms is reserved for troops in formation and for sentinels on post.

Marines armed with weapons normally carried slung use the hand salute only and, when so saluting, carry the piece at sling arms, with the left hand grasping the sling to steady the weapon.

✦ Sword Salutes

The Marine Corps Drill and Ceremonies Manual details the complete manual of the sword, but you will find below information on sword salutes as well as additional information on the sword. Every Marine officer takes pride in being precise, dexterous, and at ease with the sword.

When armed with the sword, you render or return salutes in the following ways (see figure 11-3):

- If your sword is sheathed and you are not in formation, execute the normal hand salute.
- If your sword is drawn and you are halted, either in or out of formation, execute present sword as prescribed in the manual of the sword. If commanding a formation, which will usually be the case if your sword is drawn, bring your troops to attention before you do so.
- If your sword is drawn and you are under way in formation, execute the sword salute, having first brought your command to attention, if necessary.

Carrying Sword When Not in Formation. Your sword is not a fishing pole, a hoe, or a golf club, so you should carry and handle it in a military way even when you are not in formation and the sword is unrigged. The proper way to do this is to crook your left arm at a right angle, with your forearm resting across the front of your body, and to place the sword (sheathed in its scabbard) in the crook, curve of the blade downward and hilt rearward. The sword will ride easily here if you hold your forearm steady, and the appearance will be formal and soldierly.

Marching. When under way with sword drawn, the scabbard will hang and move naturally. Despite jokes to the contrary, it is next to impossible to trip over

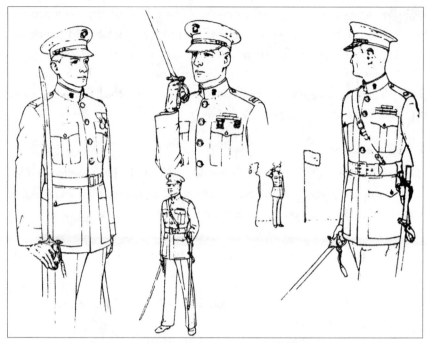

FIGURE 11-3. Sword Salutes and Manual

a scabbard. Few things make you appear more unsure of yourself than clutching at your scabbard while carrying or saluting with your sword.

❧ ❧ Rigging Your Sword

Correct wearing of your sword is a point of professional refinement. Derived from "Rig It Right," an excellent article in the *Gazette* (June 1961) by Majors T. N. Galbraith and R. N. Good, here is an account of how you should rig and wear your badge as a commissioned officer.

The first step is to get your sword knot squared away. The way to begin assembly of the knot is to reeve its small end through the eye of the pommel, slip it back through the two keepers, and hook it to the small metal eye adjacent to the large end. Draw one keeper tight against the pommel, the other over the hook and eye, and you are ready to tie the knot.

Now loop the large end of the knot under the cross guard of the hilt and tie a hitch as shown in figure 11-4. If you check this diagram closely, you will see that the knot shown is a clove hitch, not the double half-hitch specified in regulations. The fact is, a double half-hitch will not hold the knot tight to the cross guard, whereas a clove hitch will. Note which side of the clove hitch should face outboard when the sword is sheathed and worn.

When the hitch is fastened, draw it taut and, at the same time, work the knot so that the large end does not hang below the upper ring mounting on the scabbard. Depending on the length of your knot, the portion from the eye of your pommel to the cross guard will possess some degree of looseness. This is all right: the determining factor is the length hanging free below the guard. If the knot hangs down farther than it should, you may find yourself slapped in the face when you present sword.

Nomenclature of the Sword and Accessories. Attaching the knot may be the most troublesome part of rigging the sword, but the nomenclature of the sword also may be a source of confusion (see figure 11-5). Sword and scabbard are suspended from the sword sling. If you are wearing a blouse, the sword sling is attached to your Sam Browne belt by the frog or, if using a cloth belt, to the shoulder sling; if you are not wearing a blouse, the sword sling is attached to the frog on your belt. In either case, the frog and shoulder sling serve the single purpose of providing a D-ring to which you attach the sword sling.

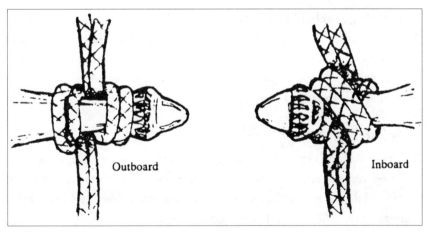

FIGURE 11-4. Rigging the Officer's Sword Knot

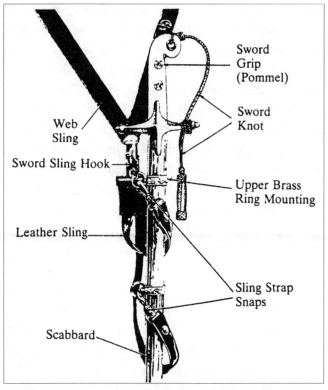

Figure 11-5. Officer's Sword, Scabbard, and Sling

Attaching Scabbard to Sword Sling. Attach your scabbard to your sword sling as shown in figure 11-5. With the sword sling on and its straps hanging free, attach the sling strap snaps to the scabbard rings. Holding the scabbard by its upper ring, give it a half twist toward the body (clockwise) and hang the upper ring over the sword sling hook.

❯ ❯ *Saluting the National Anthem*

When the National Anthem is played or "To the Color" is sounded, all military personnel come to attention, face toward the music, and salute. You hold your salute until the last note of the music but remain at attention until "Carry On" is sounded. If the anthem or call is being played incident to a ceremony involving the Color, face toward the Color rather than the music.

Troops in Formation. Troops in formation are halted (if on the march) and brought to attention, then the commander salutes, facing in the direction of the unit's original front. If participating in a ceremony that includes a rendition of the National Anthem or "To the Color," troops present arms.

Personnel Mounted in Vehicles. During the playing of the National Anthem, all vehicles within sight or hearing of the ceremony stop. Passengers do not debark but remain seated at attention and do not salute. If the passengers compose a military detail in an official vehicle, the person in charge debarks, faces toward the flag or music, and salutes.

Personnel on Horseback. Those on horseback halt and salute without dismounting.

Sentries. Sentries halt, face in the direction of the flag or music, and render the hand salute or present arms as appropriate (see the section above on individual saluting etiquette).

In Civilian Clothes. If wearing plain clothes, face in the direction of the flag or music and come to attention. If wearing headgear, remove and hold it with your right hand over your left breast.

Indoors. When the National Anthem is played indoors, you come to attention and face the music. Only those under arms salute.

Foreign National Anthems. Accord the national anthems of friendly foreign powers the same courtesies as your own.

❖ ❖ *Courtesy to the Flag*

Military personnel render the following courtesies to the National Color (or National Ensign).

Saluting the Flag. Except at Morning and Evening Colors and on board a warship at anchor or pierside, the flag is not saluted when displayed from a mast or flagstaff, nor is any flag saluted unless it is a National Color or Standard as defined in chapter 10. When the Color is encased in a protective cover (and said to be "cased"), it is not saluted. The tenth general order (see chapter 16), which enjoins Marines to "salute all officers, and all colors and standards not cased," has, at times, created some confusion on the issue of saluting the flag. But there is no routine requirement to salute the National Color when it is flown from a stationary flagstaff, such as in front of a headquarters building.

Colors and standards not cased and not displayed from a mast or flagstaff (for example, when borne by a color guard) *are* saluted when either you or they approach or pass within six paces. Hold your salute until the Color has passed or been passed by that distance.

In the field or camp, it is customary to display the National Color and unit battle color in front of the CO's tent. According to one's wishes, this may be done every day or only on Sundays and national holidays. All hands who approach within saluting distance (six paces) execute a hand or rifle salute as appropriate, holding the salute until six paces beyond. If a color sentinel is posted, he or she acknowledges salutes rendered by enlisted Marines; when officers salute the Color, the sentinel holds his or her salute or present arms until the officer has completed the salute.

Motor Vehicles Passing the Color. When passed by an uncased National Color, all persons embarked in a vehicle remain seated at attention. Vehicles approaching and passing the Color reduce speed; mounted personnel remain seated at attention but do not salute.

Individuals Not in Formation. At the approach of the Color, persons not in formation come to attention, face it, and salute when within saluting distance; if you are passing the Color, continue at attention and salute within the proper distance. Construe this distance literally. Hold your salute and keep your head and eyes turned smartly toward the Color until it has passed or has been passed by six paces. In civilian clothes, render the civilian salute with headgear held over your left breast.

Dipping the Battle or Organizational Color. In military ceremonies, battle and organizational colors (see chapter 10) are dipped in salute during the playing of the National Anthem or "Retreat" (in place of the National Anthem), "To the Color," or "Hail to the Chief"; when rendering honors to the organizational commander or an individual of higher rank; and, during military funerals only, on each occasion when the funeral escort presents arms.

On these occasions, when passing in review, the battle color or organizational color (but never the National Color) is dipped when six paces from the individual receiving the salute and remains dipped until six paces beyond.

Dipping the National Ensign. The National Color or Ensign is never in any circumstances permitted to touch the ground or deck. At sea, however, it is customary for merchantmen to dip their Colors when passing close aboard a warship, and, in reply, the warship runs its Ensign halfway down and then back up again. This is the only time when a National Color or Ensign may be dipped.

You will find additional information dealing with flags, colors, and standards in chapter 10, while a section below covers the execution of Morning and Evening Colors, the daily ceremonies that take place when the flag is raised and lowered.

⋄⋄ *Displaying the Flag*

Routine Guidelines. Throughout the Navy and Marine Corps, the National Ensign is displayed from 0800 to sunset (ships under way, however, fly the Ensign continuously). On shore, the flag is flown at base or station headquarters, at other major command headquarters, and/or at the headquarters of the most senior officer when two or more commands are located so close together that separate flags would be inappropriate. Outlying commands or activities display the National Color to make clear their governmental character.

Except when intentionally lowered to half-staff (some may be more accustomed to the interchangeable British term "half-mast," which in American usage refers primarily to the flag's position when flown on board ship) the flag must be "two-blocked" at all times—that is, it must be hoisted and secured at the very top of the staff, or gaff, since any flag not so secured is technically considered to be at half-staff (see figure 11-6). Display of the flag at half-staff indicates official mourning. On Memorial Day, the flag is at half-staff until the completion of the required gun salute or until noon, if no salute is fired.

The position of half-staff is midway between the peak (or truck) and the base of the flagstaff except when the latter has yardarms or is supported by guys, stays, or shrouds, in which case half-staff is halfway between the peak and the yardarm or the point at which guys, stays, or shrouds join the staff.

The church pennant is the only flag ever flown above the Ensign. It is hoisted at the sounding of "Church Call" for divine services on shipboard, and the National Color is lowered to a position just under the church pennant. When divine services have concluded, the church pennant is hauled down and the National Color is two-blocked.

Colors must never be allowed to become fouled. It is an important responsibility of the guard to prevent this. To avoid fouling, they should be raised or lowered from the leeward side of the pole. Should it become necessary to exchange a National Color already hoisted, a new one is first run up on a second halyard, which is why flagpoles have two sets of halyards, and the original is lowered as soon as the new one has been two-blocked.

It is a recognized international distress signal afloat or ashore, as sanctioned by law, to fly the National Ensign upside down.

In Battle. It is a very old tradition, although no longer prescribed by Navy Regulations, that on joining action, ships break out the National Ensign at the truck of each mast. The spirit of this tradition should be observed on shore. Any position under attack at which the Color is normally flown should keep the Color flying throughout action, night and day, just as the original star-spangled banner flew throughout the night over Fort McHenry at Baltimore (where Marines formed one of the defending units).

Half-Staffing the Flag. First, two-block the flag at the truck (top) of the staff, keeping it there until the last note of the National Anthem or "To the Color," then lower it to the half-staff position. When lowering the flag from half-staff, hoist it smartly to the truck at the first note of the music, then lower it in the regular manner (as described in the next section).

Displaying the Flag. The National Color is always on the right (to your left as you face the displayed flags). If other flags are flown from adjacent poles, the American flag will be the first one raised and the last one lowered.

When displayed from crossed staffs, the National Color is on the right, and the staff is in front of the staff of the other flag with which it is crossed.

When displayed over a street, the blue field (or "union") of the flag should point north on a street running east–west and point east on a street running north–south.

When used to drape a coffin, the flag should be placed so that the union would cover the head and left shoulder of the body within.

Foreign Flags. Except in cases of official ceremonies, the carrying of foreign flags by members of the U.S. armed forces is not authorized. An example of an official ceremony would be the arrival or departure of a foreign head of state. Rulings as to whether given events may be considered official ceremonies should be obtained from Marine Corps Headquarters.

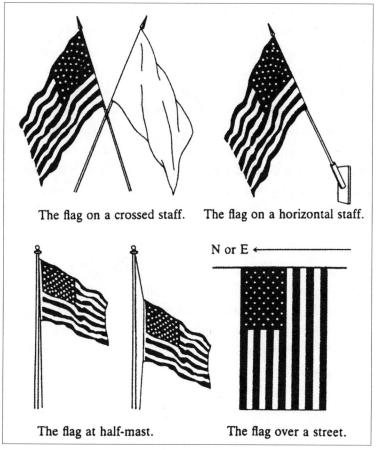

The flag on a crossed staff.   The flag on a horizontal staff.

The flag at half-mast.   The flag over a street.

FIGURE 11-6. Displaying the Flag

⅄ ⅄ *Morning and Evening Colors*

Colors are the most important daily ceremonies and must be conducted with precision and formality. Executing Colors is the responsibility of the guard of the day and should be personally supervised by the commander of the guard (see chapter 16). Honors to be rendered by individuals and formations are described in the present chapter.

Raising the Flag (Morning Colors). The color detail, a noncommissioned officer and two junior Marines, forms at the guardhouse, with the NCO (carrying the folded Color) in the center. The color guard marches to the flagstaff, halts, and fastens the flag to the halyards. The halyards are manned by the two Marines, and the NCO holds the flag until it is hauled free of his or her grasp. The NCO must see that the Color never touches the ground.

At precisely 0800, the signal to execute Colors is given from the guardhouse by the corporal of the relief on watch. The field music then makes eight bells, and, after the last stroke, the National Anthem or "To the Color" begins, and the flag is hoisted smartly. When the flag is clear, the NCO comes to hand salute. As soon as the flag is two-blocked, the Marines manning halyards likewise come to hand salute and hold this position. Hand salutes and present arms, if any, end on the last musical note, after which "Carry On" is sounded, and the halyards are secured. In saluting during Colors, members of the color detail should salute normally and avoid looking up at the Color.

In the absence of a band, the National Anthem or "To the Color" is sounded by field music. If no music is present, the signals for attention, hand salute, and carry on must be given by whistle, which should be regarded as a procedure of last resort. Even if your unit does not rate or include music, you should make every effort to obtain a bugle and train a nonrated Marine to sound the calls required for Colors.

Lowering the Flag (Evening Colors). Evening Colors is executed by the same guard detail as Morning Colors, and the ceremony is virtually a reverse performance of the latter. The flag is lowered precisely at sunset, the exact daily time of which should be kept in a table in the guardhouse. Beginning with the first note of the music, the flag is slowly lowered, in time with the music, so that it will be in the hands of the NCO of the color guard as the last note sounds. In the absence of a band, "Retreat" is sounded by field music.

After being lowered, the flag is folded in the shape of a cocked hat. Figure 11-7 depicts the correct procedure for folding the National Color.

Standing lights (such as streetlights and aircraft obstruction lights) throughout the base should not be turned on until after the last note of Evening Colors.

❯ ❯ *Displaying Personal Flags or Pennants*

At Commands Ashore. The personal flag or pennant of a general or flag officer is displayed, day and night, in the headquarters area (usually from a staff on the

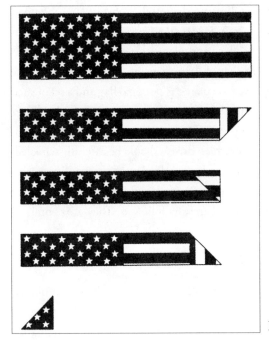

FIGURE 11-7. Folding the Flag

headquarters building). When an officer entitled to a personal flag makes an official visit or inspection at some other activity of the command, the personal flag is hauled down and shifted to the activity that the officer is visiting. If this latter activity is commanded by a flag or general officer, the senior officer's personal flag displaces that of the local commander.

When a foreign ensign or personal flag is displayed ashore during an official visit by, or gun salute to, a foreign officer or civil official, it is broken at the normal point of display of the local commander's flag or pennant, and the latter is shifted to some other point within the command.

If the points of display of two or more personal flags are so close together that it would be inappropriate to fly them in competition, so to speak, the senior officer's personal flag is displayed alone. Similarly, if two or more civil officials who rate personal flags are present officially at the same time, only the flag of the senior is broken.

On Vehicles. Any officer entitled to a personal flag or pennant may display this forward on a vehicle in which he or she is riding officially. Alternatively, one may mount plates, forward and aft, bearing the number of stars appropriate to rank. Marine Corps and Army generals have scarlet plates (but the arrangement of stars on Marine general officers' flags and plates corresponds to that of flag officers of the Navy rather than to that of Army generals). Navy and Air Force flag officers and general officers have blue plates. A personal flag and a set of such plates are never displayed at the same time from the same car. When the officer who rates the flag or plates is not in the car, the flag should be furled and cased, and the plates cased. This is a point on which drivers should be carefully schooled.

On Board Ship or in Boats. The rules for display of personal flags and pennants afloat are beyond the scope of the *Guide*. It suffices to say that they are complex and precise, and they must be carefully followed. They are contained in Navy Regulations.

➤ HONORS, VISITS, AND CALLS

As a junior officer, your first contacts with honors, official visits, and official calls will probably occur on board ship or when you find yourself detailed to command a guard of honor. Like all military etiquette, the subject demands precise attention and compliance with every rule. Because the Marine Corps prides itself on being the most military of the services, make a point to know and observe all the ins and outs of honors and official visits.

The following definitions relate to honors, official visits, and official calls.

Honors: A formal ceremony performed to honor an important person.

Official visit: A formal visit of courtesy that requires special honors and ceremonies.

Official call: An official but informal visit of courtesy that does not require honors or ceremony. Note the distinction between official calls, discussed in this chapter, and personal calls, which are covered briefly in chapter 21.

Guard of the day: For rendering honors, Navy Regulations provides that the guard of the day (normally not part of the interior guard except on board ship) shall be not less than one rifle squad.

Full guard: Not less than one rifle platoon.

Guard of honor: Any guard not part of the interior guard that is paraded ashore for rendition of honors. When the interior guard turns out in compliment to an individual, it is spoken of as "the guard," not as a guard of honor.

Compliment of the guard: This honor consists of an interior guard turning out and presenting arms as a compliment to visiting officers or civilian dignitaries.

Shipboard compliments: In addition to honors by a guard, shipboard compliments may include any or all of the following elements, which are normally dispensed with ashore:

- Manning the rail on weather decks by the ship's company
- Piping alongside and over the side
- Side boys

Because Marines *in a ship's company* are fully occupied with other elements of rendering honors to visitors, these shipboard compliments are performed only by Navy officers and enlisted personnel. Embarked Marines often *do* participate in manning the rail on board ship.

❖ ❖ *Rendering Honors*

Arrangements for rendering honors ashore are usually coordinated by the commanding general's aide. At a base or unit not commanded by a general officer, arrangements are made by the adjutant. Ashore and afloat, we render the same salutes, honors, and ceremonies, as practical, at Marine Corps bases and stations and in naval ships and stations.

Wherever Marines are present, they provide the honor guard. It goes without saying that troops paraded as honor guards must be the best. See to it that your guard is correct, precise, and immaculate—a reflection of the Corps at its smartest.

Preparations. The general's aide (or the adjutant) normally has ample advance notice to prepare for an official visit that requires honors and to notify those concerned. Ashore, the casual or surprise official visit is rare.

When detailed to command an honor guard, you should immediately visit the aide (or report to the adjutant) and obtain all possible information. Check with the bandmaster on the timing of ruffles and flourishes and with the NCO in charge of the saluting battery. If the saluting guns are remote from the honor guard's parade, see that absolutely foolproof communications are established between the parade and the saluting battery. It is elementary—but vital—that the saluting battery knows how many guns are to be fired. Additionally, ensure that a standby piece (if available) and spare rounds are in instant readiness to fire in the event of hangfire or malfunction of a saluting gun.

Reconnoiter the honor guard's parade, and know exactly where the guard and band and the recipients of honors are to be posted. Determine what markers and guidons are required and who will supply and locate them. If possible, give your platoon leaders and leading NCOs an opportunity to look over the ground. If you are going to provide an escort of honor, verify the route of march.

As to the guard itself, spare no effort to make it the finest in the Marine Corps. See that every person is immaculately turned out, that the guard is perfectly sized, and that the entire formation, if possible, is adequately rehearsed. If troops for the guard come from units other than your own, have no hesitation in returning substandard individuals to their units, reporting this action (and why) to the adjutant.

Procedure for Honors on an Official Visit Ashore. The following general procedure can serve as a guide for rendering honors ashore. Remember, however, that almost every organization has its ground rules and standing operating procedures, so be sure to consult these when preparing to render honors.

1. Well before the time of arrival of the visiting official, complete the preparations discussed above, parade your guard and band, have the color detail standing by to break or haul down personal flags involved, and have the saluting battery manned and ready. If possible, especially on a large base, have communications that can apprise you, up to the last moment, of the visitor's movements and approach.

2. When the recipient of honors arrives and debarks from boat, train, car, plane, or helicopter, "Attention" is sounded by bugle. The local commander (or whoever is receiving the dignitary) greets that individual and conducts him or her to the post front and center of the guard.

3. When the official takes post, the commander of the honor guard brings the guard to present arms. All hands in the vicinity, but not those in formation, come to hand salute, following the motions of the guard.

4. When the guard has been presented and the commander has executed the salute, the band sounds off with ruffles, flourishes, and other musical honors. The personal flag or National Color, as specified for the dignitary, is broken on the first note of the music.

5. The guard is brought to order arms after the last note of the music, or when the commander of the guard has exchanged salutes with the official, if there is no music. If a gun salute is rendered, the first gun is fired immediately after the last note of the music, and the guard remains at present arms throughout the salute, as do all hands in the official party who hold salutes throughout the gun salute. Persons not in the official party, but in the immediate vicinity, remain at attention during the gun salute. If the National Color, or a foreign flag or ensign, is to be displayed during the gun salute only, it is broken on the first gun and hauled down on the last.

6. On completion of the musical honors or the gun salute, if fired, the honor guard commander brings the guard to order arms, executes present sword to the person being honored, and reports, "Sir, the honor guard is formed." If the personage desires neither to inspect the guard nor that it pass in review, the honor guard remains at attention. For the procedure to be followed for marching the guard in review or for its inspection by the personage, see the *Marine Corps Drill and Ceremonies Manual*.

Honors on Departure from an Official Visit Ashore. In general, departure honors reverse those given on arrival.

1. Departure honors commence when the visiting official has completed personal leave-taking from the senior officer present. Either the latter officer or the aide will signal this to the commander of the guard.

2. Gun salutes, if rendered on departure, must begin before the individual actually leaves (that is, while within earshot). The personal flag, or any national ensign displayed, is hauled down on the last gun.

3. An honor guard is not normally inspected on departure. Hold the guard on parade until the official is out of sight.

Pointers on Honors, Ashore and Afloat. Your "bible" for honors incident to official visits and calls is Navy Regulations. The table of honors and ceremonies here (table 11-2) is a compilation of the information in those articles, assembled for quick reference. You must be meticulously familiar with the *Drill and Ceremonies Manual*, which gives detailed instructions for rendering all types of honors.

In addition to guards paraded in receiving the president, any foreign sovereign or chief of state, or member of a reigning royal family, all officers not required elsewhere form on the left of the honor guard, in dress uniform with swords. Troops not otherwise occupied should form on parades adjacent to the guest's route of inspection and also line the route. On board ship, persons not manning the rail fall in at quarters.

The officer of the day or officer of the deck attends the arrival and departure of any distinguished visitor, whether or not the visit is official.

Afloat, side honors only (that is, side boys only, no guard or band) are rendered when a general officer, flag officer, or another commanding officer comes on board without flag or pennant flying. If so requested, full honors may be rendered on departure; otherwise, side honors only are again the rule. While side honors are being rendered, all hands on deck and in view of the gangway stand at attention, facing the gangway; they salute as the officer reaches the top of the accommodation ladder or brow and remain at the hand salute until the end of the boatswain's pipe, following the motions of the side boys.

Honors are dispensed with

- when the visiting dignitary visits the base unofficially;
- between sunset and 0800 (except that foreign officers may be rendered honors at any time during daylight);
- during meal hours for the troops (except in the case of foreign officers);
- when a ship is engaged in maneuvers or general drills, undergoing overhaul in a navy yard, or in action;
- when a unit or installation ashore is carrying on tactical exercises or emergency drills; or
- on Sundays or national holidays (except in the case of foreign officers).

Honors in the Field. Despite the rigors of field service, Marine units make every effort to render appropriate honors even when so serving. The spirit, if not the letter, of the preceding paragraphs must be faithfully observed. It is the distinguishing mark of high-spirited, professional troops that when in the face of handicaps and obvious obstacles to smartness, they nevertheless remain smart and military and do the best they can with what they have. Marines in the field may well remember what was said of England's Brigade of Guards: "They die with their boots clean."

TABLE 11-2. Honors for Official Visits

| | | Gun salute | | | | | | | | | Flag | | |
Rank	Uniform	Arrival	Departure	Ruffles and flourishes	Music	Guard	Side boys	Crew	Within what limits	What	Which truck	During
President	Full dress	21	21	4	National anthem*	Full	8	Man rail[1,2]	....	President's	Main	Visit
President or sovereign of a foreign country	do.	21	21	4	Foreign national anthem	do.	8	do.	....	Foreign ensign	do.	do.
Member of reigning royal family	do.	21	21	4	do.	do.	8	do.	....	do.	do.	Salute
Ex-president or president-elect	do.	21	21	4	Admiral's march	do.	8	Quarters	....	National	do.	do.
Secretary of state when acting as special foreign representative of the president	Full dress	19	19	4	National anthem	Full	8	Quarters[3]	....	Secretary's	Main	Visit
Vice president	do.	...	19	4	Admiral's march	do.	8	do.	....	Vice president's	do.	do.
Speaker of the House of Representatives	do.	...	19	4	do.	do.	8	....	....	National	Fore	Salute
Governor of a state of the United States	do.	...	19	4	do.	do.	8	....	Area under governor's jurisdiction	do.	do.	do.
Chief Justice of the United States	do.	...	19	4	do.	do.	8	....	....	do.	do.	do.
Ambassador, high commissioner, or special diplomatic representative whose credentials give him or her authority equal to or greater than an ambassador	do.	...	19	4	National anthem	do.	8	....	Nation or nations to which accredited	do.	do.	do.
Secretary of defense	do.	19	19	4	Honors march†	do.	8	Quarters	....	Secretary's	Main	Visit
Deputy secretary of defense	do.	19	19	4	do.	do.	8	do.	....	Dep. secy.'s	do.	do.
Prime minister or other cabinet officer of a foreign country	Dress	...	19	4	Admiral's march	do.	8	....	....	Foreign ensign	Fore	Salute
Cabinet officer other than secretary of defense	do.	19	19	4	do.	do.	8	Quarters	....	National	do.	do.
Secretary of the Navy	Full dress	19	19	4	Honors march†	do.	8	do.	....	Secretary's	Main	Visit
Secretary of the Army or Air Force	Dress	19	19	4	do.	do.	8	do.	....	National	Fore	Salute
President pro tempore of the Senate	do.	...	19	4	do.	do.	8	....	....	do.	do.	do.
Assistant secretary of defense	Dress	17	17	4	Honors march†	Full	8	Quarters	....	Asst. Secy.'s	Main	Visit
Under secretary and assistant secretaries of the Navy	do.	17	17	4	do.	do.	8	do.	....	Under or asst. secy.'s	Main	Visit

TABLE 11-2. Honors for Official Visits (continued)

Rank	Uniform	Gun salute Arrival	Gun salute Departure	Arrival on Board or Departure Ruffles and flourishes	Music	Guard	Side boys	Crew	Within what limits	Flag What	Flag Which truck	Flag During
Under or assistant secretary of the Army or Air Force	do.	17	17	4	do.	do.	8		Area under official's jurisdiction	National	Fore	Salute
Governor general or governor of territory, commonwealth, or possession of the U.S. or area under the administration of the U.S.	do.		17	4	Admiral's march	do.	8			do.	do.	do.
Committee of Congress	do.		17	4	do.	do.	8			do.	do.	do.
Envoy extraordinary and minister plenipotentiary	Dress		15	3	Admiral's march	Full	8		Nation to which accredited	National	Fore	Salute
Minister resident	do.		13	2	do.	do.	6		do.	do.	do.	do.
Charge d'affaires	do.		11	1	do.	do.	6		do.	do.	do.	do.
Career minister or counselor of embassy or legation	do.			1	do.	do.	6		do.			
Consul general or consul or vice consul when in charge of consulate general	do.		11	1	do.	do.	6		District to which assigned	National	Fore	Salute
First secretary of embassy of legation	Of the day with sword					Of the day	4		Nation to which accredited			
Consul or vice consul when in charge of consulate	do.		7			do.	4		District to which assigned	National	Fore	Salute
Mayor of an incorporated city	do.					do.	4		Within limits of mayoralty			
Second or third secretary of embassy or legation	do.						2		Nation to which accredited			
Vice consul when only representative of the U.S. and not in charge of consulate or consulate general	do.		5			Of the day	2		District to which assigned	National	Fore	Salute
Consular agent when only representative of the U.S.	do.						2		do.			
Military and Naval Officers, United States and Foreign[4,7]												
Chairman of the JCS	Dress	19[8,9]	19[8,9]	4	Admiral's march[10]	Full	8	Quarters				
Chief of Staff, U.S. Army	do.	19	19	4	General's march	do.	8	do.				
Chief of Naval Operations	do.	19	19	4	Admiral's march	do.	8	do.				
Chief of Staff, U.S. Air Force	do.	19	19	4	General's march	do.	8	do.				
Commandant of the Marine Corps	do.	19	19	4	Admiral's march	do.	8	do.				
Fleet Admiral or General of the Army or the Air Force	Dress	19	19	4	Admiral's march[10]	Full	8	Quarters		For United States officers, personal flag at the main during the salute		
Admiral or general	do.		17	4	do.	do.	8					
Naval or other military governor, commissioned as such by the president, within area under jurisdiction	do.		17	4	do.	do.	8					
Vice admiral or lieutenant general	do.		15	3	do.	do.	8[11]					

TABLE 11-2. (continued)

| | Arrival on Board or Departure | | | | | | | | | | | |
| | Gun salute | | Ruffles and flourishes | Music | Guard | Side boys | Crew | Within what limits | Flag | | |
Rank	Uniform	Arrival	Departure							What	Which truck	During
Rear admiral or major general	do.	....	13	2	do.	do.	6	....	....	For officers of foreign nations, the foreign ensign at the fore during the salute		
Rear admiral (lower half) or brigadier general	do.	....	11	1	do.	do.	6	....	....			
Captain, commander, colonel or lieutenant colonel	Undress					Of the day	4	....	....			
Other commissioned officers	Of the day with sword					do.	2	....	....			

Official not herein provided for .... Honors as prescribed by the senior officer present; such honors normally shall be those accorded the foreign official, when visiting officially a ship of own nation, but a gun salute, if prescribed, shall not exceed 19 guns.

Foreign officer of the armed forces, diplomatic or consular representative in country to which accredited, or other distinguished foreign official — Honors for an official or officer of the United States of the same grade, except, that equivalent honors shall be rendered to foreign officers who occupy a position comparable to Chairman JCS, CNO, Chief of Staff Army, Chief of Staff Air Force, or CMC.

NOTES

1. All other ships present man rail and fire national salute at official reception or departure of president.

2. For president of United States, president of a foreign republic, foreign sovereign or member of reigning royal family, officers assembled on quarterdeck in full dress, crew man rail, and other officers unemployed formed forward of guard, personnel not occupied fall in at quarters.

3. For others for whom full dress uniform is prescribed designated officers assembled on quarterdeck and formed forward of guard.

4. When side honors only are rendered to a flag or commanding officer, officers and personnel on deck and in view from the gangway shall stand attention facing the gangway, and salute as the officer appears over the side and shall remain at the salute until the end of the pipe.

5. All honors except attendance at the gangway by the officer of the deck, except as social courtesy may demand, shall be dispensed with:
   a. When officers are in plainclothes.
   b. From sunset to 0800 (except that for foreign officers, side shall be piped during daylight).
   c. During meal hours of the crew for officers of U.S. Navy or Marine Corps.
   d. When exercising at general drills or when undergoing Navy Yard overhaul, for officers of USN and USMC.
   e. For ships with less than 180 personnel in the seaman branch, for officers of USN, USMC, USCG, USA, and USAF, except when advance notice of an official visit had been received.

6. The guard and band shall not be paraded on Sunday for USN, USMC, USCG, USA, or USAF officers.

7. All sentries on the upper deck or in view from outside shall salute all commissioned officers passing them close aboard, in boats or otherwise.

8. If a flag or commanding officer comes on board without flag or pennant flying, only side honors shall be giving unless officer should request full honors on departure. All persons on the quarterdeck shall stand at attention by command without bugle.

9. No officer in civilian clothes shall be saluted with guns or have a guard paraded in his or her honor.

10. Admirals and Marine Corps generals recieve the "Admiral's March", generals (Army/Air Force) recieve the "General's March."

11. The officer of the deck shall attend at the gangway on the arrival or departure of any commissioned officer or distinguished visitor.

* "Hail to the Chief" may be used in lieu of national anthem on either arrival or departure. When specified by the president, "Hail to the Chief" may be used while the president and immediate party move to or from their places while all others stand fast.

† Honors march is a 32-bar medley in the trio of "The Stars and Stripes Forever."

For rendering honors in the field, here are the most important points:

- Marines should be in clean, homogeneous uniforms.
- Equipment (especially weapons) should be first class and serviceable.
- Individuals should be smart, alert, and clean.
- The place for rendering honors should not be subject to enemy observation.
- Military readiness or combat operations should not be interrupted.

❯ ❯ *Official Visits and Calls Ashore*

Official visits and official calls, as we discuss them here, are paid only by officers in command. Generally speaking, official visits are more often paid by commanders afloat, whereas on shore, official calls are substituted.

On taking over a command, you must make an official call on the senior to whom you have reported for duty. This call is at the senior's headquarters and is not the domestic "visit of courtesy" that is customary.

Additionally, unless the senior indicates otherwise, there are traditionally five other occasions when official calls are required:

1. By the commander of an arriving unit on his or her immediate superior, if present, and on the senior Marine or Navy officer present
2. By commanding officers on an immediate superior in the chain of command upon arrival of the latter
3. By an officer, who has been senior officer present, upon his or her successor
4. By the commander of a unit or ship arriving at a Marine Corps installation or naval station upon the commander of such activity; when the arriving commander is senior, however, the local commander makes the call
5. On high civil officials (state and territorial governors and U.S. diplomatic and consular officials) as prescribed in Navy Regulations

When in the vicinity of a command ashore belonging to another U.S. armed service or to a friendly foreign power, the senior Marine officer present in command arranges with the other commander concerned for an exchange of official visits or calls as appropriate. Check Navy Regulations for calling procedure on foreign officials.

Official calls or visits must be paid expeditiously as they become due or on the first working day thereafter. They must be returned within twenty-four hours or on the first subsequent working day.

Circumstances permitting, flag officers personally return official visits or calls by officers of the rank of colonel or higher. The chief of staff or deputy commander returns official calls or visits by officers below colonel. Officers below flag rank return all calls and visits in person. High foreign officials (other than chiefs of state) personally return visits or calls by a general or an admiral; otherwise, they return such visits by a suitable representative.

Before making or returning an official visit or call, check both Navy Regulations and *Marine Corps Uniform Regulations* for the proper uniform. If unable to get access to these publications, or if you cannot find your answer, you will never be far wrong wearing undress blue or white, according to season and climate.

Before you make or receive an official call or visit ashore, be sure to have all arrangements taken care of well in advance. This requires liaison between the maker and the recipient of the call, which is up to the aide or the adjutant, as the case may be. Coordinate the following details especially:

- Time and exact place for the call
- Uniform
- Entrance to base, station, and headquarters that caller will use
- Transportation
- Honor guard, if required
- Use of calling cards (somewhat archaic, but may still be in fashion in some locales)
- Refreshments to be served, if any
- Specific units, places, or installations to be visited
- Arrangements to break or haul down personal flags or to fire gun salutes

❯ CEREMONIES

Ceremonial duties are written deep into the Corps' history. Marines have always excelled in this field, and we have good reason to be proud of and carry on this record. Every officer taking part in a ceremony—especially when, as is often the case, little time is available for practice—should realize how broadly revealing of wider professionalism our parade ground performance can be. Precision drill, immaculately turned-out troops, disciplined marching, and fine bearing—all these furnish, for the public to see, evidence of Marine Corps alertness, determination, and pride in Corps and selves. It is no coincidence that among the units and corps famous for ceremonial prowess are also found some of the world's most redoubtable fighting formations.

❯ ❯ *Types of Ceremonies*

The Marine Corps and Navy have eight military ceremonies that may be performed on shore. These ceremonies are in the form prescribed by the *Marine Corps Drill and Ceremonies Manual* and may be modified only when the nature of the ground or exceptional circumstances require that changes be made.

The title and a brief description or discussion of each ceremony follow.

Review. This is a ceremony at which a command or several commands parade for inspection by, and in honor of, a senior officer or in honor of a visitor or a civilian dignitary. In a review, the individual being honored passes on foot or in a vehicle throughout the formation, which is then marched past the honoree.

Presentation of Decorations. This ceremony follows, in part, the procedures prescribed for a review; it is noteworthy in that regardless of rank, the individuals who have been decorated receive the review side by side with the reviewing officer. In modified form, this ceremony can be adapted for such occasions as presentation of commissions or enlisted warrants, commendations, and so forth.

Parade. Here, the CO of a battalion or larger unit forms and drills the entire command and then marches them in review. The battalion parade is the most common form of periodic ceremony, and under normal garrison conditions in days past, it was traditionally performed each Saturday morning. Together with guard mounting, described below, the parade is probably the most important ceremony for you to know by heart. "Memorize every comma in it!" Captain Lewis "Chesty" Puller used to enjoin his Basic School lieutenants.

Escort of the National Color. It is also known less formally as "Marching on (or off) the Colors." When the Color are to take part in a ceremony, be presented to a unit, or turned over to some institution or person for safekeeping, they are ceremonially received and transported from their place of safekeeping (usually the CO's headquarters), and are similarly returned there, by a picked escort. The ceremony for this occasion corresponds somewhat to portions of the famous British ceremony Trooping the Color, from which it is derived.

Escort of Honor. This is the ceremonial escorting of a senior officer or other dignitary during an official visit or on arrival or departure.

Military Funerals. Covered thoroughly in the *Drill and Ceremonies Manual*, the present chapter and chapter 20 of the *Guide* describe selected aspects of this solemn ceremony. The ceremonial forms followed in military funerals are among the oldest in the profession of arms; some parts, such as the firing of volleys (originally to frighten away evil spirits) can be traced to pagan times.

Inspections. As described in chapter 15, inspections run to all types. The ceremonial inspection of troops in ranks has as its object the general military appearance and condition of individual uniforms and equipment within a command. Officers headed for sea duty should note that personnel inspection on board ship follows considerably different lines and frequently varies from ship to ship. Be sure you know your ship's ground rules and inspection procedure.

Guard Mounting. Through this ceremony a guard is organized from guard details, is inspected, and then relieves an outgoing or "old" guard. This is a very old ceremony, portions of which antedate the Revolutionary War and go back to the British Army. Guard mounts may be *formal* or *informal*, according to weather, size of guard, availability of music, or local conditions.

Morning and Evening Colors. As described earlier, these ceremonies are sometimes regarded as parts of the daily routine. They should, however, be conducted with the same gravity as all ceremonies, if only out of respect to the significance of the daily raising and lowering of the National Ensign.

In addition to the foregoing ceremonies of general character, Marines employ specific ceremonial forms on the occasions of *change of command, relief of the sergeant major*, and the *celebration of the Marine Corps birthday*.

Another form of ceremony not covered in any official regulations is the *tattoo*, sometimes called the searchlight tattoo. A tattoo is an evening parade conducted under floodlights or searchlights; embellished with traditional, historic, or display drills and special musical features; and usually climaxed by lowering of the Color, playing of "Taps," and sometimes singing a traditional evening hymn. The Friday Evening Parades at Marine Barracks Washington ("Eighth and Eye"), though not so named, are in fact a form of tattoo.

❧ ❧ *Precedence of Forces in Parades or Ceremonies*

To avoid conflicts at parades or ceremonies, places of honor are allocated in order of service seniority. Because you may readily find yourself at the head of a Marine detachment on such occasions, you should know your own place and those of other components relative to your own. Army Regulation 600-25, *Salutes, Honors, and Visits of Courtesy*, is a good reference. The precedence of U.S. forces in parades or ceremonies is as follows (reading from the head to rear of column, or from right to left in line):

1. Cadets, U.S. Military Academy
2. Midshipmen, U.S. Naval Academy
3. Cadets, U.S. Air Force Academy
4. Cadets, U.S. Coast Guard Academy
5. Midshipmen, U.S. Merchant Marine Academy
6. U.S. Army
7. U.S. Marine Corps
8. U.S. Navy
9. U.S. Air Force
10. U.S. Coast Guard
11. Army National Guard of the United States
12. Army Reserve
13. Marine Corps Reserve
14. Naval Reserve
15. Air National Guard of the United States
16. Air Force Reserve
17. Coast Guard Reserve
18. Other training organizations of the Army, Marine Corps, Navy, Air Force, and Coast Guard, in that order

When the Coast Guard is serving as part of the Navy in time of war or emergency, the precedence of its units and personnel shifts to position immediately after Navy units and personnel.

As a Marine, you should bear in mind that although the Air Force is one of the three larger services, it is nevertheless junior in ceremonial precedence to the Marine Corps. Never accept erroneous assignment of fourth, or junior, place to Marines following Air Force units, as is sometimes carelessly done on the basis of size.

The place of honor is the head of column or right of the line, and foreign units should be assigned that post of honor in any American ceremony or procession. Where several foreign units of mixed nationality are present, they should be placed in alphabetical order and ahead of any U.S. forces if the ceremony is conducted by U.S. forces or on American soil.

The official who organizes and coordinates a street parade or procession is known as the grand marshal, or sometimes, the marshal. If your unit is misplaced, this official should rectify the mistake.

❖ ❖ *General Appearance of Troops and Units*

The Marine Corps has long enjoyed a worldwide reputation for smart appearance and soldierly performance of every task. This reputation has been enhanced by continually demonstrating to the American public that our execution of peacetime functions is excelled only by our performance in battle.

During peacetime, the reputation of the Corps is maintained to a considerable degree by creating favorable, highly military impressions in parades, ceremonies, and other functions. It is therefore a responsibility of all officers, and especially commanding officers, that marching units in the public eye fully meet the standards by which the Marine Corps is measured. Those in key positions must have perfect posture, troop leaders must excel in command presence, and uniforms and equipment must be outstanding in condition and appearance. All such public displays should be preceded by ample drill and specific rehearsal as needed.

❖ ❖ *Pointers on Ceremonies*

Close-Order Drill. The object of drill is to teach troops by exercise to obey orders and to do so in the correct way. For this reason, slovenly drill is harmful. Close-order drill is one foundation of discipline and esprit de corps. Well-executed, confident, precise ceremonial close-order drill is therefore the foundation of success in ceremonies.

Know Your Parade Ground. If possible, you should personally reconnoiter the parade ground or area where a ceremony is to be held and conduct a rehearsal there. At a minimum, be sure your leading NCOs and unit guides know the layout and how the field will be marked.

Markers. Dress guidons (see chapter 10) mark the boundaries and the reviewing point for a parade ground. In addition, it is sometimes customary to place small metal discs on the ground to mark the posts of unit guides and other key personnel. The adjutant places markers and guidons, but every officer and NCO must know this system and its layout. In addition, guides and leaders should know the lineup of "landmarks" adjacent to and visible from the parade ground so as to be able to march in exactly straight lines and columns without wavering to right or left. Guides and leaders should keep their heads up and their lines of sight directly to the front and well out so as to be able to "navigate" on guidons, markers, and landmarks.

"Officers Center." This challenging precision movement should be rehearsed until all concerned can execute it perfectly. Every individual participant is on display, and this evolution comes at the high point of the parade. Properly executed, "Officers Center" should seem to be the movement of a single Marine. Manuals of sword and guidon count here as at no other time.

Cadence. The regulation cadence is 120 steps per minute, and this is the "tempo" at which a military band plays marches. That is, the bass drummer hits the drum 120 times per minute, with a heavier downbeat or thump on the first and succeeding alternate beats. For parades or ceremonies, it makes for smarter appearance to have a short, snappy step and, if possible, a slightly accelerated cadence. When the band is not playing, individual foot movements during a ceremony, notably those by the adjutant when taking post, are traditionally executed at markedly accelerated cadence with short steps.

Stepping Off in Time with the Music. Units must step off on the left foot, as is well known, and must accomplish this on command of the leader and on the first beat of the music, a combination that often defeats inexperienced junior leaders—but one that you, as a Marine, must perfect.

One method of achieving this result, which requires briefing your unit and some worthwhile rehearsing, is to give your preliminary command just in advance of the music and have all hands drilled to step off automatically on the first note of the music without any command of execution from you; in other words, to let the *first note of the music be the command of execution*. This is particularly effective on parade after the commands have been given to pass in review.

For guard mounting, as well as for many other ceremonies where units march on to their parades to music, troops must be brought to right shoulder arms at the first note of "Adjutant's Call" and marched off at the first note of march music. This, too, requires coordination by leader and unit. A recommended sequence for these evolutions—"by the numbers"—is summarized as follows:

- Bear in mind that "Adjutant's Call" is a sixteen-beat call, and the first note of march music therefore will be count seventeen.
- The signal for the first note of "Adjutant's Call" is given by the drum major, who brings down the baton and can thus be seen by all hands.
- Give your commands in time with "Adjutant's Call," on successive beats as shown in the diagram, in which numbers correspond to beats in the call.

1	2	3	4
Right	Shoul-	der	*Arms*
5	6	7	8
(troops execute the movement)			
9	10	11	12
(pause)			
13	14	15	16
For-	ward	(pause)	*March.*

Rehearse this a few times with music, and in the old Marine phrase, "You've got it made."

Music Played during "Sound Off." At a review or parade, when a foreign visitor or officer of another service is being honored, the march played during "Sound Off" should, if possible, be one traditional to the officer's country or branch of service. At ceremonies conducted by Marine artillery units, "The Caisson Song" is normally played at this time. For a parade on the occasion of a Marine's retirement, it is a pleasant and appropriate courtesy to ascertain whether there is any particular march the officer would like to have played on "Sound Off." When several individuals are being so honored, the senior, of course, gets the choice. At the very end of a retirement ceremony, the band should play "Auld Lang Syne."

Command of Mixed Detachments of Sailors and Marines. When a mixed (or composite) detachment of Sailors and Marines is formed for a parade, the Marines occupy their post of seniority and honor at the head of column or on right of line. But the senior line officer present, whether of the Marine Corps or the Navy, according to date of rank, commands the entire detachment. This rule does not apply when Navy and Marines form separate detachments. It usually occurs when a ship parades as a unit of which the Marines form part.

Uniform for Inspections, Parades, and Ceremonies. Where possible, undress or dress uniforms should be prescribed for inspections, parades, and ceremonies. Additionally, swords should be worn on such occasions in preference to pistols and belts. If blues are not authorized for the command, large medals may be prescribed on ceremonial occasions for wear with the service blouse.

Use of Public Address Systems and Amplifiers. In general, except for the largest ceremonies and under special conditions, it is unmilitary to employ a public-address system for commands or other purposes as part of military ceremonies. Regimental and battalion commanders and adjutants should pride themselves on their voice of command and should, if necessary, practice to strengthen its carrying power. Ideally, only the narrator, if the ceremony includes one, will rely on a public-address system.

Photographers. Photographers, both official and otherwise, can do more to detract from the formality and solemnity of a military ceremony than anyone else. Keep them under strict control, preferably in a suitably located, controlled vantage point, from which they can get good pictures but will not mar the occasion by roaming freely and potentially interfering with the ceremony.

❯ ❯ *Military Funerals*

Navy and Marine Corps funerals are conducted in accordance with Navy Regulations and the *Marine Corps Drill and Ceremonies Manual*, both of which you should check carefully if, in any role other than that of principal, you are to take part in a military funeral. Chapter 20 of the *Guide* contains administrative information on funerals and burials.

Classification. Military funerals are classified by size and location. The rank and status of the deceased will determine the size of escort and type of ceremony—for example, full, simple, or modified honors. Some next of kin may wish only gravesite honors or a reduced escort; some may not wish the firing of volleys. Such wishes are, of course, governing. Other circumstances and next-of-kin preferences usually determine the location of the military ceremony, that is, church or chapel service (remains received at church and escorted to gravesite), transfer (remains received at station, airport, or cemetery gate and escorted to gravesite), or gravesite (remains conveyed to gravesite by civilian undertaker, with military participation and ceremony at gravesite only).

Uniforms and Equipment. If the organization providing the funeral escort is authorized blues, then the uniforms should be the seasonal blue dress "A" or "B" with mourning band on the left sleeve, if available. Otherwise, the uniform should be service dress with large medals instead of ribbons, if blouse is worn.

Body bearers should not wear bayonets or scabbards.

For difficult terrain, mud, or foul weather, units and individuals—such as body bearers, musicians, and firing party—who must leave paved areas may wear shined boots instead of dress shoes.

Officers of funeral escorts wear a mourning band and mourning sword knot, as do the pallbearers. NCOs armed with the sword wear mourning sword knot only (except if acting as a pallbearer, when a mourning band will also be worn).

When sanctioned by the denomination concerned (as in the case of the Episcopal Church), the officiating clergyman, if so entitled, should wear military ribbons on vestments.

Unit rehearsals obviously cannot be conducted at the church or gravesite, although the various evolutions can be adequately rehearsed on the parade ground. Careful but unobtrusive reconnaissance, however, should be conducted by the adjutant (who acts as officer in charge unless otherwise prescribed) and by the escort commander. All Marines assigned to funeral details—especially the bugler, firing party, and body bearers—must have attained the necessary high standards of individual proficiency in their duties for these occasions.

Musical Honors. If prescribed by Navy Regulations, musical honors are rendered during each transfer of remains into or from hearse or caisson to church (and vice versa) and from hearse or caisson to gravesite. Next of kin should have an opportunity to select hymns or funeral music to be played by the band, but the "Navy Hymn" ("Eternal Father, Strong to Save") always should be included.

Dependents' Funerals. Military honors (firing of volleys and sounding of "Taps") are reserved for deceased military or former military persons. For the funerals of Marine dependents, body bearers may be assigned, and, if desired, the funeral service may be conducted by a Navy chaplain.

Marine Corps body bearers of Marine Barracks Washington prepare to fold the National Color during a full-honors funeral at Arlington National Cemetery, Virginia, for three Vietnam veterans previously unaccounted for.

❯ ❯ *Funeral Escorts*

Officers' Funerals. The basic escort for a deceased officer comprises an escort commander (same rank as deceased, if possible), staff (colonels and flag officers only), band, color guard, body bearers, firing party (eight riflemen with NCO in charge), field music, and personal flag bearer (flag officers only).

Troop escort is as follows for the respective officers.

Major general or senior: Three ceremonial companies (two platoons of three eight-person squads each).

Colonel or senior: Two ceremonial companies composed as above.

Major or senior: One ceremonial company composed as above (escort commander commands company and has no staff).

Company and warrant officers: One ceremonial platoon (three eight-person squads; escort commander serves as platoon leader and has no staff).

Enlisted Marines' funerals. The funeral escort for a deceased enlisted Marine consists of a noncommissioned escort commander (same rank as deceased, or senior), body bearers, firing party (eight riflemen), field music, and, in the case of gunnery sergeants or above, troop escort consisting of a rifle squad.

Simple honors funerals. When next of kin does not desire full honors, the simple honors funeral escort, for all ranks, consists of an escort commander (not above rank of captain), body bearers, firing party, and field music.

⟩ AIDES-DE-CAMP, DUTIES, AND RELATIONSHIPS

Duty as an aide-de-camp (usually shortened as "aide") is one of the most exacting details that a young officer can receive. If you are so assigned, you may take it as a compliment to your military and personal character—one that you must do your best to live up to.

As an aide, you are always on duty, and it is always official, personal, and confidential. Your duties include only those the general you serve personally directs. On the other hand, to succeed you must learn quickly to anticipate your general's desires and needs and take care of them without having to be told. Regardless of the circumstances, your first thoughts should be for your general's safety, reputation, and convenience. Any duty asked of you should therefore be promptly performed.

An aide's duties are diverse and may vary from one general officer to another. Virtually all arrangements that concern the general end up as the aide's responsibilities. Functionally, your job breaks down into scheduling and preparation, paperwork, protocol, and personal needs.

Keeping your general on schedule is of overriding importance; it is also one of your most difficult tasks. Remembering that "punctuality is the politeness of kings," you must stay on top of the itinerary or other program for each hour and minute. For briefings, ensure the general has good background on the subject. For visits, see that he or she is prepared for and familiar with the people one can be expected to meet and, where appropriate, with the missions and general situation of units concerned.

The main job in the realm of paperwork is to keep track of all documents going in or out and, in coordination with the chief of staff, set them into proper priority, depending on deadlines, actions required, and importance.

The responsibilities of protocol and personal needs are covered below.

Aside from your general, the two most important persons with whom you routinely deal are the chief of staff and spouse. Establishment of a cooperative, deferential, helpful relationship with the chief of staff—while being careful never to betray any confidence of the general—is essential.

Intelligence, tact, loyalty, absolute discretion, and military smartness are the most important characteristics of a good aide, with sensible frankness not far behind. Although, by direction, an aide must often serve as an extra pair of eyes and ears for the general, the aide must avoid becoming a "gossip" and should, whenever consistent with loyalty and fairness toward the boss, do the utmost to protect other officers' chance indiscretions from reaching the attention of higher authorities.

Finally, courtesy and thoughtfulness are indispensable attributes in an aide. You should be courteous to all and especially avoid a self-important attitude toward fellow officers.

Because you are expected to be the social arbiter and expert on the staff, you should know and possess a copy of *Service Etiquette* by Cherlynn Conetsco and Anna Hart (Naval Institute Press, 2013), and a copy of *Naval Ceremonies, Customs, and Traditions* by Royal W. Connell and William P. Mack (Naval Institute Press, 2004). These books can be relied on for tested and correct advice in virtually any situation involving service-related social usage or protocol. You should also keep an up-to-date Combined Lineal List, being careful to annotate all promotions, retirements, changes of status, and yearly promotion zones.

❧ ❧ *Duties of an Aide in Garrison*

The following is a useful, albeit incomplete, list of an aide's most significant duties in garrison.

Make a daily appointment schedule for your general (and, if the general desires, save it for record). Keep track of engagements, commitments, and calls to be returned, providing reminders as necessary.

Be responsive by staying as much as possible within earshot of your general.

Whenever anyone calls on the general officially or semiofficially, meet the visitors on arrival and accompany them until their departure.

It is not only proper but also completely in order for you to tactfully invite your boss's attention to anything that may be amiss as to uniform or dress as well as to remind the general of any social amenities or courtesies that may have been overlooked. It is up to you to learn your general's shortcomings and to protect him or her against them.

In cooperation with the chief of staff, supervise the performance of drivers, enlisted aides, and all others who serve the general. Keep them on their toes personally and professionally and weld them into a team. See that the general's office and the outer office are attractive and efficient.

Assist your general and spouse in preparations for all social functions to be given by them. Learn how engaged the general's spouse prefers to be in these functions and ensure your actions complement his or her efforts in their preparation. Supervise the issuance of all invitations, making sure that dates and times are correct and that the desired uniform or costume is correctly specified, and keep track of RSVPs.

On social occasions, keep close by and see that your general and the persons with whom he or she may be talking are supplied with refreshments. In a receiving line, post yourself next to your general, on the approach side. You need not shake hands except with guests you know. The most important thing is to get each name correctly and announce it clearly and distinctly to your boss, even in the cases of people he or she knows well.

Acquaint yourself with aides assigned to other flag or general officers in the immediate area. By close coordination and mutual support, you may be able to prevent many omissions or blunders.

❧ ❧ *Duties of an Aide in the Field*

An aide's duties to a general officer in the field are quite different from those in garrison, although the spirit in which they are performed and the basic relationships remain unchanged.

Subject to the general's wishes, you must accompany your chief everywhere. In any case, you must always keep a personal situation map and other maps or status boards absolutely up to the minute. Pay particular attention to locations of front lines, of installations to visit, and, above all, of unit command posts. The lastest information is important not only to the general and driver but also to you, as the general may often use you to convey personal messages to other commanders.

Be alert as to the military situation and be ready to obtain any information the general wishes, either from staff sections and subordinate headquarters or, if necessary, by personal reconnaissance.

See that your general's personal wants are met. Have arrangements been made for laundry? For keeping weapons and gear in shape? For the fighting position?

Introduce visiting officers, official visitors, correspondents, and other persons having business with the general.

Arrange and control all transportation for the general.

Oversee the security arrangements for the general's area.

Supervise the general's drivers, orderlies, cooks, and stewards as you would in garrison, but be sure these people are reminded that, in the field, they are combat Marines. They must be prepared to defend the command post area in the event of attack or enemy penetration.

Supervise and act as caterer for the general's mess. Be sure that any fatigued, wet, or cold officer or enlisted Marine who sees the general (especially people from frontline units) always gets a cup of hot coffee or other refreshment. Have plenty of coffee available for drivers and runners, day or night.

Work closely with the headquarters commandant in such arrangements as digging a suitable head, erection of tentage, digging in tents, camouflage of the area, water supply, electricity, and facilities.

Above all, do everything in your power to protect and defend your general and to shelter him or her from unnecessary strain and fatigue.

❖ ❖ *Travel Arrangements*

An aide's responsibilities with respect to travel merit special attention.

Before Leaving. Prepare an itinerary or see that one is prepared, giving hours and modes of arrival and departure at the destination and all intermediate stops, and furnish a copy to the chief of staff and any other interested parties.

Obtain a program for each official stop that includes a schedule of events, uniforms required, times, and other necessary information. This program, of course, must have been coordinated with the host activity.

Inform your general of the uniforms required throughout the trip.

Obtain your general's orders and transportation requests (if required), and see that transportation is arranged.

Issue instructions for forwarding email or phone messages.

See that all baggage for the official party is suitably tagged and identified. Determine what, if any, papers or files the general will require on the trip and arrange for their handling and stowage, especially that of any classified material. Additionally, be sure to inventory accessories—spare batteries (if applicable), chargers, adapters for international travel—for cell phones and laptop computers.

To be sure the general can be reached rapidly during any part of the trip, confirm that key command personnel have current cell phone numbers for both you and the general.

During Travel. If traveling commercially, keep timetables handy for your mode or modes of transport (including possible alternatives), and, no matter how you travel, know hours scheduled for arrival and departure. Know places and times for connections.

Keep track of time-zone changes and the dateline. Remind the general to set his or her watch.

Prescribe uniforms for aircrew and stewards and ensure that other members of the party are informed as to correct uniform during travel, on arrival, and for scheduled events.

When on board government aircraft, be sure the pilot sends a message ahead stating the composition of the party, estimated time of arrival, and transportation required on arrival. If traveling commercially, send such a message yourself. Be sure that the host activity is informed if any guests are in the party or of changes in schedule.

Take care of all tickets, baggage checks, baggage handling, and transportation. In this capacity, your first responsibility is to take care of the general's gear and keep track of it at all times. This particularly includes official and classified papers.

Based on the circumstances, consider taking with you the following: station lists or rosters of officers at activities to be visited; a copy of the Blue Book, officially known as Marine Corps Bulletin 1400; official and personal stationery and postage stamps as required; notebook, pen, and sharp pencils; a supply of the general's business and visiting cards; ample cash and a supply of personal checks on the general's bank, if you have been granted access to these; cleaning gear; refreshments as may be required; spare insignia and ribbons; and the general's personal flag and vehicle plates (if visiting an activity where such are possibly not available).

Keep a running record by name, rank or title, and address of all persons to whom thank you notes or letters of appreciation should be sent; if you have time, rough out such notes before memory fades.

After Return. Write or prepare for the general official and personal letters of appreciation to all who extended special courtesies.

Obtain and deliver all personal mail held for your boss.

Prepare, for the general's signature, the itinerary and travel claim, ensuring it is scrupulously accurate and being careful not to omit miscellaneous expenses that can be properly claimed.

—» Part II «—

AN OFFICER
OF MARINES

⦃ 12 ⦄

BECOMING A
MARINE OFFICER

*An officer is much more respected than any other man
who has as little money.*

— Samuel Johnson

AN OLD MARINE CORPS YARN tells of a young man from the hinterland who, upon entering the Marine Corps, was asked if he intended to try for a commission.

"I don't think so," the recruit answered. "I'm not a very good shot. I'd better work on a straight salary."

There are many ways to obtain a commission as a U.S. Marine officer. The variety of approaches ensures a broad base of experience, background, and education among Marine officers. It also means that regardless of your origin, once you qualify for a Marine commission, you stand on equal footing with every other officer candidate, regardless of source or education.

⟩ PREREQUISITES AND PATHWAYS

⟩ ⟩ *Initial Requirements to Become an Officer*

To be eligible for a commission in the Marine Corps, you must be morally, mentally, and physically qualified, and Marine Corps Headquarters must approve your application. If already a veteran, you must, of course, have an honorable discharge, and if you are a member of the reserve component of any other service, you must obtain a conditional release from that organization. Under limited conditions, officer transfers are authorized from the other services into the Marine Corps; for such transfers, special regulations and procedures apply that are beyond the scope of the *Guide*.

The following specific requirements apply to all officer candidates:

• Must be a citizen of the United States
• Must be at least eighteen years of age upon application
• Must not have reached one's twenty-eighth birthday upon commissioning, although HQMC *may* waive this requirement
• Must pass a physical examination
• Must possess a bachelor's degree or be a full-time student at a regionally or nationally accredited college or university
• Must attend and graduate from Officer Candidates School (OCS)

Officer candidates who satisfy all requirements and graduate from OCS are commissioned as second lieutenants and attend a rigorous six-month training and education program at The Basic School (TBS) at Quantico, Virginia. Later sections in this chapter provide additional details on both OCS and TBS.

❧ ❧ *Paths to a Commission*

The process of becoming a Marine officer begins with your application as an officer candidate, typically submitted in coordination with a Marine Corps officer recruiter known as an officer selection officer (OSO). Your specific path to a commission depends on where you are in your college education, your qualifications, and your ultimate occupational specialty preferences. To obtain a commission in the Marine Corps, you may follow any one of the paths described in the following paragraphs and summarized in table 12-1.

Platoon Leaders Class (PLC). This undergraduate commissioning program enables college freshmen, sophomores, and juniors who are currently enrolled full time in any accredited college or university to pursue a Marine Corps commission without interrupting their academic careers. PLC is the most common path to becoming a Marine officer. No military uniforms, training, or other work are required during the academic year, and all summer training takes place at Marine Corps Base Quantico, Virginia.

This path has two summer training options: two six-week training sessions for college freshmen and sophomores or one ten-week training session for college juniors. Training for both ground and aviation candidates is intensive, with initial emphasis on the basic instruction and careful screening required for all Marine officers. Aviation candidates, however, take flight examinations as part of their program, and, if found qualified, they are ultimately sent to flight training upon graduation from TBS for all newly commissioned officers.

During each training session, you receive the basic pay—but not the allowances—of a sergeant. In addition to pay while training and expenses for transportation to and from Quantico, you receive living quarters, meals, uniforms, and medical and dental care. And during off-duty hours, you have full privileges at Quantico's many venues and services.

Upon completion of training and graduation with a four-year degree, you are eligible to receive commission as a second lieutenant. PLCs may also request deferral of their required active duty to obtain a master's degree in most recognized major fields.

If you are headed for law school, you should investigate the special PLC (Law) program. Through this, individuals who have successfully completed PLC may attend law school in inactive status as second lieutenants in the Marine Corps Reserve until they obtain their degrees. Upon graduation, these officers complete their required active duty as Marine lawyers.

Officer Candidate Course (OCC). An intensive ten-week commissioning program, OCC is conducted at Quantico for college seniors and graduates interested in serving as a Marine officer. In addition to screening officer candidates, the course provides the practical military training needed to prepare for the specialized training to be received as a second lieutenant and, in the case of aviation officer candidates, for flight training. Upon successful completion, newly commissioned second lieutenants will immediately begin active duty at TBS.

Following the initial screening and training already described, both OCC and PLC candidates attend TBS at Quantico as commissioned officers before follow-on assignment to a military occupational specialty school or unit. Aviation

Marine Corps officer candidates navigate the Combat Course at Officer
Candidates School on Marine Corps Base Quantico, Virginia, in 2021.
The Combat Course simulates a battlefield environment.

officer candidates, if found qualified, go on from TBS to between fifteen and
eighteen months of preflight and flight training.

   U.S. Naval Academy. Each graduating class from the Naval Academy at
Annapolis, Maryland, includes midshipmen who have been selected for Marine
Corps commissions. Entrance into the Naval Academy, the first step toward a
commission via this route, is open to civilian preparatory school and high school
graduates and to qualified enlisted personnel from active duty and the reserves.
If you are already in the Marine Corps or Reserve, consult your commanding
officer. Otherwise, information regarding appointment to the Naval Academy
may be obtained online (https://www.usna.edu/Admissions/index.php). The
Admissions Office encourages queries using its online form to ensure questions
are routed directly to the appropriate person.

For Naval Academy midshipmen, the Marine Corps selection process can begin at any point during the first three years at the academy. During freshman and sophomore years (4th and 3rd Class years in academy parlance), it is important to gain as much information as possible about the Corps, with the goal of making a well-informed decision. The junior, or 2nd Class, year is critical, as those interested in a Marine officer commission interact with a Marine officer mentor, take several required fitness tests, and prepare for "Leatherneck," the screening and training session at OCS for academy midshipmen during the summer before their senior, or 1st Class, year.

In recent years, approximately 20–25 percent of each graduating class of midshipmen have been commissioned in the Marine Corps. All Naval Academy graduates have a five-year service obligation.

U.S. Military and Air Force Academies. Limited numbers of graduates of both West Point and the Air Force Academy are also eligible for regular commissions in the Marine Corps, with preference going to former Marines or children of Marines. Information regarding appointment to these academies may be obtained from the Departments of the Army and the Air Force, respectively.

Naval Reserve Officers Training Corps (NROTC). Any college student enrolled either as a scholarship midshipman in the NROTC or as an NROTC "college program student" may, if selected, obtain a commission in the Marine Corps. The NROTC scholarship midshipman, when selected and approved, attends college with tuition and mandatory fees paid by the Navy. He or she also receives all required uniforms, an annual $750 stipend for books, and a monthly allowance of $250 to $400 (amounts as of 2020) during the academic year. Midshipmen also spend summer "cruises" afloat with the fleet and ashore for training at various naval stations. During the summer prior to their senior year, every Marine-option midshipman completes "Bulldog," the screening and training session at OCS for NROTC midshipmen. Upon graduation from college with a B.A. or B.S. degree, he or she is commissioned and enters TBS.

A limited number of entry-level NROTC scholarships are earmarked for the Marine Corps. Civilian high school seniors and graduates may apply for these through a local OSO.

The NROTC college program student does not receive the scholarship benefits but takes the same naval-science instruction in college as the scholarship midshipman and participates in NROTC unit activities. If selected for a Marine commission while in college, the college program student completes OCS alongside other Marine-option midshipmen.

Complete information on NROTC, including the application procedures, is available online (https://www.netc.navy.mil/NSTC/NROTC/). If you are already in NROTC and want to become a Marine officer, see the Marine officer instructor attached to your NROTC unit.

— ❧ ❦ —

The Marine Corps pioneered the award of officer commissions to meritorious enlistees long before the practice was accepted among the other services. In the Corps, this door remains open through several programs.

Enlisted Commissioning Program (ECP). An enlisted-to-officer commissioning program, ECP provides outstanding enlisted Marines the opportunity to become Marine officers. The program also provides an aviation option to qualified applicants. ECP is not intended to serve as a commissioning program for Marines who are better suited to serve as warrant officers. It is open to active Regular and active Reserve Marines who meet the following eligibility requirements:

• Must possess a B.A. or B.S. degree from a regionally or nationally accredited college or university
• Must have at least twelve months remaining on the current enlistment beyond the convening date of the ECP selection board
• Must have at least one year of active Marine Corps service, although this requirement may be waived for truly exceptional recruit training graduates
• Must be found physically qualified
• Must have attained the rank of lance corporal

Additional requirements apply to active Reservists. They must be approved for augmentation into the Regular Marine Corps, meet time-in-service requirements, and be within six months of the end of their active service. Participation is contingent upon conditional release from the Active Reserve program.

Successful applicants receive orders to OCS and receive their commissions upon its completion. They attend TBS following commissioning.

Marine Corps Enlisted Commissioning Education Program (MECEP). Like ECP, MECEP is an enlisted-to-officer commissioning program that provides outstanding enlisted Marines the opportunity to become Marine officers. This program also provides an aviation option to qualified applicants. MECEP is open to active Regular and active Reserve Marines who meet the following eligibility requirements:

- Must be a high school graduate or must have completed at least two years of high school and passed the General Educational Development high school–level exam
- Must have already completed at least twelve hours of college credits, including three credit hours of entry-level math or science and three credit hours of entry-level English
- Must agree to six years of obligated service in the Regular Marine Corps upon graduation from OCS
- Must be found physically qualified
- Must be a sergeant or above at time of application
- Must be between twenty and thirty years of age for ground candidates or between twenty and twenty-seven and a half years of age (or twenty-nine with a waiver) for aviation candidates on anticipated commissioning date

Additional requirements for active Reservists mirror those of ECP.

Selected Marines will be eligible to receive a commission after successful completion of a baccalaureate degree and OCS. They attend TBS following commissioning.

Warrant Officer (WO). Exceptional noncommissioned officers may compete for appointment as WOs in specialized fields. Because qualifications for WO are quite specific and vary appreciably from time to time, the requirements for such appointments are not summarized here.

Limited Duty Officer (LDO). WOs of the Marine Corps may apply for LDO commission in specialized fields, such as administration, intelligence, infantry, logistics, artillery, engineers, tanks, amphibian tractors, ordnance, communications, supply, food, motor transport, and aviation.

Former Regular Officers. Former Regular officers of the Marine Corps who have not attained their thirtieth birthday at time of appointment and who resigned from the Corps in good standing may be reappointed with the approval of the Secretary of the Navy. Former officers of the other armed forces may, within certain limits, be appointed by transfer in the Marine Corps Reserve.

TABLE 12-1. Avenues to a Career as a Marine Officer

Program or Source	Age Limit	Education Requirements	Open to	Leads to
U.S. Naval Academy		Graduation from USNA	Midshipmen USNA	2nd Lt. USMC
U.S. Military Academy U.S. Air Force Academy[1]		Graduation from USMA or USAFA	Cadets USMA or USAFA	2nd Lt. USMC
NROTC (Scholarship Program)	Be at least 17 but not 21 years of age by 30 June of the year entering college	B.A. or B.S. degree[2]	NROTC midshipmen	2nd Lt. USMC
NROTC (College Program)	Be at least 17 but not 21 years of age by 30 June of the year entering college	B.A. or B.S. degree[2]	NROTC midshipmen	2nd Lt. USMC
Platoon Leaders Class (Ground or Aviation)	Be at least 17 but less than 28 years of age (27½ for aviation) at time of commissioning	B.A. or B.S. degree[2]	College freshmen, sophomores, and juniors	2nd Lt. USMC
Officer Candidate Course	Be at least 20 but less than 28 years of age (27½ for aviation) at time of commissioning	B.A. or B.S. degree	Regularly enrolled senior in good standing, or graduate, of an accredited institution granting a 4-year baccalaureate degree in a field other than medicine, dentistry, chiropody, optometry, osteopathy, pharmacy, veterinary medicine, hospital administration, or theology[3]	2nd Lt. USMC

TABLE 12-1. (*continued*)

Program or Source	Age Limit	Education Requirements	Open to	Leads to
Marine Corps Enlisted Commissioning Program	Be at least 20 but less than 26 years of age by 1 July of the year entering college	B.S. degree[2]	USMC enlisted with GCT 120 or higher and 6 years' obligated service remaining	2nd Lt. USMC
Enlisted Commissioning Program	Be at least 19½ and less than 27½ on date of application	High school graduate (or GED certificate) and have satisfactorily completed not less than 1 year of unduplicated college work at an accredited institution	Privates and above, who have completed recruit training, with GCT 120 or higher and at least 12 months remaining on current enlistment	2nd Lt. USMC
Limited Duty Officer	Have a minimum of 10 and maximum of 20 years' active service and have not reached one's 46th birthday by 1 January of the fiscal year in which the appointment is to be made	EL 110 (ASVAB)	Permanent warrant officers in grades of W-2 through W-4	1st Lt. USMC
Warrant Officer	Must be of an age to allow 30 years of total active service by age 62	GCT 110 or higher	Sergeant or above with 5–12 years' active service, unless a waiver is approved	Warrant Officer (W-1) USMC

[1] Military Academy and Air Force Academy graduates may, by law, be commissioned in the Marine Corps, but the Departments of the Army and Air Force will only grant approval in exceptional cases.

[2] Successful college graduation and completion of program are prerequisites for commissioning.

[3] Aviation candidates must meet flight physical standards and will be sent to flight training on completion of required ground training. Current regulations require all to attend Basic School prior to reporting to flight training.

❯ FORMATIVE TRAINING AND EDUCATION

❯ ❯ *Officer Candidates School*

Whether pursuing a commission via PLC, NROTC, ECP, MECEP, or any of the feeders to the Officer Candidate Course, you will attend OCS. Conducted at old Brown Field, Quantico's original air station and later the post–World War II site of TBS, this rigorous training provides officer candidates the knowledge and skills required of the basic enlisted Marine. At the same time, OCS rigorously evaluates and screens all candidates to ensure they possess the leadership, moral, mental, and physical qualities required for commissioning as a Marine Corps officer. In effect, OCS is an officer candidate's boot camp—and a very exacting one.

OCS ensures all future second lieutenants pass a stringent assessment covering academics, leadership, and physical fitness. Training at OCS includes combat conditioning, close-order drill, academics, and graded completion of the Obstacle Course, Stamina and Endurance Course, Fire Team Assault Course, Leadership Reaction Course, and Small-Unit Leadership Evaluation.

❯ ❯ *Commissioning*

No matter how you earn your appointment as a Marine officer, the day finally arrives when you will be sworn in as a second lieutenant.

Your commission and orders will be forwarded to your CO (if you are already serving in some capacity) or to a Marine activity near your home for presentation. The swearing-in ceremony and required administrative steps will ordinarily be handled by the presenting officer. Bear in mind, however, that pay and allowances do not begin for officers until they are sworn in and commence active duty, nor can you assume title and status as an officer until you have taken your oath and formally accepted your appointment.

Of that oath, Arleigh A. Burke, one of the Navy's greatest and best-loved fighting admirals, wrote,

> It is a responsibility that should not be taken easily. And its phraseology is disarmingly simple. When an officer swears "to support and defend the Constitution of the United States against all enemies, foreign and domestic"—he is assuming the most formidable obligation he will ever

encounter in his life. Thousands upon thousands of men have died to preserve for him the opportunity to take such an oath. What he is actually doing is pledging his means, his talent, his very life, to his country. This is an obligation that falls to very few men.

The U.S. Supreme Court has more succinctly ruled that "the taking of the oath of allegiance is the pivotal fact which changes the status from that of civilian to that of soldier."

As you raise your right hand and stand at attention to take your oath, you are at a turning point in your life. In a matter of seconds, you will become an officer in a Marine Corps whose valor, renown, and honor are second to none. From the moment you complete your oath "*to support and defend the Constitution of the United States of America against all enemies, foreign and domestic*," you are a lieutenant of Marines responsible to the president and your superior officers and fully amenable to military justice. It is a great moment!

❖❖ *Your Commission*

After you are sworn in, you receive your *commission*. This is the formal written authority, issued in the name of the president of the United States, that confers on you the rank and authority of a Marine officer. It is signed for the president and by the SECNAV, issued under the seal of the Department of the Navy, and countersigned by an officer at HQMC, normally the commandant. Your commission states your rank and the date from which it is effective (your date of rank) and enjoins "those officers and other personnel of lesser rank" to obey any lawful order you may give. You receive a new commission for each rank to which you are promoted.

❖❖ *"Special Trust and Confidence"*

Before you file away or even frame (as many do) your first commission, reread and reflect upon its opening phrase: "*Know ye, that reposing special trust and confidence in. . . .*"

With these words, the president of the United States certifies, via the SECNAV, that you, as a commissioned officer, have been set apart from your fellow citizens as one in whom "special trust and confidence" are placed. Based on this special trust, you as an officer are granted special privileges; on the same basis, you are subject to special responsibilities and obligations.

The old French term *noblesse oblige*—literally meaning "nobility obligates"—conveys the idea that nobility extends beyond mere entitlements and requires the individual who holds such status to fulfill certain responsibilities, particularly in leadership roles, and to exceed minimal standards of conduct, performance, and appearance. Similarly with officers, the *Marine Corps Manual* states, "The special trust and confidence which is expressly reposed in each officer by his commission is the distinguishing privilege of the officer corps." As a commissioned officer, you should be vigilant to discharge and, where necessary, enforce the performance of all responsibilities, thereby meriting and guarding the privileges of rank.

❯ ❯ *The Basic School*

The orders that accompany your appointment and initial commission will direct you to proceed to Quantico, Virginia, and report as a student at The Basic School, sometimes simply called Basic School. The oldest Marine Corps school, TBS is an institution whose importance to the Corps is matched only by that of the two recruit depots. It traces its history to 1 May 1891, when it was founded as the School of Application at Marine Barracks Washington by Colonel Charles Heywood, ninth commandant. Since then, the school has been variously located at Annapolis, Maryland; Port Royal, South Carolina (now known as Parris Island); Norfolk, Virginia; Philadelphia Navy Yard; and, finally, Quantico.

Today, TBS is located approximately twelve miles from the main-side area of Quantico. The school's headquarters is located at Camp Barrett, one of the outlying camps of Quantico's Guadalcanal area, which constitutes the greater part of the 57,000 acres of the training reservation. The TBS mission is to "train and educate newly commissioned or appointed officers in the high standards of professional knowledge, *esprit de corps*, and leadership to prepare them for duty as company-grade officers in the operating forces, with particular emphasis on the duties, responsibilities, and warfighting skills required of a rifle platoon commander."

No matter how you earned your commission, your first assignment as a second lieutenant will be as a student in the Basic Officer Course, a course lasting approximately twenty-eight weeks. In addition to this, Basic School conducts a Warrant Officer Course for newly appointed Marine Corps WOs.

Ordinarily, your orders specify a date by which you must report. It is vital that you *comply carefully with your orders*, and, above all, that you *report on time*, normally between 0700 and 1700 on the designated date. There is no poorer way to start a Marine career than by being late for TBS!

In reporting, pay attention to the guidelines in chapter 13 of the *Guide*, which explains the procedure for joining a new station. Reporting to TBS varies somewhat from the norm, but the general rules apply.

Tips on Reporting to Basic School. When first reporting to TBS, you will wear a pressed, well-fitting business suit or the service "A" uniform if you have it from prior service. You are specifically not required to possess any uniforms or accessories upon reporting, aside from any issued at OCS and your commissioning uniform. You should, however, ensure that your hair is recently trimmed and that you present a neat appearance. Be sure your level of physical fitness is at its peak!

Before reporting, visit the TBS website (https://www.trngcmd.marines.mil /Northeast/The-Basic-School/) to find information about the school, read the current commanding officer's intent, peruse any other available information, and begin to absorb it. If possible, request access to and scan all TBS student handouts in electronic form. Forewarned is forearmed!

You should have enough money available for living and other expenses until your first payday, which will be about three weeks after you join. Instructions that accompany your orders should suggest minimum amounts of cash that single or married new lieutenants should have.

Travel light and bring little baggage, as stowage space is limited.

Outside working hours, like any other officer, you may wear civilian clothing. This, however, must conform to accepted standards within the officer corps: clothes of eccentric design or color are not tolerated. You should have at least one suit of conservative cut and color (charcoal gray and navy blue are best options) as well as appropriate casual attire.

Except for your commissioning uniform and camouflage utilities, do not purchase or contract for uniforms before you report to TBS. Occasionally, well-intentioned students report with uniforms and accessories only to find them ill fitted, nonregulation, and too costly. Beware of high-pressure salespeople and so-called package deals for uniforms. There is one exception: WOs are encouraged to have a complete set upon reporting. One of the first items of business after you join TBS will be a uniform orientation conducted by the school. Only after this session should you begin acquiring your uniforms. Note that over the course of TBS, you will be required to purchase the full complement of Marine officer uniforms and accessories, an outlay of several thousand dollars. Ensure that you have a plan to finance this purchase at the outset.

Initial Actions. After you report to TBS, you will turn in your orders to the personnel officer, who will then assign you to a student company. The average student company numbers about 250 members, including young officers from various allied countries around the world. The company is commanded by a major, with a captain as executive officer and captains and first lieutenants as staff platoon commanders. Upon reporting to your company, you will receive an orientation on the course: what will be expected of you and what you can expect from the school. You will be assigned to a platoon and quarters. You will then be issued field equipment, individual weapons, and textbooks for your forthcoming courses.

TBS curriculum, including intense and rugged fieldwork, provides graduates with a foundation of leadership and professional knowledge. While it emphasizes the skills needed to lead an infantry platoon, the lessons apply to Marine officers in every leadership role. You will do theoretical work in the classroom and then go into the field to apply it practically. About one-half of your training is in the field, and about one-fifth of this takes place at night. Training progresses through four phases. The first focuses on the individual technical and tactical skills required of an officer. In the second and third phases, you will build on these skills and prepare to lead by example in command of a platoon. Finally, in the fourth phase, you will study the strategic organization that makes the Marine Corps our nation's expeditionary force in readiness and will prepare to apply your leadership skills in action.

Within the foregoing academic framework, the objectives of TBS are twofold: first, to instill the Marine Corps attitude and, second, to teach new lieutenants the basic professional techniques that every Marine officer must know. In other words, while you became a Marine at OCS, it is up to TBS to make a Marine officer of you. The extent to which the school succeeds, however, is largely up to

Second lieutenant students at Basic School fire an M240 medium machine gun during a crew-served weapons live-fire exercise. Lasting eight months, the Basic Officer Course at Marine Corps Base Quantico, Virginia, trains and educates newly commissioned officers in the high standards of professional knowledge, esprit de corps, and leadership to prepare them for duty as company-grade officers in the Corps, with particular emphasis on the duties, responsibilities, and warfighting skills required of a rifle platoon commander.

you. Student officers who do not measure up to the standards set by the Marines are dropped from TBS, their commissions are revoked, and they are returned to civilian life. Remember that, at TBS, you are under continual, experienced observation.

Administrivia. Heywood Hall is the main administration building of TBS. Adjoining it are four modern, air-conditioned classrooms with a total seating capacity of 1,150. Conveniently located between these classrooms is the snack shop.

Bachelor officer quarters (BOQ) for the officer students at TBS are found in O'Bannon and Graves Halls. These quarters are not luxurious, although you will find them clean and comfortable. This BOQ also houses TBS's dining hall and bar, snack bar, television lounge, library and reading room, and reception room. Married students who are accompanied by their spouses will find housing on or off base. When in training, however, they will be assigned a room as a "Brown Bagger," using this room only to store field equipment, organizational gear, and uniforms.

Additional facilities at Camp Barrett include a small Marine Corps exchange, barber shop, snack bar, post office, gymnasium, outdoor theater, chapel, armory, additional classrooms, gas chamber, combat-conditioning facilities, clinic, and a lighted playing field for baseball, softball, or football.

Next Steps. Immediately after TBS, every officer goes to follow-on training in some specialty school or course—for example, flight school or the artillery officer basic course—to qualify in his or her new military specialty. Rarely, a few officers will receive orders from TBS directly to their first unit, where they will commence work while awaiting a seat at their specialty school. Officers with an infantry military occupational specialty remain at Quantico for advanced infantry training. Thus, in all, your professional apprenticeship, including TBS, lasts more than six months—much longer in some cases, such as naval aviation.

⸭ FINAL THOUGHTS FOR NEW OFFICERS

⸭ ⸭ *What to Do, What Not to Do, and Some Pointers*

As a Marine officer, you represent the Corps. Conduct yourself with dignity, courtesy, and self-restraint.

From the moment you become a Marine, you should cultivate the habit of punctuality. Along with discipline, dedication, obedience, and loyalty, it should be a matter of pride never to be late. *Always be five minutes early* for any meeting, formation, or professional commitment.

On joining a new organization, you will be scrutinized by all hands, both officer and enlisted. First impressions can make (or break) you. Be natural and courteous, prompt and punctilious, and "squared away" in uniform and bearing.

Avoid displays of self-importance. Generally, Marine officers should avoid boastful or overbearing talk, especially among civilians or enlisted personnel. As a new second lieutenant, you should also normally avoid making an assertion that begins with the phrase "In my experience"—unless, for example, the topic of discussion happens to be roofing, and you spent most summers during high school and college as part of a crew installing new roofs. At all costs, avoid the impression of being a brash young know-it-all.

Be wary of situations beyond your depth. A new lieutenant is not expected to be all wise. You are expected to keep your head and possess enough common sense and knowledge of your own limitations to prevent you from overextending yourself. If you are asked a question and are unfamiliar with the answer, do not bluff. The proper answer from a young officer in such circumstances is, "I don't know, but I'll find out."

Something else will be expected of you—*not to make the same mistake twice*, particularly after having been told about it by a senior. Learn to accept criticism positively and with grace.

Avoid the habit of complaining or whining, and steer clear of those who do. Refrain from criticizing unless you are ready and able to provide a better solution. One of the great sayings of the greatest of all naval officers, Lord Nelson, was, "I am not come forth to find difficulties, but to remove them." By the same token, cultivate the habit of optimism. An optimist is like a breath of fresh air, and his or her positive attitude motivates others to follow suit.

Never, under any circumstances, speak ill of the Corps or of your own organization in the presence of enlisted Marines, civilians, or members of the other services. Before you voice any criticism, however merited or carefully thought out, be sure it cannot be construed by outsiders as disparaging to the Corps. Likewise, avoid criticizing other units or services—at least in public.

Be industrious and persevering, attentive to duty, and attentive to essential detail. Whether ashore or afloat, in garrison or in the field, the best officers are those who possess powers of acute observation and, having those powers, know how to use them. Akin to observation are the power and habit of forethought.

Whatever you do, do it thoroughly, and do it with enthusiasm and imagination. Do not confine yourself to doing only what you are told to do. Do more. Exceed standards and expectations. And bear in mind that it is the smart, quick, and, if possible cheery voice that gets the job done and urges others to prompt action.

Get into the habit of being systematic and methodical. In Lord Chesterfield's words, "Dispatch is the soul of business, and nothing contributes more to dispatch than method. Fix one certain day and hour in the week for your accounts, keep them together in their proper order, and you can never be much cheated." You will thus be able to accomplish two or three times as much as an equally capable but unsystematic officer.

Do not procrastinate. When you have a job to do, do it at once. If you have several items to be accomplished, prioritize and do the important thing first. If you find yourself stymied, do not shove the matter aside or report back that you cannot do it; try some other way, and keep on trying. Remember that, in the service, results count; if you can acquire the reputation of a capable officer, you are on your way to success.

When answering a phone call at work, answer smartly, in Marine Corps fashion, with your unit, name, and rank: "Charlie Company, Lieutenant Burrows"—not "Hello." When you make a call, identify yourself immediately: "This is Lieutenant Wharton, Marine Corps." Be sure to add "Marine Corps" if the call is to an external organization; it prevents mix-ups with the other services.

As an officer embarking on your new career, you should do everything possible to match your living arrangements to your new position as an officer of Marines. This should not be misconstrued as encouraging extravagance, but your pay is given to you for a purpose, and you owe it to the service to dress and live, however simply, like an officer.

❧ ❧ *Reputation and Professionalism*

Always reflect upon the reputation that you are acquiring within the service and build upon it daily. An officer's reputation for character and efficiency is his or her vested capital. Take this away, and the officer's usefulness is gone. And remember: you cannot fool your contemporaries. Working closely together, officers soon learn the ins and outs of each other's lives and character.

Conduct all business through proper channels. "Channels" is an important word in the service. The phrase "go through channels," which you may hear, simply means "don't go over people's heads." In giving instructions or in doing or getting things, be careful not to go over someone's head or infringe on his or her areas of responsibility. Doing so is a sure way to trouble in the Marine Corps.

Know where to find information. Make time to go through all the basic professional publications—for example, become familiar with Navy Regulations as well as the *Marine Corps Manual, Uniform Regulations, Drill and Ceremonies Manual,* and, of course, all the basic Marine Corps doctrinal publications and reference manuals relating to Marine weapons, tactics, and your military occupational specialty. TBS will direct your attention to the most important knowledge, but, by going through these publications on your own, you will learn where to find information that lazy or inattentive young officers neglect.

Professionalism also includes maintaining professional associations. Since you are now a member of the profession of arms and naval service, you should join the Marine Corps Association and subscribe to several professional journals, such as the association's *Marine Corps Gazette* and the Naval Institute's *Proceedings.* If you intend to make a career, you should also consider immediately joining the Army and Navy Club in Washington, especially while you can still do so as a newly commissioned officer on advantageous terms; see chapter 21 for details.

❖❖ *Military Bearing and Appearance*

Personal appearance is most important in the service, and although most young officers must and should economize wherever possible, purchasing inferior uniforms is a false economy. The ideal way to economize on uniforms and equipment is to get the best and then take meticulous care of them. Economize on your bar bill rather than your tailor's bill. Nobody in the world looks shabbier than a shabby officer. Male officers should never appear unshaven after the start of the workday.

Military bearing is equally important. Stand straight. In addition to being alert, always try to look alert. Keep your hands out of your pockets. Never chew gum or smoke in public while in uniform.

Learn to manage your feelings and emotions.

Keep fit. The Marine Corps will help you with this by periodic physical fitness tests and by vigorous training all year, but fitness is a continuous matter and must be a continuous concern to every officer. No Marine can afford to become fat.

For additional details on military appearance, refer to the sections on wearing the uniform and grooming and appearance in chapter 10.

❖❖ *Relations with Others*

In relations with your fellow officers, avoid joining factions and, if there are any bad feelings between others, avoid taking sides. Do not gossip; gossip always boomerangs. Only say of a fellow officer who is absent what you would say to his or her face.

Be extremely circumspect in any kind of financial transactions and relations with fellow officers. "Neither a borrower nor a lender be" is golden advice. Also, do not cosign another's loan; many an officer has discovered that his or her signature on the note of a "friend" resulted in the loss of both the friendship and the amount of the loan. Other than in the line of duty, you are expressly prohibited by Navy Regulations from any financial dealings with enlisted persons, and this prohibition must be strictly observed.

Do not intrude among enlisted persons. They are entitled to privacy among themselves as you are. Do not enter NCOs' messes except by specific invitation of the senior NCO present or for official unit functions. If you have been commissioned from the ranks, remember this prohibition now that you are an officer. Both WOs and LDOs have occasionally undermined their positions by maintaining overly familiar relationships with past peers.

Finally, now that you are a Marine yourself, keep your eyes open for likely recruits and for potential officers among your friends. Such individual recruiting of new Marines by convinced and loyal old Marines is one of the principal ways in which the Corps maintains its quality.

⦃ 13 ⦄

NEW STATION

One fresh man in action is worth ten fatigued men.
— John Stark

NO STATISTICIAN has ever totaled the endless adages about the importance of first impressions and good beginnings, but one thing is certain: as far as your Marine Corps career is concerned, all of them are true.

The instant you show your face on a new station, you come under close observation and appraisal. And when you report for duty at your first station—whether in garrison, in the field, at sea, or at school—you begin to lay the foundation of the service reputation that will make or break your future.

How you conduct and carry yourself, how you wear your uniforms, how you behave, how much you know, pretend to know, or do not know—by all these details you are judged.

⏵ REPORTING IN GARRISON

⏵ ⏵ *Preliminaries*

After completing Basic School and military occupational specialty (MOS) training, you will have received your primary MOS (see chapter 14) and orders to your first station. In most cases, this will be a unit in the Marine Corps Operating

Forces. You also will have been authorized some delay in reporting, which will give you an opportunity to catch your breath after training and to square yourself away for further adventures. If you are ordered to one of the Marine divisions, aircraft wings, or logistics groups, your first assignment will be predetermined by your MOS. If, however, you are ordered to a non–Operating Forces unit or command, it is good practice to write ahead to introduce yourself and assist your new commanding officer in deciding where and how to employ you to greatest advantage. A good email or letter, which should be formal but unofficial, should address the following details:

- When you plan to arrive in the vicinity of your new station and report for duty
- Marital status, whether you have children, and whether your family will accompany you or join you later
- Brief description of any special knowledge, skills, abilities, or experience that may assist in making your initial assignment within the command or unit
- Request for general information to help you familiarize yourself with your new station, command, or unit
- Request for any specific instructions from the command or unit
- Expression of enthusiasm for your upcoming assignment

It has become a standard practice for a new officer to call the adjutant or executive officer of the new unit to which he or she will be assigned, particularly when the battalion is already known. If there are multiple officers proceeding to the same unit, as may happen after completing a course, they should make a concurrent call so as to conserve the time of the officer thus contacted at the new organization.

Frequently, the unit will assign a sponsor to an inbound officer. The sponsor is usually an experienced officer of the same rank, MOS, and marital status. This officer can provide much helpful information on the unit's schedule, assist with settling into a new base, and otherwise orient the incoming officer on arrival. Almost all bases and stations operate homepages on the Internet, and these remain excellent sources of information. Links to these and more can be found at the official Marine Corps website (www.usmc.mil).

Remember you will be reporting to your new station or unit in the service uniform (normally service "A," although some commands direct the wear of a different uniform when first reporting for duty). This requires prior planning to ensure that you have a complete uniform while traveling between duty stations. You should also have enough uniforms (for example, utilities) so you can go to work immediately if the need arises. In no case should you ship all your uniforms and assume they will be ready and waiting at your new station.

❥❥ *Plan for Arrival and Reporting*

There are as many ways to report to a new station as there are individuals. During your career, you will see them all: "The Procrastinator," tearing out in a taxicab five minutes before midnight on the last day his orders allow; "The Not-So-Dynamic Duo," travel-worn parents with two overloaded cars, children, and wilted clothes; "The Pro," a careful officer who arrives two days early and reconnoiters the area before reporting.

Without considering the trouble in store if you miscalculate your reporting date or if you arrive late for any reason, legitimate or not, you should know that last-minute arrival is a risky business. Even under the best of circumstances, it can start you out off balance. So allow ample time, whatever else your personal logistics call for.

Let us assume, then, that you have correctly budgeted "proceed, travel, and delay" (if any), that you have arrived at a city near your first station, and that you are there in plenty of time—at least a day to spare.

So here you are, at the threshold of your first station.

The day before you intend to officially report, you will essentially conduct a reconnaissance. Put on appropriate civilian attire, and get a fresh haircut. Drive out to the base, show your identification card (or orders, if you have not yet been issued an ID card) to the sentry at the main gate, and ask the sentry to direct you to the adjutant's office for the command you will be joining. The adjutant is the staff officer who, among other responsibilities, traditionally receives newcomers to the command. Large bases and stations (such as Camp Lejeune), which include several commands, now have a joint reception center or personnel administration center where all company-grade officers report initially. After leaving such a center, you proceed as described herein, reporting to the adjutant of the command to which you have been assigned.

Before you enter the adjutant's office, have your orders handy and knock (or hesitate in the doorway until invited to enter). Introduce yourself informally; "Sir/Ma'am, I'm Second Lieutenant Nicholas. I have orders to report tomorrow, and I would like to confirm where and when I report, the uniform, and any information you may have on my assignment."

The adjutant probably will have advance information of you and will know a good deal about your immediate future. In any case, the adjutant will look over your orders and, unless extremely busy, chat a few minutes, if only to size you up and get you off to a proper start.

Find out the exact time and place for reporting, the name and title of the officer to whom you report, and the required uniform. This last information allows you to visit the Marine Corps exchange to purchase any items you may have overlooked.

An officer usually reports for duty toward the beginning of working hours or at such other time as the CO desires. This information can be ascertained in advance of reporting. If, to comply with the letter of orders, you must report at night or after working hours, the officer of the day or staff duty officer will receive you, log you in, and, if necessary, provide overnight accommodations. Next day, you then report formally to your new CO.

From the moment you step on board, you must be alert, fit, and ready to do whatever may be required.

Your service "A" uniform should be freshly cleaned and pressed. Your shoes should shine, your brass gleam. Your personal grooming should be immaculate. Check to make sure that pockets are buttoned and that all insignia are in place and correct. Look yourself over in the mirror for a final check.

You should carry your original orders with a half-dozen copies, personal records, and miscellaneous papers that have to do with the day's business (documentation of travel expenses, check-in sheet, information booklet, and so on).

If you are staying off base and have no personal transportation, you are normally authorized to take a taxi and claim reimbursement on your travel orders. Alternately (rarely in the United States but more common overseas), you may telephone the motor transport dispatcher at your new installation or command and request transportation.

Once on board, enter your command's headquarters and present yourself at the time and place previously ascertained, if you have conducted a preliminary reconnaissance. If you have doubts, report to the adjutant, who will take your orders and have them endorsed. The adjutant will show you to the office of the CO or XO (or, if you are reporting to a large installation or major command, possibly the chief of staff, the deputy chief of staff, or the G-1).

On cue from the adjutant, step smartly into the office, uncovered, halt at attention two paces before your senior's desk, and say, "Sir/Ma'am, Second Lieutenant Zeilin reporting for duty." *Do not salute*; Marines do not salute uncovered or indoors (except when under arms).

The officer to whom you are reporting will usually have you sit down, put you at ease, and chat with you a few minutes, both as a matter of courtesy and to fix you in mind. Do not get flustered; answer questions briefly and directly, and sit erect without slouching or fidgeting. The end of the interview usually will be indicated by instructions that you report to some lower headquarters or commence the prescribed check-in procedure. Unless you are urgently needed, your CO will almost always ask whether you have had time to "get squared away or settled in" and will allow you reasonable opportunity to attend to such personal matters as housing, administration, and so forth.

After you leave, retrieve your orders with their reporting endorsement. You will need them all day.

If you have not already arranged for quarters, this should be an early step in the reporting process. At large bases, there is usually a housing office, which not only assigns government quarters but also can give you leads on off-base housing. Because government quarters are assigned (with few exceptions) on a first-come, first-served basis and there are often waiting lists for such housing, present yourself immediately to the person who runs the quarters list and see that your name is placed on that fateful roster, which determines when you move in. (Typically, housing offices today permit you to apply for quarters as soon as you receive orders to your new station, and your control date on the quarters list is determined by the date of detachment from your previous station; it is, of course, in your interest to verify that this date is accurate.) Before making any arrangements, let alone signing leases, for off-base housing, be sure to get your change-of-station orders endorsed to the effect that government quarters are not available. If you lease "ashore" before getting an endorsement, you may find yourself being moved into government quarters anyway and, in any case, losing your quarters allowance.

Once you have gotten housing arranged, the finance office or section will be your next destination. Ask for the NCO or officer who handles officers' personnel accounts. Here you will provide certain personal information and data, and here, also, the NCO will likely audit your personnel records with you to ensure all information is accurate and updated. In addition, the finance office arranges to pay you whatever travel allowances are due—a much-needed bonus that helps reimburse you for the expenses of getting there.

With orders endorsed, quarters arranged, and "pay in your pocket," you will be ready to claim whatever baggage and belongings you shipped from your home or former station. The distribution management office (DMO) takes care of this by holding your gear until you report in and claim it. Again, your orders are necessary for this. You are entitled to temporary storage of your personal effects. If they have not arrived, leave word with DMO where you wish to be notified when your gear appears. DMO will deliver it to government quarters or to any point off base within a reasonable radius.

Under most circumstances, military health records are mailed between military treatment facilities when you transfer, although there are exceptions (for example, when traveling overseas on permanent change of station or transferring to a remote duty station). If you hand carried your health records, your next task should be to leave them at the clinic, aid station, or sick bay that will provide your health services. Find out where this is before you leave station or unit headquarters. If your new station has a standard check-in procedure for officers newly reporting, the check-in sheet will normally tell you where to find the sick bay. With health records in hand, enter and ask for the records office. Here a Navy hospital corpsman will accept your health record, enter you into the health system, and, likely, audit your record to verify that you are up to date on your immunizations. If you need dental work or any routine medical assistance, now is the time to make your needs known.

By the time you have accomplished the tasks just described, you will more than likely be ready for a bite to eat. This can usually be obtained at the commissioned officers' mess. If you are pressed for time, most Marine Corps exchanges have a short-order restaurant or food court where you can eat on the run. Lunch at the mess, however, will enable you to take care of another traditional obligation, that of joining the mess. Here you may activate your membership, pay dues if necessary, and ascertain the privileges and obligations of the mess.

Last, but by no means least, if driving your own car, find the office of the provost marshal to register your car at the station. Marine Corps installations require that privately owned vehicles carry a proper state registration, be insured according to state laws, and be able to pass safety examinations. Nothing can be more troublesome than not being able to meet installation requirements for registration of a car; without registration, you may be required to park outside the installation and walk from there. Advance planning to have your car in good shape and fully insured can save you days of headaches. Never park in a space reserved for someone else. Such spaces are usually marked by signs or numbers painted on the curb or road surface. Few events annoy a senior more than to find his or her parking space preempted by a junior.

❧ ❧ *"Snapping In"*

As you settle in to your outfit and assignment, your success will depend largely on your common sense, application, willingness to learn, and skill in human relations. Here, however, are a few tips:

- Learn quickly to associate as many names, faces, and jobs of the officers and enlisted Marines around you as you can. Study your Marines' records and their backgrounds.
- Read bulletin boards—not only the current items but also all the past accumulation that most bulletin boards display. It may be old hat to the unit's plankowners, but it is useful history to you.
- Memorize the mission of your organization if you were previously unable to do so.
- Study the tables of organization and equipment for your organization. The S-1 and S-4 can provide these.
- Study your organization's general orders and standard operating procedures. Your first sergeant can help you find copies.
- Read installation regulations; they can keep you out of much trouble.

- Learn the geography of your installation and training areas by map and personal reconnaissance. "I'm a stranger here myself" is a poor reply for an officer to give.
- Above all, strive to know your Marines. As you begin this ceaseless and vital Marine Corps task, crack open your copy of the *Marine Corps Manual* and read the article entitled "Relations between Officers and Men."

❧ ❧ *Orienting Yourself*

As you snap in, the sergeants in your unit can be a new lieutenant's best *professional* friends. An officer—especially a new one—should never be too proud or pretentious to learn from anybody who knows more about a particular subject. Both parties, however, must observe proper military courtesy and maintain mutual respect.

Some COs work out an informal orientation dealing primarily with internal administrative matters—command policies and procedures, supply and maintenance, paperwork—for new junior officers. If nothing of the kind is directed, you may find it useful, after touching base with your company commander or immediate supervisor, to take care of the following priorities:

1. Ask the first sergeant to direct you toward standing orders and manuals you ought to read—and then read them carefully. Respect and develop a professional friendship with the first sergeant.
2. Visit the unit supply operation and find out the basics of obtaining, caring for, and accounting for supplies, equipment, and other property. There is a lot to learn about these topics. Find out how weapons are safeguarded and about ammunition stowage. (Incidentally, refamiliarize yourself with safety regulations.)
3. Visit the battalion or other mess that feeds your unit. Catch the mess sergeant during some downtime and ask how the mess and galley are operated, how rations are drawn, and how the mess force is handled. Although most Marine Corps mess halls are operated by contractors today, this action bears special importance if your unit does operate or have responsibilities for the mess hall, as it will then become part of your

duties as officer of the day to monitor. In fact, study the orders governing your duties as officer of the day (staff duty officer, if more senior) well before you stand such duty for the first time.

Besides all the foregoing, read up on your job. Use the excellent professional manuals from the Marine Corps and other services that bear on your duty and unit. You will be surprised how soon you become recognized as professionally qualified.

❯ REPORTING IN THE FIELD

❯ ❯ *Actions upon Arrival*

Although reporting in the field is now somewhat rare, the circumstances under which you might join your first command in the field are as various as the world's geography and climate. A force conducting peacekeeping and stability operations leads a different life from a MARDIV, MAW, or MLG at the peak of a campaign. And joining an embarked MEU during deployment presents its own set of challenges. Nevertheless, in preparing for field duty, here are some useful rules.

Get all the briefing you can, especially from those who have recently returned from your assigned area of operations. Accept guardedly any advice or information from anyone who has not been there recently. Focus on gathering basic information, especially on the following:

- Local climate
- Uniforms worn and whether these may be procured after you arrive or should be brought with you
- Correct email address and mailing address, which will enable correspondence to meet you rather than lag weeks behind
- Local shortages or hard-to-get items—these are the things you will want to bring with you

Do not delay in moving forward. The "pipeline" affords many obstacles. Overcome them, and press forward to your destination.

Travel lightly. For a junior officer, this usually means some combination of military backpack, seabag, and hanging bag; briefcase or helmet bag; and little else. Keep your baggage tagged with your name, unit, and destination.

Keep your travel orders and service records, if not mailed, on you. Get a notebook and pencil, and keep them handy.

Try to reach your destination with two or more hours of daylight to spare. Night is no time for strangers to be stumbling about a new unit. When you report, follow the procedure described in the section on reporting in garrison as closely as circumstances permit. As soon as operational circumstances allow and administrative formalities are complete, you should take care of the following tasks:

- Find out where and when you wash, sleep, and eat.
- Ascertain immediately the likelihood of enemy attack and the degree of readiness being maintained. This includes blackout rules, where and when you wear sidearms and personal protective equipment, and what to do if an enemy attack takes place.
- Learn the password and countersign and the location of minefields and entanglements.

❧ ❧ *Taking Command in the Field*

If you are taking over a command, especially one in contact with the enemy, you must do the following:

- Understand your mission and know the degree of readiness required of your unit.
- Meet your subordinate leaders so that you can identify them and they can identify you. Meet your leading NCO and keep him or her nearby.
- Walk your front lines or perimeter. In doing so, locate your unit's boundaries on the ground, inspect individual positions, identify adjacent units, locate the enemy, and show yourself to your Marines.
- Inspect your unit's weapons and equipment. If the situation permits, hold emergency alerts and battle drills.
- Check your interior and exterior guard and security.
- Verify your communications. Be sure you are familiar with all emergency signals.
- Ascertain what supporting arms are available. Know how to obtain them.
- Check your supply situation. This includes, at minimum, ammunition, water, and rations—"beans and bullets," as the old phrase goes.

- Make a thorough sanitary inspection of heads, urinals, garbage and trash disposal, and water supply. Field hygiene is vital to unit readiness. Do not overlook general policing of your area.
- Know how to get medical assistance and how to evacuate casualties.

And, finally, remember that you can count on the Marines around you, just as they are depending on you.

❯ OVERSEAS TRAVEL AND FOREIGN STATIONS

About a fifth of your career (outside any expeditionary or war service) is spent on foreign stations.

You probably will be serving in a country that is new to you. You may miss some conveniences and facilities to which you are accustomed at home. Language, customs, national characteristics, and living habits may well differ markedly from your own.

Learn to view foreign usages and characteristics with understanding and enthusiasm and without arrogance, insularity, or provincialism. If only for the success of our missions overseas, Marines must earn the friendship of the people in whose countries we serve. Self-discipline, courtesy, tolerance, generosity, and good humor are the best ambassadors.

Finally, remember Laurence Sterne's dictum on foreign travel: "An Englishman does not travel to meet English men." When abroad, meet the people and live the life of the country where you are stationed. Otherwise, you might just as well never leave home.

❯ ❯ *Personal Effects*

Military life, including overseas duty and travel, demands flexibility. Even though ordered to sea or foreign service in one part of the world, you may suddenly find yourself on the way to some place quite different. You must therefore select clothing and personal effects that, with minimum weight and bulk, keep you prepared for duty anywhere—from the Arctic to the Caribbean, from Asia to Alaska.

Your maximum personal travel baggage should typically comprise seabag, hanging bag, and briefcase. You may allow yourself additional baggage when the mission requires that you travel with substantial tactical and organizational equipment. To be sure none of your essential gear goes adrift, there is but one safe rule, as voiced by a well-seasoned old-timer in the Corps: "Sit on your baggage and keep your orders in your pocket."

Common sense and the advice of fellow officers who are familiar with your destination are the surest guides on what to take overseas. Regardless of destination, however, never be without a complete service uniform (with garrison cap, to save space) and accessories, at least one set of camouflage utilities, rainproof parka, and regulation raincoat.

Do not take valuable papers, such as insurance policies, car titles, or deeds; irreplaceable jewelry; or anything else you cannot afford to lose. Leave such items in a safe-deposit box. And be sure your spouse's or next of kin's power of attorney contains authority to get into the safe-deposit box. Consult chapter 20 for further information.

❯ ❯ *Moving Family Overseas*

Overseas travel by your family on an accompanied tour via government transportation is usually contingent on your having adequate housing (or good assurance thereof) for them at the destination.

When possible, the Marine Corps tries to arrange for you and your family to travel together to an overseas station. If there must be delay and separation before the overseas area commander allows your family members to join you, the Corps will do its level best to get them moving quickly.

Get the latest information on living conditions in the overseas area, including climate, housing, food, education, shopping, recreation, and health care. Such data will help you decide what to take. Chapter 8 provides some details on overseas installations to which Marines are most often assigned, but this type of information is perishable, so check your destination installation's Internet homepage for the latest information.

❯ ❯ *Preparations for Travel Overseas*

Planning for, traveling to, and settling in at a new station overseas can be a daunting prospect, especially for the less traveled. Take the following preparations seriously.

Passports. You and each member of your family will require passports unless you are ordered to one of a few areas where this rule is waived. Your change-of-station orders will normally include instructions for obtaining an official passport, and the duty station you are leaving should have an office (normally the office that also issues ID cards) that will usually obtain it with minimum delay. It is also advisable to obtain a standard tourist passport at your own expense. Apply to one of twenty-seven Department of State regional passport agencies located around the country in major metropolitan areas—or, if no other source is at hand, apply to the designated clerk at the nearest branch of the United States Post Office. Regardless of what agency you deal with, have the following items with you when you apply:

- Birth certificate for yourself and for each family member
- Evidence of naturalization if you or your family members are not native U.S. citizens
- Old passport or, at a minimum, the number(s) of past U.S. passports held
- Your ID card and other supporting identification
- Two passport-size photos, full face and uncovered, of each person

Visas. Be sure you have all visas required by countries en route and at your destination. Again, your most reliable source is the Manpower Department, Marine Corps Headquarters through your command's personnel officer or adjutant. The Department of State maintains an informative website (https://travel.state.gov/content/travel.html) with a vast amount of information for overseas travelers. The nearest consulates of the countries on your itinerary can also answer your questions and issue visas when needed. Remember that you cannot get a visa until you have your passport.

Physical Examinations and Immunizations. You and your family members must have physical examinations and complete certain immunizations before going overseas. The requirements for both vary from time to time. Have your immunizations recorded and certified on the appropriate international certificate of inoculation and vaccination, if required, and be sure that every shot is recorded in your health records. Otherwise, you may find yourself getting a double dose of inoculations every time you step ashore.

You can get the necessary physical examinations and immunizations from your primary care manager at the naval hospital or clinic. If your family members are moving alone from an area without a Navy surgeon nearby, have them consult the nearest armed forces medical facility. Under outpatient provisions for family medical care, they may alternatively receive examinations and immunizations from civilian sources.

Medical service for families is usually variable overseas, as is dental service. This largely explains why some overseas assignments carry restrictions on dependent family members. Both you and your family should make every effort to be in top health before going overseas.

Baggage. Before you pack, contact your local DMO to confirm your weight allowances for overseas assignment—that is, how much baggage may accompany you and how much you may ship—as well as what items may accompany you personally and the precise address to which baggage must be shipped. Mark and tag your gear clearly. It is wise to put a copy of your basic orders inside each piece of baggage.

Forwarding Mail. Find out your new email address and mailing address in advance and submit address changes, via the Internet if possible, to all correspondents, businesses, and publications with which you have relationships. If updating addresses online is not an option for a particular correspondent or business, send change-of-address cards, which are available from your unit mail clerk or the nearest post office branch. If you are not sure of your new addresses, wait until you arrive, then handle the changes without delay.

When stationed in a foreign country, have your magazines, parcels, and any dutiable articles sent to you via the nearest Fleet Post Office (FPO) or Army Post Office (APO). This gets you domestic rather than appreciably higher overseas subscription and shipping rates.

❯ ❯ *On Foreign Station*

Here are some final considerations as you anticipate your overseas assignment.

Arrival. Because you are traveling under orders (and with an official or perhaps a diplomatic passport), you should have few, if any, problems with foreign customs or immigration authorities. Upon arrival, you probably will be met by some representative of the military community that you are joining. The commander responsible for your area or port of entry will try to move you expeditiously to your destination. If delay is unavoidable, the commander will normally arrange accommodations. But keep in touch with the officer you are relieving (if you know him or her)—that is the person directly interested in your safe and speedy arrival.

Language. Where your duties make it desirable, the Marine Corps makes every effort to give you language training before sending you to a foreign billet. Your spouse should also enroll in some type of language instruction. Your young children will have the opportunity to pick up the language of the country soon enough from other children through recreational opportunities and perhaps even in school. To enable them to learn the country and its ways, as well as the language, give serious consideration to enrolling your children in local schools, if this is safe and feasible. In certain overseas areas where there are no U.S. schools operated by the Department of Defense Education Activity, DOD will pay all or part of the cost of private schooling in eligible local schools for your children. This is an opportunity you should not overlook.

Regardless of whether you are in a U.S. service community or on detached service alone, you will be working with the citizens of the country where you are serving, and you must perfect your abilities with the local language. Some commands maintain language tutors and conduct regular classes. If you cannot avail yourself of them, you can almost always hire your own tutor for a nominal fee. Educate the entire family. The ability to speak the language vastly extends your opportunities and earns the respect of all with whom you deal.

Sanitary Precautions. Depending on the country, sanitation and public health abroad may not attain the levels to which you have been accustomed at home. Gain an understanding of the local public health situation as soon as you arrive. Take nothing for granted. Be especially careful against insect-borne and enteric diseases. Maintain current immunizations. If circumstances demand it, drink only pasteurized or boiled milk as well as water that has been boiled. Avoid raw fruits and vegetables unless you are quite sure "night soil" is not used as the local fertilizer. Make your own ice at home, using purified water. Your medical officer can advise you on what you can get away with and what you must watch.

Shopping. The "bargains" you and your spouse may find on foreign station will sometimes seem unbelievable. If you are unfamiliar with the quality, values, and local market conditions, take along a friend who knows these things.

Look into the foreign exchange, currency, and tax situations. Find out where you can get the best legal rate of exchange; although hotels will almost always change money, they usually charge a commission or give you a poor rate. In some countries, dollar purchasers are accorded purchase-tax exemptions; in others, some types of currency are more readily negotiable and thus get better rates of exchange. Know these fine points and take advantage of them. On the other hand, never demean your country or your Corps by black marketeering. This sort of thing is emphatically not done by Marines and is sternly dealt with in the few cases that arise. If you know quality, style, and value, a relatively small outlay may obtain furniture, linens, rugs, silver, chinaware, and other fine goods you might never be able to afford at home.

Take it easy at first, however. Look for a while before you begin to buy. Do not bypass your military exchange. Purchase through an exchange gives you some assurance of quality and equity in price. Often, in fact, exchanges can do better in obtaining values than you as an individual because of mass purchasing and bargaining experience.

⊰{ 14 }⊱

PROFESSION OF ARMS

In no event will there be money in it; but there may always be honor and quietness of mind and worthy occupation—which are far better guarantees of happiness.

— Alfred Thayer Mahan

MILITARY PROFESSIONALS exist to provide effective armed forces to the nation for use as an instrument of policy. In peacetime, this demands that every officer prepare the military organization to fight a war that he or she hopes will never be fought. That feature leads to the salient way in which the profession of arms stands apart from all others. Although the armed forces use many terms in common with the learned professions—rights, duties, rewards, and privileges—only the profession of arms carries the obligation to surrender life itself if duty so demands. That liability is not often called upon in time of peace, but Marines of every epoch have faced considerable violence and borne many casualties in operations short of war.

Order also distinguishes the profession of arms. Because the military operates by applying force and even violence toward the resolution of a political question, properly vested authority exists at all levels of the military structure. Within this structure, however, officers do enjoy latitude and exercise initiative in carrying out their duties. The increasingly complex and sophisticated skills that a Marine must acquire throughout active service exert a fascinating challenge for those intent upon mastering the nuances of military art and science. Many officers remain Marines simply because of the satisfaction gained in attaining a high degree of expertise in association with a likeminded cohort.

The professional officer continually seeks education and increased levels of qualification. Unlike other professions where a lengthy period of initial education qualifies a practitioner for life, the military professional's initiation merely suffices for the "apprentice" years. Thereafter, the officer returns to school frequently for specialist, command, and staff courses. Perhaps up to one-fifth of an officer's career will be spent studying, gaining experience, and preparing for greater responsibilities. This amount far exceeds the preparation for law and significantly exceeds that for medicine. In addition to formal courses, the officer reads relevant periodicals and books and seeks out ideas and innovative methods in an ongoing process to acquire knowledge and extend abilities.

In fact, the skills required for military purposes know no real bounds. The Marine Corps encourages intellectual endeavors of all sorts and frequently provides time and funds in their support. Officers may work toward a doctorate in physics or master a foreign language. The Corps can and will make direct use of such qualifications. There also seems no doubt that learning to paint, ski, sail, ride, play a musical instrument, or climb mountains will prove of benefit to the Corps, indirectly if not directly. Provided you strive to improve your military skills, your fellow officers will respect and support your most eccentric hobbies and activities. This freedom of individual expression within a highly structured profession is unique to the military. The Corps remains a closely knit group with high values, fairness, and consistency. People are at the heart of the profession of arms.

❧ MONITORING YOUR PROFESSIONAL DEVELOPMENT

❧ ❧ *A Balanced Career*

To have a successful career, you must have a balanced career. Such a career guarantees decisiveness, judgment, steadiness, and practicality at the top. Raw material for these attributes is found in most officers. But the extent to which you develop those qualities results largely from the kind of career you pursue.

You should seek the following for a balanced Marine career:

- Duty with the Operating Forces
- Experience in command
- Professional education
- Combat experience
- Joint and high-level staff experience

As you proceed from duty to duty, remember that it is the commandant who assigns you, but it is still your career. You must monitor it intelligently without earning the pejorative label "careerist"—one whose offense is placing career before Corps. Watch your career as carefully as a chemist compounding a critical formula or a free solo climber planning a route. Your career is your critical formula or El Capitan.

⋙ *Assignment and Detail*

The right balance in your career results largely from assignments, or "details" as they are sometimes still called in the Marine Corps. Your assignments send you to school, overseas, and to the Operating Forces and determine which of the thousand-and-one Marine jobs you fill. Thus, a balanced career can be attained only through a sound pattern of assignment. It is one of the important functions of Marine Corps Headquarters to see that during the first twenty years of service, every officer gets assignments designed to develop his or her potentialities, to afford equal opportunity for advancement, and to qualify the officer for command responsibility appropriate to rank.

Figure 14-1 represents the "typical career pattern" often spoken of by career counselors, although too many suitable variations exist to speak inflexibly these days of such patterns. Typically, after starting in the Operating Forces, a ground officer will progress in some capacity through the Supporting Establishment, career-level school, and staff duty as a captain, typically followed by more Operating Forces and then more Supporting Establishment duty. Aviation officers tend to spend much more time in flying tours and comparatively less time on staff duty than do ground officers. Over an officer's career, staff tours are intermingled with intermediate and perhaps top-level schools and high-level staff duty as a field-grade officer.

Managing your career while at the same time meeting the needs of the Corps is the job of the Officer Assignment Branch, HQMC. This branch distributes

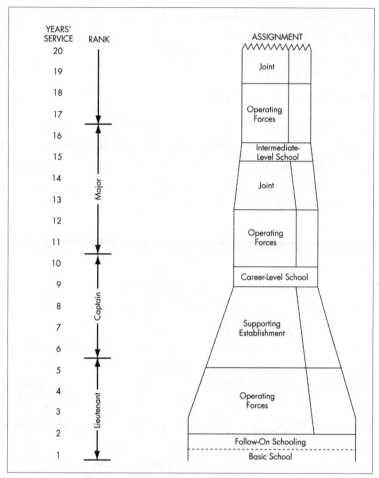

FIGURE 14-1. Typical Assignment Patterns for Marine Officers

officers to all Marine commands immediately subordinate to Headquarters. These commands in turn assign you according to your experience and military specialty.

Assignments are classed as follows:

- *Command*: duty as commanding officer or executive officer of any Marine organization
- *Staff*: duty on the general, special, or executive staff of any organization above company level

- *Instructor*: duty on the staff or as an instructor at any U.S. or foreign military school
- *Student*: duty under instruction at any school
- *Joint service*: duty on the staff of a joint command or component of the Department of Defense
- *Special duty*: a range of varied and miscellaneous duties, such as sea duty, recruiting duty, and naval attaché duty

The normal tour for Marine officers on duty ashore is three years, although the demands of the service sometimes require departure from this or any other standard duration of tour.

Overseas (and certain other) tours are classed as either "unaccompanied" (without family) or "accompanied" (with family). It is reasonable to anticipate one accompanied foreign tour during your career and around two unaccompanied.

Although it is up to HQMC, and every CO, to balance your assignments, the fact remains (as has been emphasized) that it is your career. This is well recognized in the Corps, and you have ample opportunity to communicate your wishes for assignment.

On each fitness report, you state your preference for your next duty, and your reporting senior must in turn give his or her own recommendation as to what assignment should be made. In addition, any officer may write an official letter (usually an administrative action form) to the commandant to request a future assignment.

HQMC weighs several factors in determining who moves where and when: date of last unaccompanied overseas tour, school requirements, moves precipitated by school and/or unaccompanied tour completions, career development, time on station, and, of course, special requirements—the exceptional cases—as well as economy. Timing and individual availability for assignment also bear heavily on final decisions.

You can generally expect to be assigned to overseas unaccompanied tours on the basis of your date of return from previous unaccompanied duty relative to all other officers of your grade and military occupational specialty (see the section below on military occupational specialties).

The normal process of detailing officers to the various billets of the Corps revolves around annual preparation of "slates," the lists showing the assignments in each rank that are planned for the forthcoming year. Based on a normal three-year turnover, about one-third of the officer corps should be transferred each year, but because some billets have shorter tours than three years, a larger percentage usually moves.

Slating is essentially a cross-matching of Marine Corps officer requirements (based on tables of organization, approved manning levels, school quotas, and so on) with those available for transfer in a given calendar year. The decisions on individual assignments in each case are based on optimum career pattern (including need for schooling), individual qualifications (such as MOS, college degree, and language skills), present station (to avoid costly, time-consuming cross-country or Atlantic to Pacific moves), and, of course, the individual's requests.

The factor of overriding importance in slating (and thus in shaping careers) is performance. No matter what duty you have had in the past, the singular consideration that will shape your future assignments is an established record of and reputation for consistently high performance across the range of your career.

You often hear it loosely said that "nobody pays any attention" to individual officers' requests. This is not true; contrary to all rumor, the Officer Assignment Branch does have a heart.

The core of the process lies with carefully selected officers at HQMC called monitors (or, in Navy parlance, "detailers"). The responsibility of a monitor is to assign officers under his or her cognizance in the most efficient manner to meet the needs of the Marine Corps. At the same time, your monitor tries to harmonize your best interests and expressed desires with the requirements of the Corps—not an easy job.

To accomplish the above, the Marine Corps maintains an open-door policy in which informal, frequent contact between individual officers and their respective monitors is encouraged. You can always email, call, or, when in the Washington metropolitan area, visit your monitor. In addition, the Manpower Department normally sends a team of monitors to visit major commands and schools on the East and West Coasts each year, together with a special trip to the western Pacific. These "road shows" provide an opportunity for a face-to-face meeting with your monitor if you are approaching the end of an assignment.

So never hesitate to make your desires known, especially when you feel your career might be broadened by some assignment that may seem professionally necessary to you, such as in a particular Marine Forces unit or schooling. Fortunately, the Corps is small enough to accommodate its own needs and the desires of its officers rather consistently. But you must do your part.

❖❖ *Initial Detail*

Undoubtedly, one of your major concerns is where you will be detailed upon graduating from Basic School. In virtually all cases, lieutenants and warrant officers graduating from TBS are immediately ordered to follow-on training to qualify them in their MOSs. They are then ordered to their new permanent installations or organizations. The following describes the steps and procedures leading to assignment of your MOS and first permanent duty station.

Early in the course, you will have a chance to submit a form showing your preference for duty. Here you indicate, in order, choices of occupational field, preferences of geographic area, and any reasons to support these choices. Your company officers recommend, assign, and endorse this form, affixing a summary of your record at TBS and their appraisal of your attitude, motivation, and general value to the service. The form then goes to the Officer Assignment Branch, HQMC.

The officer assignment section controls the detailing of officers into the occupational fields. Just before receipt of TBS preference statements, the monitors review their respective quotas based on projected requirements. On arrival of the preference forms, they consult and tentatively select candidates for their respective occupational fields.

How do the monitors make up their minds? As to occupational field, their choice depends on several factors:

- Current requirements of the Marine Corps
- Previous military education and experience
- Civilian education and experience
- Your desires
- TBS staff recommendations

Concerning geographic area, you will be ordered where the Marine Corps needs you, with your preference taken reasonably into account if possible. In any case, you can usually expect orders to the Marine Corps Operating Forces.

❯ ❯ *Initial and Permanent Precedence*

Every new second lieutenant is assigned a date of rank. Those with the same date of rank are assigned temporary initial precedence, which governs their seniority until publication of the first lineal list, or Blue Book, after they have finished TBS (see the section on precedence in chapter 17). At this time, their names are rearranged in permanent precedence within groups having the same date of rank, according to TBS standing.

❯ ❯ *Military Occupational Specialties*

As you look down a roster of officers, you may at first be puzzled to see an entry such as this: 1STLT JOHN HEYWOOD 0302/8023/2712. Those mysterious numbers listed after the rank and name, you will soon realize, are individual designators of a Marine's specialties, which reflect their knowledge, skills, and abilities. Those four-digit numbers indicate the MOSs of the individual concerned.

Your *primary* MOS describes your primary specialty and, by extension, the type of unit you are considered primarily qualified to command. Any *secondary* MOSs correspond to additional specialty skills and may indicate other command or staff qualifications.

The MOS system thus provides the Marine Corps with a running inventory of talent and indicates at a glance the professional qualifications of each officer and enlisted Marine. For example, returning to Lieutenant Heywood above, a translation of the entry would run as follows:

1STLT JOHN HEYWOOD: rank and name
0302: infantry officer
8023: parachute officer
2712: linguist, Arabic (Modern Standard)

Obviously, those MOSs and the skills they represent are extremely important to you. When you report to a new station, those numbers generally determine your assignment because every position, or "billet," in the Marine Corps carries the MOS appropriate to it.

When you report to TBS, you are classified as a basic officer (MOS 8001). You retain this classification until you complete about three-fifths of TBS, by which time the Marine Corps has had the opportunity to evaluate you. At that point you are generally assigned a primary MOS based on several factors, including your type of commission or appointment. There are three groups of MOSs that are assigned as primary to officers: Group I MOSs, suitable for assignment to unrestricted Regular or Reserve officers; Group II MOSs, for limited duty officers; and Group III MOSs, for warrant officers.

Historically, the Marine Corps assigned officer MOSs based solely on lineal standing at TBS. In 1977, however, the commandant of the Marine Corps opted to employ a quality spread in MOS assignments. The objective was to ensure every occupational field received a comparable share of the most competitive lieutenants. This policy still applies today. TBS assigns MOSs based on four prioritized factors: MOS quality distribution; student suitability, including satisfying certain prerequisites for several specialties; unique or additional considerations, such as specialized education, training, or experience or demographic characteristics; and student preferences. Quality distribution effectively meets the needs of the Corps while considering the desires of the student officers.

If you are an unrestricted officer, the Marine Corps will normally assign you one of the following Group I *primary* MOSs:

- 0102 Manpower Officer
- 0203 Ground Intelligence Officer
- 0204 Counterintelligence/Human Source Intelligence Officer
- 0206 Signals Intelligence Officer
- 0207 Air Intelligence Officer
- 0302 Infantry Officer
- 0402 Logistics Officer
- 0602 Communications Officer
- 0802 Field Artillery Officer
- 1302 Combat Engineer Officer
- 1702 Cyberspace Officer
- 1802 Tank Officer
- 1803 Assault Amphibious Vehicle Officer
- 3002 Ground Supply Officer
- 3404 Financial Management Officer

- 4402 Judge Advocate
- 4502 Communication Strategy and Operations Officer
- 5803 Military Police Officer
- 6002 Aircraft Maintenance Officer
- 6602 Aviation Supply Officer
- 7204 Low-Altitude Air Defense Officer
- 7208 Air Support Control Officer
- 7210 Air Defense Control Officer
- 7220 Air Traffic Control Officer
- 7315 Unmanned Aircraft System / Electronic Warfare Officer
- 7599 Flight Student (upon completing aviation training, pilots and naval flight officers will receive a final primary MOS in occupational field 75 based on their assigned airframes—for example, 7532 Pilot VMM, V-22 Qualified)

With the Marine Corps' recent divestment of its tanks and the approaching retirement of its assault amphibious vehicles, occupational field 18 is entering a period of flux. While the list above containing MOSs 1802 and 1803 reflects current information at the time of writing, it is reasonable to presume that MOS 1802 will be eliminated. Furthermore, with the coming acquisition of a new amphibious combat vehicle and possibly an advanced reconnaissance vehicle, it is likely the Corps will modify or eliminate MOS 1803 and create a new primary MOS for unrestricted officers in occupational field 18.

WOs follow a different path to their primary specialties. They are assigned primary MOSs from a much broader and more diverse set of occupational fields, their expertise is deeper and more narrowly focused, and they receive their MOSs largely based on their enlisted experience and the competitive accession process.

If you later qualify for other occupational fields or specialties, you receive *secondary* MOSs to denote this fact. As you acquire staff specializations (for example, as a force deployment and planning officer; chemical, biological, radiological, and nuclear defense officer; or civil affairs officer), these are reflected by secondary MOSs.

Be advised that although your MOS labels you for certain duties and patterns of assignment, never let it be a pair of blinders. Avoid overspecialization in fact or attitude. Remember that every Marine, regardless of MOS, must always be

A CH-53E Super Stallion externally lifts a Joint Light Tactical Vehicle during training at Marine Corps Base Hawaii in 2021. Such operations are conducted to train both landing support specialists and pilots to transfer heavy equipment and supplies from one location to another.

prepared for all duties appropriate to his or her rank. The genius of the Corps lies in the fact that Marine officers have never let themselves be "compartmentalized" into competing branches, occupational silos, or professional cliques.

You are, first and foremost, an officer of Marines; secondary to that, you pursue a major professional specialty. Command and leadership are the only universal military occupational specialties of all Marine officers and NCOs.

❯❯ *Assignment of Female Officers*

Successive revisions of Title 10, U.S. Code, have provided an integrated career for male and female officers through the grade of general. In 1981, the lineal lists of male and female officers merged, and all were selected for promotion under direct competition among contemporaries. In 1994, policy changes removed restrictions on women serving in combat units, in combat aircrews, and on board combatant ships. Until 2015, policy stipulated that women could serve in all units except those primarily concerned with "engaging the enemy on the ground with individual or crew served weapons, while being exposed to hostile fire and to a high probability of direct physical contact with the hostile force's personnel." This translated into policies that permitted women to be assigned to any occupational field except 03, 08, and 18. During 2015, changes in America's political and cultural climates crossed a threshold, and the push to open all MOSs to women gathered momentum. Occupational fields 03, 08, and 18 opened to women in 2016, and the first female officers joined their male counterparts in Marine infantry, artillery, and armor disciplines in 2017.

Pregnancy may not bar assignment or retention of women in the Marine Corps. Those who become pregnant have the option to remain on active duty or be discharged. If they elect to remain on active duty, they are treated the same as their counterpart male parents in terms of assignments. There are no special considerations based solely on the fact of family responsibilities regardless of gender.

A request for separation by reason of pregnancy may be denied if a woman has incurred an additional active duty obligation following receipt of special compensation, funded education, or advanced technical training, or when she serves in an MOS requiring her retention based upon the needs of the service. A request for separation will be considered under any of the above conditions if the woman provides overriding or compelling factors of personal need.

❧ PROFESSIONAL EDUCATION

It is impossible to overemphasize the importance of professional education.

In school, you learn from the hard-won knowledge and experience of others, and you develop your own professional skills. The education you pursue and your application to professional studies probably exercise more immediate leverage on your career than any other factors.

❧ ❧ *Professional Schools*

Professional schools are classified by instructional level and other characteristics: resident or nonresident, general or specialized in curriculum, and Marine school or a school of another service. The levels of schooling for Marine officers are *basic* (followed immediately by training in MOS), *career*, *intermediate*, and *top*.

The section below on resident schools contains typical examples of professional schools sorted by level.

So far as capacity permits, it is Marine Corps policy that every permanent unrestricted officer goes to school at the basic, career, and intermediate levels. You may not attend two schools on the same level. For the top-level schools (such as the National Defense University), only the most qualified officers are selected. If you aspire to attend such a school, you must accumulate a record of performance that competes favorably with your equally ambitious fellow officers.

In addition to resident schooling, the Marine Corps encourages all officers to enroll in nonresident (online or extension) courses. You can pursue these on your own time, thus adding to your professional knowledge and better preparing yourself for resident instruction when the time comes. It is the advice of many successful officers that during your first fifteen years of service, you should always be enrolled in some course (see the section below on distance learning).

Schooling Outside the Corps. Many Marine officers attend schools conducted by other U.S. services and foreign nations. This ensures a wide base of professional thinking throughout the Corps and fosters insight by Marines into every aspect and domain of the profession of arms.

It is a Marine tradition, which you should never forget, that when you attend the school of another service or country, you should return at or near the head of the class, or—as is said half-jokingly—not return at all.

Marine Corps Schools. Although many Marines attend school outside the Corps, Marine Corps University at Quantico, Virginia, provides the bulk of the professional education for Marines. Quantico is home to schools at all levels, together with several specialist schools. Its students come from all officer ranks of the Corps, from other U.S. services, and from numerous foreign countries. Quantico is the goal of every Marine officer who wants to make the most of his or her career. For more information about the schools, read the sections on Marine Corps Combat Development Command in chapter 6 and Basic School in chapter 12.

❭ ❭ *Resident Schools*

A resident school is one that you attend in person, as distinguished from a nonresident school, whose instruction is distributed by correspondence or via the

Internet. Marine officers attend resident professional military education (PME) at Quantico, several schools run by the other services, several civilian schools, and a few schools conducted by foreign countries. The list varies from time to time, and HQMC periodically lists each course or school open to officers or enlisted Marines.

Here are some of the typical courses and schools that you might attend at each education level. You may find still more names in the current directive on this subject and in the annual naval messages announcing school board results.

Basic Level
> The Basic School, Quantico, Virginia

Career Level
> Expeditionary Warfare School, Quantico, Virginia
> Air Defense Artillery Captains Career Course (USA), Fort Sill, Oklahoma
> Engineer Captains Career Course (USA), Fort Leonard Wood, Missouri
> Field Artillery Captains Career Course (USA), Fort Sill, Oklahoma
> Logistics Captains Career Course (USA), Fort Lee, Virginia
> Maneuver Captains Career Course (USA), Fort Benning, Georgia

Intermediate Level
> Marine Corps Command and Staff College, Quantico, Virginia
> Army Command and General Staff College (USA), Fort Leavenworth, Kansas
> Naval War College (USN), Newport, Rhode Island
> Air War College (USAF), Maxwell Air Force Base, Alabama
> Joint Forces Staff College, Norfolk, Virginia

Top Level
> Marine Corps War College, Quantico, Virginia
> Army War College (USA), Carlisle, Pennsylvania
> Naval War College (USN), Newport, Rhode Island
> Air War College (USAF), Maxwell Air Force Base, Alabama
> National War College, Washington, D.C.
> Dwight D. Eisenhower School for National Security and Resource Planning, Washington, D.C.

Limited assignments at intermediate and top levels are made to other foreign schools in Australia, Brazil, Canada, France, Japan, Norway, South Korea, Spain, the United Kingdom, and others according to current bulletins. Language training at the Defense Language Institute, Monterey, California, normally precedes any foreign professional military education. Additionally, each year there are several fellowships with graduate-level programs at various U.S. universities and Washington-area think tanks that qualify as intermediate- and top-level schooling.

The duration of resident courses generally increases with the level of the school. In quiet times, instruction is more leisurely, whereas during times of war or emergency, courses are compressed to the maximum extent. The average length of a peacetime resident course is from seven to nine months.

The resident schools of the Marine Corps at Quantico are open without distinction to all commissioned line officers, both ground and aviation.

⋄ ⋄ *Distance Learning*

In years past, Marines could pursue professional education and development by correspondence course—a course of study in which students and instructors or administrators communicated by mail. The Marine Corps Institute (MCI) at Marine Barracks Washington administered the Corps' correspondence courses until 2015. MCI was the oldest correspondence school for the U.S. armed forces, having been founded in 1920 to permit World War I Marine veterans to complete interrupted education. Over the years, it changed from a general, semiacademic correspondence school to one that focused primarily on the professional development of enlisted Marines. In 2015, the Corps transferred the distance education mission and functions to the College of Distance Education and Training (CDET) at MCU.

The mission of CDET is to design, develop, deliver, evaluate, manage, and resource distance-learning products and programs across the Marine Corps training and education continuum to increase operational readiness. CDET is a total force educational institution. Through a variety of distance-learning delivery systems, it serves all U.S. military forces and DOD agencies as well as selected international military forces around the globe. CDET's online-learning management system, MarineNet, provides education to all Marines wherever they are stationed. Additionally, the college's worldwide seminar program supports the PME Distance Education Programs (DEPs) through a network of satellite campuses and learning resource centers.

All Marine Corps distance education is free of charge. In addition, Marine officers are eligible to take similar courses conducted by the U.S. Naval War College, Newport, Rhode Island, and, if no equivalent Marine distance education course exists, similar instruction offered by the Army and Air Force war colleges and the National Defense University.

The following personnel are eligible for enrollment in MarineNet courses once they are registered in the Defense Enrollment Eligibility Reporting System (DEERS):

- Active-duty servicemembers
- Reservists
- Military family members
- Retirees
- DOD civilian employees
- DOD contractors

CDET also distributes officer PME through its distance education programs. The Expeditionary Warfare School Distance Education Program (EWSDEP) provides Marine captains, as well as their equivalent WOs, international officers, and civilian employees, career-level professional military education and training on the warfighting capabilities of a Marine air-ground task force operating within a complex and distributed naval expeditionary environment. This enables captains to command or to serve as primary staff officers in their MOSs, integrate the capabilities resident within their element of the MAGTF, integrate their element within the MAGTF, and understand the functioning of the other elements of the task force. The Command and Staff College Distance Education Program (CSCDEP) provides Marine majors and their eligible equivalents graduate-level education to develop critical thinkers, innovative problem solvers, and ethical leaders who will serve as commanders and staff officers in service, joint, interagency, and multinational organizations confronting complex and uncertain security environments. Officers interested in enrolling in EWSDEP or CSCDEP should pursue enrollment through MarineNet.

CDET does not offer any top-level school programs, but there are distance education programs available that offer Marine Corps officers a unique opportunity for high-quality nonresident education. Nonresident top-level schools open to Marine officers include the Army War College and the Air War College.

Naval War College. The College of Distance Education (CDE) represents the Naval War College's outreach program. An alternative to the resident programs offered at the campus in Newport, Rhode Island, CDE provides executive-level education to officers of the various military services and to senior DOD and other federal employees. Its programs are delivered online or through faculty-led seminars on location. Students may pursue Joint Professional Military Education Phase I credits or a master's degree. If you wish to enroll, or if you seek further information, visit the CDE website or contact the college directly by email.

Other Service Courses. If you are interested in distance education and training offered by the Army, Navy, Air Force, or DOD for which the Marine Corps does not have an equivalent, apply directly to the school of interest.

For younger officers of marked ability, the White House Fellows Program is worth considering. There are no formal age restrictions, but the program was created to give selected Americans the experience of government service early in their careers. In this program, officer college graduates, as well as civil servants, educators, and journalists, are given a year of firsthand, high-level experience in the workings of the U.S. government at the White House and cabinet level.

❯❯ *Graduate Education*

For many billets, the Marine Corps requires officers who possess postgraduate-level education, experience, and training, that is, study undertaken after obtaining an initial baccalaureate degree. In the past, the Corps satisfied these requirements through its special education, advanced degree, and tuition assistance programs. In 2019, however, it reorganized and consolidated all advanced-education programs into the Marine Corps Graduate Education Program (MCGEP).

Under MCGEP, the Marine Corps annually screens and selects officers who meet various eligibility and qualification criteria to participate in a variety of postgraduate programs. These include resident intermediate- and top-level PME, as described above, along with a variety of fellowships, scholarships, graduate education, special assignments, and training with industry. For those eligible and qualified, the screening is automatic; no application is necessary. Eligibility and qualification criteria are published annually via naval message in advance of the selection boards.

Naval Postgraduate School (NPS) at Monterey, California, is the principal source of graduate education for the Marine Corps. Its naval-focused curricula are central to the development of an educated, knowledgeable, and adaptable officer corps. Each program at NPS provides specific education to equip the officer with the knowledge, skills, and abilities required for specialized billets at major commands across the Corps.

Through its resident and nonresident programs, Marine Corps University is the Corps' principal provider of graduate-level service and joint PME. It is accredited to award master's degrees. Its curricula are central to the development of MAGTF leaders who are operationally and strategically minded, critical thinkers, and skilled naval and joint warfighters prepared to function at the operational and strategic levels of war.

Because NPS and MCU lack sufficient capacity and because the Marine Corps values graduate education from diverse sources, the annual selection boards also assign officers to an array of other institutions. Officers may participate in various fellowships, such as with the Department of State, Department of Justice, and Congress; train with industry, such as with Federal Express and Morgan Stanley; attend various U.S. and foreign civilian universities, such as Harvard University, Stanford University, and Humboldt University in Berlin, Germany; and attend U.S. and foreign military colleges, such as Naval War College, Army War College, and the Israel National Defense College.

The various graduate education programs permit officers to pursue studies in a variety of disciplines. Most common is some variation of national or international security studies, but the following disciplines are also among those that have been recently available to Marines:

- History
- International, environmental, labor, procurement, criminal, and cyber law
- Aeronautical, electrical, and environmental engineering
- Operations analysis
- Defense systems analysis
- Modeling and simulation
- Computer science

- Combat systems science and technology
- Information systems and technology
- Information warfare systems
- Manpower management
- Financial management
- Material logistics-support management
- Public affairs management
- Space systems operations
- Special operations (irregular warfare)

In addition to all the organized, formal schooling just described, there remains a place for the traditional battalion or squadron officers' school, conducted by

Officers with advanced degrees in such disciplines as operations analysis and defense systems analysis help develop future Marine Corps capabilities, such as this experimental Navy-Marine Expeditionary Ship Interdiction System (NMESIS) launcher, seen deploying into position at Pacific Missile Range Facility Barking Sands, Hawaii.

the CO and best-qualified officers of the unit. A well-tested arrangement is to hold it each Friday afternoon, followed immediately by a happy hour.

❧ ❧ *Professional Reading*

Great military leaders throughout history have recognized the importance of continuous reading in the profession of arms. Napoleon Bonaparte wrote, "Read and re-read the campaigns of Alexander, Hannibal, Caesar, Gustavus Adolphus, Turenne, Eugene, and Frederick. Make them your models. This is the only way to become a great general and to master the secrets of the art of war."

A few officers attain high rank without having mastered the history of war, but they are few indeed. The habit of systematic, planned reading of history, biography, and literature enables you to live up to your profession and to apply the lessons of the past to the future. Remember Prince Metternich's remark: "The past is chiefly useful to me as the eve of tomorrow—my soul wrestles with the future." Professional reading means more than studiously applying oneself to military regulations and field manuals that guide daily operations. This type of reading should be taken for granted, as should the reading of service journals. Professional reading even transcends military matters; remember Georges Clemenceau's barbed dictum, "War is too important a matter to be left to the generals." Your professional reading ought to embrace military and naval history and biography, U.S. and world history, literature, international affairs, economics, and psychology.

This sounds like a large order. It will not seem so large once you begin. The most important part of a professional reading program can be summed up in one verb—Read!

Subscribe to your professional journals: the Marine Corps Association's *Marine Corps Gazette* and the U.S. Naval Institute's *Proceedings*. If you have a bent for military history, take the *Journal of Military History*. Additionally, there is now an assortment of cutting-edge online journals focused on military and national security issues that merit a look.

The Commandant of the Marine Corps Professional Reading Program provides an engaging list of recommended reading, updated annually via naval message, that every officer must master. Recommended works fall into many categories, such as leadership, strategy, and the profession of arms. The Gray Research Center at Marine Corps University maintains the current reading list on its website (https://grc-usmcu.libguides.com/). Additionally, it maintains an archive of all of the commandant's reading lists since the reading program's establishment in 1989. Works in this archive are also well worth the effort to engage.

A final must are the high-quality Marine Corps operational histories prepared by the Marine Corps History Division at Marine Corps University. Every officer should become familiar with them.

So now it is time to build your professional library and get in the habit of reading professional journals. The Marine Corps packs and ships your professional library from station to station at no charge against your weight allowance and at no cost to you.

❯ PROFESSIONAL COMMUNICATIONS

❯ ❯ *The Service Author*

Every officer with professional ideas worth expressing should support his or her service journals by contributing. There are three good reasons why you should do this. First, you support the publications that spread military knowledge, promote professional discourse, and raise professional standards; second, you give readers the benefit of your ideas and experience; and third, you acquire a service reputation for professional keenness.

It is widely believed that elaborate and drastic regulations hamper an officer who chooses to write for publication. This is certainly not the case for reputable journals such as *Proceedings* or the *Gazette*. Additionally, online journals focusing on national security and military affairs, such as *War on the Rocks* and *Task and Purpose*, offer welcoming venues for military writers. Be aware, however, that material prepared by active officers for outside publication may require clearance by the SECNAV and DOD. It is usually wise to consult your security manager and staff judge advocate before submitting a manuscript for publication.

In any case, you cannot reveal classified information in an article for publication any more than you can disclose the same information in a letter or in careless conversation. Nor can you represent that you are an official spokesman of the Marine Corps or the Department of the Navy or give such an impression. Finally, whatever you write for publication should constitute a constructive contribution to the primary missions of DOD.

If you are ever in any doubt as to the classification or general propriety of an article or manuscript, you may always submit it to the director of the Office of U.S. Marine Corps Communications (formerly Public Affairs), HQMC, who will advise you as to its suitability for publication.

Public Speaking

Distinct, forceful speech is an essential quality for a successful officer. Public speaking is a primary tool of leadership. Because a large part of your career will be devoted to explaining, announcing, and teaching, you should learn at least the fundamentals of speaking techniques—and the sooner, the better.

Some believe that public speaking ability is a magic gift, bestowed on some but denied to others. This is far from true. Although some individuals are indeed naturally gifted, public speaking, like the technique of shooting a rifle, can readily be—and must be—learned.

But how do you become a good public speaker? What individual qualities do effective military speakers cultivate and possess?

Be Purposeful. You must have a clear view of your objective—that is, of what you are trying to convey. You must be able to balance the speaking time allocated to the various aspects of your topic against achievement of your objective. Avoid digression into irrelevancy.

Know Your Stuff. You must have a thorough grasp of your subject, backed up, if possible, by practical experience. Conversely, avoid, if you can, having to talk about matters in which you lack experience.

Prepare. Even if you have all the knowledge, skill, and experience needed to address your topic, there is no shortcut in preparation. Choose the right approach and method of presentation; arrange your material in logical phases, each one followed by a summary; and use visual aids, if you are instructing, to help your audience see your points. Psychological studies show that 75 percent of all we learn is taken in through the eyes, whereas only 13 percent comes through hearing and the rest through other senses.

Be Enthusiastic. Enthusiasm is as infectious as boredom. It is the driving force of a good speech or lecture. But your enthusiasm must be balanced and seasoned. If you make your listeners feel that you are a fanatic with a wild gleam in the eye, they will discount what you say and let their attention wander. And enthusiasm unseasoned by intelligence and humor soon exhausts the listener.

Cultivate a Dramatic Sense. Do not be content with dull, stodgy presentations; instead, cultivate what people in show business call a "sense of staging." Get in touch with the mood of your audience. Vary the pace, and use surprise, and emotional and dramatic appeal to drive home your points. If you can tell a funny story well, do not be afraid to use it—but do not indulge in a gag just for the gag's sake. Remember, also, that there are other (and usually more effective) ways to introduce a subject than by telling an *irrelevant* "funny" story.

Have a Confident, Easy Manner. Give your listeners confidence in what you say by having that confidence yourself. Speak clearly and distinctly. Remember that distinctness of speech stems from distinctness of ideas. One way to maintain a confident, easy manner is to stick with language in your "comfort zone." Avoid flowery language and obscure jargon.

Have the Right Approach. Your approach should be tailored to the audience. Regardless of the kind of audience you face, however, avoid the following:

- *Flippancy*. A flippant speaker displays disrespect for his or her subject and, by extension, for the audience.
- *Cheap humor and vulgarity*. Do not play the clown to get a cheap laugh. Vulgarity offends most listeners and, if repeated, bores all. By cheapening your remarks, you cheapen yourself and the Marine Corps.
- *Excessive slang*. Judiciously used, slang can be quite effective. But if you use slang indiscriminately, you lose your effect and grate on the audience's nerves.
- *"Big words" and pedantry*. Overuse of technical terms or of involved, long-winded constructions wraps your subject in a fog. Hundred-dollar words used merely for effect do not impress your listeners.

Make the Most of Your Voice and Body. Voice is your basic tool. To exploit your voice, develop power, distinctness, and variety of delivery. Your body supports your voice through erect and confident posture, natural movement, meaningful gesture, and eye contact. Make it a rule to look every listener in the eye while you speak to a group.

⊁ ⊁ *Public Affairs*

Intelligent and candid relations with the public form an important part of every Marine's career, from private to general, regardless of specialty.

The Marine Corps has long benefited from an aggressive and positive public affairs program in which attention is drawn to the mission, capabilities, and security that the nation derives from the Corps' existence. Public affairs specialists assist commanders in handling community and media relations to present and explain Marine activities to broaden the public view of the Corps. In many cases, this means that prompt attention is paid to good and bad news so that the unsparing eye of the citizenry will see that the Corps measures up to the high standards of discipline, devotion to duty, individual smartness, and valor—hallmarks of the Corps.

Despite your not being a public affairs specialist, know that your every action in public view will enhance or degrade the carefully won reputation the Marine Corps enjoys today. The Corps' best advertisement is the individual Marine. Deal truthfully, pleasantly, and respectfully with the public and its media representation. Be aware of what the public affairs program has outlined for appropriate remarks to the press and public. The Corps belongs to the nation, and your individual contribution, however isolated, will only enhance public knowledge and appreciation.

⟨ 15 ⟩

LEADERSHIP AND MANAGEMENT

It's not hard to be an officer, but it's damn hard to be a good officer.
— Gunnery Sergeant Daniel Daly

MILITARY SERVICE—in peacetime and especially in wartime—places great demands on the mental, moral, and physical strength of the individual Marine. In battle, character traits weigh more heavily than intellectual acuity. Even in this age of high technology, humans must still stand the test. Leadership thus assumes extraordinary importance, for it convinces the Marine of the necessity of service and encourages faithful performance of duty. The Marine's readiness to serve and, in wartime, to risk his or her life contributes to the integrity of the nation and the survival of its free and democratic order.

The foundations of an individual's performance as a Marine are discipline, courage, self-assurance, a sense of duty, and cooperative thinking. These qualities sustain a Marine as he or she endures hardships and strives to accomplish the mission. Establishing such foundations remains the salient objective of leadership. Of them, discipline plays the indispensable role in maintaining the combat power of a unit. Undisciplined behavior must be countered immediately and appropriately. In well-disciplined units, a sense of comradeship emerges, and soldierly values—such as confidence and unselfishness—predominate. Commanders at all levels must gain the trust of subordinates and establish solidarity in their units. This is accomplished primarily through the demonstration of knowledge and wisdom, fairness, patience, and thoughtfulness as well as setting the example and strictly enforcing standards. Most destructive to comradeship are leaders who display misguided ambition, selfishness, and insincerity.

In wartime, troops face enormous psychological pressures brought on by the effects of enemy weapons and disinformation, isolation from friendly forces, and disruption of communications. The natural fear resulting from any of these factors can escalate into unrestrained, unreasoning, and self-destructive fear—in a word, panic. Leaders must nip all signs of panic in the bud before losing influence over the troops. Prevention, however, is the best course of action. By providing the unit with up-to-date, factual, and objective information and by reiterating that their fight is meaningful and their political and military leadership sound, the leader can psychologically equip the troops to withstand the pressures of war.

Certain characteristics, techniques, and procedures contribute to both effective leadership and sound management. Leadership is fundamentally about motivating people, whereas management typically involves the direction, control, and administration of programs, systems, and organizations. The best officers are both inspiring leaders and adept managers.

❯ THE MARINE LEADER

❯ ❯ *Attributes of a Marine Leader*

Major General John A. Lejeune summarized the attributes of a Marine leader: "The young American responds quickly and readily to the exhibition of qualities of leadership on the part of his officers. Some of these qualities are industry, energy, initiative, determination, enthusiasm, firmness, kindness, justness, self-control, unselfishness, honor, and courage."

Lejeune's list can scarcely be improved, but it is worth amplifying and explaining.

Contagion of Example. This is the central thought in Lejeune's passage. It is not enough that you merely know a leader's qualities and not enough that you proclaim them; you must *exhibit* them. To exact discipline, you must first possess self-discipline, and to demand unsparing attention to duty, you must spare none yourself.

Command Presence. Much of the power of example in turn stems from "command presence," or the kind of military appearance you make. This is the product of dignity, military carriage, firm and unhurried speech, and self-confidence. Command presence is one useful adjunct of leadership that can be systematically cultivated. "Spit and polish" alone should not be confused with it.

Resolution and Tenacity. The fuel of leadership, together these show an unfaltering determination to achieve the mission assigned to you.

Ability to Teach and Speak. This combined ability usually denotes an effective leader and enhances whatever latent leadership talents you possess. Cultivate this gift at every opportunity. It is a lever that can decisively influence your career.

Protect and Foster Subordinates. Marine Corps leaders assume responsibility for their subordinates' actions (their mistakes, too) and see to it that credit is received where it is due. This distinguishing Marine leadership trait means looking out for your people.

Encouragement of Subordinates. A tradition of Marine leadership is to give subordinates all the initiative and latitude they can handle. Encourage them also in professional studies and reading and make sure they seek professional schooling.

Professional Competence. Whether your Marines like you, they will surely respect you if you know what you are doing. "You can't snow the troops" is an old Marine saying. If you are technically and tactically proficient, your enlisted Marines will be the first to get the word. Conversely, they will be mercilessly quick to spot a fraud. Demonstrate competence and keenness as an officer, and your Marines will be content to be led by you. Never be ashamed to be known as a "hard charger," as long as your aim is the best interest of the Corps.

Here is a classic remark by one of the Marine Corps' hardest-charging generals, Graves B. Erskine: "The first thing, a man should know his business. He should know his weapons, he should know the tactics for those weapons, and he should not only be qualified for the grade he is assigned to, but at least for the next higher grade."

Education. Learning contributes to professional competence. Education and study give you technical proficiency, help you think clearly, enable you to express yourself, and allow you to command respect from all.

Physical Readiness. Although not an end in itself, being in shape is essential for every Marine and thus doubly so for every leader. Unless you can confidently face your physical fitness test, you are not fit for active command.

"Can Do" and "Make Do." The spirit embodied in these phrases is as old as the Corps itself. To do the best you can with what you have, to do it promptly, cheerfully, and confidently, marks you as a leader in the best traditions of the Marine Corps. The world is divided into "can-do" and "can't-do" types. Be sure you are in the former class.

Adaptability. The mark of a seasoned Marine, it keeps you loose as a leader, lets you roll with the punches, and helps you cultivate that most admirable trait, "grace under pressure."

Devotion to the Marine Corps and Its Standards. This commitment begets equal earnestness and devotion from subordinates. Take the Corps and its time-honored ways with full seriousness, and so will your command. That is the Marine Corps attitude.

As both summary of and comment on the traits and values just discussed is this thought-provoking list of attributes: aggressive, austere, authoritative, compassionate, competent, courageous, disciplined, inventive, knowledgeable, loyal, proud, purposeful, resolute, sensitive, serious, tenacious, and tough. How do you measure up?

Based on the views and example of one of the Marine Corps' foremost leaders, Lejeune, the foregoing is a somewhat historical but timeless discussion of leadership. It is meant to supplement, not supplant, formal teaching on leadership within the Corps. Every Marine officer must also know, embrace, and embody the Corps' leadership traits: dependability, loyalty, justice, judgment, integrity, unselfishness, tact, bearing, courage, initiative, knowledge, decisiveness, endurance, and enthusiasm.

❯ YOU AND YOUR SUBORDINATES

Whether your subordinates are officers or enlisted Marines, support and back them to the hilt. They will turn to you for encouragement, guidance, and support. Never let them down. Nothing should ever be "too much trouble" if it is needed for your outfit. Protect, shelter, and feed your men and women before you think of your own needs.

LEADERSHIP TRAITS

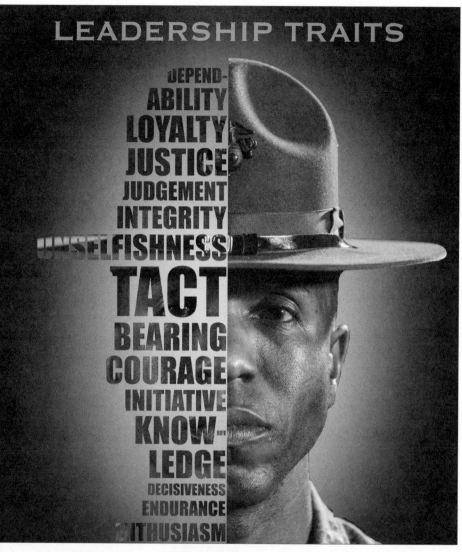

DEPEND-
ABILITY
LOYALTY
JUSTICE
JUDGEMENT
INTEGRITY
UNSELFISHNESS
TACT
BEARING
COURAGE
INITIATIVE
KNOW-
LEDGE
DECISIVENESS
ENDURANCE
ENTHUSIASM

Marines learn—and learn to embody—the fourteen leadership traits during both recruit and basic officer training. Demonstrating the leadership traits in daily activities helps one earn the respect, confidence, and loyal cooperation of other Marines.

❧ ❧ *Dealing with Subordinates*

Demand the highest standards and never let those standards be compromised. Field Marshal Erwin Rommel stated this in slightly different words: "A commander must accustom his staff to a high tempo from the outset, and continually keep them up to it. If he once allows himself to be satisfied with norms, or anything less than an all-out effort, he gives up the race from the starting post, and will sooner or later be taught a bitter lesson."

Live, lead, and exercise command "by the book." Let this be understood by your Marines.

Keep *responsibility* centralized—in you. Decentralize *authority*. Give subordinates wide authority and discretion. Tell them what results you want, and leave the "how" to them. Never oversupervise.

Avoid overfamiliarity of manner or address. If you have limitations—and all humans do have some weakness or character flaw—overfamiliarity with subordinates is the surest way to reveal it.

Develop a genuine interest in your Marines as individuals. Study each personality. Seek out background information from service records. Learn names, and address your Marines by proper names. Never let any Marine picture himself or herself as "a mere cog" in the machine. No Marine is a cog.

In your daily exercise of command, avoid the "hurry up and wait" tendency that characterizes ill-run commands. That is to say, think twice before you apply pressure to speed up something if the result is simply that your people will have to stand around waiting at some later stage. Do not get them out unduly ahead of time for formations and parades, especially if every other echelon has added its few minutes of anticipation, too. Always be on time and on schedule as far as you yourself are concerned. One of the most basic rules of military courtesy is to never keep the troops waiting.

Respect the skill and experience of your noncommissioned officers. Learn from their wisdom, but never let them mislead you. Do everything in your power to enhance the skill, prestige, and authority of NCOs except at the expense of your own authority. In public, address NCOs by name and rank. In private, you may call them by their last names only. *Never address an enlisted person by his or her first name or nickname.*

Be accessible to any subordinate who wishes to see you. It is a tradition of the Corps that any enlisted Marine who desires an interview with the commanding officer must obtain the first sergeant's permission. It is equally a tradition of the Corps that permission is unhesitatingly given unless the Marine is drunk or flagrantly out of uniform. In connection with such requests, you should give your first sergeant direct and positive instructions that he or she must report to you, the CO, every complaint received from an enlisted Marine. Most of these need never come to your attention otherwise or in any official form, but this rule helps avert trouble before it becomes serious.

❧ ❧ *Issuing and Enforcing Orders*

"In carrying out a mission, the promulgation of the order represents not over 10 percent of your responsibility. The remaining 90 percent consists of assuring, by means of personal supervision on the ground, by yourself and your staff, proper and vigorous execution." So wrote Lieutenant General George S. Patton in instructions to his corps, division, and separate unit commanders in 1944. Issuing and enforcing orders thus constitute one of the main functions of an officer.

Before you issue an order, ask yourself if it can be reasonably carried out and equally enforced. If, in the circumstances, an order cannot be executed or enforced as given, it should not be given.

Never give an unlawful order—that is, an order that contravenes law or regulations or demands that your subordinates break the rules. A good test of a lawful order is asking, "Could a subordinate be court-martialed for failing to comply?"

Issue as few orders as necessary. Keep them concise, clear, and unmistakable in purpose. Anything that can be misunderstood will be.

Never contravene the orders of another officer or NCO without clear and pressing reason. If possible, make this reason evident when you countermand the order in question. If orders to you conflict, seek guidance immediately or obey the last one.

When you have once given an order, be sure it is executed as you give it. Your responsibility does not end until you have assured yourself that the order has been carried out. Never shrug off half-hearted, perfunctory compliance. "If anyone in a key position appears to be expending less than the energy that could properly be demanded of him," wrote Rommel, "that man must be ruthlessly removed."

An order received from above should be passed on as your order and should be enforced as such. Never evade the onus of an unpopular directive by throwing the blame on the next-higher echelon.

It cannot be too often repeated that when you issue an order, make clear what you want done and who is to do it—but avoid telling subordinates how it is to be done. Remember the old promotion exam question for lieutenants in which the student is told that he or she has a ten-person working party, headed by a sergeant, and must erect a seventy-five-foot flagpole on the base parade ground. Problem—How to do it? Every student who works out the precise calculations of stresses, tackle, and gear, no matter how accurately, is graded wrong. The correct answer is simple: The lieutenant turns to the sergeant and says, "Sergeant, put up that flagpole."

❧ ❧ *Looking Out for Your Marines*

In the final analysis, the essence of Marine leadership is looking out for your people.

For the sake of your unit, you must be tireless, you must be imaginative, and you must be willing to shoulder responsibility. Your Marines' well-being must be your first preoccupation. Their interest and advancement must be always on your mind. Looking out for your Marines demands that you hold several questions foremost in your mind:

- Are they comfortably clothed, housed, and sheltered?
- Are they well fed?
- Are they getting their mail?
- Is their pay timely and accurate?
- If sick and wounded, can they rely on help?
- Are they justly treated?
- Are they trained to accomplish their mission?
- Are you available to everyone who needs counsel?
- Are you alert to help each one in his or her career?

As an officer, you demand a great deal of your Marines. But they, in fact, demand much more of you. If you let down one of your Marines, you are letting down the entire Corps.

⁂ MILITARY DISCIPLINE

⁂ *The Object and Nature of Discipline*

Effective performance by Marines in combat is the direct result and primary object of military discipline. Discipline may be defined as prompt and willing responsiveness to orders and unhesitating compliance with regulations. Since its ultimate objective is effective performance in battle, discipline may, in a very real sense, spell the difference between life and death—or, more important to the Marine, between victory and defeat. It is that standard of deportment, attention to duty, example, and decent behavior that, once indoctrinated, enables Marines, alone or in groups, to accomplish their mission.

To many persons, discipline simply means punishment. This is misguided. In fact, discipline is a matter of people working and getting along well together—even if there is a lack of harmony among them, discipline is a means of cementing them as a fighting organization. In the Marine Corps, as in any military organization, it is necessary for people to do certain things in prescribed ways and at given times. If they do so, then they are well disciplined.

Discipline exists in everyday life, too: people obey traffic signals, drive on the correct side of the road, go in through marked entrances and out through exits. Nevertheless, military discipline differs fundamentally from those of civilian life because a Marine, having taken an oath to serve an allotted time, is committed to his or her duty, while a civilian worker is free to quit a job at any time. For this reason, "management," a popular word in the civilian sector, is an incomplete, and at times unsatisfactory, term in military circles compared with "leadership."

⁂ *The Basis of Discipline*

The best discipline is self-discipline. To be well disciplined, a unit must be made up of individuals who are self-disciplined. In the ultimate test of combat, the leader must be able to depend on the Marines to do their duty correctly and voluntarily whether anyone is checking on them or not. If time and the situation permit, you should make known to your subordinates the reasons for a given order because this knowledge will increase the desire of your people to do the job and enable them to do it intelligently. You must know what you want of your people, let them know, and then demand it of them.

❧ ❧ *Characteristics of Effective Discipline*

Until severely tried, there is no conclusive test of discipline. Troops remain relatively undisciplined until subjected to *physical and mental stress*, a fact that shapes much of the programs of training for recruits and officers. No body of troops could possibly enjoy the dust, the heat, the blistered feet, and the aching back of a road march. Nevertheless, hard road marching is a necessary and sound foundation for the discipline of combat troops. The rise in spirit within any unit, which is always marked when Marines rebound from a hard march or after a record day, does not come from a feeling of physical relief but from a sense of accomplishment.

Other key factors in sound discipline are *consistency* and *firmness*. You cannot wink at an infraction one day and put a person on the report for the same offense another day. You must establish and make known your standards of good discipline, then be consistent—firmly consistent—every day.

Discipline imposed by fear of punishment will inevitably break down in combat or any other severe test. If you threaten your troops, it will also break. Discipline will not break under stress, however, if troops understand why they are enduring hardship and danger.

❧ PRAISE AND REPRIMAND

❧ ❧ *Occasions for Praise*

A basic rule is to *praise in public and reprimand in private.*

Never let a praiseworthy occasion pass unrecognized. This means more than the occasional pat on the back. Here are ways in which you can make the most of opportunities to praise subordinates.

Promotion. When an officer is promoted, he or she should be sworn in at Office Hours (see the section below) by the senior Marine officer present. Administration of the oath adds greatly to the solemnity of the occasion and enables the officer to reaffirm the original oath taken upon receiving his or her first commission. If practical, the spouse and children should be invited. All fellow officers certainly should attend. The officer administering the oath should always give a set of insignia to the individual being promoted—if possible, a set of his or her own insignia from an earlier rank, a gift that is always appreciated.

Enlisted promotions are effected by presentation of the individual's warrant for the next higher rank. This should be done at a formation. If a formation cannot be arranged, the person should receive the warrant from the CO at Office Hours in the presence of his or her immediate leadership. If enlisted offenders are to appear at the same Office Hours, form them in the rear to give them occasion to reflect on "the other side of the coin."

Under no circumstances should a Marine be called into the company office and receive the warrant from the first sergeant or clerk. This is the wrong way of marking the occasion and reflects directly on you if you permit such procedures.

Reenlistment. When a number of Marines ship over on the same day, arrange a formation in their honor. Otherwise, individuals should be reenlisted at Office Hours. If practical, make this the occasion for a day off. And, if warranted and possible, there is no better moment to effect a promotion—nothing starts a new enlistment so handsomely as another chevron.

Presentation of Decorations. The *Marine Corps Drill and Ceremonies Manual* describes the ceremony for presenting decorations. Even at some inconvenience to the unit, decorations—particularly those earned in combat or awarded for heroic action—should be presented with utmost formality at a parade or review, as the manual describes. Avoid the easy solution of calling in the Marine to Office Hours and presenting the medal with a handshake. A fundamental purpose of awards is to inspire emulation. To do this, you must present medals or commendations in the presence of all members of the command or unit.

A modified version of the awards ceremony can serve equally well for such occasions as presentation of Good Conduct Medals, civilian commendations, commissioning of meritorious NCOs as WOs or second lieutenants, and so on.

In combat, when an award can be made immediately, it is sometimes effective for a senior commander to visit the recipient at the unit, call together comrades, and give the medal on the spot. With decorations, even more than other rewards, "he gives thrice who gives quickly." As a combat leader, be alert for every deserving act, especially by an enlisted Marine. Know the criteria and standards for every award and how to initiate proper recommendations (see the section on initiating an award in chapter 10).

Retirement. The honorable retirement or transfer to the Reserve of any officer or enlisted Marine should be habitually effected at a parade or review. In the case of an officer, it is also appropriate for the officers of the unit to "dine out" at a mess night (as described in chapter 21).

Completion of Distance-Learning Course. Any Marine who completes a distance-learning course should receive the diploma from the CO at Office Hours or formation.

❧ ❧ *Reprimand*

One basic rule of reprimand is worth reiterating—*do it in private.*

A second rule is found in the Marine proverb "Never give a Marine a dollar's worth of blame without a dime's worth of praise," which is to say that it can be useful, when feasible, to begin and end a reprimand on a positive note.

And avoid collective reprimands, let alone collective punishments. Nothing so rightly infuriates an innocent person as to be unfairly included in an all-hands blast or all-hands punishment.

Before you issue any reprimand or censure, be sure that an offense or dereliction of some kind actually has been committed. This is basic. Before chastising any individual, ask yourself if what that person has done, pushed to the limit, would sustain charges under any article in the Uniform Code of Military Justice. This can save you much embarrassment and injured innocence at the hands of sea lawyers, while it sometimes cuts the other way to protect a subordinate against hasty rebuke when not warranted.

Know what you intend to say before you launch into a reprimand. A sputtering, inconclusive rebuke only makes an officer look silly.

Avoid uncontrolled anger, profanity, or abuse. Many experienced Marines, both officer and NCO, know how to vent anger into indignation. Make this your object, but at all costs avoid "acting tough."

Never make a promise or threat that you are not capable of fulfilling or that you do not intend to fulfill. Never bluff, or you will be quickly called.

Like reward, the effectiveness of admonishment is in direct proportion to its immediacy. When you spot something amiss, take corrective action at once.

Never let a wrongdoing Marine slide by with the thought, "Well, he's not one of my troops. Let his own outfit handle it." *Every* U.S. Marine is one of *your* troops.

If you have occasion to correct a Marine not under your command, find out who the Marine is and inform his or her CO, who will appreciate knowing when his or her Marines fail to measure up. Moreover, the derelictions of an individual are the responsibility of the immediate senior. A Marine with a dirty rifle is a black eye for the squad and fire team leader; a Marine in your platoon who fails to salute is a discredit to your leadership. Napoleon's dictum "There are no bad regiments—only bad colonels" applies with equal force to fire teams, squads, platoons, companies, and battalions.

⇥ ⇥ *Office Hours*

Office Hours, the Marine Corps equivalent of Captain's Mast, is the occasion when the CO awards formal praise or blame, hears special requests, and assigns nonjudicial punishment. As pertains to military justice, detailed treatment of Office Hours procedure and nonjudicial punishment is contained in chapter 19.

Remember that Office Hours is a ceremony and that much of the desired effect depends upon the manner in which it is conducted. When you hold Office Hours, do so with the greatest respect for each person's individuality. Not only must the punishment fit the crime, but it must also fit the person. Never let anyone leave Office Hours with a sense of injustice or frustrated misunderstanding.

A special and important variation of Office Hours is Request Mast, an occasion set aside for individuals who may have special requests or grievances that they wish to present to the CO. It is one of the responsibilities of command to keep this opportunity open to any Marine who, *in good faith*, wishes to utilize it. In holding Request Mast, it is important to remember that the individual is entitled to complete privacy. Unless requested otherwise, you should see individual Marines alone and take all necessary steps to avoid any prejudice to their interests that might arise out of a bona fide complaint or special request.

⇥ INSPECTIONS

Inspection is one of the most important tools of leadership and command. Throughout your Marine Corps career, you will be continually inspected or inspecting. This serves two purposes: first, to enable commanding or superior officers to assess conditions within an organization; second, to impart to an organization the standards required of it.

There are several types of inspection, varying from personnel in ranks to matériel, supplies, equipment, records, and buildings. Each inspection has a particular purpose, which the inspecting officer will keep foremost in mind. Thus, when inspected, it is up to you to ascertain or forecast the object of the inspection and to prepare yourself and your command accordingly. For example, if the inspection is to deal with the crew-served weapons and transportation in your unit, it does no great good to emphasize clean uniforms and haircuts at the expense of matériel upkeep. On the other hand, good-looking vehicles do not excuse greasy, worn clothing at a personnel inspection.

❯ ❯ *Preparation for Inspection*

Once you know the purpose of an inspection, you must prepare your outfit. The best way to do this is by putting yourself in the inspector's shoes. Be sure your leading NCOs also understand the "why" of the inspection so that they can cooperate intelligently during their preparations. Many an inspection crisis has been averted by a quick-witted, loyal NCO with a ready answer.

While your unit prepares for inspection, move about with a leading NCO, usually your first sergeant, platoon sergeant, and/or police sergeant, depending on the nature of the inspection. This enables you to see that preparations are what you want and reminds your people that you have direct interest in the hard work in which they are engaged. It also lets you discover weak spots early enough to address them.

Time the preparation for inspection so that everything is ready about thirty minutes before the appointed hour. This gives your Marines a final opportunity to get themselves ready. It also gives you a margin to handle last-minute emergencies.

Ten minutes beforehand, have your responsible subordinates standing by their respective posts, or, if the inspection is to be in formation, have your troops paraded, steady, and correct. You should be either at the head of the troops or at the entrance to your area, poised to meet the inspecting party. As a platoon leader, you should have your platoon sergeant and guide assist you in the inspection. If you are the company commander, you should have your first sergeant and gunnery sergeant in your inspection party. One of these NCOs should have a notebook and pencil ready to take notes. The police sergeant should have a flashlight. All rooms, compartments, sheds, and so forth should be unlocked and open.

When the inspecting party arrives, salute and report your unit prepared for inspection. Post yourself at the left rear of the inspecting officer. Answer questions calmly and with good humor. Avoid alibis. Remember, there is only one inspector, and you should take no actions or make comments yourself except to attend the inspector. Do not reprimand your troops during inspection for shortcomings the inspection brings out. It is your outfit; the shortcomings are yours. Be alert for the inspecting officer's comments. These will help you better prepare for the next inspection.

Afterward, if results have been notably good or notably poor, assemble your people and tell them about it. Give every Marine a personal stake in the success of each inspection.

❖ ❖ *Conduct of the Inspection*

Nothing else can raise the standards of a command like an intelligent program of inspection carefully followed up. Some officers unwisely discount the value of formal inspections, believing that they result in unbalanced, artificial impressions and that COs ought to observe informally to find out "real" conditions. While it is certainly true that every CO must keep on the move and keep his or her eyes open, the periodic formal inspection is vital because it requires all hands to overhaul their areas of responsibility. Moreover, formal inspection is the only way to determine accurately the degree of progress being made by a unit.

Before *conducting* an inspection, you, like the unit being inspected, must also make careful preparations. There are several considerations that should guide every inspector:

- Know what you intend to concentrate on—in other words, the purpose of the inspection.
- Have a planned route and sequence of inspection designed to cover the entire unit and area.
- Organize your inspecting party. This should include one Marine to take notes, one with a flashlight, plus the requisite specialist talent (such as hospital corpsman, technicians, and so forth) needed to advise and assist.

Inspections are routine but vital tools in leading and managing a unit. Prior to training and operations, inspections ensure that weapons are fully operational and ready for use.

- See that you and your party are perfectly turned out and neatly uniformed. Inspections also operate in reverse.
- Be up to date on details of the maintenance and function of any matériel you are to inspect. If matériel is on the program, leaf through the appropriate technical manual, which will contain a checklist for inspection. Become familiar with the nomenclature, functioning, and maintenance indicators associated with the equipment.
- When you inspect, do so impartially and pleasantly. Avoid a fault-finding spirit; the object of inspections is to help and inform, not to antagonize. Praise individuals when you properly can. As you uncover defects, be sure that the responsible individuals understand what you have discovered and why it constitutes a defect.
- Inspect yourself. Never walk in front of Marine you are inspecting at less than your best. The Marines you look at are inspected once, by you. All of them, on the other hand, inspect you as you pass down the ranks. Do not be found lacking.

- Inspect in cadence and at attention. Have a leading NCO—sergeant major, first sergeant, or platoon sergeant—precede you.
- Never overlook the individual Marine regardless of the purpose of the inspection. See that he or she is smart and military. Look the Marine in the eye. Make the Marine feel that he or she is the ultimate object of the inspection and that you are deeply interested in him or her as a person and a Marine.

❖ ❖ *Inspection Follow-up*

An inspection loses value if you fail to follow it up. This is the main reason for keeping careful notes on the comments of the inspecting officer.

Inspection notes should be disseminated to everyone concerned, broken down into items for corrective action so they can serve as a checklist. When you reinspect, review previous inspection notes as a guide for follow-up. On the receiving end, you can use past notes to prepare for future occasions. It is a grave reflection on you as a leader if the same defects continue to show up on consecutive inspections.

❖ ❖ *IG Inspections*

Via the longstanding previous title, "the adjutant and inspector," the inspector general of the Marine Corps can trace the title's roots back to 1798. Today, the IG's job is to assist and examine by periodic inspections the effectiveness of Marine commands in terms of ability to carry out their missions; unit leadership, economy, policies, and doctrine; work and health conditions; and discipline.

After a visit to a command by an IG team, one of three grades is awarded: satisfactory, noteworthy, and unsatisfactory. Although it may seem difficult for a unit under such searching inspection to believe, the IG is there to help: inspections are always a search for causes, not an inventory of symptoms.

❖ OTHER ASPECTS OF LEADERSHIP

❖ ❖ *Weapons Proficiency*

Given that the Marine Corps is a profession of *arms*, a Marine leader has few better ways of setting the right example to his or her troops than by maintaining high proficiency with infantry weapons—notably, the rifle and pistol. Marines respect a good shot and an officer who is handy with small arms. Do your best each year when you go to the range. Every enlisted Marine will be watching to see how you do. Make yourself a model of marksmanship technique. Demand no special favors: behind a rifle, on the firing line, all Marines are equals. Clean and maintain your own weapon, pick up your own brass, keep your own scorebook, and keep your mouth shut.

Never violate a safety precaution. Remember the shooter's proverb: "There is no such thing as an accidental discharge."

Although you will never match your best enlisted Marines, you should also seek knowledge and skill in firing and employing crew-served weapons, such as machine guns and assault and antitank weapons.

❯ ❯ "R.H.I.P."

As an officer, you are generally entitled to take precedence ahead of your juniors and all enlisted persons. This privilege is admitted in the service proverb "Rank has its privileges," or R.H.I.P. Just when and where you "pull rank," though, is a matter of some delicacy.

Generally speaking, you may assert your privilege when your time is circumscribed by duty or when failure to do so would demean your status as a commissioned officer. For example, an officer should not waste his or her own time and the government's by falling in line behind privates in a clothing storeroom or hesitate to claim the attention of an administrative functionary hemmed in by enlisted persons. Conversely, in situations where all persons are equal, take your place with the others regardless of rank. In the mess, at the barber shop (unless there is an officer's chair), or at the post exchange, avoid taking advantage of rank.

Finally, every Marine officer pulls rank in reverse when it comes to looking out for the troops. In the field, before you yourself eat, every enlisted Marine must have had a full ration. Before you take shelter, your Marines must have shelter. "There is no fatigue the soldiers go through," said Baron Friedrich von Steuben in 1779, "that the officers should not share."

❯ MANAGEMENT

In contrast to leadership, and in the military context and vernacular, management involves the sometimes monotonous but necessary stewardship of administration, services, and maintenance that a unit requires for day-to-day existence. In military units, it embraces such matters as supply and property; police and maintenance; food services; morale, welfare, and recreation; and such essentials as clothing, equipment, transportation, and pay.

Poorly managed and administered organizations are perpetually plagued with irksome disorders and nagging minor problems. Streamlined and effective management is a prerequisite to tactical efficiency so that the unit can pursue its military missions unhampered by distracting administrative demands.

❥ ❥ *Supply and Property*

Handling and accounting for supplies and property consume much of the energy of the Marine Corps. The golden rules on these topics are found in the current Marine Corps order on consumer-level supply policy. You, and every officer in the Corps, should be familiar with these rules and definitions, the most important of which are summarized here.

Anyone who possesses government property or who commands those who possess it, whether it is in use or in storage, has *responsibility* for that property, regardless of whether that individual has signed a receipt for it. Responsibility—in the supply sense—means the obligation of anyone who is required to have personal possession of, or supervision over, public property to ensure that it is procured, used, and disposed of only as authorized. When you have public property in your custody, you assume, as a public trust, responsibility that this property will be utilized only as authorized by law or regulations.

The CO of any base, station, or unit, however, has *command responsibility* over all the public property therein. It is the CO's job to ensure that all such property is safeguarded, maintained, and accounted for. An officer has *accountability* (and is known as an *accountable officer*) when specifically detailed to duty involving pecuniary responsibility for government funds and property. An accountable officer—as distinguished from a *responsible officer*—must keep formal records and stock accounts subject to audit by higher authority.

As you can see, virtually every Marine officer has some type of responsibility for government property, whereas relatively few officers are accountable. It is unlikely that you will become an accountable officer unless you specialize in supply; you may well be a responsible officer tomorrow.

As a *responsible officer*, you have certain basic obligations concerning public property. You are personally (and pecuniarily) responsible for all nonexpendable property issued to you. You are also responsible that all nonconsumable but expendable property issued to you be used only for the purposes authorized. Most such items, like individual combat equipment, which, owing to its nature, may often be in short supply and is always pilferable, require control by individual memorandum receipt.

Responsible officers have the following duties:

- Inspect property frequently to ensure serviceability, safekeeping, and proper use.
- Conduct physical inventory at least quarterly and adjust discrepancies with the accountable officer (usually the unit's supply officer).
- Maintain in serviceable condition all equipment shown on the unit's table of equipment, which is provided by the supply officer and lists all items a unit is authorized to possess.
- Maintain records reflecting the status of equipment and property on the T/E, normally using a consolidated memorandum receipt (CMR), a computerized printout that the accountable officer produces.
- Return to the appropriate supply agency any property that exceeds authorized allowances or is not needed for mission accomplishment.

As a responsible officer, you should designate in writing at least one representative, officer or enlisted, who is authorized to receipt for property in your name. An officer representative is called the property officer, and an NCO, the property sergeant.

When relieved by another officer, you must conduct a joint inventory, normally using your CMR, and adjust any discrepancies with the accountable officer. Your relief must then sign for all nonexpendable property carried on the CMR and any other equipment custody records. If you are relieving, and circumstances prevent joint inventory and immediate signature, you are nevertheless responsible for all property on hand. Before you sign any equipment custody records, however, be sure to make a complete inventory of all property.

Ensure that your officers and enlisted persons are instructed in the care, use, and maintenance of government property and that all hands are totally cost conscious. The persons you select for safekeeping property—your property sergeant, in particular—must be chosen with great care. Do not entrust keys of storerooms or chests to others without providing for officer supervision.

Expenditures of Property. Even with the most careful stewardship, property wears out and supplies are expended. The Marine Corps recognizes and provides for this. The supply system permits expenditure of matériel, and there are procedures for fixing responsibility for unusual or improper loss or damage to government property.

Nonconsumable expendables and consumables are expended on issue by the supply officer. Thus, no formal accountability exists for these items. Nevertheless, you must ensure that there is sufficient control over such matériel to guarantee proper use as well as ordinary economy.

If nonexpendable property is unavoidably lost or destroyed, this fact should be brought immediately to the attention of the supply officer, who may drop the property, with the approval of the CO, through a special adjustment to the account. If culpability or negligence is the suspected cause of loss of a nonexpendable item, an investigation should be held to determine the exact circumstances surrounding the loss (find details in the current Marine Corps order on consumer-level supply policy).

"Checkage" of individual pay is a means by which the government recovers the value of lost, damaged, or destroyed property from anyone who acknowledges responsibility therefor. An individual cannot be compelled to reimburse the government but can be subjected to disciplinary action, which most Marines are anxious to avoid.

Tips on Property. In addition to the advice in the current Marine Corps order on consumer-level supply policy, a few tips on the management of your property are in order:

- Maintain good, friendly relations with your accountable officer. Keep that officer candidly informed on the state of your property account. The relationship can be symbiotic. Though you may have shortages, the accountable officer in turn may have overages.
- Keep in touch with salvage and reclamation activities. It is often possible to adjust an awkward debit balance through assists from reclamation.

- Look and plan ahead. Nothing is worse than getting caught short because of the lack of ordinary foresight.
- Be cost conscious. The money available to your unit is not limitless, and supplies cost your unit money.
- Follow through. Your responsibility does not end with registering a requirement. It ends only when the needed items are physically either in the hands of the user or in your storeroom.
- Enforce responsibility for government property among your subordinates. When one of your Marines loses or damages property, institute pay checkage against that person. This not only reimburses the government for the loss and thus clears your books, but also reminds all hands that property is to be respected and cared for.
- Keep a neat, uncluttered storeroom. Allow no "grab-bag" accumulations in dark corners. Inspect your storeroom frequently—and unannounced.

Finally, attention to detail is vital when supply and property are concerned. As the Duke of Wellington wrote in 1810, "It is very necessary to attend to all this detail and to trace a biscuit from Lisbon into a man's mouth on the frontier and to provide for its removal from place to place by land or by water, or no military operations can be carried out." And remember also the old tongue-in-cheek saying that supposedly covers every known category of government property: "If it's small enough to pick up, turn it in; if you can't move it, paint it."

❯ ❯ *Police and Maintenance*

Police and maintenance are the "custodial" side of management. *Police* has to do with tidiness and good order; *maintenance* refers to the upkeep of property or equipment. Every organization or unit has at least some responsibilities for police and maintenance. Except on large installations or in major commands, both functions normally come under a single individual. The following discussion applies most directly at the company, battalion, or squadron level.

Every unit, afloat or ashore, designates a *police sergeant*, a noncommissioned officer who supervises cleaning details, trash collection, minor repair, and upkeep. Despite the title, the police sergeant may be any rank from corporal up. This NCO should be selected by virtue of cost consciousness, powers of observation, forceful character, ability to work independently, resourcefulness, and ingenuity. The police sergeant is a key person in your unit.

The police sergeant's workshop is known as the "police shed." This is anything from a storeroom to a separate building that houses tools, scrap materials, cleaning gear, paint, and salvaged items, which an energetic police sergeant will habitually recover wherever found adrift. As can be realized, the police shed, properly administered, may resemble a small hardware store.

The labor force for police details comes from varying sources. Except in small organizations, the police sergeant has one or more assistants, ordinarily amateur craftsmen known collectively as "the police gang." The police gang is supplemented by working details—sometimes prisoners from the brig, but more often those assigned extra duties at Office Hours. Much of the effectiveness of extra duties as a disciplinary measure depends on the personality and executive abilities of the police sergeant. If the supply of wrongdoers is inadequate, the first sergeant supplies working parties from those available. Close liaison should be maintained among the first sergeant, the police sergeant, and the gunnery sergeant.

When police and maintenance efforts are substantial, a unit, base, or station maintenance officer or public works officer is detailed (see the discussion in chapter 8 of how installations are organized). The duties, on an enlarged scale, are much the same as those of the police sergeant. Whenever the CO conducts an inspection, he or she is accompanied by, among others, the maintenance officer (if there is one) and the police sergeant.

❖ ❖ Subsistence and Mess Management

"An army travels on its belly," wrote Napoleon, and so does the Marine Corps. This being the case, every officer will benefit by some familiarity with the rules and arts of food service management, which are set forth in the *Marine Corps Manual* and presented in greater detail in the *Marine Corps Food Service and Subsistence Program* and current Corps order on consumer-level supply policy.

Today, most fixed mess operations are contractor operated; still, a word is in order to describe how messes are organized because a commander's responsibility for the mess can never be delegated. The term "mess" refers to the enlisted dining facility, where enlisted members of the command are fed, rather than any of the various types of officers' mess. Marine Corps messes today mainly operate on a cafeteria system.

The dining facility and its management represent one of the most important responsibilities of command. The CO must ensure without fail that the troops are served meals that, in the traditional officer-of-the-day logbook phrase, are "well served and well prepared, of good quality, and sufficient in quantity."

On large installations with several separate messes, and in Marine divisions and aircraft wings, a consolidated food service system is employed. This simply means that all messes are centralized for operations under a single food service officer; that central storage is provided for perishables, dry stores, and other mess supplies; and that they typically support multiple units in a designated area of the installation. In addition, the food service officer supervises training of mess personnel, advises the CO and supply and commissary officers on mess matters, and systematically inspects all messes. On small bases, there is often no food service officer, and the responsibilities may fall to the supply officer or another officer as a collateral duty. For that matter, on many small bases, Marines eat in the Navy mess.

The food service officer is a specialist, but *unit mess officers* are not—and that is where you come in. Every unit with its own mess (for example, a field mess) has a mess officer, usually a lieutenant. This officer in turn has a noncommissioned assistant, the mess sergeant, who is a specialist. The quality and standing of any given mess usually reflect the energy, imagination, and capability of the mess officer and mess sergeant working as a team.

You may be a unit mess officer at some time in your career, and the experience will be invaluable in preparing you for command. Thus, you should know how a typical mess is organized and how it operates.

The *mess sergeant* is the leading NCO of the mess. This billet demands a capable executive, a good cook, and an efficient culinary planner.

The *chief cook* is senior cook in the galley force and supervises all other cooks in the preparation of food.

The *chief messman*, usually an NCO, is in charge of the messmen. He or she is responsible for the cleanliness of the galley and mess hall. The chief messman is a key billet assignment. Although most tables of organization do not contain a chief messman billet, you should nevertheless try to find the right person and detail that individual permanently. A slipshod mess hall manned by idle, unclean messmen usually can be traced back to an inefficient chief messman.

The *storeroom keeper* assists the mess sergeant by keeping the galley stores and provisions.

Cooks are divided into watches, regulated by the chief cook. Each watch should be headed by a rated cook, known as the *cook on watch*. Depending on the size of the galley and galley force, the cook on watch may be assisted by other cooks or by "strikers," as apprentice cooks are known. Messmen who show a bent for cooking are sometimes assigned as strikers.

Messmen provide the "muscle" for the operation. They serve food, wash dishes, "wallop" pots, police the mess hall and galley, and function as the mess sergeant's labor force. On bases where civilian messmen are not authorized, messmen are detailed monthly from the nonrated Marines of the command in accordance with the *Marine Corps Manual*. The normal assignment of messmen is one for every twenty-five to thirty members of the command. An NCO should never serve as a messman except as chief messman.

The duties of the *unit mess officer* are as prescribed by the CO. If you are detailed as unit mess officer, immediately look up appropriate references in the *Marine Corps Manual, Marine Corps Food Service and Subsistence Program*, and Marine Corps order on consumer-level supply policy. Despite some variations from unit to unit, all unit mess officers should make frequent spot checks and inspections of the galley and mess hall, paying particular attention to the following factors:

- Personal cleanliness of cooks and messmen (clean, regulation clothing; clean hands and fingernails; obvious general health)
- Cleanliness and good order of cooks' and messmen's quarters, including condition of weapons and individual equipment
- Contents of garbage cans (to eliminate waste and to spot badly prepared food)
- Good order and sanitary condition of storerooms and "reefers" (look especially for signs of spoilage or evidence of rodents or insects)
- Cleanliness of mess halls (properly washed dishes and utensils, immaculate decks and tabletops, condiments covered)
- Sanitary garbage stowage and disposal

In addition to frequent spot checks, unit mess officers should attend at least one meal daily and attend breakfast at least once a week. They must ensure that food is appetizing, plentiful, and served at the appropriate temperature, and they must enforce wearing of the prescribed uniform by troops being fed.

Subject to unit policies and space constraints, it is preferable to provide separate messing sections in the general mess for officers, when they are subsisting in the mess; for staff NCOs; for sergeants and corporals; and for nonrated enlisted. Special tables for staff NCOs and sergeants and corporals—screened off, if possible—are most important and should be provided whenever physically possible.

Along with the mess sergeant, a unit mess officer must be prepared at all times—especially if responsible for an Operating Forces mess—to take the field and serve rations under such conditions.

Finally, no Marine must ever go hungry or miss a meal because of a conflict of duties. This means that special servings, both group and individual, may be frequently required for those on watch and for drivers, travelers, and the like. The mess force must embrace the idea that any Marine who has unavoidably missed a meal must receive hot chow and hot coffee, day or night. A proper galley has hot coffee available to all comers, all the time.

❧ ❧ *Morale, Welfare, and Recreation*

Morale, welfare, and recreation (MWR) concerns—once commonly called special services—embrace several nonmilitary Marine Corps Community Services activities within the Corps, chief among which is unit recreation. Remember, however, that no matter what machinery may be set up for MCCS purposes, nothing can supersede or diminish the CO's paramount responsibility to lead, care for, counsel, and educate those under his or her command.

The mainstay of the base, station, or unit MWR program is the recreation fund, which provides for the recreation, amusement, and welfare of all hands. Each battalion has an area coordinator who, along with the MWR officer, holds responsibility for the administration of these funds. The recreation fund obtains income from exchange system profits and the central MCCS fund. These are "non-appropriated funds." Some latitude exists in spending them for items not covered by official grants but nevertheless desirable for the welfare and morale of the command. Some examples of allowable expenditures include athletic equipment; athletic and marksmanship prizes; dances, picnics, and parties for the unit; and washers, dryers, irons, and televisions for the barracks.

Before seeking to make a purchase from the recreation funds, consult your area coordinator and MWR officer, not only to ensure that your project has authorization but also to preclude a prohibited transaction.

The MCCS division of your base or station also provides health, fitness, and recreation activities and facilities for use by you and your family.

❧ ❧ *Clothing Your Marines*

Instructions for wearing the uniform and specifications of all articles of uniform are found in *Marine Corps Uniform Regulations*. Procurement, issue, and inspection of clothing are covered by *Individual Clothing Regulations*.

It is your responsibility, as a Marine officer, to see that every Marine under your command is always properly uniformed and always possesses the required regulation clothing correctly marked.

Supervision of Uniforms. Here are time-tested ways to keep your Marines properly uniformed:

- Carry out frequent, systematic clothing inspections with careful follow-up of deficiencies. This means keeping written individual records.
- Place full-length mirrors in passageways and exits of barracks and in headquarters entrances to encourage the habit of self-inspection.
- Rotate the command through various uniform combinations on successive days or at troop inspections.
- Obtain cleaning, washing, and pressing equipment (irons and ironing boards) for squad rooms and barracks.
- Inspect unit laundry rooms to ensure that washers and dryers are in good working order and the spaces are in a good state of police.

Every unit has periodic clothing inspections for all hands. When inspecting, you must ensure the following:

- Each person has the required quantities of clothing.
- Clothing is marked as required by *Uniform Regulations*, bearing correct name and rank insignia.

- Clothing is in the hands of the person whose name appears thereon.
- Clothing is serviceable or that there is evidence that any unserviceable items are being replaced.

Whenever a Marine is transferred or joins, the platoon leader should hold an individual clothing inspection.

At stated intervals, each Marine receives a *clothing replacement allowance*, a pay record credit to permit replacement of worn-out items. If a Marine needs clothing but does not have enough money, the issue is made and checkage entered against future pay. This system makes it impossible for a Marine to have an excuse for not having the required and serviceable uniforms. It is your responsibility to make this system work.

Special clothing, such as cooks' and messmen's uniforms, cold-weather gear, flight gear, and chemical warfare clothing, is organizational property and issued to individuals on receipt, like equipment. If someone loses clothing, the Marine must then replace it by cash purchase.

Overall, inculcate officers and NCOs with their responsibility to always enforce proper wearing of the uniform by Marines. You have no excuse for disregarding a breach of uniform regulations with the famous last words "He/she isn't one of my Marines. It's up to that Marine's outfit to police its own." When you encounter an individual out of uniform, require immediate correction. If the violation is egregious, report the incident to the Marine's CO.

❧ ❧ *Individual Equipment*

In addition to uniforms, every Marine is issued a weapon and individual combat equipment, once called 782 gear or deuce gear on the original custody receipt form. It is one of your first responsibilities to see that the arms and equipment of your Marines are on hand, ready, and serviceable.

Upon joining the unit, a Marine is issued a rifle or pistol. It is up to that Marine to keep that weapon (and any successors) in top condition since all will have to depend upon it in combat. Even when temporarily armed with other organizational weapons, the Marine is responsible for that individual weapon's safekeeping and maintenance. A Marine's rifle is a mirror of its owner; the rifles of a platoon or a detachment are the mirror of the platoon leader or detachment commander.

In addition to the weapon, a Marine's individual combat equipment (ICE) comprises other items that one needs to fight and survive in the field. The major items are load-bearing equipment, cartridge belt, ammunition pouches, canteens, canteen cup, first aid packet, poncho, helmet, helmet cover, bayonet, and entrenching tool. Marines obtain their ICE from a centrally managed, contractor-run issue facility strategically located at Marine Corps bases, stations, and base clusters around the world. In addition to ICE, the issue facility also issues and recovers chemical, biological, radiological, and nuclear defense equipment; special training allowance pool gear; and soft-walled shelters and camouflage netting.

Your responsibility for your troops' equipment is the same as your responsibility for their clothing. It is a matter of constant supervision and inspection. Remember that each item of equipment is government property, bought and paid for by the taxpayers—including you and the Marine who carries it. Equipment wears out during field service and combat, which is to be expected. What is not to be expected—and will not be tolerated in the Marine Corps—are carelessness and negligence toward the weapons and equipment on which Marines' lives depend.

❧ ❧ *Transportation*

Every unit, station, or base that has vehicles includes a motor transport officer, who, under the S-4, is responsible for the upkeep and operation of the organization's transportation. The motor transport force includes drivers and mechanics. These operations are supervised by an NCO, who assigns vehicles to particular runs and keeps the unit's transportation operating in accordance with policy and regulations. When you need transportation, you normally contact the dispatcher, the "front man," so to speak, of the motor transportation organization, although many organizations will have more specific procedures for arranging transport.

When dealing with transportation and drivers, keep the following pointers in mind.

Cars and drivers are for official business; use them accordingly. Misuse of government transportation is a serious matter.

Driving a Marine or Navy vehicle requires a government motor vehicle operator's license. In addition, some commands require a unit driver's license. Other commands prohibit any officer from driving official vehicles except in an emergency.

If you are the senior officer in an official vehicle, you are responsible for its safe operation and proper employment. If the driver breaks rules, you are responsible. Never, except in an emergency, order a driver to violate a regulation or safety precaution. If you do, be ready to explain.

Treat the dispatcher and drivers well, and they will return the courtesy. Cancel scheduled transportation in advance if not needed. Avoid keeping vehicles waiting; instead, send them back to the motor pool with instructions to return at a specified time (or call when you need a return trip). When using an official vehicle in connection with an official social function, avoid having your driver wait outside at your pleasure. Be punctual, and keep to schedule.

Require drivers to be military and correct in manner and uniform. When not otherwise employed, see that the drivers perform routine checks, upkeep, and maintenance on their vehicles, regardless of whether they are normally assigned to you.

When the mission requires a driver to make a run during meal hours, it is your responsibility to see that arrangements are made to feed that Marine not just a snack, but a proper meal. Always ask your driver if he or she has been fed, and see the matter through. If you are not satisfied, call the dispatcher or, if necessary, the motor transport officer. In extreme cases, you may have to arrange directly with the mess sergeant. Regardless of how you do it, see that your driver is fed.

❧ ❧ *Pay*

Detailed information on pay is contained in chapter 18. From a management perspective, interest lies in the command responsibilities involved in paying the troops. These responsibilities are simple. The most important responsibility of an officer, as far as this is concerned, is to see that Marines are paid correctly. When a Marine finance officer is present, this will present fewer problems. For outlying detachments, or for units dependent on other services or on visiting finance officers, the problem sometimes requires close supervision.

Officers also have the duty of advising their people in money matters and encouraging them to save and take advantage of the financial opportunities that the government provides.

⁎{ **16** }⁎

WATCHSTANDING

A Marine on duty has no friends.
— Marine Corps proverb

ONE OF THE MOST stirring guard orders ever received by U.S. Marines was issued on 11 November 1921 by Secretary of the Navy Edwin Denby, himself a former Marine. The nation was in the grip of a crime wave, which had been highlighted by armed robberies of the U.S. Mail. Four days before Secretary Denby penned his letter of instruction, President Warren G. Harding had directed that the Marine Corps take over the job of safeguarding the mail. Accordingly, fifty-three officers and 2,200 enlisted Marines were already on watch in post offices, railway mail cars, and postal trucks throughout the country.

To the Men of the Mail Guard,

    I am proud that my old Corps has been chosen for a duty so honorable as that of protecting the United States mail. I am very anxious that you shall successfully accomplish your mission. It is not going to be easy work. It will always be dangerous and generally tiresome. You know how to do it. Be sure you do it well. I know you will neither fear nor shirk any duty, however hazardous or exacting.

This particular work will lack the excitement and glamor of war duty, but it will be no less important. It has the same element of service to the country.

I look with proud confidence to you to show now the qualities that have made the Corps so well-beloved by our fellow citizens.

You must be brave, as you always are. You must be constantly alert. You must, when on guard duty, keep your weapons in hand and, if attacked, shoot and shoot to kill. There is no compromise in this battle with the bandits.

If two Marines, guarding a mail car, are suddenly covered by a robber, neither must hold up his hands, but both must begin shooting at once. One may be killed, but the other will get the robber and save the mail. When our men go in as guards over mail, that mail must be delivered or there must be a Marine dead at the post of duty.

To be sure of success, every Marine on this duty must be watchful as a cat, hour after hour, night after night, week after week. No Marine must drink a drop of intoxicating liquor. Every Marine must be most careful with whom he associates and what his occupations are off duty. There may be many tricks tried to get you, and you must not be tricked. Look out for women. Never discuss the details of your duty with outsiders. Never give up to another the trust you are charged with.

Never forget that the honor of the Corps is in your keeping. You have been given a great trust. I am confident you will prove that it has not been misplaced.

I am proud of you and believe in you with all my heart.

/s/ Edwin Denby

Mail robberies ceased within a matter of days after Secretary Denby penned his order. Not a single piece of mail was lost to a robber while Marines stood watch.

❧ WATCHSTANDING BASICS

❧ ❧ *Importance of Watchstanding*

In the Marine Corps and Navy, the safety and good order of the entire command depend on those who stand guard. Thus, watchstanding is a routine but strict duty. The importance of guard duty is underscored by the fact that sleeping on watch can be punished by death in time of war and by heavy penalties in peacetime.

In addition to combat missions, the Marine Corps is the combat security force for the naval establishment and is thus responsible for the good order and protection not only of its own bases and stations but also, when assigned, of naval stations and vessels (see the section on Marine Corps Security Forces in chapter 6). As a Marine officer, you are therefore expected to be an authority on watchstanding and guard duty as well as a model watch officer, ashore or afloat.

Status of Marines on Watch. Any Marine on watch or guard, whether officer or enlisted, represents the commanding officer. In the execution of orders or the enforcement of regulations, the Marine guard's authority is complete. When you receive a lawful order from a member of the guard, comply without hesitation and ask questions afterward. Remember that an armed sentry has full authority to enforce instructions.

❖ ❖ *Types of Guards*

Marines maintain four types of guard: an exterior guard ashore, an interior guard ashore, a ship's guard afloat, and special guards.

An *exterior guard* is maintained only in combat or when danger of attack exists. It protects the command against outside attack and is organized and armed according to the tactical situation.

Interior guards have the fourfold mission of protecting life, preserving order, enforcing regulations, and safeguarding public property.

Ship's guards carry out the same general missions afloat as interior guards do ashore but differ in details of organization and duty because of shipboard conditions.

Special guards include all guards organized for special purposes (for example, train or boat guards). Additionally, most posts having custody of special weapons have a separate main guard for that purpose alone, leaving other normal security functions at the installation to the main guard.

In addition, Marines frequently perform military police and shore patrol duties for the regulation and assistance of Marines and Sailors on liberty.

❧ THE INTERIOR GUARD

Established to protect life, preserve order, enforce regulations, and safeguard public property (as noted above), the interior guard derives its authority directly from the CO. Figure 16-1 shows the organization of a typical interior guard. The guard comprises a main guard and, when needed, special guards.

❧ ❧ *Organization and Duties of the Guard*

The general organization and duties of the interior guard (and the CO's responsibilities in connection with it) are as follows.

The CO establishes the guard and ensures that it functions properly. Either the CO or a representative (usually the executive officer or adjutant) receives the daily reports from and relieves the officers of the day, examines the guard book, and issues whatever special instructions may be needed.

The position of *staff duty officer* (or, in some places, command duty officer) may be required at a large organization or installation where subordinate or tenant commands maintain separate guards. This individual coordinates subordinate guards and acts for the commander in an emergency.

The *officer of the day* (OD) supervises the main guard, executes all orders that pertain to it, and is responsible that the guard performs effectively. While OD, you are the direct representative of the CO.

The *commander of the guard*, a staff NCO, is responsible for the proper instruction, discipline, and performance of the guard. This position is usually required only for a large guard.

The *sergeant of the guard*, whatever his or her actual rank, is the senior NCO of the guard. This individual either assists the commander of the guard or, if the guard does not include one, performs that position's duties. The sergeant of the guard supervises the enlisted members of the guard and is responsible for government property charged to it.

Nonrated members of the guard are organized into three reliefs, each of which includes a sentry—alternately, sentinel—for each post and one supernumerary and is commanded by a *corporal of the guard*. This individual instructs and supervises the relief, which takes its successive turn on guard throughout the tour of duty.

❧ ❧ *Daily Guard Routine*

The daily routine of an interior guard varies somewhat according to the wishes of the CO and the size and missions of the base. The normal tour is twenty-four hours. Anyone detailed for guard duty must be on board and fit for duty at least four hours before commencement of the tour.

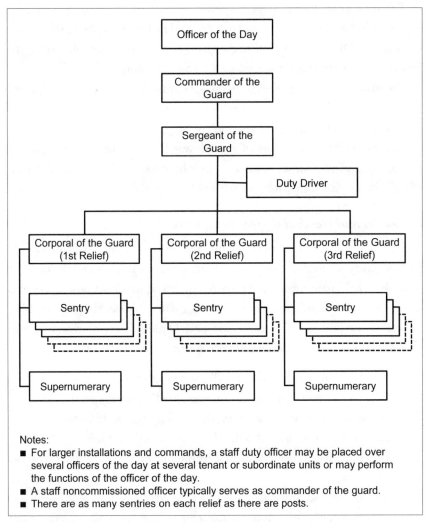

Notes:
- For larger installations and commands, a staff duty officer may be placed over several officers of the day at several tenant or subordinate units or may perform the functions of the officer of the day.
- A staff noncommissioned officer typically serves as commander of the guard.
- There are as many sentries on each relief as there are posts.

FIGURE 16-1. Organization of a Typical Interior Guard

Details for guard duty should be published well in advance, by written order, and should specify uniform and equipment as well as any other information not covered in standing orders. Officers detailed for guard duty must be notified *in person* or *by written order*, preferably both. This is the adjutant's responsibility. The adjutant also keeps the OD roster, which determines the order in which officers stand watch.

A tour on guard begins in formal situations with *guard mounting*, when the outgoing and incoming guards are paraded and inspected. After guard mount, old and new ODs and sergeants of the guard relieve each other, whereupon the former report to the CO, and the new OD assumes duty.

The guard's routine includes execution of Morning Colors and Evening Colors, posting and relief of sentinels, supervision of meal formations, and rendition of honors to the CO, visiting officers, and civilian dignitaries.

Each of the three reliefs normally stands watch for four hours before turning over to the next relief. Thus, in a twenty-four-hour tour, each relief stands a total of eight hours on watch—four by day and four by night.

❧ ❧ *Duties and General Orders for Sentries*

The sentry is the workhorse of the guard. The universal respect accorded a U.S. Marine sentry is based on that person's high military efficiency and the fact that he or she is habitually armed and prepared to defend his or her post and person in the execution of orders. A sentry's duties are to carry out the general orders for a sentry on post as well as applicable special orders. Every Marine, officer or enlisted, must know the eleven standing general orders by heart:

1. To take charge of this post and all government property in view.
2. To walk my post in a military manner, keeping always on the alert, and observing everything that takes place within sight or hearing.
3. To report all violations of orders I am instructed to enforce.
4. To repeat all calls from posts more distant from the guardhouse than my own.
5. To quit my post only when properly relieved.
6. To receive, obey, and pass on to the sentry who relieves me, all orders from the commanding officer, officer of the day, and officers and noncommissioned officers of the guard only.

7. To talk to no one except in line of duty.

8. To give the alarm in case of fire or disorder.

9. To call the corporal of the guard in any case not covered by instructions.

10. To salute all officers and all colors and standards not cased.

11. To be especially watchful at night, and, during the time for challenging, to challenge all persons on or near my post, allowing no one to pass without proper authority.

In addition to routine sentry duties, nonrated members of the guard are assigned to certain special duties, such as the following.

Guardhouse Sentinel (Post No. 1). If one is assigned, this sentinel assists the corporal of the guard in carrying on guardhouse routine. The guardhouse sentinel should be picked for intelligence, reliability, and smartness.

Main Gate Sentinel. This sentinel ensures that only authorized persons enter or leave the base through the main gate; he or she also directs traffic and assists visitors. Your main-gate sentry stands watch in the show window of the station; therefore, select the sentry for soldierly appearance, judgment, and thorough knowledge of the base. The main gate is a spot for outstanding Marines.

Supernumerary. One additional sentry stands by as a supernumerary to replace anyone who must be relieved. The supernumerary can be kept busy as a messenger and general assistant in the guardhouse.

Driver. A motor transport operator or licensed incidental driver is assigned to the guard to drive the guard vehicle. Always keep the driver up to standard in uniform and appearance; it is a notorious and shameful failing among guard drivers to lag behind the rest of the guard in this respect.

— ❖❖ ❖❖ —

The general policy of the Marine Corps is that all sentries will be armed. Detailed safety instructions, as well as restrictions on the use of the weapon, should be known to all members of the guard, from OD to sentry. Improper or careless use of firearms is an extremely serious matter.

The security environment both at home and abroad is exceedingly complex today, with the expanded reach of international criminal and terrorist organizations; advent of so-called lone wolves, often inspired by ideologies spread by social media; and proliferation of advanced technologies and increasingly lethal weaponry. Although certainly not the only novel security challenge in this environment, the active shooter—an individual engaged in killing or attempting to kill people in a populated area, such as on a base or station— is of particular concern to members of an interior guard, who may be first on the scene. Sentries must be well trained to identify an active shooter situation, take appropriate immediate action, and coordinate with specialized response teams, if any, when they arrive. For such situations, vigilance, clear procedures, and thorough training are keys to their successful resolution.

❈ ❈ *Challenging and Countersign*

"Halt! Who goes there?" This traditional *challenge*, has been employed by Marines since 1775. As an officer, you should know exactly how to challenge and reply because a faulty challenge or reply may not only embarrass you but, in combat, also cost one's life.

The challenge is used at night or in low visibility to identify anyone approaching a sentinel.

On hearing any suspicious noise, the sentinel brings his or her weapon to a ready position and commands, "Halt! Who goes there?" The person challenged halts and then identifies himself or herself either by a countersign or by some such answer as "friend" or "officer of the day." The sentinel traditionally replies, "Advance, friend, and be recognized." The person is allowed to approach near enough to the sentinel to be recognized and is halted again, at which time the sentinel examines the person. When satisfied, the sentinel commands, "Pass, friend." If being visited by the OD, the sentry reports, "Post Number _____ secure, sir/ma'am."

It is extremely important, not only as military etiquette but also for your own safety, to reply audibly and promptly when challenged and to comply exactly with the sentry's orders. The sentry is the person behind the weapon. You are in front of it.

Challenge and *countersign* (sometimes called the "password") are used to distinguish between friend and enemy. In the use of this procedure, which takes place only when prescribed by the CO, the person or party approaching a sentry is challenged in the usual way. Then, after advancing the person for recognition, the sentry repeats the secret challenge, an agreed code word to which the person being challenged must respond with the countersign, a second code word that validates the reply. Challenge and countersign change daily and must be kept secure.

❥ OFFICER OF THE DAY AND COMMANDER OF THE GUARD

❥ ❥ *Officer of the Day*

Because OD duties will take up much of your energies as a company-grade officer, you must be clear about the responsibilities of that job. In addition to what you read here, however, you must be thoroughly familiar with the *Interior Guard Manual* as well as base, station, and unit standing orders that deal with guard duty and the watch.

❥ ❥ *Duties of the Officer of the Day*

As OD, you must attend to several routine duties. More important, however, as the CO's representative, you must be ready to act promptly and sensibly in any contingency not covered by the letter of your orders.

Inspect each relief of the guard by visiting sentries at least once while that relief is on post. One inspection must take place between midnight and reveille. When visiting sentries, cover the following points:

- Verify that the sentry is on post, alert, in correct uniform, and correctly armed and equipped.
- Verify that the sentry knows verbatim and understands the eleven general orders. Have the sentry repeat a few and explain them in his or her own words.
- Question the sentry on special orders, checking particularly that he or she knows the limits and designation of the post, the location of fire-fighting gear on the post and how to sound a fire alarm, any recent changes in special orders for his or her post, the reason the post is required, and restrictions, if any, on use of a weapon.

Supervise and coordinate the inspections to be made by your commander of the guard and sergeant of the guard. See that these do not conflict with or duplicate yours.

Take immediate steps in an emergency to protect life and public property and to preserve order. As soon as the situation permits, report what has happened and what you are doing about it to the CO (or to the XO or staff duty officer, if your command has one).

Always inform the guard where you can be reached when not in the guard-house. If possible, leave a telephone number.

Abstain from alcohol throughout your tour.

Unless otherwise authorized, *remain fully clothed* at all times. This enables you to act immediately in case of emergency. Nothing can get an OD into more trouble than arriving late and drowsy at the scene of trouble.

Inspect galleys and messes, in accordance with local orders, at each meal during your watch.

Finally, *review the OD logbook before guard mount and correct any mistakes.* In it, record the times when you visited sentries along with any other information you think proper to place on record. Then attest to the correctness of all entries by signing the logbook, which constitutes your official report.

❧ ❧ *Relieving as Officer of the Day*

After guard mount, old and new ODs both report to the XO (or another staff officer as designated by command policy) for relief and posting.

March in at attention, covered and wearing side arms (as prescribed by command policy), and halt in front of the XO (the old OD on the right). You both salute together. Thereupon, the old OD says, "Sir/Ma'am, Lieutenant _____ reports as old officer of the day," and hands the logbook to the XO. The latter reads the report, asks any questions that come to mind, and comments as necessary. Then the XO informs the old OD, "You are relieved." Thereupon the old OD salutes and withdraws. Then the new OD again salutes, and says, "Sir/Ma'am, Lieutenant _____ reports as new officer of the day." The XO gives the new OD instructions, whereupon the latter salutes and withdraws.

All movements during relief and posting as OD are carried out at attention and in cadence.

❧ ❧ *Duties of the Commander of the Guard*

As you have seen, the duties of commander of the guard, if one is not detailed, are carried out by the sergeant of the guard. Regardless of whether performed

Sentries of an interior guard must remain constantly vigilant and alert. Here, a Marine surveys the sector in front of his observation post at a patrol base in Helmand Province, Afghanistan, in 2012.

by a staff NCO or an NCO, the duties listed here constitute a useful checklist by which, as OD, you can ensure that your guard is running smoothly.

The commander of the guard carries out the following functions:

- Inform the OD of any orders received from anyone else and passes on to his or her relief all instructions and current information.
- See that the guard is properly instructed and that it performs properly.
- Ensure that the guard performs its duties with the prescribed uniforms and equipment.
- Make certain that all inspections (by both the commander or the guard and sergeant of the guard) are carried out on time and as directed by the OD.
- See that sentinels are relieved, Colors executed, the proper bugle calls sounded, bells struck, and guard routine followed.

- Ensure that legible copies of general and special orders for each post are mounted both in the guardhouse and under shelter on each post.
- Inspect the guardhouse and brig thoroughly at least once during each tour.
- Inspect each relief of the guard while it is on post and, just as the OD, make one inspection of sentinels between midnight and reveille.
- Parade the guard for inspections as required.
- Report to the OD if any member of the guard takes sick, quits his or her post, or has to be relieved for any reason.
- In an emergency, turn out the guard, sound the appropriate call or alarm, and promptly notify the OD.
- Detain any suspicious persons, reporting the circumstances to the OD.
- Write a report in the guard book and, at the end of the tour of duty, present the log to the OD.

Additionally, the commander of the guard must send help immediately if any sentry calls out, "The guard!" This is the SOS for a sentinel on post.

Duties relating to Colors are traditionally of sacred importance. The commander of the guard must form the details to execute Morning Colors and Evening Colors, attend Colors to be certain that the ceremony is correctly performed, and ensure that the National Color is properly stowed and handled only in performance of duty (see chapter 11 for further details). Additionally, he or she must report to the OD if a set of colors is unserviceable.

Finally, like the OD, the commander of the guard must also keep the guard informed of his or her whereabouts whenever out of the guardhouse—if possible, by providing a telephone number.

❧ ❧ Tips for the Officer of the Day

Of all officers, the OD is the one who can least tolerate any discrepancy or violation of orders. *Never overlook a dereliction or infraction* however minor. Be especially alert for the following:

- Unmilitary behavior
- Marines out of uniform
- Traffic offenders
- Safety hazards

• Unsanitary, unusual, or unsightly conditions
• Security of restricted areas

Stay meticulously informed on the movements and whereabouts of the CO and the XO.

Be meticulous in bearing and conspicuous by your neatness when on watch. A neat OD has a well-turned-out guard. Keep your leather shining. Polish your brass. Wear your best uniforms. Set an example for the whole command.

No matter how many times you have stood watch before, review the guard orders as soon as you take over. Changes have a way of sneaking in without warning. "That isn't the way it used to be" is no excuse.

Prevent your guard from growing idle and complacent. Ensure it is instructed in guard orders and routine—and especially in weapon safety. More so-called accidental discharges of firearms take place while on guard duty than anywhere else. Sad but true, the overheads of many guardrooms are pockmarked by 9-mm bullet holes.

Make sure that reliefs and sentinels are posted in military fashion.

Keep an eye on the colors. Such avoidable fumbles as colors unwittingly hoisted upside down have, on occasion, provided the hapless OD an earful from the XO. Never allow colors to become fouled or snarled about the pole or halyards.

If serving as staff or command duty officer for a base or station, visit the main gate during rush hours. Let the main-gate guards know you are on hand to back them up.

Avoid making your rounds surreptitiously. Being seen is one of the main functions of the OD.

Be unfailingly courteous, especially to civilians and visitors. The good name of the command or installation and, in fact, the Marine Corps is in your hands when you are on watch.

Avoid personal dealings with drunks. Let enlisted members of the guard deal with them while you keep in the background. This will not only save you potential embarrassment but may also save the drunken person from some offense much more serious if done toward an officer. But never allow a drunk to be roughly treated, and, above all, *never detain a supposed drunk without medical examination*. It is easy to confuse apparent intoxication with the symptoms of a serious head injury.

Be immediately accessible at all hours. Do not let members of the guard, however well meaning, interpose themselves between you and any sober caller, whether in person or by telephone. You never know who may be calling.

Finally, run your guard the way you know it should be run. You have the responsibility, backed up by almost unlimited authority. If the guard is below standard, you have only yourself to blame.

❯ MILITARY POLICE AND SHORE PATROL

❯ ❯ *Concept of Patrols*

Whenever enlisted personnel go ashore on liberty, it is customary to provide military police, whose job is to

- assist civil authorities in dealing with members of the armed forces;
- maintain discipline and good behavior among Marines and Sailors ashore, getting them back in good order; and
- aid and safeguard personnel on liberty in every possible way.

This duty is described as MP when performed by a Marine organization. When a ship or Navy shore station provides such a guard, it is known as shore patrol (SP). Embarked Marines or Marines assigned to tenant organizations aboard naval stations often participate in SP with their Navy brethren. Its routine and duties are covered in the *Navy Shore Patrol Manual*.

Never resist, obstruct, or fail to cooperate with an SP or an MP, even if he or she comes from the Army or Air Force. Under joint regulations, MPs and SPs have all-service authority, with power to enforce any lawful acts or instructions. If you have any complaints, make them through military channels to the proper superior authorities.

❯ ❯ *Tips on MP and SP Duty*

When assigned to MP or SP duty, remember that you are functioning as a *military* police officer. Do not assert police authority over civilians—that is a job for the civilian police. By the same token, often remind your charges that they are Marines first and foremost, police only in an auxiliary and qualified sense. Do not tolerate any symptoms of "highway-patrol swagger" on the part of any of your Marines.

Never consume alcohol while on MP or SP duty. It is a longstanding naval custom that even the most minor evidence that an MP or SP has partaken of alcohol while on duty demands a court-martial.

Make yourself and your MPs or SPs conspicuous. This helps deter violations and gives assurance to all that the situation is well in hand.

If possible, have medical assistance ready at hand. Should your patrol not include a doctor or corpsman, know where you can get medical aid without delay.

Develop a working relationship with the local police. Cooperate sincerely with them, and they will do the same with you. Be unfailingly courteous toward civilians.

If in a foreign port, obtain a trustworthy interpreter who knows the local customs. Try to select enlisted Marines who know the language.

Remember, let your enlisted people deal with drunks.

Ensure that anyone taken into custody is handled "by the book." Allow no undue force or abusive behavior toward these individuals, no matter how infuriating their behavior may be. Unauthorized treatment of a detainee is unworthy of a Marine officer.

Avoid disorderly public scenes, prolonged disputes, or heated brawls. Get troublemakers back under military control quickly and deal with them in private.

Above all, exercise common sense and tact. It is your job to prevent trouble as much as it is to quell it. When you see a Marine or Sailor in difficulty, ask yourself, "How can I help this person?"

❧{ 17 }❧

INDIVIDUAL ADMINISTRATION

*My Lord—If I attempted to answer the mass of futile correspon-
dence that surrounds me, I should be debarred from all serious
business of campaigning.*

*I must remind your Lordship—for the last time—that so long
as I retain an independent position, I shall see that no officer under
my command is debarred, by attending to the futile drivelling of
mere quill driving in your Lordship's office, from attending to his
first duty—which is, and always has been, so to train the private
men under his command that they may, without question, beat
any force opposed to them in the field.*

— Duke of Wellington (attributed)

ALTHOUGH A FEW ADMINISTRATORS may convey the reverse impression, there is nothing inherently complicated or darkly mysterious about individual administration. It merely comprises several administrative matters that concern you personally: your record, rank, promotions, retirement, official correspondence, leave, and liberty. Pay and allowances as well as official travel, closely related, are covered in chapter 18.

To give you working familiarity and ready reference with military administration, and to prevent it from seeming an esoteric art known only to a chosen few, become familiar with Navy Regulations, *Department of the Navy Correspondence Manual, Marine Corps Manual*, and pertinent Marine Corps orders. Let individual administration serve and help but never get the better of you.

❖ OFFICERS' RECORDS

❖ ❖ *Your Official Record*

Throughout your career, documents and correspondence concerning you accumulate at Marine Corps Headquarters. These become part of your official record. The *vital importance of your official record to you and your career* cannot be overstressed. Entries in your record form the basis of your service reputation.

Your official record in Washington comprises a multipart, electronic administrative record; an official military personnel file, also in electronic form; and certain additional files, some of which may be kept by the judge advocate general (JAG) of the Navy. You have access to most of your record via secure login to Marine Online.

The administrative portion of your record kept at Marine Online includes the following major components.

Basic Individual Record (BIR). This record contains information relating to your service "contract," including your commissioning source, date of entry into service for pay purposes, date that any obligated service ends, and so forth. The BIR also includes both service information, such as current grade, date of rank, military occupational specialties, and details relating to your current tour and combat tour(s); and personal information, such as home of record, citizenship, blood type, current contact information, and information on your dependent family members.

Basic Training Record (BTR). Documenting your current annual training status and containing your career service training and education records, the BTR includes selected special training records; education records, documenting military and civilian schools attended and formal MOS and PME courses completed; foreign language training; martial arts training; and miscellaneous test scores.

Chronological Record. This electronic document lists your career assignments sorted chronologically, including the units or organizations you have been assigned to, your primary duty at each, and any additional remarks.

Individual Medical Record. This record summarizes some important information from your more comprehensive health records, which are kept separately in both physical and electronic form by Navy Medicine. It notably provides status of key immunizations, physicals, and required periodic health assessments.

Record of Emergency Data (RED). This record contains current information on marital status, spouse, children, and next of kin as well as essential addresses, phone numbers, and notification instructions, if any. *It is vitally important to keep your RED completely accurate and up to date.*

This administrative portion of your official record also includes some additional minor sections further addressing education, operational cultural information (that is, foreign language skills and test results, self-professed language skills, and self-reported unofficial foreign travel), and pay amounts and leave balances.

The second major part of your official record, your *official military personnel file* (OMPF), is a document collection that serves as your record of performance from initial entry through final separation. The OMPF is divided into sections:

- *Master Brief Sheet*, summarizing your record of performance
- *Performance evaluations*, detailing your performance in each assignment
- *Commendatory/derogatory information*, encompassing personal awards, school transcripts, and other items
- *Reporting senior and reviewing officer profiles*, providing a cumulative snapshot of how you performed your responsibilities when evaluating the performance of your subordinates

The Manpower Management Division, Records and Performance Branch (Code MMRP) within the Manpower and Reserve Affairs Department at HQMC, recommends that you perform a self-audit of your OMPF in advance of a scheduled performance-counseling interview, in preparation for any selection board, and in advance of contacting Records and Performance Branch customer service (Code MMRP-20) to review your record. The webpage that serves as the table of contents to your OMPF provides a link to instructions on performing a self-audit.

There are several ways to update your OMPF:

- *Email*: This is the preferred and fastest method. Again, the webpage that serves as the table of contents to your OMPF provides current instructions for preparing and submitting update material and email addresses to use depending on needs and circumstances.

- *In person*: You may drop off update material at the Records and Performance Branch customer service window located on the first deck of Building 2008 at Marine Corps Base Quantico, Virginia.
- *Mail*: You may mail update material to HQMC (Code MMRP-20), 2008 Elliot Road, Quantico, VA 22134-5030. If board eligible, you should indicate on the outside of the envelope "Update material for the FYxx [insert board name]."

Finally, there are a few additional files that are part of your official record. The *confidential file* contains any correspondence to or about an officer that must be kept confidential. Few officers have material on confidential file.

Proceedings of courts or boards that affect your record are filed by the judge advocate general of the Navy. You may examine these records in the JAG files. If unfavorable, such matter is referred to you before being filed.

The only persons who enjoy access to your official record are you (via Marine Online); your personal representative, bearing proper documentation; designated headquarters personnel; and, when authorized by the Secretary of the Navy, the courts. No person (including you or your agents) without proper authority can withdraw official records and correspondence from the files or destroy them.

Make it a habit to review your record at Marine Online at least annually. Inaccurate information, albeit seemingly minor, can sometimes prove as detrimental to your service reputation as serious missteps.

In closing this topic, it is important to emphasize that adverse matter cannot be placed in your official record without your knowledge and must always be referred to you for statement. If you wish to give your side of the matter, you may do so; if you have nothing to say, so state it in writing. In either case, the adverse matter goes back to the commandant of the Marine Corps via the reporting officer and thence through normal channels. Whether favorable or unfavorable, correspondence once rightfully included in your record cannot be removed without authorization by the SECNAV.

❧ ❧ *Your Personal Record*

The only administrative records that physically accompany you now throughout your career, as distinct from records filed in Washington, are your *officer qualification record* (OQR), *health record*, and *dental record*.

Marine Online provides all Marines direct access to their individual administrative, training, and performance evaluation records maintained centrally at Headquarters, U.S. Marine Corps.

Your OQR contains, at a minimum, a NAVMC 763 (Appointment Acceptance)—essentially the officer version of a contract—NAVMC 118(3) (Chronological Record), NAVMC 118(11) (Administrative Remarks), RED, and Servicemembers Group Life Insurance Beneficiary Election Form. In addition to this, if the officer is a "Mustang" (that is, prior enlisted), his or her enlistment contract(s) and DD Form 214 are in the OQR. A NAVMC 10922 (Dependency Affidavit) is also included for married officers.

Your health and dental records are held by the Navy's Bureau of Medicine and Surgery and contain a summary of your health history prior to accession, the results of your physical examinations, and the medical history of every ailment that befalls you during your career.

❧ ❧ *Your Personal File*

The day you are commissioned, start a personal file. This should contain, in one folder, all original travel orders and, in another, all official correspondence from, to, and concerning you. In addition, remember that some unofficial emails, letters, or notes you write or receive are just as important to your career as the official ones. And depending on your experiences and achievements, your writings and musings during your career may interest a wider audience. The Marine Corps Archives at the Alfred M. Gray Marine Corps Research Center encourages retired officers to donate personal files and papers for preservation.

> > *Fitness Reports*

Fitness reports provide the periodic documentation of your professional performance and character for the Marine Corps performance evaluation system. The system provides for the reporting, recording, and analysis of the performance, potential, and professional character of all Marines in the grade of sergeant and above. The fitness report form, when properly completed, constitutes the principal record of your performance of duties and conduct during a designated time period. Together, these reports assist selection boards of all varieties in determining which officers are best suited for the services desired. They also provide the commandant and staff with information as to your desired duty assignments and locations for the future.

The authoritative source for complete information on this topic is the *Performance Evaluation System Manual* (PES).

Completed and maintained electronically within the automated Performance Evaluation System, the fitness report consists of several distinct sections:

- *Section A* contains administrative information that identifies you individually; describes your unit and duty assignment; denotes the occasion of and period covered by the report; lists your most recent physical fitness score, small-arms qualifications, and preferences for future assignments; and identifies your reporting senior, normally that officer immediately above you in your chain of command (unless he or she is of the same grade), and reviewing officer, normally the officer to whom your reporting senior reports. It remains your responsibility to provide the report to your reporting senior with the information in this section correctly stated.
- *Section B* contains a complete description of your billet, focusing on key functions and responsibilities. This section is technically the reporting

senior's responsibility, but many reporting seniors will have you prepare a draft, which they will refine.

- *Section C* lists your key accomplishments in the billet during the period covered by the report. Again, your reporting senior will often expect you to prepare a draft of this section.
- *Sections D through H* are used by the reporting senior to rate your personal attributes in categories (for example, "Mission Accomplishment," "Leadership," and "Intellect and Wisdom") of particular interest to the Marine Corps. For each category, your reporting senior matches his or her appraisal of you to a provided word description. Elaboration, if needed, is added at the bottom of each section or to a later section.
- *Section I* is labeled "Directed and Additional Comments." Your reporting senior uses this section to add his or her own concise, personalized word picture of you, which is mandatory; any additional comments needed to elaborate on ratings of your personal attributes (Sections D through H); and any other comments or information needed to complete the evaluation.
- *Section J* contains the reporting senior's signature (and yours if the report contains adverse material).
- *Section K* contains your reviewing officer's marks and comments evaluating your performance and character, placing your reporting senior's evaluation in a broader context. The reviewing officer also affixes his or her signature in this section.
- *Section L* is purely administrative. It merely indicates if there is addendum material included.

General officers are evaluated by letter reports, occurring annually for brigadier generals.

Your fitness reports obviously will constitute a running record of your performance of duty throughout your career as seen through the eyes of your various commanders and supervisors. It is the most vital single source of your personal and professional record. It will merit your attention and review through your last day of service.

Occasions for Reports. There are thirteen occasions when a fitness report must be prepared on Marines in the grades of sergeant through colonel. These occasions normally correspond to changes in professional status, such as upon promotion to the next higher grade, when a billet or duties change, or when the reporting senior changes. The PES contains the complete list of reporting occasions.

The annual fitness report periods for Marines—ending on the last day of the month—vary by grade (as shown in table 17-1), corresponding to the needs of the promotion boards.

Reporting Senior. Normally, the reporting senior is the first commissioned or warrant officer (civilian GS-09 or above under certain circumstances) in the chain of command who is senior to the Marine reported on. The reporting senior may be in the same grade as the Marine reported on under rare circumstances specified in the PES. The performance evaluation system values the reporting senior's viewpoint as the best position from which to observe a Marine's performance and that officer as the person most responsible for setting the Marine's daily tasks and the standards to which they are performed.

Reviewing Officer. The reviewing officer, who is the next receiving one's fitness report, is normally that officer (or civilian in grade GS-12 or above) next senior in the chain of command to the reporting senior. This officer occupies a critical link in the system by ensuring adherence to the stated regulations and exerting the leadership, supervision, and detached point of view to obtain unbiased and accurate reports. The reviewing officer bears ultimate responsibility for the accuracy, completeness, and correctness of the fitness report. Errors by either the Marine reported on or the reporting senior are returned to them for correction. The reviewing officer completes the portions requiring his or her certification to indicate agreement or disagreement with the report. Written remarks based upon the reviewing officer's personal knowledge of the Marine are encouraged, especially to determine the Marine's potential to serve at a higher grade and his or her general value to the service as compared with the other officers of the same grade serving below the reviewing officer. Remarks must be provided to clarify disagreement with the reporting senior or, in the case of adverse reports, to adjudicate the respective positions of the Marine and the reporting senior.

Initial reports on Marines joining the organization within ninety days of the end of the fitness report period are normally omitted (annual) or completed as "not observed" (all other occasions). This rule is inoperative when, in the view of the reporting officer, sufficient observation has occurred, and the report remains

TABLE 17-1. Fitness Report Periods by Grade

Rank	Active Component	Reserve Component	Active Reserve
	Period Ends Last Day of	Period Ends Last Day of	Period Ends Last Day of
Sgt	March	September	September
SSgt	December	September	September
GySgt	June	September	September
1stSgt/MSgt	June	September	September
SgtMaj/MGySgt	September	May	June
WO/CWO	April	October	October
2ndLt	January/July	April	N/A
1stLt	October/April	October	October
Capt	May	September	June
Maj	May	September	June
LtCol	May	June	June
Col	May	July	July

fair to the Marine thus observed. A typical case would be during high-intensity or combat operations where close, daily, and detailed personal observation occurs.

Adverse reports contain any one of several possible ratings or phrases reflecting unsatisfactory performance and require special handling. Generally, any of the following cases would constitute an adverse report:

- A report of failure of physical fitness testing or weight control program
- Any rating of "adverse"
- Any comments in Section I of a derogatory nature relating to unsatisfactory performance of duty or failure to measure up to norms and expectations
- Similar adverse material contributed by the reviewing officer

Records. A few months after you have seen your fitness report online, you will receive a computer-generated receipt from HQMC that contains a recapitulation of the tabulated markings. Keep this in your personal file and verify its later transfer to your Master Brief Sheet. The latter is mailed annually to all officers and can be requested anytime from the HQMC Manpower Management Division, Records and Performance Branch (Code MMRP).

With the migration online of Marine Corps personnel records and administrative systems, including performance evaluation, you can audit your performance record at any time. Look at your trends, as displayed in the reports by your seniors, and objectively strive to improve the noted weaknesses, many of which you likely share with most other officers. If you desire professional help in interpreting or planning your career, seek the guidance of the HQMC Officer Career Counseling Section (Code MMRP-50) via appointment. That section's counselors have the advantage of knowing how the other officers of your grade and year group are performing and can advise you in clear and dispassionate terms.

If you believe a report reflects errors or injustice on the part of the reporting senior or reviewing officer, you should first attempt to resolve the issue directly with that individual. But you always have the final recourse of an appeal to the Board for Correction of Naval Records (BCNR) of the Department of the Navy. Any officer seeking such redress should obtain first the advice and recommendations of the HQMC Officer Career Counseling Section, which can advise as to the wisdom of proceeding with such an appeal and provide details on the exact procedure to follow.

❖ ❖ *Marking Fitness Reports*

Because fitness reports are decisive in the career of a Marine, the preparation of a fitness report is one of the most weighty tasks you will perform. This is also an opportunity for you to contribute materially to the overall improvement of the Corps. Instructions governing fitness reports are found in pertinent Marine Corps orders, most notably the PES, which you should review before you complete a report or a recommended report.

Performance appraisal should be a continuous process rather than an intermittent one performed only at fitness report time. Shortcomings should be pointed out as they arise—not saved up. Counseling policy, now distinct from performance evaluation, requires you to sit down periodically with the Marine reported on and candidly discuss his or her general performance and personal qualities. This is not always an agreeable session for either party, but it is a responsibility of leadership at every level.

The suitability of an officer or noncommissioned officer for future assignments, selection, or retention is based in large degree on the evaluations made by reporting seniors. For most officers and NCOs in today's large services, there is little else on which decisions can be based.

You must therefore prepare fitness reports carefully, impartially, and with a full appreciation of the task at hand and the responsibility that goes with it. A report that is unduly negative or fails to accent the positive might cost the Marine Corps a fine officer or NCO. On the other hand, your failure to point out weaknesses can cause the selection and promotion of a Marine unsuited for higher rank at the expense of one who is. Thus, as a reporting senior, you can add luster to a career or destroy it. This is a burden officers must bear with utmost care.

Put aside prejudice or partiality as you evaluate. Compare the Marine being reported on with others of the same rank and experience. Consider fully the circumstances and context of the reporting period. Guard particularly against the attitude of the moment; you are grading an individual's total performance during the entire period covered. Make initial drafts of the report, then review it for consistency and fairness.

Bear in mind that any group contains a few individuals at the top or at the bottom who stand out, respectively, favorably or unfavorably. The majority represents a fairly level standard of performance in between. If you find that your ratings tend to put most officers at the top or at the bottom, be quite sure you can justify this departure from the normal distribution (as you are specifically required to do in the case of certain outstanding or unsatisfactory marks). Remember that most officers are average officers, or nearly so. It is the easy way out to give high ratings to all officers, rationalizing that "everyone else does." But overrating an average officer leaves no scope for the brilliant one.

The final written Section I of the fitness report carries somewhat less weight than the former Section C, a single space furnished for all written comments under the old system. Because the report under the current system contains sections on the billet description, billet accomplishments, and an evaluation of some thirteen attributes among four categories, comments in this section must be clear, objective, and to the point—not superlative descriptions and superfluous statistics.

In Section I, you must include mandatory comments to provide a word picture of the Marine reported on for all observed reports. While these comments must be concise, they should provide a complete and detailed evaluation of the individual's professional character. You may also address any entry made in Sections A through H or as you deem appropriate. Next, you will insert the phrase "directed comments" and/or "additional comments" and, under each heading, supply objective, clear, and concise statements either required by the evaluation system (refer to the PES) or considered necessary by you to complete an accurate picture of the officer or NCO you are evaluating.

❯ PROMOTION AND PRECEDENCE

❯ ❯ *Marine Corps Promotion System*

The Marine Corps and Navy share a system of officer promotion that has been under continuous evolution since 1915 and, in past years, has served as a model for the other services. Under this system, officers who are judged "best qualified" are selected for advancement, while others are passed over and must eventually leave active service through resignation or retirement. Determination of who is best qualified for promotion is accomplished by selection boards composed of of senior officers.

Promotion never comes automatically. To qualify for promotion, you must not only perform effectively and loyally in your present rank, but you must also develop and prove your capacity to handle the increased responsibilities of higher rank. And you must excel in ways that best satisfy the needs of the Marine Corps.

❯ ❯ *Officer Distribution*

The Defense Officer Personnel Management Act of 1981, as amended, provides the officer promotion machinery for the Army, Marine Corps, Navy, Air Force, Space Force, and Coast Guard. The Navy and Marine Corps provisions are generally similar. One of the most important things that this law does is to establish certain categories of officers for promotion purposes. It also regulates the number of officers who may be assigned to each grade. This is known as "officer distribution" and determines how many vacancies for promotion each rank contains.

Officer Categories. All Marine officers are line officers. Some commissioned officers, however, are designated "restricted in the performance of duty" in contrast to all other Marine officers, who are described as *unrestricted officers*.

Existing law provides for two categories of *restricted officers*: permanent Regular limited duty officers and permanent warrant officers. All other officers in the Corps are considered for promotion and assignment purposes as not being restricted in the performance of duty.

Limited duty officers are former warrant or noncommissioned officers who have been commissioned for duty in the fields in which they have specialized, such as administration, ordnance, motor transport, and so on. Their assignments are normally limited to their designated fields. If the officer so applies and is judged to be qualified, an LDO may be redesignated as an unrestricted officer, and the limited duty designation ceases.

Like LDOs, *warrant officers* are also appointed for duty in particular fields and are thus restricted to performance of duty in the appropriate area(s). WOs selected from certain "line duty" MOSs carry the title of "Marine gunner" and wear the gunner's bursting-bomb insignia. The occupational fields from which Marine gunners are usually appointed are 03 (infantry), 08 (field artillery), 18 (tank/assault amphibian, although this may change given the Corps' recent divestment of tanks), 25 (communications), and MOS 4915 (range officer).

Reserve officers, unless on active duty with the Regular establishment, are selected separately. If on Regular active duty, Reserve officers are selected and promoted along with Regular contemporaries. The Marine Corps has a continuing requirement for Reserve officers on active duty beyond their obligated service and now offers them a career program comparable to that of Regular officers.

Distribution of Officers by Grade. The number of officers who may be promoted above first lieutenant depends on the authorized numbers for each grade. These ceilings are computed by HQMC and approved by the SECNAV. They vary periodically with the laws that establish the authorized strength of the Marine Corps. If the SECNAV decides that fewer officers than those computed are required in any grade, the secretary can establish that lower figure as the authorized number for that grade.

LDOs are not "additional numbers," but the actual number of them may not exceed a modest fixed percentage of the total number of unrestricted officers at each grade.

General Officers. Examining all provisions of the Officer Personnel Act dealing with general officers demands an extensive and even technical understanding of officer personnel management and is thus beyond the scope of the *Guide*. Yet awareness of the following highlights is worthwhile:

- Federal law limits the number of four-, three-, two-, and one-star generals on active duty in the Marine Corps.
- The commandant and assistant commandant of the Marine Corps are four-star generals. A Marine chairman of the Joint Chiefs of Staff or commander of a combatant command also is a four-star general.
- Lieutenant generals in the Marine Corps typically fill the positions of deputy commandant at HQMC; commanding general, Marine Corps forces; commanding general, Marine expeditionary force; and, when assigned, certain deputy commander and principal staff officer billets at certain major joint commands.
- Major and brigadier generals typically serve as commanders, deputy commanders, and principal staff officers at divisions, wings, and other major Marine Corps commands as well as at lower joint commands and task forces.

❯ ❯ *Promotion Procedure*

Promotion to first lieutenant is by seniority on completion of twenty-four months' service in grade. From captain to major general, inclusive, promotion is by selection. The standard of selection is "best qualified"; eligibility requirements, selection procedures, and so forth are the same for all candidates within a rank. The Marine Corps selects officers for promotion using a board process.

Eligibility for Selection. You become eligible for selection when you have completed service, approximately, as follows: first lieutenant, two years; captain, four; major, ten (plus or minus one); lieutenant colonel, sixteen (plus or minus one); and colonel, twenty-two (plus or minus one). Note that wartime exigencies can drop as much as two years from these criteria, as happened for 2007–8 promotions.

Eligibility for selection does not necessarily mean you enter a promotion zone, as described below. Once you become eligible, though, it remains valid, regardless of failure of selection, as long as you remain on active duty.

Selection Boards. Marine selection boards usually consist of at least nine active or reserve officers and are convened by the SECNAV annually. The board is usually balanced in numbers of ground and aviation officers along with those representing service support MOSs; if LDOs and Reservists are to be considered by the board, it includes at least one of each as members.

No officer may be a member of two successive boards for the same grade. This ensures that at least eighteen different officers must pass on your case before the possibility of your twice failing selection.

Members of selection boards are sworn to act without prejudice or partiality and, like members of a court-martial, may not disclose their deliberations. Specifically, their sworn duties and obligations are as follows:

- To recommend the best-qualified officers for promotion
- To give equal weight to performance of duty in the Operating Forces and the Supporting Establishment or duty in any technical specialty
- Not to consider as prejudicial the fact that an officer under consideration may have been previously passed over
- Not to select more officers than the number set by the SECNAV (but the board need not select the full number if there are insufficient qualified personnel under consideration)

Mechanics of Selection. Each selection board receives the names and official files of officers who are eligible for consideration. In addition, each panel is informed of the names of the eligible officers who constitute the primary promotion zone for that grade. Whenever a selection board convenes, the SECNAV determines how far down the eligible list members must go in making selections to ensure a satisfactory flow of promotion.

Beginning with the most senior officer of the grade under consideration who has not previously failed to be selected, the promotion zone goes down to the last unrestricted officer needed to maintain the flow of promotion "up or out" as determined by the SECNAV.

A separate promotion zone is established for LDOs, and the selection board is allocated separate quotas of limited duty vacancies to be filled by selection. These officers are considered only upon their specialist qualifications. They do not compete for selection with unrestricted officers.

All officers senior to or in a promotion zone "fail of selection" (that is, are passed over) if not recommended for promotion. The effects of failing of selection, in terms of mandatory retirement, are covered below in the section on retirement and separation.

Except for LDOs, a selection board may go below the promotion zone, among those eligible, and select outstanding officers for accelerated promotion. But no officer below the promotion zone is considered passed over, even if an officer junior to him or her is selected for accelerated promotion. Only a small percentage of the total number of officers the board is authorized to select may come from below the zone except in the case of colonels and brigadier generals being considered for the next higher grade.

Once selected, your name is submitted by the board to the CMC, SECNAV, and finally the president. If all names are approved and the Senate confirms, as is usual, you are promoted according to vacancies.

Effecting Promotions. When selected for promotion, your name goes on a promotion list in normal order of seniority. As vacancies occur, you are then promoted. All officer promotions, Regular and Reserve, are subject to such physical, mental, moral, and professional qualifications as the SECNAV may prescribe. On promotion, you rate the pay and allowances of the higher grade from the date of the appointment.

❖ ❖ *Precedence*

Precedence is your right of seniority over other officers as based on grade and the date of your appointment within that grade. The rank and precedence of officers on active duty is shown in numerical order in Marine Corps Bulletin 1400, *Officer Lineal Precedence*, informally known as the Blue Book. Your date of rank is also stated on your commission. Although complex methods previously determined the order of precedence of officers appointed to the same date of rank, today, class standing at Basic School remains the sole criterion for that order, which will change thereafter only as officers are selected, "deep selected," or passed over for promotion.

Precedence of officers of different services is in accordance with their relative grades and, within each grade, in accordance with respective dates of rank, the senior in date of rank taking precedence. Among officers of different services of the same relative grade and the same date of rank, precedence is determined according to the time each has served on active duty as a commissioned officer.

❧ RETIREMENT AND SEPARATION

❧ ❧ *Basics*

Retirement is removal from active duty following completion of certain service and longevity requirements, after which the retired officer receives retired pay. Although no longer on duty, a retired officer remains a member of the Marine Corps, retains his or her rank and status as an officer (being entitled to all military courtesies of that rank), and may under certain conditions be recalled to active duty.

In contrast, *separation*, or *discharge*, is an absolute termination of officer status. Depending on the character of discharge, the officer being separated may or may not receive lump-sum separation pay. A form of separation distinct from retirement, *resignation*, is total, voluntary separation from the service. There is also a disability severance pay for persons holding less than twenty years' service. *Revocation of commission* may separate any officer who has been on continuing active duty for less than three years as a commissioned officer in the Marine Corps or Navy. An officer whose commission is revoked does not receive any advance pay or allowances or separation pay.

❧ ❧ *Involuntary Retirement and Separation*

Except for physical reasons, you retire upon reaching a certain age, on completing certain periods of service, or after failure of selection for promotion.

Retirement Based on Age. Officers still on the active list must retire at age sixty-two (sixty-four in the case of flag officers), unless the president in a particular case authorizes deferral. Such retirement may not be deferred beyond age sixty-eight.

Retirement Based on Length of Service. Lieutenant colonels and above normally must serve three years in grade to retire at that grade. The Marine Corps grants waivers to this rule under rare circumstances. The following paragraphs summarize provisions for mandated retirement based on grade and length of service.

Major generals retire after thirty-five years of active commissioned service or five years in grade, whichever is later; *lieutenant generals*, after thirty-eight years of active commissioned service; and *generals*, after forty years of active commissioned service.

Brigadier generals not on a promotion list to major general retire after thirty years of active commissioned service or five years in grade, whichever is later.

Colonels not on a promotion list to brigadier general retire after thirty years of active commissioned service except for certain officers who are either LDOs or permanent professors at the U.S. Naval Academy.

Lieutenant colonels not on a promotion list to colonel retire after twenty-eight years of active commissioned service except for certain officers who are either LDOs or permanent professors at the U.S. Naval Academy.

Majors, captains, and *first lieutenants* who are twice failed of selection and are within two years of qualifying for retirement with twenty years of active commissioned service are permitted to stay until retirement eligible. Otherwise, they are honorably discharged (not retired) six months following the second failure, with separation pay based on length of service. An LDO, however, has the option of reversion to prior enlisted status.

Warrant officers who are twice passed over for promotion to the next higher permanent warrant grade and decline reversion to enlisted status are discharged with separation pay if they have less than eighteen years' active service since initial appointment as a WO; any passed over having eighteen but less than twenty years' service since the original appointment will be retired (unless picked up in the interim) two months after completing twenty years. Any Regular WO who has at least twenty years' active service in the armed forces will be retired at age sixty-two or, short of that age, on completing thirty years' active service in the armed forces.

LDOs, if not otherwise subject to retirement, must retire after completing thirty years' active Marine Corps or Navy service.

Selective Early Retirement. Defense Department policies authorize the services to convene boards to select officers for retirement in advance of the statutory limits of service. Such measures seek to retain the desired annual vacancies in grade and allow promotion opportunities for juniors at desired rates. The boards convene when directed by the service secretary and have the same composition normally as those convened to promote to the next higher grade. Officers so selected by the panel will be retired on the date seven months after the results are approved. Such officers who choose to retire before the seven months elapse are considered "voluntary" retirements. Normally, such retirement boards perform their duties only in time of forced personnel reductions by the services.

Revocation of Commission. The SECNAV may revoke the commission of any officer who has less than three years' continuous service. Discharge of this type does not include separation pay. The most usual causes for revocation of commission are academic failure at TBS, general low-caliber or unsatisfactory performance of duty, or temperamental unsuitability.

❧ ❧ *Voluntary Retirement*

After a Regular or Reserve officer completes twenty years' active duty in the Marine Corps, Army, Navy, Air Force, or Coast Guard (including Reserve), ten years of which must have been active commissioned service, he or she may, at the discretion of the president, retire with the highest grade satisfactorily held as determined by the SECNAV.

When an officer has thirty year's active service, he or she may retire with 75 percent of active duty base pay.

Retirements take effect on the first day of the month after the SECNAV approves the request *except* in cases of voluntary retirement for which a later date has been approved.

If you are considering voluntary retirement or are subject to involuntary or statutory retirement and you have any doubt as to your physical qualification for release from active duty, obtain a preliminary physical examination approximately *nine months ahead of the estimated retirement date*. If a disability is discovered, you might be eligible for physical retirement. Information as to your physical condition must be received by HQMC in time to modify action on your retirement papers.

After the president or SECNAV approves a request for retirement or involuntary retirement proceedings, and the retirement has become effective, there is no process of law whereby the retired status can be changed except through disciplinary action or because of physical disability incurred subsequently while serving as a retired officer on active duty.

❖❖ *Disability Retirement*

Disability retirement is governed by Title 10, U.S. Code. Servicemembers who have been determined to be unfit for duty with a disability rated by the military service at 30 percent or greater are eligible for disability retirement. A service-member whose condition is not stable may, at first, be placed on the *temporary disability retired list* (TDRL) for up to five years, at which point he or she must be either returned to duty, discharged, or retired. Cases of individuals on the TDRL are reevaluated periodically. Those whose condition has stabilized at a disability rating of 30 percent or higher may be placed on the *permanent disability retired list* (PDRL).

Persons whose disability is less than 30 percent may instead be discharged with separation pay.

Retired pay for individuals on either of these retired lists is a function of retired base pay, which varies depending on when one first entered military service (discussed in some detail in chapter 18) and a multiplier percentage. The individual may choose between two multiplier percentages: either the percentage of disability assigned or the years of creditable service times 2.5 percent. In either case, the multiplier is limited by law to 75 percent. In the case of a person on the TDRL, the minimum percentage is 50 percent while on this list. Disability retirement pay is tax exempt.

❖ CORRESPONDENCE AND MESSAGES

❖❖ *Official Correspondence*

Both the Marine Corps and Navy employ the same forms and procedures for official correspondence. These are prescribed in the *Department of the Navy Correspondence Manual*, Navy Regulations, and the *Marine Corps Manual*. "Correspondence" embraces letters, endorsements, memoranda, email (both formal and informal), and facsimile transmissions. Correspondence is filed and maintained in accordance with the *Department of the Navy Records Management Manual*.

As an individual, you may originate official correspondence that pertains to you personally, including any recommendations for improvement or innovation that may benefit the Marine Corps. Correspondence pertaining to a whole command may be originated only by, or in the name of, the commanding officer.

Official correspondence must be promptly forwarded through appropriate channels. Failure to do so if the correspondence is in proper form and language is a very serious dereliction.

Avoid unnecessary, imprecise, or verbose correspondence. Joseph Pulitzer's rule for the staff of the old *New York World* applies with considerable force to military correspondence: "Accuracy, brevity, accuracy!"

During recent decades, government correspondence has grown less precise and less effective. Vague expressions, superlatives, affectations, jargon, and clichéd prose have become commonplace, replacing, in many cases, clear and understandable terms. Complex language is used, not because it contributes to clarity, but because it makes the user feel self-important. It is not consistent with the character of the Marine Corps or with efficiency to dilute correspondence with unmilitary expressions or unnecessary language. Bumper-sticker phrases have no place in Marine Corps documents; leave them to the bumper stickers.

You will find admirable advice regarding official correspondence, and military writing in general, in the *Navy Correspondence Manual*. Read and heed.

❧ *Official Letters*

According to the nature of the correspondence, official letters may follow either the naval form, which is used throughout the naval establishment, or the business form. Examples and detailed instructions covering each can be found in the *Navy Correspondence Manual*.

Sooner or later, every officer serves as a staff officer, and writing is an essential survival skill during such duty. In addition to taking the initiative and following through, which are keys to success in any Marine Corps assignment, writing *well* will distinguish you from your peers. Here is some advice for preparing official naval correspondence.

Tips for Official Letter Writers. Until you are quite familiar with the prescribed forms for official correspondence, do your writing within arm's reach of the *Navy*

Correspondence Manual. See that your unit clerks do likewise. And keep an up-to-date dictionary at hand. English is a delightfully idiosyncratic language, filled with exceptions, contradictions, and even confusion. Sometimes words sound the same but mean different things, and sometimes words are spelled the same but sound differently and mean different things; for example, there's a difference between "lead" (lēd), "led" (led), and "lead" (led). The dictionary is your friend.

Avoid pointless letters. Correspondence with higher authority should be confined to specific requests, reports, and concrete recommendations.

One letter should normally deal with one subject only. Cover separate subjects to the same addressee in separate documents. Answer official letters by letter, not by endorsement on the letter received, unless specifically directed to do so.

Write in concise, unadorned, direct, and clear language. Generally, use short sentences and paragraphs. Use the passive voice sparingly—"Please arrange the following," not "It is requested that the following arrangements be effectuated." Do not be afraid to use the first person.

Be as temperate and courteous in writing as you would be in discussing the subject face to face with your correspondent.

Organize your facts and ideas before you write. The standard sequence for a staff study or estimate is a good one for almost any kind of official correspondence:

1. Statement of the problem
2. Facts bearing on the problem
3. Discussion
4. Conclusions
5. Recommendations

Do not send official letters to other officers in the same command. Correspondence within units and headquarters should be by email or occasionally printed memorandum.

Block out important official letters in double-spaced rough draft. This permits you to make legible corrections and interlineations.

Use "Marine" or "Marines," "officer," "enlisted person," or "all hands" instead of the more generic and bureaucratic "personnel" or "members" wherever possible in official correspondence or directives.

In expressing time, use the naval twenty-four-hour system and never add the superfluous word "hours"—for 2:30 p.m., write "1430," not "1430 hours."

Always choose a short, simple word over a long one. Write "begin," "help," "mistake" instead of "commence," "assistance," "inadvertency." Here are a few examples of gobbledygook, jargon, and canned language excerpted from a sampling of official correspondence. We would all be better off if most of these were never used again:

above-named personnel
appraise—where "apprise" is intended
as appropriate
at the earliest practicable moment
considered opinion
definitive—where "definite" is meant
deobligate
effectuate
forward—where "foreword" is intended
frame of reference
full impact
in conformance with
infeasible of accomplishment
in light of the foregoing
interface incompatibility (except in information management)
lead, the bluish-white lustrous metal that is very soft, highly malleable, and a relatively poor conductor of electricity (with symbol Pb and atomic number 82)—as a misspelling of "led," the past participle of the verb "to lead"
logisticswise
management—as a substitute for "command" or "leadership"
marshall—as a misspelling of "marshal"
materially impaired effectiveness
outload, offload, onload—"load" and "unload" work fine
personnelwise
pertinent facts

preventative—as "preventive" will do (the extra syllable adds nothing)

pursuant to

rendered mandatory

salient data

thorough and complete investigation

top management

unprecedented—as a substitute for "unusual."

▸▸ *Official Mail*

Official correspondence may be mailed with official franked envelopes bearing an official return address and the notation *Official Business* in the upper left-hand corner. You are entitled to use such envelopes for correspondence that clearly involves government business and for government parcels within prescribed weight limits. Be scrupulous in exercising this privilege. Remember you also are a taxpayer.

▸▸ *Personal Correspondence*

Because you change stations every few years, keeping correspondents advised of your correct mailing address requires effort. Update your address with your regular correspondents online, if possible, or get change-of-address cards from your mail clerk or station post office and send them every time you are detached. For guidance of your family or parents at your permanent home address, postal laws and regulations permit postage-free forwarding of any class of mail addressed to a member of the armed services if marked, "Change of Address Due to Official Orders, Postal Reg. 157.9."

Fleet Post Office and Army Post Office. Mail may be sent to units and persons afloat or overseas at domestic postage rates via East Coast and West Coast military postal centers. This privilege merits your use, as it saves you and your correspondents considerable money in postage charges, especially for publications and parcels. Units that deploy or are at sea receive their mail via the tracking and routing efforts of military postmasters in the shortest time possible.

If a ship or Marine Corps deployed unit is on the East Coast, the Atlantic, Europe, or Africa and adjacent waters, its mail normally goes via FPO AE or

APO AE (plus zip code), with domestic postage charges to New York. Ships and units in the Pacific, Far East, or Indian Ocean normally receive mail via FPO AP or APO AP (plus zip code), with domestic charges paid to San Francisco or Seattle. A ship or unit based in one geographic area but deploying temporarily to another will retain its original address, even though the postmasters will route the mail through different theaters. Finally, be aware that current postal privileges allow free mailing of letters and small parcels *within* a given postal theater by writing "MPS" in the corner normally reserved for stamps. Be sure to obtain specific instructions, however, before attempting to use this procedure.

❯ SECURITY OF INFORMATION

❯ ❯ *Operational and Personal Security*

After taking your oath and becoming a Marine officer, in your profession and status you receive access to information not generally available to civilians. One of your most important responsibilities then becomes the safeguarding and proper use of this information so that it never falls into the hands of unauthorized individuals. Remember that, during both war and peace, the battle for information goes on continually. Success in this struggle will determine whether the odds of physical combat favor Marines or their adversaries.

Indiscreet communications—conversations, emails, and letters—are potential threats to operational security. Guard against unthinking discussion of classified "shop talk," even with your family and friends. Avoid loose talk in public places. When you are on the telephone, you can never tell who may be listening. Automatic self-censorship is a responsibility of all Marines.

❯ ❯ *Security of Classified Matter*

Classified matter is anything—either information or matériel—that, in the public interest, must be safeguarded against unauthorized or improper disclosure. Navy Regulations as well as the *Department of the Navy Personnel Security Program* and the *Department of the Navy Information Security Program* contain detailed instructions that you must follow to the letter when you handle classified matter.

Classifications. The categories of security classification are *Top Secret, Secret,* and *Confidential.* In addition, regulations classify certain information regarding nuclear weapons and related subjects as *Special Information.* It is up to a designated, original classification authority to assign matter the appropriate classification, and he or she as well as higher authorities may reclassify it when appropriate. Reclassification can involve either "upgrading" or "downgrading" the security status.

Handling of Classified Matter. The precautions regarding preparation, marking, custody, handling, transmitting, storage, disclosure, control, accounting for, and disposal of classified matter may be found in the references mentioned earlier, and, of course, you must follow them to your utmost. If, however, you find yourself in a situation where you cannot physically comply with certain of these rules, you are bound simply to do your utmost, with common sense and zeal, to safeguard whatever may be entrusted to you. Should you have reason to believe classified information has been compromised, either through your fault or anyone else's, you must inform your security manager or CO at once.

No one, regardless of rank, position, or clearance level, is automatically entitled to knowledge or possession of classified matter. Such information goes only to those who have both an appropriate *clearance* and a *need to know*.

❯ LEAVE AND LIBERTY

❯ ❯ *Leave of Absence*

Subject to the needs of the service, *leave of absence*, or more simply and commonly "leave," provides time off for mental and physical relaxation from duty and gives you the opportunity to settle your affairs when the time comes for change of station. Every officer on active duty accrues leave at the rate of 30 days a year (that is, 2½ days per month).

Your CO sometimes cannot grant every officer all the leave he or she rates without jeopardizing the readiness of your command. Whatever leave is not taken "goes on the books" until you have a maximum of 60 days' unused, or accrued, leave. Earned leave that accrues above 60 days must be automatically dropped on 30 September each year and when you retire. As you approach retirement, under certain circumstances it may be beneficial to let leave build up to a minimum of 30 days since you receive a lump-sum payment for such accrued leave when you retire. Short of final years, however, take leave as you can; regular leave keeps you sharp for the next mission. And you can never recover the unused leave days that are dropped each 30 September.

Leave describes authorized vacation or absence from duty, as distinguished from *liberty,* which is merely authority to be away from your place of duty for short periods and is not charged to leave.

Accrued leave is the unused leave "on the books" to your credit each 1 October. You cannot bank more than 60 days' accrued leave except in extraordinary circumstances when authorized by HQMC.

Annual leave is an absence taken as routine vacation from duty. Annual leave is limited to your total accrued leave plus up to 45 days' advance leave, with approval, but may not exceed periods of 60 days.

Advance leave is an accounting term to describe leave granted in advance of accrual.

Sick leave is given to convalescents on recommendation of the medical authorities or to repatriated prisoners of war. Sick leave does not count against accrued leave.

Emergency leave may be granted to help alleviate some personal emergency, such as death or serious illness in the immediate family. Emergency leave is charged against accrued leave and may not exceed 105 days.

Excess leave is leave in excess of all your accrued leave plus 45 days' advance leave. Avoid taking excess leave whenever possible because your pay and allowances are checked while you are on excess leave.

Delay in reporting, or more simply "delay," is leave authorized to be taken after detachment from one permanent station and before reporting to another. It is normally charged against your leave balance.

Graduation leave is granted to officers newly commissioned from one of the service academies (not to officers from any other source). It is 30 days, not chargeable to the officer's leave account, and you must take it prior to reporting to the first permanent duty station (ordinarily TBS) or port of embarkation in the continental United States if ordered to permanent overseas duty.

❧ ❧ *Computing Leave and Delay*

Accurately calculating leave and, when changing duty stations, delay requires some low-order bookkeeping and occasional finger counting. But such calculations are relatively straightforward.

Your day of departure, normally after 1600, counts as a day on duty (and hence is not charged as leave). If your commander authorizes a departure earlier than 1600, the day still counts as a day of duty, not as a day of leave.

If you return after the beginning of working hours on shore station or on board ship, the calendar day of return counts as a day of leave. For leave-accounting purposes, the beginning of the formal workday varies by command, but it is typically 0700, 0800, or 0900. If you return after the designated start of the workday, your day of return counts as a day of leave. If you return before working hours, however, the calendar day of return is a day of duty.

All the days in between count as days of leave.

Finally, regulations require Marines to begin and end leave periods at or in the vicinity of their duty locations. They also prohibit the combination of leave periods with liberty periods. The implications of these regulations for computing leave periods are somewhat nuanced. Check with your adjutant or personnel officer for clarification.

❖ ❖ *Leave Requests and Records*

Requesting Leave. When you want leave, give your immediate supervisor or commanding officer advance notice. Some organizations have an annual leave plan that permits all officers to schedule absences well in advance. After you have informal approval for your projected leave, submit a leave request via Marine Online to the officer who is authorized to grant it—usually your battalion commander, squadron commander, officer in charge, or one of their designated subordinates, such as the executive officer, adjutant, or personnel officer. Your leave request should include the number of days and type of leave desired, the number of days' leave you have already taken during the fiscal year, your address while away, whether you are a member of any military court or board, and any other pertinent information or special justification for the request.

If approved, your leave request is returned by electronic endorsement, which you then print and keep with you throughout your leave.

Officers are typically entrusted to sign themselves out on and in from leave by annotating their leave papers directly. Some commands may require them to report the start and end of leave with a telephone call to the officer of the day or S-1.

Address during Leave. It is your responsibility to keep your command always apprised of your address while on leave. If your plans change, inform your command by telephone. If you are touring, provide addresses for hotels where you expect to stay or homes of friends or relatives. You have no leg to stand on if, while on leave, your command tries to communicate with you and cannot reach you. The ubiquity of cell phones today has made this responsibility easier to fulfill.

Your Leave Record. Every officer has a leave record, part of your leave and earnings statement (LES), on which all leave taken is debited and all leave earned is credited each month. This record is compiled and kept current by the headquarters that administers you, but it is your responsibility to see that your leave record is correct.

❧ ❧ *Foreign Leave*

Foreign travel while on leave is subject to certain controls and restrictions for reasons of personal and operational security. In general, Marines desiring to take leave or travel outside the United States, or outside the territory or foreign country of current assignment, must obtain approval from their CO; there are exceptions, however, for visits to certain foreign areas specified from time to time in current directives for which blanket authorization is granted.

Marines going on foreign leave may travel, on a space-available basis, in government aircraft. Unless you are specifically authorized to wear a uniform while on foreign leave, you must wear civilian clothes.

❧ ❧ *Liberty*

Liberty is local free time, within limits, that does not count as leave. Normal weekends are considered periods of liberty. It may also be granted at any time for up to forty-eight hours. If the period includes a legal holiday, any CO can extend a "forty-eight" to a "seventy-two."

COs so authorized by the commandant may grant ninety-six-hour liberty, which normally encompasses a weekend. But, as previously mentioned, liberty cannot be used as a device to extend leave.

Unless you have specific permission to the contrary, while on liberty you must remain within the general vicinity of your duty station. Almost all bases, stations, and units have standing orders that designate "liberty limits"—normally functions of the length of the period—beyond which ordinary liberty does not extend. The purpose of this is to prevent Marines from going so far afield that they cannot count on returning safely within the prescribed time.

❖ IDENTITY DEVICES

❖ ❖ *ID Card*

The armed forces identification (ID) card is the most important identifying document you have. Today's ID card, the common access card (CAC) identical for active duty and inactive reserve forces, features bar coding, a magnetic strip, and an embedded integrated circuit chip. It identifies you as a Marine officer and must be safeguarded with great care. The Corps now issues retired Marines an ID card similar to a CAC (in place of what used to be a simple green photo ID card). Loss of an ID card is serious and must be reported immediately because they are controlled items.

Always carry the card, and never surrender it. If somebody asks you to surrender your ID card in exchange for a temporary pass or badge—for example, to access a building or space—they are doing so in violation of regulations; after showing them your CAC, politely offer them another form of identification to hold "hostage."

❖ ❖ *Identification Tags*

Every Marine on active duty is issued two "dog tags" for identification should he or she be killed or wounded in action. These tags are items of equipment. When not required to be worn, they must remain in your possession. Note that when tags are required, both tags must be worn.

❖ ❖ *Dependents' ID Cards*

Your spouse and each family member over age ten are entitled to an armed forces dependent's card. This card, like your CAC, is an identity device and does not in itself entitle the bearer to anything. It ordinarily serves, however, to establish identification for medical care, military exchange, and similar privileges extended to dependents.

⁌{ **18** }⁊

PAY, ALLOWANCES, AND OFFICIAL TRAVEL

If love of money were the mainspring of all American action, the officer corps long since would have disintegrated.
— The Armed Forces Officer

A MARINE CORPS ANECDOTE relates that during the early days of World War II, a lofty-minded civilian visited Guadalcanal. During his tour, war aims were mentioned. Addressing Lieutenant Colonel L. B. Puller, one of the most hard-bitten professionals on the island—or, for that matter, in the Marine Corps—the visitor inquired, "And what, colonel, are you fighting for?"

Colonel Puller reflected for a moment, then answered, "$649 a month."

In contrast, more than a century and a half earlier, George Washington shared his thoughts on remuneration with Congress upon his appointment as commander in chief in 1775: "As to pay, I beg leave to assure the Congress that, as no pecuniary consideration could have tempted me to accept this arduous employment at the expense of my domestic ease and happiness, I do not wish to make any profit from it."

It is immaterial whether you are inclined to Puller's view or to the sentiments of the Father of the Nation. The importance of knowing about pay and allowances is self-evident.

❯ MILITARY COMPENSATION

The military term for your pay and benefits is "military compensation." There are various types of pay. *Basic pay* is received by all and is the main component of a Marine's salary. Some receive other *pays*, often referred to as special and incentive pays, for specific qualifications or events. For example, there are special and incentive pays for aviators, parachutists, and qualified linguists, and Marines are entitled to special pays for dangerous or hardship duties.

Allowances are the second-most-significant element of military compensation. These add to and complement basic pay for specific needs, such as food or housing. Monetary allowances are provided when the government does not provide for a specific need. For example, the quantity of government housing is not sufficient to house all military members and their families. Those who do not occupy government housing receive an allowance to assist them in obtaining commercial housing off base.

Most allowances are not taxable, which is an additional imbedded benefit of military compensation.

Pay and allowances are periodically adjusted in line with cost-of-living increases in the private economy.

Significance of Family Members. Although basic pay is not affected by marital status or family members (alternately referred to as "dependents"), some allowances do vary according to family composition. The law defines "family" as follows:

- Your spouse (whose financial dependency is presumed)
- Unmarried children under age twenty-one (twenty-three if enrolled in higher education) or over age twenty-one if incapable of self-support
- A parent (or one who has stood in loco parentis), if chiefly dependent on you for over half of his or her support
- Stepchildren and adopted children, if financially dependent

Except for your spouse and any unmarried minor children, you must prove financial dependency for any persons for whom you claim allowances.

You will find complete, up-to-date coverage of military compensation online (https://militarypay.defense.gov/) as part of the Defense Department website.

❖ ❖ *Basic Pay*

Your basic pay is the core of your military compensation, and it is a function of your pay grade and longevity—that is, the length of your service creditable for pay purposes. Regardless of whether your grade is temporary or permanent, you are paid at the rates prescribed for it. You are normally paid twice monthly.

Service Creditable for Pay Purposes. In determining your length of service for pay purposes, you receive credit for all service, active or inactive, in the Marine Corps, Navy, Army, Air Force, Coast Guard, and the Reserve components thereof; the National Guard; and certain federal agencies such as the Public Health Service and the National Oceanic and Atmospheric Administration. Active service in the appointive grade as aviation cadet and officer candidate (Platoon Leaders Class) *may* be counted as service for pay purposes.

Service not creditable for longevity purposes includes service as cadet or midshipman; service in the inactive National Guard or State, Home, or Territorial Guard; service in ROTC; and time spent in voided fraudulent enlistment.

Besides basic pay, officers whose duties or status so qualify them are entitled to special and incentive pay, including flight pay (discussed in a later section).

❖ ❖ *Subsistence Allowance*

Every officer on active duty receives a basic monthly subsistence allowance, known officially as the *basic allowance for subsistence* (BAS), regardless of his or her family status. The law exempts subsistence allowance from income tax.

❖ ❖ *Quarters Allowance*

Quarters allowance, known officially as the *basic allowance for housing* (BAH), comes in many forms to satisfy various housing situations that occur among servicemembers. If you are on permanent duty within the fifty states and are not furnished government quarters, you are normally entitled to an amount of BAH calculated as a function of duty location, pay grade, and whether you have dependents. Under most circumstances, you receive BAH for the geographic location where you are stationed, not where you live. Additionally, you may be entitled to different BAH amounts if you are residing separately from your dependents. This occurs, for example, if you are assigned to an unaccompanied overseas tour or have a dependent child who resides with a former spouse. The rules regarding these situations can become quite complex. Consult your local finance office if you are in such a situation.

If stationed overseas, including U.S. protectorates, and not furnished government quarters, you are entitled to an *overseas housing allowance* (OHA), calculated based on your dependency status, pay grade, and permanent duty station. If serving an unaccompanied overseas tour, you normally receive BAH at the "with dependents" rate, based on the zip code where your spouse or family actually resides, plus OHA at the "without dependents" rate if you are not furnished government quarters.

If you live in quarters managed under the public-private venture program, which operates at many U.S. installations, you remain entitled to and continue to receive quarters allowance. Under normal circumstances, you in turn surrender this same amount to the private partner (for example, Lincoln Military Housing) as if you are paying rent.

Officers without family members who do not qualify for a full quarters allowance because they are at sea or living in government quarters are entitled to a partial quarters allowance.

If uncertain about your entitlement to quarters allowance, consult your unit's personnel officer or the local finance office. Inattentive or careless officers have unwittingly drawn quarters allowances exceeding their entitlements and, after several months or even years, found themselves deeply indebted to the federal government.

The law exempts quarters allowance from income tax.

The Defense Travel Management Office maintains a handy online BAH calculator (https://www.defensetravel.dod.mil/site/bahCalc.cfm) that will help you verify your entitlement to quarters allowance at your present or any future duty station.

❥ ❥ *Family Separation Allowance*

If your dependents are not authorized to live with you at or near your permanent duty station, whether inside or outside the United States, you may be entitled to *family separation allowance* (FSA) payable at the rate of $250 per month (as of 2021).

FSA is intended to provide compensation for added expenses incurred because of an enforced family separation under one of the following circumstances:

1. Movement of dependents to the permanent duty station at government expense is not authorized. This presupposes that the dependents do not already live at or near that station.
2. The servicemember is on duty on board a ship away from the ship's home port for a period of more than thirty continuous days.
3. The servicemember is on temporary duty away from the permanent duty station for a continuous period of more than thirty days, and the dependents do not live at or near the temporary duty station.

If you opt to serve an unaccompanied tour of duty at a permanent duty station where the movement of dependents at government expense is authorized, you are not entitled to FSA under the first condition noted above.

❧ ❧ Dislocation Allowance

When an officer with family has completed a permanent change of station (PCS) move, he or she gets a *dislocation allowance* (DLA) to help pay the numerous extra expenses of relocating a household. DLA is payable only once in any fiscal year except by special authorization or when the officer is ordered to or from a course of instruction. It is not payable on orders to or from active duty. An officer without family is authorized DLA on a PCS if not assigned government quarters at the new station.

❧ ❧ Uniform Allowances for Officers

All Marine officers, regardless of source of commission or previous enlisted status, are entitled to an *initial uniform allowance* of $400 (as of 2021). Except as noted below, the initial uniform allowance is payable only once to an officer

- upon first reporting for active duty (other than for training) for a period of more than ninety days;
- upon completing at least fourteen days of active duty or active duty for training as a member of a Reserve component;
- upon completing fourteen periods of inactive duty training as a member of the Ready Reserve; or

- upon reporting for the first period of active duty required of a member of the Armed Forces Health Professions Scholarship Program.

Upon transfer to a different component that requires a different uniform, a Reserve officer may receive another initial uniform allowance. Regular officers may not receive this allowance when transferring to another military service.

Civilian clothing allowances for officers depend on an assignment to a high-risk area, certified as such by the Department of State or DOD. In such a case, where officers wear civilian clothing for all or a substantial part of their duties, a one-time allowance is paid for the two- or three-year tour length.

The subject of uniform allowances remains complex. For the final word, consult *DOD Financial Management Regulations*, volume 7A.

⤮ *Special and Incentive Pay*

Basic pay and allowances are only a part of military compensation. Many Marines qualify for various special and incentive pays that are part of the Corps' recruitment and retention efforts. Some of these compensate Marines for assignment to hazardous or difficult duty conditions. Examples include additional pay for undertaking an aviation career, maintaining needed foreign language proficiency, or performing hazardous duty in obedience to competent orders.

Current law authorizes more than sixty special and incentive pays, although not all may be available to Marines. By way of example, the following hazardous duties currently rate incentive pay:

- Duty involving parachute jumping as an essential element
- Duty involving frequent and regular participation in flight operations on the flight deck of an aircraft carrier or any other ship from which aircraft are launched
- Duty involving the demolition of explosives as a primary duty (including training for such duty)
- Duty inside a high- or low-pressure chamber
- Duty as a human acceleration or deceleration experimental subject
- Duty as a human test subject in thermal-stress experiments
- Duty involving the servicing of aircraft or missiles with highly toxic fuels or propellants

- Duty involving fumigation tasks utilizing highly toxic pesticides
- Duty involving laboratory work utilizing live dangerous viruses or bacteria
- Duty involving handling of chemical munitions
- Duty involving maritime visit, board, search, and seizure operations
- Duty involving use of ski-equipped aircraft on the ground in Antarctica or on the Arctic ice pack

You may not receive hazardous duty incentive pay for more than two purposes at the same time.

In addition to hazardous duty incentive pay, Marine officers frequently qualify for two other types of incentive pay:

- *Career sea pay* (CSP) compensates persons assigned to a ship performing missions while primarily under way. Payment ranges from $50 to $150 per month depending on pay grade. More than thirty-six months entitles you to CSP premium.
- *Foreign language proficiency pay* (FLPP) provides up to $1,000 per month for persons demonstrating and maintaining proficiency in one or more foreign languages, validated by examination on an annual basis (see the current Marine Corps order on this program for detailed information). Only those assigned to billets requiring language proficiency or holding an MOS that requires language skills will receive FLPP.

Special and incentive pays such as these are normally *not* exempt from income tax.

❥ ❥ *Flight Pay*

To qualify for flight pay—or, as it is now technically termed, "aviation career incentive pay" (ACIP)—you must either be designated as a student naval aviator or student naval flight officer or be rated as a naval aviator or naval flight officer and be assigned to an aviation unit having aircraft. During your first twelve years' service, besides having a minimum number of operational flying assignments, you must also meet annual and semiannual prescribed minimum required flight hours. After your initial twelve years in flight status, your continued qualification to fly for pay depends on satisfactory passage of "gates" set by law, which are contained in volume 7A of *Department of Defense Financial Management Regulation* and updated in annual Marine Corps issuances. Determining continued entitlement to ACIP beyond twelve years is somewhat complex, but the *Marine Corps Assignment, Classification, and Travel System Manual* (ACTSMAN) contains two handy flowcharts to aid in understanding the process.

❯ ❯ Advance Pay

An advance of pay—a "dead horse" in slang—incident to a PCS provides funds to meet the extraordinary expenses of a government-ordered relocation. It assists with out-of-pocket expenses that exceed or precede reimbursements incurred during a PCS move and are not typical of day-to-day military living.

You may draw advance pay up to 90 days prior to departure from the old permanent duty station until 180 days after reporting to a new permanent station, provided the orders are not incident to separation from the service or trial by court-martial. Temporary duty en route is no bar to drawing advance pay. The amount advanced normally does not exceed one month's pay, but with approval, you may draw as much as three months' basic pay (less income tax, deduction for Social Security, and any indebtedness to the government).

❯ ❯ Pay of Enlisted Persons

The monthly basic pay of enlisted persons in the Marine Corps, Army, Navy, Air Force, Space Force, and Coast Guard may be found in current pay tables and is the same, grade for grade, in all services.

Under certain circumstances, enlisted Marines may be authorized a subsistence allowance in lieu of rations in kind at a current rate determined by law and regulation. Regulations give commanding officers some latitude in authorizing this allowance. Leave rations are granted to enlisted Marines on leave, if they are not furnished rations in kind, at the current BAS rate.

In general, enlisted Marines are entitled to a quarters allowance, with or without family, under the same conditions as officers.

❯ ❯ Enlisted Clothing Allowances

An initial, in-kind clothing allowance is granted to each enlisted person. Six months after assignment to active duty, a monthly basic clothing replacement

A U.S. Marine with the Force Reconnaissance Platoon gathers his parachute during operations on Ie Shima Training Facility, Okinawa, Japan, in 2021. Marines are entitled to special pay for parachute duty provided they are filling a parachutist-designated billet and maintain jump proficiency.

allowance accrues to each enlisted person. The first payment of this allowance is made on the Marine's enlistment anniversary month, after completing one year of uninterrupted service. After three years of service, an increased standard clothing maintenance allowance accrues.

❧ ❧ *Enlisted Retention Bonuses*

Retention bonuses encourage enlisted Marines, particularly those with costly or specialized skills, to reenlist. To provide you an idea of the magnitude of these bonuses, during fiscal year 2021, so-called first-term Marines who reenlisted after completing their first enlistment in one of forty-five high-demand MOSs were eligible for "shipping over" bonuses ranging from $2,000 to $47,500. Retention bonuses change annually according to the needs of the Corps. Be aware of current reenlistment bonuses so that you can intelligently advise your Marines and promote their reenlistment.

✵ Retired Pay

Since 1980, there have been several revisions to retired pay, with multiple retirement plans being in force simultaneously depending on a servicemember's initial date of entry into military service. Past retirement plans have gone by various names: Final Pay, for those entering service before 7 September 1980; High-36, for those entering after 7 September 1980 but before 1 August 1986; and REDUX, for those entering after 1 August 1986. The *Guide* is designed for officer candidates and junior officers, so this section will focus on the current retirement plan.

Today, the *Blended Retirement System* (BRS) is the only retirement plan for servicemembers with an initial date of entry into military service on or after 1 January 2018. As the name implies, BRS blends a traditional *defined benefit plan* with a modern *defined contribution plan*. Generally, a defined benefit plan is a type of retirement plan in which an employer promises a specified pension payment upon retirement that is predetermined by a formula based on the employee's age, earnings history, and tenure of service. A defined contribution plan is a type of retirement plan in which the employee, employer, or both make contributions to a retirement account on a regular basis. These accounts normally offer employees certain investment opportunities that enable contributed funds to grow. Individual accounts are set up for plan participants, and benefits in retirement are ultimately based on the sum of contributions to these accounts plus any investment earnings on the funds in the account.

Defined Benefit Component. After serving twenty or more years, Marines are eligible to receive a defined benefit upon retirement based on a percentage of basic pay. Those who qualify for this longevity-based retirement will receive a defined benefit each month that is 2 percent multiplied by the number of years of service multiplied by the average monthly basic pay of the servicemember's highest thirty-six months of basic pay. Reservists are also eligible for this defined benefit upon retirement after accumulating twenty qualifying years of service.

Defined Contribution Component. BRS also incorporates a defined contribution component—a retirement savings and investment plan called the Thrift Savings Plan (TSP) that offers the same types of savings, investment, and tax benefits many private corporations offer their employees through 401(k) or similar plans. The TSP is the same defined contribution plan available to thousands federal government civilians for their retirement savings. Beginning sixty days after entering the Corps, Marines automatically receive a monthly service contribution to a tax-advantaged TSP account that equals 1 percent of basic pay. They may also contribute pretax dollars from their basic pay to their TSP accounts, thus reducing their tax burden. When they do so, the service will make additional matching contributions up to 4 percent of basic pay beginning after the second year of service through the twenty-sixth year of service.

Retired Marines are not entitled to any allowances.

Persons retiring on or after 1 January 2007 may receive credit for years of active service exceeding thirty years under conditions authorized during a period for such purposes as designated by the secretary of defense. In theory, this new act provides for computing retired-pay percentages from 75 to 100 percent of active-duty basic pay (paragraph [3], section 1409[b], Title 10, U.S. Code, as amended).

Retired Pay Accounts. The Defense Finance and Accounting Service (DFAS), an agency under the Office of the Secretary of Defense, operates Retired and Annuitant (R&A) Pay, which manages pay accounts for all military retirees. R&A Pay establishes and maintains the accounts and disburses funds from them to military retirees and their surviving spouses and other family members.

Income tax continues to be withheld on retired pay except for wholly exempt physically disabled officers. Unless otherwise requested, all allotments are automatically continued when you retire.

Not to be confused with retired pay, separation pay is a lump-sum payment made to an officer involuntarily discharged from the service. It is based on 10 percent of active duty pay for each year of commissioned service.

❧ ❧ *Settlement for Unused Leave*

If you have unused leave upon discharge or separation from active duty, you are compensated for it. You receive one month's basic pay per thirty days of unused leave on a pro rata basis. Payment is made for up to sixty days' unused leave.

Thus, as retirement approaches, you may consider it advantageous to keep the maximum accrued leave on the books.

❧ ALLOTMENTS AND TAXES

❧ ❧ *Allotments*

As a matter of convenience and to facilitate regular monthly payments, you may make allotments of your pay for certain purposes. When you do so, your pay is checked that amount, and the Marine Corps transfers the funds monthly to the designated recipient. Individuals can start and stop allotments conveniently themselves using the MyPay website (https://mypay.dfas.mil/).

You may grant allotments to a bank and to pay life insurance premiums. You may also make allotments for purchase of U.S. Saving Bonds or other investment purposes. Allotments are credited on the last day of the month of checkage.

You should register an allotment for support of your family as soon as you are ordered overseas so that your family can rely on uninterrupted support—especially if you are headed for combat.

❧ ❧ *Income Tax*

Your basic pay and any special pays are taxable income, subject to federal and state withholding tax at its source. Not taxable, however, are disability retired pay and most allowances, including quarters, subsistence, and family separation allowances. (Tax exemptions for Marines and Sailors serving in combat zones during hostilities are covered below in the section on combat pay.)

Marine Corps withholding tax procedure provides that the finance officer establishes your withholding rate based on your rate of pay; this rate changes as your pay changes. Tax deductions are checked on your pay record in the same fashion as allotments. At the end of the year through MyPay, DFAS furnishes you a withholding statement, or Internal Revenue Service W-2 form, to be filed with your income tax return. You in turn must inform the personnel officer of your tax-exemption status by filing a W-4 form so that the correct rate is applied.

When hospitalized in a naval hospital as a result of wounds, disease, or injury *incurred while in a combat zone*, you may, if certain conditions are met, exclude from taxable income a certain portion of your pay, known as "sick pay." Check with your legal assistance officer (or that of the naval hospital) to determine eligibility.

❧ ❧ *Social Security Tax*

Social Security coverage extends to Marine officers on active duty and requires the withholding of Social Security deductions from pay. These taxes are computed on your basic pay and are deducted at rates prescribed by law. The amount subject to withholding and the amount of tax withheld are reflected on the W-2 form furnished to you by DFAS at the end of each year as well as your monthly leave and earnings statement.

❧ ❧ *Combat Pay and Tax Exemptions*

Combat pay—technically termed "hostile fire pay" (HFP)—is provided for all military personnel serving within geographic limits established by the secretary of defense during hostilities and meeting certain criteria of exposure to hostile fire or enemy action. This pay is the same for all grades and is taxable to the same extent as other pay. The rate was $225 per month as of 2021. Your finance officer can advise you as to eligibility.

Income tax exemption for officers and enlisted persons serving in combat areas may be placed in effect by executive order of the president. This exemption extends to all military pay of enlisted men and warrant officers. For commissioned officers, the amount of pay eligible for combat zone tax exclusion equals the sum of the monthly basic pay for highest enlisted pay grade plus the amount of HFP that the officer rates for the qualifying month. Here again, your finance officer can advise you as to eligibility and the precise provisions of the effective executive order. Note that the geographic areas of this tax exemption do not necessarily coincide with the combat pay geographic limits just mentioned.

❧ ❧ *Pay System*

Marines, both active and reserve, are paid through the centralized, automated Marine Corps Total Force System (MCTFS). Under MCTFS, a master pay account is maintained for each Marine by DFAS. For your use, DFAS produces a monthly LES from information in your master pay account, available to you online at MyPay. Your LES reflects what you are due, tax withholding, leave balance, and any deductions, and it forecasts the amount payable for the next two paydays.

By Department of the Treasury mandate, all Marines receive their semi-monthly pay by electronic funds transfer, also called direct deposit, to their designated bank account.

❥ TRAVEL

❥ ❥ *Travel Orders*

Travel status is travel away from your duty station, under orders, and on official business. When you apply for reimbursement for travel performed, or for transportation for travel to be performed, you must have travel orders.

Authority to issue travel orders rests with the commandant, who delegates this authority to certain commands.

All travel orders normally contain the following information:

- Marine's name
- Reference to authority other than the commandant
- Place or places to which the Marine is ordered to travel
- Date on which the Marine will proceed
- Delay authorized in reporting, if any
- Modes of transportation authorized
- Duty (official/public) to be performed
- Person to whom the Marine shall report (if so required)
- Accounting data for cost of travel

Omission of any of these items can delay reimbursement and might cause rejection of a travel claim as invalid. Be sure you understand your orders before departure, and carry them out exactly.

You should be familiar with several types of travel orders.

Permanent Change of Station. This includes travel to your first duty station after appointment; transfer from one permanent station to another; call to active duty; change in home port or home yard of a ship (for family members); and travel home from your last duty station upon retirement, separation, or relief from active duty.

Temporary Duty (TD). This is detachment to a place other than your permanent station, under orders that direct further assignment to a new permanent station. While on TD—as distinguished from *temporary additional duty*—you have no permanent station.

Temporary Additional Duty (TAD). This includes travel away from your permanent station, performance of duty elsewhere, and return to the permanent station.

Blanket or Repeat Travel Orders. These are TAD orders issued to individuals for regular and frequent trips away from their permanent duty stations in connection with duty.

⟩ ⟩ *What to Do about Your Orders*

Upon receipt of orders—here TAD orders, as these are the most frequently encountered—there are several steps to follow. First, immediately read through them and check the following points:

- Correct rank, name, Social Security number, and MOS
- Departure date
- Place or places to be visited
- Whether you are to report to a given headquarters or command
- Mission you are to accomplish
- Security clearance
- Modes or options of transportation
- That the orders are signed
- First (receiving) endorsement completed
- Statement on requirement to use government quarters and meals

If your orders appear incorrect, or if it appears that you cannot carry them out as directed, return them immediately to the issuing officer with an explanation of the difficulty.

Check out before departing and check in upon return with your adjutant/S-1 or possibly the Installation Personnel Administration Center, depending on duty station policies, during working hours or with the officer of the day or staff duty officer at all other times.

Upon arrival at your temporary station, and if your orders so direct, you will have to report to some other headquarters or command; these are known as "reporting orders." When your TAD is completed at the distant place or station and before returning, be sure your orders are endorsed and signed, stating the time and date you reported, the date your TAD was completed, and the availability or nonavailability of quarters and messing facilities.

If your orders do not direct you to report (that is, are "nonreporting orders"), you intend to claim full per diem, and your TAD at a place is twenty-four hours or longer, you must still obtain a certificate of endorsement from the command representative at that place. The endorsement should indicate whether government quarters and mess were available to you while there on TAD. When they are not, you are entitled to a higher per diem to cover your expenses for lodging and meals.

If, while away from your parent command, you find you cannot carry out your orders as written without incurring additional expense, or if some unforeseen contingency arises that is not provided for in the orders, request instructions by telephone (which can be reimbursed at government expense) or email before proceeding further. Reimbursement for unauthorized additional expenses or unauthorized travel might be denied if prior approval from the command is not received.

If orders specify travel by government aircraft where available, you must use government air unless a transportation officer certifies that such transportation is not available. Under current regulations, government air is considered "available" if there is a scheduled government plane departing for your destination that will permit you to execute your orders in a timely manner. If no special mode of transportation—or some other option—is specified in your orders, take your choice, but make it one that is most economical for your command.

Keep an accurate itinerary and a record of authorized travel expenses for which you can claim reimbursement.

Turn in your orders for return endorsement and then complete your travel claim within five working days after returning to home base.

❯❯ *Travel Time*

Travel time allowed in connection with a PCS is either the actual time required or "constructive travel time," whichever is less.

Actual travel time is computed in whole days regardless of the length of time actually spent traveling in any given day. This requires completion of an itinerary showing all stops of one calendar day or more.

Constructive travel time for commercial transportation is one hour for each forty miles of travel by rail or bus, with a proportionate part of one hour allowed for any fraction of forty miles, and one hour for each five hundred miles of air travel, with similar proportionate allowances for fractions of five hundred miles. One day of travel time is allowed for each eighteen hours of commercial constructive travel time.

Constructive travel time for travel by privately owned vehicle (POV) is based on one day for each 350 miles and for any fraction above 50 miles (that is, 350 miles equals one day, 400 miles equals one day, but 401 miles equals two days).

Regardless of the actual sequence of travel, constructive travel time is computed in order of POV, commercial surface, and commercial air. It is computed based on the official distance between the points of duty contained in the Defense Table of Official Distances (DTOD).

Regardless of the mode or modes of transportation, only one day of travel time is allowed if the ordered travel is four hundred miles or less.

Government and commercial vessel travel time is the actual time required to complete the trip.

Proceed, delay, and travel time are covered in detail in chapter 4 of the ACTSMAN. There are few parts of the ACTSMAN more important for a young officer to know thoroughly.

❧ ❧ *Travel Guidelines*

The guidelines and norms for official military travel are complex and vary somewhat with the type of travel you are executing, but here are some of the highlights.

On PCS, except when traveling in a group or with troops, you normally enjoy some flexibility for travel within the United States. When executing PCS orders, you may elect one of the following modes of transportation (listed from most common to least common):

- POV, which entitles you to mileage expense at a prescribed rate
- Common carrier transportation (scheduled air, rail, or bus) on government travel request (GTR), which means the government procures the ticket(s) at no expense to you
- Government or government-contracted transportation, if available, which the government funds directly

- Common carrier transportation at your initial expense (when authorized and quite rare), which means that after you submit your travel claim, the government reimburses you the authorized expense of the ticket(s) you purchase

When executing PCS travel by POV, the authorized travel days are calculated using 350 miles per day (based on the DTOD distance between the authorized points). One travel day is allowed for each 350 miles of official distance of ordered travel. If the excess distance is 51 or more miles after dividing the total official distance by 350, one additional travel day is allowed.

For travel in connection with TD, reimbursement for travel is generally similar to PCS as shown above.

For travel under TAD orders, which permit per diem reimbursement, transportation is normally furnished in kind or by GTR, and reimbursement is at specified per diem rates. If, for whatever authorized reason, you opt not to accept transportation in kind or by GTR and travel by POV, you will be reimbursed for the actual cost of the conveyance or at a given prescribed rate per mile for the official distance. If travel by POV is authorized and used—as more advantageous to the government—you are entitled to a different mileage rate.

If the TAD orders authorize you to travel by private conveyance (normally when it is advantageous to the government), you are entitled to travel time for the actual time necessary to make the trip within certain parameters. In this case, the authorized travel days are calculated using 400 miles per day (again based on the DTOD distance between the authorized points). One travel day is allowed for each 400 miles of official distance of ordered travel. If the excess distance is 1 or more miles after dividing the total official distance by 400, one additional travel day is allowed. When the total official distance is 400 or fewer miles, only one day of travel time is allowed. If POV use is for the traveler's convenience, the traveler is only authorized one travel day (based on a typical flight time of one day) for each leg.

When orders direct a specific mode of transportation but you perform travel via another mode, including privately owned conveyance, for your own convenience, you will not be entitled to reimbursement of full mileage expense, or to a monetary allowance in lieu of transportation, unless the authority responsible for furnishing the transportation requests certifies that GTRs were not available or the mode of transportation directed was not available at the time and place required in time to comply with the orders.

In all cases, travel time in excess of that authorized by the directed mode in your orders is chargeable as annual leave.

❧ ❧ *Reimbursement of Travel Expenses*

The law provides for reimbursement of authorized travel expenses for military personnel and, when applicable, their authorized dependents who travel by private conveyance, bus, rail, or aircraft. The allowances for travel are computed based on some combination of actual expenses, mileage rates, and/or per diem expenses. Basically, the regulations authorize reimbursement of four broad categories of travel expenses:

1. **Transportation**. This covers the expense of your conveyance from origin to destination (and return, if applicable). It is provided for by transportation in kind, transportation by GTR (for example, a plane ticket procured on your behalf by the government), reimbursement thereof when you purchase it yourself (if authorized), or a monetary allowance in lieu of the cost of transportation based on distance in official mileage tables (normally when you use a POV).

2. **Lodging**. This covers your cost of overnight lodging for the nights authorized, which must fall within strict guidelines for reimbursement. Rates of reimbursement vary by locale.

3. **Meals and Incidentals**. This covers your expenses for daily meals and certain minor expenses while traveling. It is based on established per diem rates that also vary by locale.

4. **Reimbursable Expenses**. These include certain expenses (see the section below on reimbursable expenses) that do not fall within the previous three categories but nevertheless are authorized, such as fuel expense for an authorized rental vehicle. Such reimbursements normally require receipts.

The term "per diem" is generally understood to comprise lodging expense and meals and incidental expenses.

Regulations governing authorization for and reimbursement of travel, as well as the actual rates of reimbursement, are contained in the *Joint Travel Regulations*

(JTR) and *Marine Corps Travel Instructions Manual*. Check with your local finance officer for guidance, as the regulations can be complex, and claiming reimbursement for unauthorized expenses can land you in trouble.

❖ ❖ *Per Diem Allowances*

Per diem allowances are designed to offset the cost of lodging, meals, and incidental expenses incurred by a member while performing travel away from the permanent duty station or while changing duty stations. You receive per diem for TAD or TD, including periods of necessary delay while awaiting transportation and at ports during PCS.

In the United States. Per diem policies and rates within the United States are given in the JTR. Where government quarters and/or mess are available, the allowance is reduced proportionately. If you claim maximum per diem, you must secure a certificate from the local commander stating that government quarters and/or mess were not available.

Outside the United States. Per diem allowances vary widely from country to country and are subject to frequent change. They are discussed in chapter 4 of the JTR.

The Defense Travel Management Office also maintains current per diem information and rates on its website (http://www.defensetravel.dod.mil/), which is a great resource.

❖ ❖ *Reimbursable Expenses*

Certain travel expenses, described above among the four main categories of expenses, are separately reimbursable. The following list, although not exhaustive, includes some of the most common reimbursable expenses:

- Taxi fares or other local transportation between places of abode and terminals as well as between terminals when free transfer is not included; also taxi fares between terminal and place of duty
- Fees for checked baggage and excess baggage, when approved
- Fares and tolls
- Registration fees at technical, professional, or scientific conferences and so forth, when approved

U.S. Marines with Alpha Battery, Battalion Landing Team 3/5, 11th Marine Expeditionary Unit, fire an M777-towed 155-mm howitzer in the Philippines during Exercise Kamandag 3 in 2019.

- Passport and visa fees, including cost of associated photographs
- Mandatory taxes and fees upon arrival or departure from foreign countries
- Incidental expenses that can be justified as necessary for mission accomplishment

On all the foregoing items, you may be required to produce receipts, especially to support claims exceeding $75. If in doubt on any point, consult the JTR as well as your finance officer. If you and the finance officer disagree as to whether a given item is reimbursable (or if you differ on any computation of pay and allowances), you have the right to submit a claim for adjudication by the comptroller general. The finance officer will explain how to go about this.

❧ ❧ *Travel Advance*

Before departure under orders on PCS, you may, if you request, draw an advance on mileage allowance, known as a travel advance. An advance of per diem on TD or TAD orders is also considered a travel advance. But advances are no longer extended to individuals who are required to possess and use the Government Travel Charge Card (GTCC), which includes most officers.

Do not confuse these advance payments with a "dead horse" (described earlier).

❧ ❧ *Travel Claim*

Upon completing travel, you will submit your travel claim electronically using the Defense Travel System (DTS), a DOD-wide software application (https:// dtsproweb.defensetravel.osd.mil/dts-app/pubsite/all/view) that allows service-members, as well as federal government civilians, and their supervisors to manage their travel from start to finish. DTS enables you to accomplish the following:

- Book your travel, estimate expenses, and request advanced payments, if eligible.
- Receive approval for your travel plans and known expenses before and after you travel.
- Keep records updated with your travel plans and expenses before and during your trip.
- Input final expenses and attach required receipts and records after you complete your trip.
- Get reimbursed to your bank account, GTCC, or both.

Upon completing travel to your first duty station and until you become proficient with DTS, you may seek assistance with your travel claim from a designated administrative NCO, who will help you prepare and submit your claim for mileage (if applicable), per diem, and other reimbursable expenses on your orders. You must normally submit your completed claim within three working days, depending on local policy.

❧ ❧ *Travel by Family Members on Permanent Change of Station*

The government pays authorized travel expenses for family members on PCS.

If you are not traveling by private vehicle, it is simplest to obtain tickets for family members by GTR. You may, however, transport family members at your own expense, although this is unusual, and *it is wise to seek authorization before doing so.* Using DTS, you claim reimbursement for your family's travel expenses afterward at prescribed mileage and per diem rates within certain maximum ceilings.

In the event you plan to marry while en route to a new duty station, (for example, en route to your first station after graduating from Basic School) your proceed time, leave, and excess travel time are added to your date of detachment to determine the effective date of your orders for the purpose of entitlement to dependent's travel. It will be to your advantage to *discuss this with your finance officer* and ask for his or her advice.

❖ TRANSPORTATION OF HOUSEHOLD GOODS

❖ ❖ *Household Goods Defined*

Household goods (HHG) are items associated with the home and all personal effects belonging to you and your dependents on the effective date of your PCS or TD orders. To qualify, they must be legally transportable by an authorized commercial transporter. In addition to clothing, furniture, and other normal household items, the following items are normally considered to be HHG:

- Professional books, papers, and equipment (PBP&E) needed for the performance of official duties at the next or a later destination
- Spare POV parts and a pickup tailgate when removed
- Integral or attached vehicle parts that must be removed due to their high vulnerability to pilferage or damage (for example, seats, tops, winch, spare tires, portable auxiliary gasoline cans, and miscellaneous associated hardware)
- Vehicles other than POVs, such as motorcycles, mopeds, hang gliders, golf carts, jet skis, and snowmobiles (and/or their associated trailers)
- Boats (and/or their associated trailers)
- Utility trailers, subject to certain limitations

The following items are not considered HHG and are therefore normally not eligible for transportation at government expense:

- Personal baggage when carried free on commercial transportation
- Automobiles, trucks, vans, and similar motor vehicles; airplanes; mobile homes; camper trailers; horse trailers; and farming vehicles

- Live animals, including birds, fish, and reptiles
- Articles that otherwise would qualify as HHG but are acquired after the effective date of the PCS order
- Cordwood and building materials
- Privately owned live ammunition
- Hazardous articles, including explosives, flammable and corrosive materials, poisons, and propane gas tanks (see DOD 4500.9-R, *Defense Transportation Regulation*, part IV, *Personal Property*, for examples of hazardous materials)

Note that if returning from foreign-shore duty overseas, your legitimate HHG are allowed to enter the United States duty free.

❧ ❧ *Professional Books, Papers, and Equipment*

PBP&E merit further discussion because failure to properly identify and account for them can contribute to exceeding your weight allowance. As noted above, PBP&E are articles of HHG in a member's possession needed for the performance of official duties at the next or a later destination. Subject to limits, such items are not counted against your weight allowance and therefore must be weighed separately and identified on the inventory at the origin as PBP&E. Examples of these materials include

- references that may be used in professional education, development, and/or writing;
- instruments, tools, and equipment peculiar to technicians, mechanics, and members of the professions;
- specialized clothing, such as diving suits, astronauts' suits, flying suits and helmets, band uniforms, chaplains' vestments, and other specialized apparel that is not normal or usual uniform or clothing;
- individually owned or specially issued field clothing and individual combat equipment;
- official awards given to a member by a service (or a component thereof) for duties performed in the member's capacity, by a professional society or organization, or by the United States or a foreign government for significant contributions in connection with official duties; and

- personal computer and accompanying equipment used for *official government business.*

Excluded from PBP&E are sports equipment and office, household, or shop fixtures or furniture (such as bookcases, study/computer desks, file cabinets, and racks), even though perhaps used in connection with the PBP&E.

❧ ❧ *Weight Allowance*

There are weight limits, based on pay grade, on the amount of HHG that you may ship at government expense. Current tables of weight allowances show the maximum weight of HHG that you may ship on either permanent or temporary change of station. To illustrate, the 2021 weight allowances for a second lieutenant were 10,000 pounds (without dependents) and 12,000 pounds (with dependents) for PCS. In addition, the government ships up to 2,000 pounds of PBP&E without charge to your allowance.

On PCS, you may ship "by expedited mode" (in most instances, simply a phrase for express shipment) up to 1,000 pounds net weight of personal property classified as unaccompanied baggage if shipped via commercial air. This shipment should include only high-priority items necessary to permit you to carry out your duties or to prevent undue hardship to you or your family. The net weight is charged against your total weight allowance. This type of shipment is invaluable for uniforms—but be sure to hand carry a complement of essential uniforms you will need—and effects required immediately after reporting.

HHG exceeding your weight allowance may be shipped, but excess costs will be charged to you. Be careful; these excess costs can mount quickly. Remember, however, that weight allowances shown are net—that is, they do not include packing materials.

❧ ❧ *Shipment of Household Goods*

Subject to weight allowances and other limitations, you may ship HHG at government expense (including packing, crating, unpacking, uncrating, drayage, and hauling as necessary) on PCS under the following circumstances:

- Entrance into the service or orders to more than twenty weeks of active duty

- Orders to sea or duty overseas, where family may not follow
- PCS orders while on active duty
- Orders to duty under instruction of twenty or more weeks' duration
- Orders to or from prolonged hospitalization
- Honorable separation or retirement
- Death on active duty or reported dead, missing, or interned
- Transfer between ships having different home ports
- Orders changing home port of ship to which attached
- Transfer between ship and shore, where shore installation is not ship's home port

But shipment is not authorized in the following circumstances:

- Before receipt of orders, unless specially authorized by competent authority
- If separation is other than honorable or if transfer is incident to trial
- For change of station by Reservists on duty for less than six months

There is also a "do-it-yourself" HHG shipment program under which you move your own items by personal, commercial, or rental vehicle and are paid up to 75 percent of what it would have cost the government to ship the goods. Before doing this (which requires specific authorization), you should get the advice of your installation's distribution management office. Based on the experience of some officers, this is not the money-making prospect that it might, at first, seem.

Finally, before your first experience shipping HHG, you will normally meet with a counselor (or possibly attend a special class) at the DMO, during which extensive details on entitlements, limitations, and procedures for HHG shipping, storage, and claims will be covered. This session is invaluable, and it will maximize your chances of having a successful move. The official DOD customer moving website (https://www.militaryonesource.mil/moving-housing/moving/pcs-and-military-moves/) also provides comprehensive information on military moves.

⊁ ⊁ *Storage of Household Goods*

Temporary Storage. You are entitled to temporary storage at government expense for up to ninety days in connection with any authorized shipment of HHG.

Under certain conditions arising from circumstances beyond your control—unavailability of quarters at the new station, arrival of your effects before you do, early surrender of quarters, and so forth—competent authority may authorize an additional ninety days' storage. This added time is not automatic; to arrange it, you should consult DMO.

Nontemporary Storage. The term "nontemporary storage" refers to storage for longer periods, typically in the range of six months to three years. There are many situations under which an officer may be entitled to nontemporary storage of household effects, not exceeding prescribed weight limitations. Because the length of storage at government expense varies and you are subject to excess costs beyond the authorized time limit, you should check with DMO. Among the most common situations under which you are entitled to nontemporary storage are the following:

- TD pending detail overseas
- Change of station from within the United States to outside the United States
- PCS with TD en route
- Retirement, discharge with severance pay, or reversion to inactive duty with readjustment pay (up to one year's storage allowed)
- Assignment to government quarters

Prohibited Articles. You may not store automobiles, flammables, ammunition, or liquor.

❯ ❯ *Household Goods Loss, Damage, and Transit Insurance*

You may suffer loss or damage to your personal property during shipment or storage; this is an unfortunate risk inherent in changing duty stations. When moving with the military, your items are insured at "full replacement/repair value" at no additional cost to you. Essentially, this means that if an item is lost or destroyed during the move, the transportation service provider (TSP) is obligated to pay the lesser of the cost to replace or repair the item. If replacement cost is offered, it should replace the item with an identical or similar one. The replacement could be new or used. The TSP will still require proof of the item's value, quality, and cost to replace. If it can be repaired as determined by a qualified inspector and the repair cost is less than the replacement cost, the TSP may pay for the repair.

Although the development of the Internet-based Defense Personal Property System in recent years has somewhat improved the moving experience and claims process, collection of claims against a TSP remains a complicated, time-consuming, often frustrating, and sometimes fruitless process. Thus, for hard-to-value or hard-to-replace items and those with sentimental value, you may be wise to purchase additional protection in the form of a commercial transit insurance policy.

Should you take out such a policy, be careful to know exactly what type of coverage you are getting. It is well to note, for example, that most such policies expire when your effects are delivered. Thus, when items are delivered by van to a warehouse for temporary authorized storage, your policy will very likely expire as soon as the goods are accepted by the warehouse unless you have made special arrangements to extend your coverage.

Ultimately, if you are unhappy with the resolution offered by the carrier, you have the option to transfer your claim for lost or damaged HHG to the regional military claims office with responsibility for your new duty station.

❧ ❧ *Checklist for Shipping Household Goods*

The following short paragraphs summarize key things you should do and think about when you ship HHG.

Become familiar with resources, tools, and brochures on military moves available from DMO or the Defense Personal Property System website.

Have enough certified copies of your orders, usually ten copies for each shipment, and see DMO at least three months before you plan to move. Earlier is better if you are contemplating a summer move. If your orders are "short-fused," see DMO within a day or two of receiving them.

Tell DMO if you have professional books and papers to be shipped so that they may be weighed separately and packed without being charged against your weight allowance.

If you plan to depart for your new station before shipping your HHG, designate your spouse or someone you trust *completely* as your agent when you arrange your move, leave or send this individual enough certified copies of orders to initiate shipment, and consider leaving him or her a *limited* power of attorney or written authority to make the shipment.

If you have high-value items to be shipped, inform DMO so that special arrangements can be made.

Get all possible information about your housing situation at the new station before you request shipment of your goods.

Request storage at the point of origin (your old station) if you are in doubt as to where to ship your goods. You have up to ninety days of storage on either end.

If goods go by van, be sure to get a copy of the inventory sheet from the driver.

Never sign a blank "certificate of packing" that the driver might present you.

If your orders are modified or canceled, or a change of destination of the shipment is desired, notify DMO immediately.

Get from DMO the estimated time of arrival of your goods at the destination as well as the destination DMO telephone number.

Be at home on the day of the expected move.

If possible, turn over all your HHG for the same destination at the same time except items to be shipped by express.

Let the movers know about fragile items, such as chinaware and delicate glassware.

Keep nonperishable food supplies together for proper packing.

Walk through every room of your home and check in every drawer, cabinet, and closet before releasing the movers.

Arrange for receipt of your HHG at the destination. If you cannot be there yourself, check with your DMO to find out whether storage is authorized. In cases of direct delivery by van, you or your agent must be at the new home to receive it. Plan where (in what room) you want your items to be placed.

Here is a summary of things not to do:

- Do not request shipment to some place other than your new station without finding out first how much it will cost you.
- Do not contract for shipment with commercial concerns unless you have been authorized in writing to do so by DMO.
- Do not be upset if the movers do not show up at your quarters exactly at the appointed hour. It is hard to schedule a move by the minute.

- Do not try to get special services from the carrier unless you have checked with DMO.
- Do not, in general, disassemble or pack anything yourself in preparation for your move. Leave this to professional packers. Usually, commercial firms will not pay claims on items they did not pack. Any exceptions to this general rule should be covered with you when you arrange your shipment.

Finally, although Marines have scant option as to when they move, the best time of year to schedule the movement of household effects is from October through May, when only about 30 percent of all moves take place. In any given month, according to the Defense Department's Military Surface Deployment and Distribution Command, which is responsible for the Defense Personal Property System, the best time to move is between the third and the twenty-fifth of the month. In other words, if you want better, quicker, more careful handling of household effects, do not move in the summer or at the end of a month—if you have a choice.

❧ ❧ *Excess Charges*

Knowing and adhering to your applicable weight allowance are vitally important, as costs can mount rapidly. Gaining at least a basic understanding of your entitlements associated with PCS is equally important. You will be financially responsible for all transportation costs under the following circumstances:

- Exceeding authorized weight allowance
- Transportation between non-authorized locations
- Transportation of articles that are not HHG
- Transportation in more than one lot with the exception, when authorized, of unaccompanied baggage transported separately from the HHG shipment, shipment to storage, and shipment of expedited items of extraordinary value
- Special services (for example, covering the cost of increased valuation liability)
- Transportation-related costs that are charged to the government due to negligence by the servicemember or the servicemember's agent (for example, attempted pickup and/or delivery charges)

⦗ 19 ⦘

MILITARY JUSTICE

Law is a regulation in accord with reason, issued by
a lawful superior, for the common good.
— Thomas Aquinas

MILITARY LAW GOVERNS individual conduct and performance of duty
in the naval services. It also provides means—nonjudicial punishment (NJP)
and trial by court-martial—for enforcing the rules. As a Marine officer, you
must be familiar with military law and its sources. It is part of the tradition of
Marine Corps discipline that legal proceedings are conducted expeditiously,
firmly, and expertly. Marine officers are frequently called upon to perform
various legal functions, and they must set an example with their competence
and knowledge.

This chapter contains a general description of the system of military justice
in force in the U.S. Marine Corps and, with minor differences, throughout
all the U.S. armed forces. This is not intended as an exhaustive review or as
a source of legal authority; it merely covers some major points in military
law. Because the military justice system is complex, technical, and, at times,
inflexible, there can be no substitute for consultation with a staff judge advocate
or legal officer.

❭ FUNDAMENTALS

❭ ❭ *Sources of Military Law*

The sources of military law include the Constitution of the United States, the Uniform Code of Military Justice (UCMJ), and other acts of Congress. The implementation and administration of these laws in the military are carried out by the president, who promulgates the *Manual for Courts-Martial, United States* (MCM), and the Secretary of the Navy, who promulgates the *Manual of the Judge Advocate General* (JAGMAN). These two manuals constitute the primary sources of military law that applies to the Navy and Marine Corps. You must be generally familiar with these publications and pertinent general orders.

Other sources of military law include decisions of the Court of Appeals for the Armed Forces and the Navy–Marine Corps Court of Criminal Appeals; directives from the president, secretary of defense, SECNAV, and commandant of the Marine Corps; and customs and usage of the service.

❭ ❭ *Civil and Military Law*

In addition to being subject to the federal and state laws that bind all citizens of the United States, members of the armed forces are subject to a second body of law and a separate jurisprudence. This includes the statutes and regulations setting forth the rights, liabilities, powers, and duties of officers and enlisted persons in the military services. Thus, members of the armed forces may be brought before civil or military tribunals and are generally answerable to both bodies of law. Breaches of the peace and other minor offenses by service personnel that violate both civilian and military law will often be tried by court-martial, although this does not exclude exercise of civil jurisdiction as well. When an offense violates state, federal, and military law at the same time—for example, a serious crime, such as murder—the authority that first obtains control over the offender may try him. Just as civil courts may not interfere with military courts (other than by writ of habeas corpus), military authorities do not have the power to interfere with civil courts.

A member of the Marine Corps accused of an offense against civil authority may, upon proper request, be delivered to the civil authority for trial. Regulations promulgated by the SECNAV covering this are found in the JAGMAN.

In foreign countries, Marines are subject to the laws of those countries and may be tried and punished by foreign authorities. In certain countries, the United States has status of forces agreements, which, among other things, prescribe conditions under which U.S. military personnel may be delivered to local authorities for trial in local courts (or, alternatively, tried by U.S. military courts). These agreements vary from country to country.

❯ ❯ *Uniform Code of Military Justice*

On 5 May 1950, President Harry S. Truman approved the UCMJ. The authorities who administer military justice under the present revised Code are shown in table 19-1. You should be familiar with some of the basic principles, provisions, and features contained in the Code.

Instructions and Publication. Certain articles of the UCMJ must be carefully explained to every enlisted person entering active duty, then again after six months, and once again when reenlisting. A complete text of the Code must be available to every person on active duty in the armed forces of the United States.

At frequent intervals, the punitive articles, those dealing mainly with offenses and punishments, must be published to troops and posted so they may read them. This is known by the old Navy phrase as "reading the Rocks and Shoals."

Jurisdiction. All persons in the armed forces are subject to the Code. Reciprocal jurisdiction between services is provided, but the exercise of jurisdiction over a member of another service is limited to those circumstances prescribed by the president in the MCM, that is, when a joint service command is specifically authorized to refer such cases or when manifest injury to the armed forces will result from the delivery of the accused to the accused member's service.

Rights of the Accused. In addition to the constitutional rights enjoyed by all U.S. citizens, an accused person under the UCMJ has (1) the right to be warned before interrogation of any suspected offense; (2) the right to a preliminary investigation before trial for an offense; (3) the right to challenge members of the court, both for cause and peremptorily; (4) the right, if convicted, to testify under oath or to make an unsworn statement to the court regarding extenuating or mitigating matters; (5) the right to forward a brief of matters that should be considered in review of the case; and (6) the right to counsel at specified stages of the foregoing proceedings.

Rights of the Victim. In addition to the constitutional rights enjoyed by all U.S. citizens, a victim of an offense under the UCMJ has (1) the right to be reasonably protected from the accused; (2) the right to reasonable, accurate, and timely notice of hearings, courts-martial, and public proceedings relating to the offense as well as of the release or escape of the accused from confinement; (3) the right not to be excluded from any public hearing or proceeding relating to the offense except under certain specific circumstances; (4) the right to be reasonably heard at a public hearing, sentencing hearing, or public proceeding relating to the offense; (5) the reasonable right to confer with counsel representing the government at any public hearing or proceeding relating to the offense; (6) the right to receive restitution as provided by law; (7) the right to proceedings free from reasonable delay; and (8) the right to be treated with fairness and with respect for his or her dignity and privacy.

Review and Appeals. The UCMJ establishes elaborate machinery and channels for review and appeal of courts-martial. In all cases, the convening authority—that is, the commander, at a given level, empowered to send a case to a court-martial—must take action to approve, remit, or suspend an adjudged sentence. The convening authority may not, however, adjust any findings of guilt for felony offenses where the sentence is longer than six months or contains a discharge, nor may the convening authority change findings for any sex crime, regardless of sentencing time.

The accused may waive appellate review by higher authority. If not waived, the case may be reviewed by various officers in the chain of command, by the *Navy–Marine Corps Court of Criminal Appeals* (composed of not less than three appellate military judges), by the *judge advocate general of the Navy*, by the *Court of Appeals for the Armed Forces* (composed of five civilian judges), and by the U.S. Supreme Court.

Approval. Sentences of death must be approved by the president. Those dismissing an officer, cadet, or midshipman must be approved by the SECNAV. Sentences to a dishonorable or bad conduct discharge (BCD) are not executed until appellate review is completed and the trial case affirmed by the Navy–Marine Corps Court of Criminal Appeals (unless appellate review has been waived).

Legal Duties. Officers who perform legal duties include the following.

The *staff judge advocate* is the senior Marine officer-lawyer, certified in accordance with the Code, who performs the staff legal duties of a command.

TABLE 19-1. Administration of Military Justice under the Uniform Code of Military Justice

	Nonjudicial — Commanding Officer's Office Hours		Judicial — Courts-Martial		
	By commanding officer (Art. 15)	By officer in charge (Art. 15)	Summary (Art. 16)	Special (Art. 16)	General (Art. 16)
Members			One commissioned officer (Art. 24)	Four or more members plus a military judge (Art. 23)	Eight or more members plus a military judge (Art. 22)
Convening Authority			(Art. 24) (1) Any person who may convene a general or special court-martial (2) Commanding officer of a detached company or other detachment of the Army (3) Commanding officer of a detached squadron or other detachment of the Air Force or a corresponding unit of the Space Force (4) Commanding officer or officer in charge of any other command when empowered by the secretary of the department	(Art. 23) (1) Any person who may convene a general court-martial (2) Commanding officer of a district, garrison, base, or similar military installation where members of the Army, Air Force, or Space Force are on duty (3) Commanding officer of a brigade, regiment, detached battalion, or corresponding unit of the Army (4) Commanding officer of a wing, group, or separate squadron of the Air Force or corresponding unit of the Space Force (5) Commanding officer of any naval or Coast Guard vessel, shipyard, base, or station; any Marine brigade, regiment, or detached battalion; any Marine group, squadron, or corresponding unit; any Marine barracks, base, station, or other place where members of the Marine Corps are on duty (6) Commanding officer of any separate or detached command or group of detached units of any of the armed forces placed under a single commander for this purpose (7) Commanding officer or officer in charge of any other command when empowered by the secretary of the department	(Art. 22) (1) President of the United States (2) Secretary of defense (3) Commanding officer of a unified or specified combatant command (4) Secretary of the department (5) Commanding officer of an Army group, an army, an Army corps, a division, a separate brigade, or a corresponding unit of the Army or Marine Corps (6) Commander of a fleet or commanding officer of a naval station or larger shore activity of the Navy beyond the United States (7) Commanding officer of an air command, an air force, an air division, or a separate wing of the Air Force or Marine Corps, or the commanding officer of a corresponding unit of the Space Force (8) Any other commanding officer designated by the secretary of the department (9) Any other commanding officer in any of the armed forces when empowered by the president
Jurisdiction	Officers and other personnel under his or her command (Art. 2)	Enlisted personnel under his or her charge (Art. 2)	All enlisted persons subject to the Code for any noncapital offense made punishable by the Code, BUT no person may be tried before a summary court-martial if he or she objects (Art. 20)	All persons subject to the Code for any noncapital offense made punishable by the Code and, under such regulations as the president may prescribe, for capital offenses (Art. 19)	All persons subject to the Code for any offense made punishable by the Code, under such limitations as the president may prescribe (Art. 18)

Punishments and Limitations	Art. 15	Art. 18	Art. 19	Art. 20	Art. 25
	Punishments, including admonitions and reprimands Upon officers of his or her command: (1) Restriction to specified limits, with or without suspension from duty, for up to 30 consecutive days (2) If imposed by an officer exercising general court-martial jurisdiction or an officer of general or flag rank in command: (a) Arrest in quarters for up to 30 consecutive days (b) Forfeiture of up to 1/2 of 1 month's pay per month for 2 months (c) Restriction to certain specified limits, with or without suspension from duty, for up to 60 consecutive days (d) Detention of up to 1/2 of 1 month's pay per month for 3 months Upon other personnel of his or her command: (1) Confinement for up to 3 consecutive days, if imposed upon a person attached to or embarked in a vessel (2) Correctional custody for up to 7 consecutive days (30 days if imposed by an officer of the grade of major/lieutenant commander or above) (3) Forfeiture of up to 7 days' pay (if imposed by O-4 or above, 1/2 of 1 month's pay per month for 2 months) (4) Reduction to the next inferior pay grade, if the grade from which demoted is within the promotion authority of the officer imposing the reduction (if imposed by O-4 or above, reduction to the lowest or any intermediate pay grade, if the grade from which demoted is within the promotion authority of the officer imposing the reduction, but an enlisted member in a pay grade above E–4 may not be reduced more than 2 pay grades) (5) Extra duties, including fatigue, for up to 14 consecutive days (if imposed by O-4 or above, extra duties, including fatigue, for up to 45 consecutive days) (6) Restriction to certain specified limits, with or without suspension from duty, for up to 14 consecutive days (if imposed by O-4 or above, restrictions to certain specified limits, with or without suspension from duty, for up to 60 consecutive days) (7) Detention of up to 14 days' pay (if imposed by O-4 or above, detention of up to 1/2 of 1 month's pay per month for 3 months)	Under such limitations as the president may prescribe, any punishment not forbidden by the Code, including the penalty of death when specifically authorized	Under such limitations as the president may prescribe, any punishment not forbidden by the Code except death, dishonorable discharge, dismissal, confinement for more than 1 year, hard labor without confinement for more than 3 months, forfeiture of pay exceeding 2/3 pay per month, or forfeiture of pay for more than 1 year Note: Neither a bad conduct discharge, confinement for more than 6 months, nor forfeiture of pay for more than 6 months may be adjudged if tried at a special court-martial consisting of a military judge alone.	Under such limitations as the president may prescribe, any punishment not forbidden by the Code except death, dismissal, dishonorable or bad conduct discharge, confinement for more than 1 month, hard labor without confinement for more than 45 days, restriction to specified limits for more than 2 months, or forfeiture of more than 2/3 of 1 month's pay	Qualifications of Members (that is, who may serve on courts-martial) For the trial of any person who may lawfully be brought before such courts for trial (1) Any commissioned officer on active duty (2) Any warrant officer on active duty for the trial of any person other than a commissioned officer (3) Any enlisted member on active duty for the trial of any other enlisted member by general or special court-martial Note: Before a court-martial is assembled for trial, an accused enlisted person may personally request, orally on the record or in writing, that (1) the court-martial membership be composed entirely of officers; or (2) enlisted members compose at least 1/3 of the court-martial membership, regardless of whether enlisted members have been detailed to the court-martial.

A *judge advocate* is a Marine officer-lawyer certified in accordance with the Code to perform duties as trial and/or defense counsel. In addition, the judge advocate is authorized to review trial records of summary, special, and general courts-martial.

A *military judge* is a judge, appointed by the judge advocate general of the Navy, who serves on general and special courts-martial in a capacity similar to that of a civilian judge. If the accused requests and the military judge consents, a military judge may sit as a one-officer court-martial to determine the issue of guilt or innocence and adjudge sentence if found guilty.

An *initial review officer* is a disinterested and detached officer who reviews command decisions to confine individuals prior to trial by court-martial. Not later than seven days after imposition of pretrial confinement, the initial review officer must determine whether confinement will continue or the Marine will be released.

A *legal assistance officer* is a Marine officer-lawyer designated by the commander to give legal advice to members of the command on personal legal problems involving civilian law.

A *legal officer* is an officer (nonlawyer) designated by a commanding officer to perform legal duties of purely military nature within the command. This officer does not render legal assistance (see above) but can answer questions regarding the Code.

❯ ❯ *Common Offenses and the Small Unit*

The Punitive Articles. Articles 77–134, the "Rocks and Shoals" of the UCMJ, divide punishable offenses into three general groups: (1) crimes common to both civil and military law, such as murder, rape, arson, burglary, larceny, and frauds against the United States; (2) purely military offenses arising out of military duties and having no counterpart in civilian life, such as desertion, willful disobedience of lawful orders of superior officers and noncommissioned officers, misbehavior before the enemy, and sleeping on watch; and (3) a general group of offenses based on two articles that do not specify any particular acts of misconduct but cover a variety of transgressions harmful to the service in general terms.

Article 133, the first in the general group of articles, applies only to officers and midshipmen. It makes punishable "conduct unbecoming an officer."

The second, Article 134, applies to all persons who are subject to military law. Offenses punishable under this article include disorders and neglects prejudicial to good order and discipline, conduct tending to bring discredit upon the armed forces, and crimes and offenses covered by federal laws other than the UCMJ. This general article ensures that there will be no failure of justice simply because an offense is not specifically mentioned in an article of the Code.

Offenses in the Small Unit. As a company-grade officer, you should familiarize yourself with the most encountered offenses, mainly order violations, that arise within the platoon, company, or battery:

- 86: Absence without leave
- 87: Missing movement; jumping from vessel
- 89: Disrespect toward superior commissioned officer; assault of superior commissioned officer
- 90: Willfully disobeying superior commissioned officer
- 91: Insubordinate conduct toward warrant officer, noncommissioned, or petty officer
- 92: Failure to obey order or regulation
- 95: Offenses by sentinel or lookout (typically, being drunk or asleep on watch)
- 112: Drunkenness and other incapacitation offenses
- 112a: Wrongful use, possession, and other mishandling of controlled substances
- 113: Drunken or reckless operation of a vehicle, aircraft, or vessel
- 120: Rape and sexual assault generally
- 121: Larceny and wrongful appropriation
- 128: Assault
- 134: General article (conduct prejudicial to good order and discipline; scandalous conduct)

With increased emphasis on preventing and combatting sexual assault and sexual harassment in all its forms in the military, it is worth highlighting several changes to the UCMJ over recent years. These changes affect Article 120, covering rape and sexual assault. Those accused of violating this article must appear before a general court-martial; there is no opportunity to be tried at a summary or special court-martial. Those found guilty of rape or sexual assault are subject to mandatory minimum punishments, including dishonorable discharge for enlisted personnel and dismissal for officers. Prior to the National Defense Authorization Act of 2014, which enacted these changes, there had been a five-year statute of limitations on rape and sexual assault cases under Article 120; now, there is no such limit. Congress also repealed the offense of *consensual* sodomy to bring the Code in line with Supreme Court rulings.

To deal effectively with all offenses encompassed by the punitive articles, you should familiarize yourself with the elements that form each, together with the possible defenses against such charges. Otherwise, you cannot effectively use the Code as a tool for maintaining effective discipline.

❧ ❧ *Investigations, Warnings, and Evidence*

Criminal investigations of felonies and other serious offenses are normally performed by the Naval Criminal Investigative Service (NCIS). Some serious and less serious offenses may be investigated by the Criminal Investigation Division of an installation's provost marshal's office or by a duly appointed member of the command. There are two types of investigations relating to offenses that are frequently performed within the chain of command: preliminary inquiries, prior to an Article 15 hearing (see below), and Article 32 investigations, preliminary to a general court-martial. Since the latter must normally be performed by a judge advocate, detailed discussion of Article 32 investigations lies beyond the scope of the *Guide*.

Preliminary inquiries are a common occurrence within units and should thus be understood by all officers. Typically, within the Marine division, a company commander who receives a report of misconduct directs that a preliminary inquiry be conducted by an officer or staff NCO of the command. The purpose is to provide the CO with sufficient information so that he or she can intelligently dispose of the case. Depending on the CO's wishes, the inquiry may be oral or written.

What you are looking for in a preliminary inquiry boils down to three elements: (1) Has any offense chargeable under the Code been committed? (2) Who committed it? (3) What is the gravity of the offense considering the circumstances?

Your job is not to perfect a case or "hang" an accused but to collect all evidence, favorable or unfavorable, to enable your commander to dispose of the matter.

A preliminary inquiry is inherently informal. It is up to you to go out and get the information. Likely places to start include the logbook of the officer of the day, military police "blotter," civilian police, hospitals and dispensaries, judges advocate, and witnesses otherwise identified. What you learn should be distilled into findings of fact, together (if requested by the CO) with any opinions or recommendations arising out of the inquiry.

Warnings. Because both the Constitution and Article 31 of the UCMJ protect a Marine from being forced to incriminate himself or herself, every accused or suspect must be fully warned of certain rights. Such a warning should make clear the following:

- The nature of the offense of which the individual is suspected
- That the individual has an absolute right to remain silent
- That any statement made may be used against the individual in any subsequent trial or proceeding
- That the individual has the right to consult a lawyer and have counsel present during all questioning and that he or she may seek counsel's advice before answering any question
- That the individual may obtain a civilian lawyer at his or her own expense
- That if the individual cannot afford or does not desire civilian counsel, he or she may have a military lawyer at no cost
- That the individual may discontinue an interrogation at any time at his or her own option

Evidence. Without attempting to summarize the laws of evidence, which are precise and complex, it is enough to say that even junior officers should be familiar with them for two reasons: (1) evidence that is obtained in any manner contrary to law generally cannot be used against an offender; and (2) much evidence is originally uncovered, either at first instance (for example, by an OD) or during preliminary inquiry, by junior, nonlawyer line officers—that is, you. Thus, the admissibility (which is to say, the usability) of evidence often depends on legally correct decisions at the outset based on your knowledge of the rules.

Two kinds of searches that frequently turn up evidence are the limited search of an individual and the immediate area, incident to a lawful apprehension based upon probable cause, and a search authorized by a CO, based on probable cause, of areas within the command (for example, a barracks). The laws of search, which are part of those of evidence, are also precise and complex, and you should be acquainted with them. Many an otherwise well-founded case has failed because an officer has conducted an overly broad or otherwise improper search, which in turn denies admissibility of evidence so obtained.

❯ NONJUDICIAL PUNISHMENT

❯ ❯ *Convening Nonjudicial Punishment (Office Hours)*

COs and officers in charge are authorized by Article 15 to impose NJP upon members of their command at Office Hours in the Corps, known as Captain's Mast in the Navy. Under Article 15, a CO is defined as a commissioned or warrant officer who, by virtue of rank and assignment, exercises primary command authority over a military organization or prescribed territorial area that, under pertinent military directives, is recognized as a command. Under the law, distinctions are made between officers in command, with progressively increased limitations on their powers, as follows. Flag and general officers in command and officers having general court-martial jurisdiction have the greatest scope of NJP. Among COs not in the foregoing class, those of or above the rank of major / lieutenant commander have considerably increased authority over that possessed by COs of company grade and officers in charge (see table 19-1).

NJP is a disciplinary measure more serious than administrative corrective measures but less serious than trial by court-martial. It provides an essential and prompt means of maintaining good order and discipline and promotes positive behavior in Marines without incurring the stigma of a court-martial.

Preliminary Report and Investigation. The customary procedure for putting a Marine on report is as follows. An officer may submit a report against a Marine directly to the executive officer or adjutant of the command concerned. Otherwise, a written report is sent up the accused's chain of command to the XO or the adjutant, giving the name of the offender, the offense charged, the name of the individual making the charge, and any witnesses.

The XO or adjutant makes—or causes to be made by the offender's company commander, the provost marshal, or other responsible person—a thorough investigation of the charges (see the preceding section for details on the conduct of the preliminary inquiry or investigation into an offense). For company-level proceedings, see figure 19-1.

At company level each morning, the first sergeant informs the CO of Marines placed on report during the preceding day. At battalion level, this is done by the XO or adjutant.

Officer offenses, when they occur, are by custom the province of battalion commanders or higher. They are dealt with by special reports and handled separately and privately.

Unit Punishment Book (UPB). Every unit whose commander has Article 15 powers must keep a UPB, a record of each case considered at Office Hours. The book also records each individual's acknowledgment that he or she has been apprised of their rights under Articles 15 and 31 and his or her waiver of right to trial by court-martial. The first sergeant or sergeant major takes care of this prior to Office Hours and obtains the individual's initials in the appropriate spaces in the UPB. At this time, the accused is also told that although he or she has no right to legal representation at Office Hours, they may obtain a personal representative to speak on their behalf and call witnesses and cross-examine witnesses against them.

The UPB is an important administrative record that is liable to inspection at any time incident to a case or by higher authority or the IG. A sloppy or improperly kept UPB can get you into trouble.

◆ ◆ *Office Hours Procedure*

Office Hours, as we have seen, is the Marine Corps equivalent of Captain's Mast. Like Mast, it can be, and frequently is, devoted to nondisciplinary matters, such as praise, special requests, and the like. Here the discussion centers only on the legal and disciplinary aspects of Office Hours. Bear in mind that Office Hours is not merely an administrative procedure but also a ceremony intended to dramatize praise and admonition. Like any ceremony, it should be dignified, disciplined, set apart in the daily routine, and carefully planned.

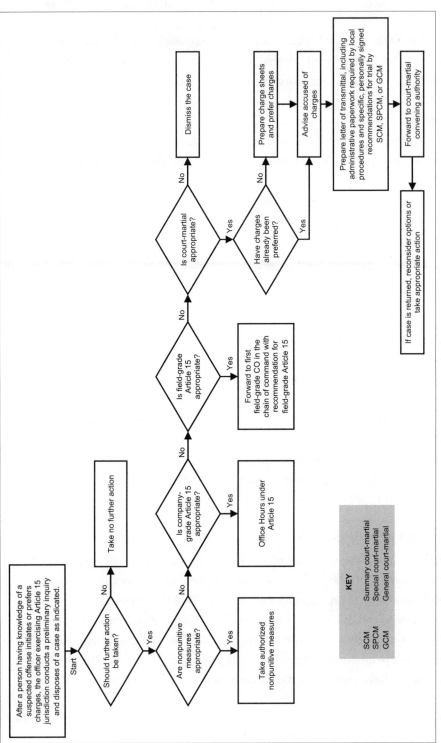

FIGURE 19-1. Decision Flowchart for Company Commander's Disposition of

Office Hours should be

- held at a set time and in a set place, usually the office of the commanding officer;
- attended by immediate COs and first sergeants (or platoon sergeants if within a company) of those required to appear, whether for praise, for reprimand, or by request;
- supervised by the adjutant and sergeant major if at battalion level, otherwise by the company first sergeant; and
- held in the full, immaculate uniform of the day.

Every officer attending Office Hours should review the cases of personal concern. If one of your Marines is up, take a careful look at the individual's service record and talk with the squad leader and platoon sergeant. Assure yourself that your Marine is in tip-top condition as to uniform, cleanliness, and military demeanor. If you yourself hold Office Hours, be sure to review the service records and individual cases before you call in the individuals concerned. This does not mean that you should prejudge the case. But it does ensure that you focus your thoughts on the Marine and on the case.

A Marine receiving Office Hours has the right to personally appear at the hearing or waive appearance and submit written matters for the CO's consideration. To make an impression on the Marine, the CO may desire that the individual be present for the hearing or at least for announcing punishment, even when appearance has otherwise been waived. In such cases, the Marine will be ordered to be present but cannot be forced to participate in the proceedings.

A typical procedure for Office Hours is as follows.

Ten minutes before the scheduled time, the sergeant major (or first sergeant, if a company-level proceeding) assembles all who are to appear, together with any enlisted witnesses and the respective first (or platoon) sergeants, who bring the service records (if these are not already in the hands of the sergeant major). At the same time, immediately subordinate commanders and any officer witnesses report to the adjutant, who conducts the officers into the commanding officer's office, where they are then seated.

At the appointed time, the adjutant (or company XO) stands on the left of the CO with relevant documents; these should be opened and tabbed appropriately for ready reference. First (platoon) sergeants stand in a group to one side. The sergeant major (first sergeant) escorts in the first accused and reads aloud the charge or report against them, while the adjutant (company XO) places the documents before the CO. The accused stands uncovered and at attention throughout, one pace in front of the commanding officer's desk.

After the charges have been read, the CO must be satisfied that the accused understands his or her rights under Articles 15 and 31, UCMJ and, as a matter of prudence, should again warn the Marine as follows: "Private, you do not have to make any statement regarding the offense of which you are accused or suspected. I must warn you that under Article 31 of the Code any statement made by you may be used as evidence against you in a trial by court-martial. Also that, if you so desire, you have the right to a trial by court-martial rather than accept NJP here at Office Hours. Do you understand?"

Next, the CO will ask the individual if he or she has anything to say. This gives the accused a chance to tell his or her side of the case, if desired. Witnesses may be called—usually the reporting officer and witnesses to the offense. The accused must not be compelled to make a statement, nor does the accused have to admit guilt or produce evidence.

After all explanations have been heard and the CO has considered the report of preliminary investigation, the CO has four courses of action (see figure 19-1): (1) dismiss the accused, either accepting the explanation or giving a warning; (2) impose NJP; (3) order the accused to be tried by special or summary court-martial (or recommend such trial, if the CO is not authorized to convene these courts); or (4) for a very serious offense, order or recommend that an investigation be conducted under Article 32 to determine whether the accused should be tried by general court-martial. An Article 32 or pretrial investigation must be conducted before a case can be referred to general court-martial.

At the conclusion of the hearing, the sergeant major (first sergeant) commands: "About, FACE. Forward, MARCH." On the command, "MARCH," the person marches out of the office. The process then is repeated with the next case.

When meritorious cases (such as presentation of Good Conduct Medals, promotions, or special commendations) are involved, disciplinary cases should first be paraded in the rear of the commanding officer's office to watch the meritorious proceedings. They are then marched out and individually brought in again as described above.

❖ ❖ *Appeal from Nonjudicial Punishment*

When NJP is imposed at Office Hours, the Marine must be informed of the right to appeal the punishment to the next immediate superior in command if he or she feels that the punishment is unjust or that it is disproportionate to the offense. This appeal must be in writing and must be presented within five days. A Marine who has appealed may be required to undergo any punishment imposed while the appeal is pending unless action is not taken on the appeal within five days after the appeal was submitted, and if the Marine so requests, any unexecuted punishment involving restraint or extra duty will be stayed until action on the appeal is taken. The immediate superior in command (or the officer who imposed punishment) may, at any point, suspend probationally any part of the unexecuted punishment or remit, mitigate, or set it aside.

❖ ❖ *Limits of Nonjudicial Punishment*

At Office Hours, under Article 15, the CO may impose, in addition to or in lieu of admonition or reprimand, one or certain combinations of the sentences outlined below.

Upon *officers and warrant officers*:

- By any commander: restriction to certain specified limits, with or without suspension from duty, for not more than thirty consecutive days
- By an officer exercising general court-martial jurisdiction or an officer of general or flag rank in command: (1) arrest in quarters for not more than thirty consecutive days; (2) forfeiture of not more than one-half of one month's pay per month for two months; (3) restriction to certain specified limits, with or without suspension from duty, for not more than sixty consecutive days; and/or (4) detention of not more than one-half of one month's pay per month for three months

Upon *other military personnel of the command*:

- By any commander: (1) if imposed upon a person attached to or embarked in a vessel, confinement for not more than three consecutive days; (2) correctional custody for not more than seven consecutive days; (3) forfeiture of not more than seven days' pay; (4) reduction to the next inferior pay grade, if the grade from which demoted is within the promotion authority of the officer imposing the reduction or any officer subordinate to the one who imposes the reduction; (5) extra duties, including fatigue or other duties, for not more than fourteen consecutive days; (6) restriction to certain specified limits, with or without suspension from duty, for not more than fourteen consecutive days; and/or (7) detention of not more than fourteen days' pay

- By an officer of the grade of major or lieutenant commander or above: (1) if imposed upon a person attached to or embarked in a vessel, confinement for not more than three consecutive days; (2) correctional custody for not more than thirty consecutive days; (3) forfeiture of not more than one-half of one month's pay per month for two months; (4) reduction to the lowest or any intermediate pay grade, if the grade from which demoted is within the promotion authority of the officer imposing the reduction or any officer subordinate to the one who imposes the reduction, but an enlisted member in a pay grade above E–4 may not be reduced more than two pay grades; (5) extra duties, including fatigue or other duties, for not more than forty-five consecutive days; (6) restrictions to certain specified limits, with or without suspension from duty, for not more than sixty consecutive days; and/or (7) detention of not more than one-half of one month's pay per month for three months.

Although the law permits reduction of more than one pay grade, Navy Department regulations provide that no person can be reduced more than one grade through NJP. Even more important as far as Marines are concerned, *no staff NCO may be reduced nonjudicially* at Office Hours under Article 15 of the Code, *except by the commandant,* as the CMC is the only one who has the authority to promote a staff NCO.

On the point as to who may impose commanding officer's punishment on board ship, only the captain has such power over members of the ship's company (the Marine detachment included), even though the title of the leader of a Marine detachment is also that of commanding officer. On the other hand, the disciplinary authority of the CO of an embarked, separate organization of Marines (a floating battalion, for example) remains unaffected whether afloat or not insofar as members of that officer's command are concerned.

Office Hours punishment is not considered a conviction insofar as the offender's record is concerned. Remember, also, that under no circumstances may an offender awarded extra duty be placed on guard to work it off. And do not forget to keep the unit record of NJP as required by the UCMJ and departmental regulations.

❧ NAVAL COURTS-MARTIAL

❧ ❧ *Summary Courts-Martial*

Summary courts-martial may be convened by any person who may convene a general or special court-martial, the CO of any battalion or squadron, and the CO or officer in charge of any other command when empowered by the SECNAV.

Commissioned officers, WOs, cadets, midshipmen, and those accused of capital offenses cannot be tried by summary court-martial.

A summary court-martial consists of one commissioned officer, whenever practical not below the rank of captain, USMC, or equivalent. This officer will be of the same armed force as the accused, although the Navy and the Marine Corps are considered the same service for this purpose. When only one officer is attached to a command, the CO will conduct the summary court-martial, in which case no convening order is required. The summary court-martial officer is not sworn but performs his or her duty under the overall sanction of the oath of office.

Witnesses testify under oath. Examination is conducted by the summary court-martial officer. Rules of evidence are binding. A finding of guilt at a summary court-martial is not recorded as a federal criminal conviction; thus, it is aimed at promptly addressing relatively minor offenses.

Right to Counsel. The accused at a summary court-martial does not have the right to counsel. If the accused hires civilian counsel, that counsel will be permitted to represent the individual if it will not delay the proceedings unreasonably and if military exigencies do not preclude it.

Limits of Punishment. Summary courts-martial may adjudge any sentence not more than confinement at hard labor for one month, forfeiture of two-thirds pay for one month, and reduction to pay grade E-1. Within specified guidelines, restriction for up to sixty days or hard labor without confinement for forty-five days may be substituted for confinement at hard labor. Enlisted Marines above pay grade E-4 will not be reduced more than one pay grade and cannot be adjudged confinement or hard labor without confinement. An admonishment or reprimand may be adjudged in all cases.

Objection to Trial by the Accused. No person may be tried by summary court-martial over his or her objection. Each person must consent to the trial, or the case is returned to the convening authority for further action.

Record. The record of a summary court-martial is written on a standard form (DD Form 2329). Detailed instructions and examples of the record of trial are found in the MCM. The accused has seven days after the sentence is announced to submit matters to the convening authority. The convening authority can then act to approve or disapprove the findings and sentence, subject to the previously discussed constraints. An entry reflecting trial by summary court-martial is also made in the Marine's service-record book.

❯ ❯ *Special Courts-Martial*

Special courts-martial may be convened by any of the officers shown in table 19-1 or, specifically insofar as the Marine Corps is concerned, by any officer with general court-martial authority; general officer in command; CO of any battalion or squadron; directors of Marine Corps districts; CO of any Marine brigade, regiment, detached battalion, or corresponding unit; CO of any aircraft group, separate squadron, station, base, or Marine barracks; CO of any independent Marine Corps unit or organization where members of the Corps are on duty; any inspector-instructor; and any other CO or officer in charge when so designated by the SECNAV. A special court-martial may try officers or enlisted persons for any offenses (except capital) that the convening authority deems appropriate.

A special court-martial is composed of a military judge and four members, who may be commissioned officers, WOs, or (if the accused is an enlisted person and so requests) enlisted persons of any of the services, including members of the National Oceanic and Atmospheric Administration and the Public Health Service when assigned to and serving with the armed forces. An accused has the option in both general and special courts-martial to request trial by military judge alone, in which case the judge alone hears arguments, adjudges guilt, and hands down the sentence; there are no other members of the court.

When a full special court-martial sits, the function of the members (sometimes called the panel) is to determine guilt or innocence and adjudge sentence, if the accused elects sentencing by members after the findings are announced. The senior member of the court—usually a major or higher—is called the president, even though no longer presiding, which is the judge's duty.

No member of a court-martial should be junior to the accused, and WOs or enlisted persons may not, under any circumstances, sit as members for the trial of a commissioned officer. While the law provides for a variant form of special court without military judge and with diminished powers, it is the policy of the Marine Corps that all Marine special courts shall have military judges and full powers. For that reason, the *Guide* omits other references to the lesser type of court.

If an accused enlisted person requests in writing that enlisted members be included in the special court-martial trying the case, at least one-third of the members must be enlisted, unless that many cannot be obtained. Enlisted members cannot be from the same unit as the accused. When such members cannot be obtained, the trial may still be held, but convening authority must give the reasons in writing.

The *trial counsel* conducts the prosecution's case; the *defense counsel* acts as defense attorney for the accused. In the naval services, a reporter transcribes the testimony and keeps the record under guidance of the trial counsel. The bailiff acts as guard and messenger and, if need be, escorts the accused.

❥ ❥ General Courts-Martial

The highest naval court, the general court-martial, may be convened by the president; the SECNAV; the CMC; the commanding generals of the Fleet Marine Forces; the commanding general of any corps, division, aircraft wing, or brigade; the commander of a fleet; the CO of a naval station or large shore activity beyond the continental limits of the United States; any general officer or immediate successor in command of a unit or activity of the Marine Corps; and such COs as may be authorized by the president and the SECNAV. General courts-martial may try anyone who is subject to the UCMJ and award any punishment authorized by law (see table 19-2).

Composition. A general court-martial comprises a military judge and eight members in noncapital cases—that is, when the accused does not face the death penalty. Alternately, it may consist of a military judge alone if trial by a military judge is requested and approved. Capital cases require a military judge and twelve members. The senior officer among members serves as the president. Unless unavoidable, all members should be senior to the accused. As with a special court-martial, if the accused is enlisted, he or she may request enlisted members named to the court.

Investigation of Charges. Charges may not be referred to a general court-martial unless they have been formally investigated or such investigation has been waived by the accused. The court-martial convening authority orders this investigation. The officer conducting the investigation must, with rare exception, be a judge advocate, preferably a field-grade officer possessing substantial legal training and experience. The investigating officer's job is neither to develop nor to whitewash a case but simply to ascertain the facts thoroughly and impartially under Article 32 of the Code.

Proceedings. A general court-martial is conducted with special military formality. The military judge presides, while trial counsel prosecutes, and defense counsel defends.

Although special courts have jurisdiction to try officers, by custom of the Marine Corps, officer cases are reserved for general court-martial. Article 66 requires automatic review by the courts of criminal appeals only in cases that include death, dismissal, a dishonorable or bad conduct discharge, or confinement for two years or more. In cases involving confinement for six months or more but less than two years, an accused may petition for review. All cases involving a death sentence must be approved by the president of the United States before that portion of the sentence is executed. Dismissal of a commissioned officer, cadet, or midshipman may be approved and ordered executed only by the secretary of the service concerned or a designated undersecretary.

❧ ❧ *Duty as a Court Member*

Second lieutenants rarely serve as court members, but first lieutenants and captains often do. Despite the importance of this duty, no special preparation

TABLE 19-2. Court-Martial Punishments

Type of Punishment	General Court-Martial	Special Court-Martial	Summary Court-Martial
Bad conduct discharge (enlisted only)	Yes	Yes	No
Confinement	Yes	Yes (enlisted only; not in excess of 12 months)	Yes (enlisted only below 5th pay grade; not in excess of 1 month)
Bread and water*	Yes	Yes	Yes
Death	Yes	No	No
Dishonorable discharge (warrant officers and enlisted only)	Yes	No	No
Dismissal (officers only)	Yes	No	No
Fines	Yes	Yes	Yes
Forfeiture	Yes	Yes (not in excess of ⅔ pay per month for 12 months)	Yes (not in excess of ⅔ of 1 month's pay)
Hard labor (without confinement–enlisted only)	Yes (not in excess of 3 months)	Yes (not in excess of 3 months)	Yes (not in excess of 45 days; only enlisted below 5th pay grade)
Life imprisonment	Yes	No	No
Loss of numbers, lineal position, seniority	Yes (seniority only)	No	No
Reduction of officer	No	No	No
Reduction to lowest enlisted grade	Yes	Yes	Yes (only enlisted below 5th pay grade)
Reprimand	Yes	Yes	Yes
Restriction to limits	Yes (not in excess of 2 months)	Yes (not in excess of 2 months)	Yes (not in excess of 2 months)

*Subject to various administrative limits; enlisted personnel only.

is required. Your one big responsibility as a member is to be there, smartly turned out in the prescribed uniform, prepared to be alert and attentive. From the court's convening to adjournment, your duty as a member is primary and comes first regardless of how pressing your regular duties may be.

As trial progresses, the military judge will explain all applicable points of law. Your job is to listen to the evidence presented by both sides, determine the facts fairly and impartially, and then apply the law, on which the judge will have instructed you, to the facts as you see them. Every member has an equal vote regardless of grade. You may not divulge your deliberations.

❯ ❯ *Role of Counsel*

Counsel on both sides before Marine Corps courts-martial must be qualified judge advocates.

Trial counsel prosecutes cases for the government, but he or she is more than a prosecutor, having a responsibility to help the court determine the truth and safeguard the rights of the accused. You will often have dealings with trial counsel in preparation for cases for which you may have conducted an inquiry or investigation. You may also be called as a witness.

Defense counsel conducts the defense, to which every accused is entitled. The defense counsel's duties include the following:

- To undertake the defense regardless of opinion as to the guilt of the accused
- To disclose to the accused any interest he or she may have in connection with the case, any ground of possible disqualification, and any other matter that might influence the accused in the selection of counsel
- To represent the accused with undivided fidelity
- Not to divulge the secrets or confidences of the accused

❯ RELATED ADMINISTRATIVE MATTERS AND PROCEEDINGS

❯ ❯ *Arrest, Restriction, and Conditions on Liberty*

When charged with an offense, anyone subject to the UCMJ may be subjected to pretrial restraint (moral or physical restraint) by having conditions placed on liberty, arrest, restriction in lieu of arrest, or confinement. These are administrative acts, not punishment.

Conditions on liberty are imposed by orders directing a person to do or refrain from doing certain acts.

Restriction in lieu of arrest is the restraint of a person by oral or written orders directing the individual to remain within specified limits. A restricted person *shall perform full military duties* unless otherwise directed.

Arrest is the restraint of a person by oral or written orders directing the individual to remain within specified limits. A person in the status of arrest *may not be required to perform full military duties.*

Confinement is physical restraint depriving a person of freedom.

Pretrial restraint should be no more rigorous than the circumstances require. It is not punishment and should not be used as such. Personnel should not be placed in confinement pending trial by court-martial unless it is foreseeable that (1) the individual will not appear at trial or will engage in serious criminal conduct and (2) less severe forms of restraint are inadequate. Those in pretrial confinement may not be subjected to punishment (including hard labor) during that time. Additionally, a command representative must visit them periodically to ascertain their condition and see to their needs.

An officer under arrest must remain within the limits assigned. He or she should not ordinarily be deprived of the use of any part of the ship or installation to which he or she had access before arrest. But on board ship, if suspended from duty, an arrested officer may not visit the ship's bridge or quarterdeck except in case of danger to the ship. An arrested officer also cannot officially visit the CO or other superior officer unless summoned or on approval of a written request for a meeting.

Physical Restraints. As an OD, you will occasionally have the decision of arresting, apprehending, or confining enlisted people and, on rarer occasions, of applying such physical restraints as irons or even straitjackets, the use of which is carefully restricted by Navy Regulations and other instructions.

On probable cause to believe that an offense has been committed, any of the following may apprehend (arrest) any enlisted person: officers, WOs, NCOs, and enlisted personnel on duty as MP. As OD, you may apprehend and confine. Orders for confinement, which you may receive from a CO, may be oral or written, direct or conveyed through a staff officer.

You (as an OD) are required by the Code to accept any prisoner brought to you by a commissioned officer with a signed, written report of an offense. Not later than your relief as OD, you must report to the CO the full details of any such confinements.

Instruments of restraint (handcuffs, for example) can never be used for punishment. They are authorized only for safe custody and for no longer than is strictly required to prevent escape during transfer; on medical grounds certified by the medical officer; or by order of the CO or officer in charge to prevent a Marine from injuring himself or herself.

❯ ❯ *Administrative Investigations*

It is important to be familiar with several forms of administrative investigation convened by commanders under the regulations of the JAGMAN and sometimes called JAGMAN investigations. These proceedings perform no direct judicial function and are in no sense the trial of an issue or of an accused person. They are convened and conducted to inform the convening authority of the facts involved.

It is also important to be aware that, in addition to the administrative investigations governed by the JAGMAN, other investigations may be required by other regulations. These have different purposes, and both JAGMAN investigations and other investigations may be appropriate under certain circumstances. Examples of investigations required by other regulations include the following:

- Investigations conducted by an IG
- Investigations of aviation mishaps
- Investigations concerning security violations, in particular those that may involve the compromise of classified information
- Safety and mishap investigations
- Investigations conducted by NCIS

The important thing to remember here is that to avoid potential conflicts, commanders must be aware of the conduct of adjacent or parallel investigations and coordinate appropriately.

Under the JAGMAN, there are four types of administrative investigations: courts or boards of inquiry, litigation report investigations, command investigations, and lost, damaged, or destroyed government property investigations.

Court or Board of Inquiry. The court of inquiry and the board of inquiry are formal fact-finding bodies in the naval services. The court of inquiry is the most formal option and is used for the most serious matters: for example, loss of life under peculiar circumstances; a serious fire; loss, stranding, or serious casualty to a ship of the Navy; or major loss or damage to government property.

In case of loss of life, a medical officer should be a member of the court of inquiry or investigation. The investigating body must determine, if possible, whether death was caused through the intent, fault, negligence, or inefficiency of any person in the naval services. No opinion will be expressed, however, regarding the misconduct or line of duty status of an individual in the investigation report of his or her death or any endorsement thereon.

Courts of inquiry have the following characteristics:

- Convened by a general court-martial convening authority or other person designated by the SECNAV
- Convened by written appointing order, which should direct that all testimony be taken under oath and all open proceedings, except counsel's argument, be recorded verbatim
- Consist of at least three commissioned officers as members, with appointed legal counsel and other advisers as needed
- Follow a hearing procedure
- Designate as parties to the proceeding any persons subject to the UCMJ whose conduct is subject to inquiry
- Designate as parties to the proceeding those persons subject to the UCMJ or employed by and who have a direct interest in the subject under inquiry
- Have the power to order military personnel to appear, testify, and produce evidence as well as the power to subpoena civilian witnesses to appear, testify, and produce evidence

Courts of inquiry return findings of fact and do not express opinions or make recommendations unless required to do so by the convening authority.

Boards of inquiry have the following characteristics:

- Convened by a general court-martial convening authority
- Convened by written appointing order, which should direct that all testimony be taken under oath and all open proceedings, except counsel's argument, be recorded verbatim
- Consist of one or more commissioned officers as members, with appointed legal counsel and other advisers as needed
- Follow a hearing procedure
- May designate as parties to the proceeding those persons whose conduct is subject to inquiry or who have a direct interest in the subject of the inquiry
- Do not possess power to subpoena civilian witnesses unless convened under Article 135, UCMJ but can order naval personnel to appear, testify, and produce evidence

Do not confuse reports of such proceedings (or of individual investigations) with certain reports required by Navy Regulations or with reports of investigations conducted by the IG.

Litigation Report Investigation. Commanders use a litigation report investigation to investigate an incident or event (1) that has the potential to result in claims or civil litigation against the Department of the Navy for damage to real or personal property, (2) involving personal injury or death caused by Navy personnel acting within the scope of their employment, or (3) on behalf of the department as an affirmative claim for damage caused to department property by non-DON personnel or caused by DON personnel not acting in the performance of their duties. The primary purpose of a litigation report is to document facts and gather evidence to protect the legal interests of the department and the United States.

It is enough to be aware of this type of administrative investigation, as you are unlikely to encounter a litigation report investigation early in your career.

Command Investigation. A command investigation functions as a tool to gather, analyze, and record relevant information about an incident or event of primary interest to the command. Most investigations will be of this nature. It is an informal proceeding conducted by one or more officers, and it is ordered by any commander with Article 15 powers. It resembles the preliminary inquiry into an offense (described earlier) except it is nonpunitive and thus outside the disciplinary process.

Though an informal proceeding, a command investigation is not a minor affair. For example, an important part of any investigation dealing with death, injury, or individual performance of a Marine (for example, a serious traffic accident involving a government vehicle) is to determine whether it took place in line of duty or involved individual misconduct. Such findings have wide repercussions in the subsequent handling of claims against the government, determinations by the Department of Veterans Affairs, and so on. For this reason, the responsibility of an investigation is heavier than it may seem at first.

The conduct of a command investigation may well be one of your earliest legal assignments on your own, so it behooves you to handle it in competent fashion.

Lost, Damaged, or Destroyed Government Property Investigation. A common form of investigation often falling to junior officers is an investigation into the loss, damage, or destruction of government property. When tasked with such an investigation, it is imperative that you first consult the current Marine Corps order on consumer-level supply policy, which supplements the JAGMAN with much special information.

❖ ❖ *Administrative Discharge Boards*

These boards, convened by officers with general court-martial jurisdiction, hear cases of individuals whose separation from the Corps by administrative discharge (as distinct from a punitive discharge) has been recommended. The *Marine Corps Separation and Retirement Manual* requires that the board consist of at least three officers, one of whom must be field grade. Junior officers may serve as board members and frequently must appear before such boards as witnesses.

In general terms, this board, like an investigation, seeks to determine facts. Based on its findings, the panel recommends either that a Marine be retained in the Corps or that he or she be given an administrative discharge of a character and type recommended by the board.

–» Part III «–

PERSONAL, FAMILY, AND SOCIAL MATTERS

⁓{ 20 }⁓

PERSONAL AND
FAMILY MATTERS

Provide in advance for the needs of thy growing age
and the protection of thy family.
— George Samuel Clason

YOUR FIRST RESPONSIBILITIES as a Marine officer are to country and Corps. Hardly second, however, are your responsibility to your family and your responsibility to organize your affairs so that they can continue undisturbed through all the ups and downs and sudden turnings in a service career.

Sudden death is only one contingency you must anticipate. What if you are captured, prematurely retired, or ordered overseas where your family cannot follow?

Reflect on these possibilities. Put your house in order. Keep it in order.

⋗ FINANCIAL MATTERS

Under the selection system of promotion and owing to the rigors of military service, most officers retire from active service between the ages of forty-two and fifty-two, and all must retire by age sixty-four. Thus, a military career is shorter than that in many other professions. Today's laws have considerably lessened assurance of adequate retirement income, even for the physically retired. If you are over age fifty or physically disabled when you retire, your prospects for employment are regrettably diminished. For all these reasons, you must lose no time in laying the foundations of a balanced estate—one that reflects well-planned objectives; combines a prudent insurance program, wise investments, and property ownership; and protects against the unexpected.

❧ ❧ *Banking*

You should open and maintain checking and savings accounts with a reputable national bank or credit union, preferably one with multiple branches—or, at a minimum, automated teller machines—located near naval installations around the country. Your chosen institution should be accustomed to handling accounts on a worldwide basis. This will help avoid the administrative burden of continually opening and closing local bank accounts when transferring from one duty station to the next.

You should also begin systematic savings with your first paycheck, aiming for a minimum of 10 percent of gross pay throughout your career.

❧ ❧ *Social Security*

Social Security coverage is extended to all hands in uniform. You contribute through an automatic deduction of a percentage of your basic pay. In addition to your military retirement pay, assuming you complete a military career, and any disability compensation paid by the Department of Veterans Affairs, Social Security provides monthly income for

- you, upon reaching full retirement age, which is currently sixty-seven for those born in 1960 or later (or age sixty-two, if you apply early to receive reduced payments);
- your spouse, if you die and your minor children remain in your spouse's care;
- you, your spouse, and children, if you should be totally disabled;
- your spouse, if not entitled earlier, on attaining age sixty;
- your children under age eighteen, or older if incapable of self-support, after your death or while you are disabled; or
- your dependent parents.

The payments for a family group may go as high as the legal maximum even if you have only paid into the Social Security program through taxation of your basic pay for a few years. The amount of your benefit is determined by your "average monthly wage" during the years you were contributing. The exact amount differs in almost every case. You must apply for Social Security benefits; they are not paid automatically. You should get in touch with the local Social Security Administration office on attaining age sixty-seven, or when your spouse reaches age sixty, or at any time if disabled before reaching age sixty-five. When you die, your next of kin should check with the Social Security office to see if there is an entitlement to survivor's insurance.

Your Social Security number is important for both you and your family to know, and it must, of course, accompany claims or inquiries. Moreover, it is used for several military administrative purposes and is used by the Internal Revenue Service in connection with all your tax returns and related records. Record it with any emergency papers you keep, such as insurance policies and so forth, and safeguard it carefully.

To assist in understanding your situation and entitlements, the Social Security Administration encourages every insured individual—you—to create an online account at its website (https://www.ssa.gov). In this way, you can determine whether the records are complete and you are getting credit for all earnings on which Social Security tax has been paid. There are also calculators available online to help with financial planning.

You can get full information on these and other matters of interest by searching online, applying at the nearest Social Security Administration office, and usually from your unit personnel officer. Before retirement, investigate your Social Security rights and credits, and be sure your spouse is acquainted with his or her rights under the law.

❖ ❖ *Life Insurance*

From the moment you take out life insurance, you create a cash estate of the amount of that policy, an estate whose proceeds are not taxable under the inheritance laws of most states. Life insurance provides an estate while you are in a low-income bracket and before you have had time to accumulate sizable savings, and it protects the future of your spouse and family during your younger years against the occupational hazards of your profession. Finally, certain types of life insurance give a modest return on your investment and can help maintain your standard of living after retirement.

The *Guide* does not advocate one type of insurance over another; it merely summarizes several options that the informed officer might consider.

Broadly speaking, there are two categories of life insurance: *permanent*, which provides insurance for the entire life of the insured party, and *term*, which insures an individual for a defined period of time, the "term." Each of these categories contains a number of variations.

Whole life insurance is basic permanent insurance. It covers the insured for his or her entire life. This type of policy includes a cash value component that grows tax deferred at a contractually guaranteed rate. The premiums are usually level for the life of the insured, with part of the premium applying to the insurance portion of your policy, part covering administrative expenses, and the balance contributing to the investment, or cash, portion of the policy. The death benefit is guaranteed for the insured's lifetime.

Universal life insurance, which is sometimes called *flexible premium* or *adjustable life*, is another form of permanent life insurance. Like whole life, it provides cash value benefits based on prevailing rates of return. The principal feature distinguishing this policy from whole life is that the premiums, cash values, and the level of insurance protection may be adjusted up or down according to the insured's changing needs.

Variable life insurance is similar to whole life, though more complicated. It combines whole life's traditional protection and savings features with the growth potential of investment funds in lieu of the savings component.

Variable universal life insurance is still more complex, for it combines features of universal life and variable life insurance. In simplified terms, it provides the insured the flexibility of selecting and adjusting premiums, death benefits, and investment choices. Be aware that, under these types of policies, the policy owner bears significant investment risk, and the death benefit may rise or fall depending on the performance of the underlying investments.

Term life insurance, the second broad category, is the most economical and straightforward form of insurance. Term life pays a clearly stated amount on the death of the insured, but it is distinguished from permanent life in that it provides coverage only during a clearly defined, but fixed, period of time—typically from one to thirty years. Nor does it include a cash-value component. Term life is particularly useful when the period of needed protection is known and limited and when the funds available to pay premiums are limited, as premiums for term life are the among the lowest available. Premiums for term life increase (in most cases) with the age of the insured, usually in five-year increments.

Level term life insurance is characterized by a fixed death benefit and a guaranteed premium for specified periods—the longer the guarantee, the higher the premium. These policies are normally renewable at the end of the term, although at increased premiums as the insured ages.

Another variation of term life, *decreasing term life insurance*, combines a level premium with a decreasing death benefit over time. Individuals often use this form of term life to protect mortgage debt by roughly matching the declining death benefit with the declining mortgage liability, thus enabling the policy's beneficiary to pay off a home mortgage upon death of the insured.

Finally, *annual renewable and convertible term insurance* is one of the more complex forms of term insurance. It normally protects the insured for a single year but permits him or her to renew the policy at higher premiums for successive periods thereafter without the need to resubmit evidence of insurability. The policy holder may also convert these term policies into permanent life insurance under specified terms.

Your Life Insurance Program. A sound life-insurance program varies with income, age and number of your children, your own age, and your probable number of years remaining on the active list. Periodically, you must overhaul your program and consider carefully many variables, such as the scope and duration of your spouse's and children's needs, your spouse's employment opportunities, and your income after retirement.

Consider the needs of your family five, ten, and twenty years from now and your probable income. Think about retirement income, education, and cash for the down payment on a house. Contrary to some opinion, not all permanent policies are bad; they can satisfy certain needs efficiently and effectively. In some instances and for certain needs, term policies are the ideal choice.

Life insurance is a complicated but necessary financial instrument that protects family members and loved ones. Selecting life insurance is a very personal decision, and you would be wise to carefully assess your needs and then research and understand your options before selecting an insurance product. If you find this important task daunting, it may be wise to consult a financial professional who takes seriously a *fiduciary duty* to provide advice in your best interest.

But, first, consider joining the *Navy Mutual Aid Association*, a mutual, non-profit, tax-exempt, and voluntary membership association of sea service personnel and their families. Navy Mutual offers life insurance and other financial products to its members. The association gives more than helpful assistance to the beneficiaries of its members. Only second to Navy Mutual, you should also consider the *Group Insurance Plan* of the Marine Corps Association (MCA), which pays an active duty death benefit up to $500,000. Details on Navy Mutual and the Group Insurance Plan are given below and later in this chapter.

At least every five years, review your program. You may well find that changes in income or employment and a different family situation indicate modifications. Look through a sound guide on insurance.

Government Life Insurance. Military service entitles you to *Servicemembers' Group Life Insurance* (SGLI), which provides term life insurance in $50,000 increments up to the maximum of $400,000 while on active duty. Your pay is checked monthly for this coverage, and you are covered for the full amount until and unless you cancel all or part of your coverage or until you elect to convert SGLI into a veterans policy (see below) upon separation or retirement. Death claims are handled by Marine Corps Headquarters and by the commercial company that is the prime insurer.

Veterans' Group Life Insurance (VGLI) is a five-year term policy that has no cash, loan, paid-up, or extended values. VGLI automatically covers Marines who are separated or retired (or Reservists released from active duty over thirty days). It takes effect at the end of the 120-day free coverage period under SGLI following separation or retirement as above if payment for at least the first month of the required premium is made before the end of the free period. Depending on age, monthly VGLI premiums vary and must be paid directly to the Office of Servicemembers' Group Life Insurance.

At the end of the five-year term, VGLI may be renewed or converted to an individual insurance policy with an eligible company *without medical examination*.

On government insurance matters, refer to the *Handbook for Retired Marines*, published by HQMC and frequently updated.

Navy Mutual Aid Insurance. The Navy Mutual Aid Association (https://www.navymutual.org), a nonprofit group, offers quality life insurance to members at close to net cost, helps members obtain all government benefits to which they are legally entitled, and educates members and their families on matters of financial security. Individuals in the following categories are eligible for membership: active duty servicemembers, those recently separated honorably from active duty (if contacted within 120 days of separation), military retirees, members of the Reserve or National Guard, and employees of the U.S. Public Health Service or National Oceanic and Atmospheric Administration. Also, all honorably discharged veterans residing in any of the following states are eligible for membership: Arizona, Connecticut, Florida, Hawaii, Maryland, North Carolina, Oregon, Rhode Island, South Carolina, Texas, and Virginia.

On receipt of notice of your death from the Navy Department, Navy Mutual pays 10 percent of the death benefit up to $10,000 to your beneficiary overnight; the remainder of the benefit will be paid in accordance with the desires of the beneficiary. Navy Mutual will also render help to your surviving dependents in settlement of all other claims. Perhaps the most important service performed by the association (and described later in this chapter) is the assistance provided in securing service-connected compensation for spouses, children, and dependent parents of deceased members. In the event compensation is disallowed initially (as sometimes happens), the association provides, without charge, competent legal representation before the Veterans Administration Board of Appeals to obtain the best possible settlement. Navy Mutual membership merits serious consideration by every Marine officer.

Marine Corps Association & Foundation Group Benefits Program. This incorporates term insurance plans and other beneficial programs designed and operated by Marines. It is open to any member of the Marine Corps Association and Foundation (MCA&F) under age eighty. Depending on the plan chosen and on the age of the insured, benefits may go as high as $500,000. Rates are very competitive. One of the attractive features of this plan is that unlike most group insurance products, you may, after separation or retirement, continue your low-cost protection until age seventy so long as you retain MCA membership (another good reason to take the *Gazette*). Visit the MCA&F website (https://www.mca-marines.org) for details on this program (as well as membership).

Final Thoughts on Life Insurance. If you hold government insurance, do not let it lapse. In service or out, it is the best insurance you can get.

Do not take out insurance haphazardly. Include it as part of a comprehensive personal financial plan.

Do not overload yourself with insurance against remote dangers, but be sure your policies protect against all expected military hazards. Many insurance companies have restrictions, sometimes included in the proverbial "fine print," as to war, flying hazards as a pilot or crew member of a military aircraft, and so on.

Pay premiums by allotment. Regulations permit indefinite allotments for insurance premiums that continue after retirement. Doing this prevents lapse of policies due to unpaid premiums.

Keep your listed beneficiaries up to date, and be sure to name contingent beneficiaries. Remember to look for or include the phrase "or to the survivor or survivors thereof," which covers most eventualities. If a beneficiary dies, make a prompt change in recipient. Consider the consequence if both you and your beneficiary should die in the same accident.

Ensure your insurance program includes provisions to make some funds available immediately to family members upon your death.

Review settlement arrangements with your insurance agent or broker periodically to ensure that they are adapted to your present circumstances.

Do not arrange all your insurance with a single company. Protection is enhanced by diversification among several good companies, although this does complicate the bookkeeping.

Although insurance is something you should attend to promptly, perform due diligence before you sign insurance contracts. Be extremely cautious in dealing with companies and insurance agents who hover about newly commissioned lieutenants. Deal with sound, well-known companies, and select an agent with discrimination.

❧ ❧ *Insurance Death Claims*

Government Insurance Death Claims. If you are on active duty at the time of your death, the VA will mail the relevant claim forms to your beneficiary. The VA is notified by HQMC; no further proof of death is required. Your beneficiary must fill out the forms and return them.

If you die when retired or separated from the service, however, your beneficiary should apply at the nearest VA regional office for the necessary forms or see the legal assistance or personal affairs officer at the nearest Navy or Marine Corps installation; if these are inaccessible, the beneficiary should seek assistance from his or her nearest state or other service organization. Proof of death must be furnished; the beneficiary should get certified copies of the public death record, coroner's report, death certificate by the attending physician, or death certificate from the naval hospital.

Delays in processing VA claims are not uncommon. The Navy Mutual Aid Association, if you are a member, can keep them moving.

The beneficiary should keep possession of your government policy until the claim is paid; it should not be sent with the claim.

Commercial Insurance Policy Death Claims. Your beneficiary should consult local representatives of each company or write directly to the head office. The following actions are normally required:

- Provide the insured's (your) name.
- Provide insurance policy numbers.
- Request necessary forms to make a death claim.
- Return by *certified mail* the completed forms, with return receipt requested.
- Send a certified copy of the death certificate, affidavit of death as described above, or, if death occurred at sea or abroad, a certified copy of the official notification of death.

You should list the commercial companies that insure your life in the Record of Emergency Data in your personnel file at HQMC. Headquarters will notify the companies in case of death. Most companies accept such notification as proof of death.

Some companies require submission of the policy before paying the claim. Your insurance agent will assist your beneficiary with this paperwork. In general, it is unwise for your family to put claims for government benefits in the hands of private attorneys, as this may simply cause unnecessary delay and will certainly entail added expense.

⇥ *Other Kinds of Insurance*

Automobile Insurance. Your car can cause you much grief if not properly insured. Many states and all Marine Corps installations require public liability and property damage insurance before you can obtain the required registrations for your car.

Auto insurance is available to cover liability for bodily injury, property damage, medical payments, collision, fire and lightning, and transportation, theft, windstorm, earthquake, explosion, hail, or water damage. Liability awards for bodily injury and property damage are very high and are rising. Your insurance agent can recommend how much coverage you should carry in each category. Collision coverage is also expensive; you should therefore take out a "deductible" policy (for example, $500 deductible for each accident, as nearly every accident now costs that much or more). This protects you against heavy damage to, or total loss of, your vehicle.

Homeowner's and Personal Liability Insurance. Take out homeowner's insurance on any house or other real property you own. Another valuable coverage is personal liability insurance, which protects you against claims for injuries by guests or workers visiting your home; damage done by pets, children, spouse, or self (usually including damage arising out of sports); and damage done to the property of others by such accidents as falling trees or fire originating on your property. This insurance is inexpensive but invaluable should trouble come.

Renter's Insurance. Those who are not homeowners should arrange renter's insurance to protect personal belongings, such as uniforms, clothing, and home furnishings. Renter's insurance covers the contents of your dwelling but not the dwelling itself, so it is ideal for those occupying the bachelor officer quarters or renting a commercial apartment or private house.

Valuable Personal Property Insurance. Expensive personal property (valuable jewelry, computers, and so on) should be covered against fire, theft, and breakage or other damage at home or during transportation. Many companies write affordable "floater" policies for officers.

One highly regarded underwriter is United Services Automobile Association (USAA) of San Antonio, Texas, an association of servicemembers who mutually insure each other against losses and liabilities. USAA has grown to offer a full range of competitive financial products, which are available at its website (https://www.usaa.com).

❧ ❧ *Investments*

The complexity of the financial environment, particularly considering the many new investment instruments that have become available, may initially seem overwhelming to you. In investments, as in your military career, you must remain informed and consistent in your approach. A good place to begin your familiarity with this world is the library or bookstore, where generally accepted references can help you navigate the reef-strewn waters of high finance.

Investments should be viewed as a part of a well-conceived and comprehensive personal financial plan (see figure 20-1). Your aim should be threefold: to save a portion of your income (10 percent is a good starting point), beginning early in your career and increasing the share saved as your income grows; to preserve what you have saved by investing conservatively; and to select investment packages that have a record of providing a positive, long-term return at relatively low cost. The adage that it is tough to make something out of nothing is never more applicable than in the area of investments.

❧ ❧ *Real Estate*

While you are young, with limited income and few obligations, it is probably better to rent quarters given the "nomadic" lifestyle of military service. As you mature and your family grows, however, you may decide it is advantageous to own a home, particularly if there is a duty station or locality you expect to return to throughout your career. For example, a ground officer would serve most stateside duty in the vicinity of Camp Lejeune, Camp Pendleton, or

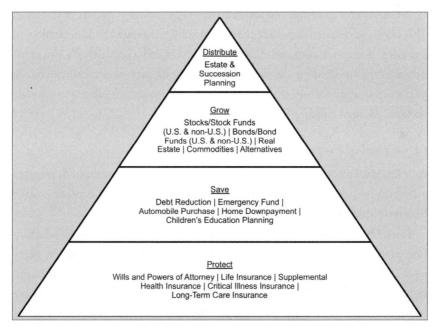

FIGURE 20-1. Personal Financial Pyramid

Washington-Quantico; an aviator would have maximum service in the vicinity of Miramar, Yuma, Cherry Point, Beaufort, or Washington-Quantico.

Some officers find it financially advantageous to buy a house where they have duty and are not assigned quarters, then either sell or rent when ordered to other shore duty or leave the family in their own home while on sea or expeditionary service. Although being an absentee landlord is certainly a difficult role, it is worthwhile to have a home available when you return, and you can approach retirement with something besides canceled checks and rent receipts. When retirement comes, you have an asset that will permit you to buy a house wherever you decide to settle. And if you die on active duty, your family will have a home or an income from the real estate you leave.

Carefully consider the terms of ownership of any real property before the deed is prepared. Joint ownership or transfer of property to your spouse by deed may offer material advantage to your estate. Leave among your valuable papers a list of your real estate holdings that gives the description and location of all properties; location of deeds, mortgages, or other papers; and original cost, depreciated cost, estimated present value, and present ownership status.

If you do rent housing, you should insist on a "military clause" in the lease. This clause generally states that the tenant may terminate the lease subject to payment of a certain sum and allows the tenant to end it on thirty days' written notice to the landlord for any one of several reasons, such as permanent change of station or release from active duty. Your legal assistance office can provide you with desired wording and other details.

❧ ❧ *Control of Property*

An individual may use or control an estate himself or herself or through an agent acting under power of attorney. Remote control of one kind or another is often necessary during a service career.

Joint Ownership. To facilitate use of property and to provide for its disposition after the owners death, that individual may arrange for most property to be held in joint tenancy with his or her spouse or other beneficiary with right of survivorship, thus enabling the joint tenant to also use and control the property jointly during the individual's lifetime. After the individual's death, the joint tenant obtains full title as survivor. Property held jointly cannot be disposed of by will if your joint tenant survives you, but it is wise to include provision for its disposal should your joint tenant die before (or at the same time as) you do.

The advantages of joint tenancy are less expense, less inconvenience, and less time required to dispose of property after a death. But there are also disadvantages. Be aware that the provisions of the Servicemembers' Civil Relief Act (SCRA) exempting military personnel from state or municipal taxation where they are temporarily stationed do not apply to your spouse's interest in property.

Real estate is not the only property that can be held in joint tenancy. Joint bank accounts and joint ownership of securities, with right of survivorship, have some advantages.

Joint Bank Accounts. If suddenly ordered to deploy or upon sudden death, an officer who carries a bank account solely in his or her own name may temporarily deprive the family of access to funds at a time when they are most needed. Investigate the advantages of joint accounts—at least during times when you are separated from your family.

Automobiles. Joint ownership of the family car also has advantages. Serious loss may result if your spouse or another family member drives your individually owned vehicle after your death. The best plan is to hold the title to the car in joint tenancy. The certificate of title and the insurance policy should bear the names of the joint owners.

Although joint ownership of automobiles is desirable, your spouse's interest in this personal property is taxable. Payment of taxes in a state where you live temporarily can be avoided under the SCRA if the car is registered in your name alone and in your own state of legal residence. A power of attorney to your spouse, however, will enable him or her to transfer title, secure registration, and sell or buy a car during your lifetime.

❧ ❧ *Borrowing Money and Loans*

Because the first few years of a junior officer's career may be spent paying off debts, it may be wise to underscore Shakespeare's advice to "neither a borrower nor a lender be," if you can help it. Avoid loan sharks, and equally avoid private loans to fellow officers, however deserving the case may appear; particularly avoid acting as cosigner to any note, which makes you just as liable as the actual borrower.

Interest Rates. The amount of interest you pay on a loan is a matter of vital concern and often a source of confusion. This is because lenders often charge different rates from those they quote. Whenever you borrow, ask what kind of interest is being charged, and carefully read the load disclosures. When comparing loans, ensure the terms (interest rate, compounding period, and so on) are similar, and compare interest costs and other charges to determine which lender offers the best terms.

It is particularly important to understand the difference between *annual percentage rate* (APR) and *annual percentage yield* (APY). The former, APR, is the simple annual rate of interest without taking into account the compounding of interest within the year. The latter, APY, accounts for the effects of compounding and rises as the compounding period shortens. This difference has important implications for borrowers, who actually pay back their loans at the latter rate. For example, a borrower with a loan at 5 percent APR actually pays 5.06 percent APY if compounding is semiannual; 5.09 percent APY, quarterly; and 5.11 percent APY, monthly.

If you must borrow, investigate the Navy Federal Credit Union or Marine Federal Credit Union. Both for borrowing and saving, whether by Internet, mail, or in person, these nonprofit organizations are tailored to the needs of the young officer: charges are comparatively low, and interest earned on deposits is generous.

❧ ❧ *Servicemembers' Civil Relief Act*

Building on the Soldier's and Sailor's Civil Relief Act of 1940, civil protections for military personnel were completely revised and updated in the SCRA of 2003. It is designed to relieve servicemembers from worry over certain civil problems and obligations.

The SCRA temporarily suspends enforcement of some civil liabilities of military personnel on active duty if their inability to meet their obligations results from their military status. Additionally, the act protects personnel from a form of double taxation that can occur when they have a spouse who works and is taxed in a state other than the one in which they maintain their permanent legal residence. The law prevents a state from using the income earned by a servicemember in determining the spouse's tax rate when the couple do not maintain their permanent legal residence in that state.

Legal advice is necessary in any application of the SCRA because of the many technicalities. The act is designed to provide a shield against hardship; *it is not a device to evade civil liabilities.* Information and advice may be obtained from your legal assistance officer, who is located at the legal services center at your base or station.

❯ FAMILY MATTERS

❯ ❯ *Medical Care for Family Members*

Medical care for service families and for retired officers and their families is provided by the government on a space-available basis in military health-care facilities. TRICARE is the military health insurance program that provides for medical care and hospitalization of military family members. A small fraction of the typical cost of a dependent family member's medical care and hospitalization is borne by the individual service family or individual through an annual premium payment and "copays" for some procedures.

Eligibility. Virtually all family members (spouse and unmarried children under age twenty-one, subject to a few exceptions) of Marines on active duty are eligible for civilian medical care and care in military medical facilities. To receive such care, however, armed forces personnel first must enroll their families in the Defense Enrollment Eligibility Reporting System. Check with your personnel officer or, on larger bases, the DEERS Office for appropriate forms and actions. You should update your family's enrollment in this system immediately with every change in family status. Do not put this off, as your family cannot be treated without DEERS certification.

Retired officers and their dependents likewise have such eligibilities, although under differing provisions (see the section below on retiree benefits). If you die, whether on active duty or after retirement, your surviving dependents remain eligible for care at armed forces or U.S. Public Health Service medical facilities (subject to availability of space and staff) as well as for certain civilian medical care and hospitalization.

Civilian Medical Care. Under TRICARE, routine doctor visits, prescribed medicines, laboratory and X-ray tests, outpatient care by civilian facilities, civilian semiprivate hospitalization, and so forth are available to active duty personnel and their family members on a cost-sharing basis. There are basically two plans to choose from, TRICARE Prime and TRICARE Select, with variations of these for remote and overseas duty stations. (Information can be found on TRICARE's website, https://www.tricare.mil.) In general, depending on the plan you select, you pay some combination of a minimum annual fee per person or family, copays per visit, and/or cost-share per medical service or procedure. Given the differences in cost, flexibility, and level of service between the plans, it is wise to consult a TRICARE benefits adviser when making a selection.

Financial assistance is also available for active duty personnel whose spouse or children are mentally or physically handicapped. This program authorizes diagnostic services, treatment, and use of private nonprofit and nonmilitary institutions for such family members. You, the sponsor, pay a varying amount according to rank, and the government pays the remaining portion of the cost up to a given maximum.

Medical Care at Military Health-Care Facilities. When medical staff, space, and facilities are available, the Navy Medical Department will provide the following care for your family:

- Preventive health care (also known as wellness care)
- Immunization
- Diagnosis
- Treatment of acute medical or surgical conditions, contagious diseases, and acute emergencies of any kind
- Maternity and infant care

All care received for and during a pregnancy that results in hospitalization is considered, for payment purposes, as part of that hospitalization, while oral contraceptives are considered to be prescription drugs.

Family members (including your parents, if legally dependent upon you) are normally able to receive outpatient services—that is, medical care provided without hospital admission. Most medical activities on board military installations in the continental United States have dependent outpatient service.

The extent and quality of medical services for family members vary widely not only due to the limitations of local hospitals and clinics, but also the medical workload as a whole. Regional military health-care facilities generally offer full services. Isolated outlying bases may provide basic medical and dental services, relying on a regional medical center for more comprehensive care. In appropriate cases, the government will normally provide or fund transportation for family members from outlying bases where medical care is inadequate to centers where proper care can be provided (with roundtrip expenses for attendants when they are found to be required).

In some regions, available health services are coordinated among various government health providers. In effect, you and your family may be assigned to a specific primary clinic for all outpatient and referral services. Consult your unit or base medical department or retired affairs office, as appropriate, to obtain information on local procedures.

A few cautionary words are in order on the subject of family medical care.

First and foremost, the medical needs of military personnel are the primary concern of the Medical Department. This means that care for family members takes second place and always gives way, when conflict arises, to military medicine functions. That said, the medical needs of family members will be met; it is just that the arrangements may not always be optimal.

Second, although members of the Marine Corps and Navy receive free dental care, dependents do not (except on remote overseas installations or as otherwise required in connection with medical or surgical treatment). As compensation, you are offered the TRICARE Dental Program, a government cost-sharing program equivalent to TRICARE.

Third, to receive medical assistance from any Navy (or other armed forces) establishment, your family member must possess and present a family member identification card (discussed in the next section). Obtain these cards and have each family member carry one at all times.

Finally, if you wish and can afford the more personal attentions of a private practitioner and civilian hospital, you are free to obtain such services according to the policies and procedures of your TRICARE plan, although usually at increased personal expense.

❧ ❧ *Identification and Privilege Cards for Family Members*

The Department of Defense issues a standard Identification and Privilege Card (Form DD 1173) for family members (except children under age ten) of all active duty personnel. This card is essential for your family to be able to use the

Families and friends await the emotional homecoming
of their Marines and Sailors from a challenging
overseas deployment.

medical facilities, commissary, exchange, and other services provided at military
installations. It is honored not only on Marine and Navy installations, but also
on those of the other services. If your family expands, apply immediately for
their identification and privilege cards and DEERS enrollment.

⟩ LEGAL MATTERS

⟩ ⟩ *Powers of Attorney*

A power of attorney authorizes someone else, your "agent," to act in your name
in the same manner and extent as you yourself could act. This power permits
your agent to do only acts expressly authorized within the document.

When you are deployed, a power of attorney enables your family to carry
on your affairs without interruption. Thus, when ordered overseas, you should
consider whether to execute a power of attorney covering your affairs generally
and permitting an agent to manage your affairs on your behalf.

Powers of attorney come in two forms, *general* and *special* (or sometimes
limited). A general power of attorney permits your agent to take any action on
your behalf. While this is straightforward, flexible, and convenient, it also has

drawbacks. It requires an unquestionably trustworthy agent. And some businesses may not accept a general power of attorney or may do so for only basic transactions. A special, or limited, power of attorney applies only to specific transactions or business relationships. You may arrange special powers of attorney for specific financial accounts, real estate, vehicles, or limited actions, such as the sale of designated property. The weakness of special powers of attorney is that you need to have one for each business relationship or activity.

You must prepare and execute a power of attorney in the presence of required witnesses, and it must be acknowledged by a notary public or, if outside the United States, by any officer of the United States authorized to administer oaths. Your unit adjutant is normally vested with notary powers.

Bear in mind that *not everyone needs to execute a power of attorney*. It can be a dangerous tool in the hands of the uninitiated or untrustworthy.

❖ ❖ Wills

Considering the occupational hazards of military service, it is important that you have a will. A will simplifies settlement of your estate, reduces expenses, conserves assets, and enables your last wishes to be carried out.

Definitions. A *will and testament* is the legal document by which an individual leaves instructions for the disposition of property after his or her death. A holographic will (rare today) is one that has been entirely handwritten and signed by the testator.

A *testator* is a person who leaves a will. An *intestate* is a person who dies without a will.

Settling an estate refers to the entire process of identifying assets, filing inventories and accounts, paying claims, distributing assets in accordance with the will or laws of descent and distribution, and filing final accounting with the court.

An *executor* is appointed by your will to execute its provisions after your death. If you die intestate, the court appoints an *administrator*, who discharges the duties of an executor in settling the estate.

A *codicil* adds to, or qualifies, a will and is drawn up in the same way. Will and codicil are taken together. When possible, it is best to make a new will rather than to add a codicil to an old will.

Probate is the process of presenting the will for record to the proper authority in the county where the deceased had legal residence. If executed according to the law of your legal domicile, a will made anywhere in the world will be admitted to probate in the jurisdiction of your domicile without question. Probate establishes the validity of the will and evidences the right of beneficiaries to succeed to title to property in the estate. The place of probate is usually the county and state in which you are domiciled at the time of death; the will must also be probated in any other county and state where you own real property.

Before Making a Will. Analyze your estate, estimate state and federal taxes, and plan to minimize them. Then, if not sooner, confer with a competent legal adviser. See your legal assistance officer or a member of the local bar for this advice. It is wise at this time to discuss, and document, the lawyer's expected charges for settling the estate.

List the property that you cannot dispose of freely—property limited by joint tenancy, community property, your share of trust funds, life insurance already assigned to individuals, and so on—and put down opposite each item the amount that you are entitled to distribute:

- Cash
- Real estate
- Securities
- Life insurance payable to the estate
- Business interests
- Automobiles in your name
- Household furniture and furnishings that are not community property
- Personal effects
- Other property

Estimate expenses, debts, and taxes to be paid from your estate:

- Expense of last illness
- Funeral expenses
- Unpaid household bills
- Personal debts
- Mortgage or notes payable (just your share, if joint)
- Expense of administering the estate
- Taxes, such as real estate, estate, and inheritance

Provide liquid assets, if possible, in your estate to meet expenses, debts, and taxes. Be careful in making cash bequests. If your estate decreases, you may cut off residual legatees with little or nothing.

For a small estate, it is probably best for husbands and wives to make the other the executor of each other's estate. For a large estate or a complicated will, consider your bank as executor or coexecutor, for banks provide several advantages. The trust department of a bank has officials trained to handle large or complicated estates. A bank is normally a durable, financially responsible institution; has a fiduciary responsibility to act in your best interests; and receives no more for its services than an individual. Seek advice from your lawyer and banker.

You may technically prepare a will yourself, but depending on your legal domicile, an attorney, witnesses, or notary may be required to execute it properly. To avoid complications, it is best to rely on the expertise of the installation's legal assistance office or a competent private attorney.

File the original of your completed will in a safe deposit box or other secure location (or with the Navy Mutual Aid Association, if you belong), but be sure that your spouse and your executor possess copies of your latest will and know the location of and have access to the original.

During your lifetime, you will probably make a new will several times. Certain milestones indicate when to reconsider your will and bring it up to date:

- Change of legal residence
- Removal of the named executor to another state or his or her death
- Radical change in your estate
- Sale of property mentioned in your will
- Major changes in tax laws
- Marriage, divorce, or remarriage
- Birth or death of a child
- Death of your spouse

It is wise, in any case, to review your will every few years. You should certainly check it when changing legal residence (not change of station) to another state, as the provisions of your will may not be legal in that state and your executor may not be able to function there.

❯ DEATH AND BURIAL

Contemplating one's own demise has little appeal, but given the hazards of military service, taking a few moments to do so is time well spent. Knowledge and preparation can bring peace of mind.

❯ ❯ *Marine Corps Casualty Procedures*

The Marine Corps notifies the next of kin recorded on your RED in case you are seriously injured, wounded, killed, or missing. Your next of kin is kept advised of your condition while you are on the critical list.

When a Marine dies or is missing in action, a casualty assistance calls officer (CACO) is appointed from a nearby Marine Corps organization to advise and assist survivors. It is the CACO, usually accompanied by a chaplain and perhaps another command representative, who makes personal notification of the death or missing status to family. In the ensuing weeks, the CACO meets periodically with the next of kin and outlines the rights and benefits of survivors, helps prepare claims, and so forth.

Chaplain. The survivors of a deceased Marine (active or retired) should not fail to seek assistance from the chaplain of the nearest Marine Corps or naval activity. Not only can chaplains minister spiritually at this difficult time, but they are also ready to help with burial arrangements, transportation, and all the problems that arise after a Marine's death. Chaplains may assist the CACO with arrangements for burial in government or civilian cemeteries and, upon request, will normally conduct the funeral service, unless the next of kin prefer other arrangements.

Marine Officials. The nearest Marine commanding officer, recruiting officer, or inspector-instructor is competent and eager to assist families of deceased Marines with their problems.

❯ ❯ *Burial Arrangements*

When Death Occurs near a Navy or Marine Activity. When a Marine on active duty dies at or near his or her station, the CO takes charge and arranges for local burial or for shipment of the body at government expense.

Death at a Remote Place. When an officer on active duty dies at some distance from a military installation or hospital, the next of kin should contact the nearest Marine Corps or Navy activity for aid. If unable to contact a local activity, he or she should telephone the deceased's CO or HQMC, giving the deceased's full name, rank, and Social Security number; the date, place, and cause of death; and the place where burial is desired. Request instructions as to burial arrangements and provide current contact information.

Death in a Naval, Military, or Veterans Hospital (while in Inactive Status). When the death of a veteran or a retired or inactive officer occurs in a naval or military hospital or similar facility, the hospital authorities will make necessary arrangements upon request of the next of kin.

The Navy Mutual Aid Association has an outstanding pamphlet, *What to Do Immediately in Case of Death*, which is available on request. Obtain a copy of this and keep it with your important papers, as it is a complete checklist of essential information and actions required.

❖ ❖ *Burial Allowances*

Expenses for burial or shipment of the remains of a Marine who dies on active duty that are borne by the surviving spouse or another individual may be reimbursable. When the place of death is remote from a Marine Corps or naval installation or hospital, the surviving spouse or individual is well advised to consult carefully with the CACO, whom the Corps will assign. When it is impossible to obtain instructions from the CACO or other Marine or Navy authorities, the surviving spouse or individual may employ a local funeral director or, if necessary, arrange shipment of the body to the place of burial; in such cases, he or she should obtain itemized bills and receipts. Authorized categories of expenses are described below. Allowances are reasonable but may not cover charges for top-tier services. Because the precise allowances can change, it is best to consult the CACO, who will have access to the prevailing reimbursable amounts listed in the *CACO Guide to Benefits and Entitlements*.

Primary Expenses. Allowances will normally cover reasonable costs for removal of remains, embalming, casket, clothing, dressing, cosmetic/restorative procedures, permits, air tray, cremation, urn, and engraving.

Secondary Expenses. Allowances will normally cover reasonable costs for professional services, facilities, staff, church, limousines, gratuities, obituary notice, memorial items, one grave space, cemetery labor, headstone or marker, vault or outer enclosure, and columbarium.

Reimbursable amounts differ based on the following factors:

- Interment in a private cemetery
- Interment in a national cemetery
- Direct disposition to a national cemetery
- Cremation
- Whether there is government involvement with burial in a national or private cemetery

Transportation Expenses. Subject to limits, the cost of transportation is normally reimbursed in addition to primary and secondary expenses.

In the case of an honorably discharged, inactive, or retired veteran, the VA pays burial allowances, which are flat-rate monetary benefits generally paid at the maximum amount authorized by law for an eligible veteran's burial and funeral costs. The allowed amounts depend on whether the death is considered "service connected," whether the veteran was hospitalized in a VA medical facility at the time of death, and when the veteran died.

Allowances for burial and other services vary, depending on whether the death is service connected. You can find details on current allowances at the relevant VA website (https://www.va.gov/burials-memorials/).

Generally, no expenditure is authorized for shipping the remains of an officer who dies on inactive duty, such as in a retired status. Yet if the death occurred while the officer was properly hospitalized by the VA or under VA-contracted nursing-home care, some or all of the costs for transporting the remains may be reimbursed.

There is no interment expense for burial in one of the many national cemeteries situated around the country.

If next of kin have paid funeral expenses, they can claim reimbursement in writing with the assistance of the assigned CACO, stating the name and rank of the deceased and date and place of burial, and enclosing itemized bills in triplicate, receipted to show by whom payment was made and the dates when rendered. If funeral expenses have not been paid, unpaid bills in triplicate are forwarded as above.

If remains are claimed at the place of death for private burial, and the service of the government is declined, the next of kin thereby relieves the government of any obligation for funeral or transportation expenses.

❯❯ *Place of Burial*

You may be buried at the place of death, in a private cemetery near your home, or in an open national cemetery. Leave written instructions as to your choice. If burial is to be in a national cemetery, the funeral director should contact its superintendent. If your family lives near the selected national cemetery, the next of kin may request burial directly from the superintendent. Remains are cremated only on written request from the next of kin.

Arrangements for burial at sea may be initiated via either HQMC or local naval authorities. Burial at sea is not a right but a privilege. Under certain circumstances, it may not be feasible to accommodate such a request. Expenses incurred for delivery of remains to the point of embarkation on board a naval vessel must be paid by your survivors.

Military Funerals, Arlington National Cemetery. Funeral arrangements for burial in Arlington National Cemetery are made with the superintendent by the shipping activity, funeral director, or next of kin. HQMC can make hotel reservations for family and friends, meet transport, explain the different types of military funeral, and assist in the selection of honorary pallbearers and furnish their transportation. HQMC will also put the surviving spouse in touch with any organization that can assist in preparing applications for pensions, compensation, or other claims on the government.

After the next of kin has received confirmation from Arlington of the request for burial, he or she should contact the superintendent's office (and also pass the information on to HQMC), stating the number in the funeral party, the means of transportation, the date and hour of arrival, and whether local transportation and hotel reservations are required.

When you think of burial, remember that Quantico now has a national cemetery, a special place for those of us in the Corps.

❯❯ *Other Information*

Funeral Flag. A U.S. flag accompanies the remains and may be retained by the family. When death is remote from a naval or Marine activity, the postmaster of the county seat may furnish a flag.

Honors. When practical, and if requested, full military honors will be provided at the funeral of an officer (see *Marine Corps Manual*). But at cemeteries remote from both Marine Corps installations and Marine Corps Reserve activities, military honors are not always practicable, and relatives must make their own arrangements for funeral services. Veterans organizations usually can assist.

Gravestones. The government will provide a standard white headstone inscribed with the name, rank, and branch of service of the deceased. If burial is in a national cemetery, do not order a private monument until the design, material, and inscription have been approved by the National Cemetery Administration. The superintendent of the national cemetery concerned should be informed of plans for the headstone when you apply for the burial lot; many national cemeteries allow private markers only in certain areas.

Government headstones are provided for officers' dependents buried with the sponsor in national cemeteries.

Transportation for Family. One person may escort the body of an officer who dies on active duty to the place of burial. The escort may be a relative or friend (not in the service), with the government providing transportation in kind. If private burial is desired, a military escort usually accompanies the remains.

Household Effects. The household and personal effects of an officer who dies on active duty may be shipped from the last duty station or place of storage to the place the next of kin selects as home. Arrangements are made in the usual manner with the local traffic or distribution management officer. Shipment must take place within a year of death.

Death Certificates. For a death on inactive duty, the funeral director will obtain as many certificates as may be requested at a nominal cost ($1 to $2 each, depending on the locality). One is needed for each insurance company, for the will, for each claim, for HQMC, for the pay office carrying your accounts, and usually for the transfer of each account or asset held in joint ownership. For deaths on active duty, HQMC furnishes five copies of the official Report of Death, which will serve as a legal death certificate. Additional copies may be obtained on request.

➤ SURVIVOR BENEFITS AND ASSISTANCE

Current laws, which took effect in 1957 and have since been amended and extended, provide a greatly improved structure of benefits for eligible survivors of all officers and enlisted Marines who die on active service or, after separation from active service, die due to results from a condition incurred or aggravated

PERSONAL AND FAMILY MATTERS ❖❖ 581

during active duty. These benefits—federal government life insurance and Social Security (both already discussed above); Survivor Benefit Plan; death benefits (including back pay, death gratuity, dependency and indemnity compensation, pension for non-service-connected death, and compensation for unused leave); and other benefits—are described briefly.

❖ ❖ *Survivor Benefit Plan*

In the past, surviving members of a retired Marine's family often found themselves with little or no income after the retiree's death. The Survivor Benefit Plan (SBP) fills this gap, providing survivor income of up to 55 percent of your retired pay to your surviving spouse and dependent children. Until the plan's enactment, retired pay had ended with the retiree's death unless he or she had elected to take part in the old Retired Servicemen's Family Protection Plan.

If you have a spouse or dependent child at retirement time, you will be automatically enrolled in the SBP with maximum coverage when you retire, unless you specifically elect a lesser coverage or decline participation. You may only decline *with concurrence of your spouse.*

If you have no spouse or dependent child when you retire, you may either join the plan at that time by naming someone else as beneficiary or begin participation later if you acquire a spouse or child after retirement, although you must join within one year of acquiring said family members.

SBP survivor benefits are based on your retired pay at the time of death, not what you initially received or elected when you began. The cost of SBP will be checked from your retired pay (6.5 percent of that portion of retired pay you elect to cover). Because the government pays a substantial part of the SBP costs, your rate for participation might be considerably lower than if you purchased the same commercial coverage upon retirement.

The decision whether to elect the SBP is a big one. It is a complement to life insurance, not a substitute—it is taxable as an annuity, you have no equity in the plan, and you cannot cash it in or borrow against it. Whether it is best for you depends on your personal situation. Basically, if you have a long life expectancy upon retirement, adequate life insurance, and a solid estate, the plan has the disadvantages that you will probably receive reduced retired pay for many years, your surviving spouse may remarry (at which time payments cease unless remarriage is after age fifty-five) or die soon afterward (at which time payments cease), and he or she would receive little benefit in the end. On the other hand, if you have a relatively shorter life expectance, find additional life insurance costly, or simply value the peace of mind it affords, SBP may be an excellent means of augmenting insurance and other survivor benefits at a relatively small cost. The decision whether to participate should be carefully pondered.

❧ ❧ *Death Benefits*

Back Pay. Pay and allowances due to a deceased are payable to the persons designated to receive them on the RED. If the deceased did not make such a designation or if the person designated dies first, this payment is made to the surviving spouse or, if predeceased, to the children, then the parents. HQMC will send the necessary form to the person(s) eligible to receive this payment.

Compensation for Unused Leave. Your spouse or estate is eligible to claim and receive compensation for any unused leave to your credit should you die on active duty.

Death Gratuity to Active Personnel. The Marine Corps pays a death gratuity of $100,000 to the next of kin of Marines who die while on active duty (including those who die within 120 days of separation) because of service-connected injury or illness. If there is no surviving spouse or child, then parents or siblings designated as next of kin may be provided the benefit. The payment is normally arranged by the last command of the deceased. If the beneficiary is not paid automatically, application may be made to HQMC.

In case of financial distress, your spouse may apply to the nearest Marine command for help. The Navy and Marine Corps Relief Society may also help with either a grant or loan. (For further information, see the section addressing aid from other organizations.)

Dependency and Indemnity Compensation (DIC). DIC is a tax-free, monthly monetary benefit paid to eligible survivors of servicemembers who die in the line of duty or eligible survivors of veterans whose death resulted from a service-related injury or disease. The surviving spouse and/or children must meet certain eligibility requirements published by the VA and must submit proof of eligibility when applying.

Eligible survivors may apply for DIC in a variety of ways:

- Consult the CACO, who will assist in completing and submitting the Application for Dependency and Indemnity Compensation, Death Pension and Accrued Benefits by a Surviving Spouse or Child (VA Form 21-534)
- Work with an accredited representative or agent
- Go to a VA regional office and obtain the assistance of a VA employee
- Complete VA Form 21-534 and mail it to the Pension Management Center that serves the state or region

Based on 2020 figures, the VA pays DIC to the surviving spouse at the monthly rate of $1,357.56. This amount is increased by $336.32 for each eligible child under eighteen years of age. Eligible survivors are entitled to additional amounts if they meet certain criteria.

⁘ ⁘ *Other Benefits*

Hospital and Medical Care. Dependent parents, spouses, and children under age twenty-one of deceased Marines are eligible for certain civilian medical care on a cost-sharing basis and, in general, for space-available treatment at armed forces hospitals. They may receive outpatient medical service where such service is available.

Exchange and Commissary Privileges. Armed forces exchange and commissary privileges are available to the families of Marine Corps personnel upon presentation of a valid identification and privilege card. Before going overseas, be sure that these ID cards are current for each family member and that anyone over ten years of age has received a card.

Educational Assistance for Children of Marine Corps Personnel. From time to time, the Department of the Navy publishes a list of schools, colleges, universities, and other organizations that grant concessions and scholarships to children of servicemembers.

Navy Relief Educational Loans. The Navy–Marine Corps Relief Society may offer interest-free loans and grants ranging from $500 to $3,000 per academic year for undergraduate/postsecondary education at an accredited two- or four-year educational, technical, or vocational institution in the United States. This financial assistance is available for children of active duty, retired, or deceased Marines and Sailors and for spouses of active duty and retired Sailors and Marines. Information may be obtained from the Navy–Marine Corps Relief Society.

Family Educational Assistance. Administered by the VA, this program provides up to thirty-six months of schooling for spouses of deceased veterans, spouses of living veterans, and children of either (ages eighteen to twenty-six) when death or total, permanent disability arose from service. Spouses and children of Marines who were missing in action (MIA), prisoners of war (POWs), or forcibly detained or interned by a foreign power for more than ninety days are also eligible.

In certain cases, children with disabilities may begin special courses as early as age fourteen. In most cases, a child's eligibility ends with the twenty-sixth birthday.

Generally, eligibility for a spouse extends to ten years from the veteran's date of death or total, permanent disability, whichever is later. For spouses of MIAs or POWs, eligibility extends to ten years from the date the servicemember was so listed.

Naval Academy Preparatory Scholarships. The U.S. Naval Academy Foundation awards preparatory school scholarships to enable high school seniors who are the children of active, retired, or deceased Marine Corps, Navy, or Coast Guard personnel to prepare for entrance to the Naval Academy.

Employment. Important preferences are granted to surviving spouses, not remarried, in connection with examinations, ratings, appointments, and reinstatements under civil service and in connection with government reductions in force. Those interested should contact the U.S. Office of Personnel Management for information.

❧ ❧ *Aid from Organizations*

Several organizations offer advice and assistance to families of deceased Marines.

American Red Cross. This organization assists families with all types of government claims as well as other problems. Family members should consult the Red Cross field director at the nearest installation or the Red Cross chapter in their town. Proof of dependency is normally necessary.

Navy Mutual Aid Association. In case of death of a member, next of kin should contact the secretary of the association. Navy Mutual can be depended upon to handle all matters pertaining to pensions and other government claims.

Navy–Marine Corps Relief Society. This organization provides aid to members of the naval services and their dependents. Aid includes financial assistance (loan or grant); services of a Navy Relief nurse; help with transportation and housing; information about dependency allowances, pensions, and government insurance; location of and communication with naval personnel; and advice about community services. Apply to the local branch or through the website of the national office (http://www.nmcrs.org).

Tragedy Assistance Program for Survivors (TAPS). This program began with a group of bereaved military families who lost their loved ones in a military plane crash in Alaska in 1992. Formally founded in 1994, TAPS employs best practices found in peer-based support programs to assist anyone who is grieving the death of a servicemember, regardless of where or how he or she died. Grief counseling, case work, peer mentors, and care and support groups are a few of the services TAPS offers. Contact information for TAPS is available online (https://www.taps.org).

United Service Organizations (USO). Known for its centers at transportation hubs providing respite to traveling servicemembers and its entertainment programs for those deployed, the USO also supports families of deceased servicemembers. It often assists by making special travel accommodations for grieving families in transit at its airport centers around the world. The USO also supports families through partnerships with organizations like TAPS. Contact information for USO is available online (https://www.uso.org).

Veterans' Groups. The Military Officers Association of America, American Legion, Veterans of Foreign Wars, Disabled American Veterans, Military Order of the World Wars, Marine Corps Scholarship Foundation, and other veterans' groups may also render aid to survivors of Marine veterans.

❯ RETIRED OFFICER BENEFITS

When you retire, you automatically rate various Marine Corps benefits. You may also be entitled to various veterans' benefits if you apply for them. Some of these have already been mentioned, so this section sums up the most important ones. In connection with most veterans' benefits, it is important to know that, although your retired pay is taxable, it is not classified as "other income" and thus does not bar you from receipt or limit the extent of benefits for which you are otherwise eligible. But if you receive disability compensation from the VA, your retired pay is reduced by the amount of the VA disability payment.

❯ ❯ *Medical Care and Hospitalization*

As a retired Marine, you benefit from several health-care alternatives. These include TRICARE, VA-provided medical benefits, and other supplemental health-care insurance options.

TRICARE for Retirees. Retirees and their authorized family members remain eligible to use military treatment facilities, depending on availability, and civilian health-care facilities under TRICARE. Your eligibility remains in force until you are sixty-five years of age. Upon reaching that age and becoming eligible for Medicare, TRICARE ends, and you become eligible for TRICARE for Life, a supplemental insurance program.

TRICARE currently offers retirees two health-care options: TRICARE Prime and TRICARE Select. *TRICARE Prime* is a managed-care program. Retirees are required to pay an annual enrollment fee. They and their eligible family members are assigned a primary-care manager, who determines the most appropriate, available source of care at either a military treatment facility or a civilian network provider. Enrollees pay little or no copayment and are usually not required to file claims for their care.

TRICARE Select is a self-managed, preferred-provider network plan. Enrollment is unnecessary for retirees, but to minimize out-of-pocket costs, they and their eligible family members must obtain care from a TRICARE network provider. Retirees will be responsible for paying a small annual enrollment fee, annual deductible, and cost shares at a reduced rate. The network provider will normally file the health-insurance claims.

When they turn sixty-five years of age, retirees transition to *TRICARE for Life*, which is wraparound coverage that complements Medicare Parts A and B.

Retirees should contact a health-benefits adviser or beneficiary counselor at a nearby military treatment facility or stop by a TRICARE service center for more information and assistance.

U.S. Department of Veterans Affairs Health Care. Retired Marine officers continue to be eligible for VA medical care. The Veterans Health Administration is America's largest integrated health-care system, with over 1,700 health-care sites serving more than eight million veterans each year.

Obtaining VA-provided medical care requires enrollment during the annual enrollment process. It is wise to plan ahead, because this process can be lengthy, as the VA evaluates a variety of factors when determining and verifying a veteran's eligibility for enrollment. Once accepted, however, he or she remains enrolled in the VA health-care system and maintains access to VA health benefits.

This may be a good option if there is a well-regarded VA medical center nearby.

Federal Employees Dental and Vision Insurance Program. TRICARE's dental insurance program was discontinued, but military retirees are now eligible for the Federal Employees Dental and Vision Insurance Program (https://www .benefeds.com/), which is a voluntary dental and vision program available to federal employees and annuitants, retired uniformed servicemembers, and others. Participants pay an annual premium, copays, and cost shares that vary with the dental and vision services obtained.

Finally, *a word to the wise*: At the time of retirement, when your active duty health record is closed out, make a copy for personal retention in case of future VA claims or whenever you need attention from any other medical facility.

❧ ❧ *Veterans' Benefits*

As a veteran of military service, whether in time of war or peace, you have certain privileges and benefits. Although some of these are subject to expiration, Congress adds others from time to time. The following are the most important current benefits.

Department of Veterans Affairs. The VA offers a multitude of benefits to persons honorably discharged from the armed forces: special care and pensions for the physically and mentally impaired; hospital and domiciliary care; vocational rehabilitation; family benefits, including financial and education support; loans or loan guarantees for acquiring homes or farms and their upkeep and improvement; home remodeling for the disabled; nursing-home care; alcohol and drug rehabilitation; counseling services; and burial and funeral expenses. Consult your nearest VA field office. Once you are admitted to any program, including active duty VA loans and educational benefits, retain your VA file number for easy access to all future transactions.

Educational Assistance. The VA also provides education benefits to eligible servicemembers, veterans, and certain dependents and survivors. You may receive financial support for undergraduate and graduate degrees, vocational and technical training, licensing and certification tests, apprenticeships, on-the-job training, and more.

Post-9/11 GI Bill. The Post-9/11 GI Bill provides to eligible servicemembers and veterans up to thirty-six months of education benefits. These benefits may include financial support for school tuition and fees, books and supplies, and housing. Eligible veterans may also receive reimbursement for license or certification tests (such as broker, private investigator, and CPA), national tests (for example, Scholastic Aptitude Test, College Level Examination Program, American College Testing, Graduate Management Admission Test, and Law School Admission Test), or assistance for apprenticeships or on-the-job training. A one-time payment to support relocation from certain rural areas to attend school is also available.

Each type of benefit, such as tuition or books, has a maximum rate. Based on the length of your active service, you are entitled to a percentage of the maximum total benefit.

Montgomery GI Bill. The Montgomery GI Bill–Active Duty (MGIB-AD) provides eligible veterans up to thirty-six months of financial assistance for educational pursuits, including college, vocational or technical training, correspondence courses, apprenticeships or on-the-job training, flight training, high-tech training, licensing and certification tests, entrepreneurship training courses, and national examinations. Generally, your MGIB-AD benefits are paid directly to you on a monthly basis.

You may be eligible for MGIB-AD benefits while on or after separating from active duty. To receive benefits after separating, you must have received an honorable discharge. You generally have ten years from your last date of separation from active duty to use your MGIB-AD benefits.

Reserve officers are eligible for different VA educational benefits. They should investigate the VA benefits website for the most up-to-date information.

❥ ❥ *Travel on Government Aircraft*

Retired officers, and family members when accompanied by the sponsor, may travel, space available ("Space-A"), in government aircraft both within the continental limits of the United States and overseas. Yet be aware that there is no guaranteed space for any Space-A traveler. DOD is not obligated to continue an individual's travel or return him or her to the point of origin or any other point. Travelers must have sufficient resources to support themselves while awaiting transportation or pay for commercial transportation to return to their home or duty station if Space-A transportation is not available. Such travel is a privilege, not an entitlement.

Retired officers and accompanying family members who desire to travel Space-A may gather information and register to do so by contacting the Air Mobility Command passenger terminal from which they plan to depart. AMC personnel there are best positioned to provide the most current information about policies, procedures, routes, schedules, and waiting lists. Registration may be submitted in person or by fax, email, Internet, or mail. On the day of the desired flight, all passengers are required to be ready for travel at the designated "show time." To be considered travel ready, each prospective passenger must have all required documentation (with ID card and, of course, passport, visas as required, and immunization record, if required) and checked baggage; all accompanying family members must be present.

Routes and schedules vary, so, as mentioned, contact the various AMC terminals directly for the latest Space-A travel opportunities. Still, if your destination is the Pacific or the Far East, the AMC terminal at Travis Air Force Base, California, is perhaps the best option, although other West Coast terminals, such as Joint Base Lewis-McChord, Washington, may provide travel options. For destinations in Japan or Alaska, travelers have found flights available at Lewis-McChord and the AMC terminal at Seattle-Tacoma International Airport, Washington. For the Mediterranean or Latin America, the AMC terminal at Joint Base Charleston, South Carolina, has traditionally been a good source. And for Europe, the terminals at Joint Base McGuire-Dix-Lakehurst, New Jersey, and Dover Air Force Base, Delaware, have been good options.

Space-available travelers—especially retirees, who travel with the lowest priority—are subject to being "bumped" by official travelers and travelers on emergency orders at any point en route. Each passenger may check two pieces of luggage up to seventy pounds each plus one small hand-carried item. Finally, it bears repeating that Space-A travelers must have sufficient funds to proceed via commercial means if "bumped."

Detailed policies and procedures are available on the AMC Space-Available Travel website (https://www.amc.af.mil/AMC-Travel-Site/).

⁅ 21 ⁆

MARINE CORPS SOCIAL LIFE

We are all members of the same great family. . . . On social occasions the formality of strictly military occasions should be relaxed, and a spirit of friendliness and good will should prevail.
— Major General John A. Lejeune

YEARS AGO, officers and their families lived, worked, and socialized within a rather insulated community of fellow servicemembers. Most officers and families lived on board bases, and the nearby civilian communities often offered less in the way of social attractions and recreational diversions than did the bases. With World War II, the military services expanded, and the separate military and civilian societies blended. In the postwar period, the United States continued to be internationally engaged, and the peacetime military remained robust and active globally. Civilian communities surrounding military bases grew and prospered. These phenomena brought that old insular military society to a gentle close. Today, military officers live, commute, and mix freely with their civilian counterparts.

Many enjoyable trappings of that traditional military society remain, and you may even want to share them occasionally with civilian friends. While a few of these traditional events have become extinct for practical purposes, they are discussed here for reference in case they are revived in isolated instances or celebrated in a foreign country in which you serve.

As you become a Marine and join the corps of officers, you must also be prepared to share the time-honored and pleasant social traditions of your Corps. As you do, remember one thing above all: the phrase "an officer and a gentleman/ gentlewoman" remains a current one in the Marine Corps. It means what it says.

➤ SOCIAL OCCASIONS

➤➤ *Marine Corps Birthday*

As every Marine knows, the Corps was founded on 10 November 1775. From that day to the present, 10 November has been the climax of the Marine Corps year and the occasion for the top social event of the Corps.

A friend, colleague, and great Marine—albeit not renowned outside of aviation circles or sparsely attended Operation Desert Storm reunions—somewhat irreverently refers to this date as the beginning of "Marine Corps Ramadan," so dubbed because it begins a period filled with observances, holidays, and annual leave. During this period, Marines struggle to balance these "rites" with normal work. "Marine Corps Ramadan" ends with the New Year.

The birthday of the Corps is celebrated officially and socially by all Marines throughout the world. Not only do Marine units carry out the prescribed ceremony but also wherever one or more Marines are stationed—on board ship, at posts of other services, even in the field—10 November is celebrated.

How a Command Observes 10 November. For a Marine command, the birthday celebration includes prescribed or customary features that are observed as circumstances permit. For Marines on duty with other services, many of these items cannot be fulfilled exactly, but this list may serve as a guide:

• Hold a troop formation (preferably a parade and cake-cutting ceremony) for publication of Article 38 from the *Marine Corps Manual* (see appendix IV). The uniform should be a blue dress "A" or an authorized variation thereof that is appropriate to the climatic conditions. If blues cannot be worn, the service uniform is acceptable. On board ship, hold a special formation of all Marines and get permission from the captain to pipe the birthday article over the public-address system. If you are with some other service and only a few Marines are present, you may defer publishing the article until the evening social function.

The ceremonial cake cutting is the traditional highlight of the annual Marine Corps birthday celebration.

- Provide holiday rations, which should include a main course of roast beef or steak, accompanied by a lobster tail or shrimp.
- Authorize maximum liberty and minimum work consistent with the missions of the command.
- Hold a birthday ball for officers and one for enlisted Marines. At each, a cake-cutting ceremony takes place. Circumstances sometimes dictate (for example, at smaller commands) a single, all-hands ball.

Any training or instruction scheduled for 10 November should emphasize the traditions and history of the Corps.

The Birthday Ball. Marines celebrate the annual birthday ball with pride, forethought, and care. Whenever possible, every Marine command must have one. If on detached service away from the Corps, the senior Marine officer present must take charge and make every effort to arrange a suitable birthday ball, and every Marine must chip in to support it.

The birthday ball is formal, which means evening dress for officers who possess it or blue dress (with large medals) as a substitute. Those who are not required to possess either evening dress or blues wear service uniform.

As a command performance, unless duty prevents, you attend the birthday ball. If resources permit, distinguished civilian guests and officers from other services should be invited, although not too many. It is also customary to include retired Marine officers and any marine officers present from other countries.

Most commands have well-established procedures for conduct of the birthday ball. If your current command does not, you can easily borrow one from a previous or adjacent command. Details may vary according to facilities, numbers of officers and guests, and local traditions. There is only one ironclad rule for the birthday ball: Make it a good one!

⋗ ⋗ *Mess Night*

A mess night (also called a guest night or a dining-in, in some circles) is a formal military dinner. Mess nights may be held to acknowledge special anniversaries, such as that of a battle in which the unit participated, to recognize officers being detached, or to honor a distinguished guest or guests from another unit, service, or country. The dinner includes a set agenda, and, by custom, attendance by all officers (or sometimes all members) of the command or unit is obligatory.

A variation of the mess night, a "dining-out" includes spouses and often omits some of a mess night's more formal and traditional elements.

In the U.S. armed forces, mess nights date back to the Army's regimental messes of the pre–World War I days and, among the naval services, to the days of the wine mess in the wardroom afloat, which ended abruptly in 1914 when Secretary Josephus Daniels imposed prohibition on the Navy. In this early era of a small Corps with only several hundred officers, the only permanent Marine officers' mess was at "Eighth and Eye," where the officers of Headquarters (HQMC) and The Marine Barracks Washington had their mess nights in the Old Center House (torn down in 1908).

Chapter 8 of the *Social Usage and Protocol Handbook* provides a useful, official discussion of the major features of a mess night.

Preparation. The first step in preparing for a mess night is to designate the officer who will act as vice president. In some units, the vice president is traditionally the junior lieutenant present. Yet it is good practice to rotate the post among all company officers on board so that all may gain experience. In any case, the function of the vice president, at least beforehand, is to make all preliminary arrangements—guest list, seating diagram, and menu, all to be approved by the mess president; catering details; music; decorations; and so forth. The success of the evening depends on this officer, who is typically addressed as "Mister Vice" or "Madame Vice" as appropriate.

Subject to local or unit customs and available facilities, these are the specific arrangements that should be made for a mess night:

- Unless the commanding officer desires to preside, a field-grade officer— often the executive officer—is detailed as president of the mess for the occasion; a company-grade officer acts as vice president.
- After approval of the guest list, invitations should be prepared and mailed or delivered at least two weeks in advance of the mess night. Each person, regardless of organization or of sponsoring officer in the host unit, is a guest of the mess and should be so treated.
- Uniform is evening or mess dress, blue dress "A," or blue-white dress "A." Civilians invited to a mess night should wear full dress with miniature medals if uniform is evening or mess dress; dinner jacket with miniatures if blues or blue-whites.
- The table is set with complete dinner service, including wine glasses, candles, and flowers.
- The National Color and the Marine Corps Color are placed behind the president's chair. Guidons and drums may also be used as decorations.
- The mess president sits at the head of the table, the vice president at the foot. Other guests and members take seats by rank (as in the wardroom on board ship), except that guests of honor are on the right and left of the president. A seating diagram should be posted in advance, and place cards and menu cards prepared. The vice president supervises all preliminary arrangements.
- If available, a three- or four-piece military band detachment should be detailed to provide dinner music. The orchestra should know the national anthems and regimental marches of guest officers. If suitable

"live" music is not available, a good-quality public-address system with recorded selections will serve as a substitute. The musical program should be checked and timed by the vice president and should always include "Semper Fidelis" and the regimental march of each guest.

- In some messes and commands, the custom of emulating the Continental Marines endures by drinking toasts of rum punch rather than port. Here is the mix for "1775 Rum Punch": four parts dark rum, two parts lime juice, one part pure maple syrup. Add a small amount of grenadine syrup to taste. Ice generously and stir well. The maple syrup was originally used during the Revolution because of the British blockade that cut off supplies of West Indies sugar cane.

Procedure. Officers assemble in an anteroom at least thirty minutes before dinner for cocktails and to greet guests. This provides all officers the opportunity to welcome and become acquainted with guests of the mess. It is also the occasion for each officer to pay respects informally to the senior officers present.

Dinner is announced according to local custom. In some messes, "Semper Fidelis" is played; elsewhere, Officers' Call is sounded followed by a march, and when drum and bugle corps is available, "Sea Soldiers" is a suitable march. Still another variation is to play "The Roast Beef of Old England" (known previously as "Officers' Mess Gear") on fife and drum. Whatever the signal, officers and guests proceed to their places. A member of the mess should escort each guest. The chaplain, if present, says a brief grace; otherwise, the president of the mess fulfills this role. Officers then take their seats. The ranking guest, seated at the mess president's right, is served first, then the president, and so on counterclockwise without further regard to seniority. Appropriate wines are served with each course. There must be no smoking during dinner, and no officer may leave the table until after the toasts except by permission from the president. (If for any reason, official or otherwise, you arrive late, you should express your regrets to the mess president before taking your seat.)

After dessert, there is a short concluding grace, the table is cleared, and preparations are made for a succession of formal toasts, speeches, and informal toasts. Port decanters and glasses are placed on the table in preparation for a series of formal toasts. The port passes clockwise until all glasses are charged. When

After a long hike, Marine officers at Camp Pendleton, California, build comradery during an informal mess night in the field in 2017.

the decanter has completed the circuit (or both decanters, if two are used), the president raps for silence. If a foreign officer is present, his or her head of state is toasted first; otherwise, toasts begin with the president of the United States.

To begin, the president rises, lifts a glass, and says, for example, "Mister (or Madame) Vice, His Majesty, King _____ of _____." The vice president then rises, glass in hand, waits until all have risen, and gives the toast. "Ladies and gentlemen, His Majesty, King _____ of _____." The orchestra plays the appropriate foreign national anthem, following which all say, "King _____ of _____," drink, and resume seats. Good-natured conversation may resume. After about a minute, the president again raps for silence, the senior foreign officer rises and says, "Ladies and gentlemen, the president of the United States," and the orchestra plays the National Anthem. Subsequently, there is a series of additional formal toasts, the subjects of which may depend on the occasion or circumstances surrounding the mess night. Normally, designated members of the mess offer formal toasts in preplanned succession, with each one seconded by the vice president. If the guest of honor is from another service, a toast to that service is in order.

After the formal toasts, coffee is typically served, the smoking lamp is lighted, and the president rises and introduces the guest of honor, who then addresses the mess. If the impending departure of an officer occasions the mess night, the CO makes brief, usually humorous remarks, whereupon the officer being honored replies in the same vein. In some messes, the orchestra remains and plays the regimental march of each guest, during which the individual stands. After this, or whenever the orchestra is released, the president may send for the orchestra leader and offer a drink.

Following speeches, the president may open the floor to informal toasts offered by members of the mess. During this period, any member of the mess who wishes to initiate a toast rises and addresses the president. On being recognized, the member briefly presents his or her rationale for the toast, followed by the toast itself. Inspired wit and subtle sarcasm are much appreciated in these presentations. If the president deems the toast justified, he or she will direct the vice president to second it in the same manner as in the formal toast.

The concluding traditional toast is always to the Marine Corps, during which, if music is available, "The Marines' Hymn" is played. The wording of this toast should be, "Mister (or Madame) Vice, Corps and Country," and the custom has grown up (proposed long years ago by Colonel A. M. Fraser) that the vice president reply in words taken from a Revolutionary War recruiting poster of the Continental Marines: "Long live the United States, and success to the Marines!"

Apart from the evening's concluding traditional toast, formal and informal toasts are not "bottoms up." Do not be caught in the position of having an uncharged glass!

The traditional toast ends the formal part of the evening. At this point, the president announces, "Ladies and gentlemen, will you join me in the bar?" and the senior officers rise and depart the dining room, following which the remaining members of the mess adjourn individually to the bar and anteroom, where songs may be sung and games played. All hands should remain until the ranking guest and the CO leave, after which anyone may secure at discretion.

Concluding Thoughts. Circumstances often do not permit a mess night with all formalities as to uniform, catering, and table service that are outlined above—or all of them might not be desired. Organizations should nevertheless make the effort. The idea is to make the best of what you have and let the spirit of the occasion take care of the rest. Do not let yourself be overcome or stultified by the apparent formality of mess nights; the object is the pleasure and comradeship of all hands. There have been reports that a few commands have actually rehearsed mess nights; if true, this surely drained every drop of enjoyment from the occasion.

The costs of a mess night, like other "chip-in" Marine Corps social functions, should be prorated by rank so that officers who make the most, pay the most.

Finally, it is better not to schedule mess nights too regularly. It is much preferable that officers begin asking when the next one will take place. Thus, a mess night will be looked forward to with anticipation and never become a burden.

❖ ❖ *Military Wedding*

As a Marine officer, you enjoy the privilege of having a military wedding. This is simply a formal wedding with traditional service embellishments. The following describes the characteristic features and ground rules of a military wedding.

Uniform. Marine members of the wedding party wear blue dress "A" with sword. Dress "A" uniforms call for medals, not ribbons. If the weather requires, wear boat cloak rather than overcoat, if available. Even though wearing sword, and thus under arms, the bride and groom should not wear gloves, whereas the ushers should wear gloves throughout the ceremony.

Naturally, all servicemembers of the wedding party wear the same uniform. If officers from other services are included, they wear their nearest equivalent uniform. For an evening wedding, evening dress is worn. Civilian members of the wedding party wear civilian formal.

Wedding Party and Ushers. Since your wedding is to be military, members of the wedding party and ushers may be Regular or Reserve officers. Inactive Reserve officers may don uniforms for the occasion. It is usual for ushers to be the same rank as the bride or groom, although this is not mandatory. The senior usher coordinates or signals for movements by the ushers and for the arch of swords.

The best man looks out for the groom. The maid/matron of honor performs the same function for the bride. Although a brother or close friend customarily serves as best man, it is permissible and considered a nice compliment for a male officer to ask his immediate commander (if close in rank and on those terms) to be the best man. Under analogous circumstances, a female officer could appropriately ask her immediate commander to be the maid/matron of honor. In any case, however, your CO and fellow officers should be invited to the wedding, and all should attend.

In the unlikely event the wedding takes place away from the bride's home and her parents or near relatives cannot attend—as is sometimes the case in the service—it is appropriate for the CO or other senior officer to give away the bride.

The Clergy. You may choose either a chaplain or a civilian member of the clergy. A chaplain performs the ceremony in uniform or vestments, according to the customs of the denomination. In some denominations (such as the Episcopal Church), ministers, whether chaplain or civilian, are permitted to wear military ribbons on their vestments and will do so at your request. The best man should see to this.

Do not pay a chaplain for officiating at a military wedding. If you have a member of the civilian clergy officiate, follow civilian custom regarding fees. Again, this is something the best man traditionally handles. The same applies to fees for an organist and music at the church.

Wedding under the Colors. If you wish and your denomination permits, the National Color and Marine Corps Color of your unit may be crossed above and in the rear of the chaplain or displayed in the chancel of the church during the ceremony. This is known as "a wedding under the colors." It is an old tradition, signifying your spouse's acceptance into the Corps.

Handling the colors for this ceremony is the responsibility of the senior usher, who, with designated ushers, receives the colors (cased) from the adjutant, places them before the ceremony, and removes, cases, and returns them immediately afterward.

Arch of the Swords. This is probably the most distinctive feature of a military wedding, and the tradition represents a salute to the newly married couple. It is executed in the following manner:

1. After the ceremony, the senior usher forms the ushers—normally numbering six or eight—in two columns immediately outside the exit of the church, facing inboard. Wedding guests assemble outside to view the event before it begins.
2. As the newly married couple passes through the portal, the senior usher introduces the them appropriately.

3. The senior usher then gives the preparatory command, "Officers, draw," pauses briefly, and then commands, "Swords."

4. At the command of execution, ushers carry out only the first count of the movement and leave their swords raised, with tips touching and blades pointed upward, to form an arch under which the couple passes.

5. After the newlyweds have passed, swords are returned on command by the senior usher.

Cutting the Wedding Cake. The wedding cake is cut by the bride and groom together, using the servicemember's sword. If two Marine Corps officers are marrying, it is proper to use the senior's sword. After the cake has been cut, the best man proposes a toast to the bride and groom, and, as the guests drink, the orchestra plays "Auld Lang Syne."

❯ ❯ *Calls*

A *call* is a brief, usually formal social visit. The exchange of calls once received emphasis in military society far exceeding that in civilian life, although the practice has somewhat fallen into disuse. If only for historical interest, it is worth briefly discussing calls here, especially if one day you rise to levels of the defense establishment or serve in a foreign country where the practice is still observed.

There are two types of calls: official and personal. Official calls are still practiced in some circumstances (see chapter 11). These are rendered only between COs, officers of state, and officers' messes.

Personal calls are exchanged among officers and their families. Although a bit ritualistic, they serve several functions. Such visits break down barriers of seniority, widen one's circle of acquaintances, and reveal mutual interests that might otherwise remain undiscovered. Making calls—for example, on one's CO—is no longer common practice. Instead, the function formerly served by calls is largely accomplished during a "hail and farewell," a periodic command gathering during which the CO introduces newly joined officers and their families and recognizes the contributions and achievements of officers departing for a new permanent posting.

Should you find yourself in a situation warranting a personal call, it is worthwhile to do some research. Service customs govern personal calls, but some COs have special preferences as to when and how calls are paid. Thus, before making any personal calls, check with the adjutant and, if necessary, with the general's aide (or, if serving with the Navy, the flag lieutenant) to find out the local policies. Twenty minutes (or "one drink") is the accepted duration of a formal personal call.

❯ ❯ *Hail and Farewell*

A hail and farewell is an informal command gathering at which the CO welcomes—or "hails"—officers and their families who have recently joined the unit and bids farewell to departing officers and their families. It is a casual social event that builds camaraderie within the command and, among other aims, accomplishes what personal calls formerly achieved. It also provides the opportunity to publicly recognize the service to the command of departing officers and their families. A hail and farewell is meant to be an enjoyable event you attend enthusiastically; you should nevertheless consider it a place of duty unless you are otherwise engaged in a time-sensitive mission or task important to the command.

Although there is no fixed periodicity for a hail and farewell, commands commonly hold them quarterly. If held more frequently, the event may be perceived as burdensome. When less frequent, they often fail to serve their purpose: newly joined officers are no longer "new," and departing officers may have departed without appropriate recognition from the command.

Likewise, there is no prescribed format for a hail and farewell. There are as many styles for this ceremony as there are commands and commanders. The one overarching rule is that they should be casual, enjoyable gatherings that renew the bonds of camaraderie and friendship among the unit's officers and their families. Here are a few ideas to consider should you be involved in planning a hail and farewell:

- Hold the event at a convenient, pleasing location. The officers' club or lounge is an ideal venue.
- Consider the schedules of those to be hailed or bid farewell—officers and their families—when selecting date and time. It is often a good idea to schedule the hail and farewell during the latter part of the workday on a Wednesday or Thursday, although consideration in scheduling should also be given to the needs of working spouses and school-age children.
- The XO must ensure that all officers attend.

- For attire, uniform of the day normally suffices.
- Allow some time for libations and socializing before commencing the informal agenda of the hail and farewell.
- Hails are brief introductions by the CO of the new officers. When bidding farewell to an officer, the CO will normally speak a bit longer on the contributions and achievements of the departing officer and, if applicable, spouse, then turn the floor over to the departing officer for brief remarks.
- Depending on the size of the unit, a well-run hail and farewell need last no more than about two hours.
- It is a failure of leadership when an officer is permitted to depart for a new posting without a proper farewell.

Typically, the XO or adjutant will help orchestrate a hail and farewell. Where it is a command practice, the adjutant is additionally responsible for procuring mementos for departing officers.

❧ CLUBS AND MESSES

Every base or station has a commissioned officers' mess in some form. It acts as a social focus for the officers and spouses of the installation, serves meals, and sometimes provides accommodations for visiting officers.

Today, the commissioned officers' mess is most often referred to as the "club" or the "officers' club." Like any club, the mess is a private association operated for the convenience of its members on Marine bases and stations by Marine Corps Community Services, a department or division of the installation. Although you are not automatically a member of every commissioned officers' mess at every station just because of your rank and status, it is nonetheless habitual to extend privileges of a station mess to any visiting officer and family. At your home station, you are automatically a member the commissioned officers' mess upon payment of the required membership fees, if any, as membership fees are rare today.

❧ *Officers' Clubs and Bachelor Officer Quarters*

Officers' clubs and unmarried or bachelor officer quarters, when available, have three main functions: social recreation, meal service, and housing for bachelor, temporary bachelor, and visiting officers. Any officer assigned temporarily or permanently to a BOQ normally pays a fixed charge to take care of cleaning services, linen, and so forth. In certain BOQs with messing facilities, officers living therein pay for and take meals at given rates on a menu catered by the base officers' club. In a few cases (for example, Camp Barrett at Quantico), the base central mess operates the officers' dining facility and serves (and charges for) the basic ration. Where a BOQ does not have a messing capability, you may take your meals at the officers' club (or possibly in an officers' section of a unit mess hall).

Closely related to the BOQ are its derivatives, married officer quarters (MOQ) and transient officer quarter (TOQ). An MOQ is usually an apartment building.

❧ ❧ *The Wardroom Mess*

A wardroom mess is a commissioned officers' mess on board ship. The wardroom is the common room, recreational space, and dining room for the officers of a Navy warship. The wardroom mess, or simply "wardroom," is the organization through which the ship's officers cater their meals and meet most of their social and recreational needs while on board. Like any closed mess, it is a private association whose operation is paid for by members. Because they fulfill essential functions of feeding and accommodation, wardroom messes receive some government support. You will find notes about wardroom-mess etiquette in chapter 9. If you are going to sea duty, be sure to look up these rules—and observe them.

❧ ❧ *Mess Etiquette*

Before leaving the subject of clubs and messes, here are some general rules of conduct and etiquette that have always maintained the tone and correctness of Marine officers' messes.

Remember that the mess belongs to the members who support it. As a guest, defer to their ways and rules; as a member, assume responsibility for it and support it as your mess.

Dress conservatively and correctly at the club. You cannot go wrong, ordinarily, if you wear full uniform of the day or complete civilian clothes. What is considered appropriate civilian attire at the officers' mess varies around the country and around the world. Clubs in Hawaii and on the West Coast tend to be more casual; clubs on the East Coast and overseas, less casual. The dining room in an officers' mess may require more formal attire than an adjacent officers' lounge. Most messes publish and post their uniform rules. You, your guests, and your family members must abide by them if you expect to use the club.

If your officers' mess still maintains member accounts, sign chits legibly and accurately, pay your bills promptly, and always be sure your bank account is in shape to meet any checks you write. The officers' mess is founded on the proven concept that a Marine officer's word or signature is his or her bond. Dishonorable disregard of your obligations as an officer will destroy your personal standing, weaken your mess, force irksome restrictions on other members, and bring swift retribution—and it will mar your record.

Tip mess employees as you would in a civilian restaurant or bar unless the mess rules specify otherwise.

When you bring guests to the mess, be sure they are people you would entertain in your own home or introduce, as your friends, to the commanding general and spouse.

Whether in a private club or a service mess, remember that an officer of Marines is well mannered. If in doubt as to some nicety or ground rule, be gracious.

⋗ WASHINGTON DUTY

⋗ ⋗ *White House and Diplomatic Functions*

The White House is a focus of social and official Washington. Although rare for junior officers, some officers on duty in Washington may find themselves invited to the White House, and a few are detailed to additional duty as Marine aides-de-camp at the Executive Mansion.

Because a White House invitation constitutes a presidential command, it takes precedence over any other social commitment, previous or not. If you receive such an invitation, consult one of the aides to the commandant at Marine Corps Headquarters. The aide will tell you the appropriate uniform and give you whatever briefing may be in order.

Second only to White House functions in their requirement for fine attention to dress and etiquette are those conducted by the diplomatic corps. Uniform is ordinarily worn for official parties at embassies or legations or those given by a military or naval attaché. The general rule is some variation of blues for afternoon receptions and cocktail parties and evening dress for formal evening parties.

When at a diplomatic party, be alert for and familiar with foreign badges and insignia of rank and with the host country's national anthems. On occasions of this kind, your dignity, courtesy, and smartness set you apart not only as a Marine but also as a representative of the United States.

Service Etiquette is an invaluable reference if your duties immerse you in the Washington social scene.

❯ ❯ Recreation in the Washington Area

Private Clubs. The Washington area boasts two of the foremost military and naval clubs in the country: The Army and Navy Club (the "Town Club") and the Army and Navy Country Club (the "Country Club").

The Army and Navy Club, located on historic Farragut Square in Washington, is one of the senior private clubs in the United States and provides all amenities (including rooms for members and guests). The Town Club is a traditional meeting place for officers and their friends. The Army and Navy Country Club, in Arlington, Virginia, overlooking the capital city, is one of the nation's top-quality country clubs (with a first-rank golf course).

Both the Town Club and Country Club allow newly commissioned officers to join, as nonresidents, on very advantageous terms. If you fail to take advantage of this privilege at the outset of your career, you must later negotiate waiting lists and pay relatively large initiation fees, which may make it impossible for you to be a member of these fine clubs. Membership on these inviting terms is one of the best bargains open to a new officer; lose no time in taking advantage of it.

❯ MARINE CORPS SOCIAL CUSTOMS

❯ ❯ Standing Social Customs

Having existed for hundreds of years, the Marine Corps has many customs and traditions—some borrowed, some evolved. Certain social customs and traditions are observed throughout the Corps and deserve mention here.

Wetting Down Your Commission. Whenever you are promoted, you are obligated to host a "wetting-down party." At this affair, the new commission (which was once traditionally displayed at some conspicuous but safe vantage point) is said to be "wet down." When several officers are promoted together, they may join in a single wetting-down party.

Cigars. If you are a new parent, it is common and appreciated to distribute cigars or candy to all officers and staff NCOs of your unit.

Five Aces. Dice games are common in Marine Corps officers' clubs. Any officer who rolls five aces when throwing dice for refreshments in a mess is obliged to buy a complete round of drinks for all who are present in the bar. In large, crowded messes, this custom is eased to the extent that you must buy drinks only for your own party.

Entering a Mess Covered. Unless you are on duty and under arms, if you enter a mess covered, you are liable to buy all present a round of drinks. Most messes adhere to and post the old rule, "He who enters covered here buys the house a round of cheer." In fact, some even have a bell and lanyard that may be rung by anyone present who spots an offender against this rule, thus signaling a free round.

Placing Your Cover on the Bar. Those who place their headgear on the bar are also liable to buy the house a round of drinks.

Drawing Your Sword in a Mess. The seagoing rule that any officer who unsheathes a sword in the wardroom must buy a round also applies on shore, if you are so unwary as to draw sword in any public room of an officers' mess. The custom goes back to the days of dueling, when this was one method of cooling off hotheads and restricting indiscreet sword play.

Send-Off. When a unit leaves, the CO, band, and friends see them off. If the move is routine, the band plays "Auld Lang Syne" as aircraft embarkation is completed, the transport casts off its last line, or the train gets under way. If the unit is bound for war or expeditionary service, "The Marines' Hymn" is the send-off. In either case, the departing unit should be played down to the airfield, dock, or loading platform by "Semper Fidelis."

Special Courtesy to Commanding Officers and Senior Guests. At any social functions—cocktail parties and receptions especially—you have certain special obligations to your CO and his or her spouse and to the guest of honor, if any. On your arrival (or on the CO's arrival, if later than yours), both you and your spouse should make it a point to approach and speak to the CO and spouse as soon as practicable. This was once known as "making your number." Except when absolutely necessary, you should not depart before your CO and the guest of honor do so. If you must leave early, however, express your regret to your CO and ask permission. It is a mark of poor military courtesy and social manners if either you or your spouse fails to observe these courtesies.

❧ ❧ *Social Dos and Don'ts*

Common sense, tact, and ordinary courtesy are the fundamentals of social success in the Marine Corps. For fine points and unusual situations, you may wish to refer to the tested references listed in the next section or some other recognized social guide such as *Emily Post's Etiquette*. The following pointers are supplementary but worth bearing in mind.

When you are on board a base, station, or ship, in uniform ashore, or otherwise recognizable as a Marine officer, your conduct must be impeccable. "If you must raise hell," goes an old Marine proverb, "do it at least a mile away from the flagpole."

It was once written, "The ideal income is a thousand dollars a day—and expenses." Obviously, you stand no chance of attaining this on military pay, although a few inexperienced or improvident officers try to live as if they had it. You cannot fool anybody as to how much you make, so live within your means.

"Good clothes open all doors"—be sure yours are correct both for style and occasion. Always check to see which uniform is prescribed before you attend a social function.

"It is easier to be critical than correct"—avoid criticism about other officers, and never vent destructive criticism of your service, your unit, or your superiors.

Be punctual. It is never wrong to arrive exactly on time for a social function, although it is sometimes considered a courtesy to the host or hostess to arrive perhaps ten minutes after the appointed start time. For large parties and receptions, you may arrive not later than a half hour after the announced time. For seated meals, it is best to be exactly on time. "Punctuality is the politeness of kings."

Do not fill up social conversation with technical language, and refrain from applying Marine Corps terms to civilian matters. On the other hand, as a professional, learn the talk and nomenclature of the Corps. Use precise terms to convey precise meanings. Avoid undue shop talk and thus avoid becoming the character whom Joseph Addison so well described: "The military pedant always talks in a camp, and is storming towns, making lodgements [*sic*] and fighting battles from one end of the year to the other. Everything he speaks smells of gunpowder; if you take away his artillery from him, he has not a word to say for himself."

Polite society is no place to play "the tough Marine." Courtesy and personal modesty are never more becoming than in an officer. Rudeness, abruptness, gory tales of blood and guts, and coarse language usually show up the greenhorn or counterfeit—certainly the ill-mannered.

At a mess or at any official function, politics, religion, and sex are discussed (if at all) only with the greatest discretion. Whatever you do, never speak ill of your Corps or of any fellow officer in the presence of outsiders, civilians, or members of any other service. And remember always, insofar as public utterances are concerned, an American soldier has no politics and espouses no political party or cause.

Remember that your spouse does not and cannot wear your rank. Be certain that he or she understands this quite clearly and does not exhibit a tendency to dominate the juniors or subordinates. This will only belittle your rank in the eyes of others. Insist, however, that your spouse receive due courtesy.

"Be prepared" is just as good a social motto for Marine officers as for Boy and Girl Scouts. Before you attend any social function, ascertain the dress, whether there will be a receiving line, who will receive, when the line closes, and who of importance to the Marine Corps may attend. All of these are the essential elements of information that help place you at ease and prepare you for any social eventuality.

❥ ❥ *Helpful References*

This chapter was not intended to thoroughly cover etiquette and protocol for Marine officers, but simply to deal with the military—and more especially the Marine—aspects of service social life. For more general and complete reference, consult the latest editions of the following publications:

- *Service Etiquette* (Naval Institute Press, 2013). This classic is a sound general guide, indispensable in certain matters.
- *Social Usage and Protocol Handbook: A Guide for Personnel of the U.S. Navy* (Department of the Navy). This government publication, for many years withheld from general circulation by DON civil servants, is a

comprehensive, useful handbook. Any officer going on attaché, military assistance group, or naval mission duties should obtain a copy.

• *Protocol for the Modern Diplomat* (Department of State). Although not specifically designed for the military community, this remains a useful compilation containing many excellent suggestions and much good advice.

Appendix I

"The Marines' Hymn"

From the Halls of Montezuma
To the shores of Tripoli,
We fight our country's battles
In the air, on land, and sea.
First to fight for right and freedom,
And to keep our honor clean,
We are proud to claim the title
Of United States Marine.

Our flag's unfurl'd to every breeze
From dawn to setting sun;
We have fought in ev'ry clime and place
Where we could take a gun.
In the snow of far-off northern lands
And in sunny tropic scenes,
You will find us always on the job—
The United States Marines.

Here's health to you and to our Corps
Which we are proud to serve;
In many a strife we've fought for life
And never lost our nerve.
If the Army and the Navy
Ever look on Heaven's scenes,
They will find the streets are guarded
By United States Marines.

Appendix II

Commandants of the Marine Corps

Major Samuel Nicholas, 1775–81
Lieutenant Colonel William Ward Burrows, 1798–1804
Lieutenant Colonel Franklin Wharton, 1804–18
Lieutenant Colonel Anthony Gale, 1819–20
Brigadier General Archibald Henderson, 1820–59
Colonel John Harris, 1859–64
Brigadier General Jacob Zeilin, 1864–76
Colonel Charles G. McCawley, 1876–91
Major General Charles Heywood, 1891–1903
Major General George F. Elliott, 1903–10
Major General William P. Biddle, 1911–14
Major General George Barnett, 1914–20
Major General John A. Lejeune, 1920–29
Major General Wendell C. Neville, 1929–30
Major General Ben H. Fuller, 1930–34
Major General John H. Russell Jr., 1934–36
Lieutenant General Thomas Holcomb, 1936–43
General Alexander A. Vandegrift, 1944–47
General Clifton B. Cates, 1948–51
General Lemuel C. Shepherd Jr., 1952–55
General Randolph M. Pate, 1956–59
General David M. Shoup, 1960–63
General Wallace M. Greene Jr., 1964–67
General Leonard F. Chapman Jr., 1968–71
General Robert E. Cushman Jr., 1972–75

General Louis H. Wilson Jr., 1975–79
General Robert H. Barrow, 1979–83
General Paul X. Kelley, 1983–87
General Alfred M. Gray Jr., 1987–91
General Carl E. Mundy Jr., 1991–95
General Charles C. Krulak, 1995–99
General James L. Jones, 1999–2003
General Michael W. Hagee, 2003–6
General James T. Conway, 2006–10
General James F. Amos, 2010–14
General Joseph F. Dunford Jr., 2014–15
General Robert B. Neller, 2015–19
General David H. Berger, 2019–

Appendix III
Fellow Marines

STRONG BONDS of comradeship-in-arms link many of the corps of marines in today's world. As a member of the world's largest (though not the oldest) of these military organizations, you should know of the other sea soldiers serving under foreign flags. Many of these—the older corps in Europe and the Latin American, East Asian, and Southeast Asian corps of marines and naval infantry—enjoy active relations with the U.S. Marine Corps.

Numerical estimates of marine corps and naval infantry organizations existing worldwide range from forty-one to sixty-two. The disparity in these figures results from analysts' varying judgments of the roles, missions, and capabilities of these organizations and their somewhat "elastic" definitions of what constitutes a corps of marines. This appendix provides a brief orientation to some of these organizations. It focuses on the larger and more capable ones that resemble in many respects our own Corps as well as on some smaller marine corps with whom our Corps has close and longstanding relations. A few included here have been regarded as adversaries, depending on the vicissitudes of diplomacy.

➤ EUROPE
➤ ➤ *The Royal Marines*
Britain's Royal Marines, elder brothers of the U.S. Marine Corps, were III years old in 1775, when our own Corps was founded. From inception, the infant American Corps was modeled after its illustrious British prototype, and many of the traditions of our Corps can be traced to the Royal Marines. Camaraderie between American and British marines is a tradition of both Corps, and every U.S. Marine should possess some knowledge of the Royal Marines.

The Royal Marines were "born" on 28 October 1664, when King Charles II commissioned a regiment of 1,200 sharpshooters, originally the Duke of York and Albany's Maritime Regiment of Foot, to deploy on board Royal Navy vessels to target enemy sailors manning heavy guns. Since the Duke of York was the Lord High Admiral, the organization became known as the Admiral's Regiment. Throughout history, the Royal Marines have fought, often alongside the British Army, in several major wars involving the United Kingdom, including the Seven Years' War, Napoleonic Wars, American Revolutionary War, War of 1812, Crimean War, World War I, World War II, Korean War, Falklands War, Gulf War, Bosnian War, Kosovo War, Iraq War, and Afghanistan War.

U.S. and Royal Marines have served side by side on many occasions, but both corps traditionally cherish associations stemming from the Boxer Uprising and the Korean War. In the Boxer Uprising, American and British marines formed the backbone of the Western troops defending the Legation Quarter in Peking (Beijing) throughout a long and bloody siege in 1900. They additionally served together in the International Brigade, which finally relieved both Peking and Tientsin (Tianjin). Fifty years later, a unit of Royal Marines was attached to the 1st Marine Division in Korea and served with the division throughout the Chosin Reservoir campaign.

Like the U.S. Marine Corps, the Royal Marines are an elite amphibious force maintained at very high readiness for rapid worldwide deployment. Unlike our Corps, they are the nation's commando force, and they reside within the Royal Navy. They are organized, trained, and equipped to deal with a wide spectrum of security threats and challenges. Fully integrated with the Royal Navy's amphibious ships, Royal Marines can deploy globally to conduct expeditionary operations from the sea. Additionally, they are experts in ship-to-ship operations.

The Royal Marines number roughly 7,000 and consist of 3 Commando Brigade, the Special Boat Service, and the Royal Marines Band Service. Headquartered at Stonehouse Barracks in Plymouth, 3 Commando Brigade comprises 40 Commando, 42 Commando, and 45 Commando, each an elite battalion-sized, light infantry unit; 43 Commando Fleet Protection Group, which protects the United Kingdom's strategic nuclear deterrent capabilities; 47 Commando (Raiding Group), which provides training in the use of landing craft and boats and serves as a parent unit for the three assault craft squadrons; 30 Commando Information Exploitation (IX) Group, which provides intelligence, surveillance, and target acquisition capabilities as the brigade's "eyes and ears"; and the Commando Logistic Regiment, Commando Engineers, and 29 Commando Royal Artillery, which provide, respectively, the brigade's organic logistical, engineering, and fire support capabilities.

Formed at the height of World War II, the Special Boat Service was the Royal Navy's answer to the Special Air Service. The Special Boat Service is an elite, maritime counterterrorism unit comprising small, highly trained teams that primarily conduct convert operations.

The Royal Marines Band Service includes the Royal Marines School of Music and five bands situated throughout the United Kingdom, providing musical support to the naval service.

The Royal Marines' motto is *Per Mare, Per Terram* (By Sea, By Land). Their Birth of the Corps Day, which corresponds to our 10 November, is 28 October of each year.

⋗ ⋗ *French Marines (Fusiliers Marins)*

In contrast to the Anglo-American evolution, French marines started out as sailor-infantrymen rather than soldiers of the sea. This was the inspiration of Cardinal Richelieu, who founded the Sea Company in 1622 for landing party duties in the French navy. He later raised a full regiment in 1627, the official year of origin. The Régiment de La Marine eventually became the Troupes de marine of the modern French army. The Fusiliers Marins were created by an imperial decree of 5 June 1856, which confirmed their status as seagoing specialists. They have fought in all of France's modern conflicts, with particularly distinguished service in the world wars and Indochina.

These fusiliers must be distinguished from members of the French army's Troupes de marine, considered by some as "French marines." The latter are the former colonial infantry that protected and fought in the outposts of the French empire. In the modern order of battle, Troupes de marine units form motorized and parachute battalions of the French army's 9th Light Armored Marine Brigade. While this unit can execute amphibious landings, it is not designed for regular service with the French navy.

The Fusiliers Marins protect key vessels, installations, and facilities of the French navy; provide security for naval forces; execute advance force and reconnaissance operations from the sea; and conduct maritime special operations.

Today, roughly 2,700 marines are assigned to the Force maritime des fusiliers marins et commandos (FORFUSCO), which is one of five major elements of the French navy. These operating forces are formed in seven companies of fusiliers marins and two larger groups for the security of various naval facilities and the large naval bases at Brest and Toulon. Additionally, there are five commando companies based at Lorient, and other marines serve in the naval school, also at Lorient.

❯ ❯ *Spanish Marines (Infantería de la Marina Española)*

Established on 27 February 1537 by Charles V and dating from the Tercios de la Armada Naval (of Spanish Armada days), Spain's Infantería de la Marina can claim almost five centuries of service and is regarded as the world's oldest corps of marines. Its men fought at Lepanto in 1571 and with the Armada in 1588, defended Cartagena in 1741, took Sardinia in 1748, and served gallantly in the Peninsular War, Cuba, the Philippines, Guam, Morocco, Cochin China, the Spanish Civil War, and Western Sahara. In recent years, Spanish marines have participated in various NATO operations, including the war in Afghanistan.

Spanish marines conduct amphibious and expeditionary operations and protect naval vessels and facilities.

The Infantería de la Marina today numbers roughly 5,300 and includes a brigade, security forces, special forces, and company of the Royal Guard. Maintained at San Fernando (Cádiz) for duty with the fleet, the Tercio de la Armada is a marine expeditionary brigade composed of a headquarters battalion; three landing battalions, one of which is mechanized; an amphibious mobility group; an artillery landing group; and a service support group. It is situated with the development and education center. Security forces comprise five *agrupaciones* (light infantry battalions) at El Ferrol, Cartagena, Cádiz, Las Palmas, and Madrid; each contains guard companies and an expeditionary company. Consisting mostly of Spanish marines, the Fuerza de Guerra Naval Especial (Special Naval Warfare Force) executes special operations in mainly maritime and coastal environments. Finally, the Compañía Mar Océano de la Guardia Real, essentially a marine rifle company, was created in 1981 and became part of the Royal Guard.

❯ ❯ *Royal Netherlands Marines (Korps Mariniers)*

The Korps Mariniers, as the Dutch marines are officially known, was founded on 10 December 1665 during the Second Anglo-Dutch War. One of their most important early operations was the amphibious raid up the River Thames in 1666, one of a few occasions since the Norman Conquest when foreign troops have landed in Great Britain. Subsequently, the Korps Mariniers performed normal sea and garrison duty throughout the Dutch empire. During World War II, after Holland was overrun by the Germans, several thousand Dutch marines trained at Camp Lejeune as the basis for reconstitution of the corps, and the relationship between our two corps has since been close. In recent decades, the Korps Mariniers have fought in Cambodia, Bosnia, Kosovo, Afghanistan, and Iraq.

The Korps Mariniers are trained to execute special maritime operations, amphibious landings, and expeditionary land operations with light infantry units. They also serve in detachments for ships and naval stations. Dutch marines provide physical, military, and ceremonial training for all Royal Netherlands Navy personnel.

Today, the Korps Mariniers numbers about 3,100 and continues to serve as an integral part of the Royal Netherlands Navy. It comprises a deployable brigade with a command element and two combat groups; a surface assault and training group; a sea-based support group; a maritime special operations force; and a separate raiding squadron, which is essentially a reinforced company responsible for the defense of the Netherlands Antilles. Within the brigade, a combat group includes three raiding squadrons (each essentially a light infantry company), a combat support squadron, a combat service support squadron, and a reconnaissance, surveillance, and target acquisition squadron. The 1st Marine Combat Group is the main contribution of the Korps Mariniers to the combined United Kingdom–Netherlands Landing Force, which manifests the close relationship between the Royal Marines and Korps Mariniers in modern times.

Qua Patet Orbis (To the Ends of the World) is the motto of the Korps Mariniers.

❯ ❯ *Russian Marines*

Formally named Morskaya pekhota Rossii (Russian Naval [or Sea] Infantry), the turbulent history of the Russian naval infantry began with Peter the Great in

November 1705. Soviet practitioners later used the term "naval infantry" loosely for large detachments of sailors thrown into land battles as well as specialized permanent troops. But Peter, from the start, plainly called his marines *morskoi soldaty*, or sea soldiers, and assigned them to sea regiments. By 1715, experience gained in campaigns against Sweden caused him to more than double the force to five large battalions. Steady growth under Peter's successors came to an abrupt halt when Napoleon's invasion caused a permanent transfer of all the sea regiments to the Imperial Russian Army. Not until the early 1960s did the Soviet Union reestablish the naval infantry. Each of the four Soviet naval fleets received base-security units and a landing battalion. A later expansion created a combined arms brigade in each fleet, complete with armored vehicles and heavy weapons. Reports indicate that Russian marines saw action most recently in the Syrian Civil War.

The Morskaya pekhota Rossii is organized, trained, and equipped to conduct amphibious operations and maritime special operations as part of the Russian navy.

Today, the force includes roughly 12,000 personnel organized into five naval infantry brigades and three separate naval infantry battalions distributed across the Baltic, Black Sea, Northern, and Pacific Fleets. Sizes and configurations of the brigades vary according to mission, region, and specialization, but they typically include a combination of two or three naval infantry, air assault, and armored battalions; a reconnaissance battalion; one or more field artillery battalions; and additional integrated combat support and combat service support units.

The Russian naval infantry's motto translates to "Where We Are, There Is Victory!"

❯ LATIN AMERICA

❯ ❯ *Brazilian Marines (Corpo de Fuzileiros Navais)*

The Fuzileiros, as the Brazilian marine corps is known throughout Brazil, trace their lineage to the Portuguese marines, founded in 1797. Units of this organization first came to Brazil in 1808, and 7 March, the date of their landing, is considered the birthday of the corps in Brazil, an overseas dominion of Portugal until its formal independence in 1825. The Fuzileiros fought in their country's wars throughout the nineteenth century, including major riverine operations along the River Paraguay. The most recent expeditionary service of the Fuzileiros was as part of the Inter-American Peace Force, which kept order in the Dominican Republic for fifteen months in 1965 and 1966. During part of that time, they served side by side with U.S. Marines. In recent years, Brazilian marines have served extensively in United Nations missions.

The Fuzileiros specialize in amphibious operations, maritime special operations, counterinsurgency operations, coastal reconnaissance, and unconventional warfare.

Part of the Brazilian navy and including roughly 15,000 personnel, the corps is divided into operating forces, which include a Fleet Marine Force and regional security forces, and a supporting establishment, which functions like our own. The Fleet Marine Force includes a headquarters battalion, a brigade-size amphibious "division" of three infantry battalions, and separate field artillery, armored vehicle, and air defense battalions. In support, there are also a logistical group and a special operations battalion. The regional security forces include base garrisons and a group or battalion in each of nine naval districts.

The motto of the Fuzileiros is *ADSUMUS*, which signifies "Here We Are, and We Are Ready."

›› *Colombian Marines (Infantería de Marina Colombiana)*

The first combat landing by Colombian marines took place on 11 November 1811, less than a year after their organization during their country's war of independence. Throughout the nineteenth century, the corps had its ups and downs, but it was permanently constituted as amphibious and expeditionary troops in 1937. Since 1948, during Colombia's prolonged struggle to defeat banditry, the Infantería de Marina has been continually engaged in riverine, amphibious, and pacification duties.

Colombian marines focus on riverine, counterinsurgency, and counternarcotic operations. Like our own Corps, they carry out operations in both the Atlantic and the Pacific Oceans.

The Infantería de Marina Colombiana numbers roughly 22,000, thus making up more than half of the Colombian navy. The force includes one infantry brigade, consisting of a mix of rifle, counterguerrilla, and commando battalions; three riverine infantry brigades, each of four to seven battalions; a riverine task group; and a supporting training establishment.

Voluntas Omnia Superat (Will [or Willpower] Overcomes All) is the motto of the Colombian marines.

❯ ❯ *Venezuelan Marines*
(División de Infantería de Marina General Simón Bolívar)

The Venezuelan marines formed on 22 July 1822, during their country's war of independence, as is the case with many of the South American corps of marines. It was dissolved just a few years later. During the remainder of the nineteenth century, they were inactive. A company of marines reformed in 1938 to provide ship's detachments, and the corps was officially reconstituted on 11 December 1945. Venezuelan marines have been active in the country's defense against guerrillas and bandits over the years. Over a third of its officers are graduates of U.S. Marine Corps schools.

The missions of the Venezuelan marines include amphibious operations, riverine operations, counterinsurgency, and naval base security.

With a strength of roughly 7,000 personnel, the División de Infantería de Marina fields four amphibious brigades, a riverine brigade, two riverine border brigades, a special operations brigade, an air-defense battalion, and a communications battalion, plus supporting logistical units. The amphibious brigades typically include a headquarters and headquarters company, one or more infantry battalions, and a battalion each of field artillery, assault amphibians, and logistics. The riverine brigades include a headquarters and service company, an infantry battalion, a maintenance company, and a service support company. Naval police fall under the command of the Venezuelan marine corps, as do naval base security units.

The Venezuelan marine corps motto is *Valor y Lealtad* (Valor and Loyalty).

❯ ❯ *Argentine Marines*
(Infantería de Marina de la Armada de la República Argentina)

The Argentine marine corps dates from 1807, when a naval battalion was organized to defend Buenos Aires against British attack. Subsequently, during Argentina's war of independence, marines served on board warships and conducted landing operations. In 1879, an artillery battalion was formed to man coastal defenses at Argentina's seaports and naval bases. Following World War II, the Corps was reorganized in 1947 along modern amphibious lines, with the United States providing an ongoing U.S. Marine adviser. That officer did not accompany the battalion that spearheaded Argentina's seizure of the Falklands/Malvinas Islands by amphibious assault in 1982. In recent years, Argentine marines have taken part in the Gulf War and served with the United Nations as military observers and peacekeepers.

The Infantería de Marina specializes in amphibious and special operations, and it secures naval installations.

With a strength of approximately 5,500, the Infantería de Marina is composed of infantry battalions assigned to the fleet amphibious brigade and the southern district, plus additional battalions and groups of commandos, field artillery, air defense artillery, coastal defense artillery, amphibious vehicles, and service support troops. Additionally, there are two security battalions and several separate security companies to protect naval bases.

Patriae Semper Vigiles (Always Vigilant for Country) is the motto of the Argentine marines.

❯ EAST ASIA

❯ ❯ *Republic of Korea Marine Corps*

Moving to the other side of the globe, the Republic of Korea Marine Corps (ROKMC) was founded on 15 April 1949 at Chinhae, destined to become the Quantico of Korea. In less than two years, the 1st Korean Marine Regiment became an integral part of the 1st U.S. Marine Division and performed admirably in three years of hard fighting during the Korean War. In addition to fighting alongside U.S. Marine forces on the peninsula, ROK marines deployed to Vietnam in the latter stages of the war and fought beside their American counterparts. Since the 1980s, the ROKMC has experienced several organizational changes, but throughout this period, it has maintained a high state of readiness to counter any North Korean adventurism.

The primary ROKMC mission is to conduct amphibious operations as part of the national mobile striking force. Like the U.S. Marine Corps, it also performs security duty for the naval shore establishment and develops amphibious warfare doctrine, tactics, techniques, and matériel.

Numbering roughly 29,000, the ROKMC is organized into two divisions and two separate brigades, together with supporting forces. Each division contains three infantry brigades of three battalions each, a field artillery brigade, and armor, assault amphibian, reconnaissance, engineer, signal, supply, and maintenance battalions. The separate brigades each include three or four infantry battalions, with supporting field artillery, reconnaissance, and engineer units. In addition to maintaining a brigade in the mainline of resistance at Kimpo, the ROKMC has two main bases, Chinhae and Pohang.

The ROKMC motto translates to "Once a Marine, Always a Marine."

❧ ❧ *Chinese Marines*

The question of Chinese sovereignty, the one China principal, and the One China policy are among the more complex and debated geopolitical issues of the day; thus, there is no simple and straightforward discussion of Chinese marines. Given this state of geopolitics, it is unsurprising that there effectively remain two Chinese corps of marines, separated by tradition, politics, and the Taiwan Strait. Both corps can trace some lineage to the earlier Chinese marines of 1917, with antecedents dating to 1433.

❧ ❧ ❧ *Republic of China Marines*

Although no longer recognized diplomatically by the United States, Taiwan, formally the Republic of China, continues to field one of the larger corps of marines in the world. Founded on 16 September 1947 during the Chinese Civil War, the Republic of China Marine Corps, or ROC Marine Corps, expanded with U.S. assistance after 1951 and oriented themselves to the Marine Corps organization of their advisers. After the tough Kinmen Island defense of 1958, the Taiwanese marines settled into a taut peacetime training and readiness regimen that continues today.

Taiwanese marines conduct amphibious warfare, counterlanding operations, and security of naval installations. They also function as a rapid reaction force and a strategic reserve.

With a strength of more than 10,000, the ROC Marine Corps comprises three brigades, the Vanguard, Iron Guards, and Iron Force Brigades; one amphibious armor group, including amphibious artillery and transport units; and one amphibious reconnaissance and patrol unit. In addition, it fields security and support units.

The ROC Marine Corps shares the U.S. Marine Corps motto, Always Faithful.

❥ ❥ ❥ People's Republic of China Marines

The Marine Corps of the People's Republic of China operates under the somewhat awkwardly translated moniker People's Liberation Army Navy Marine Corps, or PLAN Marine Corps. It has precursors in the Chinese Civil War, when the Communists formed units to conduct amphibious operations against islands held by the Nationalists, but these units later disbanded. The PLAN Marine Corps officially celebrated its twenty-fifth birthday in 2005. This suggests that no such corps existed in China prior to 1980, when on 5 May, the 1st Marine Brigade was activated on Hainan Island. The corps has not accumulated an extensive operational history in recent decades; instead, its preoccupation has been organizational growth, training, and exercises.

Considered elite troops in China, PLAN marines typically focus on two principal missions in the country's near periphery: spearheading amphibious operations and garrisoning island chains. Based on China's most recent national strategy, however, the PLAN Marine Corps aims to broaden its mission set to include longer-range expeditionary operations.

Still somewhat obscure are the size and composition of the PLAN Marine Corps. Records indicate that it added a second brigade of 6,000 marines in the Guangzhou military region in 1990, and reports in early 2017 indicate that China planned to expand the corps to number 100,000. A January 2020 report in the *Business Standard*, an English-language Indian daily newspaper, suggests a roughly 36,000-strong PLAN Marine Corps now comprises six brigades, two each with the Northern Theater Navy, Eastern Theater Navy, and Southern Theater Navy. Yet *Military and Security Developments involving the People's Republic of China 2020*, an annual report to Congress by the secretary of defense, indicates that the PLAN Marine Corps has grown to include not only six combined arms brigades but also an aviation brigade and a special operations brigade. Each combined arms brigade typically includes three infantry battalions supported by separate battalions of field artillery, air assault, air defense, reconnaissance, combat support, and service support.

The PLAN Marine Corps motto translates to "Tiger of the Land, Dragon of the Seas."

> ## SOUTHEAST ASIA

> > ### Royal Thai Marines

The Royal Thai Marine Corps was formally organized on the U.S. Marine Corps model on 30 July 1955, but it also traces its existence to 1932, with further historical antecedents to 1824. Its combat operations include the 1941 conflict with France, border conflicts with Cambodia since 1961, counterinsurgency actions throughout the 1970s, and action against a Vietnamese incursion in 1985. More recently, Thai marines have supported United Nations peacekeeping in Southeast Asia and Africa.

The Royal Thai Marines' missions are amphibious operations, counterinsurgency, base defense, and support of the Royal Thai Army.

Operating as part of the Royal Thai Navy and numbering roughly 23,000, the Royal Thai Marine Corps consists of a combat division, security regiment, and a few smaller task groups. The division comprises three infantry regiments, a field artillery regiment, a service support regiment, and separate armor, reconnaissance, signal, assault amphibian, and combat engineer battalions. Additionally, the corps operates its own education command and a special operations center.

> > ### Indonesian Marines (Korps Marinir Republik Indonesia)

The Indonesian marine corps traces its lineage from the Corps Mariniers in 1945 through the Korps Komando, a corps of naval commandos established in 1949. Throughout the 1950s and 1960s, forces of the Korps Komando conducted amphibious and counterinsurgency operations mainly within Indonesia. On the thirtieth anniversary of the corps in 1975, the chief of staff of the navy restored the Indonesian marine corps' original name, Korps Marinir, and implemented a substantial reorganization. Further reorganization and expansion followed in 1984, 1999, 2001, and 2004. Indonesian marines saw action fighting separatist movements and quelling sectarian conflicts during 1990–2000. Since 2016, they have also participated in operations conducted jointly by the national police and armed forces to capture or eliminate members of Mujahidin Indonesia Timur, an Indonesian terrorist group linked to the Islamic State.

Missions of the Korps Marinir include amphibious warfare, land warfare, special operations, and counterinsurgency.

With approximately 20,000 personnel, the Korps Marinir comprises three divisions, a separate brigade, and a special operations unit. Each division includes an infantry brigade, artillery regiment, cavalry regiment, and combat support regiment. The separate 4th Marine Infantry Brigade includes four infantry battalions and a combat support battalion. The Korps Marinir also maintains a special operations unit, including an amphibious reconnaissance battalion and a joint navy-marine counterterrorism unit.

The motto of the Korps Marinir translates to "Glorious on the Land and Sea."

❖ ❖ *Philippine Marines*

The story of the Philippine Marine Corps began on 7 November 1950, with the establishment of A Company, 1st Marine Battalion at Naval Base Cavite. With training and support from both the U.S. Marine Corps and U.S. Army, Philippine marines conducted their first amphibious landing in April 1951 and, two months later, saw first combat against Communist insurgents. In subsequent decades, the Philippine Marine Corps expanded and reorganized several times while deploying to Korea, securing land features in the Spratly Islands, and continuing to combat Communist insurgents and Islamic militants within the country—operations that continue to the present.

The Philippine Marine Corps executes amphibious, expeditionary, and special operations; provides coastal defense; and secures naval installations and vital government facilities.

Numbering approximately 12,500, the Philippine Marine Corps encompasses three maneuver brigades, each with three infantry battalions; a combat service and support brigade, which supports the maneuver brigades; a coastal defense regiment, newly established in 2020 to protect the nation's territorial integrity, territorial waters, and exclusive economic zone; and independent units, such as the Marine Special Operations Group and the Marine Security and Escort Group.

The motto of the Philippines Marine Corps is *Karangalan, Katungkulan, Kabayanihan* (Honor, Duty, Valor).

Appendix IV

Article 38, *Marine Corps Manual,* 1921

EVERY 10 NOVEMBER, the central part of the ceremony to celebrate the Corps' anniversary is the distribution to all hands of Article 38, *Marine Corps Manual,* 1921, which was written especially for this purpose by Major General John A. Lejeune, thirteenth commandant. While this text and its introduction are found in the *Marine Corps Manual* today, it is reproduced here as a matter of convenience for those who do not have a manual within easy reach.

On November 1st, 1921, John A. Lejeune, 13th Commandant of the Marine Corps, directed that a reminder of the honorable service of the Corps be published by every command, to all Marines throughout the globe, on the birthday of the Corps. Since that day, Marines have continued to distinguish themselves on many battlefields and foreign shores, in war and peace. On this birthday of the Corps, therefore, in compliance with the will of the 13th Commandant, Article 38, *United States Marine Corps Manual,* Edition of 1921, is republished as follows:

"(1) On November 10, 1775, a Corps of Marines was created by a resolution of the Continental Congress. Since that date many thousand men have borne the name Marine. In memory of them it is fitting that we who are Marines should commemorate the birthday of our Corps by calling to mind the glories of its long and illustrious history.

"(2) The record of our Corps is one which will bear comparison with that of the most famous military organizations in the world's history. During 90 of the 146 years of its existence, the Marine Corps has been in action against the Nation's foes. From the Battle of Trenton to the Argonne, Marines have won foremost honors in war, and in the long era of tranquility at home, generation after generation of Marines have grown gray in war in both hemispheres, and in every corner of the seven seas that our country and its citizens might enjoy peace and security.

"(3) In every battle and skirmish since the birth of our Corps, Marines have acquitted themselves with the greatest distinction, winning new honors on each occasion until the term 'Marine' has come to signify all that is highest in military efficiency and soldierly virtue.

"(4) This high name of distinction and soldierly repute we who are Marines today have received from those who preceded us in the Corps. With it we also received from them the eternal spirit which has animated our Corps from generation to generation and has been the distinguishing mark of the Marines in every age. So long as that spirit continues to flourish, Marines will be found equal to every emergency in the future as they have been in the past, and the men of our Nation will regard us as worthy successors to the long line of illustrious men who have served as 'Soldiers of the Sea' since the founding of the Corps."

The inspiring message of our 13th Commandant has left its mark in the hearts and minds of all Marines. By deed and act from Guadalcanal to Iwo Jima, from Inchon to the Korean Armistice, from Lebanon to Taiwan, the Marines have continued to epitomize those qualities which are their legacy. The success which they have achieved in combat and the faith they have borne in peace will continue. The Commandant and our many friends have added their hearty praise and congratulations on this, our _____ birthday.

Abbreviations

THE ACRONYMS AND INITIALISMS included here either were used in the text or refer to common terms, phrases, or organizations with which Marine officers should be familiar. This list can be used as a reference like the *DOD Dictionary of Military and Associated Terms*, which can be found in the Joint Electronic Library (https://www.jcs.mil/Doctrine/DOD-Terminology-Program/).

1stLt	first lieutenant
1stSgt	first sergeant
2ndLt	second lieutenant
ACC	Air Combat Command
ACE	aviation combat element
ACIP	aviation career incentive pay
ACMC	assistant commandant of the Marine Corps
AC/S	assistant chief of staff
ACTSMAN	*Marine Corps Assignment, Classification, and Travel System Manual*
ADC	assistant deputy commandant
AETC	Air Education and Training Command
AFC	U.S. Army Futures Command
AFCEC	Air Force Civil Engineer Center
AFDW	Air Force District of Washington
AFGSC	Air Force Global Strike Command
AFIA	Air Force Inspection Agency
AFLMA	Air Force Logistics Management Agency
AFMAA	Air Force Manpower Analysis Agency

AFMC	Air Force Materiel Command
AFOSI	Air Force Office of Special Investigations
AFOTEC	Air Force Operational Test and Evaluation Center
AFPC	Air Force Personnel Center
AFRC	Air Force Reserve Command
AFRL	Air Force Research Laboratory
AFRS	Air Force Recruiting Service
AFSA	Air Force Services Agency
AFSC	Air Force Safety Center
AFSOC	Air Force Special Operations Command
AFWA	Air Force Weather Agency
AMC	U.S. Army Materiel Command; Air Mobility Command (Air Force)
ANC	Arlington National Cemetery
ANGLICO	air naval gunfire liaison company
ANGRC	Air National Guard Readiness Center
APO	Army Post Office
AQI	al-Qaeda in Iraq
AR	Active Reserve
ARG	amphibious ready group
ASN(EI&E)	assistant secretary of the Navy (Energy, Installations, and Environment)
ASN(FM&C)	assistant secretary of the Navy (Financial Management and Comptroller)
ASN(M&RA)	assistant secretary of the Navy (Manpower and Reserve Affairs)
ASN(RD&A)	assistant secretary of the Navy (Research, Development, and Acquisition)
ASVAB	Armed Services Vocational Aptitude Battery
ATEC	U.S. Army Test and Evaluation Command
AWC	U.S. Army War College
BAH	basic allowance for housing
BAS	basic allowance for subsistence
BCNR	Board for Correction of Naval Records

BICMD	Blount Island Command
BIR	basic individual record
BLT	battalion landing team
BOQ	bachelor officer quarters
BRS	Blended Retirement System
BTR	basic training record
BUMED	Bureau of Medicine and Surgery (Navy Medicine)
CAC	common access card
CACO	casualty assistance calls officer
CAG	civil affairs group
Capt	captain
CATC	Combined Arms Training Center
CCDR	combatant commander
CCMD	combatant command
CDD	Capabilities Development Directorate
CDE	College of Distance Education (Navy)
CDET	College of Distance Education and Training
CE	command element
CHINFO	chief of information
CHRA	U.S. Army Civilian Human Resources Activity
CIA	Central Intelligence Agency
CIO	chief information officer
CIS	communications and information systems
CJCS	chairman of the Joint Chiefs of Staff
CLB	combat logistics battalion
CLR	combat logistics regiment
CMC	commandant of the Marine Corps
CMR	consolidated memorandum receipt
CNIC	commander, Navy Installations Command
CNO	Chief of Naval Operations
CNR	chief of naval research; chief of Navy Reserve
CNRF	commander, Navy Reserve Force
CO	commanding officer
Col	colonel

COMMARFOR	commander, Marine Corps Forces
COMNAVRESFOR	commander, Navy Reserve Force
CONUS	continental United States
COT	commander of troops
CS	combat support
CSA	chief of staff of the Army
CSAF	chief of staff of the Air Force
CSCDEP	Command and Staff College Distance Education Program
CSO	chief of space operations
CSP	career sea pay; Consolidated Storage Program
CSS	combat service support
CWO	chief warrant officer
DARPA	Defense Advanced Research Projects Agency
DC	deputy commandant
DCAA	Defense Contract Audit Agency
DC Aviation	deputy commandant for aviation
DC CD&I	deputy commandant for combat development and integration
DC I	deputy commandant for information
DC I&L	deputy commandant for installations and logistics
DC M&RA	deputy commandant for manpower and reserve affairs
DCMA	Defense Contract Management Agency
DCNO	deputy chief of naval operations
DCO-IDM	defensive cyberspace operations–internal defensive measures
DC P&R	deputy commandant for programs and resources
DC PP&O	deputy commandant for plans, policies, and operations
DCSA	Defense Counterintelligence and Security Agency
DECA	Defense Commissary Agency
DEERS	Defense Enrollment Eligibility Reporting Service
DEP	distance-education program
DFAS	Defense Finance and Accounting Service
DHA	Defense Health Agency

DHRA	Defense Human Resources Activity
DHS	Department of Homeland Security
DIA	Defense Intelligence Agency
DIC	dependency and indemnity compensation
DIRINT	director of intelligence
DISA	Defense Information Systems Agency
DLA	Defense Logistics Agency; dislocation allowance
DLSA	Defense Legal Services Agency
DMA	Defense Media Activity
DMCS	director of the Marine Corps staff
DMO	distribution management office
DNI	director of national intelligence
DNS	director of Navy Staff
DOD	Department of Defense
DODD	Department of Defense directive
DODEA	Department of Defense Education Activity
DOE	Department of Energy
DON	Department of the Navy
DON/AA	Department of the Navy Assistant for Administration
DPAA	Defense POW/MIA Accounting Agency
DPC-RSU	deployment processing command–reserve support unit
DSCA	Defense Security Cooperation Agency
DTIC	Defense Technical Information Center
DTOD	Defense Table of Official Distances
DTRA	Defense Threat Reduction Agency
DTS	Defense Travel System
DTSA	Defense Technology Security Administration
DUSN	deputy undersecretary of the Navy
EABO	expeditionary advanced base operations
ECP	Enlisted Commissioning Program
EOTG	expeditionary operations training group
EWSDEP	Expeditionary Warfare School Distance Education Program

FAST	fleet antiterrorism security team
FCC	U.S. Fleet Cyber Command
FFC	U.S. Fleet Forces Command
FLPP	foreign language proficiency pay
FM	field manual
FMCR	Fleet Marine Corps Reserve
FMF	Fleet Marine Forces
FMFLANT	Fleet Marine Force Atlantic
FMFPAC	Fleet Marine Force Pacific
FOA	field operating agency
FORFUSCO	Force maritime des fusillers marins et commandos
FORSCOM	U.S. Army Forces Command
FPO	Fleet Post Office
FSA	family separation allowance
GC	general counsel
GCE	ground combat element
GCM	general court-martial
GCT	General Classification Test
GTCC	government travel charge card
GTR	government travel request
GySgt	gunnery sergeant
HHG	household goods
HMH	Marine heavy helicopter squadron
HMLA	Marine light-attack helicopter squadron
HMX-1	Marine Helicopter Squadron 1
HQMC	Headquarters, U.S. Marine Corps
HRC	U.S. Army Human Resource Command
I&I	inspector-instructor
ICE	individual combat equipment
IG	inspector general
IMA	individual mobilization augmentee
INSCOM	U.S. Army Intelligence and Security Command
IRR	Individual Ready Reserve
ISIS	Islamic State of Iraq and Syria

JAG	judge advocate general
JAGMAN	*Manual of the Judge Advocate General*
JCD	Joint Capabilities Directorate
JCS	Joint Chiefs of Staff
JGSDF	Japan Ground Self-Defense Force
JTF	joint task force
JTR	*Joint Travel Regulations*
LCE	logistics combat element
LDO	limited duty officer
LES	leave and earnings statement
LOCE	littoral operations in a contested environment
LOGCOM	Marine Corps Logistics Command
LtCol	lieutenant colonel
MAG	Marine aircraft group
MAGTF	Marine air-ground task force
MAGTFTC	Marine Air-Ground Task Force Training Center
Maj	major
MAJCOM	major command
MALS	Marine aviation logistics squadron
MARCENT	U.S. Marine Corps Forces Central Command
MARCORLOGCOM	Marine Corps Logistics Command
MARCORSYSCOM	Marine Corps Systems Command
MARDET	Marine detachment
MARDIV	Marine division
MARFOR	Marine Corps forces
MARFORCOM	U.S. Marine Corps Forces Command
MARFORCYBER	U.S. Marine Corps Forces Cyberspace Command
MARFOREUR-AF	U.S. Marine Corps Forces Europe and Africa
MARFOR-K	U.S. Marine Corps Forces Korea
MARFORPAC	U.S. Marine Corps Forces Pacific
MARFORRES	U.S. Marine Corps Forces Reserve
MARFORSOUTH	U.S. Marine Corps Forces South
MARFORSTRAT	U.S. Marine Corps Forces Strategic Command
MARSOC	U.S. Marine Corps Forces Special Operations Command

MARTD	Marine air reserve training detachment
MAW	Marine aircraft wing
MAWTS-1	Marine Aviation Weapons and Tactics Squadron 1
MB	Marine barracks
MCA	Marine Corps Association
MCA&F	Marine Corps Association and Foundation
MCAF	Marine Corps air facility
MCAGCC	Marine Corps Air-Ground Combat Center
MCAS	Marine Corps air station
MCB	Marine Corps base
MCCDC	Marine Corps Combat Development Command
MCCS	Marine Corps Community Services
MCESG	Marine Corps Embassy Security Group
MCGEP	Marine Corps Graduate Education Program
MCI	Marine Corps Institute; Marine Corps installation
MCIA	Marine Corps Intelligence Activity
MCICOM	Marine Corps Installations Command
MCIEAST	Marine Corps Installations East
MCINCR	Marine Corps Installations National Capital Region
MCIOC	Marine Corps Information Operations Center
MCIPAC	Marine Corps Installations Pacific
MCIRSA	Marine Corps Individual Reserve Support Activity
MCIWEST	Marine Corps Installations West
MCLB	Marine Corps logistics base
MCM	*Manual for Courts-Martial, United States*
MCRC	Marine Corps Recruiting Command
MCRD	Marine Corps recruit depot
MCSCG	Marine Corps Security Cooperation Group
MCSF	Marine Corps security force(s); Marine Corps support facility
MCSFR	Marine Corps Security Force Regiment
MCTFS	Marine Corps Total Force System
MCU	Marine Corps University
MCWL/FD	Marine Corps Warfighting Lab / Futures Directorate

MCWP	Marine Corps warfighting publication
MCX	Marine Corps exchange
MDA	Missile Defense Agency
MDW	U.S. Army Military District of Washington
MEB	Marine expeditionary brigade
MECEP	Marine Enlisted Commissioning Education Program
MEDCOM	U.S. Army Medical Command
MEF	Marine expeditionary force
MEU	Marine expeditionary unit
MGIB-AD	Montgomery GI Bill–Active Duty
MGySgt	master gunnery sergeant
MHG	MEF headquarters group
MIA	missing in action
MLG	Marine logistics group
MMRP	Manpower Management Division, Records and Performance Branch
MOQ	married officer quarters
MOS	military occupational specialty
MP	military police
MPF	maritime prepositioning force
MSC	major subordinate command; Military Sealift Command
MSG	Marine security guard
MSgt	master sergeant
MSO	mandatory service obligation
MSOAG	Marine Special Operations Advisor Group
MSOB	Marine Special Operations Battalion
MSOSG	Marine Special Operations Support Group
MTU	mobilization training unit
MWR	morale, welfare, and recreation
MWSS	Marine wing support squadron
MWTC	Mountain Warfare Training Center
NASA	National Aeronautics and Space Administration
NATO	North Atlantic Treaty Organization

NAVAF	U.S. Naval Forces Africa Command
NAVAIR	Naval Air Systems Command
NAVCENT	U.S. Naval Forces Central Command
NAVEUR	U.S. Naval Forces European Command
NAVFAC	Naval Facilities Engineering Systems Command
NAVSAFECEN	Naval Safety Center
NAVSEA	Naval Sea Systems Command
NAVSOUTH	U.S. Naval Forces Southern Command
NAVSUP	Naval Supply Systems Command
NAVWAR	Naval Information Warfare Systems Command
NAWDC	Naval Aviation Warfighting Development Center
NCA	National Command Authority
NCIS	Naval Criminal Investigative Service
NCO	noncommissioned officer
NCR	National Capitol Region
NECC	Navy Expeditionary Combat Command
NETC	Naval Education and Training Command
NFO	naval flight officer
NGA	National Geospatial-Intelligence Agency
NIC	Navy Installations Command
NIOC	Navy Information Operations Command
NJP	nonjudicial punishment
NLSC	Naval Legal Service Command
NMOC	Naval Meteorology and Oceanography Command
NPC	Navy Personnel Command
NPS	Naval Postgraduate School
NRO	National Reconnaissance Office
NROTC	Naval Reserve Officers Training Corps
NSA/CSS	National Security Agency / Central Security Service
NSC	National Security Council
NSWC	U.S. Naval Special Warfare Command
NUC	Navy Unit Commendation
OAD	Operations Analysis Directorate
OCC	Officer Candidate Course

OCS	Officer Candidates School
OD	officer of the day
ODNI	Office of the Director of National Intelligence
OEF	Operation Enduring Freedom
OGC	Office of General Counsel
OHA	overseas housing allowance
OIE	operations in the information environment
OIF	Operation Iraqi Freedom
OLDCC	Office of Local Defense Community Cooperation
OMB	Office of Management and Budget
OMPF	official military personnel file
ONI	Office of Naval Intelligence
OOD	officer of the deck
OPCON	operational control
OPNAV	Office of the Chief of Naval Operations
OPTEVFOR	Operational Test and Evaluation Force
OQR	officer qualification record
OSD	Office of the Secretary of Defense
OSO	officer selection officer
PACAF	Pacific Air Forces
PACFLT	U.S. Pacific Fleet
PBP&E	professional books, papers, and equipment
PCS	permanent change of station
PDRL	permanent disability retired list
PEO LS	Program Executive Office, Land Systems
PEO MLB	Program Executive Office, Manpower, Logistics, and Business Solutions
PES	*Performance Evaluation System Manual*
PFPA	Pentagon Force Protection Agency
PLC	Platoon Leaders Class
PME	professional military education
PNT	position, navigation, and timing
POV	privately owned vehicle
POW	prisoner of war

RCT	regimental combat team
RED	Record of Emergency Data
REIN	reinforced
RLT	regimental landing team
ROK	Republic of Korea
ROKMC	Republic of Korea Marine Corps
ROTC	Reserve Officers Training Corps
SBP	Survivor Benefit Plan
SCM	summary court-martial
SCRA	Servicemembers' Civil Relief Act
SDA	Space Development Agency
SDDC	Military Surface Deployment and Distribution Command
SECNAV	Secretary of the Navy
SELRES	Selected Reserve
SGLI	Servicemembers' Group Life Insurance
Sgt	sergeant
SgtMaj	sergeant major
SMCR	Selected Marine Corps Reserve
SMMC	sergeant major of the Marine Corps
SOP	standard operating procedure
SORM	Ship's Organization and Readiness Manual
SP	shore patrol
SPCM	special court-martial
SPMAGTF	special purpose Marine air-ground task force
SPMAGTF-CR-AF	Special Purpose Marine Air-Ground Task Force–Crisis Response–Africa
SPMAGTF-CR-CC	Special Purpose Marine Air-Ground Task Force–Crisis Response–Central Command
SpOC	Space Operations Command
SSgt	staff sergeant
SSP	Strategic Systems Programs
SYSCOM	Marine Corps Systems Command
TAD	temporary additional duty

TAPS	Tragedy Assistance Program for Survivors
TBS	The Basic School
TD	temporary duty
TDRL	temporary disability retired list
T/E	table of equipment
TECOM	Marine Corps Training and Education Command
TF	task force
TG	task group
TMO	traffic management office
T/O	table of organization
TOQ	transient officer quarters
TRADOC	U.S. Army Training and Doctrine Command
TRAP	tactical recovery of aircraft and personnel
TSP	Thrift Savings Plan; transportation service provider
TU	task unit
UCMJ	Uniform Code of Military Justice
UPB	unit punishment book
USAA	United Services Automobile Association
USAASC	U.S. Army Acquisition Support Center
USACE	U.S. Army Corps of Engineers
USACIDC	U.S. Army Criminal Investigation Command
USAFA	U.S. Air Force Academy
USAFE-AFAFRICA	U.S. Air Forces in Europe and Air Forces Africa
USAFRICOM	U.S. Africa Command
USARAF	U.S. Army Africa
USARCENT	U.S. Army Central
USARCYBER	U.S. Army Cyber Command
USAREUR	U.S. Army Europe
USARNORTH	U.S. Army North
USARPAC	U.S. Army Pacific
USARSOUTH	U.S. Army South
USASMDC	U.S. Army Space and Missile Defense Command
USASOC	U.S. Army Special Operations Command
USCENTCOM	U.S. Central Command

USCYBERCOM	U.S. Cyber Command
USEUCOM	U.S. European Command
USFK	U.S. Forces Korea
USINDOPACOM	U.S. Indo-Pacific Command
USMA	U.S. Military Academy
USNA	U.S. Naval Academy
USNO	U.S. Naval Observatory
USNORTHCOM	U.S. Northern Command
USO	United Service Organizations
USSOCOM	U.S. Special Operations Command
USSOUTHCOM	U.S. Southern Command
USSPACECOM	U.S. Space Command
USSTRATCOM	U.S. Strategic Command
USTRANSCOM	U.S. Transportation Command
VA	Department of Veterans Affairs
VCNO	vice chief of naval operations
VGLI	Veterans' Group Life Insurance
VMA	Marine attack squadron
VMM	Marine medium tiltrotor squadron
VMU	Marine unmanned aerial vehicle squadron
WAVES	Women Accepted for Volunteer Emergency Service
WHS	Washington Headquarters Services
WO	warrant officer
XO	executive officer

Glossary

THIS GLOSSARY compiles terms both historically and currently used within the Marine Corps. The list is far from exhaustive, but it includes many widely used terms and colloquialisms. Readers may recognize certain of these as being shared with the other services. Nevertheless, the terms are incorporated here because of their long inclusion in the Marines' distinctive vocabulary.

The authoritative source for all military terminology, acronyms, and initialisms is the *DOD Dictionary of Military and Associated Terms*. It is worth becoming familiar with this document, which can be found in the Joint Electronic Library (https://www.jcs.mil/Doctrine/DOD-Terminology-Program/). Marine Corps Reference Publication (MCRP) 1-10.2 (formerly MCRP 5-12C), the *Marine Corps Supplement to the DOD Dictionary of Military and Associated Terms*, complements the *DOD Dictionary*. This official collection of Marine Corps terminology resides in the Marine Corps Publications Electronic Library (https://www.marines.mil/News/Publications/MCPEL/).

COMMON TERMS, PHRASES, AND USAGES

782 gear or **equipment**: individual combat equipment. References the numeric designation of the memorandum receipt used in issuing it.

airdale: aviator.

all hands: all members of a command; everybody.

alphas: Service "A" uniform, based on the letter *A* in the phonetic alphabet.

ant farm: area where a unit's radio antennae are emplaced, usually remote from its main position.

ashore: (1) on the beach, as differentiated from on board ship; (2) any place off a Marine Corps or government reservation. GO ASHORE: go on liberty; leave the reservation.

aye, aye, Sir/Ma'am: required official acknowledgment of an order, meaning, "I have received, understand, and will carry out the order or instructions."

B&W: solitary confinement on bread and water, now only authorized on board ship; colloquially, "cake and wine."

barracks cover (or **cap**): frame type, visored headgear, so called as the traditionally prescribed cover for organizations not part of the Operating Forces.

BCD: bad conduct discharge; colloquially, "Big Chicken Dinner."

Benotz: reference to a generic junior Marine; sometimes spelled "Benotts."

binnacle list: roster of Marines placed on light duty by the surgeon; in the old days, posted on or near the binnacle, a waist-high case or stand on the deck of a ship, generally mounted in front of the helmsman.

Blue Book: *Combined Lineal List of Officers of the Marine Corps on Active Duty*; also the *Register of Commissioned and Warrant Officers of the U.S. Navy and Marine Corps*; so called because original print editions were bound in a blue cover.

blues: generic reference to the blue dress uniform in any of its forms.

boondocks or **boonies**: woods, jungles, faraway places; semifacetiously, "that portion of the country that is fit only for the training of Marines."

boot: (1) a recruit; (2) any new person of limited experience.

boot camp: recruit depot.

boots and utes: utility uniform worn without the uniform blouse; typical dress for physical training or a *working party*.

brassard: armband, piece of cloth, or other material worn around the upper arm as a temporary insignia or emblem.

break out: (1) to unfurl; (2) to remove from storage; (3) to rouse.

brig: place of confinement on board ship or ashore at a Marine Corps or naval installation; the base or station prison.

brig rat: one who has served much brig time; habitual offender.

brig time: confinement.

bug juice: (1) insect repellant; (2) any syrupy, sweet drink made by adding artificially flavored powder, such as Kool-Aid, to water.

bulkhead: (n) wall; (v) to complain against or asperse a superior while pretending not to.

cammies: camouflage utility uniform.

campaign cover: broad-brimmed felt hat with four-dent crown, formerly worn on Marine expeditionary service, now only at rifle ranges and recruit depots; colloquially, "Smokey the Bear" cover; "field hat" (obsolete).

cannon-cocker: artillery Marine.

Captain's Mast: Navy equivalent of *Office Hours*, normally having the negative connotation of nonjudicial punishment for a Sailor.

CG: commanding general.

charger: highly motivated, aggressive Marine; short for *hard charger*.

charlies: Service "C" uniform, based on the letter C in the phonetic alphabet; sometimes called "chucks."

chaser: short for *prisoner chaser*.

checkage: electronically drawing funds from a servicemember's pay account in reimbursement for advance pay, lost/destroyed items, meals, or other services.

chew out (or **on**): reprimand severely.

chief messman: permanently detailed assistant to the mess sergeant, supervising all messmen and responsible for the policing and good order of the mess hall.

chit: (1) acknowledgment of indebtedness to a mess; (2) receipt or authorization; (3) any small piece of paper.

chopper: helicopter.

chow: food, rations.

chow down: to eat heartily.

chow hound: one who appreciates food.

civvies: civilian clothing; "mufti."

Class Six (or **VI**): (1) personal demand items in the military supply system; (2) alcoholic beverages of any kind.

clutch: serious, sudden emergency.

CMC: commandant of the Marine Corps.

CO: commanding officer.

color sergeant: distinguished noncommissioned officer given the privilege of carrying the National Color and leading the color guard.

colors: both national and organizational colors when referred to collectively (that is, "the colors"); *cap*: ceremony when the *National Color* is raised or lowered or when the national and organizational colors together are posted and retired.

combat service support: essential capabilities, functions, activities, and tasks necessary to sustain all elements of all operating forces in theater at all levels of warfare; "CSS." See also *combat support*.

combat support: fire support and other operational assistance provided to combat elements; "CS." See also *combat service support*.

commission: (1) the rank and authority officially conferred upon military officers; (2) the formal written certificate or warrant conferring military rank and authority.

communicator: officer or enlisted Marine assigned to or specializing in communication duties.

company-grade officer: any officer second lieutenant through captain, normally also covering the first three grades of warrant officer.

corpsman: enlisted sailor of the Navy Hospital Corps.

cover: Marine cap or hat; headgear.

crying towel: something used by those with many troubles or complaints to wipe away their tears (and said to hang in every chaplain's office).

cut it: See *hack it*.

D&D: drunk and disorderly; entry formerly made beside the name of anyone on the liberty list returning in that condition.

DD: dishonorable discharge.

dead horse: pay advance, which the Marine must repay via monthly *checkage* over a prescribed period.

deck: (n) floor; surface of the earth; (v) to knock down with one blow.

deuce gear: See *782 gear*.

DI: recruit depot drill instructor, ordinarily an experienced drillmaster.

dinged: hit, as by a bullet ("to be *dinged* by enemy fire").

doc: Navy hospital corpsman. DEVIL DOC: term of respect for Navy hospital corpsmen who are Fleet Marine Force qualified.

doggie: enlisted Army soldier (diminutive for "dog-face").

donkey dick: spout for a fuel can.

dope: (1) information; (2) sighting and/or wind correction for a rifle under given conditions. BAD DOPE: misinformation.

drug deal: obtaining a posting, equipment, supplies, or services outside of normal channels.

dungarees: Marine Corps utility uniform (obsolete).

eight-ball: worthless, troublesome individual; one who deservedly remains "behind the eight-ball."

Eighth & I or **Eighth & Eye**: Marine Barracks Washington, located at the intersection of Eighth and I Streets SE, Washington, D.C.

Emblem, the: Marine Corps Emblem, or Corps badge, adopted in 1868; *Globe and Anchor*; Eagle, Globe, and Anchor.

EPD: extra police duties, such as cleaning or tidying up heads, offices, or other areas.

fall in: command to members of a unit to form into ranks and come to attention.

fall out: (1) to assemble outside barracks immediately prior to a formation; (2) after a formation, to break ranks and remain in the general area, resume what one was doing, or proceed to the next activity of the day.

fallen angel: Marine officer who failed flight school and was assigned another military occupational specialty.

fart sack: mattress cover made of cotton or some other fabric.

field day: (n) day or portion of a day set aside for thorough cleaning of a space or area; (v) act of conducting a field day.

field meet: organized competition between military units, usually including athletic and military skill events and often culminating with a barbeque or picnic.

field-grade officer: any officer major through colonel.

float: deployment on board a ship.

FMF: Fleet Marine Force.

fore-and-aft cap: green garrison cap worn with the service uniform; *piss cutter*.

foul up: (n) mistaken, botched, bungled, or confused situation; (v) to confuse, bungle, or botch. FOULED UP: badly confused or botched.

frock: to grant official permission for an officer selected for promotion to assume the title, uniform, and authority of the next grade before they make their number.

frost-call: procedure within a command whereby all officers and other key personnel may be alerted by sequential telephone calls or other notification.

galley: (1) kitchen of a mess hall; (2) mobile field kitchen; (3) ship's kitchen.

gangway or **gangplank**: movable bridge or passage used in boarding or leaving a ship at a pier.

gear: equipment. PACK THE GEAR: measure up to Marine standards.

gedunk: (1) candy and other junk food; (2) location where such food is sold, such as a store, snack bar, or vending machine. See also *pogey bait*.

general mess: the enlisted mess.

gizmo: any miscellaneous, nondescript, unidentified thing, widget, or gadget.

Globe and Anchor: Marine Corps *Emblem*; sometimes Eagle, Globe, and Anchor.

greens: Marine Corps service uniform.

grinder: drill field.

ground pounder: See *grunt*.

grunt: an infantry Marine; originally a pejorative term, but now of a neutral or even complimentary tone.

gung-ho: (1) possessing aggressive esprit de corps; (2) hard-charging.

gunner: short for Marine Gunner, a nickname for an infantry weapons officer; may be used to refer informally to any warrant officer.

gunny: nickname for gunnery sergeant.

gunship: armed helicopter.

hack: arrest of an officer. TO BE IN HACK or TO BE UNDER HACK: to be under arrest, although the phrase sometimes refers to merely having one's liberty secured for a time.

hack it: to be competent or successful in a job or assignment ("Do you think Corporal Calkoff can *hack it* as a squad leader?").

hard charger: aggressive, dynamic, zealous, indefatigable officer or enlisted Marine; one who is professionally keen; *charger*.

hashmark: service stripe worn on the service uniform sleeve by enlisted Marines for completion of each honorable four-year enlistment in any of the U.S. armed services.

head: toilet facility; latrine.

head shed: unit headquarters or command post.

heel-and-toe watch: condition during which watchstanders alternate tours, one individual relieving the other and vice versa, for an indefinite period.

high and tight: type of military haircut—a variant of a buzz cut—in which hair on the top of the head is cut extremely short, then gradating, or "fading," to skin high up on the sides and back of the head.

hill, to go over the: to desert.

hill, to run over the: to force an individual to desert or apply for a transfer or retirement ("Captain Hardnose certainly *ran* that brig rat *over the hill*.")

holiday routine: period during which routine drills, instruction, training, and work are *knocked off* throughout a command, normally followed on weekends and authorized holidays.

I&I: inspector-instructor, a regular officer assigned to supervise the training and readiness of a reserve unit.

ID card: identification card issued to every member of the U.S. armed forces.

IG: inspector general of a major command.

IG inspection: official inspection of a command or unit (usually biennially) by the inspector general or representatives.

IPAC: Installation Personnel Administration Center, a single, consolidated personnel center servicing the administrative needs of all Marines assigned to the base or station.

Irish pennant: loose thread or string on a uniform detracting from a correct military appearance.

Iron Mike: (1) nickname for the statue of a World War I Marine in front of old Post Headquarters, Quantico (now the Marine Corps Association offices); (2) tough, inspiring, can-do Marine or soldier (as a result of which at least eight statues named Iron Mike stand on Marine Corps and Army bases around the world).

jarhead: pejorative term for a Marine.

JO: junior officer.

joe: coffee.

joe pot: coffeepot; percolator.

JORG: junior officer requiring guidance, the most junior O-1.

junk on the bunk: periodic inspection of equipment, or more loosely, of clothing and equipment, displayed on one's bunk.

kevlar: combat helmet and body armor fabricated with Kevlar, a strong, antiballistic, heat-resistant synthetic fiber.

khakis: summer service uniform, obsolete in the Marine Corps (but Navy officers and chief petty officers still wear a version as a working uniform).

knock off: to cease immediately.

ladder: (n) stairs or stairway; (v) to adjust gunfire by a series of graduated spots in range.

leather personnel carriers: combat boots.

leatherneck: longstanding nickname for a Marine, arising from the leather stock, or neckpiece, that was part of the Marine uniform from the late 1700s to late 1800s.

leave: period of time when one is permitted to be absent from work or place of duty; vacation.

liberty: authorized free time ashore or off base not counted as *leave*. Standard periods of liberty are usually denoted in hours and referred to as a **48**, **72**, or **96**, corresponding to liberty periods of two, three, and four days.

lifer: Marine who intends to make a complete career out of the Marine Corps.

line company: narrowly, any of the lettered Marine rifle companies within an infantry battalion, as opposed to the Headquarters and Service Company and Weapons Company, which are not considered line companies; generally, a company within a unit that spearheads execution of that unit's mission, rather than playing a supporting role.

lock up: to confine in a brig (enlisted); to place under arrest in quarters (officer). LOCKED UP: confined or under arrest.

Maggie's drawers: a red-disk signal for a miss on the rifle range from "the butts," or downrange location of the targets. The signal was originally a red flag.

main gate: main entrance to a post, station, reservation, camp, or compound at which a guard post is maintained.

mainside: main or traditional center of a naval installation, usually near the base or station headquarters.

***Manual*, the**: *Marine Corps Manual*.

Marine Online: Internet resource for individual Marines, providing secure access to electronic individual administrative and personnel records; abbreviated as *MOL*.

mast: upright spar supporting the signal yard and antennas on a naval ship.

MCRD: Marine Corps recruit depot; either of the boot-camp facilities located at Parris Island, South Carolina, and San Diego, California.

mess sergeant: noncommissioned officer in charge of an enlisted mess.

messman: nonrated enlisted personnel assigned to additional duty in the mess hall, typically for a period of one month; on board ship, called "mess cook."

MOL: See *Marine Online.*

mount out: to load and embark for expeditionary service in amphibious shipping or transport aircraft.

mustang: Marine officer who began his/her career in the enlisted ranks.

National Capital Region: geographic area encompassing the District of Columbia and eleven local jurisdictions in the state of Maryland and the commonwealth of Virginia.

National Color: U.S. flag when mounted on a staff (or pike) and either carried by an individual on foot or displayed or cased in a fixed location; sometimes simply called the "Color."

National Ensign: U.S. flag, or alternately the canton or Union—the blue background and the fifty stars—when flown from the stern of a ship or craft of the Navy or from a flagstaff at commands ashore; sometimes simply called the "Ensign" (distinguished by context from the identical term for the most junior Navy commissioned officer rank).

NCO: noncommissioned officer.

nervous in the service: jittery, fearful, and apprehensive, especially when in forward areas.

nonrated: servicemember in pay grade E-3 or below.

number, to make: (1) to be promoted, when a vacancy occurs, to a higher grade for which previously selected; (2) colloquially, to pay one's respects to a senior.

OD: officer of the day; sometimes abbreviated as OOD.

Office Hours: periodic, usually weekly or monthly, occasion when the commanding officer receives requests, investigates offenses, reenlists and discharges enlisted Marines, and awards commendations (the last now less common, as commanding officers normally prefer to decorate Marines at all-hands formations). See also *Captain's Mast.*

officers' country: (1) officers' living spaces on board ship; (2) any portion of a base or station allocated for the exclusive use of officers.

oh-three: vernacular for "infantry"—that is, occupational field 03. Other large occupational fields include "oh-two" for intelligence; "oh-four," logistics; "oh-six," communications; and "oh-eight," field artillery.

old man: commanding officer.

old salt: (1) old-timer; (2) experienced Marine; (3) sardonically, person who thinks he knows all the answers.

oorah: (1) Marine exclamation expressing motivation, agreement, or excitement; (2) battle cry common in the Marine Corps since the mid-twentieth century.

organizational color: organizational flag of a military unit.

out-of-bounds: area or space restricted from use by normal traffic or prohibited to enlisted men; sometimes called "restricted area." The equivalent Army/Air Force term is "off limits."

outside: civilian life ("Sergeant Boatspace is now on the *outside*.").

overhead: ceiling of a room (ashore) or compartment (on board ship).

pass over: to omit an officer or staff *NCO* from a promotion list by advancing someone junior in rank.

passed over: having failed selection for next-higher commissioned or staff *NCO* rank.

people: (1) enlisted Sailors or Marines; (2) one's subordinates, regardless of rank.

pick up: to promote an officer who has previously been *passed over*.

picked up: having been selected for next-higher rank after having been passed over one or more times.

piece: (1) Marine's rifle; (2) artillery gun.

pipe up: to speak up.

piss cutter: green garrison cap worn with the service uniform; *fore-and-aft cap*.

platoon sergeant: senior *NCO* in a platoon, executive to the platoon leader.

pogey bait: candy or other junk food, often sold from a vending machine. See also *gedunk*.

pogey rope: French fourragère worn by members of the 5th and 6th Marine Regiments.

police: (v) to straighten or tidy up an individual, area, or structure; (n) condition of neatness or cleanliness.

police gang: permanent working force assigned to the police sergeant, who oversees the *police* and upkeep of a unit's area and facilities.

police shed: structure or space assigned to the police sergeant for stowage of tools, gear, and supplies; police sergeant's workshop.

prisoner chaser: escort, sometimes armed, for a prisoner or detail of prisoners. See also *chaser*.

property room: storeroom for unit property; sometimes called a "property shed." **PT**: physical training.

pull butts: to mark and score targets on a rifle range from behind a berm where the targets are located.

PX: post exchange, a retail store selling articles necessary for the health, comfort, and morale of the command (inherited from Army lingo and still used today); also, MCX, for the Marine Corps exchange on board Marine installations.

qualify: (1) to attain a qualifying score in weapons proficiency; (2) to attain the qualification of marksman with the service rifle or pistol.

quarter deck: (1) raised deck behind the main mast of a ship; (2) area near the stern of a modern ship where ceremonies may be performed, guests may be received, or personnel may embark and disembark the vessel; (3) location of prominence in a naval building, office, or barracks.

quarters: (1) government housing at a base or station for officers and *NCOs* with authorized dependents; (2) periodic—usually daily—muster of a ship's company (Navy).

rack: bed, bunk; *sack*.

rated Marine: noncommissioned officer.

rating: similar to a military occupational specialty in the Marine Corps, and occupational field or specialty in the Navy or Coast Guard, characterized by achievement of specific skills and abilities, each having its own specialty badge, which is worn on the left sleeve by all persons qualified in the relevant field.

reading, take a: to sound out.

record day: when a Marine fires an individual weapon for qualification; sometimes called "qual day."

recruiter: Marine assigned to recruiting duty.

reefer: refrigerator in a mess hall.

reeve: to pass (something, such as a rope) through a hole or opening.

regulation: (1) strictly in accordance with regulations or adopted specifications; (2) issued from government sources. Avoid *GI*.

RHIP: "rank has its privileges."

Rock, the: Okinawa, Japan.

rock-happy: eccentric or mildly deranged as the result of long overseas duty at a remote installation, often on an island (such as *the Rock*).

rocks and shoals: punitive articles of the Uniform Code of Military Justice.

runner: messenger.

running guard: duty in which individuals have one tour on guard duty, one off, and then back on again with no intervening free period.

rust bucket: old, worn-out ship; pejorative for any Navy transport.

sack: See *rack*.

saddle up: to put on individual combat equipment and prepare to move out; "gear up."

salty: confident and experienced; seasoned ("That Corporal Brass sure is one *salty* team leader.").

Schmuckatelli: friend and *liberty* buddy of *Benotz*; sometimes spelled "Smuckatelli."

scoop, the: latest news, information.

scope out: to check out; to ascertain or verify a piece of information ("I'm not sure whether that's good or bad *dope*—you'd better *scope it out*.").

scuttlebutt: (1) drinking fountain; (2) unconfirmed rumor.

sea soldier: Marine.

sea story: anecdote calculated to impress recruits and gullible individuals.

seabag: canvas duffel bag issued to each Marine for storage and transportation of uniforms and personal gear.

seagoing: (1) sea duty; (2) pertaining to or assigned to sea duty.

secure: (1) to anchor firmly in place; (2) to lock up, thus rendering a space physically secure; (3) to cease or terminate an activity or exercise; (4) to seize by force ("*secure* a beachhead [or objective]").

semper gumby: colloquialism associated with flexibility and adaptability to changing circumstances, often used as a response or exclamation upon receiving changed orders or instructions. The term references the pliable American

Claymation character Gumby of the 1950s and 1960s television program *The Gumby Show.*

shanghai: to get rid of an individual by involuntary or surprise transfer.

ship over: to reenlist.

shoot the breeze: to chat or to engage in casual conversation.

shooter: Marine whose avocation is marksmanship with the rifle or pistol; loosely, one who has displayed special prowess with rifle or pistol or has served with distinction on a Marine Corps rifle or pistol team.

short-fused: (1) having a deadline for completion very near in time; (2) very quick tempered; sometimes used derivatively in the nominative sense ("Gunnery Sergeant Piledriver sure has a *short fuse.*").

short timer: one who will soon complete an enlistment or tour of duty.

shove off: to depart or leave; to get under way.

sick bay: ship or unit aid station, dispensary, or infirmary.

sick bay commando: individual who spends undue time in hospital or at sick call; malingerer.

sick call: daily period when routine ailments are treated at the *sick bay.*

sight in: to aim a weapon at a target; loosely used as synonym for *zero.*

skipper: (1) ship's captain in the Navy; (2) colloquially, commanding officer of a company, battery, or squadron.

skivvies: underwear.

slop chute: base or station exchange restaurant (similar to a *gedunk* on board ship).

slop down: to rapidly drink a large quantity, especially beer.

slop up: to rapidly eat a large quantity, without regard to table manners.

smoking lamp is lighted (or **out**): smoking is permitted (or is not); originally, a lamp on board ships used by men to light their pipes.

snap in: (1) to conduct sighting and aiming exercises with an unloaded weapon; (2) to try out for, or break in at, a new job.

snow: to fool, bewilder, mislead, or exaggerate.

snow job: misleading or grossly exaggerated report or sales talk.

snuffy: generic reference to a nonrated Marine; sometimes spelled "snuffie."

soup sandwich: (1) description of a disheveled, disorganized, unprepared Marine; (2) reference to a messy, chaotic military operation; (3) a gaggle.

spit and polish: (1) extreme individual or collective military neatness; (2) extreme devotion to the minutiae of traditional military procedures and ceremonies.

spit shine: (v) to shine leather, employing spittle or tap water to remove excess grease and produce a high polish; (n) an extremely high polish on a piece of leather.

squad bay: barracks space occupied by nonrated Marines and, under some circumstances, junior NCOs.

square away: to align, set in place, or correctly arrange an article, articles, or living space; to take in hand (an individual) and direct.

squid: pejorative for a Sailor.

staff NCO: *NCO* above the grade of sergeant.

stand by: command to wait.

striker: (1) apprentice or aspirant, attempting to learn a military specialty; (2) on board ship, the Marine entrusted with the ordnance maintenance of a single gun; sometimes called a "gun-striker."

survey: (n) medical discharge; examination by authorized competent personnel to determine whether a piece of gear or equipment, stores, or supplies should be discarded or retained; (v) to effect discharge or retirement of an individual for medical reasons; to dispose of an item of government property for unserviceability.

swabbie: pejorative for a Sailor.

sympathy chit: *chit* supposedly issued by those in authority, or by chaplains, authorizing an individual with many woes to obtain a prescribed amount of sympathy. Used derisively to indicate lack of sympathy or concern over the exaggerated plights of another.

TAD: temporary additional duty.

take off your pack: relax.

thirty-year Marine: Marine who intends to make the Corps a career. See also *lifer*.

top: nickname for "master sergeant." Avoid the Army term "top-kick."

topside: weather deck or, more generically, the upper areas of a ship.

troop and stomp: morning troop inspection, followed by close-order drill.

two-block: (1) to hoist a flag or pennant to the peak, truck, or yardarm; (2) to tighten and center a regulation Marine Corps necktie.

UA: unauthorized absence; naval version of absent without leave (AWOL).

under way, to get: (1) to depart on board ship; (2) to depart or to start out for an objective or destination.

UNQ: unqualified, usually in reference to annual rifle or pistol qualification but occasionally applied to other training events. Pronounced "unk."

utilities: green or camouflaged field and work uniform, first issued in World War II. Now officially termed the combat utility uniform in both woodland and desert camouflage patterns.

voluntold: to be volunteered by a superior for an assignment, task, or chore without having a choice.

watch: official tour of duty of prescribed length, such as guard or officer of the day.

wet down: to serve drinks in honor of one's promotion.

wetting down: party in honor of a promotion.

whites: Marine Corps or Navy white dress uniforms. In the Marine Corps, worn only by officers until discarded in 2000, although the white trousers are retained as part of the blue-white dress uniform.

wing-wiper: enlisted aviation Marine.

wooly pully: green wool service sweater optionally worn over the khaki shirt as part of the service "B" uniform or under the blouse of the utility uniform.

word, the: latest news, usually considered to be well verified and reliable.

work your bolt: to resort to special measures, either by energy, persuasion, or connections, to attain a particular end.

working party: a group of Marines assigned a particular chore or task. Often associated with cleaning up an area.

yut: a motivational exclamation like *oorah*. Short for "yelling unnecessarily things."

zapped: killed in action. Occasionally used as a verb ("Corporal Buttplate sure *zapped* that sniper.").

zero: (v) to determine by trial and error the sight setting required to strike a target with an individual weapon at a given range (synonymous with "zero in"); (n) the sight setting required to strike a target with a weapon at a given range.

TERMS AND USAGES TO AVOID

Increased interaction between the services has led some individuals to adopt certain undesirable expressions from outside the naval services to the detriment of the authentic Marine Corps way of talking. Avoid the following unfortunate usages:

career (as in "career officer"): Say "regular."

E-4 (and other similar ways of speaking of enlisted rank): Never refer to an enlisted person as "an E-4," "an E-6," and so forth, as these are pay grades. Refer to Marines and all servicemembers using their correct grades and titles.

EM: Just say "enlisted Marine," or, even better, simply "Marine."

GI: Use *square away* or *regulation* instead of this Army term. Never speak of an enlisted Marine as a "GI."

hitch: Use "enlistment" instead of this Army term dating from the horse cavalry.

insignia (when you mean *emblem*): Even though unified clothing procedures have designated the Marine Corps *Emblem* as "insignia, branch of service," this terminology should be absolutely avoided. The only acceptable word is *Emblem*. The term "insignia of rank" is okay.

medic: This is an Army and Air Force term for a hospital *corpsman* or "aid man or woman" (also an Army and Air Force term). Always say *corpsman* when referring to Navy hospital corpsmen.

TDY (for "temporary duty"): This Army and Air Force term now appears on many joint forms. Always use the Navy and Marine *TAD*.

trooper: Army airborne soldier (originally, cavalry). This term is taken as an insult by Marines. Refer to an individual Marine as a Marine, never a "trooper." "Troops" as a plural is acceptable, but not "troopers." "Marine" or "Marines" is best, "people," second best.

WM: Woman Marine (obsolete). Avoid using this term, as it is now considered pejorative.

Index

About the Author

COL CHRISTIAN HALIDAY, USMC (RET.), received his commission through the Naval Reserve Officers Training Corps Program after graduating from Duke University in 1984. During his twenty-eight years on active duty, he served in a variety of Marine Corps and joint assignments, including company, battalion, and installation command. Along the way, he earned a master's degree in security studies from Marine Corps University and completed additional graduate work at the Institut d'Etudes Politiques de Paris, better known as Sciences Po.